D1192233

Date Due

*

AMERICAN WRITERS SERIES
*
HARRY HAYDEN CLARK
General Editor

*

⋆ AMERICAN WRITERS SERIES ⋆

Volumes of representative selections, prepared by American scholars under the general editorship of Harry Hayden Clark, University of Wisconsin. Volumes now ready are starred.

AMERICAN TRANSCENDENTALISTS, *Raymond Adams, University of North Carolina*

*WILLIAM CULLEN BRYANT, *Tremaine McDowell, University of Minnesota*

*JAMES FENIMORE COOPER, *Robert E. Spiller, Swarthmore College*

*JONATHAN EDWARDS, *Clarence H. Faust, University of Chicago, and Thomas H. Johnson, Lawrenceville School*

*RALPH WALDO EMERSON, *Frederic I. Carpenter, Harvard University*

*BENJAMIN FRANKLIN, *Frank Luther Mott, University of Iowa, and Chester E. Jorgenson, Wayne University*

*ALEXANDER HAMILTON AND THOMAS JEFFERSON, *Frederick C. Prescott, Cornell University*

BRET HARTE, *Joseph B. Harrison, University of Washington*

*NATHANIEL HAWTHORNE, *Austin Warren, Boston University*

OLIVER WENDELL HOLMES, *S. I. Hayakawa, University of Wisconsin, and Howard Mumford Jones, Harvard University*

*WASHINGTON IRVING, *Henry A. Pochmann, Mississippi State College*

HENRY JAMES, *Lyon Richardson, Western Reserve University*

*HENRY WADSWORTH LONGFELLOW, *Odell Shepard, Trinity College*

JAMES RUSSELL LOWELL, *Norman Foerster, University of Iowa, and Harry H. Clark, University of Wisconsin*

*HERMAN MELVILLE, *Willard Thorp, Princeton University*

*JOHN LOTHROP MOTLEY, *Chester P. Higby and B. T. Schantz, University of Wisconsin*

THOMAS PAINE, *Harry H. Clark, University of Wisconsin*

*FRANCIS PARKMAN, *Wilbur L. Schramm, University of Iowa*

*EDGAR ALLAN POE, *Margaret Alterton, University of Iowa, and Hardin Craig, Stanford University*

WILLIAM HICKLING PRESCOTT, *Michael Kraus, College of the City of New York, and William Charvat, New York University*

*SOUTHERN POETS, *Edd Winfield Parks, University of Georgia*

SOUTHERN PROSE, *Gregory Paine, University of North Carolina*

*HENRY DAVID THOREAU, *Bartholow Crawford, University of Iowa*

*MARK TWAIN, *Fred Lewis Pattee, Rollins College*

*WALT WHITMAN, *Floyd Stovall, University of Texas*

JOHN GREENLEAF WHITTIER, *Harry H. Clark, University of Wisconsin, and Bertha M. Stearns, Wellesley College*

Pen drawing by Kerr Eby, after a photograph

FRANCIS PARKMAN

ÆT. CA. 35

Francis Parkman

REPRESENTATIVE SELECTIONS, WITH
INTRODUCTION, BIBLIOGRAPHY, AND NOTES

BY

WILBUR L. SCHRAMM

Assistant Professor of English
University of Iowa

AWS

AMERICAN BOOK COMPANY
New York · Cincinnati · Chicago
Boston · Atlanta

PREFACE

It is no longer necessary to defend Francis Parkman's right to be the subject of a book of exposition or selections. That battle was won long ago. Almost with one voice, American historians have acknowledged Parkman foremost among them, and literary historians have long included his with the few great names of American letters. Critics and writers of all schools have paraded under his banner. The most scientific of modern specialists on the history of the West agree with "cosmic philosophers" like John Fiske; writers like Vernon L. Parrington, who had no love for New England but who honored Parkman's work above that of any other "Brahmin," are aligned with writers like Barrett Wendell, for whom the horizon of American literature coincided for the most part with the horizon of New England.

And yet the very extent and unanimity of this verdict have not been good for Parkman scholarship or Parkman students. The chorus of appraisal has rolled up in two great waves—one in the decade after the historian's death, when writers sought to define his accomplishment and do honor to his gallant life; the other in the neighborhood of the centennial year, when the customary centennial eulogies quite out-sounded a few reservations from later specialists and analysts to whom Parkman's narrative history had come to seem old-fashioned. Most of this criticism has been tucked away in periodicals. There are only two full-length studies of Parkman, and none since 1904; and there has been no extended systematic attempt since 1900 to work out the logical articulation of Parkman's ideas and to evaluate them. The years following 1900 have produced much new evidence on Parkman's life, on his milieu, and on the ages, men, and events he wrote about. We have only recently come to realize the importance of some of his writings apart from his great histories—

his ventures into contemporary politics, for instance, his literary criticism, his novel. Furthermore, a new age, both in history and in literature, has come to America since the studies of 1900 and 1904; and the test of history is, how does it stand up under investigation and amidst new fashions and attitudes? The time has come, therefore, for a new interpretation and a new evaluation.

Perhaps it is the fixed quality of Parkman's reputation, the very inertia of success, that has prevented the issuing of a comprehensive book of selections for students. There have been "reductions" of *France and England in North America*, it is true, but most of these have been made up of fragments of narrative joined by editorial comment so as to make a continuous story; they have sacrificed the distinctive qualities of Parkman to the necessity of telling of the conflict between France and England in short compass. These have been mostly for young people. So also have been the volumes of "thrilling tales from Parkman." But, in general, the teacher has had to take his choice between assigning to his students *The Oregon Trail* as a whole, or a chapter, reprinted in an anthology, from one of the histories. *The Oregon Trail*, charming though it is, is not Parkman's greatest work, nor is it a representative work; his great reputation is not based on that book. Nor is a single chapter from one of the histories a satisfactory representation of the man, his ideas, or the reasons for his fame. The situation has not been conducive to the best teaching.

These selections have been chosen in an attempt to resolve such a difficulty. They include the divisions of Parkman's writing of which we have only recently begun to see the importance: his fascinating diary, his own story of his struggle against ill-health, some of his reviews, three of his vigorous essays on current problems, and early attempts at fiction (including a chapter from the novel) which helped to form his historical style. The teacher, of course, and the advanced student will find these readings essential; the ordinary student in a college or high school class will want to read a few of them and will find them both interesting and illuminating. But the ordinary student will have his chief pleasure in the rest of the book. Here he will find the heart of *The Oregon Trail*, the great chapters from *Pontiac*, and many comprehensive selections from the volumes of *France and England in North America*, so chosen as to give the high points of the narrative, to exhibit Parkman's style and insight at their best, and to give in Parkman's own words his interpretation of the struggle for a continent.

This volume attempts to combine intensive scholarship with usability. The bibliography, for instance, is practically exhaustive, but the most important titles are starred. The usual scholarly mechanisms are available for the scholar who wants to use them, but they need not be utilized, and the references are given, wherever possible, to the books which will be available in most libraries.

The selections from *Montcalm and Wolfe* and the early theme on "Studies of Nature" are reprinted by permission of and special arrangement with Little, Brown and Company. The excerpts from Parkman's diaries are reproduced by permission of the Houghton Mifflin Company. The quotations from Parkman's letters are made by permission of the Massachusetts Historical Society.

Professor Harry Hayden Clark has read the introduction and notes and has been more than generous with advice and suggestions.

W. L. S.

CONTENTS

INTRODUCTION

I. PARKMAN'S MILIEU

Francis Parkman was born in the year when the Monroe Doctrine was formulated and died in the year of the Columbian Exposition. When he was born, the railroad was a curiosity and the telephone was unheard of; when he died, the first automobiles and moving pictures were being made.[1] When he was born, the new author was Cooper; when he died, the new authors were Garland and Crane. In his seventy years, 1823–1893, he saw the frontier move from the Alleghenies to the Pacific; the Machine Age grow from gawky adolescence into smooth-muscled maturity; the United States pass through their greatest age of idealism and their wildest orgy of materialism; the literary careers of Poe, Cooper, Emerson, Thoreau, Longfellow, Lowell, Melville, Whitman, Hawthorne, Whittier, Howells, James, and Mark Twain.

Parkman's life-span, that is to say, covers almost exactly the years which Lewis Mumford has called the Golden Day and the Brown Decades.[2] Parkman contributed two noteworthy books[3] to the age of romantic idealism which came into being after "the long winter of the seventeenth century, a sturdy battle with the elements, had given way to the slow spring of the eighteenth; . . . the ground was ploughed and the country made ready. . . . Then, in the few warm weeks that elapsed between 1830 and 1860, there had come a quick leafing and

[1]Bell's telephone was introduced in 1876, the first moving picture was shown in 1894, and the internal combustion engine was being tried on horseless carriages as early as 1885.

[2]In his books, *The Golden Day* (New York, 1926) and *The Brown Decades* (New York, 1931).

[3]*The Oregon Trail* (magazine publication begun in 1847, published as a book in 1849) and *The Conspiracy of Pontiac* (1851). His novel, *Vassall Morton* (1856), might also have been mentioned.

efflorescence."[4] This was the age when the voices of Rousseau, Wordsworth, and Scott came loudly across the Atlantic and the words of Jefferson to the farmers still debated the words of Hamilton to the capitalists; the age of Transcendentalism, Brook Farm, simple living and high thinking; the age of "Elizabethan daring on the sea, of a well-balanced adjustment of farm and factory in the East, of a thriving regional culture operating through the lecture-lyceum and the provincial college";[5] the age of springtime in New England. Parkman fretted over the ill health that kept him from joining the four years of bloodshed which, under the name of a humanitarian crusade, brought New England's spring to an end. With the greatest barrier to capitalism fallen, with the machine in the saddle, with idealism sated and the acquisitive instinct shamelessly bared, America forgot restraint for three mad decades. The War between the States, says Mumford, "shook down the blossoms and blasted the promise of spring. The colours of American civilization abruptly changed. By the time the war was over, browns had spread everywhere: mediocre drabs, dingy chocolate browns, sooty browns that merged into black. Autumn had come. . . . The Brown Decades . . . began with the mourning note of Lincoln's funeral, . . . ended, like a sun thrusting through the clouds, in the golden portal of Sullivan's Transportation Building at the Chicago World's Fair in 1893."[6] In these brown years, Parkman accomplished his largest and greatest work, but his voice was loud against the materialism of the age. His thought and method, as we shall see later, were crystallized before the War of 1861. But he gave his heart wholly to neither age, Golden or Brown; his basic allegiance was rather to an earlier age—to the eighteenth-century doctrine of rationalism and to the doctrine's Federalistic spokesmen.

[4]Lewis Mumford, *The Brown Decades*, pp. 4–5.
[5]*Idem, The Golden Day*, pp. 158–9.
[6]*Idem, The Brown Decades*, pp. 5, 9.

It remains here briefly to sketch the background of his life and thought.

Two physical aspects of 1823–93 America dwarfed all others in their importance. These were the rise of the machine and the progress of the frontier. One depended on the other. The frontier rode westward on the wheels of the machine, and the machine rose in importance because the frontier provided an almost insatiable market for it.

The frontier took two hundred years on foot and animal-back to reach the Alleghenies. Then the rivers suddenly awakened to the whistles of steamboats, narrow ribbons of steel rail unwound over the prairies, the telegraph carried its staccato voice into the most remote mining camp, and the frontier in less than a century conquered a whole continent. Cold numerals tell a dramatic story of the industrial revolution in America. The United States Patent Office recorded an average of 77 patents annually between the years 1790–1811; in the year 1830 alone it recorded 544; in the decade before the War of 1861, 28,000 were issued.[7] In 1800 there were only eight cotton mills in the country; in 1840 there were 1,369.[8] A steamboat first descended the Ohio and Mississippi in 1812, but could not return against the current; by 1825 there were 125 steamboats on those two rivers, and by 1860 there were more than 1,000.[9] In 1830 there were 32 miles of railroad in the country; in 1840 there were 2,800, and in 1860, 30,000.[10] Samuel Morse worked fourteen years to get private firms interested in his new telegraph. Congress built a line from Baltimore to Washington in 1844, and a private company connected Philadelphia and Newark in 1846; by 1861, 50,000 miles of telegraph lines were in operation.[11] When the cotton

[7] H. U. Faulkner, *American Economic History*, p. 275.
[8] *Ibid.*, pp. 275–6.
[9] *Ibid.*, p. 317.
[10] *Ibid.*, p. 327.
[11] *Ibid.*, pp. 334–5.

gin was invented the average annual production of cotton in the
United States was about four thousand bales; in 1800, it rose
to 73,000, and thereafter until 1861 approximately doubled
every ten years.[12] Between 1840 and 1870 the population of the
section we now call the Middle West quadrupled, the production of wheat was multiplied by seven, and the cash value of
the farms increased tenfold.[13] When Parkman was born, the
population of the country was about 10,000,000, and five per
cent of these lived in cities; in 1860, the population was 31,000,-
000, and 16 per cent lived in cities.[14]

These figures hide a drama—the drama of more and more
blueprints registered in the Patent Office, more and more iron
roaring out of the West into Eastern mills and returning in the
form of steel tools, engines, machines; the drama of a civilization moving relentlessly westward. During all of Parkman's
life this trek from the East to the West continued, draining the
East of some of its most adventurous souls, draining the immi-
grant ships that docked at New York and Philadelphia. Some
Americans went west for gold, some for furs, some for free
land and thick black soil, some for adventure. A few went for
liberty, and a great many went because they needed a new
start and had heard that in the West was to be found equality.[15]
Whatever the reason, they went, in numbers that increased
impressively from year to year and jumped phenomenally when
each new gold strike was announced and when the war ended
with a bankrupt South and a tired New England. The West
was the land of opportunity. That assurance profoundly
affected the thought and action of Parkman's America.

[12] *The South in the Building of the Nation* (Richmond, 1910), V, 211.
[13] Bureau of the Census, Decennial Reports for 1840 and 1870. See also
Faulkner, *op. cit.*, p. 231.
[14] Bureau of the Census, Decennial Reports for 1820 and 1860. See also
Faulkner, *op. cit.*, p. 338.
[15] See F. J. Turner, *The Frontier in American History* (1920), pp. 1–38;
also F. L. Paxson, *The History of the American Frontier, 1763–1893*
(Boston, 1922).

Parkman's America was offered the choice of two antagonistic philosophies. One was the romantic humanitarian thought imported from Europe, thought which was based on the assumption that man is perfectible, that the way to perfection is to be found through a cultivation of natural goodness, and that the ultimate function of the state is the service of the common good. The other was the thought denominated politically by the name Federalism, which trusts in rational civilization rather than a benevolent nature, which recognizes the inequality of men and the ineradicableness of the acquisitive instinct, and which aims toward a state which would allow the pleasant exercise of that instinct, especially by a privileged class. This latter way of thinking was closely related to the hardheaded rationalism of the American eighteenth century, and it was taken up by Hamilton and spoken in the Federalist manifestoes. Hamilton's traditional opponent, Jefferson, chose the other doctrine and preached it in terms of agrarian democracy.[16]

Some, not all, of the writers of the Golden Day gave their hearts to Jefferson's choice. They opened the floodgates of European romantic literature and heard ad infinitum the phrases of the day: natural goodness, back to nature, the natural man, corrupt civilization, intuition, glamour of the past, sentimentalism, wonder of the supernatural, unimpeded imagination, free expression, liberty, equality, fraternity. But American romanticism was not to be a mirror held up to European. In America the seeds of romanticism fell on Puritan soil, and a long training in Puritanism had taught New Englanders the necessity of restraint. Furthermore, the seeds fell among a race of Yankees whose faith in native shrewdness and common sense was too fundamental to be blown away with every wind from

---

[16]For a good exposition of these philosophies see V. L. Parrington, *Main Currents in American Thought*, Vol. II (*The Romantic Revolution in America*).

Europe. The seeds fell in a country where passion for quality and respect for aristocracy were already strong. In New England the Brahmin class, in the South the First Families, stood as a bulwark against the growth of equalitarian government and against humanitarian faith in the natural goodness of the masses. Longfellow, Cooper, Holmes, Motley, Prescott, Lowell in his later years, and Parkman himself might have joined Poe in his statement that "democracy is the best government in the world —for dogs!" Most important of all, the European influence fell on a country which still had a mobile frontier. As long as the frontier existed, America enjoyed what Vernon L. Parrington has appropriately called "a fluid economics"; there could be no fixed economic system as long as free land, free opportunity, and unlimited natural resources remained in the West. This Thor's flagon of wealth encouraged a hopeful attitude, and the problems of frontier life encouraged a robust individualism. In such a man as Emerson these native factors joined with the European ones to create the highest expression of the Golden Day: an optimistic outlook, a stout individualism, a love for nature tempered with a healthy respect for the past, a desire to know one's self combined with a perception of the necessity of controlling one's self, and good mixtures of the ethical and the artistic, of mysticism and Yankee common sense.

Emerson rode the crest of the wave. There were other riders. Longfellow looked on his contemporaries and his history books with a mellow, dignified sort of sentimentalism. Poe sang in his wonderful style of Love, Beauty, Death, the Nevermore. Lowell sat like a humanistic statue amidst a romantic renaissance. Whittier combined his Quaker training with the new gospel of freedom and equality and achieved a humanitarian fanaticism against slavery; freedom bought, he retired to write of the simple life. Thoreau approximated the perfect individualism, and his conception of man's relation to the state has had recent echoes as far away as India. Hawthorne wrote deep-etched chronicles of solitude and sin. Melville tried to put together the jigsaw puzzle of life, tried desperately to find meaning and end to Ahab's quest. Walt Whitman loved his fellow men, preached the gospel of democracy, loved and glorified life, chanted the doctrines of the Enlightenment in the ears of the money changers of the Gilded Age.[17]

For by the time Whitman spoke out loud and clear the Golden Day was over. The war, as one writer says, had "cut a white gash through the history of the country."[18] Bankruptcy followed close upon Appomattox—financial, spiritual, emotional. The Southern dream of an agrarian democracy was dead. The optimism of New England was deflated when the bubble of romantic economics burst. The idealism of Concord ran a sad race with the realism of land speculation. The last barriers to a capitalistic dominance of American life had been cleared away, and the great middle class seized the throne room, enthroned a plutocracy in place of an aristocracy or a democracy, and celebrated the occasion with a great barbecue.[19] The scene of the barbecue was the West.

We have seen another such postwar barbecue in our own day, but since 1890 we have had no unsettled frontier land to give as prizes. In the years after 1865 the frontier was pushed mercilessly forward toward the oil, the gold and silver, the coal, the rich wheatland, there for the man who was smart enough to get it away from his neighbor. The men who were

---

[17] Students wishing more complete and scholarly treatments of these men and other American writers mentioned in this chapter will find the introductions and annotated bibliographies in the other volumes of the American Writers Series very useful.

[18] Mumford, *The Golden Day*, p. 158.

[19] V. L. Parrington, in Vol. III of *Main Currents in American Thought* (*The Beginnings of Critical Realism in America*), pp. 7 ff., was extremely successful in capturing the spirit and the appearance of this period. See especially pp. 12–16.

smart enough were of the stamp of Boss Tweed, Jay Gould, Jim Fisk, Phil Armour, Mark Hanna, John D. Rockefeller, and Andrew Carnegie. In the ears of this group the quiet voice of Emerson and the impassioned song of Whitman went unheard. Mark Twain grinned sardonically and wrote *The Gilded Age*. And out of this materialistic orgy grew a new realism.

The frontier at a distance is romantic; the frontier at hand is realistic. There is no place for romantic dreams in an existence of constant danger and hardship, where life and happiness and success depend solely on the individual. It was easy for the Beadles in New York to publish romantic paper-bound tales telling how "three more redskins bit the dust";[20] but in the instant when one is faced with the necessity of making three redskins fall, in order not to fall oneself, there is mostly realism. The frontier came nearer American life in the years after the war because it was so bound up with American economics. Furthermore, as the amount of free land grew steadily less, as the frontier gobbled up mile after mile of the supposedly inexhaustible West—until the Bureau of the Census could declare in 1890 that there was no more frontier—the stock of American optimism steadily fell. As the end of the frontier grew nearer, there came an end to the fluid economics, the romantic notions of endless opportunity. The facts had to be faced realistically; there was no escape to the West; the battle had to be fought with the weapons and on the battlefield at hand.

About this time the country became very conscious of science. Applied science had hastened westward expansion; now theoretical science had its inning. John Fiske explained Darwinian evolution; William James developed a pragmatic psychology;

---

[20]Erastus F. Beadle, of Otsego, New York, published the first dime novel in June, 1860. This book, *Malaeska, or the Indian Wife of the White Hunter* (128 pp., paper-bound), by Ann Sophia Winterbotham Stevens, is said to have sold 300,000 copies the first year. Beadle advertised "a dollar book for a dime." Soon other publishers took notice. By 1866, dime novels were selling by the millions.

from the lecture platform and the magazines Americans heard over and over again: "Examine things as they are, collect all the evidence, and generalize therefrom." This, of course, implied a natural basis, a *real* basis.[21] Such thinking encouraged the movement toward realism in writing, monism in theology. It encouraged the revolt from the teleological view of life. And its evolutionary conception of the survival of the fittest began to be used to explain and condone the existence of the commercial superman, the buccaneer of business.

Thus realism came to literature. Howells brought out of Ohio a new idea of writing about ordinary life unadorned— realism, pale and diluted and expurgated, to be sure, but nevertheless realism of the commonplace. Howells became a literary lion of Boston. Henry James fled from Boston and found refuge in England (as Henry Adams found refuge in the Middle Ages), away from the great barbecue, but he extended the use of realism to a penetrating analysis of human thought and behavior. Mark Twain made use of a realistic method even as he looked backward through the clouds of romance to his youth. And an army of short-story writers discovered unsuspected individual differences in America and Americans, and used the new technique of realism to record the local color of the mountains and the plantations and the towns of New England and the gold fields.

While literature played with its new real toys and economics completed its rape of the West, a few murmurs of dissatisfaction were heard. They were directed not against the new

[21]See Parrington, *op. cit.*, III, 203–11. See also B. J. Loewenberg's Harvard dissertation on the impact of evolution, published in part in the *New England Quarterly* (VIII, 232–57, June, 1935) under the title, "The Controversy over Evolution in New England, 1859–1873." The history of scientific thought in the America of 1865–95, and especially of evolutionary thought, has never been satisfactorily written, and deserves more attention. For the student, a good beginning is to be found in John Fiske's essay, "Darwinism Verified," in his *Darwinism and Other Essays* (Boston, 1879).

fashions in literature, but against the middle-class capitalism, the plutocracy that existed in the name of democracy. The spirit of Jefferson came to life again in a small but determined revolt by agrarian democrats of the Middle Border. Certain socialistic theories came from Europe and were rather timidly caught up. Mark Twain and Charles Dudley Warner wrote their sardonic portrait of *The Gilded Age*[22]—marvelous title! Edward Bellamy found time to describe a Utopia far different from the goal toward which American civilization seemed to be heading.[23] Hamlin Garland spoke bitterly of injustice to prairie farmers.[24] Edwin Markham's poem about the farmer was heard as the trumpet of an humanitarian crusade.[25]

Thus, with realism triumphant, with the frontier at an end, with a growing social disquiet and a growing distrust of the ruling theories of economics and government, the century drew toward an end. The great New England Romantics died off, one by one, and the pioneer realists passed their peaks and started the downward path. There were signs of something new on the horizon, indicated in literature by Garland, Markham, Hovey, and Crane. Meanwhile, the Standard Oil Company, Carnegie Steel, and Armour and Company continued to grow, and some Americans began to entertain imperialistic ideas.

From this America, for which he had little sympathy, Francis Parkman was taken in 1893, in the seventy-first year of his life. He had outlived the movements and most of the men for whom he felt real sympathy. In many points of view

[22]Published in 1873.

[23]Edward Bellamy, *Looking Backward, 2000–1887* (Boston, 1887). For discriminating discussion of fifty-odd utopian novels at the end of the century see Allyn Forbes, "The Literary Quest of Utopia, 1800–1900," *Social Forces*, VI, 179–89 (Dec., 1927).

[24]Hamlin Garland, *Main-Travelled Roads*, 1891; *Prairie Folks*, 1893; *Crumbling Idols*, 1893; *Other Main-Travelled Roads*, 1910.

[25]Edwin Markham, "The Man with the Hoe," published in the San Francisco *Examiner* and in his first volume, *The Man with the Hoe, and Other Poems* (New York, 1899).

he had felt akin to the romantic lovers of the glamorous and distant past—the Irving of *Granada*, the Prescott of *Mexico*, the Longfellow of *King Olaf*, the Hawthorne of "Endicott and the Red Cross," the Lew Wallace of *Ben-Hur*. But we shall see in later sections of this Introduction how he recoiled against most of the manifestations of the French romantic regime in America, how he borrowed its interest in the past, high colors, and dramatic events, and repudiated its humanitarian interest in the natural man, its faith in mysticism and natural goodness, its dislike of restraint. That part of him which was anti-romantic kept him from Motley's preoccupation with liberty, Prescott's capitulation to glamour, and Longfellow's romantic sentimentality (Parkman was disgusted by the inaccuracies in *Evangeline*). In fact, Parkman found himself much less in sympathy with romanticism than with the romantic survivors of a still earlier dispensation—the rational Federalism which found its chief expression during Parkman's day in the Brahmin mind of New England. His critical attitude toward the democracy of his age was akin to that of Holmes, the later Lowell, the Cooper of *The American Democrat*, the Bryant of the dignified editorials in the *Evening Post*, and Charles Eliot Norton. If we must put him in only one group, we must put him with those Brahmins of New England; and if we must connect him with only one movement in thought, that movement must be Federalism. But yet he was more than a Brahmin and a Federalist, and he was somewhat less Brahmin and Federalist than many who bore those names. To clarify his position in regard to fundamental questions is the province of the following sections of this Introduction.

II. THE RELATION OF HIS LIFE TO HIS WRITING

If Emerson had known Francis Parkman as well as we do, he might have found in Parkman an excellent illustration of the theory of compensations. For we do know Parkman even better than his contemporaries did,[26] thanks to the autobiographical letters that reticent man left behind him and to nearly half a century of biographical scholarship; and as the chorus of funereal and anniversary praise is succeeded by calmer judgments we begin to see that only half the truth has usually been told about Parkman's equipment for his lifework. We have done no more than justice to him when we have praised his gallant fight to complete his work in the face of almost insurmountable physical handicaps; on the other hand, we have done rather less than justice to Parkman scholarship when we have neglected to mention the elements in his physical, mental, and economic equipment which were so strongly on his side during that life struggle. In certain physical qualities he was far below the average man; in certain other physical qualities and in many mental, social, and economic qualities he was well above the average. Let us list debit against credit and see how the ledger balances.

Debit: His health. Exactly what was wrong with Parkman's health?

On the few occasions when he could be brought to speak of his ailments, he described the symptoms with great vividness and clarity. His "childhood was neither healthful nor buoyant."[27] Early in his life he was taken to the country for his health. During his senior year in college he sailed to Europe for his health. On the Oregon Trail he was attacked by dysentery; he counterattacked by starvation and will power—when "to have worn the airs of an invalid would certainly have been an indiscretion, since in that case a horse, a rifle, a pair of pistols, and a red shirt might have offered temptations too strong for aboriginal virtue."[28] He hunted buffalo on horseback, "over a

[26]For interesting examples, see the articles by Justin Winsor and John Fiske, *Atlantic Monthly*, LXXIII, 660–74.

[27]Autobiographical letter to Dr. George E. Ellis, 1868; most easily available in C. H. Farnham's *A Life of Francis Parkman*, p. 318—hereafter referred to as "Farnham."

[28]Letter to Ellis (Farnham, p. 324).

broken country, when, without the tonic of the chase, he could scarcely sit upright in his saddle." He won his fight, "gained rather than lost strength, while his horse was knocked up and his companion disconsolate with a painful cough." He returned in better condition, but "to the maladies of the prairie succeeded a suite of exhausting disorders, so reducing him that circulation at the extremities ceased, the light of the sun became insupportable, and a wild whirl possessed his brain, joined to a universal turmoil of the nervous system. . . . All collapsed, in short, but the tenacious strength of muscles hardened by long activity."

In 1851, an effusion of water on the knee added to his discomfort. After this, "a partial recovery was followed by a relapse, involving a close confinement of two years and a weakened and sensitive condition of the joint from which it . . . never recovered."[29] Then, "all the irritability of the system centred in the head. The most definite of the effects produced was one closely resembling the tension of an iron band, secured round the head and contracting with an extreme force, with the attempt to concentrate the thoughts, listen to reading, or at times to engage in conversation. This was, however, endurable in comparison with other forms of attack. . . . The brain was stimulated to a restless activity, impelling through it a headlong current of thought which, however, must be arrested and the irritated organ held in quiescence on a penalty to avert which no degree of exertion was too costly. The whirl, the confusion, and strange undefined torture attending this condition are only to be conceived by one who has felt them. Possibly they may have analogies in the savage punishment once in use in some of our prisons, where drops of water were made to fall from a height on the shaved head of the offender. . . ."[30]

[29] Letter to Ellis (Farnham, p. 328).
[30] *Ibid.*

Insomnia was another symptom. "Sleep, of course, was banished during the periods of attack,"[31] he said, and his sister reported that for him to sleep none at all at night was uncommon, to sleep about an hour was common, and, "by the aid of sulphonal, trional or some other hypnotic," it was sometimes possible for him to sleep four or five hours.[32]

His disorders reached two crises, in 1853 and 1858. "In the latter case it was about four years before the power of mental application was in the smallest degree restored." In 1868, he was able to write that for eighteen years he had been forced to observe "extreme caution" in regard to mental application, whenever he had been able to endure it at all. During all this time his eyes had seldom permitted reading or writing continuously for much more than five minutes, and often not at all.[33] Parkman fought like the good soldier he was. He constructed a grill—a frame with horizontal wires to guide his pencil—by means of which he could write in the dark. He employed countless copyists, readers, stenographers. He kept his notes in his head when necessary. When he was able to dictate only six lines a day, he forced himself to be content with that. When he was unable either to dictate or to listen, he betook himself to horticulture, returning to his twilit study when he was again able. For his gathering of material and his writing he used every minute when his tortured eyes and nerves would permit the activity, and yet he was able to say, in 1886, that, "Taking the last forty years as a whole, the capacity of literary work which during that time has fallen to my share has, I am confident, been considerably less than a fourth part of what it would have been under normal conditions."[34]

[31] *Ibid.*
[32] Miss Parkman's statement is quoted in George M. Gould, *Biographic Clinics*, II, 173.
[33] See evidence cited in Gould, *loc. cit.*
[34] Letter to Martin Brimmer, in H. D. Sedgwick, *Francis Parkman*, p. 338 (hereafter referred to as "Sedgwick").

To his wretched eyesight, his throbbing head, and his insomnia were added other discouraging infirmities[35]—palpitations of the heart, and rheumatism and arthritis which lamed him so that he was often able to walk only a few steps.[36] All these infirmities waxed and waned by cycles. At times he would be—to all outward appearance—wholly well. In general, his visual and nervous troubles lessened as he grew older, whereas the arthritis and rheumatism became progressively more troublesome.[37]

The attitude of the medical profession toward Parkman's maladies was not very reassuring. He whimsically described it: "Meanwhile the Faculty of Medicine were not idle, displaying that exuberance of resource for which that remarkable profession is justly famed. The wisest, indeed, did nothing, commending his patient to time and faith; but the activity of his brethren made full amends for this masterly inaction. One was for tonics, another for a diet of milk, one counselled galvanism, another hydropathy; one scarred him behind the neck

[35] See the letter to Dr. Silas Weir Mitchell, reproduced in Sedgwick, pp. 296–7.

[36] *Letters from Parkman to Squier*, ed. Don C. Seitz (1911), pp. 23–4 (letter of Oct. 15, 1849). Nothing was so hard for Parkman to bear as inactivity. His autobiographical letters and the two biographies, already referred to, are full of his craving for intense activity. When he was confined to a wheel chair, he still found means to exercise the upper part of his body; when he was attacked by arthritis and both legs and arms were crippled, he practiced deep breathing in bed.

[37] Parkman said little about his trouble. Only in his autobiographical letters, in his letters to such physicians as Silas Weir Mitchell (Sedgwick, pp. 296–7), all of which were revealed only after his death, and in an occasional letter to such a good friend as Squier (Seitz, *op. cit.*) did he speak of the symptoms or their effect on his life. To Squier he wrote: "My eyes I don't mind. I can get along without them, but to have one's brains stirred up in a mush, may be regarded as a decided obstacle in the way of intellectual achievements. Give me the tithe of a chance, and I will do it" (p. 22, letter of May 13, 1849). And again, "I can bear witness that no amount of physical pain is so intolerable as the position of being stranded and doomed to be rotting for year after year" (pp. 23–4). And in his earlier letter to Ellis he particularly described his enforced procedure as "combining the slowness of the tortoise with the uncertainty of the hare" (Farnham, p. 331).

with nitric acid, another drew red-hot irons along his spine with a view of enlivening that organ."[38] Opinion, he smilingly added, was as divergent as practice. One physician "said in a low and solemn voice that his duty required him to warn me that death would probably follow within six months";[39] another said he would recover in six years; and still another predicted that he would speedily go insane.[40] In other words, the medical profession did little or nothing to assuage Parkman's sorest physical tribulations.

Since Parkman's death there has been one medical study of his case, by Dr. George M. Gould, a well-known physician of Philadelphia.[41] Dr. Gould begins by discounting two of the most common explanations of Parkman's malady. It was not, he says, due to "inherited weakness," as both Parkman and his biographers so often declare;[42] a man can inherit only what his ancestors have, the Doctor says bluntly, and he was able to discover no hint of such maladies in Parkman's ancestors. In the second place, he scoffs at the idea that Parkman's health was ruined by the trip over the Oregon Trail.[43] "Parkman came home from the Oregon trip, essentially without any permanent injury," declares Dr. Gould. "His subsequent ill-health had nothing whatever to do with the hardships and temporary intestinal troubles of the outing among the Indians."[44] What, then, was the cause of the illness? Answers Dr. Gould: "The cause of all his succeeding illness (except of course the arthritis and rheumatism that came on later) . . . was

[38] Letter to Ellis (Farnham, p. 329).

[39] Sedgwick, p. 335.

[40] Farnham, pp. 317, 330.

[41] In an article published in the *Boston Medical and Surgical Journal*, Sept. 17 and 24 and Oct. 1, 1903. Reprinted as a chapter in *Biographic Clinics* (1904), II, 131–202.

[42] Parkman makes the statement in both the autobiographical letters. For an example of the biographers' opinion, see Farnham, p. 127.

[43] Farnham (p. 136): "The Oregon Trail trip thus cost Parkman his health for life."

[44] Gould, *op. cit.*, II, 142.

eyestrain."[45] Dr. Gould finds that Parkman had "a low degree of unsymmetric astigmatism and anisometropia,"[46] or, as he elsewhere states it, "hyperopic astigmatism, probably unsymmetrical,"[47] or again, "unsymmetric astigmatism, hyperopia of eyes different, probable difference in amount of astigmatism of two eyes."[48] This means, in nonmedical language, that Parkman was shortsighted, that he had a certain amount of fuzziness (astigmatism) in his sight, and that the amounts of shortsightedness and astigmatism were not the same in the two eyes.

Furthermore, says Dr. Gould, "this unsymmetric astigmatism and anisometropia was not corrected by any of the glasses that were ordered for him"[49] (i. e., any of the prescriptions which have been preserved). Therefore, "the effort of overcoming [this ocular condition] was so great and so expensive of nerve force that it resulted in the ocular and cerebral symptoms enumerated. The almost unexampled severity of these symptoms was exceptional, because of the heroic resolution of the man and his indomitable perseverance in his chosen work."[50]

If this explanation is true, it is a lamentable picture that Dr. Gould presents: Parkman suffering all his life, reducing his working time 75 per cent, merely because he was not given the right kind of glasses. Parkman's later biographers, however, have repeatedly shied away from Dr. Gould's diagnosis, and the medical profession, despite its traditional unwillingness to criticize one of its members before a popular audience, has been noticeably cool toward the book in which the diagnosis appears—a book which attempts to trace the maladies of

[45] *Ibid.* On pp. 173–7 Dr. Gould lists Parkman's symptoms which appear to point toward the diagnosis of eyestrain.
[46] Gould, *op. cit.*, II, 182.
[47] *Ibid.*, p. 184.
[48] *Ibid.*, p. 189.
[49] *Ibid.* Dr. Gould's statement is as quoted. He makes no allowance for the fact that undoubtedly not *all* the prescriptions and lenses were preserved.
[50] *Ibid.*, p. 190.

many famous men to faulty eyes. Dr. Gould's article on Parkman appeared first in 1903. In an effort to get a later interpretation of the facts, a well-known specialist in disorders of the
eyes, a man who has been honored by election to the American
College of Surgeons, was asked to re-examine the facts for this
book.[51] He did so not without reluctance, because, as he took
care to explain, it is somewhat unsatisfactory to diagnose an illness over the space of half a century and the distance of a good
many miles. When the pertinent facts were all before him,
however, he gave this report:

The preserved facts are insufficient for a positive diagnosis.
It is evident, however, that some aspects of the treatment of
the case are not sufficiently explained. For example, I have
never known a patient who with proper correction [eyeglasses]
could use his eyes for a few minutes a day, who could not use
them regularly. The described cerebral symptoms are probably
neurotic. Eyestrain is a possible explanation of these symptoms, but it is by no means the only possible explanation. None
of the corrections preserved indicate that Parkman's eyes were
bad enough to cause the cerebral symptoms he described.

The same facts were laid before a psychiatrist. He objected that
literary scholars seem to be the only people who want to
psychoanalyze a man after he is dead, but said that Parkman's
symptoms, such as the oppressive iron band around the head,
are common psychoneurotic manifestations, and that the cause of
the neurosis is hardly determinable at this distance and this date.

It may be suspected, then, that Dr. Gould's interpretation of
Parkman's malady in terms of eyestrain is somewhat too
simple. Whether the medical faculty of today could have done
more to relieve Parkman than did the physicians of his own
day is a question we should like but hesitate to answer in the

[51]He requested that his name, for obvious reasons, not be used with
this statement. With the assistance of the present writer, however, he is
planning a full-length study of the medical aspects of Parkman's case.

affirmative. The facts remain that in his own day Parkman solicited the best medical aid available and received almost no relief; that from his late adolescence until his death he was never wholly free from "the enemy," as he called it, which might take away his sight for a period of a few minutes or years, and which might make the mere act of thought the occasion for almost insupportable agony.

Credit: His physique. It is not quite true, however, to say that Parkman had "poor health." He had weak eyes and he had some neurotic symptoms, but he had a tough, wiry physique. Upon the first attack of "the enemy," he said, "all collapsed, in short, but the tenacious strength of muscles hardened by long activity."[52] Despite his attack of dysentery he bore the remarkable exertions on the Oregon Trail with better success than many of his companions. All through his life he was capable of the most strenuous activity. Even when his arthritis kept him in a wheel chair, he pushed the chair hither and yon, tending his flowers, sickling the grass, shooting at targets. He was quite unable to move slowly, mentally or physically; when he was walking with the aid of canes, he would sometimes hurry for a few steps, then stop for a second to recruit his strength. No, Parkman was no weakling. When he was past sixty he still loved to paddle a woodsman's canoe. J. M. Le Moine humorously described one incident late in Parkman's life:

Mr. Parkman pressed me to take a seat in his diminutive Rice Lake canoe, and return to camp with him some miles below the railway bridge, where I was: however, not being an expert swimmer, I had to decline the honor of being paddled through the furious eddies of the Batiscan by the most eminent historian of Massachusetts in a canoe evidently intended for one man only.[53]

[52] Letter to Ellis (Farnham, p. 324).
[53] J. M. Le Moine, "Reminiscences of Francis Parkman at Quebec," *Canadian Magazine*, III, 496 (Oct., 1894).

Parkman's last words, it is said, were to say that he had just dreamed of shooting a bear. And one of his most characteristic remarks, made when a friend expressed sympathy, was, "Damn it, I'm not feeble!"[54]

Credit: His intellect. It is almost unnecessary to say that Parkman was equipped with a brain amazingly keen, penetrating, retentive, and vigorous. It is perhaps more necessary to point out that the firmness and solidarity of his intellect kept him from following the predictions of some of his physicians and going insane under the mental strain of his malady.

Credit: His economic status. It was a fortunate thing for Parkman and his books that he inherited sufficient money to keep him in comfort. Just how much money he had, we do not know, but it was enough to let him devote all his time, when his health permitted, to his writing. Parkman never had to potboil; everything he wrote he could be serious about. He never had to work all day for someone else and steal spare time in the evening for his own writing. He had sufficient money for education, a great deal of travel both in Europe and America, and the limited social contacts he was interested in. He could afford the great expense of having manuscripts copied in little-accessible libraries, and he could buy the books he needed. He could hire persons to be his eyes and fingers, when he needed them. He could afford sometimes to have his own books set up in type before he sold them to a publisher. He was never a rich man, even when royalties increased, but he was virtually free from economic worry. With a perfectly clear conscience, he could make writing his main business.

Credit: Right emotional and volitional structure. It sounds suspiciously like second-guessing to say that Parkman was ideally constituted to be an historian. Yet, if we could make to order an historian of France's and England's struggle for the New World we should have to make his emotional line-

[54] Quoted in Farnham, p. 237.

up and his qualities of will much like Parkman's. We should have to reproduce Parkman's love for the outdoors, for the wilderness, for the past, especially the dramatic past. We should have to reproduce his perseverance, thoroughness, untiring ambition; his insatiable desire for truth; his capacity for making friends of the people he needed to help him; his calm, cheerful temper in the face of discouragements. In these respects, Parkman was ideally equipped for the task he had in mind.

Credit: Favorable reflexes from his poor health. One more credit we have to record on our ledger. The maladies which took Parkman's eyes from him and racked his head with torture were not an unmixed disadvantage. It is unquestionably true that his books improved as he grew older. His illness, by retarding his labors and requiring fifty years for work which he thought would take twenty, deepened his experience before writing and lengthened the years before publication. His enforced leisure gave him time for planning and contemplation that many incessantly active men neglect. The malady provoked him, but it made him write slowly, and slow writing is careful writing. When a man can write but six lines a day he is very likely to write six good lines.

Thus our ledger adds up. To Parkman the things we have mentioned may have been poor compensation for the mental delays and physical torture he suffered, but we, who have read his books, feel that in the final result his illness was not uncompensated.

The second biographical element which affected Parkman's writing was the amazing depth and thoroughness of his preparation.

Parkman was fortunate in his early choice of vocation and subject matter. "Before the end of my sophomore year," he wrote to Martin Brimmer, "my various schemes had crystallized into a plan of writing the story of what was thus known as the

'Old French War;' that is, the war that ended in the conquest
of Canada; for here, as it seemed to me, the forest drama was
more stirring and the forest stage more thronged with appropriate actors than in any other passage of our history. It was
not till some years later that I enlarged the plan to include the
whole course of the American conflict between France and
England; or, in other words, the history of the American forest;
for this was the light in which I regarded it. My theme fascinated me, and I was haunted with wilderness images day and
night."[55] Even before this, he had shown signs of his inclination. At "the critical age of fifteen . . . a complete change"[56]
came over him; he abandoned his boyish chemical experiments
in favor of books and the first-hand study of the backwoods,
and soon the backwoods "mixed itself with all my literary
aspirations."[57] This new passion, he remarks, "was no doubt
traceable in part to fond recollections of the Middlesex Fells,
as well as to one or two journeys which I was permitted to
make into some of the wilder parts of New England."[58] L. H.
Vincent even suggests (somewhat naïvely) that Parkman's interest in the Indian may have been inherited from Puritan
ancestors like John Cotton, and it is true that two of his maternal
ancestors used to preach to the Indians in their native tongues.[59]
Be this as it may, we may be certain that by his second year in
college he had decided upon his lifework, and that even earlier
he had begun, whether or not conscious of his goal, to prepare
himself for that work.[60]

Once set upon his task, he wasted no opportunity to fit
himself for it. His college mates noticed that he had "Injuns

[55] Letter to Brimmer (Sedgwick, pp. 328–9).
[56] *Ibid.*, p. 328.
[57] *Ibid.*
[58] *Ibid.*
[59] See L. H. Vincent, *American Literary Masters*, p. 379.
[60] An interesting angle on Parkman's choice of his life work is to be
found in the hero's similar problem in Parkman's novel, *Vassall Morton*,
pp. 36–8.

on the brain."[61] Even when he was a junior in college he was listing names of books which he must read as soon as possible to familiarize himself with the vast field of Anglo-French relations in America—books on the Jesuits, the prairies, the West, *Frontier Life in '44*. He accepted every opportunity to visit the scenes of battles and explorations, and he tried to harden his muscles and increase his resistance against a life of rigorous mental and physical effort. At this time and later, he sought to prepare himself in four general ways: by developing his physique, by improving his technique of literary composition, by assiduously collecting and reading everything bearing on the subject, and by traveling, whenever possible, to the places he wrote about. Let us consider these preparations, one by one.

On those few occasions when Parkman talked about himself he was always his own best spokesman. Thus, in 1886 he wrote to Martin Brimmer: "Two ideas possessed me. One was . . . to realize a certain ideal of manhood, a little mediæval, but nevertheless good. Feeling that I fell far short of it, I proceeded in extreme dissatisfaction to apply heroic remedies. I held the creed that the more hard knocks a man gets, whether in mind or body, the better for him, provided always that he takes them without flinching; and as the means of forcing myself up to the required standard, I put my faith in persistent violence which I thought energy. I held that the true aim of life was not happiness but achievement; had profound respect for physical strength and hardihood when joined with corresponding qualities of character; took pleasure in any moderate hardship, scorned invalidism of all kinds, and was full of the notion, common enough with boys of a certain sort, that the body will always harden and toughen with exercise and exposure. I remember to have had a special aversion for the Rev. Dr. Channing, not for his heresies, but for his meager proportions, sedentary habits, environment of close air and female parish-

[61] Vincent, *op. cit.*, p. 380.

ioners, and his preachments of the superiority of mind over matter; for, while I had no disposition to gainsay his proposition in the abstract, it was a cardinal point with me that while the mind remains a habitant of earth, it cannot dispense with a sound material basis, and that to neglect and decry the corporeal part in the imagined interest of the spiritual is proof of a nature either emasculate or fanatical. For my own part, instead of neglecting, I fell to lashing and spurring it into vigor and prosperity."[62]

How he lashed and spurred is indicated in the autobiographical letter of 1868. In the belief, he says, that "discipline sufficiently unsparing would harden him into an athlete, he slighted the precautions of a more reasonable woodcraft, tired old foresters with long marches, stopped neither for heat nor rain, and slept on the earth without a blanket."[63] His biographers and reminiscent friends have filled in the outline.[64] Harvard established a gymnasium during Parkman's student days, and the future historian was tremendously enthusiastic over the new possibilities for physical development. He worked on the apparatus for long periods every day. The riding school provided another training to which he could give himself wholeheartedly.[65] He practiced shooting at birds and small animals. In fact, after his first year at Harvard he seems to have been considerably more interested in these informal aspects of education than in the proceedings of the classrooms.[66] By the time he started over the Oregon Trail he was a good rider and a good shot, and his muscles were sinewy and tough.[67]

[62]Letter to Brimmer (Sedgwick, pp. 329–30).
[63]Letter to Ellis (Farnham, pp. 320–1).
[64]For example, see Farnham, p. 52.
[65]He practiced riding under the direction of a former manager of a circus. See Edward Wheelwright's life of Parkman in *History of the Harvard Class of 1844;* see also Farnham, p. 130.
[66]See Farnham, pp. 75–6, and Parkman's own statement to Brimmer, quoted in Sedgwick, p. 332.
[67]For Prescott's similar physical preparations, see Rollo Ogden, *William Hickling Prescott* (Boston, 1904), p. 45.

Furthermore, he had that familiarity with nature that comes not only from the study of textbooks (zoology was one of his adolescent hobbies) but, even more, from long association with and love for nature. When he was but a boy, the flora and fauna of the Middlesex Fells were his tutors, and when he was at Harvard he went to school to the rock cliffs of the White Mountains and the gentler hills of Massachusetts.[68] In most men, as he sadly remarks, this sort of life would have resulted in magnificent health.[69]

Parkman was "a quiet, gentle, and docile boy," reported his teacher, Thomas Cushing.[70] He "seemed to appreciate the fact that school meant an opportunity for improvement, and always gave an open and willing mind to instruction. He became, according to the ideas of the day, a good Latin and Greek scholar, and excelled in the rhetorical department. I think he early set his face in the direction of a literary life of some sort, though the idea of *historical* work was probably developed somewhat later. As a means to any sort of literary work, he no doubt saw the advantage and necessity of forming a good English style and acquiring correctness in the use of language, and took great pains with all exercises tending to bring about this result. His compositions were especially good, and he used sometimes as a voluntary exercise to versify descriptions of heroic achievements that occurred in his reading. I remember that he put into verse the whole description of the Tournament in Scott's 'Ivanhoe,' and then used it afterwards in declamation, and it was so much liked that other boys used it for the same purpose. I think he might have excelled in narrative and descriptive poetry (the poetry of action) had he not early imbibed the historical idea."

Parkman gave the credit rather to William Russell than to Cushing. In a book on *The Art of Authorship*, published in

[68] For Parkman's thrilling account of one experience on those cliffs see the passage from his diary quoted in Farnham, pp. 54–7.

[69] For example, see the letter to Ellis (Farnham, p. 322).

[70] Wheelwright, *op. cit.*; also quoted in Farnham, pp. 72–3.

1890, Parkman is quoted as saying: "When fourteen or fifteen years old I had the good luck to be under the direction of Mr. William Russell, a teacher of excellent literary tastes and acquirements. It was his constant care to teach the boys of his class to write good and easy English. One of his methods was to give us lists of words to which we were required to furnish as many synonyms as possible, distinguishing their various shades of meaning. He also encouraged us to write translations, in prose and verse, from Virgil and Homer, insisting on idiomatic English, and criticising in his gentle way anything flowery and bombastic. At this time I read a good deal of poetry, and much of it remains verbatim in my memory. As it included Milton and other classics, I am confident that it has been of service to me in the matter of style. Later on, when in college and after leaving it, I read English prose classics for the express purpose of improving myself in the language. These I take to be the chief sources of such success as I have had in this particular."[71]

From these accounts we can piece together the process. Parkman learned the rules of the language, probably as much by studying Latin and Greek as from studying English grammar. He had the usual vocabulary drill. Like Franklin, he practiced turning prose into verse.[72] Like several centuries of English writers, he learned the bounds of his own language by translating from the Latin and Greek. He wrote a great deal— verse and fiction, as well as nonfiction. He practiced declamation, and thus learned the sound of his periods. He had the benefit of wise (and gentle) criticism by a man who disliked flowery, bombastic, artificial writing. He read, and remem-

[71]George Bainton, comp., *The Art of Authorship, personally contributed by leading authors of the day* (New York, 1890), pp. 181–2; quoted in part in Farnham, pp. 73–4.

[72]See Franklin's *Autobiography*, in the volume on Franklin edited by F. L. Mott and C. E. Jorgenson for the American Writers Series, pp. 14–15, and the Introduction to the same volume, pp. xlvi–lvi.

bered, a great deal of the best English poetry. And he read English prose classics as models.

What prose and poetry did he read? His chief biographer remarks that Burke is said to have been his chief model for style.[73] Bliss Perry[74] is inclined to emphasize his early immersion in the literature of the Romantic Movement—Byron, Scott, Chateaubriand, Cooper—and it is an old story that when Quincy Shaw offered Parkman his choice of three books to read at Fort Laramie in 1846—the Old Testament, Shakespeare, and Byron—Parkman chose what he said was "the worst of the three."[75] Furthermore, it is known that *Childe Harold* was the last book he read before his death. It would seem, therefore, that he was thoroughly grounded in the romantic books of his age. From Scott, says Professor Perry, Parkman learned his genius for verbal portrait-painting, picturesque grouping, and dramatic narrative. From other romantics he learned to use natural images. But his reading was by no means confined to romantic books. The quotations which head the chapters in *Vassall Morton* show a familiarity with every century of English literature from Shakespeare's century to his own.[76] In his own writing he combined the volatile dynamism of the Romantics with the solider eighteenth-century qualities of Burke, and both with a respect for the truly fine in Shakespeare, Milton, and the other older classics.

[73] Farnham, p. 74.
[74] "Some Personal Qualities of Parkman," *Yale Review*, N.S. VIII, 443–8.
[75] *Oregon Trail*, p. 345: "I chose the worst of the three [Byron], and for the greater part of that day I lay on the buffalo-robes, fairly revelling in the creations of that resplendent genius which has achieved no more signal triumph than that of half beguiling us to forget the unmanly character of its possessor." (References to Parkman's works through this Introduction are to the New Library Edition, 1902–3, which reprints the material as it stood at the time of Parkman's death. Several other editions were printed from the same plates, notably the Pocket Parkman and the Centenary Edition.)
[76] See O. B. Frothingham's sketch of Parkman in *Proceedings of the Massachusetts Historical Society*, 2d series, VIII, 520–62, for a good statement on Parkman's reading.

Parkman much preferred the woods to the libraries. When he saw that his purpose required "an unwearied delving into dusty books and papers, a kind of work which I detested," he came to "the agreeable yet correct conclusion that the time for this drudgery was not come." His first business, he felt, was to impregnate himself with his theme, fill his mind with impressions from real life, "range the woods, mix with Indians and frontiersmen, visit the scenes of the events" he meant to describe, and so bring himself as near as might be to the times with which he meant to deal.[77] This he did, joyfully and thoroughly, but when the biographical labor could no longer be postponed, when the time came that he needed documents, he abandoned the forests and the ancient battlefields and buried himself in libraries and archives.

The assiduousness with which this outdoors man collected materials is one of the marvels of scholarship. When Parkman began his study of the conflict in America, says George Willis Cooke in a magazine article, "the whole field . . . had been but little explored. . . . A few volumes of documents had been published by the state of New York, and some other labors of the same kind had been here and there undertaken; but for the most part no one had preceded him."[78] The materials were known to be rich and abundant. Letters, reports, state papers, reminiscences were available in countless libraries, public and private, American and European, and in dozens of dusty government depositories. But how to ferret them out, copy them, and fuse them into the whole scheme of his history? "He has made repeated visits to France," said George E. Ellis, "for the examination of the manuscript collections of the French government, in the national archives, the national library, and the archives of the Marine and the Colonies, with other public and

---

[77]Letter to Brimmer (Sedgwick, pp. 330–1).
[78]G. W. Cooke, "Francis Parkman," *New England Magazine*, N.S. I, 257.

many private places of deposit for valuable documents, and has sought out in the interior of the realm and its ancient seaport every trace and relic of those of whom he has made record in his pages. The journals, official relations, and private letters of the Jesuit Fathers, of the military and civil functionaries in Canada, and the correspondence of governors, intendants, and ecclesiastical dignitaries with the king and the ministry, have been brought into his service. . . . Other sources of information there are in Canadian repositories, civil and ecclesiastical, French, English and Dutch documents, which have been copied from foreign archives . . . existing still in manuscript or printed with more or less careful editing."[79]

Evidences of his industry are his books. In a more direct way, the evidence is the Parkman collection of the Massachusetts Historical Society, about seventy thick volumes, most of them folios. In these books Parkman bound the documents and copies of documents which he collected from all over the world, studied, evaluated, penciled "used" on the margin, and presented to the keeping of the Society. Seventy large volumes of original documents, wholly apart from printed records! Or, for another direct evidence, turn to the introductions and notes to his books. Thus he described the preparation of *Pontiac:* "The most troublesome part of the task was the collection of the necessary documents. These consisted of letters, journals, reports, and despatches, scattered among numerous public offices and private families in Europe and America. When brought together, they amounted to about *three thousand four hundred manuscript pages.* Contemporary newspapers, magazines, and pamphlets have also been examined, and careful search made for every book which, directly or indirectly, might throw light upon the subject. I have visited the sites of all the principal events recorded in the narrative, and gathered

[79]Remarks at a special meeting of the Massachusetts Historical Society, November, 1893 (*Proceedings*, 2d series VIII, 347–8).

such local traditions as seemed worthy of confidence."[80] "Like the rest of the series, this work is founded on original documents," he said in the preface to his last work. "The statements of secondary writers have been accepted only when found to conform to the evidence of contemporaries, whose writings have been sifted and collated with the greatest care."[81] And when he came to write of the siege of Louisbourg he could say, in a note to his chapter, that he had before him as he wrote:[82]

(1) Four long and minute French diaries of the siege,

(2) Numerous letters from the principal officers, military, naval, and civil engaged in the defense,

(3) Chief printed authorities on the French side,

(4) Chief authorities on the English side (including Amherst's journal, letters of Amherst to Pitt, Wolfe's correspondence, and two private journals),

(5) The diary of a captain or subaltern in the army of Amherst, and

(6) Plans of the siege operations.

To this material he added, of course, personal observation of the site and a thorough historical background for the events about which he wrote.

Many documents were distant, expensive, difficult of access, hard to interpret, but the most disappointing situation occurred when Parkman knew where the documents were but was forbidden to use them. Such was his experience with Margry. Parkman tells it with admirable restraint in his preface to the eleventh edition of *La Salle*.[83] Pierre Margry was director of the Archives of Marine and Colonies at Paris. For more than thirty years he had been collecting documentary material, both from his own archives and elsewhere, dealing with the early French explorers and especially with La Salle. Apparently he

[80] *Pontiac*, I, x–xi. (Italics supplied.)
[81] *A Half-Century of Conflict*, I, v.
[82] *Montcalm and Wolfe*, II, 85–6, note.
[83] *La Salle*, pp. vii–x.

had no intention of writing any history based upon these documents, but he wanted to publish the documents themselves, and he therefore refused Parkman permission to make use of his collection which was, says Parkman, of "extraordinary richness." Parkman knew that the collection contained the letters of La Salle and the narrative of his companion Joutel. This material, when it was published, might completely change his interpretation of La Salle. Should he write the book upon what information he had, or should he wait until Margry published his documents, if he ever did? Margry was adamant. He was unable to find a publisher for his book, but he would not release the material. Regretfully, Parkman wrote his book without Margry's documents.

Meanwhile, he was trying to find a publisher for Margry's book. A tentative arrangement with Little, Brown, and Company was not carried through because the United States were in a period of financial stress and a sufficient number of patrons could not be assured. An attempt to secure an appropriation from Congress failed in 1870 and 1871. Several years later the appeal to Congress was renewed, and that body set aside money to cover the purchase of 500 copies. After the usual delay of several years, the work finally appeared—three volumes devoted to La Salle, two to other explorers. Parkman warmly congratulated Margry and patiently set about rewriting *La Salle*. He published the revised edition in 1878, nine years after the first edition. The new materials, he was proud to say, "while they add new facts and throw new light on the character of La Salle, confirm nearly every statement made in the first edition." [84]

Parkman's thoroughness was evident not alone in his search for documentary evidence, but in his pursuit of every kind of information which bore on his subject. He sent his young

[84] See also Parkman's own story of his fifteen-year search for Montcalm's letters to Bourlamaque, quoted in Farnham, p. 178.

cousin, Coolidge Shaw, who had been recently converted to Catholicism and was studying in Rome for the priesthood, on a search for information about the history of the Society of Jesus.[85] He wrote this remarkable note to an eminent astronomer: "I believe there is a difference between the way of estimating latitude in the seventeenth century and now. Can you without much trouble tell me how this is? In 1685 La Salle calculated a certain point on the Gulf of Mexico at 28° 18′. What would this correspond to on a modern map? How can I ascertain if a comet—a somewhat remarkable one—was visible from the site of Peoria, Illinois, in January, 1681? Also, how can I ascertain on what day of the month Easter Monday, 1680, occurred? I want the information to test the accuracy of certain journals in my possession."[86] This was from the man who, twenty years before, had thoroughly detested the prospect of "delving into dusty books and papers"![87]

Faced with the evidence of such prodigious energy devoted to the collection of historical materials, we are amazed at three things: first, that he was able to maintain the almost fanatical quest for so many years in the face of so many physical and political handicaps; secondly, that, having gathered materials from so many sources, he was able to evaluate them, digest them, and weave them into a smooth, jointless historical narrative; and thirdly, that he, a nearly blind and otherwise sorely afflicted man, was able to accomplish the work of studying, weighting, and organizing so much material. Solutions to the first two of these problems died with Parkman, but we may profitably consider the third one.

A blind man, declared Dr. Johnson in his life of Milton, can not write history. Of course, the good Doctor was wrong: Thierry, Prescott, and Parkman all proved him wrong. But

---

[85] See Sedgwick, pp. 141–2.
[86] Quoted in Farnham, pp. 177–8.
[87] Letter to Brimmer (Sedgwick, p. 330).

it is unquestionably true that an historian without his eyes is like a one-handed ballplayer. Parkman had to hire readers. Some of these were unfamiliar with the languages of the documents. The prospect of a schoolgirl employed by the hour to read Old French documents to an eminent historian, when she had never studied even modern French, has its humorous sides—although they were doubtless more humorous for the bystanders than for the historian who was straining all his attention to understand what words lay behind the girl's weird pronunciation. To his good friend Squier, Parkman wrote in 1851: "Go to work at consulting fifteen hundred books in five different languages with the help of a school girl who hardly knows English and you will find it a bore: add to this the infantile music in the next room and you will agree that my iniquities have as good a chance of being atoned for as yours."[88]

Of Parkman's mental processes, of his method of organizing and planning, we know almost nothing. There is not a single outline among his papers, and, as far as we know, he never used an outline. But we do know how he worked in libraries and how he assimilated the documents at home.[89] When he visited archives or libraries he would take with him a reader who would read aloud the documents the titles of which sounded interesting. Parkman would take notes or order sections copied. Terrific waste of time! With his own eyes he could have scanned the manuscript at a glance and picked out the pertinent matter; without the use of his eyes, he had to listen carefully to every paragraph. Of course, he himself was not able to visit all the libraries; therefore, he maintained clerical assistants in Paris, London, and Quebec, and these persons kept a stream of

[88]Seitz, *op. cit.*, pp. 37–8 (letter of Sept. 17, 1851). It is, of course, true that no man can ever learn everything there is to know about an event in the past. And it is also true that later discoveries have modified some of Parkman's conclusions, as, for instance, his treatment of the Acadian events. But we may confidently say that he examined every source of information which was known and accessible in his own day.

[89]For a good discussion of these matters, see Farnham, pp. 170–7.

manuscripts—at great expense to Parkman—flowing back to Boston. Back in his dim study, Parkman would assemble the documents and hear them read, once, twice, sometimes three times, noting the location of essential facts and pondering the meaning of what he had heard. When he was ready to write a book he had all the pertinent materials read to him, pacing up and down in the darkened end of the study while the reader sat under the light. Occasionally, Parkman would stride over to the reader to put a cryptic mark—an X or cross bars—on the margin beside something that had just been read. His documents contain almost no verbal notes, only the marginal marks and the word "used." When he had digested the matter of the documents, he was ready to write. Sometimes six lines a day, sometimes more, according to his health, he dictated to one of his family, and the shelf of his works slowly lengthened over the space of fifty years. In the last years of his life his sight improved so much that he was able to write a great deal of *Montcalm and Wolfe* and *A Half-Century* with his own hand; his other books, from *The Oregon Trail* through *Frontenac*, were written almost entirely by the hands of others.

In the preface to his first historical work, Parkman had said proudly that he had "visited the sites of all the principal events recorded in the narrative." He could have said the same for every book he wrote. But he traveled for many other reasons. He made himself thoroughly familiar with American forests and lakes and rivers, with forest life and river travel. He met nature at first hand and the Indian at first hand. Furthermore, he visited almost every depository in Europe and America where he might expect to find useful documentary evidence. Seven times he went to Europe; more times to Canada.[90]

---

[90] A biography or such a chronological table as has been affixed to this study gives a very inadequate idea of how much Parkman really traveled. It may be useful, therefore, to set down here a brief record of his principal trips:

1841. First trip to the wilderness, with Slade, passing through Portsmouth to Alton, along Lake Winnipesaukee to Centre Harbor; on to the

What was the importance to his writing of all this traveling? Disregarding the importance of the documents he brought back, the travel was justified if it did no more than make his books live. Perhaps better than any other American historian, Parkman was able to visualize the scenes and events he wrote about. He had been on the ground; he had been able to imagine how Braddock's men felt, and Amherst's, and Wolfe's, and how the Mississippi looked first to Joliet and La Salle. He had tramped the battlefields of Louisbourg and Quebec, and knew where the troops stood at every minute of the fight. He could draw in the backgrounds, so that his histories are not only of men, but of men performing in their proper stage setting. Some of his most glamorous pages are results of his direct experience with the country he writes about. Such, among others, are the brilliant description of the flight of escaped prisoners through

---

Notch and up Mount Washington; to Franconia Notch, Lancaster, Colebrook, Dixville Notch, to the Androscoggin river near the mouth of the Magalloway, up this river to its junction with the Little Magalloway.

1842. Second trip to the Magalloway, with White. Through Albany, Saratoga, Glens Falls to Lake George. After studying the battlefields about Caldwell they hired a rowboat, camped a week along shores of the lake. At Sabbath Day Point gathered traditions of the region from old Revolutionary pensioner, Captain Patchen. Careful examination of Ticonderoga, crossed Lake Champlain to Burlington, walk to Canada, and headwaters of the Magalloway. Through Essex, Jericho, Underhill, Cambridge, Johnson, Troy, Stanstead, Barnston, Canaan, finally to Connecticut Lake.

1843. Canadian trip for historical materials, examining battlefields of Lake George and Lake Champlain, on to St. Johns, Chambly, and Montreal. Gathered notes on the Hope Gate and other important localities at Quebec. Back through White Mountains, noted stories of frontier life and border warfare. Studied Indians near Bangor and traditions of Mohawk wars. In September sailed for Europe—Sicily, Italy, Switzerland, France, Great Britain.

1844. Tramped alone with rifle over hills of western Massachusetts to study the routes followed by the French and Indians in their attacks on that region. Through Springfield, Cabotville (Chicopee), Chester Factory, Lee, Stockbridge, Great Barrington, Lebanon Springs, Stephentown, the Hopper, and North Adams.

1845. Focus on *Pontiac*. In April, trip to St. Louis, collecting materials. Visited Lancaster, Paradise, Harrisburg, Williamsport, Trout Run, Blossburg, Corning, Seneca Lake, Rochester, Buffalo, Detroit, Windsor, Sandwich, Mackinaw, Sault Ste. Marie, Palmer, Newport, Niagara, the

the forest in *Pontiac;*[91] the journey to the Mississippi in *La Salle;*[92] the several descriptions of that lake he particularly loved, Lake George. In a later edition of *The Old Régime in Canada* he was able to insert this sly footnote after a picture of the wilderness: "An adverse French critic gives as his opinion that the sketch of the primeval wilderness on the preceding page is drawn from fancy, and not from observation. It is, however, copied in every particular, without exception, from a virgin forest in a deep moist valley by the upper waters of the little river Pemigewasset in northern New Hampshire, where I

Devil's Hole, Fort Niagara, Oswego, Syracuse, Onondaga Castle. Noted scenery of historic places, examined family papers and other documents. Interviewed descendants of historic characters.

1846. The Oregon expedition; lived some weeks with band of Sioux. Winter—trip through Pennsylvania, visiting Trenton, Philadelphia, Washington, Baltimore, Harrisburg, Carlisle, Chambersburg, Pittsburgh. By the close of 1846 he had seen most of remnants of Indian tribes to be found between Maine and the Rocky Mountains, visited localities connected with his theme, gathered what could be procured of family papers, traditions, besides official and published documents.

1856. Trip to Montreal, Quebec, Nova Scotia.

1858–59. In Paris. Some investigations in the archives, arranging for copying of documents.

1865. Visited battlefields, Washington, Richmond. Brought back valuable papers to Boston Athenaeum.

1866. Journey to Montreal. Two Mountains, the Long Sault, the Chaudière; to Quebec to study scenes connected with Wolfe's attack.

1867. Journey to Fort Snelling to see Indians, visiting Keokuk, Peoria, Illinois River, Prairie du Chien, St. Louis.

1868. Winter, abroad. Some research.

1872. To Europe for historical materials.

1873. Visited several families living on seigniories along shores of St. Lawrence below Quebec, to gain personal knowledge of French Canadian people.

1877. Explored region between Lake George and Quebec, studying battlefields along route.

1879. In Quebec and Louisburg.

1880, 1881. Summer trips to Europe to get historical material.

1885. Journey to Florida to examine places of historic interest; stopping at Beaufort, South Carolina; on to Fernandina, Jacksonville, Fort George, Palatka, Ocklawaha river, Ocala, and St. Augustine.

1886. Month of camping on Batiscan River.

1887. Last journey to Europe.

[91] *Pontiac*, II, 99–102.

[92] *La Salle*, p. 64.

spent a summer afternoon a few days before the passage was written."[93]

To Francis Parkman, in the course of his preparation, came one of the grandest adventures a historian ever had. He tells of it in a note to *La Salle*. Until his time, nothing was known of the site of a great town of the Illinois Indians which played an important part in the early history of the Mississippi valley. At one time thousands of Indians had lived there; but every trace had apparently vanished with them. Parkman read the original documents of men like La Salle and Joliet and made a mental image of how the site of the town should look and about where it should be. Then he went to Utica, Illinois. But let him tell the story:

"On the way down from the hill I met Mr. James Clark, the principal inhabitant of Utica, and one of the earliest settlers of this region. I accosted him, told him my objects, and requested a half hour's conversation with him, at his leisure. He seemed interested in the inquiry, and said he would visit me early in the evening at the inn, where, accordingly, he soon appeared. The conversation took place in the porch, where a number of farmers and others were gathered. I asked Mr. Clark if any Indian remains were found in the neighborhood. 'Yes,' he replied, 'plenty of them.' I then inquired if there was any one spot where they were more numerous than elsewhere. 'Yes,' he answered again, pointing towards the farmhouse on the meadow; 'on my farm down yonder by the river, my tenant ploughs up teeth and bones by the peck every spring, besides arrowheads, beads, stone hatchets, and other things of that sort.' I replied that this was precisely what I had expected, as I had been led to believe that the principal town of the Illinois Indians once covered that very spot. 'If,' I added, 'I am right in this belief, the great rock beyond the river is the one which the first explorers occupied as a fort; and I can describe it to you

[93]*Old Régime*, pp. 378–9.

from their accounts of it, though I have never seen it, except from the top of the hill where the trees on and around it prevented me from seeing any part but the front.' The men present now gathered around to listen. 'The rock,' I continued, 'is nearly a hundred and fifty feet high, and rises directly from the water. The front and two sides are perpendicular and inaccessible; but there is one place where it is possible for a man to climb up, though with difficulty. The top is large enough and level enough for houses and fortifications.' Here several of the men exclaimed: 'That's just it.' 'You've hit it exactly.' I then asked if there was any other rock on that side of the river which could answer to the description. They all agreed that there was no such rock on either side, along the whole length of the river. I then said: 'If the Indian town was in the place where I suppose it to have been, I can tell you the nature of the country which lies behind the hills on the farther side of the river, though I know nothing about it except what I have learned from writings nearly two centuries old. From the top of the hills, you look out upon a great prairie reaching as far as you can see, except that it is crossed by a belt of woods, following the course of a stream which enters the main river a few miles below.' 'You are exactly right again,' replied Mr. Clark; 'we call that belt of timber the "Vermilion Woods," and the stream is the Big Vermilion.' 'Then,' I said, 'the big Vermilion is the river which the French called the Aramoni; "Starved Rock" is the same on which they built a fort called St. Louis in the year 1682; and your farm is on the site of the great town of the Illinois.'"[94]

III. HIS THEORY OF HISTORICAL WRITING

With his admirable resolution to write history, not write *about* it, Francis Parkman never recorded in any essay, criticism, or apologia his theory of how history should be written. Yet

[94] *La Salle*, pp. 239-41.

anyone who is familiar with Parkman's works can guess what that theory must have been. It must have been compounded of two passions: a passion for *the truth* (and Parkman meant the whole truth and nothing but the truth, about whatever subject may have been under consideration); and a passion for clear, realistic expression of that truth, in a manner dignified but vivid. This was the recipe he used for his own books, and it must have been the recipe he would have recommended to others.

But "must have been" is shifting sand on which to reconstruct a man's belief. We can do better than that by examining the prefaces to Parkman's books, his occasional critical comments, and his reviews. The last, especially, deserve our attention. It has almost been forgotten that Parkman reviewed new historical books for at least four Eastern periodicals[95] from his twenties until the last few years of his life. Many of these reviews are excellent in themselves, and all are important for their bearing on Parkman's thought and taste. By examining these reviews, side by side with other important pronouncements, and by isolating the characteristics which Parkman approved of and those he did not approve of, it is possible to formulate Parkman's theory of historical writing almost entirely in his own words.

While Parkman would doubtless have been the last man to insist that an historian should write only the history of his own country, there is a significant nationalism in his comments about subject matter. He praised Cooper because his work springs from the "deep rich soil"[96] of America. He lamented that "the highest civilization of America is communicated from without instead of being developed from within, and is therefore nerveless and unproductive."[97] The tone of the fine review

[95] *Christian Examiner, Atlantic Monthly, North American Review, Nation.*
[96] *North American Review,* LXXIV, 160. See also the comparison of English and American scenery in his diary, quoted in Sedgwick, pp. 117–18.
[97] *North American Review, loc. cit.,* p. 161.

of Cooper and the emphasis on knowledge of the subject and
background in all the reviews implied plainly that Americans
should write of America. And although Parkman justly
praised Prescott and Motley, his own choice of an American
theme is significant in view of the well-known fact that Prescott
purposely shied away from such a theme.[98] Parkman was thus
inclined probably not because of any militant nationalism, but
because of his insistence on accuracy and exact information. A
man can write a better history of a country if he is familiar with
its people, its geography, customs, and traditions. One should
write about what he knows best.

In *The Book of Roses* Parkman gave horticulturists a piece
of advice which he might also have applied to historians:
"Never attempt to do any thing which you are not prepared to
do thoroughly. A little done well is far more satisfactory than
a great deal done carelessly and superficially."[99]

In the preceding section we have seen the almost fanatical
character of Parkman's own pursuit of historical sources. It is
not surprising, therefore, that his first attack on the books he
reviews should concern the adequacy of their documentation.
He was glad to report that "M. Girouard has been untiring in
research."[100] He admired H. H. Bancroft's herculean work in
collecting native material from the Pacific slopes.[101] Charlevoix's
research was "thorough and tolerably exact."[102] In another case,
the author was "very zealous, and no less successful, in collecting material."[103]

How much does the author know of his subject? was always
his first question. He took pains, of course, to be sure that the
author had used first-hand sources. He exceedingly regretted

[98] See H. T. Peck, *William Hickling Prescott* (English Men of Letters
series), p. 50; and Rollo Ogden, *William Hickling Prescott*, pp. 82–3.
[99] *Book of Roses*, p. 53. See also Sedgwick, p. 236.
[100] *Nation*, LVII, 201, Sept. 14, 1893.
[101] *North American Review*, CXX, 34–47.
[102] *Atlantic Monthly*, XX, 125.
[103] *Atlantic Monthly*, XIX, 384.

M. Rameau's "use of second-hand sources."[104] And in his own research he accepted the statements of secondary sources only when they conformed to carefully weighted primary sources.[105]

Another requirement is that the author imbue himself with the spirit of the times, become like a spectator or a participant.[106] This will often require more than book knowledge. It will require personal inspection of the places he writes about and personal experience with the kind of life he writes about. "The subject has been studied as much from life and in the open air as at the library table," he said of one of his own books.[107]

One of Parkman's own greatest problems was to digest the enormous mass of source material he gathered and combine it into a harmonious whole. In this he was highly successful, and he required the same success of others. Thus he admired M. Gravier's "careful analysis" of a difficult mass of material,[108] and he wished that a well-known author had "digested his material, and given it to us in a more compact form."[109]

Parkman's own works are examples of full but unpedantic annotation. Of books under review he always asked the question, Where did you learn this? He regretted exceedingly that Margry's first volume had no notes,[110] and he complimented the translator of a famous work because, although "Charlevoix rarely gives his authorities," the translator has gone through the book and supplied the lack.[111] Bancroft's book, he said, "is a storehouse of facts, gathered with admirable industry and care, arranged with skill and judgment, and sustained, at all points, by copious reference to the sources whence they were drawn."[112]

[104]*Nation*, XXV, 400, Dec. 27, 1877.
[105]See note 81, above, and text.
[106]See *Pioneers*, p. xxiv.
[107]*Montcalm and Wolfe*, I, ix; see also *Pontiac*, I, x.
[108]*Nation*, XXX, 438, June 10, 1880.
[109]*Atlantic Monthly*, XIX, 384.
[110]*Nation*, XXV, 400, Dec. 27, 1877.
[111]*Atlantic Monthly*, XX, 125.
[112]*North American Review*, CXX, 37.

Once the source material is gathered and digested, the duty of the historian is to give a truthful interpretation of it. Parkman was adamant in his stand on this point. He was lukewarm toward Longfellow's poetry because Longfellow sentimentalized the Acadian peasant and the Indian.[113] He vigorously criticized Rameau: "He is the bravest of generalizers; snatches at a detached fact and spreads it over as much ground as his theories require. . . . [His] book is a curious example of the manner in which a man of confused brain and weak judgment, eager to see things in his own way, will distort some facts, overlook others, magnify others that are trifling into gigantic proportion, and all with no apparent intention to deceive anybody."[114] Parkman even objected to the grammatical revision of source materials. Justin Winsor wrote in the *Atlantic Monthly:* "In two, at least, of these contemporary historians there were symptoms of a still older school of historical writers. These had subjected historical documents, especially if the contributions of actors in the scene, to the revision of the pedagogue. It was a fashion never stronger anywhere than in New England, where the characteristics of ancestors have always been viewed tenderly. The treatment of such material was a test in Parkman's mind of what may be called an historical integrity. I remember hearing him once make a strong protest (in a way which was always more incisive in his talk than in his books) against this misuse of revision. He believed that the actual record made in the thick of a conflict, and not a decorous paraphrase of it, was the true one. 'In mending the style and orthography, or even the grammar,' he said, 'one may rob a passage of its characteristic expression, till it ceases to mark the individuality of the man, or the nature of his antecedents and surroundings.' Speaking again of editorial glosses of the letters

[113]He declared that the tale of Acadia had been "copied and improved in prose and verse, till Acadia has become Arcadia" (*Montcalm and Wolfe*, I, 268).

[114]Review of *Une Colonie féodale en Amérique*, *Nation*, XXV, 400.

of Dinwiddie, Parkman referred to their 'good English without character, while as written they were bad English with a great deal of character. The blunders themselves,' he adds, 'have meaning, for Dinwiddie was a blunderer, and should appear as such if he is to appear truly.'"[115] The unvarnished truth was always Parkman's goal. "Describe them just as they are," he once advised Farnham, "and let the reader philosophize as much as he likes."[116]

This devotion to truth was certain, sooner or later, to cause him trouble. He admitted that when he was writing on the history of the Catholic Church in America he was on "delicate ground,"[117] and he regretted the nature of some of his findings because "they cannot be agreeable to persons for whom I have a very cordial regard."[118] But he told the truth as he saw it, and let the chips fall where they might. He was always ready to recant when he was proved wrong, and at the time of his death he was still revising and enlarging on the basis of new information.[119] As a result, he could say of his most bitterly attacked book, "so far as I know, none of the statements of fact contained in it have been attacked by evidence, or even challenged."[120]

The highest praise he could give the content of a book he reviewed was to say that it showed "the results of a genuine research concentrated on an object truly historic, and producing results of a real interest and value."[121]

Oftener than any other quality except documentation and truth in the books he criticized, Parkman chose to speak of

[115] *Atlantic Monthly*, LXXIII, 662.
[116] Farnham, p. 185. Parkman quoted with approval Bancroft's remark that he had endeavored to avoid theorizing (*North American Review*, CXX, 34–7).
[117] *Old Régime*, p. 161.
[118] *Ibid.*, p. xi.
[119] See Farnham, pp. 178–9.
[120] *Frontenac*, p. vii.
[121] *Atlantic Monthly*, XIX, 764.

their sense of proportion. He accused his good friend Casgrain of lacking a sense of proportion, when the Abbé objected to Parkman's treatment of the Roman church.[122] He criticized the heterogeneity of Girouard's book, which "fills whole pages with the names of the *habitants*, or peasants, of La Chine, to the exclusion of more important matter."[123] Of another book he wrote: "If Mr. Hole could contain his vivacity within reasonable bounds, curtail his anecdotes, suppress his Greek, Latin, and French, and spare us the occasional butt end of a sermon inserted as a counterpoise to his jokes, his book would be more useful."[124] He expected writers "when so much that is trivial, crude, and superficial is daily thrust before the public" to know what material is important and what is not.[125]

Knowing Parkman's own style, we might expect him to be critical of the styles of others. And indeed he was. Crudities in style he hated. He mentioned the abundant grammatical errors in the writing of Gerald E. Hart, and suggested that the Society for Historical Studies, of which Hart was president, restrain the literary activities of its chief officer.[126] He admired the "manly directness" of Cooper's style, and commended its "freedom from those prettinesses, studied turns of expression, and petty tricks of rhetoric, which are the pride of less masculine writers."[127] On the other hand, he regretted that Cooper's style had no "glow."[128]

In order to understand what Parkman meant by "glow" and by "manly," "direct," and "vigorous," turn to his books, and read the description of the *coureur de bois* in *The Old Régime*,[129] of

---

[122]*North American Review*, CXVIII, 225.
[123]*Nation*, LVII, 201.
[124]*Nation*, XXXVI, 476.
[125]*Atlantic Monthly*, XIX, 764.
[126]*Nation*, XLVI, 308, April 12, 1888.
[127]*North American Review*, LXXIV, 149.
[128]*Ibid.*, p. 150.
[129]Pp. 377–9. Reprinted in this volume under the title, "The Canadian Frontier," pp. 372 ff.

Frontenac's expedition in *Pontiac*,[130] and of Fort Duquesne in *Montcalm and Wolfe*.[131] Such pages as these have been far better teachers for young writers than any essay on literary theory Parkman might have left.

Akin to his demand for truth was his demand for real and living characters and scenes. This was one of the main reasons for his painstaking research, for his far traveling, for his seeking to imbue himself with the spirit of the period he wrote about. But to this basic material, he realized, the writer must add imagination—not to create a fiction but to make the truth live. Thus Vincent said of Parkman's own practice: "He used imagination not to embroider the facts of history, but to give to dead facts a new life."[132] Parkman noticed that "Mrs. Grant's facts . . . have an air of fiction; while Cooper's fiction wears the aspect of solid fact."[133] He admires the vividness of Cooper's descriptions of forests and battles, although he thought that Cooper's white women and Indians were unreal.[134] The secret of the vividness of the battles and forests, he says, is in "their fidelity, in the strength with which they impress themselves upon the mind, and the strange tenacity with which they cling to the memory."[135]

---

[130]I, 73–4.
[131]I, 215.
[132]L. H. Vincent, *American Literary Masters*, p. 397.
[133]*North American Review*, LXXIV, 153.
[134]*Ibid.*, p. 154.
[135]*Ibid.*, p. 149. Parkman's theory of historical writing was not radically different from the theories of Bancroft, Prescott, and Motley, as far as those can be determined. All believed in vivid writing based upon detailed research. Parkman differed from the rest in the emphasis he put on certain parts of this theory and in the vigor with which he carried it out. His research was more far-reaching than that of any of the others, and his historical integrity has better stood the test of time. Bancroft, for example, so colored his work and so missed evidence that his books were being superseded even before he died. Motley let his passion for liberty prejudice him against the Spaniards. Prescott relied on doubtful Spanish chronicles rather than on personal observation and archaeological investigation. Thus none of these men was as successful at getting to the essential truth of events as Parkman was. Furthermore, vivid writing meant different things to the different men. To Bancroft, it meant the invitation to add many purple passages fabricated from details of his own making. To

Even Parkman's enemies admitted the vividness and the realism of his own characters and his own narration. La Salle, Joliet, Menéndez, Frontenac, Wolfe, Montcalm—all seem to live again in Parkman's pages; and the person who reads *Montcalm and Wolfe* can see the heights of Quebec flame with French guns and hear the cannon balls whistle over his head.

But Parkman's own pages are the best spokesmen for his method. For one example out of many, consider that vivid passage from *Pontiac* just referred to:

> . . . In the year 1696, the veteran Count Frontenac marched upon their cantons [the homes of the Iroquois] with all the force of Canada. Stemming the surges of La Chine, gliding through the romantic channels of the Thousand Islands, and over the glimmering surface of Lake Ontario, and trailing in long array up the current of the Oswego, they disembarked on the margin of the Lake of Onondaga; and, startling the woodland echoes with the clangor of their trumpets, urged their

---

Motley, it meant eloquence to plead the cause of his revolutionary Dutch. To Prescott, it meant a high color and glamour. To Parkman, it meant re-creating living scenes.

In general, Parkman's position in the history of historiography is at the focal point of the older tradition of history as literature with the new idea of history as science. Parkman accomplished this union more successfully than any other American historian, but he did not go so far as to consider history a science which could interpret the story of human behavior in terms of a few determinable rules (as Taine and Froude did, for example).

Parkman's theory differed interestingly from the theories of other literary men of his time mostly in the emphasis he placed upon the rational aspect of writing rather than the inspirational side. For interesting material on literary theory, see William Charvat's *Origins of American Critical Thought, 1810–35* (Philadelphia, 1936), and Norman Foerster's *American Criticism* (Boston, 1928). For historical theory, see the last chapter of J. T. Shotwell's *An Introduction to the History of History* (New York, 1922), and the somewhat unsatisfactory comments in J. A. Jameson's *History of Historical Writing in America*. See also the discussions of Motley's and Prescott's literary theories in forthcoming volumes in the American Writers Series. More general treatments which may profitably be consulted include: G. P. Gooch, *History and Historians in the Nineteenth Century* (New York, 1913); J. H. Robinson, *The New History* (New York, 1913); and H. E. Barnes, *The New History and the Social Sciences* (New York, 1925).

march through the mazes of the forest. Never had those solitudes beheld so strange a pageantry. The Indian allies, naked
to the waist and horribly painted, adorned with streaming
scalp-locks and fluttering plumes, stole crouching among the
thickets, or peered with lynx-eyed vision through the labyrinths
of foliage. Scouts and forest-rangers scoured the woods in
front and flank of the marching columns,—men trained among
the hardships of the fur-trade, thin, sinewy, and strong, arrayed
in wild costume of beaded moccason, scarlet leggin, and frock
of buckskin, fantastically garnished with many-colored em-
broidery of porcupine. Then came the levies of the colony,
in gray capotes and gaudy sashes, and the trained battalions
from old France in cuirass and head-piece, veterans of European
wars. Plumed cavaliers were there, who had followed the
standards of Condé or Turenne, and who, even in the depths
of a wilderness, scorned to lay aside the martial foppery which
bedecked the camp and court of Louis the Magnificent. The
stern commander was borne along upon a litter in the midst,
his locks bleached with years, but his eye kindling with the
quenchless fire which, like a furnace, burned hottest when its
fuel was almost spent. Thus, beneath the sepulchral arches of
the forest, through tangled thickets, and over prostrate trunks,
the aged nobleman advanced to wreak his vengeance upon
empty wigwams and deserted maize-fields.

If we want to put Parkman's theory of historical writing in
a few words, we can say this:

He advises the choice of a subject which the writer is readily
qualified to handle, preferably a national subject. Then he
insists upon the most meticulous search for all the facts bearing
upon that subject—utilizing first-hand sources whenever possible, observing as well as reading, striving to imbue oneself
with the spirit of the period. Then this material must be digested
into a harmonious whole, annotated punctiliously with the
sources of the information. The goal of all this work is to
create the basis of a truthful interpretation of all the known

facts; integrity is perhaps the most important requirement of good history. There remains, then, the question of how the interpretation and its supporting facts shall be written. Parkman says that, first of all, the writer should show a sense of proportion in arranging and discarding. Secondly, he should write in a direct, manly, vigorous, glowing style. Finally, he should make his characters and events live again in the pages of the book.

IV. HIS POLITICAL THEORY

Because he owed allegiance to the narrative school of historians who believe good history is a vivid, truthful, and proportioned retelling of events, and furthermore because he was a very modest man, Francis Parkman succeeded in most cases in keeping his personal opinions out of his books. We have seen that he did not formalize his philosophy. But with his theory of politics it was different. Realizing that the whole American conflict of France and England was the clash of two conflicting political systems, he took great pains to insert a clear analysis of those systems in every one of his books which discussed them, and in a number of shorter writings, including letters to his severest Canadian Catholic critics, he stated frankly and clearly his own point of view toward the conflict. Therefore, there is no dearth of material concerning what Parkman thought of the fundamental problems of government.

The consistency of his attitude toward these questions is amazing. In *Pioneers of France in the New World*, the first volume of his great series, published in 1865 and written and prepared at various times during the preceding fifteen years,[136] he interpreted the struggle between France and England exactly as he interpreted it in his last book, *A Half-Century of Conflict*, published in 1892. In the preface to the first edition of his first historical book, *Pontiac*, published in 1851, he developed the

[136] *Pioneers*, pp. 437–8.

same conflict between military despotism and ordered democracy, with liberty tipping the scales.[137] In the novel, *Vassall Morton*, published in 1856, appear the essential planks of the argument which he directed against woman suffrage from 1879 to 1887.[138] Even *The Oregon Trail*, his earliest book, carries the same distrust of democracy which he held until the day of his death. In studying his political theory, therefore, we may dismiss the chronological problem in a few words: there was no essential change in his opinion during all his productive career.

He stated his opinion most clearly in a letter to the Abbé Casgrain, who had reviewed *The Old Régime* and had taken exception to many of its statements. Said Parkman:

My political faith lies between two vicious extremes, democracy and absolute authority, each of which I detest the more because it tends to react into the other. I do not object to a good constitutional monarchy, but prefer a conservative republic, where intelligence and character, and not numbers, hold the reins of power.[139]

He feared the democratic ballot. "I have always declared openly my detestation of the unchecked rule of the masses," he told Casgrain.[140] Some of that feeling went into the dialogue of *Vassall Morton*:

". . . If a man wants the people's votes, it's fifty to one that he's got to sink himself lower than the gutter before he gets them."

"Yes, and when the people have turned out of office every man of virtue, honor, manliness, independence, and ability, then they will fling up their caps and brag that their day is come, and their triumph finished over the damned aristocracy."[141]

[137]*Pontiac*, I, ix.
[138]*Vassall Morton*, pp. 114 ff.
[139]Letter of May 9, 1875; quoted in Sedgwick, pp. 274-5.
[140]*Ibid*. See the discussion of natural goodness and primitivism in this Introduction, pp. lxxvii-lxxxiv.
[141]*Vassall Morton*, p. 157.

On the Oregon Trail he had not a single good word to say for the lowest class of immigrants who were seeking equality on the plains; they were ignorant, dirty, potential criminals.[142] At Harvard he embraced the long current belief that "the best class of students are those of families of inherited wealth or easy means."[143] Again and again he declared his dislike for *nouveaux riches*.[144] He remembered that the Acadians had "the social equality which can exist only in the *humblest conditions* of society."[145] He described the forests of Maine, with young trees "pressed together in struggling confusion, squeezed out of symmetry and robbed of normal development, as men are said to be in the level sameness of democratic society."[146] He noticed the dirtiness and stupidity of a group of immigrants on his boat.[147] The spectacle of democracy on vacation at Niagara, he said, "filled me with sensations of particular contempt instead of amusing me, as they would have done had not my stomach been disordered."[148] The passengers on an Ohio River boat he called "half-civilized," and the democratic Western men "a set of beasts."[149] And in his most bitter moment he drew upon all the fervor of his Puritan ancestors and called modern democracy "organized ignorance, led by unscrupulous craft, and marching, amid the applause of fools, under the flag of equal rights."[150]

Obviously, his greatest fear was that the delusion of equality will lead to the irrational rule of mobs and demagogues. Some

[142] For a comment on this, see George M. Wrong, "Francis Parkman," *Canadian Historical Review*, IV, 289–303.

[143] Wrong, *loc. cit.* See also Parkman's pamphlet on *Our Common Schools* (1890).

[144] For example, see Sedgwick, p. 313.

[145] *Half-Century*, II, 174. (Italics supplied.)

[146] *Ibid.*, I, 35.

[147] Sedgwick, p. 137.

[148] In his diary; quoted in Sedgwick, p. 138.

[149] Letter of April 9, 1846, to his mother; available in Sedgwick, pp. 144–5.

[150] Quoted in Sedgwick, p. 308.

form of restraint is necessary. This restraint, however, is not to be provided by absolutism. In the first book of his series, he wrote two eloquent pages against "the party of reaction and absolutism."[151] In the same book he describes Spain as "an athletic man penetrated with disease." Spain was "gloomy and portentous" with "tyranny" which "crushed all freedom of thought or speech. . . . Commercial despotism was joined to political and religious despotism. The hands of the government were on every branch of industry. Perverse regulations, uncertain and ruinous taxes, monopolies, encouragements, prohibitions, restrictions, cramped the national energy." Spain was "verging to decay."[152] Again and again he spoke of the fatal effects of absolutism in Canada.[153] He regretted that the government made industry "wear the ball and chain."[154] He was proud to record that Wolfe had the fear "of imbibing the tyrannical principles of an absolute commander."[155]

Yet he admitted, in referring to Virginia, that "a vigorous aristocracy favors the growth of personal eminence."[156] He complimented William Penn for having "used his feudal rights in the interests of a broad liberalism."[157] And he said that New England in 1745–55 was a democracy "ballasted *as yet* by strong traditions of respect for established worth and ability, as well as by the influence of certain families prominent in affairs for generations."[158]

[151] *Pioneers*, pp. 96–7.
[152] *Ibid.*, pp. 20–1.
[153] Among others, see *Old Régime*, pp. 342–3.
[154] *Ibid.*, p. 355.
[155] *Montcalm and Wolfe*, II, 193.
[156] *Ibid.*, I, 33.
[157] *Ibid.*, I, 351.
[158] *Ibid.*, I, 28. Parkman's attitude toward the Puritan heritage compares interestingly with Lowell's ("New England Two Centuries Ago"). Parkman would have agreed wholly with Lowell's summary of that heritage as a "regulated freedom." Parkman, however, saw more clearly the defects of the Puritan mind than did Lowell. Puritanism, as he carefully expressed it, was "not an unmixed blessing." (Italics supplied.)

What he wanted, then, was a kind of liberal Federalism, closer to Hamilton's and John Adams's idea than to Jefferson's, closer to Jefferson's than to Andrew Jackson's. He distrusted the unlimited rule of ballots; he feared the unchecked rule of a despot. He thought he would have been happy under a monarch restrained by a constitution or in a republic ruled by some sort of aristocracy of talent. In politics he followed the middle road.

But he followed his stern words about democracy and absolutism with a warning. "There are no political panaceas, except in the imagination of political quacks," he said. "To each degree and each variety of public development there are corresponding institutions, best answering the public needs; and what is meat to one is poison to another. Freedom is for those who are fit for it; the rest will lose it, or turn it to corruption." [159]

Whether Parkman used the struggle of France and England as a gigantic laboratory from which to evolve a political theory by inductive methods or as a mighty proving ground to test a theory already evolved, we do not know. The conditions were ideally set for either purpose.

On one side was extreme despotism. "Never in Europe had power been so centralized." [160] Louis XIV had been able to say, "The state is myself." [161] From Versailles the King's will went out to all corners of the kingdom. Parkman saw, as De Tocqueville had seen, that the best test of such a policy is often in colonial government. "The physiognomy of a government," De Tocqueville said, "can best be judged in its colonies, for there its characteristic traits usually appear larger and more distinct. When I wish to judge of the spirit and the faults of the administration of Louis XIV., I must go to Canada. Its de-

[159] *Old Régime*, p. 463.

[160] *Montcalm and Wolfe*, I, 367.

[161] John Fiske develops this point in his article on Parkman in the *Atlantic Monthly*, LXXIII, 674.

formity is there seen as through a microscope."[162] This "de-formity" Parkman at once picked out.

France closed the door of Canada against the foreigner and the Protestant. "England threw open her colonies to all who wished to enter,—to the suffering and oppressed, the bold, active, and enterprising. France *shut out those who wished to come, and admitted only those who did not,*—the favored class who clung to the old faith and had no motive or disposition to leave their homes. English colonization obeyed a natural law, and sailed with wind and tide; French colonization spent its whole struggling existence in futile efforts to make head against them."[163] The French Huguenots, Parkman said, "would have hailed as a boon the permission to emigrate under the fleur-de-lis, and build up a Protestant France in the valleys of the West. It would have been a bane of absolutism, but a national glory; would have set bounds to English colonization, and changed the face of the continent. The opportunity was spurned."[164] As a result, "France built its best colony on a principle of exclusion, and failed; England reversed the system, and succeeded."[165]

Had France let the Huguenots enter, Parkman repeated in *Frontenac*, "the valleys of the west would have swarmed with a laborious and virtuous population, trained in adversity, and possessing the essential qualities of self-government. Another France would have grown beyond the Alleghanies. . . . France, like England, might have been great in two hemispheres . . . but despotism was consistent with itself, and a mighty opportunity was for ever lost."[166] Furthermore, since "the zeal of propagandism and the fur-trade" were the vital interests of the feeble population of New France, "the best part was bound to

[162]*Old Régime*, p. ix.
[163]*Pioneers*, p. 441. (Italics supplied.)
[164]*Montcalm and Wolfe*, I, 24; see also *Frontenac*, pp. 416–17.
[165]*Montcalm and Wolfe, loc. cit.*
[166]*Frontenac, loc. cit.*

perpetual chastity; while the fur-traders and those in their service rarely brought their wives to the wilderness. The fur-trader,
moreover, is always the worst of colonists; since the increase
of population, by diminishing the numbers of the fur-bearing
animals, is adverse to his interest."[167] "But behind all this,"
Parkman added, "there was in the religious ideal of the rival
colonies an influence which alone would have gone far to
produce the contrast in material growth. To the mind of the
Puritan, heaven was God's throne; but no less was the earth His
footstool: and each in its degree and its kind had its demands on
man. He held it a duty to labor and to multiply. . . . On the
other hand, those who shaped the character and in great measure
the destiny of New France had always on their lips the nothingness and the vanity of life. For them, time was nothing but a
preparation for eternity, and the highest virtue consisted in a
renunciation of all the cares, toils, and interests of earth. . . .
It is the monastic idea carried into the wide field of active life,
and is like the error of those who, in their zeal to cultivate their
higher nature, suffer the neglected body to dwindle and pine,
till body and mind alike lapse into feebleness and disease."[168]
Thus it was that England kept pouring its hordes of eager
dissenters into New England, while France sent out its sparse
colonies of the faithful, each accompanied by priests.

These French colonies took all their orders from overseas.
They were "trained to subjection and dependence," "planted
in the wilderness by the hand of authority, and told to grow
and flourish."[169] "Artificial stimulants were applied, but freedom
was withheld." The colonists were the sport of "perpetual
intervention of government,—regulations, restrictions, encouragements sometimes more mischievous than restrictions, a
constant uncertainty what the authorities would do next, the

[167] *Jesuits*, p. 427.
[168] *Ibid.*, pp. 427–8.
[169] *Old Régime*, p. 461.

fate of each man resting less with himself than with another . . . the condition, in short, of a child held always under the rule of a father, in the main well-meaning and kind, sometimes generous, sometimes neglectful, often capricious, and rarely very wise."[170] On the other side of the St. Lawrence were the English colonies, consisting of people trained for centuries in "habits of reflection, forecast, industry, and self-reliance,— a training which enabled them to adopt and maintain an invigorating system of self-rule, totally inapplicable to their rivals."[171] "They were neither sent out by the King, governed by him, nor helped by him. They grew up in utter neglect, and continued neglect was the only boon they asked."[172]

The English colonies, therefore, grew up self-reliant; the French colonies grew up France-reliant, for perhaps the most insidious thing about the French absolutism was that it was exercised at long distance. There was no local power in Canada. Frontenac, used to governing men, saw the error of the system, and, when he was appointed governor of New France, established the office of syndic to present petitions in behalf of the people. He also instituted a states-general, or congress. A reproof came back from Versailles: "It is well for you to observe that you are always to follow, in the government of Canada, the forms in use here; and since our kings have long regarded it as good for their service not to convoke the states-general of the kingdom, in order, perhaps, to abolish insensibly this ancient usage, you, on your part, should very rarely, or, to speak more correctly, never, give a corporate form to the inhabitants of Canada. You should even, as the colony strengthens, suppress gradually the office of the syndic. . . ."[173] The English colonies, on the other hand, were "a republic, but by no means

[170]*Ibid.*, pp. 461–2.
[171]*Ibid.*, pp. 463–4.
[172]*Ibid.*, p. 464.
[173]*Frontenac*, pp. 23–4.

a democracy"[174] (a significant statement, in view of Parkman's political theory detailed above). "They chose their governor and all their rulers from among themselves, made their own government and paid for it, supported their own clergy, defended themselves, and educated themselves."[175]

In the brilliant twenty-fourth chapter of *The Old Régime* Parkman analyzes the two civilizations and their relative advantages and disadvantages. The English, of course, grew much faster than the French. At the end of the war, as J. T. Adams points out, the ratio of population was about twenty to one.[176] On the other hand, the French system was built for greater military efficiency. "The Canadian population sprang in great part from soldiers, and was to the last systematically reinforced by disbanded soldiers. Its chief occupation was a continual training for forest war."[177] "The people, like an army, obeyed the word of command,—a military advantage beyond all price."[178] New England could boast of no such military efficiency. "The New England man was precisely the same material with that of which Cromwell formed his invincible 'Ironsides'; but he had very little forest experience. . . . He was too busy to fight without good cause."[179] He was essentially commercial, essentially jealous or distrustful of his fellow citizen, unready to spring to arms at a moment's notice, and unwilling to fight at all unless his own interests were jeopardized.[180] But when he fought, his orders came from this side of the Atlantic; New France moved at the call of Versailles.

To Parkman the outcome of the conflict seemed inevitable. The English colonists with their "true foundations of a stable

[174] *Old Régime*, p. 464.
[175] *Ibid.*
[176] Adams, "Francis Parkman," in *Dictionary of American Biography*, XIV, 250.
[177] *Old Régime*, p. 465.
[178] *Montcalm and Wolfe*, I, 38.
[179] *Old Régime*, p. 466.
[180] *Ibid.*

freedom,—conscience, reflection, faith, patience, and public spirit";[181] their training in self-reliance; their self-government; and their power to expand—these men had a great advantage over their French fellows with their "volition enfeebled, self-reliance paralyzed";[182] dependent on orders from overseas; unfavorable toward expansion, and not sorry that their government had shut off the best source of immigration; fighting a constant internal battle between the license taught by the forest and the authority taught by their church and state. Says Parkman: "The contest on the continent between Liberty and Absolutism was never doubtful."[183]

In Parkman's books, as William Dean Howells characterizes them, "One moral is traced from beginning to end,—that spiritual and political despotism is so bad for men that no zeal, or self-devotion, or heroism can overcome its evil effects; one lesson enforces itself throughout,—that the state which persistently meddles with the religious, domestic, and commercial affairs of its people, dooms itself to extinction. In Canada the Jesuit realized his dream of a church untroubled by a heretic, obedient, faithful, devoted; in Canada the monarchist realized his dream of subjects paternally governed even to the intimate details of social and family life; and these dreams were such long nightmares to the colonists that the English conquest, and the perpetual separation of the colony from the mother-country, was a blessing instinct with life, freedom, and prosperity."[184]

The clash which his books describe, Parkman said, "was the strife of a united and concentred few against a divided and discordant many. It was the strife, too, of the past against the future; of the old against the new; of moral and intellectual torpor against moral and intellectual life; of barren absolutism

[181]*Ibid.*, p. 464.
[182]*Ibid.*, p. 463.
[183]*Jesuits*, p. 552.
[184]Howells, "Mr. Parkman's Histories," *Atlantic Monthly*, XXXIV, 602–3. See also *Old Régime*, pp. 467–8.

against a liberty, crude, incoherent, and chaotic, yet full of prolific vitality."[185] And the whole course of affairs in America
might have been different "but for one rooted error of French
policy."[186]

The historian of the French and English war let himself only
once be dragged into contemporary politics. That was in
reference to the problem of suffrage, and especially to the
problem of extending the ballot to women.

In a flaming article in the *North American Review* for July
and August, 1878, Parkman described "The Failure of Universal Suffrage." A year later in the same magazine he expressed
himself on "The Woman Question," and in 1880 answered his
critics with "The Woman Question Again." He repeated most
of these arguments in a pamphlet, "Some of the Reasons against
Woman Suffrage," which was published for wide circulation in
1887. That was all; but for Parkman such an excursion into
practical politics was noteworthy.

Why was he opposed to woman suffrage?

He based his case on two arguments: the fundamental difference between the abilities and duties of the two sexes, and his
distrust of the unrestricted ballot. He had held both these
beliefs many years before he applied them to woman suffrage.
His distrust of democracy is evident, as we have already seen,
both in *Pontiac* (1851) and *Vassall Morton* (1856). In *Vassall
Morton* he discusses also the weakness of women,[187] and to
certain other qualities of women he devotes a sparkling dialogue
which is worth quoting. Morton has said that there must be a
few rational women in the world. His friend answers:

"My dear Morton, are you demented? A woman always
rational, always sensible, always consistent; a logical woman;

---

[185] *Montcalm and Wolfe*, I, 38. In *Frontenac* (p. vi) he said: "The present volume will show how valiantly, and for a time how successfully, New
France battled against a fate which her own organic fault made inevitable."
[186] *Frontenac*, p. vi.
[187] *Vassall Morton*, p. 403.

one who can distinguish the relations of cause and effect, one who marches straight to her purpose like a man,—who ever found such a woman; or, finding her, who could endure such a one?"

"You fly into extremes; but women may be rational, as well as men."

"I like to see the organ of faith well developed—yours is a miracle. Granted, a rational woman; and, with a liberal rendering of the word, such, I admit, are now and then seen,— women always even, always cheerful, never morbid, always industrious, always practical; busy with good works,—charity, for example, or making puddings,—pious daughters, model wives, pattern mothers—"

"At last you have found a creditable character."

"Very creditable; but far from interesting. The truth is, Morton, the very uncertainty, the flitting gleams and shadows, the opalescent light, the chameleon coloring of a woman's mind are what make her fascination,—the fascination and the danger. . . ."[188]

By 1878, however, Parkman was ready to argue the question in a more logical manner. He began with the premise that men are built for conflict, women are not. By "conflict" he meant, primarily, war, but also political, governmental, economic strife.[189] Now, he continued, "the right of voting and the duty of fighting should never be divorced. . . . Neither Congress, nor the States, nor the united voice of the whole people could permanently change the essential relations of the sexes. Universal female suffrage, even if decreed, would undo itself in time. . . ."[190] Why? Because woman is not made for it. She

[188]*Ibid.*, p. 130. For interesting material on the attitude toward women in nineteenth-century America (and earlier), see Mary S. Benson, *Woman in Eighteenth Century America* (New York, 1935); Augusta S. Violette, *Economic Feminism in American Literature Prior to 1842* (Orono, Maine, University of Maine Studies, II); Belle Squire, *The Woman Movement in America* (Chicago, 1911); Elizabeth C. Stanton and Susan B. Anthony, *History of Woman Suffrage* (New York, 1881–1902, 4 vols.).

[189]Parkman, "The Woman Question," *North American Review*, CXXIX, 304–5.   [190]*Ibid.*, p. 321.

is the more idealistic, less practical part of humanity; she is above the petty brawling of politics; she has higher duties to the family and the home.[191] And "in the full and normal development of womanhood lie the best interests of the world."[192]

But the real reason why Parkman thinks woman suffrage is undesirable is his deep objection to extending the democratic ballot. "For the old monarchs we have substituted Demos!" he writes in "The Failure of Universal Suffrage." This creature, if unperverted by politicians, would be equal to the average mind of the citizens. This mind itself has been made unfit to govern by the invasion of peasants, by the growth in machines and materialism in general. As a result, there has been "a slow but ominous transfer of power from superior to inferior men." We have ignorant masses and a half-taught plutocracy. We have "wretched wire-pulling demagogues," and the spineless individual who follows them "cares not a farthing for the general good, and will sell his vote for a dollar—when, by a native instinct, he throws up his cap at the claptrap declamation of some lying knave, and turns with indifference or dislike from the voice of honesty and reason—then his vote becomes a public pest."[193]

In other words, we have confused liberty with equality. Wanting equality so desperately, we have forgotten natural inequality. We have forgotten that the masses by themselves are not capable of any progress except material progress, and that but imperfectly. We have forgotten that "any reasonable man would willingly renounce his privilege of dropping a piece

[191]See his pamphlet, *Some of the Reasons against Woman Suffrage* (1887).

[192]*North American Review*, CXXIX, 321.

[193]Parkman, "The Failure of Universal Suffrage," *North American Review*, CXXVII, 8. Parkman shared this distrust of the democratic ballot with the Puritan elect, with such Federalists as John Adams, with Poe, and even with such a modern poet as Edwin Arlington Robinson (see his "Demos and Dionysus").

of paper into a box, provided that good government were assured to him and his descendants."[194] We want, not equality, not the ballot, but good government.

So far, he has been talking about the democratic ballot in general. Where do women fit into the argument? They fit in, he said, because they are "the most impulsive and excitable half of humanity."[195] They are too impressionable, too easy for demagogues and grasping politicians.[196] Furthermore, he fears the effects of their charms upon the minds of masculine voters; is it fair to get votes by sex attraction? "If politics are to be purified by artfulness, effrontery, insensibility, a pushing self-assertion, and a glib tongue, then we may look for regeneration; for the typical female politician will be richly endowed with all these gifts."[197]

There is something of the Puritan in the grim vigor with which, in his notebook, he sums up his attitude toward the matter:

The first and fundamental requisites of women, as of men, are physical, moral, and mental health. It is for men to rear the political superstructure; it is for women to lay its foundation. God rules the world by fixed laws, moral and physical; and according as men and women observe or violate these laws will be the destinies of communities and individuals for this world and the next. The higher education is necessary to the higher order of women to the end that they may discharge their function of civilizing agent; but it should be cautiously limited to the methods and degree that consist with the discharge of their functions of maternity. Health of body and mind is the one great essential. In America men are belittled and cramped by the competition of business, from which women are, or ought to be, free. Hence they have opportunities

---

[194] *North American Review*, CXXVII, 10.
[195] "The Woman Question," *loc. cit.*, p. 316.
[196] *Ibid.*, pp. 319–20.
[197] *Ibid.*, p. 317.

of moral and mental growth better in some respects than those of men.[198]

Thus spoke Francis Parkman. Not even the War between the States aroused him so fully.

This attitude toward the political function of women, perhaps more than any other things he did or said, has brought on Francis Parkman the label of "reactionary." Thus, Bliss Perry and George M. Wrong both have pointed out that Parkman "hated change," and it is true that their statement is easily supportable. He thought traveling by steam power was "disgusting." As Perry says, he could never have accommodated himself to twentieth-century democracy, and he had too much nationalism about him, too much Yankee distrust of anything he could not watch, to have thought internationally. He was cold toward social reforms. "Excepting a vile politician," it has been said, "no one repelled him more than a reformer marked by extreme views and eccentric conduct."[199] He thought—to the horror of modern women—that woman's place is in the home.

His attitude toward abolition was a surprising and in some ways contradictory one, and as abolition was a chief problem of his day we may be justified in considering at somewhat greater length his attitude toward it.

Before the war of 1861 he was distinctly cold toward the reform. He wrote to Charles Eliot Norton: "For my part, I would see every slave knocked on the head before I would see the Union go to pieces, and would include in the sacrifice as many abolitionists as could be conveniently brought together."[200] After Sumter, however, he was torn by conflicting loyalties: his

[198] From a notebook kept in Bemis Camp in 1886; see Sedgwick, p. 309. It might be interesting to know what Parkman's wife thought of his view of the "Woman Question," but she died in 1858, long before he expressed himself vigorously on female suffrage. His utterances before her death (in *Vassall Morton*, 1856) are much gentler than the later remarks.

[199] See Farnham, p. 295.

[200] Letter of Nov. 10, 1850; available in Sedgwick, p. 221.

love for union, his rational insistence on peaceful settlement by arbitration, and, at the same time, the "rock and iron" in his blood which made him thrill to a martial tale or a bugle call and led him to regret that his health debarred him from military activities. During the war, he was surprisingly inactive. He wrote letters to the Boston *Advertiser* explaining why New England armies were "no longer the best in the world"— because "luxury and commerce have sometimes emasculated a people naturally warlike," and because "the pride of a good bargain has overborne the pride of manhood." He was impressed by the heroism of the common people, but thought little of the leaders. And in 1878 he summarized the conflict in these words:

Some half a century ago, a few devoted men began what seemed a desperate crusade against a tremendous national evil. American slavery has now passed into history. It died a death of violence, to our shame be it said; for the nation had not virtue, temperance, and wisdom enough, to abolish it peacefully and harmlessly; but it is dead.[201]

This coldness toward the "crusade" when almost all the rest of New England was aflame is not to be explained entirely by the fact of his ill-health during the years immediately preceding the war and during the war. It is to be explained rather in terms of his dislike for reform, his objection to an extension of suffrage, his faith in rational rather than physical justice, his whole reactionary attitude.

For it is undoubtedly true that his mind was firmly set in its Federalism, and it clung to those principles with Puritan vigor. Yet there is another side to the argument. He was a liberal in education, and he faithfully seconded President Eliot's attempt to remodel Harvard according to modern needs. He was a

[201]"The Failure of Universal Suffrage," *North American Review*, CXXVII, 19.

liberal in his attitude toward conservation; his review of *The Forests and the Census*[202] is a model of farsighted national policy. In religion he was more than a liberal; according to the standards of his day he was a radical. If he belonged to "the old dispensation,"[203] then, it was mostly the old, and yet surprisingly new, dispensation of political Federalism.

In the last few lines of *Montcalm and Wolfe*, Parkman gathered together the advice to America which he had been implying throughout the twelve volumes of his major work. It is a final word of friendly counsel from one who has spent a lifetime following certain principles of national conduct through history.

The British colonies along the Atlantic have become a great nation, he begins. They have become so powerful that they may overcome every foe except that most dangerous of foes, themselves. They are destined to a majestic future if they will do certain things. What are those things? First, shun the excess and perversion of the principles that made them great (by which he means freedom, self-reliance, republicanism). Secondly, prate less about the enemies of the past and strive more against the enemies of the present; and the enemies of the present, Parkman says, are the mob and the demagogue and materialism. Thirdly, "rally her powers from the race for gold and the delirium of prosperity to make firm the foundations on which that prosperity rests, and turn some fair proportion of her vast mental force to other objects than material progress and the game of party politics."[204]

It remains for this new nation to prove, "if she can," he says, "that the rule of the masses is consistent with the highest growth of the individual; that democracy can give the world a civilization as mature and pregnant, ideas as energetic and

[202]*Atlantic Monthly*, LV, 835–9 (June, 1885).
[203]Bliss Perry, "Some Personal Qualities of Parkman," *Yale Review*, N. S. VIII, 443–8.
[204]*Montcalm and Wolfe*, II, 428–9.

vitalizing, and types of manhood as lofty and strong, as any of the systems which it boasts to supplant."[205]

V. HIS PHILOSOPHY

The reader who searches Parkman's works for a formal philosophy will search in vain. There is no reason to believe that Parkman ever thought in terms of formal philosophy. As one of his critics points out, he was interested in the entire drama of life rather than the inner workings of the human spirit,[206] and the study of the abstract and the metaphysical was wholly foreign to his interests. Philosophy, therefore, meant to him a code for action, a sense of rightness and wrongness, an attitude toward life rather than an explanation of life. This attitude, however, he expressed with great frankness and clarity, and by examining his position in regard to some of the fundamental questions we may approximate what was, for Parkman, a philosophy.

Parkman was always sensitive to the charms of nature. He made his most extreme statement of this feeling in *Pontiac*, when he explained why some white captives preferred captivity to freedom. To wish to return to the Indians and the hard life of the forest may be absurd, he says;

Yet such has been the experience of many a sound and healthful mind. To him who has once tasted the reckless independence, the haughty self-reliance, the sense of irresponsible freedom, which the forest life engenders, civilization thenceforth seems flat and stale. Its pleasures are insipid, its pursuits wearisome, its conventionalities, duties, and mutual dependence alike tedious and disgusting. The entrapped wanderer grows

[205] *Ibid.* This was in 1884. For a vivid description of the excessive materialism and corruption of that era, see A. Nevins, *The Emergence of Modern America*, especially chapter VII. This book is equipped with full bibliography on the subject. See also Parrington's characterization of the age as "The Great Barbecue," in *Main Currents in American Thought*, III.

[206] G. M. Wrong, "Francis Parkman," *loc. cit.*

fierce and restless, and pants for breathing-room. His path, it is true, was choked with difficulties, but his body and soul were hardened to meet them; it was beset with dangers, but these were the very spice of his life, gladdening his heart with exulting self-confidence, and sending the blood through his veins with a livelier current. The wilderness, rough, harsh, and inexorable, has charms more potent in their seductive influence than all the lures of luxury and sloth. And often he on whom it has cast its magic finds no heart to dissolve the spell, and remains a wanderer and an Ishmaelite to the hour of his death.

There is a chord, in the breasts of most men, prompt to answer loudly or faintly, as the case may be, to such rude appeals. But there is influence of another sort, strongest with minds of the finest texture, yet sometimes holding a controlling power over those who neither acknowledge nor suspect its workings. There are few so imbruted by vice, so perverted by art and luxury, as to dwell in the closest presence of Nature, deaf to her voice of melody and power, untouched by the ennobling influences which mould and penetrate the heart that has not hardened itself against them. Into the spirit of such an one the mountain wind breathes its own freshness, and the midsummer tempest, as it rends the forest, pours its own fierce energy. His thoughts flow with the placid stream of the broad, deep river, or dance in light with the sparkling current of the mountain brook. No passing mood or fancy of his mind but has its image and its echo in the wild world around him. There is softness in the mellow air, the warm sunshine, and the budding leaves of spring; and in the forest flower, which, more delicate than the pampered offspring of gardens, lifts its tender head through the refuse and decay of the wilderness. But it is the grand and heroic in the hearts of men which finds its worthiest symbol and noblest inspiration amid these desert realms,—in the mountain, rearing its savage head through clouds and sleet, or basking its majestic strength in the radiance of the sinking sun; in the interminable forest, the thunder booming over its lonely waste, the whirlwind tearing through its utmost depths, or the sun at length setting in gorgeous majesty beyond its waves of verdure. To the sick, the wearied, or the sated spirit, nature opens a theatre of boundless life, and holds forth a cup brimming with redundant pleasure. In the other joys of existence, fear is balanced against hope, and satiety against delight; but here one may fearlessly drink, gaining, with every draught, new vigor and a heightened zest, and finding no dregs of bitterness at the bottom.[207]

Not Henry Thoreau, not John Burroughs, not even Jean Jacques Rousseau himself, ever wrote a nobler tribute to nature than that one. It was the young Parkman speaking, barely past twenty-five, fresh from happy vacations in the woods and on the mountains of New England, fresh from a vacation lark on the western prairies.[208] All the joy of youth and vigor went into the tribute, and it is true that as he grew older he wrote less and less of the joys of nature, and never again did nature tip his pen with such fire as lit that passage in *Pontiac*.

But that is not to say that Parkman was, even at that time, a follower of the "back to nature" doctrines of Rousseau. About the same time he was writing the eloquent section in *Pontiac* he was writing thus informally to his friend Squier:

Copway has recently come back from his Western tour and is now in New York preparing to publish the Traditional History of the Ogibhewas, and a collection of their legends.

Between you and me I shall have no great faith in them. Copway is endowed with a discursive imagination and facts

---

[207] *Pontiac*, II, 253–6. For an excellent study of primitivism see Lois Whitney, *Primitivism and the Idea of Progress* (see Bibliography). Interesting material on conceptions before Rousseau of the Indian as nature's nobleman may be found in G. Atkinson, *The Extraordinary Voyage in French Literature from 1700 to 1720* (Paris, 1922), and his *Les Relations des Voyages du XVIIᵉ siècle et l'évolution des idées* (Paris, 1925); Benjamin Bissell, *The American Indian in English Literature of the Eighteenth Century* (New Haven, 1925); G. Chinard, *L'Amérique et le rêve exotique dans la littérature française au XVIIᵉ et au XVIIIᵉ siècle* (Paris, 1925), and also Chinard's introduction to his edition of La Hontan's *Dialogues curieux* (Baltimore, 1931); Nicholas van Wijngaarden, *Les Odyssées philosophiques en France entre 1616 et 1789* (Haarlem, 1932).

[208] See *The Oregon Trail*, pp. 462–4.

grow under his hands into a preposterous shape and dimensions. His scheme of settling the Indians is a flash in the pan,
or rather he has no settled scheme at all, and never had any. . . .
He had a great deal to say about the forest gentlemen, nature's
noblemen, etc., but very little about the regeneration of the
tribes. . . .

. . . Hoffman, poor devil, became engaged to Schoolcraft's
daughter and took a fancy into his head that he was bound in
consequence to avenge the wrongs of the Red race against the
white men. This idea got such possession of him that his
friends rightly concluded him to be mad and the match was
broken off.[209]

A true disciple of Rousseau would never thus have scoffed at
"nature's noblemen." In later years, his aversion to Rousseau
became more open. He distrusted Jefferson because Jefferson
had followed French democracy, especially Rousseau, whom
Parkman called a "depraved and half crazy man of genius."[210]
In *A Half-Century* he spoke disparagingly of the "wild dreams"
of Rousseau.[211] In *Montcalm and Wolfe*, he several times made
fun of Rousseau's doctrines once in this fashion: "Rousseau
was sounding the first notes of his mad eloquence,—the wild
revolt of a passionate and diseased genius against a world of
falsities and wrongs."[212]

As a matter of fact, Parkman embraced neither of the two
common ideas of the day, that the white race should bring the
blessings of civilization to the Indians, or that the white race
should seek from the Indians the lessons of a life better and
happier than civilization. Toward the first idea he expressed
frank skepticism:

[209]Letter to Squier, Nov. 18, 1849, in Seitz, *Letters of Parkman to Squier*,
pp. 25–6.
[210]See Farnham, p. 278.
[211]*Half-Century*, I, 4.
[212]*Montcalm and Wolfe*, I, 18; also p. 132. Parkman was cold to the
poetry of Wordsworth, and, although he thought Thoreau a notable man,
he disliked Thoreau's extreme individualism. See Farnham, pp. 196, 347.

To reclaim the Indians from their savage state has again and again been attempted, and each attempt has failed. Their intractable, unchanging character leaves no other alternative than their gradual extinction, or the abandonment of the western world to eternal barbarism; and of this and other similar plans, whether the offspring of British or American legation, it may alike be said that sentimental philanthropy will find it easier to cavil at than to amend them.[213]

Education of the Indians spoiled them as savages and still failed to civilize them, he said.[214] They oppose change, and refuse to open their minds to possibilities of improvement.[215] Their ferocity and indolence unfit them to live in civilization, and these qualities cannot be eradicated.[216] Between the barbarian and the truly civilized man, Parkman felt, there lay a mighty chasm which a few years of education would not bridge.

Toward the other and even more humanitarian idea, that the Indians should not be disturbed, but should rather be emulated ("back to nature"), Parkman was openly scornful. He denied that civilization had taught the Indian his worst vices.[217] His realistic observation made him unable to accept Rousseau's characterization: "I dare not speak of those happy nations who did not even know the name of many vices which we find it difficult to suppress: the Savages of America, whose simple and natural mode of government Montaigne preferred, without hesitation, not only to the laws of Plato, but to the most perfect visions of government philosophy can ever suggest."[218] He deplored the "New England humanitarianism, melting into sentimentality at a tale of woe," which wept over

[213] *Pontiac*, II, 170.
[214] *Ibid.*, p. 285.
[215] *Ibid.*, p. 216.
[216] *Jesuits*, p. 418.
[217] *Half-Century*, I, 216.
[218] *Discourse on the Moral Effect of the Arts and Sciences;* quoted in H. N. Fairchild, *The Noble Savage*, p. 127.

the despoiling of the idyllic forest life of this child of nature.[219] When the white man and the savage are brought together, Parkman said in summing up the question in *Pontiac*, they are both gainers and both losers.[220] The white man gains a rugged independence; the savage gains the comforts of civilization. Yet in the white man "the dormant savage" begins to appear, and he loses the benefits of his civilized training; in the savage, the rugged independence and self-reliance are destroyed, and, too unstable for civilized life, he becomes unfit even for life in the forest.

Against the American version of the Noble Savage and the romantically idealized picture of Indian life, Parkman brings a long list of accusations. He makes fun of Charlevoix's assertion that a certain chief had nothing of the savage about him except his name and dress.[221] The Indian is deficient in the ethical sense; not the *morally* good, but the fierce, warriors go to the Happy Hunting Grounds.[222] The Indian is indolent.[223] The Indian is deceitful and treacherous: "All children, says Sir Walter Scott, are naturally liars; and truth and honor are developments of later education. Barbarism is to civilization what childhood is to maturity; and all savages, whatever be their country, their color, or their lineage, are prone to treachery and deceit."[224] The "savage lethargy of mind" makes the Indian incapable of progress. He doubts that even the Iroquois, the most advanced Indians who figured in his histories, if left to work out their destiny undisturbed, could ever have developed a civilization of their own.[225] But his fundamental objection to

[219] *Montcalm and Wolfe*, I, 294. He referred here indirectly to Long-fellow's *Evangeline*. The same sentiment expressed, in greater or less degree, his attitude toward such reforms as abolition, utopianism, etc.

[220] *Pontiac*, I, 164.

[221] *Frontenac*, p. 181.

[222] *Jesuits*, pp. 74, 76–7.

[223] *Ibid.*, p. 226.

[224] *Ibid.*, pp. 86–7.

[225] *Ibid.*, pp. 37, 59.

the Noble Savage is that he is not a rational man.[226] The savage intelligence, he says, is a mere instrument of blind frenzy.[227] "No man practically familiar with Indian character need be told the impossibility of foreseeing to what strange acts the wayward impulses of this murder-loving race may prompt them. Unstable as water, capricious as the winds, they seem in some of their moods like ungoverned children fired with the instincts of devils."[228] Over and over again he remarks on the Indian's subservience to superstition, which makes his actions the result, not of thought, but of every accident of nature.[229] And he crowns his case with the evidence that the Iroquois habitually acted upon the advice of their women; this, said Parkman, is "barbarism, not progress."[230]

"Take a savage from his woods or his prairies," Parkman said in *Vassall Morton*, "and, school him as you will, the ingrained savage will still declare itself. Take the most polished of mankind, turn him into the wilderness, and forthwith the dormant savage begins to appear. Hunt him with enemies, gnaw him with hunger, beat him with wind and rain, and observe the result; how the delicate tissues of civilization are blown away, how rude passions start into life, how his bodily cravings grow clamorous and importunate, how he grows reckless of his own blood and the blood of others. 'Men are as the times.'"[231]

Parkman's solution of the problem of evil, then, would not be a return to nature. The tissues of civilization are too delicate, too dearly won, to be given away so easily. He would admit that there are corruptions in civilization, but the way to eliminate them is to fight them, not to flee from them. The origin

[226] *Ibid.*, pp. 66 ff.
[227] *Ibid.*, p. 538.
[228] *Pontiac*, II, 306.
[229] *Jesuits*, pp. 66–8, 226. See also *North American Review*, CIII, 1–18.
[230] *Some of the Reasons against Woman Suffrage*, p. 10.
[231] *Vassall Morton*, p. 244.

of evil was not in the civilized, rational, volitional, and social control which raised the white man out of the forest. Parkman, as we shall see later, was too deeply grounded in rationalism and the stoical virtues to give up the restraints of civilization for the dubious freedom of the Noble Savage.

Yet he sincerely admired certain qualities of the Indian. He envied the savage his self-reliance, his knowledge of nature. He admitted that honor was not entirely extinct among some tribes of Indians.[232] He said that the Iroquois were examples of the highest civilization "man can reach without emerging from his primitive condition of the hunter."[233] And he never missed an opportunity to record instances of the stern, Spartan self-control which allowed the Indian silently to endure hardship and torture.[234]

Although he was the son of a minister, Parkman was never a religious man. Ostensibly he began with the early Unitarianism of Channing, changed to what his chief biographer calls "the more natural and manly religion of Parker,"[235] and soon came to rest on a position of agnosticism. But even in his Unitarian youth and the flux of his adolescence and young manhood there were signs of defection. When he was a mere boy, a pious old lady found him drawing a picture of three devils carrying off three ministers on pitchforks.[236] We have already seen his low opinion of the powerful Dr. Channing, and in his European diary of 1844 he expressed his disrespect for gentle-

---

[232] *Jesuits*, pp. 447–8.

[233] *Ibid.*, p. 36.

[234] For example, *Old Régime*, p. 387; *Frontenac*, pp. 434–5.

[235] Farnham, p. 312. The statement is Farnham's. Parker thought the purpose of religion was "to recall men from the transient shows of time to the permanent substance of religion; from a worship of Creeds and Empty Belief to a worship in the spirit and in Life" (from Parker's *Discourses on Religion;* see H. S. Commager, *Theodore Parker* [Boston, 1936], especially pp. 80–6). Parker's belief was thus a negating of creeds and organized religion in favor of individual religion based on instinct, conscience, emotion, and reason.

[236] Farnham, pp. 258–9.

men of the cloth, in general.[237] He wrote to his mother, that same year, from Rome, that "We are in the midst of the fooleries of Holy Week."[238] He described his adventures in a Roman monastery in a not very respectful manner,[239] and he congratulated an acquaintance on "so happy a conversion" from devout religion to agnosticism.[240] Even in his late years, when he wrote whimsically of a boy who had been named after him, he said: "I hope the youngster will do honor to the name. He should be brought up to some respectable calling and not allowed to become a minister."[241]

His good friend and unbending critic, the Abbé Casgrain, put his finger on the source of such opinions. "L'œuvre de M. Parkman est la négation de toute croyance religeuse," wrote the Abbé. "Il est purement rationaliste."[242] And he goes on to say that Parkman, by rejecting the supernatural, forces himself to find a human explanation for the conduct of priests and all other Catholics, and this is the source of contention between Parkman and his Catholic critics.

Of course, the Abbé is right. Parkman placed his faith in reason and distrusted everything irrational. Among his strongest characteristics, as has been noted, were a love of the real and an aversion to anything visionary and spiritual.[243] Hundreds of examples of his distrust for the supernatural can be gleaned from his works. Some of the actions of Marie de l'Incarnation, he said, were "vagaries of an insane mysticism."[244] He made fun of the habit of giving thanks to God for the slaughter of enemies.[245] Of the Jesuits he said, with his tongue

[237] Available in Sedgwick, p. 108.
[238] *Ibid.*, p. 104.
[239] *Ibid.*, pp. 96–104.
[240] *Ibid.*, p. 74.
[241] Farnham, p. 259.
[242] H. R. Casgrain, *Œuvres Complètes*, II, 316: "Parkman's work is the negation of all religious belief. He is purely rationalist."
[243] See Farnham, pp. 196 ff.
[244] *Jesuits*, p. 278.
[245] *Pioneers*, p. 177.

in his cheek: "The efforts of the missionaries for the conversion of the savages were powerfully seconded from the other world, and the refractory subject who was deaf to human persuasions softened before the superhuman agencies which the priest invoked to his aid."[246] He was none too respectful in relating the miracles which were reported to have taken place in early Canada,[247] nor in telling the beneficence of the Virgin, who made the Iroquois shoot wide of their mark.[248] In *Vassall Morton* he told how, after a wreck on the railroad, "One of the morning papers,

> 'for profound
> And solid lying much renowned,'

solemnly averred that none but Providence was responsible for it."[249]

Parkman had other quarrels with religion, and especially with the church whose early Canadian history he wrote.[250] He frequently mentioned reports of its bigotry.[251] He speaks of the medieval fervor of New-World Christianity.[252] He complains that Jesuit training does "horrible violence to the noblest qualities of manhood";[253] and that Loyola would "rob a man of volition, yet . . . preserve in him, nay, . . . stimulate, those ener-

[246] *Jesuits*, p. 197.

[247] *Old Régime*, pp. 110–12.

[248] *Ibid.*, pp. 55–7.

[249] *Vassall Morton*, p. 80.

[250] Parkman's attitude toward Catholicism was not far from the main stream of New England opinion at the time. Emerson and Thoreau never showed great sympathy for the church, although Emerson was more impressed than he expected to be, on the occasion of his first trip to Europe (see his *Journals*). Motley, fired by his sympathy for the Dutch revolution, was violently hostile to Catholicism. Holmes expressed an unfavorable opinion in *Elsie Venner*. On the other hand, Longfellow in his translation of the *Divine Comedy*, his sonnets on the *Divina Commedia*, and his *Golden Legend*, showed greater sympathy, as did Lowell—probably because of his studies in Spanish and medieval Italian literature. Hawthorne expressed a sympathetic opinion in *The Marble Faun*.

[251] *Old Régime*, p. 420, and many others.

[252] *Jesuits*, p. 301.

[253] *Ibid.*, p. 98.

gies which would make him the most efficient instrument of a great design." The novice is summoned "to the utter abnegation of intellect and will in favor of the Superior. . . . If the Superior pronounces black to be white, he is bound in conscience to acquiesce."[254] To a Catholic this simply means that the novice sacrifices his intellect and will to God, through God's representative on earth; to a rationalist and nonsupernaturalist like Parkman, it means something else.

Parkman also objected to the earthly character of the church, in terms which he set forth eloquently in chapter VIII of *The Jesuits in North America.* In other places he objects to the superficiality of conversion of the Indians,[255] and accuses the Jesuits of inciting border raids on the English.[256] "It was the mission of Canada to propagate Christianity and civilization!" he exclaims after telling the story of one of these Indian raids in which many Englishmen were killed and scalped.[257]

The Roman Catholic Church in Canada was not his only target. He was never favorable to Puritanism, although he recognized in it many of his own stern virtues. He summarized early eighteenth-century Puritanism in a remarkable passage:

A harsh and exacting creed with its stiff formalism and its prohibition of wholesome recreation; excess in the pursuit of gain,—the only resource left to energies robbed of their natural play; the struggle for existence on a hard and barren soil; and the isolation of a narrow village life,—joined to produce, in a meaner sort, qualities which were unpleasant, and sometimes repulsive. Puritanism was not an unmixed blessing. Its view of human nature was dark, and its attitude towards it one of repression. It strove to crush out not only what is evil, but much that is innocent and salutary. Human nature so treated will take its revenge, and for every vice that it loses find

[254] *Ibid.*, pp. 96–7.
[255] *Half-Century*, I, 216.
[256] *Frontenac*, pp. 393–6, and others.
[257] *Ibid.*, p. 426.

another instead. Nevertheless, while New England Puritanism bore its peculiar crop of faults, it produced also many good and sound fruits. An uncommon vigor, joined to the hardy virtues of a masculine race, marked the New England type. The sinews, it is true, were hardened at the expense of blood and flesh—and this literally as well as figuratively; but the staple of character was a sturdy conscientiousness, an undespairing courage, patriotism, public spirit, sagacity, and a strong good sense.[258]

He found many things to admire in the Catholic Church, also. He admired the zeal, energy, and self-abnegation of the Jesuits.[259] Especially did he single out their early apostleship for kind words.[260] He wrote glowingly of the Spartan fortitude of Jean de Brébeuf, "the founder of the Huron mission, its truest hero, and its greatest martyr."[261] He admired Garnier, who gave away his own life in order to give absolution to dying Indians.[262] Repeatedly he praises the manly qualities, the fearless vigor of Dollier de Casson, and that stout Sulpitian priest emerges as one of his favorite Canadians.[263] He praised Bishop Laval's sincerity, although he did not like the bishop's domineering temper.[264] And for Christian ethics in general he held the highest regard. In a letter written in 1887 he expressed the opinion that the world has outgrown the dogmatic part of Christianity, "But when one compares Christianity on its ethical side with all other religious systems, with the partial

[258] *Montcalm and Wolfe*, I, 29. The relation of Parkman's view to Lowell's has already been discussed. Longfellow, although fundamentally anti-Puritan, was inclined toward ancestor worship. Motley found the Puritan age a suitable field for two novels, and Hawthorne—although his answers to fundamental problems were not the Puritan answers—lived almost his whole literary life among the Puritan memories.

[259] *Jesuits*, p. 94.

[260] For example, in *Half-Century*, I, 219 ff.

[261] *Jesuits*, pp. 491–2.

[262] *Ibid.*, pp. 508–10.

[263] *Old Régime*, pp. 261–5, 438–9, and others.

[264] *Ibid.*, pp. 163–4.

exception of Buddhism, one cannot but feel that whether we believe in its supernatural origin or not, it is to be accepted with a reverent gratitude as a vast boon to mankind."[265] And in *The Jesuits* he mentions "that principle of self-abnegation which is the life of true religion, and which is vital, no less, to the highest forms of heroism."[266]

Yet from this religion Francis Parkman turned away. As his father had turned from eighteenth-century Puritanism to Unitarianism, so Parkman turned from his particular brand of nineteenth-century deism to agnosticism,[267] always, however, retaining a certain reverence and respect for the best parts of the beliefs he refused. One day his sister said to him: "If I should be asked about your religious beliefs, it seems to me I might say that you are a reverent Agnostic." "Yes, that's about it," Parkman answered.[268]

We have seen that Parkman declined both natural and religious roads to happiness. It is now our problem to follow his attempts to find meaning and values in life by means of rational, human processes.

The 1840's (his seventeenth to twenty-seventh years) were apparently the years in which his philosophical flux hardened into an attitude which lasted throughout the rest of his life. There was little of his later Spartanism about the letter which he wrote to a friend in 1844. He describes a gay life: "a sea-coal fire—a dressing-gown—slippers—a favorite author; all set off

---

[265] Sept., 1887; available in Farnham, p. 313.

[266] *Jesuits*, p. 199. This is thoroughly in accord with the emphasis on self-discipline and near-agnosticism of Parkman's New England. "Control thyself" was the doctrine preached by most of the major New England writers—Emerson with his emphasis on the inner check, Thoreau with his simple living and high thinking, Hawthorne with his preoccupation with sin, Longfellow with his code of restraint and gentlemanly action, Holmes with his doctrine of the "genteel."

[267] For a study of these currents of thought, see H. G. Townsend, *Philosophical Ideas in the United States*, and Woodbridge Riley, *American Thought*.

[268] See Farnham, p. 312.

by an occasional bottle of champagne, or a bowl of stewed oysters at Washburn's. . . . This is the cream of existence."[269] "After all," he continues, "a man was made to be happy; ambition is a humbug—a dream of youth; and exertion another."[270] These boyish words of his must have echoed sardonically some years later when he made that grim statement: "The true aim of life is not happiness but achievement."[271]

Barely two years after he was glorying in his Cambridge comfort, he wrote the following statement in his diary (the scene was St. Louis, the year, 1846): "The true philosophy of life is to seize with a ready and strong hand all the good in it, and to bear its inevitable evils as calmly and carelessly as may be."[272] This is the first stone he set in his philosophic structure. As he grew older, the sharp lines of the building grew softer; his viewpoint mellowed and became gentler; but the beginning was that vigorous sentence scribbled in his diary for 1846.

Perhaps the best way to round out that later belief is to see what qualities he liked and what qualities he disliked in the characters he wrote about. On both sides there is God's plenty of material. He disliked Newcastle's headlong thoughtlessness, his combination of timidity and rashness, and his lavishness with worthless promises.[273] He did not like La Barre, because he was "scared, excited, and blustering."[274] He disliked drunkenness.[275] He highly disliked egotism and vanity.[276] He had no respect for idleness and laziness, no sympathy for slackers.[277] He disliked weakness, and was disgusted by

[269]Letter to George B. Cary, Dec. 15, 1844; available in Sedgwick, pp. 130–1.
[270]*Ibid.*, p. 131.
[271]Wrong, *op. cit.*, p. 296.
[272]Quoted in Farnham, p. 309.
[273]*Montcalm and Wolfe*, I, 184.
[274]*Frontenac*, p. 92.
[275]*Old Régime*, p. 444, and others.
[276]*Montcalm and Wolfe*, I, 474–5; *Old Régime*, p. 420.
[277]*Old Régime*, pp. 338, 446; *Oregon Trail*, p. 90.

cowardice.[278] He deplored the "effusive humanitarianism of today."[279] And he had little liking for either the manners, the morals, or the lack of restraint in George II's England.[280]

On the other hand, he admired Champlain's "dauntless courage" and "unwearied patience."[281] When he dissected the character of Hale, he found that he liked the fearlessness, resoluteness, and endurance of the man, disliked his boastfulness, sarcasm, and sometimes-blind partisanship.[282] He admired Pitt's loftiness of soul, undaunted courage, proud incorruptibility.[283] He admired Frontenac because he was the sort of man who inspired trust,[284] and Wolfe because of his modesty, lack of fear, hardihood, contempt for effeminacy.[285] He admired Washington, "a name destined to stand one of the noblest in mankind," and Hamilton; Franklin was a little too materialistic for him, and Jefferson was a little too deeply infected with French democracy.[286] La Salle was a hero, he said, "not of a principle nor of a faith, but simply of a fixed idea and a determined purpose."[287] Did he "bend before the storm?"[288] No. He had the "Roman virtues."[289]

In fact, the qualities he liked both in these men and in the men of the forest and the men of religion who were discussed earlier in this section were the "Roman" virtues, the positive, masculine, soldierly ones which Rome learned from Sparta, and which, in a higher form, went into the Stoicism of Marcus

---

[278] *Frontenac*, 128 ff.; *Half-Century*, pp. 263–4.
[279] *Montcalm and Wolfe*, II, 46. Charles Sumner, who was a hero to so many New England writers, seemed only a sentimentalist to Parkman, and deficient in intelligence as well.
[280] *Montcalm and Wolfe*, I, 7–9.
[281] *Pioneers*, pp. 463–4.
[282] *Half-Century*, I, 224–49.
[283] *Montcalm and Wolfe*, I, 11.
[284] *Frontenac*, p. 324.
[285] *Montcalm and Wolfe*, II, 194–7.
[286] *Ibid.*, I, 137.
[287] *La Salle*, pp. 431–2.
[288] *Ibid.*, p. 202.
[289] *Ibid.*, p. 431.

Aurelius. The wisdom which he sought was the wisdom born of reason.[290]

For the clearest working out of this Stoic-Spartan-rational philosophy we turn to Parkman's novel, *Vassall Morton*. The novel sold sparsely. He never wrote another one, and neglected to include *Vassall Morton* when mentioning his collected works. Yet many a man has put into a novel a philosophy which he would blush to put into a history, and in this particular case the conditions were especially favorable for putting in the philosophy. Every first novel is supposed to be autobiographical; this one was interestingly so, both because it drew its scenery and some of its plot from Parkman's own experience and because its hero was much like Parkman.[291] He had the characteristics Parkman admired: frankness, openness, honesty, health, strength, vigor, love for the outdoors, firmness of purpose, modesty, dignity, sympathy, keenness. He was not materialistic, and he cared little for religion. His foil was a villain who had Parkman's pet dislikes; he was covert, sly, shrewd, sickly; he disliked the outdoors, and lived for money and publicity. Furthermore, the hero of the novel is set a problem parallel to Parkman's own life problem. That is why the book, too long neglected, is so important as a revelation of Parkman's attitude toward life.

Vassall Morton early decides that he needs some form of restraint. He tells his cousin that she is like a skyrocket without a stick; the stick is intended to "give balance and aim to the rocket—make it, as the transcendentalists say, mount skyward. . . ." If the rocket has no stick, "it sparkles, and blazes, and hisses on the ground; flies up and down, this way and that, plays the deuse [*sic*] with every thing and every body, and at last blows itself up to no purpose." And his cousin admits that he is right; she has no rational plan, no curb upon her impulses, no "rule of life."[292]

Of course, the rocket needs more than a guiding stick; it needs also a propelling force. The importance of energy, vigor, and action is again and again emphasized. "It is but a weak punishment to which Milton dooms his ruined angel," Morton cries from his prison cell:

"Action,—enterprise,—achievement,—a hell like that is heaven to the cells of Ehrenberg. He should have chained him to a rock, and left him alone to the torture of his own thoughts. ... Action! the panacea of human ills; the sure resource of misery; the refuge of bad consciences; a maelstroom [*sic*], in whose giddy vortex saints and villains may whirl alike."[293]

Might not that be the uninhibited voice of Parkman crying out from his darkened study? Like the hero in his book, he was "one of those unfortunates who are sentenced to a life of endless activity." He was one of those bulldog-like persistent individuals who never give up a task once begun until it is finished. As Morton said, "When I was in college, I laid down my plan of life, and adopted one maxim. . . . Never to abandon an enterprise once begun; to push on till the point is gained, in spite of pain, delay, danger, disappointment,—any thing."[294]

The formula stands: energy plus control. But suppose that an outside barrier, an apparently insurmountable obstacle, stands in the way of the action; suppose that the hero is cast into prison for life when his sweetheart and his career wait for him, or that Parkman is reduced almost to blindness when he wants to write the whole history of a continent and that he is troubled with such cerebral disturbances that he can seldom sleep and hardly dares think—then what is to be a man's

[292] *Vassall Morton*, p. 76.
[293] *Ibid.*, p. 208; see also pp. 209–10.
[294] *Ibid.*, p. 281.

course? The rocket is pointed into a great stone cliff; what to
do? The novel answers by defining "manhood" as

that unflinching quality which, strong in generous thought
and high purpose, bears onward towards its goal, knowing no
fear but the fear of God; wise, prudent, calm, yet daring and
hoping all things; not dismayed by reverses, nor elated by
success; never bending nor receding; wearying out ill fortune
by undespairing constancy; unconquered by pain or sorrow,
or deferred hope; fiery in attack, steadfast in resistance, unshaken
in the front of death; and when courage is vain, and hope seems
folly, when crushing calamity presses it to the earth, and the
exhausted body will no longer obey the still undaunted mind,
then putting forth its hardest, saddest heroism, the unlaurelled
heroism of endurance, patiently biding its time.[295]

And Morton said, "I will nail my flag to the mast, and there it
shall fly till all go down, or till flag, mast, and hulk rot together."[296] Marcus Aurelius the Stoic would have liked that,
and Leonidas the Spartan; and so also would Parkman's heroes,
Wolfe, Brébeuf, Champlain, and La Salle.

Furthermore, there is something to be won through adversity. "Misery is the mind-maker; the revealer of truth; the
spring of nobleness; the test, the purger, the strengthener of
the spirit. Our natures are like grapes in the wine press: they
must be pressed to the uttermost before they will give forth
all their virtue," Morton said.[297] And his sweetheart said to him,
"With a heart steeled by dangers, refined by sufferings, tempered in fires of anguish, what path need you fear to tread?"[298]
When Morton's cousin had passed through her ordeal of sorrow
and misfortune, she asked Morton whether he found her
scorched and withered. "I see," he said, "such traces as on gold
that has passed through the furnace."[299]

[295]*Ibid.*, p. 362.
[296]*Ibid.*, p. 217.
[297]*Ibid.*, p. 209.
[298]*Ibid.*, p. 321.
[299]*Ibid.*, p. 356.

What was the goal of this tempering process by which the soul was refined in the fires of misery and adversity? The heroine of the novel said of Morton: "It was a bitter schooling; a long siege, and a dreary one; but you have triumphed, and you wear its trophy,—the heroic calm, the mind tranquil with consciousness of power. You have wrung a proud tribute out of sorrow."[300]

The Stoic ideal—the heroic calm, the tranquil mind.

We could say that Parkman was a Stoic, and it is true that he was very close to the fundamental Stoical virtues and that he said in 1858 of the philosophy of Marcus Aurelius, "That's about as good a philosophy of life as you can get."[301] Yet he did not follow the metaphysics of the Stoic philosophy nor was he in agreement with many important beliefs of the Stoics. In his attitude, as has been pointed out, he was as much Spartan as Stoic.

The truth is that Parkman's attitude toward life was not Stoic, not Spartan, but personal to Parkman. It was born of his self-analysis and his own solution of his peculiar problem. Vassall Morton's philosophy holds a mirror up to Parkman's solution of his own problem. And in a sense Parkman's own criticism of life is a mirror held up to the virtues he was able to develop in himself. That is why he never formalized his belief; it was not for anyone else, it was personal to him.

His philosophy—if we may sum it up in terms of Francis Parkman, rather than Vassall Morton—is based on self-knowledge: Know thyself! In a remarkable passage he writes:

There is a universal law of growth and achievement. The man who knows himself, understands his own powers and aptitudes, forms purposes in accord with them, and pursues these purposes steadily, is the man of success. He who takes no account of his own nature, makes his will the father of his

[300] *Ibid.*, p. 383.
[301] Quoted in Farnham, p. 310.

thought, shuts his eyes to unwelcome truths, places himself in false positions, and turns from the good within his reach to strain after the unattainable, is predestined to vexation and failure. Every one has his place in the world, and the wise and fortunate find it.[302]

So one will learn to know his ship well, plot his course, and follow it to a goal. The self-knowledge, the navigation, is the task he assigns to reason. To keep the ship going requires a great deal of vital energy; to keep the course requires a great deal of ethical control, a great many of the stern Spartan and Stoical virtues. "The true aim of life is not happiness, but achievement."[303] But in achievement, in winning a hard fight fairly, there is a certain happiness—the heroic calm, the tranquil mind.

It is a manly philosophy, a brave philosophy. And we can say one thing about it which we are unable to say about many more formal, more ponderous, less individual philosophies: Its author was remarkably able to follow it.

VI. HIS PLACE

"It is in the literature of knowledge [in contrast to the literature of power] that we excel," writes Howard Mumford Jones in an article entitled "Salvaging Our Literature."[304] "We need to re-estimate the line of American historians constituted of some of our finest literary men . . . to see that Motley and Prescott, Parkman and Henry Adams are also in the great tradition."

In the case of Parkman this re-estimation is especially necessary, because the real Parkman has been nearly buried under an avalanche of extravagant praise and carping criticism. The

---

[302] Quoted, *ibid.*, p. 122.

[303] Wrong, *loc. cit.* For a similar vein of stoic heroism, see Longfellow's "Morituri Salutamus" and Emerson's essay, "Heroism."

[304] *American Scholar*, II, 361–2 (May, 1933).

criticism, far more salutary than the praise, has come mostly from groups on whose toes he stepped in his histories, notably from French Canadian churchmen,[305] and from the romantic idealizers of the Indian.[306] The praise, on the other hand, has rolled up in great waves of funeral and centennial eulogy. John Fiske linked Parkman's name, whenever he wrote or talked about him, with the names of Herodotus, Thucydides, and Gibbon.[307] Howells wrote proudly, "If we have objected to nothing in these histories, it is because we have no fault to find with them."[308] As a result, Parkman has been neatly tagged and pigeonholed almost from the minute he put his last book on the shelf. His stock has been fixed at a certain price and then taken off the market. There has been no biography of him since 1904,[309] and periodical treatments since then have mostly been concerned with special aspects of his work. Most scholars have felt, apparently, that Charles H. Farnham, in his official biography (1900), and such great contemporaries as Howells and Fiske, said the last word. The point is, not that Parkman's high reputation is unjustified, but that this sort of reputation is not good for a man. It leads toward atrophy. If Francis Parkman's work is really a part of the living, vital tradition of American letters it is time that his reputation is taken off the shelf, re-examined, and re-estimated in the light of our new knowledge and interpretation.

Let us begin by seeing how his books stand up under the various criticisms that have been made of them.

[305] Of whom Casgrain has always been the best spokesman.

[306] For example, see Theodore Parker's letter to Parkman, Dec. 22, 1851 (Farnham, pp. 374 ff.): "Yet I do not think you do the Indian quite justice," etc.

[307] For example, in the address at the commemorative service in Sanders Theatre, Harvard, Dec. 6, 1893; revised as a chapter in *A Century of Science and Other Essays;* expanded to form the introduction to the 20-volume Parkman, 1897–98—all containing the famous comparison.

[308] *Atlantic Monthly,* XXXIV, 610.

[309] Sedgwick's, in American Men of Letters series; see Bibliography, p. cxxxviii, below.

He has been accused of lack of appreciation of spiritual elements in experience, and unfairness toward the Catholic Church in Canada.

Perhaps the principal thesis in Farnham's biography is that Parkman's excellent development in the natural and rational realms of experience was not supplemented by a faith or a religion, and even Parkman's most devoted ally would have to admit the justice of this charge. Parkman was the ethical, rather than the religious, sort of man. His character and his actions were all that could have been expected of the most sincerely religious person; yet he never accepted the supernatural. If this is a fault in a historian, Parkman is guilty. The seriousness of the fault will have to be judged by its effect on his histories.

Some of his critics have found it to be a very serious fault indeed. Wisely and in good temper, his friend the Abbé Casgrain remonstrated against what Catholics thought was unfair treatment of the Catholic Church in Canada.[310] Perhaps less wisely and certainly in harsher temper, other Canadian Catholics argued likewise. The feeling led to the dramatic refusal, after a stormy discussion, to grant Parkman an honorary degree from Laval University. His more recent critics also have hinted at this defect. Joseph Schafer, for example, mentions "an occasional hint of imperfect sympathy; at frequent intervals a judgment marred by impatient harshness—these are slight defects."[311]

His Catholic critics did not think the defects were slight, and it is not hard to see what irritated those otherwise friendly readers. Parkman's complete skepticism before the super-

---

[310] See *Œuvres Complètes*, II, 294–335.
[311] "Francis Parkman," *Mississippi Valley Historical Review*, X, 364. Clarence W. Alvord (*Nation*, CXVII, 394–6) goes farther than Schafer in pointing out unfairness. He charges that Parkman had the "Anglo-Saxon superiority complex" which was so common at that time, and that this prejudiced him strongly against the French political and religious system.

natural, his arraignment of the participation of the clergy in civil affairs (inciting border raids, fomenting sedition, "vile practices" in Acadia,[312] petty politics in Quebec), his thinly veiled hostility to the spread of Catholic education, and his apparent fear that the Catholic population in the United States was growing faster than the Protestant—all these were extremely irritating to men who had been used to glorifying the deeds which Parkman holds up disapprovingly, and who had been used to reading their history in such a book as that of Charlevoix[313] whose interpretation is as nearly as possible the opposite of Parkman's.

On the basis of even a brief reading of his histories we can rightly accuse Parkman of "imperfect sympathy" with persons who believed sincerely in supernatural manifestations, and of "impatient harshness" in judging the actions of the Jesuits in Canada, but can we accuse him of intellectual and scholarly dishonesty? It was the Abbé Casgrain who pointed out the true key to Parkman's attitude—his firm rationalism which required him to find human explanations for the actions of men who, Catholics believe, were moved by supernatural inspiration. Parkman left the supernatural out of his scheme of things. Honestly, and in the best manner of the scientific historian, he interpreted events from a rational viewpoint. The "rock and iron" of his character, his stern, fierce love of truth (*rational* truth) and justice led him into impatient utterances which offended his Catholic readers even more than the facts which he reinforced with so many documents. He was not intellectually dishonest; from his own viewpoint he was not unfair. The difference between him and his Catholic critics is a fundamental clash of belief—rationalist vs. supernaturalist and religionist.

[312]For example, see *Montcalm and Wolfe*, I, 294.
[313]*History of New France* (Englished and annotated by J. G. Shea). See Parkman's reviews of these volumes in *Atlantic Monthly*, XX, 125, and XXIV, 499.

That Parkman may have been partial to New England was not mentioned in the funeral and memorial studies, for the good reason, perhaps, that most of those writers were New Englanders. In a few of the centennial essays, however, the charge is made bluntly and effectively. Thus Clarence Alvord says that Parkman fell victim to the "current Anglo-Saxon superiority complex," that he knew Western history very imperfectly, and that he neglected essential matters of other histories in favor of less essential facts concerning New England and New Englanders.[314] Likewise, James Sullivan finds that Parkman is an illustration of "Sectionalism in Writing History," that he was unduly partial to Anglo-Saxon institutions and especially New England manifestations of these.[315] And W. G. Leland implies that some such attitude is at the bottom of what he calls Parkman's misinterpretation of the French government.[316] Parkman was too fond of English institutions, he says. The despotic nature of French rule was *not* responsible for the downfall of New France. There was "as much individual freedom in Canada as in New England, and very likely more," he declares. The real reasons for the downfall were the geographical situation (Canada was too big and had access to the sea only six months of the year), the weakness of the economic life (because the fur trade absorbed energies which might otherwise have been turned to farming, and because it drew colonization ever farther into the interior and mitigated against settlements), and the failure of immigration (French Canada was outnumbered twenty to one at the end of the war with England).

Of course, Mr. Leland could be answered on his own ground. Although Parkman undoubtedly did no more than lip service to the geographical situation, he did consider the others at some

---

[314] *Nation*, CXVII, 394–6 (Oct. 10, 1923).
[315] See Sullivan's article, *New York State Historical Journal*, II, 73–88.
[316] *Ex Libris*, I, 232–3.

length. Again and again, he made the statement that if France had relaxed its despotic refusal to let the Huguenots migrate, these Protestants would have filled up the Mississippi Valley and made all North America a French colony. France let only those migrate who did not wish to, and refused permission to those who did. Likewise, the nature of France's control of its colony encouraged fur trading, rather than settlement and farming. America was not a place to settle; it was a place to make a fortune with which to return to France. In the last chapters of *The Old Régime* Parkman traces with great skill the throttling effect of the long-range control from Versailles.

However, the accusation in general has some strong evidence on its side. The constant complaint of the French critics that Parkman failed to appreciate their religious and political system is not without truth. The charge of sectionalism is emphasized by the interest Parkman took in such massacres as those at Deerfield, an interest out of all proportion to his interest in the non-New England frontiers which fairly rolled in blood. And yet there is no good reason to accuse Parkman of consciously blowing the bugle for New England. If he had wanted to do that he had a glorious chance when he wrote of Sir William Phips and his odyssey up the St. Lawrence; but he paints Phips very realistically and calmly, and remarks disapprovingly that Cotton Mather's account of the same expedition, in the *Magnalia*, is "excessively eulogistic." No, if Parkman was prejudiced toward Anglo-Saxon institutions and New England interpretations it was not because he was intellectually dishonest, but because he absorbed those prejudices from his environment. His was the age of nationalism, the age of the great bloom of New England when Anglo-Saxon traditions seemed to be vindicating themselves. His class was what Holmes called the "Brahmin class" of New England. If Parkman could look on New England with a wholly objective eye, if he could set his New England ancestors against Canada's ancestors and New

England's Anglo-Saxon republican and Protestant traditions against French Catholic and absolutist traditions, and still never reveal by the slightest emphasis whether he lived north or south of the St. Lawrence, he would be a very remarkable man indeed. And the remarkable fact is that so little evidence of prejudice —and no evidence of intentionally weighting the scales toward his prejudice—is discernible in his writing.

It is improbable that either one of the preceding charges would have much disturbed Parkman. He would have said, as he said of some of the conclusions he wrote into *The Old Régime:*

Some of them are of a character which I regret, since they cannot be agreeable to persons for whom I have a very cordial regard. The conclusions drawn from the facts may be matter of opinion, but it will be remembered that the facts themselves can be overthrown only by overthrowing the evidence on which they rest, or bringing forward counter-evidence of equal or greater strength; and neither task will be found an easy one.[317]

Indeed the task will not be found an easy one. We have seen how Parkman searched Europe and America for every document, every piece of evidence which might bear on the subjects he wrote about, how he reinforced his books with copious references to his evidence, how he hated the sentimentalizing or falsifying of material. His intellectual integrity was always more important to him than the good opinion of his critics. He was always willing to recant. He kept his books in a constant process of revision and was prevented by death from carrying out a thorough revision of the whole series. Toward new evidence he was always open-minded; in a conflict of personal opinions, he preferred his own.

Since his death, a constant search of the archives has been in progress and the most scientific tests have been applied to the fields of which he wrote. How many errors of fact has this

[317] *Old Régime*, p. xi.

prolonged and intensive investigation charged up to Parkman? There have been a few. The Canadian critics have made some dents in his story of the expulsion of the Acadians, chiefly by unearthing new documents which were not available to Parkman. Parkman's story was based on publications of the Province of Nova Scotia which have been shown to be badly garbled. Furthermore, South Dakota investigators have cast some doubt on his story of the Verendryes. But his sins have been shown to be rather of omission than of commission—lack of attention to important events outside New England, for instance, and too little attention to social and economic history. Almost nothing that he wrote has had to be written over because of errors of fact. No other American historian who covered a field of any considerable magnitude can make the same claim. Bancroft's volumes were superseded before Bancroft was in his grave. Prescott's Mexicans were soon shown to be dream creatures. Motley's partisanship for the Dutch was admitted even by him. But Parkman's work has stood up almost without blemish against nearly four decades of painstaking source study. We may take the word of James Truslow Adams, who says: "The long series of systematic archival investigations that have been carried on since the completion of his work have supplemented it and have corrected it at certain points but have not impaired its substantial validity."

That Parkman's portrait of the Indian was too unfavorable was the common feeling of the romanticists of his own day,[318] and the same opinion has recently been stated by another writer whose book is slightly reminiscent of those romantic doctrines, Albert Keiser. Mr. Keiser, in his book *The Indian in American Literature*,[319] says that "within certain limits"

[318] See Parker, *loc. cit.*
[319] Albert Keiser, *The Indian in American Literature.* See the more complete and penetrating discussion of the problem in J. A. Russell's article, "Francis Parkman and the Real Indian," *Journal of American History*, XXII, 121–9.

Parkman's characterization of the Indian, in *Pontiac*, is admirable,[320] but he takes exception to the darkness of the portrait ("Parkman as the historian of the clash of French and English interests and cultures on American soil not unnaturally was impressed by the darker side of aboriginal character which such a conflict inevitably revealed"),[321] and he defends Cooper's Indians against Parkman's incredulity.[322] He might also have pointed out that Parkman's whole theory of the rational man as superior to the natural man, his Federalism, would have tended to make him deprecate the good qualities of the Indian. And yet Parkman does not deprecate the Indian's good qualities. He makes much of them. The difference between his portrait of the Indian and the typical romantic portrait is that the romantic portrait is one-sided, whereas Parkman's portrait is rounded; he paints in both the good and the bad qualities. John Fiske summed up a historian's view of the matter when he said: "His Indians are true to the life. In his pages Pontiac is a man of warm flesh and blood, as much so as Montcalm or Israel Putnam. This solid reality in the Indians makes the whole work real and convincing."[323]

In our day, of course, we have no direct way of finding out what the Indians of the seventeenth and eighteenth centuries really were. Parkman had a better chance. There were still wild bands of Indians on the prairies, and he spent a summer with them and most of a lifetime studying about them. There is some justification for pitting Parkman's characterization of the Indian—in view of his direct experience with them, his extensive research, and his well-known hardheaded rationality in interpreting facts—against the opinions of critics who may have been swayed by preconceived notions of the nobility of the natural man.

[320] Keiser, *op. cit.*, p. 294.
[321] *Ibid.*, pp. 294-5.
[322] *Ibid.*, pp. 142-3.
[323] "Francis Parkman," *Atlantic Monthly*, LXXIII, 667.

The suggestion by modern historians[324] that Parkman lacked interest in sociological, economic, and institutional history practically amounts to saying that Parkman is not "modern," for sociological, economic, and institutional history is the kind modern historians like to write. And, in that sense, Parkman is truly not modern.

This is not to say that he completely omitted these factors. He was interested in social conditions, and wrote several brilliant chapters on them in *The Old Régime*.[325] He brought in the economic problem frequently, especially the importance of the fur trade. He wrote the history of at least one institution, the Catholic Church in Canada, although the members of that church have been loath to accept his interpretation. But he did not emphasize any of these factors in the way Charles A. Beard, for instance, might emphasize the economic elements, or Vernon L. Parrington the political viewpoints and the workings of economic determinism. As Edward Bourne said, he "belonged to the narrative school of historians, and chose to picture the past rather than reason about it."[326] He was not a speculative historian; he was a dramatic, narrative historian. And therein lay both his strength and, some modern historians would say, his weakness.

The fact that he loved the dramatic in life and possessed the ability to record it on paper led him sometimes to overwrite. This was especially true of his earlier books. Consider, for instance, this sentence from *La Salle:*

They had reached the mouth of the Missouri, where that savage river, descending from its mad career through a vast unknown of barbarism, poured its turbid floods into the bosom of its gentler sister.[327]

---

[324] For example, Schafer, *op. cit.*, p. 358.
[325] See chapters XV–XXIV.
[326] E. G. Bourne, *Essays in Historical Criticism*, p. 285.
[327] *La Salle*, p. 69.

And these from *Pioneers:*

Years rolled on. France, long tossed among the surges of civil commotion, plunged at last into a gulf of fratricidal war. Blazing hamlets, sacked cities, fields steaming with slaughter, profaned altars, and ravished maidens, marked the track of the tornado.[328]

This "labored picturesqueness,"[329] as Schafer aptly calls it, tended to disappear as Parkman grew older and farther from his romantic models. Nor is it typical of his style in general, which is vivid without losing good taste. Of his books, Howells said, "We find their style delightful always."[330] That same delightful quality, which Howells noticed, was the one which, in his younger and less stable years, led him to overwrite. It is the quality which so seldom appears on the pages of modern historians, to the regret of their readers. And of this criticism we may say that Parkman with his style was like a man with an automobile. When the car is new the man is apt to drive too fast out of sheer joy in the performance of his possession, but when that first exuberance is worn away he is likely to become a steady, able driver. And so Parkman, out of sheer joy in his ability to recreate the dramatic moments of history, sometimes drove too fast while the experience was yet a new one.

In general, Bliss Perry is right when he says that Parkman "hated change" and was unable to assimilate the new ideas of his day.[331] In considering his political theory we pointed to numerous reactionary attitudes he took, and we saw that he was a staunch Federalist in the midst of a democratic, romantic age. And yet to Parkman the struggle was not one between the present and the past, but between a certain set of general principles which he sincerely believed and the apparently more transitory intellectual currents of the day. His mind was not

---

[328] *Pioneers*, p. 233.
[329] Schafer, *op. cit.*, p. 560.
[330] "Mr. Parkman's Histories," *Atlantic Monthly*, XXXIV, 610.
[331] "Some Personal Qualities of Parkman," *loc. cit.*

the typical reactionary mind. He seldom lamented the passing of the "good old days" nor did he wish that he had been born into some other age and country. Rather, he selected his principles and beliefs out of the past and present and his own experience, wherever he found usable ones—and stuck to them. Thus he was firm in his belief in liberty, as opposed to license and absolutism, in the rational road to truth, in the importance of action and achievement; and his almost Puritan vigor in speaking those beliefs was like the vigor of many other men who uphold what they believe are permanent principles against the flux of their day. And so Parkman, like many others, was called a reactionary.

It is surprising that no more has been said of the organization of Parkman's history. Almost all the criticism has had to do with his opinions or his accuracy or his style. Faults in organization were hinted at by Theodore Parker in a letter to Parkman concerning *Pontiac*[332] and by Joseph Schafer when he remarked that the unity of the series was dramatic, rather than logical.[333] But the surprising fact is that the books are units neither in themselves nor as a series. There is a constant clash between two distinct points of view—the dramatic and the political. The dramatic point of view would interpret the history of the French-English conflict as a series of events clustered around the lives of a few important men; the other would see it as a logical series of events between the causes and the final solution, with a number of men playing interesting parts in the events. That conflict between the importance of the man and the importance of the chain of events is glaringly evident throughout *France and England in North America*. The number of the titles which bear names of men and the evident fondness of Parkman for the biographical elements of the story bear witness to his tendency to organize each book as a dra-

[332]Parker, *loc., cit.*
[333]Schafer, *op. cit.*, pp. 265–80.

matic unit, complete in itself; the scope of the series, the linking chapters, and the many cross-references indicate his wish to write of the struggle as a whole. And the final result indicates that neither one nor the other finally won out. The books are not complete and independent units in themselves, nor do they join together, without loose fitting, spare parts, and unequal emphases, to make a series. This was apparently to have been the object of the final revision, which Parkman never accomplished—to have welded the nine volumes of *France and England in North America* into a unit.

This discussion of the case against Parkman has at least indicated that his art has limitations. Now let us see what can be said of that art in the way of a more positive estimate of Parkman's place among American historians. When Parkman chose his career two new currents were powerfully altering the course of history. One was the romantic contemplation of the glories of the past, a movement which looked to literature for its inspiration in the historical novels of Scott and the romances of Chateaubriand, and in America the novels of Cooper and the stories of Irving. The other was the inductive, critical, and scientific approach to the remnants of the past, which was typified by the beginnings of scientific philology in Germany and the new historical writing of Wolf and Niebuhr, and which was brought across the Atlantic by American students from Göttingen:[334] Ticknor, Bancroft, Hedge, Everett, and others. Both currents were offshoots of the Romantic Movement and its respect for the past. One led historians to become intensely interested in some portions of the past which, less than a century before, had seemed wholly uninteresting. The other led historians to build their generalizations inductively from evidence painstakingly gathered and weighted.

---

[334] For a study of early American students at Göttingen, see O. W. Long, *Literary Pioneers: Early American Explorers of European Culture* (Cambridge, Mass., 1935).

From the one current Parkman took his love for the picturesque and dramatic, his vivid style; from the other he took his respect for sources and their honest, accurate interpretation. The rational, inductive method of the one he combined with the penetrating flashes of the other, and his whole structure was built on the solid rock of almost fanatical research and preparation.

Thus Parkman stood between the older group of American moralist-historians—represented a century before by Cotton Mather and his righteous *Magnalia* and in Parkman's own time by Jared Sparks with his twelve volumes of *Washington*[335]— and the new hybrid history of the social scientists, represented in our time by Charles A. Beard,[336] Frederick Jackson Turner,[337] and Vernon L. Parrington.[338] The older group, like Parson Weems,[339] put hatchets in George Washington's hand and then expounded the moral at great length. When Jared Sparks read a portion of the manuscript of *Pontiac* in 1850 he saw it as "a striking picture of the influence of war and religious bigotry upon savage and semi-barbarous minds."[340] And in his indignation at the murderous exploit of the Paxton Boys,[341] he complained, "Although you relate events in the true spirit of calmness and justice, yet I am not sure but a word or two of indignation now and then, at such unnatural and inhuman

---

[335]Cotton Mather's monumental *Magnalia Christi Americana, or the Ecclesiastical History of New England* was printed in England in 1702, in America in 1820. Jared Sparks's work is *The Life and Writings of George Washington* (12 vols., 1834–7).

[336]C. A. Beard, *The Economic Origins of Jeffersonian Democracy* (New York, 1915); with his wife, Mary R. Beard, *The Rise of American Civilization* (rev. 1933).

[337]F. J. Turner, *The Frontier in American History* (1920).

[338]Parrington, *Main Currents in American Thought* (New York, 1927–30).

[339]The cherry-tree story appeared first in a revised edition of M. L. Weems's *Life of Washington*, along with other folklore which helped Weems to peddle fifty editions of the book.

[340]Quoted in Sedgwick, p. 222.

[341]Described in *Pontiac*, chapter XXIV.

developments of the inner man, would be expected of a
historian, who enters deeply into the merits of his subjects."[342] The younger group, strangely indoctrinary in their
own tendency, have been trained to regard history as a
science, the rules for which may be learned through accurate investigation, and the whole of which may be interpreted by means of these fundamental rules. Thus Taine
applied his three tests to all of English literature. And thus in
our own time Turner expounds the importance of the frontier,
Beard of economic determinism, and Parrington of critical
liberalism.

From the moralist, Parkman borrowed the vigor, left the
moral. To the later historians he left his strenuous ideal of
documentation and his fervid respect for the truth, without
anticipating their interest in the social and economic aspects of
the story. He achieved an objectivity to which the moralists
had never attained, and he left a living, dramatic style which his
followers have never equaled.

Prescott and Motley were his greatest contemporaries among
American historians and yet in a sense his predecessors, for
Prescott's great works were published before Parkman's first
book and Motley's histories were out before Parkman began
his chronicle of France and England in North America. The
three men were surprisingly different although almost the same
influences acted on them all. All three had learned the value
of thorough research and convincing documentation; all three
had learned to write history as interesting as fiction; yet they
went three ways. Motley let his heart lead his head when he
told the story of the Dutch struggle for liberty from Spain. He
himself said in a letter to Prescott: "You have by nature the
judicial mind which is the *costume de regueur* of all historians. . . .
I haven't the least of it—I am always in a passion when I write
and so shall be accused, very justly perhaps, of the qualities for

[342]Sedgwick, p. 222.

which Byron commended Mitford, 'wrath and partiality.'"[343]
He has, indeed, been accused of wrath and partiality, and perhaps the greatest detriment to his reputation today is the fact that so many of his conclusions—made in the heat of his hatred of oppression—must be rewritten. Prescott, as Motley said, was a much calmer, more objective person. If his books on Mexico and Peru are today regarded as untrustworthy, it is because he followed the old Spanish sources and saw everything through their eyes; modern ethnology has told a far different story.[344] If Parkman is the superior of these men it is because of the sternly impersonal justice of his judgments, on the one hand, and because of the greater reliability of his fundamental facts, on the other.

He is perhaps superior, too, in the magnitude of his task and his product. He was extremely fortunate in his subject: a gigantic one to tax his phenomenal powers of gathering, assimilation, and interpretation; a grand one, with mighty scenery, dramatic events, powerful men. No other American historian has ever covered such a vast field so surely and finally. No other American historian has been able to breathe life so successfully into so many different and interesting men or recapture from

[343] Quoted in H. T. Peck, *William Hickling Prescott*, p. 166.

[344] "Here is the great contrast between Parkman's work and that of Prescott in so far as the latter dealt with American themes. In reading Prescott's account of the conquest of Mexico one feels one's self in the world of the Arabian Nights; indeed, the author himself, in occasional comments, lets us see that he is unable to get rid of just such a feeling. His story moves on in a region that is unreal to him, and therefore tantalizing to the reader; his Montezuma is a personality like none that ever existed beneath the moon. This is because Prescott simply followed his Spanish authorities not only in their statements of physical fact, but in their inevitable misconceptions of the strange Aztec society which they encountered; the Aztecs in his story are unreal, and this false note vitiates it all. In his Peruvian story Prescott followed safer leaders in Garcilasso de la Vega and Cieza de Leon, and made a much truer picture; but he lacked the ethnological knowledge needful for coming into touch with that ancient society, and one often feels this as the weak spot in a narrative of marvelous power and beauty." (John Fiske, "Francis Parkman," *Atlantic Monthly*, LXXIII, 667.)

oblivion so many dramatic events. "This isn't history; it is romance!" exclaimed a modern historian. And yet it *is* history.[345]

Allan Nevins has made a nice distinction among the characteristics of these three historians. "If in Prescott we are
impressed by color, and in Motley by eloquence," he says, "in
Parkman the abiding impression is of vividness." For Parkman,
perhaps more than for any other American historian, history
was what Michelet said it was—"resurrection." His great
ability lay in the resurrection of men, moments, and scenes
from the past. Perhaps because he was compelled to *listen* to
so much of his material being read in the shadows of his study,
he created for himself sharp, clear pictures of the faces, the
sounds, the forests. These pictures he transferred to his books.
The art has almost died with him. "After the Civil War,"
writes Nevins, "new historians arose. But they were trained
in a different school; their aims were primarily factual and
scientific instead of literary, and among them all Henry Adams
was the only writer whose literary gifts kept his work steadily
at the point of real distinction." [346]

Given a few wishes, we could wish many differences in
Parkman's history: more unity in the individual books[347] and
in the series, for instance, more attention to social and economic questions, greater sympathy for beliefs foreign to his
own. But there is no doubt that he succeeded in his object and
that the history he has written is firm and enduring, as well as
vivid and dramatic. He himself, with his regard for achievement, would have considered that of much greater importance
than the result of the process of relativity by which critics have
for years, and almost with one voice, named him the greatest
of American historians.

[345] C. W. Alvord, *Nation*, CXVII, 395.

[346] In John Macy (ed.), *American Writers on American Literature*, pp.
241–2.

[347] None of Parkman's series are as much units in themselves as Prescott's *Conquest of Mexico* or *Conquest of Peru*.

Born into the Romantic Movement, writing his greatest books in the Age of Realism, Francis Parkman declined allegiance to either and gave it rather to the rational Federalism of the age before. We have seen in the preceding pages that Romantic sentimentalism sickened him; what he chose to call "romantic eccentricities"—transcendentalism, individualism, utopianism, humanitarianism, back-to-Nature-ism—disgusted him. He would have argued with Emerson the sources of knowledge and the problem of evil. He disliked Thoreau's eccentric nature.[348] He had no sympathy for Longfellow's mellow sentiment.[349] He was deaf to the pleas of the abolitionists, and thought union more important than freedom of the Negroes.[350] Himself a lover of nature, he stood at sword's points with the whole Romantic Movement over the meaning of nature and over the concept of the natural man. And although he is not known to have expressed himself at length on the literature of realism, he repeatedly took his stand against the materialism of the postwar years. He feared that materialism would throttle out art itself. "The present condition and prospects of American Literature are not very flattering," he said in 1875. "A score or more of years ago there seemed a fair hope that the intellectual development of the country would not be absolutely disproportioned to its material growth; but thus far the hope has not been fulfilled, and, relatively to our vast increase in wealth and population, the value, though not the volume, of literary products is less than before."[351]

From each age he took what he wanted. From the romantic age in general he heard the call to an investigation of the past, although he never chose to look at the past through nostalgic

[348] See Farnham, p. 196.

[349] See *Montcalm and Wolfe*, I, 294, and Farnham, p. 348.

[350] See letter to Norton previously quoted, available in Sedgwick, p. 221. See also footnote 201, above.

[351] *North American Review*, CXX, 34.

spectacles. From the scientific German scholars of the age he
took a method of investigating the past. From the romantic
novelist Scott and others he learned the value of vivid pages.
If he gained anything from the realists it was support for his
realistic attitude toward facts. From the Federalists he drew
his political viewpoint and his rationalism. "Yet through the
rock and iron of his character, there ran, known to but few, a
delicate vein of poetic feeling"[352]—this characterization of one
of the figures in *Vassall Morton* might have been applied to
Parkman himself. The rock and iron—evident in his stern
vigor, his demand for justice, his uncompromising attitude—
came from his ancestral Puritanism reinforced by his Federalistic
training; the poetic feeling—evident in the glamour of his pages
and in his eye for nature—was in key with the Romantic
Movement.

His books are a compromise between his contemporary
inclination to romanticize and the restraint he learned from
Puritan and rationalist teachers. A very few pages will show
a reader that he might have liked to romanticize the Indian as
Cooper did and to glorify wild natural scenes as Scott did; but
he resisted the temptation and, as one of his critics says, "gave
so cool and objective a portrait of the Indian that it has been
criticized by philanthropic persons as lacking sympathy. . . .
This 'Passionate Puritan,' as his daughter called him, described the whole triple conflict of Indian, Frenchman, and
Briton under the same double impulse: delight in the romance
of it all, held in leash by a cool scientific interest in analyzing the defects of French institutions . . . and showing
how Anglo-Saxon practicality and democracy overthrew
them."[353]

He was too big for a pigeonhole, and yet if we have to
pigeonhole him we must call him a romantic. Basically his

[352]Said of Euston in *Vassall Morton*, p. 46.
[353]*American Writers on American Literature*, p. 240.

history was romantic: stirring events in a setting of great natural vigor (an unknown continent, mysterious forests, rivers, mountains, and savages), and the whole story told in a colorful and dramatic style. That was Prescott's formula, and Motley's, and we have seen that it was also Parkman's—up to a certain point. But the limitations of the name "romantic" are nowhere more glaringly evident than when the name is used to define the writing of Parkman.

In American literary thought he stands as the apostle of liberty, opposed to both license and absolutism; as the representative of rationalism against both natural inspiration and supernatural inspiration; as the representative of Spartan and Stoic virtues amidst an age of natural goodness and materialistic laissez faire; as a realist, searching uncompromisingly for truth; as a thinker of unusual stability who could make up his mind on the fundamental questions by the time he reached his middle twenties and plan a course of action to last throughout the rest of his life; as a man of unusual moral fibre who could early choose an object in life and pursue that object over almost insurmountable obstacles to a successful conclusion.

His books join with the Federalist papers, the best American state papers, and the works of a few other historians in triumphant proof that the literature of knowledge can be literature. For the great individual triumph of Parkman is in using—and still hiding—his vast scholarship in books that are as exciting as Cooper's, as true as Howells's, as dramatic as Melville's,[354] books that because of the character of their thought and method belong in the American tradition as surely as do *The Deerslayer*, *The Rise of Silas Lapham*, and *Moby Dick*.

Since Parkman's time only a very few historians have been admitted without question to American literature, one—Henry Adams—more for his autobiography and a book of interpreta-

---

[354] For an eloquent tribute to Parkman's style, see James Russell Lowell's unfinished essay in the *Century Magazine*, XLV, 45.

tion that is almost autobiography than for his history,[355] and another—John Fiske—as much for his work on science as his work on history.[356] Modern historians have kept Parkman's scholarship but, it seems, lost the magic elixir for which De Soto searched and which every great author has—the priceless formula which keeps men and their actions forever alive.

[355] *The Education of Henry Adams* and *Mont St. Michel and Chartres.* His great historical work was *The History of the United States* (during the administrations of Jefferson and Madison), in nine volumes.

[356] Such as *Outlines of Cosmic Philosophy*, *The Destiny of Man*, etc.

1823. Born September 16, at 4A Allston Street (then Somerset Place), Boston, to the Rev. Francis Parkman and Caroline Hall Parkman. Descendant of Elias Parkman who settled in Dorchester in 1633; on his mother's side, descendant of John Cotton.

1829. Family moved to 1 Green Street.

1831–36. At Medford, for the sake of his health, lived with his maternal grandfather.

1831–40. Attended private schools.

1837. Family moved to 5 Bowdoin Square.

1840. Entered Harvard. As a freshman, he roomed with Benjamin Gould in 9 Holworthy Hall; as a sophomore, he lived at Mrs. Ayers's house, 4 Appian Way; as a junior, he occupied 24 Massachusetts Hall; and as a senior, 21 Massachusetts.

1841. Vacation trip with Daniel Slade. Portsmouth to Alton, Lake Winnipesaukee to Centre Harbor; on to the Notch, and up Mount Washington; thence to Franconia Notch, Lancaster, Colebrook, Dixville Notch; to the Androscoggin River near the mouth of the Magalloway.

1842. Another trip to the Magalloway, accompanied this time by Henry Orne White. Albany, Saratoga, Glens Falls, to Lake George; studied battlefields around Caldwell; Ticonderoga; through Canada to headwaters of the Magalloway; Essex, Jericho, Underhill, Johnson, Troy, Stanstead, Canaan; Connecticut Lake.

1843. Winter vacation trip to Keene, N. H. Another trip to Canada; Lake George, Lake Champlain, St. Johns, Chambly; Montreal; back to Boston by way of White Mountains. Went to Bangor, Maine, to study Indian traditions. September, sailed for Europe.

1843–44. September, 1843 to June, 1844, traveled through Sicily, Italy, Switzerland, France, Great Britain. Returned to United States. Received A.B. from Harvard; entered law school. Walking trip over hills of western Massachusetts: through Springfield, Cabotville, Chester Factory, Lee, Stockbridge, Great Barrington, Lebanon Springs, Stephentown, the Hopper, and North Adams.

1845. In April began a trip to St. Louis, and spent summer collecting materials for *Pontiac*. Visited Lancaster, Paradise, Harrisburg, Williamsport, Trout Run, Blossburg, Corning, Seneca Lake, Rochester, Buffalo, Detroit, Windsor, Sandwich, Mackinac, Sault Ste. Marie, Palmer, Newport, Niagara, Devil's Hole, Fort Niagara, Oswego, Syracuse, Onondaga Castle. Contributed sketches to *Knickerbocker Magazine*, March, April, and June; poem, August.

1846. Received LL.B. from Harvard. April 28, set out from St. Louis over the Oregon Trail to Fort Laramie. Lived some weeks with band of Sioux. Visited Pennsylvania cities: Trenton, Philadelphia, Harrisburg, Carlisle, Chambersburg, Pittsburgh; also Baltimore and Washington. October, showing signs of physical breakdown, went to Brattleboro, Vermont. Dictated *Oregon Trail* to his companion Quincy Shaw.

1847. February, first instalment of *Oregon Trail* published in *Knickerbocker Magazine*.

1848. Began to write *History of the Conspiracy of Pontiac*. Spent six months on Staten Island.

1849. *Oregon Trail* published in book form.

1850. May, married Catherine Scollay Bigelow, daughter of Jacob Bigelow, Boston physician.

1851. *Pontiac* published. Much hampered in health, began to collect material for his historical project. Wrote reviews for the *Christian Examiner*.

1853. Experiencing nervous crisis, put work aside and went to Northampton. Began work on a novel.

1856. His novel, *Vassall Morton*, published. Made trip to Montreal, Quebec, Nova Scotia.

1857. Death of his only son.

1858. Death of his wife, leaving him with two daughters, Grace and Katharine. Renewed nervous crisis; consulted specialists in Paris.

1859. Returned to Boston by way of Nice and Genoa. Lived at Jamaica Pond, summers; winters, with mother and sisters in Boston until 1864. Unable to work on books, occupied himself with horticulture. Between 1859 and 1884 received 326 awards from the Massachusetts Horticultural Society.

1862. Formed partnership for business venture in horticulture. Lasted one year.

1863–74. Chairman of library committee, Massachusetts Horticultural Society. Served as vice-president, 1871–74; president, 1875–78.

1865. Published *Pioneers of France in the New World*. Visited Washington and Richmond.

1866. Published *The Book of Roses*. Visited Montreal, Two Mountains, the Long Sault, the Chaudière, Quebec.

1867. Published *The Jesuits in North America*. Trip to Fort Snelling; visited Keokuk, Peoria, Illinois River, Prairie du Chien, St. Louis.

1868. Elected overseer of Harvard; resigned 1871; re-elected 1874–76. Spent winter in Europe.

1869. Published *La Salle and the Discovery of the Great West*.

1871. Harvard appointed him professor of Horticulture in the Bussey Institute.

1872. Went to Europe to collect historical materials.

1873. Visited along shores of St. Lawrence below Quebec.

1874. Published *The Old Régime in Canada*.

1875. Chosen fellow of Harvard Corporation.

1876. Developed the *lilium Parkmanni*. Granted membership in the Royal Historical Society, London.

1877. Published *Frontenac and New France under Louis XIV*. Visited battlefields of Lake George and Quebec.

1878. Made honorary member, London Society of Antiquarians.

1879. Helped found the Archeological Institute of America. Awarded LL.D. by McGill. Visited Quebec and Louisburg.

1880. Participated in organization of St. Botolph Club, Boston. Summer trip to Europe.

1881. Summer trip to Europe.

1884. Published *Montcalm and Wolfe*. Made corresponding member, Royal Society of Canada.

1885. Southern trip: Beaufort, Fernandina, Jacksonville, Fort George, Palatka, Ocklawaha River, Ocala, and St. Augustine. LL.D., Williams.

1886. Camped for a month on Batiscan River.

1887. Last journey to Europe: Santander, Madrid, home by way of Paris.

1888. Began to spend summers in old Wentworth house, Portsmouth, N. H.

1889. LL.D., Harvard.

1892. Severe attack of pleurisy. Published *A Half-Century of Conflict*.

1893. November 8, died at Jamaica Plain.

SELECTED BIBLIOGRAPHY

I. WRITINGS

(The seven volumes of the "great history," *France and England in North America*, are numbered according to their position in that series. Entries in this section are chronological.)

The Oregon Trail. New York: 1849. (Narrative of his trip across the prairies in 1846. Originally serialized in *Knickerbocker Magazine*, beginning 1847. Called *The California and Oregon Trail* because of publicity value of title during gold-rush years. For a contemporary review see Francis Bowen's favorable critique in *North American Review*, LXIX, 182–96 [July, 1849].)

The Conspiracy of Pontiac and the Indian War after the Conquest of Canada. Boston: 1851. (The story of Pontiac told as a part of the story of English conquest in America. Follows in time immediately after *Montcalm and Wolfe*, which describes the end of the Seven Years' War and the conquest of Canada. For contemporary reviews of *Pontiac* see Francis Bowen in *North American Review*, LXXIII, 495–529 [October, 1851]; G. E. Ellis in *Christian Examiner*, LI, 376–94 [November, 1851]; *Littell's Living Age*, XXXI, 137–40 [October 18, 1851]; *Brownson's Quarterly Review*, N.S. VI, 139 [January, 1852]. *Littell's Living Age*, XXXII, 143–4 [January 17, 1852], prints extracts from the English critical notices. See also the letter criticizing *Pontiac* written to Parkman by Theodore Parker, reprinted in Farnham's *Life* [see below], pp. 374–8.

Vassall Morton. Boston: 1856. (A novel with autobiographical elements. See W. L. Schramm, "Parkman's Novel," *American Literature*, IX, 218–27, May, 1937.)

I. *Pioneers of France in the New World.* Boston: 1865. (First part deals with the struggle of French Huguenots and Spanish Catholics for Florida; second, with Champlain and his

associates. For a contemporary review see *Littell's Living
Age*, LXXXIX, 880–1 [June 23, 1866]. Parkman wrote this
book without having seen the Southern scenery it describes,
contrary to his usual practice of first-hand observation. In
later years he made a trip to the South and wrote personal
observations and new material into later editions of the book.
Chapters printed in advance of book publication in *Atlantic
Monthly*, XII, 30–5, 225–40, 537–55 [July, August, November, 1865], and XIV, 530–7 [November, 1864].)

The Book of Roses. Boston: 1866. (This is a by-product of the
middle years of Parkman's life when eyes and nerves forbade
his writing history. The first part of the book deals with the
culture of the rose; the second part describes many varieties
of roses.)

II. *The Jesuits in North America in the Seventeenth Century*.
Boston: 1867. (After an introduction on Indian tribes,
Parkman tells the story of the long struggle of Jesuit priests
to Christianize the Indians, ending with the rout of the converted tribes by the Iroquois about 1670. For contemporary
reviews, see *Nation*, IV, 450–1 [June 6, 1867]; *Littell's
Living Age*, XCV, 765–7 [December 21, 1867]—both favorable; and "Rome or Reason," in *Catholic World*, V, 721–2
[September, 1867], which declares that Parkman com-
prehends little of the Jesuits' "whole interior spiritual life."
Advance chapter in *Atlantic Monthly*, XIX, 723–31 [June,
1867].)

III. *La Salle and the Discovery of the Great West*. Boston: 1879.
(Published in 1869 as *The Discovery of the Great West*.
La Salle's name added after publication of Margry's monumental collection of La Salle material and use of that material. The story of La Salle's courageous effort to colonize
the Mississippi valley, in the face of opposition and jealousy.
Other Western explorers mentioned. Commendatory reviews in *Nation*, IX, 389 [November 4, 1869], and by George
E. Ellis in *North American Review*, CX, 260–84 [April, 1870].
The eleventh edition of the book, with its new material, is
reviewed in *Nation*, XXIX, 241 [October 9, 1879].)

IV. *The Old Régime in Canada.* Boston: 1874. (This book states, perhaps more clearly than any other, Parkman's political theory of the failure of France in the New World. The first part of the book describes the feudal chiefs of Acadia; the second deals with the mission problem; and the third analyzes with remarkable clarity the relation of colony and king. For a contemporary review, quite favorable, see *Nation*, XIX, 252–3 [October 15, 1874]. Advance chapters in *Atlantic Monthly*, XXX, 687–701 [December, 1872], XXXII, 84–91, 691–8 [July, December, 1873], and *North American Review*, CXVIII, 225–55 [April, 1874].)

V. *Count Frontenac and New France under Louis XIV.* Boston: 1877. (Frontenac portrayed as the strong man who alone could maintain France's precarious hold on her colony. For contemporary reviews see W. F. Allen, "Parkman's Frontenac," in *Nation*, XXV, 259 [October 25, 1877]; M. P. Lowe, in *Unitarian Review*, IX, 210 [February, 1878]; *Canadian Monthly*, XII, 541–4 [November, 1877]. Advance chapters in *Atlantic Monthly*, LIII, 719–32 [December, 1876].)

VII. *Montcalm and Wolfe.* Boston: 1884. (The final volume in Parkman's story of the conflict. Deals with the Seven Years' War in America and ends with the final downfall of France on the Plains of Abraham. For contemporary reviews see J. A. Doyle, in *Academy*, XXVI, 335–6 [November 22, 1884]; *Nation*, XXXIX, 506 [December 11, 1884]; E. G. Mason, in *Dial*, V, 235–6 [January, 1885]; *Athenaeum*, I, 113–5 [January 24, 1885]; *Atlantic Monthly*, LV, 265–70 [February, 1885]; *Macmillan's Magazine*, LI, 336–45 [March, 1885]; *Critic*, VI, 211–14 [May 22, 1885]. Advance chapters in *Atlantic Monthly*, LIV, 339–51, 444–56 [September, October, 1884].)

Some of the Reasons against Woman Suffrage. No date. (Printed 1887, by request of an association. This pamphlet is a succinct statement of his view of the matter, and is largely a repetition of the arguments already advanced in two articles published 1879 and 1880. See "The Woman Question" and "The Woman Question Again," p. cxxvii below.)

Our Common Schools. Boston: 1890. (A plea for the continuance of the public school, which, he says, is menaced by the rapid increase in Catholic schools.)

VI. *A Half-Century of Conflict*. Boston: 1892. (This was the last book Parkman wrote, although its place is not last in the series. Parkman put it aside while he wrote what he thought was a more important work, *Montcalm and Wolfe*. *A Half-Century* bridges the gap between the end of *Frontenac* and the beginning of *Montcalm and Wolfe*, or approximately the years 1700–1741. It deals mostly with border warfare, and such expeditions as that which resulted in the siege of Louisbourg. For contemporary reviews, see *Critic*, XX, 348 [June 25, 1892]; *Nation*, LV, 9–10 [July 7, 1892]. Advance chapters appeared in *Atlantic Monthly*, LXI, 783–93 [June, 1888], LXVII, 314–25, 514–23, 621–30 [March, April, May, 1891], and LXXI, 25–31, 201–13 [January, February, 1893].)

Among library editions of the historical works are the Champlain Edition, 20 vols., 1897; the Frontenac Edition, containing Farnham's *Life*, 17 vols., 1902; and the Centenary Edition, 13 vols., 1924. The Frontenac is perhaps to be preferred, but there is little difference in quality of text. Any authorized edition after 1893 will have a good text.

"The Ranger's Adventure," *Knickerbocker Magazine*, XXV, 198–201 (March, 1845). (Story of an old ranger's encounter with Indians.)

"The Scalp Hunter, A Semi-Historical Sketch," *Knickerbocker Magazine*, XXV, 297–303 (April, 1845). (Eight white men against the Indians.)

"A Fragment of Family History," *Knickerbocker Magazine*, XXV, 504–18 (June, 1845). (Adventures of one of the writer's ancestors in search of a girl stolen by Indians.)

"The New Hampshire Ranger, by Captain Jonathan Carver, Jr.," *Knickerbocker Magazine*, XXVI, 146–8 (August, 1845). (Poem in ballad meter, dealing with the adventures of rangers near Lake George during the "Old French War.")

"Satan and Dr. Carver, by Captain Jonathan Carver, Jr.,"
Knickerbocker Magazine, XXVI, 515–25 (December, 1845).
(Amusing adventures of a physician who thought he was about
to be attacked by Indians.)

Review of Squier, E. G. *The Serpent Symbol and the Worship
of the Reciprocal Principles of Nature in America. Christian
Examiner*, LI, 140–1 (July, 1851). (Says that the book might
be called "An exposition of the Philosophy of Symbolism as
applied to the Ideas of Religion.")

Review of Cooper, James Fenimore. *Works*, revised edition.
North American Review, LXXIV, 147–61 (January, 1852).
(Although he thinks Cooper's Indians are not true to life,
he admires Cooper for vividness, vigor, and nationalism.)

Review of French, B. F. *Historical Collections of Louisiana.
Christian Examiner*, LIV, 142–3 (January, 1853). (Praises
abundance of documents.)

"Exploring the Magalloway," *Harper's Magazine*, XXIX, 735–
41 (November, 1864). (A trip taken during one of his college vacations. Drawn mostly from his journals.)

"Manners and Customs of Primitive Indian Tribes," *North
American Review*, CI, 28–64 (July, 1866). (Material on social
and political life of Indian tribes, much of which later went
into *Jesuits*.)

"Indian Superstitions," *North American Review*, CIII, 1–18
(July, 1866). (Showing that the savage intellect was "the instrument of a blind frenzy," that the Indian was fundamentally irrational.)

Review of Read, J. M. *An Historical Inquiry concerning Henry
Hudson. Atlantic Monthly*, XIX, 764 (June, 1867).
"Genuine research concentrated on an object truly historic,
and producing results of a real interest and value.")

Review of Charlevoix, P. F. X. de. *History and General Description of New France.* Reviewed, *Atlantic Monthly*, XX,
125 (July, 1867). Again, *Atlantic Monthly*, XXIX, 499–500
(April, 1872). (Praises translator, J. G. Shea, for having
supplied the documentation the book lacked, and for having
corrected some of the errors of Charlevoix.)

Review of Riedesel, Madam General. *Letters and Journals Relating to the War of the American Revolution and the Capture of the German Troops at Saratoga. Atlantic Monthly*, XXI, 127–8 (January, 1868). (Praises translation by W. L. Stone.)

Review of Morgan, H. J. *Bibliotheca Canadensis. North American Review*, CVII, 370–1 (July, 1868). (Considers this manual indispensable to students of history, but demurs at choice of material.)

"The Tale of the Ripe Scholar," *Nation*, IX, 558–60 (December 23, 1869). (Penetrating discussion of education.)

Review of Bonnechose, Charles de. *Montcalm et le Canada Français. Nation*, XXIV, 269 (May 3, 1877). (Argues that the failure of French colonization was due not "to unavoidable causes," but to the despotic and exclusive policy pursued by the government in limiting the colonization.)

Review of Bancroft, H. H. *The Native Races of the Pacific States of North America. North American Review*, CXX, 34–47 (January, 1875). (High praise for the project and the objective quality of the scholarship.)

Review of Higginson, T. W. *Young Folks' History of the United States. North American Review*, CXX, 469–71 (April, 1875). (Favorable.)

Review of Margry, Pierre, compiler. *Découvertes et établissements des Français dans l'Ouest et dans le Sud de l'Amérique septentrionale: mémoires et documents originaux. Nation*, XXIII, 168–9 (September 14, 1876). (Parkman summarizes the contents of this first volume, which he had worked so long and hard to have published, and states its importance.)

"Cavalier de la Salle," *North American Review*, CXXV, 427–38 (November, 1877). (Portrait of La Salle, based on Margry's volume of documents, and containing much material which later went into revised edition of *La Salle.*)

Review of Rameau, M. *Une Colonie féodale en Amérique. Nation*, XXV, 400 (December 27, 1877). (Parkman declares this book is guilty of both inaccuracy and misinterpretation. Rameau retorted, and Parkman replied, *Nation*, XXVI, 230 [April 4, 1878].)

Review of Le Moine, J. M. *The Chronicle of the St. Lawrence.* *Nation*, XXVII, 30 (July 11, 1878). (Pleasant summary.)

"The Failure of Universal Suffrage," *North American Review*, CXXVII, 1–20 (July-August, 1878). (The goal is not universal balloting, but good government.)

"Mr. Parkman and His Canadian Critics," *Nation*, XXVII, 66–7 (August 1, 1878). (Answers critics of his view of religious and political history of Canada, and challenges them to bring forth facts to support their criticisms.)

Review of Stewart, George, Jr. *Canada under the Administration of Lord Dufferin.* *Nation*, XXVII, 369 (December 12, 1878).

"The Woman Question," *North American Review*, CXXIX, 303–21 (October, 1879). (Arguments against woman suffrage. The right of voting and the duty of fighting should not be dissociated. Woman has higher duties.)

"The Woman Question Again," *North American Review*, CXXX, 16–30 (January, 1880). (Restatement of his position and answer to critics.)

Review of Joliet, Louis. "Note on Joliet's Map." *Nation*, XXX, 438 (June 10, 1880). (Discusses circumstances under which map was made, and considers its accuracy.)

Review of Ellwanger, H. B. *The Rose.* *Nation*, XXXIV, 366 (April 27, 1882). (Thinks the book will be useful to the amateur.)

Review of Hole, S. R. *A Book about Roses.* *Nation*, XXXVI, 476 (May 31, 1883). ("Unequalled.")

"The Acadian Tragedy," *Harper's Magazine*, LXIX, 877–86 (November, 1884). (Expulsion of the Acadians justified on argument that they would neither take the oath of fealty to Britain nor leave the country, and that they were a constant source of danger. See H. H. Smith's reply to this article in *Nation*, XXXIX, 374–5 [October 30, 1884], and Parkman's rejoinder, *Nation*, XXXIX, 398 [November 6, 1884].)

Review of Sargent, C. S. *The Forests and the Census.* *Atlantic Monthly*, LV, 835–9 (June, 1885). (Parkman's review develops into a vigorous and farseeing essay in praise of forest conservation.)

"Revocation of the Edict of Nantes," *Critic*, VII, 205–6 (October 31, 1885). (Bicentennial of what Parkman calls an "act of bigoted tyranny.")

Review of T. C. B. *Voyage au Canada dans le Nord de l'Amérique septentrionale fait depuis l'an 1751 à 1761. Nation*, XLII, 314–5 (April 15, 1886). (This "French memoir of our colonial history" is "inaccurate.")

Review of Hard, F. G. *The Fall of New France, 1755–1760. Nation*, XLVI, 308 (April 12, 1888). (Biting criticism of poor writing and inaccurate statement.)

Review of Irving, T. J. *Indian Sketches. Nation*, XLVI, 385 (May 10, 1888). (Summary, and notations from Parkman's own experiences.)

Review of Casgrain, H. R. *Un Pèlerinage au pays d'Évangeline. Nation*, XLVIII, 232–3 (March 14, 1889). (Parkman disputes Casgrain's defense of the Acadians.)

"A Convent at Rome," *Harper's Magazine*, LXXXI, 448–54 (August, 1890). (Parkman spent a week in a Passionist convent at Rome during his college days. This account is drawn from his journals.)

Review of Lucas, F. W. *Appendiculæ Historicæ. Nation*, LII, 346 (August 23, 1891). (Brief summary of Lucas's interpretation of cartography found on an old powder horn.)

Review of Girouard, Désiré. *Lake St. Louis, Old and New; and Cavalier de la Salle. Nation*, LVII, 200 (September 14, 1893). (Mostly summary.)

Parkman contributed the following articles to the *American Journal of Horticulture:* "Spring Flowers" (January, 1867); "Flowers of May" (February, 1867); "New Dwarf Perpetual-Flowering Carnations" (October, 1868); "Comtesse de Chabrilland Rose" (June, 1869); "Variations of Flowers from Seed" (November, 1869); "How to Propagate Shrubs" (February, 1870); "Spanish Iris" (December, 1870); "Deutzia Crenata Flore Pleno" (January, 1871).

To the Boston *Daily Advertiser*, during the war years, he sent the following letters: "The Nation's Ordeal" (September

4, 1861); "To the Lingerer" (August 12, 1862); "Why Our Army Is Not the Best in the World" (October 14, 1862); "Conservatism" (October 17, 1862); "The Weak Side of Our Armies" (June 30, 1863); "The Chiefs of the Nation" (July 4, 1863); "Aristocrats and Democrats" (July 14, 1863); "Our Best Class and the National Politics" (July 21, 1863).

II. LETTERS, DIARY, MISCELLANEOUS

Articles on Frontenac, La Salle, and Montcalm for *Appleton's Cyclopedia of American Biography*, 1866–7.

Preface to William Smith's *Historical Account of Bouquet's Expedition against the Ohio Indians*. Cincinnati: 1868. (Parkman speaks of the Indian character and traces in historical background.)

Letter welcoming Carl Schurz to Boston, in *Visit of the Honorable Carl Schurz to Boston, March, 1881*. Boston: 1881.

Letter to meeting at Trinity Chapel, Boston, to organize the Boston branch of the Indian Rights Association. Published in *Critic*, VIII, 248 (May, 1886). (Favors "strong and watchful" protection.)

"Report on the Alleged Sharpless Portraits of Washington," *Proceedings of the Massachusetts Historical Society*, 2d series, III, 179–86 (1886–7). (Parkman's committee decides the portraits are not of great value.)

"French War Papers of the Maréchal de Lévis Described by the Abbé Casgrain," *Proceedings of the Massachusetts Historical Society*, 2d series, IV, 92–3 (1888). (Fifty copies of these comments were later printed in pamphlet form.)

Autobiographical letters, written to George E. Ellis, 1868, and to Martin Brimmer, 1886. Largely repetitive. The former letter is available entire in *Proceedings of the Massachusetts Historical Society*, 2d series, VIII, 349 ff. (1893), and in Farnham's biography of Parkman, pp. 318–32. It was also reprinted in the *Harvard Graduates' Magazine*, June, 1895. The latter is available in its entirety in Sedgwick's biography, pp. 327–38. Portions are reprinted in the *Proceedings, loc. cit.*, and in Farnham, *loc. cit.*

Letters from Francis Parkman to E. G. Squier, with biographical
   notes and a bibliography of E. G. Squier, by Don C. Seitz.
   Cedar Rapids, Iowa: 1911. (Twenty-four letters. Early ones
   contain interesting references to his personal condition; later
   ones mostly matter-of-fact.)

"Letters of Parkman to Pierre Margry," with introductory note
   by John Spencer Bassett, *Smith College Studies in History,*
   VIII, Nos. 3 and 4 (April-July, 1923). (Eighty-three letters from
   Parkman to Margry; four by Parkman to Spofford; two by
   Spofford to Parkman. Much information on the attempts to
   have Margry's documents published, and a few personal
   references.)

Many letters are reproduced in the biographies by Farnham
and Sedgwick.

Parkman kept a diary from 1841 to 1846. He used much of
this material in the *Oregon Trail* and the articles listed above
which are ascribed to the diary. Other parts of the diary are
plentifully excerpted by Farnham and Sedgwick.

For record of many valuable manuscripts deposited by Park-
man in the Library of the Massachusetts Historical Society, see
Transactions of the Society, 2d series, I, 360–2; III, 152, 153;
VI, 105, 391, 392; VII, 348, 349; VIII, 171.

III. BIOGRAPHY AND CRITICISM

(The most important titles in this section are starred.)

Abbott, L. F. "Francis Parkman," *Outlook,* CXXXV, 212–14
   (October 10, 1923). (Centennial tribute. Quotes letter from
   Theodore Roosevelt.)

Abbott, L. F. "Two Literary Sportsmen," *Outlook,* CXLVII,
   177 (October 12, 1927). (Emerson and Parkman as sportsmen.)

*Alvord, Clarence W. "Francis Parkman," *Nation,* CXVII,
   394–6 (October 10, 1923). (Centennial estimate by another
   historian. Romantic nature of Parkman's history. Was interested in New England more than in the West; knew inti-
   mately only two parts of Western history, those concerning

La Salle and Pontiac. Also subscribed to current Anglo-Saxon superiority complex. But still he is our greatest American historian.)

[Anonymous.] "Topographical Accuracy," *Nation*, LVII, 412 (November 30, 1893). (Parkman personally observed the land he wrote about.)

[Anonymous.] "Notes on Translations of Parkman by Madame de Clermont-Tonnerre," *Nation*, XXXVI, 213 (March 8, 1883). (She omitted certain passages in order to make the histories more pleasing to Catholic readers.)

[Anonymous.] *A Critical Review of the Works of Francis Parkman*. Boston: 1897. (Publisher's advertisement.)

[Anonymous.] "What Francis Parkman Has Done for American History," *Current Opinion*, LXXV, 549–50 (November, 1923). (Largely quotation.)

*Bassett, John S. "Francis Parkman, the Man," *Sewanee Review*, X, 285–301 (1902). (Résumé of his life, with an interpretation of Parkman as "a product of New England Puritanism and a protest against it.")

Bourne, Edward G. *Essays in Historical Criticism*. New Haven: 1913. (Chapter on Parkman, pp. 277–87, explains him as a narrative, rather than a reasoning, historian. Chapter first used as introduction to 1901 edition of *Oregon Trail*.)

Bowman, James C. Introduction to *The Oregon Trail*. Modern Student's Library. New York: 1924. (Summarizes career. Says *Oregon Trail* is important because "one learns what men of the Stone Age are like.")

Bradley, A. E. "Francis Parkman and His Work," *Macmillan's Magazine*, LXIX, 420–9 (April, 1894). (A picture of the country and history about which Parkman wrote.)

Cairns, W. B. *A History of American Literature*. New York: 1912. (Brief discussion of Parkman's works, pp. 344–5.)

Calnek, William A. *History of the County of Annapolis*. Edited and completed by A. W. Savery. Toronto: 1897. (The ninth chapter, pp. 123–44, is a defense, by the editor, against Parkman's charge that the Acadians would neither leave the country nor take the oath.)

The Cambridge History of American Literature. New York: 1917–21. (Parkman discussed briefly by J. S. Bassett, III, 189–91.)

*Casgrain, Henri R. "Biographies Canadiennes," in *Œuvres Complètes*, II. (Chapter on Parkman, II, 294–355, balances good points against what Casgrain considers Parkman's misinterpretation of the Catholic Church in Canada.)

Casgrain, Henri R. *Francis Parkman.* Quebec: 1872. (Part of the same material discussed in the previous reference.)

Casgrain, Henri R. *Un Pèlerinage au pays d'Évangeline.* Paris: 1886. (A brief in favor of the Acadians and their conduct at the period of deportation. Parkman relied on materials published by the Province of Nova Scotia; Casgrain shows that these were garbled.)

Cooke, George W. "Francis Parkman," *New England Magazine*, N.S. I, 248–62 (November, 1889). (A broad survey of his career up to 1889. Life, purpose, résumé of work. Valuable for its contemporary picture. Interestingly illustrated.)

Coolidge, Mrs. J. T., Jr. Two-stanza poem to Francis Parkman, quoted in Farnham's *Life*, p. 210. (Mrs. Coolidge was Parkman's daughter.)

Dictionary of American Biography. New York: 1932–6. (James Truslow Adams writes on Parkman, XIV, 247–50. Brief bibliography.)

Doyle, John Andrew. *Essays on Various Subjects.* Edited by W. P. Ker. London: 1911. (Chapter on Parkman, pp. 54–118, divides all American historians into three sorts—filiopietistic, cosmopolitan, and scientific—and says that Parkman transcends all groups. His history is a combination of love for England, appreciation of his own country, indefatigable toil, genuine zeal, and a love for letters.)

E. G. J. "Memoirs of an American Historian," *Dial*, XXIX, 259–61 (October 16, 1900.) (Parkman's likes and dislikes.)

Eggleston, Edward. "Notes on the Completion of Mr. Parkman's Work," *Century Magazine*, XLV, 46 (November, 1892). (Sample: "Only the other day, in a quiet library in Chestnut Street, Boston, a great scholar, who is at the same

time a charming writer, put the last touches to a work that
has cost almost a lifetime of absorbing and devoted toil.")

*Farnham, Charles H. *A Life of Francis Parkman*. Boston:
1900. (Best critical and interpretative biography. The author
wisely departs from the chronological style of writing biography, and divides his book into three parts: preparation,
reflection of personality in works, moral growth. Stresses
the fact that Parkman lacked spiritual growth. See sympathetic reviews in *Nation*, LXXI, 368–9 [November 8, 1900],
and *Critic*, XXXVIII, 415–6 [May, 1901].)

Farnham, Charles H. "Francis Parkman in Jamaica Plain and
Boston," *Critic*, VIII, 101–2 (February 27, 1886). ("Authors
at Home" series.)

*Fauteux, Aegidus. "Francis Parkman," *Bulletin des Recherches
Historiques*, XXXI, 177–83 (June, 1925). (Address delivered
at the Parkman centennial celebration in Montreal. The
French-Canadian viewpoint: gratitude to and respect for
Parkman, but dislike of his attitude toward the Church and
his pro-Anglicism.)

*Fiske, John. *A Century of Science and Other Essays*. Boston:
1899. (Chapter on Parkman, pp. 194–264. Originated as
address at Sanders Theatre, Cambridge, December 6, 1893,
on the occasion of a commemorative service. Expanded,
this material went into the *Atlantic Monthly*, LXXIII, 664–
74 [May, 1894], as an article. The chapter here listed is the
same article with the addition of much more biographical
material. In this form it was used as an introduction to the
20-volume edition of Parkman's works, 1897–8. The chapter is a thoughtful analysis of the qualities of greatness in
Parkman's work. Mentions his truthful picture of Indians,
knowledge of past civilizations, painstaking research and observation, his clear perception of issue between France and
England. Places Parkman among few greatest historians of
the world.)

Fiske, John. "Francis Parkman," in Carpenter, G. R., *American Prose*, New York: 1907. (Parkman, pp. 433–50. The
same material went into previously listed article by Fiske.)

Fitch, G. H. *Great Spiritual Writers of America*. San Francisco: 1916. ("Francis Parkman's Historical Work," pp. 103–10. Stresses ethical values of Parkman's work.)

*Frothingham, O. B. "Memoir of Francis Parkman," *Proceedings of the Massachusetts Historical Society*, 2d series, VIII, 520–62 (1894). (Useful biographical data written by a man who had known Parkman, who had access to all the manuscripts of the Massachusetts Historical Society, and who was said to have been allowed use of the diaries.)

Garland, Hamlin. Introduction to *The Oregon Trail*. Modern Reader's Series. New York: 1930. (The spirit of the West.)

Godkin, E. L. "Francis Parkman," *Nation*, LXXI, 441 (December 6, 1900.) (A brief character sketch by a friend.)

Gould, George M. *Biographic Clinics*. Philadelphia: 1904. (Study of Parkman's maladies, II, 131–202. Says that eyestrain was the cause of all Parkman's ill-health except his arthritis; see Introduction, pp. xxviii–xxxi.)

Gregory, J. G. "The Parkman Club," *Wisconsin Magazine of History*, VII, 309–19 (March, 1928). (The object of the Parkman club was to study northwestern historical subjects and publish results.)

Hale, B. B. Two-stanza poem quoted in M. A. D. Howe's *American Bookmen*, p. 152.

Holmes, Oliver Wendell. Memorial Poem, in *Proceedings of the Massachusetts Historical Society*, 2d series, VIII, 360–1. Quoted in Sedgwick's *Parkman*, pp. 339–40. (The poem was read at the commemorative meeting of the society, November 21, 1893.)

Howe, M. A. DeWolfe. *American Bookmen*. New York: 1898. (Chapter on Parkman and Prescott, pp. 125–52, appeared originally in *Bookman*, V, 383–94 July, 1897. Compares the two men.)

Howe, M. A. DeWolfe. "Two Historians," *Atlantic Monthly*, XCIV, 709–10 (November, 1904). (Uses Ogden's and Sedgwick's biographies as points of departure for a comparison of Prescott and Parkman.)

Howells, William Dean. "Mr. Parkman's Histories," *Atlantic Monthly*, XXXIV, 602–10 (November, 1874.) (Summary of Parkman's work. "If we have objected to nothing in these histories, it is because we have no fault to find with them.")

Jameson, J. A. *History of Historical Writing in America.* Boston: 1891. (Parkman is the author who most conspicuously continued the school of picturesque historians; the only American historian in the last twenty-five years who can fairly be called classical.)

J. M. R. "Francis Parkman," *National Education Association Journal*, XII, 83–4, (March, 1923). (Brief centennial summary of life and career.)

Keiser, Albert. *The Indian in American Literature.* New York: 1933. (Interesting, although undocumented, summary of the whole subject. Parkman mentioned briefly on pp. 126, 142–3, 294–5, 299. Defends Cooper's Indians against Parkman's criticism. Thinks Parkman's Indians are too evil.)

Leland, W. G. "Francis Parkman, 1823–1923, and the History of New France," *Ex Libris*, I, 227–34 (February, 1924). (Written by the director of historical research in Paris of the Carnegie Institute. Argues that the real reasons for the fall of New France were the geographical situation, the weakness of the economic condition, and the failure of immigration, rather than despotism of French government.)

Le Moine, J. M. "Reminiscences of Francis Parkman at Quebec," *Canadian Magazine*, III, 493–7 (October, 1894). (Pleasant memories.)

Leonard, W. E. Introduction to *The Oregon Trail.* New York: 1910. (A good general introduction.)

Lodge, Henry Cabot. "Francis Parkman," *Proceedings of the Massachusetts Historical Society*, 2d series, LVI, 319–35 (1923). (Read before the Society, June 14, 1923. Personal reminiscences and high praise.)

Logan, J. D., and French, D. G. *Highways of Canadian Literature.* Toronto: 1924. (P. 396, reference to the influence of Thomas Chandler Haliburton's *Historical and Statistical Account of Nova Scotia* on Parkman's books.)

Lowell, James Russell. "Francis Parkman," *Century Magazine*, XLV, 44–5 (November, 1892). (An unfinished essay more interesting as the last piece Lowell prepared for publication than as a study of Parkman. It was apparently to have been a very favorable verdict.)

MacDonald, William. "Francis Parkman," *Literary Review*, IV, 37–8 (September 15, 1923). (Compliments Parkman for clearness, vividness, simplicity.)

Margry, Pierre. "À Francis Parkman, auteur des Français en Amérique." (Poem written in honor of Parkman's birthday, 1872. Three stanzas—of the original ten—quoted in Sedgwick's biography, p. 290.)

Mayo, Lawrence Shaw. "Francis Parkman," Boston *Evening Transcript* (September 15, 1923). (An intelligent appreciation.)

Moulton, C. W., editor. *Library of Literary Criticism of English and American Authors*. New York: 1910. (Many excerpts from criticisms of Parkman's works, VIII, 218–26. A useful means of tracing his reputation.)

*Nevins, Allan. "Prescott, Motley, Parkman," in Macy, John, ed., *American Writers on American Literature*. New York: 1931, pp. 226–42. (Interesting comparisons of personality, style, and accuracy.)

Oliver, J. W. "Francis Parkman," *Western Pennsylvania Historical Magazine*, VII, 1–9 (January, 1924). (Biography and long series of critical quotations from eminent men.)

Parkman Centenary Celebration at Montreal, November 13, 1923. Montreal: 1923. (Another account in *Proceedings of the Massachusetts Historical Society*, 2d series, LVII, 190–2 [1923].)

Parrington, Vernon L. *Main Currents in American Thought*. New York: 1927–30. 3 vols. (Parkman discussed, II, 438–9. "The Brahmin mind has contributed to American letters no more brilliant work than came from the pen of Francis Parkman.")

*Perry, Bliss. "Some Personal Qualities of Parkman," *Yale Review*, N. S. VIII, 443–8 (April, 1923). (Sympathetic essay, especially valuable for its analysis of the effect of Parkman's early reading.)

Polmaise, Alan. "Parkman and the Martyrs," *Commonweal,* XII, 546–8 (October 1, 1930). (Parkman's books played important part in canonization of such martyrs as Brébeuf and Garnier.)

Richard, Edouard. *Acadia; Missing Links of a Lost Chapter in American History, by an Acadian.* New York: 1895. ("A labored and unconvincing attempt to refute Parkman's justification of the removal of the Acadians.... Involved, tedious, controversial, intemperate . . . partisan character evident."— Grace Griffin, in *Writings on American History.*)

Robinson, Doane. "Parkman Not in Dakota," South Dakota Historical Department, *South Dakota Historical Collections,* XII, 103–7 (1924). (Evidence that Parkman was not in South Dakota nor any section of the Black Hills as we now know them.)

Robinson, Doane. "Parkman's Story of the Verendryes," South Dakota Historical Department, *South Dakota Historical Collections,* VII, 380–402 (1914). (Parkman's story reprinted from *A Half-Century* "chiefly for the purpose of indicating several palpable errors" in his conclusions.)

Russell, Benjamin. "What We Owe to Francis Parkman," *Dalhousie Review,* III, 330–41 (October, 1923). (With frequent quotations from Parkman and his critics, the essay concludes that we have to thank Parkman for his vivid recreation of history and his clear insight.)

Russell, J. A. "Francis Parkman and the Real Indian," *Journal of American History,* XXII, 121–9 (1928). (Parkman's pictures were in the main accurate.)

*Schafer, Joseph. "Francis Parkman, 1823–1923," *Mississippi Valley Historical Review,* X, 351–64 (March, 1924). Also in *Wisconsin Magazine of History,* VII, 265–80 (March, 1924). (Points out some defects amidst the familiar excellences. Parkman is not a social or economic historian, is sometimes laboredly picturesque, and represents romance in history.)

Schouler, James. "Francis Parkman," in Hyde, W. D., ed., *Vocations.* Boston: 1911. VIII, 317–25. (Parkman as representative of the vocation of writing.)

Schouler, James. *Historical Briefs*. New York: 1896. (Chapter on Parkman, pp. 1–15, reprinted from *Harvard Graduates' Magazine*, II, 305–15 [March, 1894]. Pleasant summary of Parkman's career.)

*Sedgwick, Henry Dwight. *Francis Parkman*. American Men of Letters series. Boston: 1904. (Useful as a source-book, rather than as a critical interpretation. Long quotations from Parkman's diary. Many letters quoted entire. See review in *Nation*, LXXIX, 82–3 [July 28, 1904].)

Simonds, W. E. "Two American Historians," *Dial*, XXXVII, 207–8 (October 1, 1904). ("Peculiar parallelism" in the lives of Prescott and Parkman.)

Slade, D. D. "In the White Mountains with Francis Parkman in 1841," *New England Magazine*, N.S. XI, 94–9 (September, 1894). (Parkman's college chum recalls vacation trips, and illustrates with excerpts from Parkman's diary.)

Stewart, George. "The Works of Francis Parkman," *New England Magazine*, XX, 704–11 (August, 1899). Also in *Canadian Magazine*, XIII, 362–8 (August, 1899). (Parkman's careful documentation.)

Sullivan, James. "Sectionalism in Writing History," *New York State Historical Association Journal*, II, 73–88 (April, 1921). (Evidence that Parkman was not free from sectionalism. He emphasized New England matters to exclusion of other important ones.)

The Times (London) *Literary Supplement*, September 20, 1923, pp. 609–10. (His are "the most vigorous and living pictures yet produced of Canada from its discovery till its conquest by the English.")

Trent, William P. *History of American Literature, 1607–1865*. New York: 1903. (High praise for Parkman's style, pp. 553–8.)

Trent, William P., and Erskine, John. *Great American Writers*. New York: 1912. (Brief consideration of Parkman's life and writings, pp. 181–6.)

Underwood, F. H. *The Builders of American Literature*. Boston: 1893, pp. 252–4. (Parkman "has now less renown than some of his more fortunate rivals" because his books are less sensational.)

Underwood, F. H. "Francis Parkman," *Contemporary Review*, LIII, 642–60 (May, 1888). Emphasizes the importance of his subject matter.)

Vedder, Henry Clay. *American Writers of Today*. Boston: 1894. (Superficial chapter on Parkman, pp. 27–42. Makes much of physical disabilities. Parkman "secure among the immortals.")

Vincent, Leon Henry. *American Literary Masters*. Boston: 1906. (Chapter on Parkman outlines his career and work, well summarizes his characteristics, and says much of imagination and style.)

Ward, Julius H. "Francis Parkman," *McClure's Magazine*, II, 185–98 (January, 1894). (Survey of Parkman's achievement. "Who would have thought, fifty years ago, that a member of the Harvard class of 1844 . . . would grow up to be the historian of 'England and France in North America'?"—and more of the same.)

Ward, Julius H. "Francis Parkman and His Work," *Forum*, XVI, 419–28 (December, 1893). (Broad summary. Stresses his truth and fairness.)

Wendell, Barrett. "Francis Parkman," *Proceedings of American Academy of Arts and Sciences*, XXIX, 435–47. (Interesting personal reminiscences and evaluation of his style.)

Wendell, Barrett, and Greenough, Chester N. *A Literary History of America*. New York: 1904. (Parkman, pp. 225–6. "Latest and most mature of our historians.")

*Wheelwright, Edward. "Memoir of Francis Parkman," *Publications of the Colonial Society of Massachusetts*, I, 304–50 (1894). (This and O. B. Frothingham's are the best memoirs of Parkman. Well grounded in personal memories and documentary evidence and rich in biographical data.)

Williams, Basil. "The Centenary of Francis Parkman," *History*, N.S. VIII, 269–74 (January, 1924). (Summarizes centennial celebration, records an appreciation of Parkman's work, and concludes with a brief note on editions.)

Williams, Basil. "Francis Parkman," in *Annual Report* of Canadian Historical Association, 1923, pp. 39–48. (Material similar to preceding reference.)

*Winsor, Justin. "Francis Parkman," *Atlantic Monthly*, LXXIII, 660–4 (May, 1894). (High praise from a fellow historian. Parkman's Indians were real Indians. Contrast between realistic atmosphere of Parkman's books and unreal atmosphere of Prescott's.)

*Wrong, George M. "Francis Parkman," *Canadian Historical Review*, IV, 289–303 (December, 1923). (Excellent antidote to a superfluity of adoration. Points out that Parkman hated democracy, distrusted change, was interested in actions rather than in inner workings of the human spirit, that he failed to appreciate fully the characteristics of French-Canadians.)

Wuerzberger, Ruth Evelyn. *Francis Parkman as a Romantic Historian.* B. A. Thesis, University of Wisconsin, 1931. (A good unpublished thesis, although somewhat on the surface. Discusses Parkman's point of view toward French-English conflict, points out tendency toward Federalism, discusses narrative and dramatic elements in his writing.)

Wyatt, Edith Franklin. "Francis Parkman," *North American Review*, CCXVIII, 484–96 (October, 1923). (Centennial eulogy.)

Young, Alexander. "Francis Parkman," *Bookbuyer*, VII, 421–2 (November, 1890). (Brief biographical sketch.)

Obituaries may be found in the *Athenaeum*, II, 698 (November 18, 1893); *Literary World*, XXIV, 384 (November 18, 1893); *Public Opinion*, XVI, 153–4 (November 16, 1893); *Proceedings of the Massachusetts Historical Society*, 2d series, VIII, 360–9 (1894), which record a special memorial meeting of November, 1893, at which remarks were made by George E. Ellis, Oliver Wendell Holmes, Robert C. Winthrop, George S. Hale, John Lowell, Martin Brimmer, and Leverett Saltonstall; *Critic*, XXIII, 322–4 (November 18, 1893), by J. B. Gilder and E. L. Wingate; *Proceedings of the American Antiquarian*

Society, N.S. IX, 116–25 (1893–4), by J. B. Greene; in *Garden and Forest*, VI, 471 (November 15, 1893), by C. S. Sargent; in *Nation*, LVII, 365–7 (November 16, 1893), by L. J. Walker.

IV. BACKGROUND

Alvord, Clarence W. *The Illinois Country, 1673–1818*. Springfield: 1920. (Volume I of his centennial history of Illinois. It tells the history of the Illinois country, so often mentioned by Parkman, in "admirable and authoritative fashion"— W. G. Leland.)

American Writers Series (Harry Hayden Clark, general editor). New York: 1934—. (Documented interpretations of the political, religious, social, and literary theories of major American writers.)

Beard, Charles A. and Mary R. *The Rise of American Civilization*. New York: 1927. (Economic interpretation, which Parkman too often neglected.)

Cole, A. C. *The Irrepressible Conflict*. New York: 1930. (Excellent annotated bibliography covers the social history of the period.)

Cooke, George W. *Unitarianism in America*. Boston: 1902. (Useful for religious background of Parkman's Boston.)

Fairchild, Hoxie N. *The Noble Savage*. New York: 1928. (The American Indian represented to English writers the noble savage. Good background for Parkman's viewpoint.)

Faulkner, Harold U. *American Economic History*. New York: 1924. (Useful statistics on Parkman's period.)

Gettell, R. G. *History of American Political Thought*. New York: 1928. (Authoritative, comprehensive work with bibliographies.)

Gooch, G. P. *History and Historians in the Nineteenth Century*. New York: 1913. (Chapter XXI deals interestingly with American historians.)

Heinrichs, Pierre. *La Louisiane sous la Compagnie des Indes*. Paris: n. d. (The history of Louisiana from 1717 to 1731 is studied in detail, and the earlier history is sketched in. Valuable for comparison with Parkman's treatment of Louisiana.)

Jones, H. M. *America and French Culture, 1750–1848.* Chapel
    Hill, N. C.: 1927. (With extensive bibliography.)

Kellogg, Louise P. *The French Régime in Wisconsin and the
    Northwest.* Madison: 1925.

Kraus, Michael. *The History of American History.* New York:
    1937.

Lauvrière, Émile. *La Tragédie d'un peuple.* Paris: 1922. (Pas-
    sionately hostile to Parkman's viewpoint toward French
    Canada.)

Moore, Charles. *The Northwest under Three Flags.* New York:
    1900. (History of the region about Detroit.)

Munro, William Bennett. *Crusaders of New France.* In *Chroni-
    cles of America*, edited by Allen Johnson. New Haven:
    1918. (Social, economic, and institutional history of French
    Canada. Interesting comparison with Parkman's *Old Régime.*)

Nevins, Allan. *The Emergence of Modern America, 1865–1878.*
    New York: 1927. (With comprehensive bibliography.)

Parrington, Vernon L. *Main Currents in American Thought.*
    New York: 1927–30. (See Biography and Criticism, p. cxxxvi
    above. Excellent interpretation of American thought from
    viewpoint of a political liberal.)

Riley, Woodbridge. *American Thought from Puritanism to
    Pragmatism.* New York: 1923. (Useful chapters on Puri-
    tanism, deism, materialism, realism, Transcendentalism,
    evolutionism.)

Salone, Émile. *La Colonization de la Nouvelle France.* Paris:
    1905. ("Exceedingly valuable study of the process of peo-
    pling Canada and of its economic and social progress; as a
    supplement to Parkman it is indispensable."—W. G. Leland.)

Short, Adam, and Doughty, Arthur G., editors. *Canada and
    Its Provinces.* Toronto: 1914. (I, narrative history of French
    Canada; II, social, economic, political institutions; XIII, his-
    tory of Acadia; XV and XVI, history of Quebec.)

Surrey, Mrs. N. M. M. *The Commerce of Louisiana during the
    French Régime.* New York: 1916. (Detailed and definite in-
    formation gained from intensive work in Paris archives. A
    book for the student, rather than the general reader.)

Thwaites, R. G. *Early Western Travels, 1748–1846.* 32 vols. Cleveland: 1904–07. ("A series of annotated reprints of some of the best and rarest contemporary volumes of travel descriptive of the aborigines and social and economic conditions in the middle and far west during the period of early American settlement." Texts and editorial apparatus of great value.)

Thwaites, Reuben Gold. *France in America* (in *The American Nation, A History*). New York: 1905. (A good summary. W. G. Leland, however, objects to the lack of evidence of original scholarship.)

Thwaites, R. G., ed. *Jesuit Relations and Allied Documents; Travels and Explorations of the Jesuit Missionaries in New France, 1610–1791.* Cleveland: 1896–1901. (With notes.)

Townsend, H. G. *Philosophical Ideas in the United States.* New York: 1934. (Discusses successive impact of English, French, and German thought on America. Full and up-to-date bibliography. Supplements Riley.)

Turner, Frederick Jackson. *The Frontier in American History.* New York: 1920. (The viewpoint of a later school of historians toward the West.)

Whitney, Lois. *Primitivism and the Idea of Progress in English Popular Literature of the Eighteenth Century.* Baltimore: 1934. (Good background for Parkman's stand on primitivism. See reviews in *Journal of Philosophy*, XXXI, 579; *International Journal of Ethics*, XLV, 122.)

Wrong, George M. *The Conquest of New France* (in *Chronicles of America*, edited by Allen Johnson.) New York: 1920. (Chiefly military narrative.)

Wrong, George M. *The Rise and Fall of New France.* New York: 1928.

V. BIBLIOGRAPHIES

The Cambridge History of American Literature. New York: 1917–21. IV, 737. (Lists Parkman's books and seven critical and biographical titles.)

Farnham, Charles H. *Life of Francis Parkman.* Boston: 1900, pp. xii–xiii, 359–64. (Contains most complete list of works *by* Parkman printed up to the time of this bibliography, although Farnham's list is marred by a few unfortunate errors and by lack of complete biographical information. A few works *on* Parkman are mentioned in the preface.)

Hartwick, Harry. Bibliography of Francis Parkman, in W. F. Taylor's *A History of American Letters.* New York: 1936, p. 621. (Lists only five works by Parkman, sixteen biographical and critical titles.)

Johnson, Merle. "American First Editions," *Publishers' Weekly,* CXXVII, 263–4. (Some information on first publications.)

Leland, W. G. "Works Dealing with Parkman's Field," *Ex Libris,* I, 234–6 (February, 1924). (Brief annotated list.)

Ramsey, Ruth. "Francis Parkman: 1823–1893. A Bibliography." Unpublished research, available at University of Wisconsin Library School. (Although this Bibliography was practically complete before Miss Ramsey's became available, hers furnished a few items which might otherwise have been overlooked.)

For current articles on Parkman the student should consult the bibliographies in *Publications of the Modern Language Association* (annually, in the supplement), *American Literature* (brief bibliography in each issue), and Grace G. Griffin's *Writings on American History* (compiled annually).

*

Selections from
FRANCIS PARKMAN

*

[AUTOBIOGRAPHY]

[AUTOBIOGRAPHICAL LETTER*]

50 Chestnut St., 28 Nov., 1868.

My DEAR FRIEND,—Running my eye over this paper, I am more than ever struck with its *egoism*, which makes it totally unfit for any eye but that of one in close personal relations with me.

It resulted from a desire—natural, perhaps, but which may just as well be suppressed—to make known the extreme difficulties which have reduced to very small proportions what might otherwise have been a good measure of achievement. Having once begun it, I went on with it, though convinced that it was wholly unsuited to see the light.

Physiologically considered, the case is rather curious. My plan of life from the first was such as would have secured great bodily vigor in nineteen cases out of twenty, and was only defeated in its aim by an inborn irritability of constitution which required gentler treatment than I gave it. If I had my life to live over again, I would follow exactly the same course again, only with less vehemence.   Very cordially,

F. PARKMAN.

Allusion was made at the outset to obstacles which have checked the progress of the work, if the name of obstacles can be applied to obstructions at times impassable and of such a nature that even to contend against them would have been little else than an act of self-destruction. The case in question is certainly an exceptional one; but as it has analogies with various other cases, not rare under the stimulus of our social and material influences, a knowledge of it may prove of use. For this, as for other reasons, the writer judges it expedient to state it in full, though in doing so, much personal detail must needs be involved.

*Written to Dr. George E. Ellis in 1868, with the request that it be withheld from the public until after Parkman's death. [*Editor's note.*]

His childhood was neither healthful nor buoyant. His boyhood, though for a time active, was not robust, and at the age of eleven or twelve he conceived a vehement liking for pursuits a devotion to which at that time of life far oftener indicates a bodily defect than a mental superiority. Chemical experiment was his favorite hobby, and he pursued it with a tenacious eagerness which, well guided, would have led to some acquaintance with the rudiments of the science, but which in fact served little other purpose than injuring him by confinement, poisoning him with noxious gases, and occasionally scorching him with some ill-starred explosion.

The age of fifteen or sixteen produced a revolution. At that momentous period of life retorts and crucibles were forever discarded, and an activity somewhat excessive took the place of voluntary confinement. A new passion seized him, which, but half gratified, still holds its force. He became enamored of the woods,—a fancy which soon gained full control over the course of the literary pursuits to which he was also addicted. After the usual boyish phases of ambitious self-ignorance, he resolved to confine his homage to the Muse of History, as being less apt than her wayward sisters to requite his devotion with a mortifying rebuff. At the age of eighteen the plan which he is still attempting to execute was, in its most essential features, formed. His idea was clear before him, yet attended with unpleasant doubts as to his ability to realize it to his own satisfaction. To solve these doubts he entered upon a training tolerably well fitted to serve his purpose, slighted all college studies which could not promote it, and pursued with avidity such as had a bearing upon it, however indirect.

The task, as he then reckoned, would require about twenty years. The time allowed was ample; but here he fell into a fatal error, entering on this long pilgrimage with all the vehemence of one starting on a mile heat. His reliance, however, was less on books than on such personal experience as should in some sense identify him with his theme. His natural inclinations urged him in the same direction, for his thoughts were always in the forest, whose features, not unmixed with softer images, possessed his waking and sleeping dreams, filling him with vague cravings impossible to satisfy. As fond of hardships as he was vain of enduring them, cherishing a sovereign scorn for every physical weakness or defect, deceived, moreover, by a rapid development of frame and sinews which flattered him with the belief that discipline sufficiently unsparing would harden him into an athlete, he slighted the precautions of a more reasonable woodcraft, tired old foresters with long marches, stopped neither for heat nor rain, and slept on the earth without a blanket. Another cause added not a little to the growing evil. It was impossible that conditions of the nervous system abnormal as his had been from infancy, should be without their effects on the mind, and some of these were of a nature highly to exasperate him. Unconscious of their character and origin, and ignorant that with time and confirmed health they would have disappeared, he had no other thought than that of crushing them by force, and accordingly applied himself to the work. Hence resulted a state of mental tension, habitual for several years, and abundantly mischievous in its effects. With a mind overstrained and a body overtasked, he was burning his candle at both ends.

But if a systematic and steady course of physical activity can show no better results, have not the advantages of such a course been overrated? In behalf of manhood and common sense, he would protest against such a conclusion; and if any pale student, glued to his desk, here seek an apology for a way of life whose natural fruit is that pallid and emasculate scholarship of which New England has had too many examples, it will be far better that this sketch had not been written. For the student there is, in its season, no better place than the saddle, and no better companion than the rifle or the oar. A highly irritable organism spurred the writer to excess in a course which, with one of different temperament, would have produced a free and hardy development of such faculties and forces as he possessed. Nor, even in the case in question, was the evil unmixed, since from the same source whence it issued came also the habits of mind and muscular vigor which saved him from a ruin absolute and irremediable.

In his own behalf, he is tempted to add to this digression another. Though the seat of derangement may be the nervous system, it does not of necessity follow that the subject is that which, in the common sense of the word, is called "nervous." The writer was now and then felicitated on "having no nerves" by those who thought themselves maltreated by that mysterious portion of human organism.

This subterranean character of the mischief, early declaring itself at the surface, doubtless increased its intensity, while it saved it from being a nuisance to those around.

Of the time when, leaving college, he entered nominally on the study of law,—though in fact with the determination that neither this nor any other pursuit should stand in the path of his projects,—his recollection is of mingled pain and pleasure. His faculties were stimulated to their best efficiency. Never, before or since, has he known so great a facility of acquisition and comprehension. Soon, however, he became conscious that the impelling force was growing beyond his control. Labor became a passion, and rest intolerable, yet with a keen appetite for social enjoyment, in which he found not only a pleasure, but in some sense a repose. The stimulus rapidly increased. Despite of judgment and of will, his mind turned constantly towards remote objects of pursuit, and strained vehemently to attain them. The condition was that of a rider whose horse runs headlong, the bit between his teeth, or of a locomotive, built of indifferent material, under a head of steam too great for its strength, hissing at a score of crevices, yet rushing on with accelerating speed to the inevitable smash.

A specific sign of the mischief soon appeared in a weakness of sight, increasing with an ominous rapidity. Doubtless to study with the eyes of another is practicable, yet the expedient is not an eligible one, and the writer bethought him of an alternative. It was essential to his plans to give an inside view of Indian life. This then was the time at once to accomplish the object and rest his failing vision. Accordingly he went to the Rocky Mountains, but he had reckoned without his host. A complication of severe disorders here seized him, and at one time narrowly missed bringing both him and his schemes to an abrupt termination, but, yielding to a system of starvation, at length assumed an intermittent and much less threatening form. A concurrence of circumstances left him but one means of accomplishing his purpose. This was to follow a large band of Ogillallah Indians, known to have crossed the Black Hill range a short time before. Reeling in the saddle with weakness and pain, he set forth, attended by a Canadian hunter. With much difficulty the trail was found, the Black Hills crossed, the reluctance of his follower overcome, and the Indians discovered on the fifth day encamped near the Medicine Bow range of the Rocky Mountains. On a journey of a hundred miles, over a country in parts of the roughest, he had gained rather than lost strength, while his horse was knocked up and his companion disconsolate with a painful cough. Joining the Indians, he followed their wanderings for several weeks. To have worn the airs of an invalid would certainly have been an indiscretion, since in that case a horse, a rifle, a pair of pistols, and a red shirt might have offered temptations too strong for aboriginal virtue. Yet to hunt buffalo on horseback, over a broken country, when, without the tonic of the chase, he could scarcely sit upright in the saddle, was not strictly necessary for maintaining the requisite prestige. The sport, however, was good, and the faith undoubting that, to tame the devil, it is best to take him by the horns.

As to the advantages of this method of dealing with that subtle personage, some question may have arisen in his mind, when, returning after a few months to the settlements, he found himself in a condition but ill adapted to support his theory. To the maladies of the prairie succeeded a suite of exhausting disorders, so reducing him that circulation at the extremities ceased, the light of the sun became insupportable, and a wild whirl possessed his brain, joined to a universal turmoil of the nervous system which put his philosophy to the sharpest test it had hitherto known. All collapsed, in short, but the tenacious strength of muscles hardened by long activity. This condition was progressive, and did not reach its height—or, to speak more fitly, its depth—until some eighteen months after his return. The prospect before him was by no means attractive, contrasting somewhat pointedly with his boyish fancy of a life of action and a death in battle. Indeed, the change from intense activity to flat stagnation, attended with an utter demolition of air-castles, may claim a place, not of the meanest, in that legion of mental tortures which make the torments of the Inferno seem endurable. The desire was intense to return to the prairie and try a hair of the dog that bit him; but this kill-or-cure expedient was debarred by the certainty that a few days' exposure to the open sunlight would have destroyed his sight.

In the spring of 1848, the condition indicated being then at its worst, the writer resolved to attempt the composition of the "History of the Conspiracy of Pontiac," of which the material had been for some time collected and the ground prepared. The difficulty was so near to the impossible that the line of distinction often disappeared, while medical prescience condemned the plan as a short road to dire calamities. His motive, however, was in part a sanitary one, growing out of a conviction that nothing could be more deadly to his bodily and mental health than the entire absence of a purpose and an object. The difficulties were threefold: an extreme weakness of sight, disabling him even from writing his name except with eyes closed; a condition of the brain prohibiting fixed attention except at occasional and brief intervals; and an exhaustion and total derangement of the nervous system, producing of necessity a mood of mind most unfavorable to effort. To be made with impunity, the attempt must be made with the most watchful caution.

He caused a wooden frame to be constructed of the size and shape of a sheet of letter-paper. Stout wires were fixed horizontally across it, half an inch apart, and a movable back of thick pasteboard fitted behind them. The paper for writing was placed between the pasteboard and the wires, guided by which, and using a black lead crayon, he could write not illegibly with closed eyes. He was at the time absent from home, on Staten Island, where, and in the neighboring city of New York, he had friends who willingly offered their aid. It is needless to say to which half of humanity nearly all these kind assistants belonged.

He chose for a beginning that part of the work which offered fewest difficulties and with the subject of which he was most familiar, namely the Siege of Detroit. The books and documents, already partially arranged, were procured from Boston, and read to him at such times as he could listen to them, the length of each reading never, without injury, much exceeding half an hour, and periods of several days frequently occurring during which he could not listen at all. Notes were made by him with closed eyes, and afterwards deciphered and read to him till he had mastered them. For the first half year, the rate of composition averaged about six lines a day. The portion of the book thus composed was afterwards partially rewritten.

His health improved under the process, and the remainder of the volume—in other words, nearly the whole of it—was composed in Boston, while pacing in the twilight of a large garret, the only exercise which the sensitive condition of his sight permitted him in an unclouded day while the sun was above the horizon. It was afterwards written down from dictation by relatives under the same roof, to whom he was also indebted for the preparatory readings. His progress was much less tedious than at the outset, and the history was complete in about two years and a half.

He then entered upon the subject of "France in the New World,"—a work, or series of works, involving minute and extended investigation. The difficulties which met him at the outset were incalculable. Wholly unable to use his eyes, he had before him the task, irksome at best, where there is no natural inclination for it, of tracing out, collecting, indexing, arranging, and digesting a great mass of incongruous material scattered on both sides of the Atlantic. Those pursuing historical studies under the disadvantages of impaired sight have not hitherto attempted in person this kind of work during the period of their disability, but have deputed it to skilled and trusty assistants,— a most wise course in cases where it is practicable. The writer, however, partly from the nature of his subject and his plan, though in special instances receiving very valuable aid, was forced in the main to rely on his own research. The language was chiefly French, and the reader was a girl from the public schools, ignorant of any tongue but her own. The effect, though highly amusing to bystanders, was far from being so to the person endeavoring to follow the meaning of this singular jargon. Catalogues, indexes, tables of contents in abundance were, however, read, and correspondence opened with those who could lend aid or information. Good progress had been made in the preliminary surveys, and many books examined and digested on a systematic plan for future reference, when a disaster befell the writer which set his calculations at naught.

This was an effusion of water on the left knee, in the autumn of 1851. A partial recovery was followed by a relapse, involving a close confinement of two years and a weakened and sensitive condition of the joint from which it has never recovered. The effects of the confinement were as curious as unenviable. All the irritability of the system centred in the head. The most definite of the effects produced was one closely resembling the tension of an iron band, secured round the head and contracting with an extreme force, with the attempt to concentrate the thoughts, listen to reading, or, at times, to engage in conversation. This was, however, endurable in comparison with other forms of attack which cannot be intelligibly described from the want of analogous sensations by which to convey the requisite impressions. The brain was stimulated to a restless activity, impelling through it a headlong current of thought which, however, must be arrested and the irritated organ held in quiescence on a penalty to avert which no degree of exertion was too costly. The whirl, the confusion, and strange undefined torture attending this condition are only to be conceived by one who has felt them. Possibly they may have analogies in the savage punishment once in use in some of our prisons, where drops of water were made to fall from a height on the shaved head of the offender, soon producing an effect which brought to reason the most contumacious. Sleep, of course, was banished during the periods of attack, and in its place was demanded, for the exclusion of thought, an effort more severe than the writer has ever put forth in any other cause. In a few hours, however, a condition of exhaustion would ensue; and both patient and disease being spent, the latter fell into a dull lethargic state far more supportable. Excitement or alarm would probably have proved wholly ruinous.

These were the extreme conditions of the disorder, which has reached two crises,—one at the end of 1853, the other in 1858. In the latter case it was about four years before the power of mental application was in the smallest degree restored, nor, since the first year of the confinement, has there been any waking hour when he has not been in some degree conscious of the presence of the malady. Influences tending to depress the mind have at all times proved far less injurious than those tending to excite or even pleasurably exhilarate, and a lively conversation has often been a cause of serious mischief. A cautious vigilance has been necessary from the first, and this cerebral devil has perhaps had his uses as a teacher of philosophy.

Meanwhile the Faculty of Medicine were not idle, displaying that exuberance of resource for which that remarkable profession is justly famed. The wisest, indeed, did nothing, commending his patient to time and faith; but the activity of his brethren made full amends for this masterly inaction. One was for tonics, another for a diet of milk; one counselled galvanism, another hydropathy; one scarred him behind the neck with nitric acid, another drew red-hot irons along his spine with a view of enlivening that organ. Opinion was divergent as practice. One assured him of recovery in six years; another thought that he would never recover. Another, with grave circumlocution, lest the patient should take fright, informed him that he was the victim of an organic disease of the brain which must needs despatch him to another world within a twelvemonth; and he stood amazed at the smile of an auditor who neither cared for the announcement nor believed it. Another, an eminent physiologist of Paris, after an acquaintance of three months, one day told him that, from the nature of the disorder, he had at first supposed that it must in accordance with precedent be attended with insanity, and had ever since been studying him to discover under what form the supposed aberration declared itself, adding, with a somewhat humorous look, that his researches had not been rewarded with the smallest success.

In the severer periods of the disorder, books were discarded for horticulture, which benign pursuit has proved most salutary in its influences. One year, four years, and numerous short intervals lasting from a day to a month, represent these literary interruptions since the work in hand was begun. Under the most favorable conditions, it was a slow and doubtful navigation, beset with reefs and breakers, demanding a constant lookout and a constant throwing of the lead. Of late years, however, the condition of the sight has so far improved as to permit reading, not exceeding, on the average, five minutes at one time. This modicum of power, though apparently trifling, proves of the greatest service, since, by a cautious management, its application may be extended. By reading for one minute, and then resting for an equal time, this alternate process may generally be continued for about half an hour. Then, after a sufficient interval, it may be repeated, often three or four times in the course of the day. By this means nearly the whole of the volume now offered has been composed. When the conditions were such as to render systematic application possible, a reader has been employed, usually a pupil of the public schools. On one occasion, however, the services of a young man, highly intelligent and an excellent linguist, were obtained for a short time. With such assistance every difficulty vanished, but it could not long be continued.

At present the work, or rather the series of separate works, stands as follows: Most of the material is collected or within reach. Another volume, on the Jesuits in North America, is one third written. Another, on the French explorers of the Great West, is half written; while a third, devoted to the checkered career of Louis de Buade, Comte de Frontenac, is partially arranged for composition. Each work is designed to be a unit in itself, independently of the rest; but the whole, taken as a series, will form a connected history of France in the New World.

How far, by a process combining the slowness of the tortoise with the uncertainty of the hare, an undertaking of close and extended research can be advanced, is a question to solve which there is no aid from precedent, since it does not appear that an attempt under similar circumstances has hitherto been made. The writer looks, however, for a fair degree of success. Irksome as may be the requirements of conditions so anomalous, they are far less oppressive than the necessity they involve of being busied with the past when the present has claims so urgent, and holding the pen with a hand that should have grasped the sword.

[SUPPLEMENTARY PASSAGES*]

Causes antedating my birth gave me constitutional liabilities to which I largely ascribe the mischief that ensued. As a child I was sensitive and restless, rarely ill, but never robust. At eight years I was sent to a farm belonging to my maternal grandfather on the outskirts of the extensive tract of wild and rough woodland now called Middlesex Fells. I walked twice a day to a school of high but undeserved reputation about a mile distant, in the town of Medford. Here I learned very little, and spent the intervals of schooling more profitably in collecting eggs, insects, and reptiles, trapping squirrels and woodchucks, and making persistent though rarely fortunate attempts to kill birds with arrows. After four years of this rustication I was brought back to Boston, when I was unhappily seized with a mania for experiments in chemistry involving a lonely, confined, unwholesome sort of life, baneful to body and mind. . . .

My favorite backwoods were always in my thoughts. At first I tried to persuade myself that I could woo this new mistress in verse; then I came down to fiction, and at last reached the sage though not flattering conclusion that if I wanted to build in her honor any monument that would stand, I must found on solid fact. Before the end of the sophomore year my various schemes had crystallized into a plan of writing the story of what was thus known as the "Old French War"; that is, the

*From the second autobiographical letter, written to Martin Brimmer in 1886, with the request that it be withheld from the public until after Parkman's death.

war that ended in the conquest of Canada; for here, as it seemed to me, the forest drama was more stirring and the forest stage more thronged with appropriate actors than in any other passage of our history. It was not till some years later that I enlarged the plan to include the whole course of the American conflict between France and England; or, in other words, the history of the American forest; for this was the light in which I regarded it. My theme fascinated me, and I was haunted with wilderness images day and night.

From this time forward, two ideas possessed me. One was to paint the forest and its tenants in true and vivid colors; the other was to realize a certain ideal of manhood, a little mediæval, but nevertheless good. Feeling that I fell far short of it, I proceeded in extreme dissatisfaction to apply heroic remedies. I held the creed that the more hard knocks a man gets, whether in mind or body, the better for him, provided always that he takes them without flinching; and as the means of forcing myself up to the required standard, I put my faith in persistent violence which I thought energy. I held that the true aim of life was not happiness but achievement; had profound respect for physical strength and hardihood when joined with corresponding qualities of character; took pleasure in any moderate hardship, scorned invalidism of all kinds, and was full of the notion, common enough with boys of a certain sort, that the body will always harden and toughen with exercise and exposure. . . .

While engaged on these books I made many journeys in the United States and Canada in search of material, and went four times to Europe with a similar object. The task of exploring archives and collecting documents, to me repulsive at the best, was, under the circumstances, difficult, and would have been impossible but for the aid of competent assistants working under my direction.

Taking the last forty years as a whole, the capacity of literary work which during that time has fallen to my share has, I am confident, been considerably less than a fourth part of what it would have been under normal conditions. Whether the historical series in hand will ever be finished I do not know, but I shall finish it if I can.

[EARLY ADVENTURES IN LITERATURE]

STUDIES OF NATURE

(The earliest preserved composition, 1839)

Of all pursuits the cultivation of natural science tends most to enlarge the mind and improve the understanding. Nature affords for our contemplation subjects from the minutest to the most grand. We may study the animalcule contained in a drop of water, or observe the motions of the planetary bodies as they revolve in their unchanged orbits. No class of pursuits affords so vast a variety of subjects and none is capable of awakening a deeper interest. Nature cannot be exhausted. The farther we investigate her secrets the wider appears the range she opens to us. The nearer the view we take of her, the more captivating does she appear.

We all are born with an instinctive fondness for the beauties of nature. We all take pleasure in viewing a lofty mountain, a fertile valley, or a clear stream. But most of us look upon such objects as we would upon a beautiful picture, we imagine no pleasure to be derived from them farther than that which arises from the clearness of the stream or the picturesque contrast of mountain and valley.

But suppose a man who has made nature his study, who, while searching into the great laws that govern her, has not neglected the tribes of living and inanimate beings to which she is indebted for life and beauty,—suppose him to be placed where we were, and to be looking upon the same objects. The black and precipitous rocks which lie piled in confusion above him, remind him of the period when that mountain emerged from the plain impelled by some irresistible subterranean power. He notices the deposits which through successive ages have accumulated about its base, and compares the present appearance of that valley, enlivened by grazing herds and sparkling rivulets, with its aspect in former ages, when it perhaps formed the bed of a stagnant lake, the abode of monsters, now happily extinct. The plants and animals about him next engage his attention, and in observing their appearances and watching their motions, he finds an inexhaustible source of innocent gratification.

"But," say some, "of what use are such pursuits, or what man of sense can take pleasure in studying the habits of a paltry insect, or in classing and arranging an insignificant shell?" I answer that whatever tends to increase our knowledge of the globe we inhabit is of use, and that objects which appear to be too trifling to be noticed may, at some future day, be found of great benefit to mankind.

When the great chemical discoveries of Davy were published, it was said by some, "Such discoveries are curious and wonderful, but to what possible use can they be applied?" Of what use is the spring of a watch? It is the agent by which the motion of the other parts is produced, and unless it had first been invented, a watch could never have been made. The principle of the spring was known long before any one thought of applying it to the construction of time-pieces. It is the same with such discoveries. They point out the principles which sooner or later will be made the agent in some great improvement in art. The application of the principle may not immediately be discovered, but we should not on this account condemn it as useless.

Why then should the naturalist be accused of spending his time in useless pursuits? Use, of which we have no idea may yet be made of his researches, and in the meantime there is no pursuit more innocent, more interesting, or more agreeable than the study of Natural History.

THE NEW-HAMPSHIRE RANGER

(From the *Knickerbocker Magazine*, August, 1845)

In the Old French War, a body of Rangers were employed on scouting expeditions around Lake George, between the hostile military posts of Ticonderoga and Fort William Henry. Their most celebrated leader, Major Rogers, with a large part of the men, were from New-Hampshire. The service they were engaged in was of the most severe and dangerous kind. In parties varying from two or three to a hundred or more, they scoured the woods at all seasons, to seize stragglers, intercept convoys, and encounter the parties of Canadians and Indians that the French were constantly sending out to annoy the English; and whom, unless there was a great disparity of force, the Rangers almost always defeated and beat back to Canada.

> No ordered rank and measured tramp,
>   No restless flash of steel;
> Nor the long line of dancing plumes,
>   And ringing trumpet-peal!
> The soldiers of the wilderness,
>   A rough and hardy band,
> In woodland garb, with woodland arms,
>   We guard this forest land.
> 'Tis ours to breathe the battle smoke,
>   To range the trackless wood,
> To struggle with the howling storm,
>   And swim the lashing flood.
> Deep in the gloomy forest,
>   Unseen by human eye,
> We track the foe, we strike the blow,
>   And nameless all, we die.
> The scarlet coat, the waving plume—
>   Good for the triumph day!
> The hunter's frock, the cap of fur—
>   Good for the battle fray!
> Gay warrior of England,
>   Idling the whole day long,
> Drink and laugh and gaily dance,
>   And shout the camp-fire song.
> In William Henry's sheltering walls
>   Enjoy thy mirth and cheer,
> We guard the dangerous wilderness—
>   No danger can come near.
> Yet do not deem that I complain;
>   Soldier, I would not change,

For thy safe and idle slavery,
   My own free forest range.
I love the savage war-whoop,
   And the whistling of the ball;
The woods, the rocks, the boiling streams,
   I love them, one and all.
And yet their memory is entwined
   With thoughts of sore distress,
Of famine, grief, and danger,
   And bitter weariness.
For the ranger's gun has echoed
   From a thousand pathless mountains;
And the ranger's blood has stained with red
   A thousand limpid fountains.
Some of our band lie wasting
   In the dark noisome dell;
No friendly ear could their death-cries hear,
   None lived their fate to tell.
On stern and wild Agiochook
   The whitening bones are spread;
The fish of crystal Horicon
   Are feeding on our dead.
The ravens of Oswego,
   Slow settling on the plain,
Tear vainly at the sinewy limbs,
   And soar away again.
Some have died by famine,
   Some by the headlong fall,
Some by the wave, and some by frost,
   Some by the foeman's ball.
Among these wild green mountains,
   And o'er this gentle flood,
In cold and heat, by day and night,
   Have I in battle stood.
The sultry breath of August,
   December's breezes bleak;
The sleet, the snow, the rushing rain,
   Have beat upon my cheek:

And Nature, I have gazed on thee
   In thy calmest, sweetest hour;
And I have seen thy frowning face
   In all thy wrath and power:
Thy gentle smile, thy whispering voice,
   Have ever a charm for me;
But I love as well thy lowering brow
   Of angry majesty.
I love thee even 'mid winter's cold,
   When trackless lies the snow,
And the boughs of the loaded fir-tree bend
   Into the drifts below:
When in the sharp still evening
   The sky is flushed with red,
And o'er the wide white wilderness
   The crimson glow is shed;
And in the thickest forest
   We heap the snow around,
And spread the boughs of evergreen
   Upon the frozen ground.
And through the long dull night we hear,
   On that cold couch reclined,
The music of the groaning ice,
   The howling of the wind:
While high among the snowy trees
   Swirls up the roaring blaze,
And the bright swarm of dancing sparks
   Far in the darkness plays.
I lie and watch them wandering,
   And gleaming wide and bright,
Like fire-flies by the orchard side,
   On some soft summer night.
But how the blasts sweep moaning
   O'er the solid lake below,
And scatter in the bright moonbeams
   The glistening flakes of snow!
And in the tortured forest
   The pine-trees tough and old

Crack sharply with a sudden sound,
    As if rent with the biting cold.
Wo to the wretch who wanders lost
    In the drear wood to-night!
Like the sculptor's chiselled marble
    He'll be ere morning light.

But the fierce heats of August,
    The pale sun's noontide blaze,
When each hot mountain slumbers
    Dim in the sultry haze!
No song of bird, no rustling leaf,
    No stirring of the breeze;
Nought but the drowsy hum of gnats,
    Beneath the withering trees!
With the red sun's glare, the breathless air,
    And the faint and pale-blue sky,
With the sleeping flood, and drooping wood,
    The heart sinks languidly.
On yonder rich and verdant shore,
    Where the swelling forests spread,
Glistening beneath the fiery rays
    On the shrinking foliage shed,
I know a cool and limpid spring;
    Its laughing waters gay
Steal rippling through the velvet grass,
    Low murmuring on their way.
I could fling down my weary oar,
    And lay me by its side,
Bathe my hot brow and swelling veins,
    And watch the waters glide;
The cold and gushing waters,
    The pebbles clear and white,
The maples and young linden trees
    That shade them from the light!

Would, by that merry sparkling spring,
    Beneath the fresh cool shade,

I might sit and hear the sweet low voice
    Of Hampshire's blue-eyed maid!
Mark her heart's soft emotions,
    By many a sigh confest,
By the gleaming of her melting eye,
    The swelling of her breast.
Then would I loathe the bugle-note,
    And curse the battle cry,
And know no other joy on earth
    Than soft tranquillity.
But let the poet muse and moan
    In fancied desperation,
The tame voluptuary melt,
    In selfish lamentation:
Man was made to toil and fight,
    And not to dream and sigh,
And woman fires his failing heart
    To deeds of gallantry.

Best I love the clear cool morn
    Of the bright October day;
When the mountains glow, and the lake below
    Reflects the colors gay.
When the fresh woods are ringing
    With the screaming of the jay;
When, through the ruddy maple leaves,
    Pours the sun's crimsoned ray:
When the stiffened leaves are rustling,
    And dropping from the trees,
And the dark blue water ripples
    In the light morning breeze:
And far aloft against the sky
    The mountain summits rear
Their black rocks, gay with leafy plumes,
    In the sharp atmosphere.
Then, by the island's grassy bank,
    I fling me on the ground,

And snuff the breezes, like a deer
   That scents the distant hound.
'Tis then the fire of health and youth
   Burns high in every breast,
And the wild zeal to dare and do,
   And scorn of slothful rest.
'Tis then our thoughts are proudest;
   The dearest joy we know,
Would be to hear the war-whoop ring,
   To grapple with the foe.
The feelings of my earlier youth
   I may recall again,
When I was a lonely wanderer
   In the wild land of Spain.
And up the rough Sierra
   By the faint moon I rode,
And the pale light, so softly bright,
   Rock, gulf, and torrent showed.
I looked on her: it seemed to me
   That I low sounds could hear,
As if the spirits of the rocks
   Were whispering in my ear.
And strange vague thoughts came thronging,
   Thickly and dreamily;
Thoughts of loves and battles
   In ages long gone by.
O'er rock and stone my steed tramped on;
   Wild chafed the haughty beast;
He champed the bit, he shook the rein,
   And tossed his sable crest.
Mine was the youthful recklessness,
   The high presumptuous soul,
Soaring elate, defying fate,
   Disdaining self-control.
Thus up the steep and rocky path,
   Careering carelessly,
Fearing nought and heeding nought,
   Went my brave steed and I.

And then a softening memory
　　Rose up within my breast,
Of that, of all things on the earth,
　　I've longest loved and best.
It was of dear New-England,
　　Her mountains and her woods,
Her savage rocks, her headlong streams,
　　Her pure and gentle floods.
And now, from wandering returned,
　　I've trod thy shore again,
Land barren of the corn and wine,
　　Fruitful of fearless men!
Blooming with bright-eyed laughing girls,
　　The lovely flowers that spring
Luxuriant from thy rocky soil,
　　A matchless offering!
And I have armed me in her cause
　　In this her day of wo,
Nor vainly fight to shield her right
　　Against her hated foe.
But how, in such a scene as this,
　　Can thoughts of slaughter rise?
The rich green hill, the waters still,
　　The pure and amber skies:
When Nature's sweet and powerful voice
　　Whispers of peace and rest,
And to a tranquil tenderness
　　Would soothe the unquiet breast.
Our toil and wo are well nigh done;
　　Strain, comrades, at the oar!
There lie the walls that shelter us,
　　On yonder guarded shore.
I see the frowning rampart,
　　The rigid palisade,
And slowly rolled in swelling fold,
　　Old England's flag displayed.
Hark to the rolling of the drum,
　　And the gay trumpet-note,

That, softened on the greedy ear,
    O'er the calm waters float!
And see! and see! on yonder plain,
    The long and glittering line;
The red coats glow in the evening rays,
    The bristling bayonets shine;
How, 'twixt those shadowy western hills,
    Upon the bright array
The sinking sun pours duskily
    His last departing ray!
Where's the cold eye that would not glow,
    At yonder gallant sight!
Where the tame heart that would not beat
    With a high and wild delight!
I love that broad red banner,
    And the stately soldiery
That bear it on through blood and smoke.
    Always triumphantly.
Brave Briton, I could ever be
    A comrade by thy side
Around the merry camp-fire,
    Or in the battle's tide:
But I cannot brook thy haughty brow,
    Thy bearing proud and high;
Thou 'lt make a cold disdainful friend,
    But a gallant enemy!
I have dreamed it, and I know it,
    The day is coming yet,
When axe and rifle-butt shall clash
    With British bayonet!
No more through dark and pathless woods
    We'll hunt the savage foe,
Or track the flying Frenchman,
    By his foot-prints on the snow;
But hand to hand, and steel to steel,
    On the broad open field,
We'll try who blenches in the strife,
    Who shall be last to yield!

And I have dreamed it in my sleep,
  How the bullets stormed like hail,
And the red bristling ranks went down
  As wheat bends to the gale!
As I have dreamed it in my sleep,
  That sight mine eyes shall see;
And when that bloody morning comes,
  Right welcome shall it be.

CAPT. JONATHAN CARVER, JR.

Cambridge, Mass.,
  June 25, 1845.

SATAN AND DR. CARVER

(From the *Knickerbocker Magazine*, December, 1845)

My ancestor, whose exploits are recorded in a former number of "Old KNICK.," had a cousin several years his junior, who once met with an adventure, which I shall submit to the contemplation of the public. This cousin was a physician, or at least was so entitled. Not that he entered with rude zest upon the duties of that profession; in fact, he took the first plausible excuse for escaping them; and when, in the year 1755, men were enlisted in all parts of the country to serve against the French, he suddenly felt himself patriotic, and zealous for the public service. Getting commissioned as a lieutenant, he joined the army of Sir William Johnson, and the violence of his military ardor abated only on the receipt of two Indian bullets, one of which carried off a fragment of his left ear, while the other broke his shoulder-blade. Thus disabled, he retired from active service, and lay for some months disgusted with the glories of warfare, until the recovery of his health and the lapse of time revived his old propensities, and he began to hold the medical profession in as low esteem as ever.

Medicine, meanwhile, treated him better than he deserved at her hands. Two or three lucky chances combined to give him a professional reputation, on the strength of which he received pressing invitations to establish himself in a frontier village, the name of which, as a writer of fiction would say, "we shall decline, for obvious reasons, from mentioning." He was soon firmly seated in the good graces of half the old women, and engaged in such a career of small practice, that he had not an hour at his disposal. To the recommendation of novelty—he was the first doctor that ever visited that settlement—he joined those of a very handsome person and a remarkably lively and good-natured disposition, which gave him great favor with one class of patients. There were other traits of his character that did not so soon appear, but which will be made manifest before our story comes to an end.

It was now late in the summer of the memorable year 1757. Doctor Carver had resided but a fortnight in his new home, when the country was thrown into consternation by the rumor of a threatened invasion. The Marquis of Montcalm, it was said, was coming to attack the colonies with the largest army ever collected in America, backed by all the savages that he could gather from Canada and the upper lakes. The terror grew ten-fold when the news arrived that he had already passed Lake George; and close at the heels of it the announcement that he had taken Fort William Henry, the main bulwark of the colonies, and that his Indians had butchered the whole garrison. The facts of the case were bad enough, but rumor made them appalling indeed; and it was said in addition that he had descended the Hudson, and turned loose his savages upon the people of Albany. New-England would no doubt be his next victim. By destroying or carrying off the harvests along the frontier, driving away the cattle, taking the wheels from the wagons, and resorting to every other imaginable expedient, the frightened colonists tried to impede his progress. The militia held themselves ready to march against him at a moment's warning.

The village where the doctor exercised his vocation had its full share of the general consternation: nothing was heard by day but evil forebodings and anxious surmises as to the movements of Montcalm and his ferocious allies: nothing was dreamed of by night but rifles, scalping-knives and blazing houses. The vagueness of the rumors that reached them, the horrible and insidious nature of the warfare with which they were threatened, combined to produce on the women and children, and not a few of the men, all the effect of a hideous ghost-story. Frightened groups discussed the matter over the fire at night, and glanced over their shoulders at the dark window, expecting to encounter the eyeballs and grim features of the savage enemy. Most of those who dwelt beyond the skirts of the village, dreading the dangerous shadows that encompassed them at night-fall, gathered for protection in a little stockade fort, whose pickets had been quietly rotting in the ground since the war of the year '45. This was the grand rendezvous of the story-tellers and alarmists. At sunset, the women would repair to the upper apartment of the block-house at the western angle of the fort, and peer through the loop-holes at the great waste of forest that stretched full in sight for fifty miles toward Canada. Streams glistened here and there through its shadowy bosom; and they could not tell but at that moment they might bear on their swift current the canoes of the Canada savages. All the evening, and far into the night, they were gathered in the lower apartment of the building, where grey-headed woodsmen, smoking their pipes, told the adventures of former campaigns, and the anxious auditors listened in nervous attention.

The doctor cared little for the reports that he heard. In the first place, he did not believe them; and beside, as I before hinted, he had the folly to wish for a fray. One afternoon, he determined to refresh himself after his medical labors with a hunt, an amusement to which he was addicted: so, laying aside the tools of his profession, he took down his long-neglected gun, and in order to banish the more effectually all memory of his present avocations, he put on an old campaigning suit of his, which he had long before received as a present from a Cayuga chief. Thus equipped, he betook himself to the woods. His success was tolerable, considering his ignorance of the country, and he returned an hour before sunset with a reasonable load of game. He was not far from the village when he saw Eben Chipmunk approaching him. Eben was one of those personages with which a New-England village, in common with a feudal castle, was usually furnished; that is, a sort of fool, from whom every body feels privileged to extract all the amusement he can. He had in one hand a tin kettle for gathering "huckleberries," and in the other a hickory stick to drive home his brother's cows. He was light-hearted as usual, and was whistling a tune under the ragged brim of an old straw hat that covered his head to the eye-brows. Beside being a simpleton, Eben was rated as the most timid person in the village. Nobody listened so intently to the stories about the Indians, or could repeat so many of them; and nobody had such a power of frightening himself with his own narratives. One other of his peculiarities was too prominent to pass by; he was a great admirer of the fair sex. Not that this was exhibited in flatteries and gallantries, for he was rather sheepish in their presence; but he would spend whole evenings in a chimney-corner, among a group of girls, taking no part in the conversation except by grinning, giggling, and cracking his fingers, and well contented if he could engage so much notice as to be made the general butt of the company. On the old principle of judging others by himself, he was in the habit of attributing amorous motives to the most indifferent actions of his acquaintances.

"Hallo, Doctor!" said Eben, drawing near, and stuttering as he always did; "where did *you* come from, dressed up like a wild Injun? Been a-huntin', ain't you?"

Then he scrutinized the bunch of game, and looking up sagaciously in the doctor's face:

"I know who them are for!" he said.

"Who is it, Eben?" asked the doctor.

"*I* know; so do *you* too," replied Eben.

"Well, who is it?"

Eben made no answer, but with an expression more sly and penetrating than before, pointed with his thumb over his shoulder in the direction of Squire Gladwin's. The doctor's face flushed for a moment. The amorous simpleton had touched a chord which he believed concealed from every living soul. Not many days before, his fancy had been attracted by the black eyes and glowing cheek of the Squire's daughter, who, as he was jogging along on his professional hack, had passed him on a horse as young and spirited as herself. The doctor, disgusted with the figure he had made on this first interview, soon took measures for appearing before her to better advantage.

"Come," said Eben, "you're going up there—I know you be. I'll go too! She *is* a splendid gal, any how!"

The doctor was vexed, and was thinking how to rid himself of Eben's company, when the simpleton saved him the trouble of inventing an expedient:

"That 'ere's a pretty suit of clothes to go a courtin' in! I seen it hung up in your room the other day. Hold on! let's look again"; and, beginning his examination at the top, Eben took off the doctor's cap, and inspected it very carefully. He soon found a bullet hole in it. "Hallo! what's this? Did Injuns do that?"

"To be sure," said the doctor. He had himself thrown it into the air and fired a bullet through it on a wager.

"Where be they?" said Eben, getting alarmed. "How many did you see? I *told* the 'squire he'd have 'em at him if he didn't look out. Hark! that's them now!"

"No it isn't," said the doctor; "it's a cat-bird in the bushes; but you'd better run home, Eben, before they catch you!"

Eben waited no longer; but forgetting his cows and his "huckleberries," he walked off toward the village at his swiftest pace, growing more terrified every moment. The doctor turned down a by-road that led more directly to his lodgings.

He flung off his cap and seated himself by the window. He was blessed with an innate *savoir vivre;* so, drawing a table to his side, with a glass of brandy-and-water upon it, and lighting a cigar, he disposed himself at ease on his sofa; and as the wreaths of smoke rose before his dreamy eye, he saw gleaming within them the dark eyes of the Squire's dashing daughter. Thus he lay in his lazy musings for some fifteen or twenty minutes, when he was startled by a hollow and dismal sound that entered the open window. He recognized the voice of the broken conch-shell that was accustomed to summon the con-

gregation to church, but never had he known it to breathe forth
such awful and lugubrious notes. Just then, a three-pounder
was discharged from a block-house of the little stockade work
on the hill. This he knew was the signal of alarm, and, snuffing
the battle afar off, he seized his gun, which was loaded with
seven buckshot, and feeling his heart beat with a wild and not
unpleasing excitement, he leaned from the window to see what
would happen. In front of the dingy wooden church, which,
in the likeness of an overgrown barn, closed the prospect down
the street, half a dozen men were gathered with their guns, and
others were running to join them, while frilled caps, dishevelled
locks, and pale startled faces were thrust from innumerable
windows.

"Injuns! Injuns! Turn out! turn out!" roared a man, who
went dashing by the house like a frantic cart-horse.

"Where?" demanded the doctor.

"Where? Why, up to the Squire's. They've burnt the house
and scalped the whole of 'em, darter and all! Injuns!—turn
out, men! turn out!"

This was enough for the enamoured doctor. His mistress's
image was uppermost in his mind, and he bolted out of the
window, his long black hair streaming in the wind. Pausing
only to shout a malediction at the tardy warriors before the
meeting-house, and exhort them to make haste, he sprang off
like a hunted deer toward the Squire's.

The Squire was the patriarch of that settlement. He lived
beyond the outskirts of the village, on a farm by far the most
extensive, and in a house by far the most sumptuous of all that
the place could boast. It was no modern trumpery edifice of
shingles, but was dingy with the venerable antiquity of almost
twenty years, having been one of the first buildings erected in
the settlement.

The Doctor ran at full speed, swinging his gun in his hand,
and magnanimously forgetful of the jeopardy in which he was
placing his own scalp, so engrossed were all his thoughts by the
direful fate of his mistress. The road ran through a thick forest:
the impatient Doctor cursed the foliage that intercepted the

view. At length a recent clearing of the Squire's afforded an open prospect into the hollow where the mansion had stood; and there the Doctor saw it still! The massive brick chimneys, the steep double roof, the gray unpainted sides, rose amid the orchards, and fields of pumpkins and rigid Indian corn that surrounded them. No smoke or flame betokened the presence of an enemy: on the contrary, the scene was a gay and peaceful one, for the afternoon sun was looking his last upon the Squire's fields and meadows, and the wooded hills around were no less calm and smiling than the rustic scene they encircled.

The Doctor knew something of Indians, and was not to be deceived by appearances. Moderating his ardor, as best he might, he made a swift yet cautious approach, with his body bent, his hand on the lock of his gun, and his eyes glancing on every side. He soon came to the avenue that led up to the house: it was flanked by rows of clumsy water-willows, and at the end of this vista appeared the front of the house, with quaint carvings over the door; for the Squire, as already hinted, was a man of style. The Doctor listened; he looked over the fields and peered along the edge of the woods and up the avenue. No living thing was to be seen but the turtles sunning themselves around the margin of a little pond hard by; nothing to be heard but the chirruping of the crickets in the sunny meadows. He walked swiftly up to the house. All here was quiet as the grave. The milk-pans were arranged in military order at one side; a hen and her chickens were cackling round the well; and a black-and-white cat sat sleepily opening and shutting her eyes on the door step.

The Doctor unceremoniously entered. Still he could find nothing stirring but the cat, who seemed offended at his hasty intrusion, and was now arching her back and spitting at him from a corner. He called—no reply! He shouted at the top of his lungs, and got no answer but the echoes! He opened door after door, and found nobody! He burst into the sanctuary of the "best room," where in the "awful light obscure" of closed blinds and drawn curtains, he could faintly discern the great mirror gleaming darkly from amidst its paper hangings; and the sheen of the polished mahogany table, and the japanned box of marine curiosities with which the Squire used to astonish his more favored guests; and, lurking far amid the darkness, the white tops of the Squire's "London boots," which he never wore, but cherished and displayed as the most enviable article of luxury in his establishment. All this, and more, the Doctor saw at one comprehensive glance, and then bolted from the apartment. Running up stairs, he opened the first door he encountered, and was greeted by an hysterical squealing that proceeded from an old woman, no other than the old Squire's octogenarian mother, who was trying, in an agony of terror, to hide herself under the bed. "They *have* been here!" thought the Doctor, now doubly anxious; and he plied the old lady with question after question; but all in vain; and stamping his foot with impatience, he ran down stairs again. The Squire's family were, he knew, sometimes absent of an afternoon; but the silence frightened him; and then the old lady's terror! He was sure the Indians had been there.

He ran out of the front door again; and here, at last, he encountered an unequivocal token of the enemy. A gun was fired at him from the woods on the left, and another from a maple thicket near the road: at the same time, looking across the cornfield, he could discern half a dozen figures bounding like deer within the edge of the orchard! The Doctor was surrounded—fairly entrapped! The instinct of self-preservation banished for the moment every other thought from his mind. But how to escape? for no human speed could extricate him. An expedient on the instant occurred to him, exactly suiting his hair-brained disposition.

Squire Gladwin, who was famous for his love of horses, had one among the rest of such an outrageous temper that none of the villagers dared to mount him, and some of them stood in awe of his very presence. He was swifter than a dromedary, about as large as a small elephant, and so strong limbed and long winded that nothing could tire him down, or curb his furious temper; in consideration of which qualities, and of the sable hue of his coat, the neighbors had with one accord christened him Satan, to the great horror of parson Bellows.

Satan happened at this moment to be cropping the grass on the little green before the door, his vicious eyes glaring ominously through the shaggy locks of hair that fell over them. Startled at the firing, he now raised his head, and curling his swarthy nostril, snuffed gently in the wind. The Doctor approached him: twisting his hand in the tangled mane, he bounded upon his back, and as he alighted in his seat, he swung his gun aloft, and brought it down with the full sweep of his arm over the black flank of Satan. One furious snort; one bound into the air; and away he sprang like lightning down the avenue. The dents of his hoofs were visible for weeks after. He made straight for the gate, and would no doubt have carried his rider to the village, and heaven knows how much farther, had not another gun been discharged almost in his face by an enemy crouched behind the gateway. The ball was harmless; but startled at the flash and report, Satan brought up so suddenly, bracing his fore legs on the gravel, that the Doctor was pitched forward upon his arched and rigid neck, and had well nigh remained in the hands of the enemy. Then, with another snort, he turned abruptly to the right, dashed through the willows, leaped over a stone wall and ditch, and stretched away at full speed along a row of trees that the Squire had suffered to grow between his fields and the road. He soon came to the limits of the farm in that direction, when he turned to the right again and ran along a road or cart-track made for the convenience of bringing in fuel, and which, after skirting the edge of the woods for a few rods, turned suddenly and entered them. The Doctor feared, however, that the horse would keep on his course, and circle round the farm, by orchard, pasture and cornfield, thus giving his enemies so many chances for a fair shot, that his mortal career must soon be closed.

He was about to fling himself off at all risks, and run for the woods, when the bungling precipitation of his enemies saved him the necessity. Just as Satan came to the turning of the track, they set up a shout, followed by the reports of a dozen guns sending their bullets humming merrily about his ears. Then came the explosion of a carbine from the orchard, not far off: it was levelled with right good will at the Doctor's head:

but the heavy bullet, descending as it flew, came groaning solemnly through the air, and scored a deep furrow across the fore shoulder of Satan. At this, he wheeled again, toward the woods, goaded by rage, and terror, and pain. The Doctor's peculiar temperament was such that he was rather exhilarated than rendered serious by a narrow escape from sudden danger. The reckless blood now tingled to his very finger-ends. He turned round and laughed; and shaking his gun toward the enemy, gave an Indian whoop of defiance! An instant more, and he vanished from their sight.

Satan now scoured along the track, the Doctor, who was a good horseman, sitting quite at his ease, while trees and bushes fled past them like the wind. They had gone about a mile, when a dense smoke assailed their nostrils and nearly blinded them. The next moment, Satan's hoofs thumped over a rustic bridge thrown across a stream that rolled out from a dark cavern of vegetation and ran down into a new clearing of the Squire's. Satan bounded into this opening. The prostrate woods lay piled in ruin and desolation together, throwing up great volumes of smoke, with forked flames gleaming luridly in the midst. The forest stood around, with its foliage withered and scorched, and its bare trunks scathed by the fire that had made such a gap in its bosom. The Squire's men were at work among the piles of ruins not far off, and startled at the Doctor's sudden ingress, they rested on their axes, and gazed open-mouthed on the apparition. "Indians! Indians!" roared the Doctor, disappearing in the woods.

Satan had not borne him much farther, when he saw approaching him the Squire's daughter herself, who had been enjoying an afternoon's ride on her little white pony, and was now returning to superintend the affairs of the household. She hastily pressed the pony into the bushes by the side of the road, and with her rosy lips parted, fixed her great black eyes in amazement on her embarrassed cavalier: "Hide yourself! Indians! Indians!" he shouted, dashing by her like a thunderbolt. He had been for some time watching an opportunity to throw himself off the horse, an attempt which the narrowness of the road made imminently dangerous; but now the sight of his mistress disarmed all his prudential scruples. Grasping Satan's mane, he was about to leap, when Fate interposed her veto. It happened that the road divided just beyond the place of his interview: one branch of it was tolerably wide and smooth, and ran through a sufficiently level tract; but the other was newly made, and descended an abrupt hill. The headlong brute chose this latter course; and the Doctor found himself in a situation that would make the attempt to dismount no better than stark madness. He had but a moment to make his observations. All that he saw was a steep passage-way of over-arching trees above, and rocks, stumps and logs below. "I'm done for!" he thought to himself as he looked at this unenviable prospect. He held his breath! There was a rushing like a gale; a chaos of vanishing rocks and trees; and in an instant he was at the bottom. Here his self-congratulations at his escape were interrupted by a terrible switching that he got from the branches, for the track, though comparatively level, was very narrow; and soon a new danger threatened him. A tree had fallen across the way, and lay there with all its withering foliage. Satan cleared it, in spite of his furious speed; but now difficulties thickened around the hapless Doctor, as the track was constantly growing narrower and narrower, and dissipating itself into a labyrinth of little "bridle paths" that diverged in all directions. The Doctor was switched with redoubled severity. It was a joyful sight to him, when a rich flood of amber light poured through the tree-tops; and the horse, with a long bound, leaped out into the wide bed of a stream. It was rippling and gurgling quietly down through the forest, all its shallow waves reflecting the color of amethyst from the sky; and in the soft but gorgeous light, the scene had the tranquil beauty of a savage fairy-land, till Satan and the Doctor burst in upon its whispering stillness. Tired of the forest, the brute now turned and galloped up the shallow and gravelly stream, mid-way between its banks. It was a sight for a painter; the furious and unbridled horse, the helpless but still undaunted rider, in his wild Indian attire, his gun resting across his lap, and his hair flying loose in the wind.

Satan soon took to the woods again in a direction that would lead him back toward the Squire's. This time he dashed up a hollow between two hills, where, in the spring, a little brooklet ran down. Here the Doctor's troubles were redoubled. He buried his face in Satan's mane; he embraced his sturdy neck; but the branches tore away his hair by handsful, and menaced him every moment with the fate of Absalom. The horse's speed seemed not in the least abated by the ascent. He tore through the boughs as if his name-sake were behind him, till he gained the crown of the hill, which the axes of the settlers had luckily cleared of its woods, leaving it open and bare like the tonsured head of a monk. Satan jumped out into the clearing. A flock of crows were gathered at its edge, close at hand, on an old shattered oak, and alarmed by his unceremonious entrance, they swung clumsily from their perch, circled once with an ominous cawing above the Doctor's head, and then flapped away over the green forest tops. It was no very desirable place for a gallop. The stumps were still in the ground, which was beside encumbered with rocks, piles of cord-wood, and a rank growth of bushes; but any thing like an opening was grateful to the persecuted Doctor. He sat once more gallantly erect. Satan's wrath, too, seemed a little mollified, for he ceased running, and breaking into a long swinging trot along the ridge of the declivity, he shook his mane and tail, and uttered a discordant neigh. This was no doubt inspired by the sight of his stable, which, with the Squire's chimnies, was just visible over the woods, about half a mile off. The Doctor was prompt to avail himself of Satan's improved temper; but before he could throw himself to the ground, the brute set off down the hill more savagely than before.

Another track led from the clearing to the Squire's farm. Fortunately, it was a better one than the others had been; and as the Doctor reflected that he was being borne back to the tender mercies of the Indians, he resolved to get to terra firma in some manner or other. The ground was neither remarkably hard nor rough, and the track was wide enough to give him some chance to escape being dashed against the trees in the attempt. Fortune, however, tired at last of persecuting him, presented him with a more favorable opportunity of effecting his purpose: a horizontal branch projected across the road within reach of his hands. He dropped his gun and seized it, and though his arms were severely wrenched, he kept his hold while Satan vanished from beneath him, and left him swinging like a pendulum in the air!

When he had let himself drop to the earth, he felt for a moment as if it were rocking beneath him. To stand on firm ground that would not gallop away with him; to see trees and bushes that remained fixed while he looked at them, seemed a novel experience to the Doctor's faculties. He stamped, to assure himself that his bones were still whole and sound; and then sat on a log to gather his scattered ideas and reflect on what he had best do. His appetite for adventure had been satiated for the present. He had no inclination to encounter Indians or fight battles; and as he thought the enemy might still be lurking about the farm, he prudently determined to be cautious in his approaches. It was now nearly night; the woods were gray and dusky, and in a quarter of an hour it would be dark enough for his purpose. Meanwhile, he prepared as well as he could for any emergency, by making his gun ready for action and renewing the priming, which had been shaken from the pan by the blow he gave to Satan at the outset of his career. At length he rose, and cautiously proceeded toward the farm, pausing at intervals to listen. When he came to the edge of the clearing, and had a fair view upon the back of the Squire's premises, he saw nothing unusual, though the broad disk of the moon was just looking through the tree-tops. He stepped into the bushes, however, and watched the place for a moment, when, finding the lover growing importunate within him, he no longer hesitated to advance. Just before him was a newly-cleared field; beyond that, a meadow dotted with a few trees; and still farther on rose the barns and numerous store-houses of the Squire.

The Doctor soon passed the field and the meadow, and came to a high rail-fence separating the latter from the buildings; and here he stopped and listened again. All was tranquil enough: he could see the dingy backs of the cattle in the yard, and thought to himself that the Indians had not made very clean work of it. Climbing the fence, he walked through a sort of muddy lane, with the buildings on one side, and a row of old stunted willows on the other, which made it quite dark. After passing it safely, he entered a narrow space between the great barn and a projecting store-house. He was groping with some confidence through this passage, for he saw a light at a back window of the house, when suddenly a figure sprang out on each side and laid hold of him. All his troubles and perils were in vain!—the enemy had him at last. The Doctor, who was active and sinewy as a wild-cat, struggled manfully with his captors; threw one of them to the ground, and was aiming a blow at the other, when his wrist was seized with an iron gripe, and at the same time, a dozen hands were applied to his neck, arms, and body. In a moment, he was down. His arms were jerked behind him; a rope was wound about them, round and round, and the captured Doctor was lifted to his feet again. All this was most expeditiously performed in perfect silence, except the hard breathing of the earnest operators. He now found himself in the midst of them, as they stood by him, scrutinizing him intently by the light of a dark lantern which one of them produced. Judge of his astonishment, when he saw himself encircled, not by plumed and painted Indians, but by his own friends of the village—the men whom he had left gathering before the meeting-house, while he ran off to fight the enemy by himself! It was some time before he could convince them of his identity, as what with the Cayuga chief's hunting-shirt and leggins, and his own sunburnt face, he really did look more like an Indian than a Doctor of medicine. All was amazement and perplexity for a while, but at last the mystery was partially unravelled; and this was it:

The alarm was attributable, not to Montcalm or his Indians, who were by this time safe in Ticonderoga, but solely to Eben Chipmunk. He had parted from the Doctor, as will be remembered, in great terror and perturbation, which might have subsided if he had not met three old women, great cronies of his, who were boiling their kettle and washing clothes down by the brook. Eben ran to them and communicated his own terror, for they were as timid as he. The old women screamed, and made for the fort, alarming their neighbors by the way. Eben's fright was redoubled at seeing that of his listeners; he began to spread hideous stories, that his terrified imagination supplied him with, and that he fully believed to be fact. By the time he had got to the fort, he thought that the Indians were at that moment attacking the Squire's house and butchering the inmates. In the fort, as well as the houses, there were, by ill luck, none but women and children; they ran to alarm the men in the fields; the men blew the conch and fired the gun; and all the village was in a hubbub. Meanwhile, the innocent Doctor, forgetful of his meeting with Eben, sat smoking his cigar till the noise reached his ears; and in his anxiety he ran, as we have seen, to rescue his mistress before the others were ready. They soon followed, surrounded the house, and hearing a great noise within, and seeing a man in the dress of an Indian rushing out with a gun in his hand, they very naturally took him for the enemy they expected to find there, and fired at him. The Doctor, finding himself attacked, and coming on his part to the same conclusion, took the only means that seemed to offer a chance of escape.

The men now looked upon the Doctor with some wonder and admiration, which they expressed in very audible whispers to one another; but he himself was much vexed at the predicament in which his precipitation had involved him. As they passed the stable door, one of his companions opened it, and displayed Satan in his stall, whither he had come thundering at full speed from the woods about half an hour before. The Doctor looked at him with no benevolent emotions. He was chiefly vexed on account of his mistress. Though a party had gone to seek her, neither she nor the Squire's men were yet returned from the woods; probably, as he reflected, in consequence of the alarm, that he had roared at them as he rode past. He execrated himself between his teeth. He was in some degree relieved, when he and his companions came to the door, by seeing a body of men approaching over the fields, with the Squire's daughter in front, on her pony. After hearing the Doctor's warning, she had joined her brother, who was in the clearing with the men; and they all hid in the woods, till they saw the party that came to look for them.

It is not unlikely that her admirer's jeopardy had engaged her thoughts more than her own disagreeable situation; for no sooner did she learn that he was safe in the house, and the whole matter had been explained to her, than the vexation she had before expressed vanished, and she affected to treat the whole matter as a laughable joke. The Doctor got no sympathy from her; she rallied him without mercy; yet she entertained at heart a great admiration for his conduct through the whole course of the affair, not at all diminished by the conviction that she herself was the original cause of his perils and mishaps. She could see that while running away from an imaginary enemy, he had shown the impetuous daring of his character no less effectually than he would have done in assailing a real one. Yet one evil result followed the adventure; the Doctor's occupation was gone!—his flourishing practice was no more! Not an old woman in town would trust her rheumatic joints to the care of a physician who had so little regard for his own limbs. In spite of this, it may be that in the end his ride had a favorable influence on his prospects of happiness and content; but I will tell the reader all that I know myself, and he can form his own judgment. The last that I heard of him was from a gentleman who, in his college days, in the winter of 1810, visited the Squire's old homestead on a sleighing frolic. Here they found a tall erect old man, with the laughing eye and merry heart of a boy; and his lady, a stately dame, who welcomed them with the cordial and profuse hospitality of the olden time. These were the Doctor, transformed into a wealthy farmer, and the Squire's daughter; whose son, as I hear, still occupies the venerable mansion, and is ready to transfer any unfortunate gentleman from the hands of the village inn-keeper to the more agreeable entertainments of his own house.

[A STORM AT SEA]

(From *Vassall Morton*, 1856)

At one o'clock at night, in the midst of the Atlantic, a hundred leagues west of the Azores, the bark Swallow, freighted with salt cod for the Levant, was scudding furiously, under a close-reefed foresail, before a fierce gale. On board were her captain, two mates, seven men, a black steward, a cabin boy, and Mr. John White, a passenger.

The captain and his mates were all on deck. John White, otherwise Horace Vinal, occupied a kind of store room, opening out of the cabin. Here a temporary berth had been nailed up for him, while on the opposite side were stowed a trunk belonging to him, and three barrels of onions belonging to the vessel's owners, all well lashed in their places.

The dead lights were in, but the seas, striking like mallets against the stern, pierced in fine mist through invisible crevices, bedrizzling every thing with salt dew. The lantern, hanging from the cabin roof, swung angrily with the reckless plungings of the vessel.

Vinal was a good sailor; that is to say, he was not very liable to that ocean scourge, seasickness, and the few qualms he had suffered were by this time effectually frightened out of him. As darkness closed, he had lain down in his clothes; and flung from side to side till his bones ached with the incessant rolling of the bark, he listened sleeplessly to the hideous booming of the storm. Suddenly there came a roar so appalling, that he leaped out of his berth with terror. It seemed to him as if a Niagara had broken above the vessel, and was crushing her down to the nethermost abyss. The rush of waters died away. Then came the bellow of the speaking trumpet, the trampling of feet, the shouts of men, the hoarse fluttering of canvas. In a few moments he felt a change in the vessel's motion. She no longer rocked with a constant reel from side to side, but seemed flung about at random, hither and thither, at the mercy of the storm.

She had been, in fact, within a hair's breadth of foundering. A huge wave, chasing on her wake, swelling huger and huger, towering higher and higher, had curled, at last, its black crest above her stern, and, breaking, fallen on her in a deluge. The captain, a Barnstable man of the go-ahead stamp, was brought at last to furl his foresail and lie to.

Vinal, restless with his fear, climbed the narrow stairway which led up to the deck, and pushed open the door at the top; but a blast of wind and salt spray clapped it in his face, and would have knocked him to the foot of the steps, if he had not clung to the handrail. He groped his way as he could back to his berth. Here he lay for a quarter of an hour, when the captain came down, enveloped in oilcloths, and dripping like a Newfoundland dog just out of the water. Vinal emerged from his den, and presenting himself with his haggard face, and hair bristling in disorder, questioned the bedrenched commander touching the state of things on deck. But the latter was in a crusty and savage mood.

"Hey! what is it?"—surveying the apparition by the light of the swinging lantern,—"well, you *be* a beauty, I'll be damned if you ain't."

"I did not ask you how I looked; I asked you about the weather."

"Well, it ain't the sweetest night I ever see; but I guess you won't drown this time."

"My friend," said Vinal, "learn to mend your way of speaking, and use a civil tongue."

The captain stared at him, muttered an oath or two, and then turned away.

Day broke, and Vinal went on deck. It was a wild dawning. The storm was at its height. One rag of a topsail was set to steady the vessel; all the rest was bare poles and black dripping cordage, through which the gale yelled like a forest in a tornado. The sky was dull gray; the ocean was dull gray. There was no horizon. The vessel struggled among tossing mountains, while tons of water washed her decks, and the men, half drowned, clung to the rigging. Vast misshapen ridges of water bore down from the windward, breaking into foam along their crests, struck the vessel with a sullen shock, burst over her bulwarks, deluged her from stem to stern, heaved her aloft as they rolled on, and then left her to sink again into the deep trough of the sea.

Vinal was in great fear; but nothing in his look betrayed it. He soon went below to escape the drenching seas; but towards noon, Hansen, the second mate, a good-natured old sea dog, came down with the welcome news that the gale had suddenly abated. Vinal went on deck again, and saw a singular spectacle. The wind had strangely lulled; but the waves were huge and furious as ever; and the bark rose and pitched, and was flung to and fro with great violence, but in a silence almost perfect. Water, in great quantities, still washed the deck, but found ready escape through a large port in the after part of the vessel, the lid of which, hanging vertically, had been left unfastened.

The lull was of short space. A hoarse, low sound began to growl in the distance like muffled thunder. It grew louder,—nearer,—and the gale was on them again. This time it blew from the north-west, and less fiercely than before. The venturous captain made sail. The yards were braced round; and leaning from the wind till her lee gunwale scooped the water, the vessel plunged on her way like a racehorse. The clouds were rent; blue sky appeared. Strong winds tore them apart, and the sun blazed out over the watery convulsion, changing its blackness to a rich blue, almost as dark, where the whirling streaks of foam seemed like snow wreaths on the mountains. Jets of foam, too, spouted from under the vessel's bows, as she dashed them against the opposing seas; and the prickling spray flew as high as the main top. The ocean was like a viking in his robust carousals,—terror and mirth, laughter and fierceness, all in one.

But the mind of Vinal was blackness and unmixed gall. His game was played and lost. The worst that he feared had befallen him. Suspense was over, and he was freed from the incubus that had ridden him so long. A something like relief mixed itself with his bitter and vindictive musings. He had not fled empty handed. He and Morton's friend Sharpe had been joint trustees of a large estate, a part of which, in a form that made it readily available, happened to be in Vinal's hands at the time of his crisis. Dread of his quick-sighted and vigilant colleague had hitherto prevented him from applying it to his own uses. But this fear had now lost its force. He took it with him on his flight, and converted it into money in New York, where he had embarked.

At night the descent of Hansen to supper was a welcome diversion to his lonely thoughts. The old sailor seated himself at the table:—

"I've lost all my appetite, and got a horse's. Here, steward, you nigger, where be yer? Fetch along that beefsteak. What do you call this here? Well, never mind what you call it, here goes into it, any how."

A silent and destructive onslaught upon the dish before him followed. Then, laying down his knife and fork for a moment,—

"I've knowed the time when I could have ate up the doctor there,"—pointing to the steward,—"bones and all, and couldn't get a mouthful, no way you could fix it." Then, resuming his labors, "Tell you what, squire, this here agrees with me. Come out of that berth now, and sit down here alongside o' me. Just walk into that beefsteak, like I do. That 'ere beats physicking all holler."

Thus discoursing, partly to himself and partly to Vinal, and, by turns, berating the grinning steward in a jocular strain, Mr. Hansen continued his repast. When, at last, he left the cabin, Vinal found the solitude too dreary for endurance; and, to break its monotony, he also went on deck.

The vessel still scoured wildly along; and as she plunged through the angry seas, so the moon was sailing among stormy clouds, now eclipsed and lost, now shining brightly out, silvering the seething foam, and casting the shadows of spars and rigging on the glistening deck. Vinal bent over the bulwark and looked down on the bubbles, as they fled past, flashing in the moon.

His thoughts flew backward with them, and dwelt on the hated home from which he was escaping.

"What an outcry! what gapes of wonder, and eyes turned up to heaven! Gulled, befooled, hoodwinked! and now, at last, you have found it out, and make earth and heaven ring with your virtuous spite. I knew you all, and played you as I would play the pieces on a chess board. The game was a good one in the main, but with some blunders, and for those I pay the price. If I had had that villain's brute strength, and the brute nerve that goes with it, there would have been a different story to tell. Before this, I would have found a way to grind him to the earth, and set my foot on his neck. They think him virtuous. He thinks himself so. The shallow-witted idiots! Their eyes can only see skin-deep. They love to be cheated. They swallow fallacies as a child swallows sweetmeats. The tinsel dazzles them, and they take it for gold. Virtue! a delusion of self-interest—self-interest, the spring, lever, and fulcrum of the world. It is for my interest, for every body's interest, that his neighbors should be honest, candid, open, forgiving, charitable, continent, sober, and what not. Therefore, by the general consent of mankind,—the inevitable instinct of self-interest,—such qualities are exalted into sanctity; christened with the name of virtues; draped in white, and crowned with halos; rewarded with praises here and paradise hereafter. Drape the skeleton as you will, the bare skeleton is still there. Paint as thick as you will, the bare skull grins under it,—to all who have the eyes to see, and the hardihood to use them. How many among mankind have courage to face the naked truth? Not one in a thousand. Cannot the fools draw reason out of the analogy of things? Can they not see that, as their bodies will be melted and merged into the bodily substance of the world, so their minds will be merged in the great universal mind,—the *animus mundi*,—out of which they sprang, like bubbles on the water, and into which they will sink again, like bubbles when they burst? Immortality! They may please themselves with the name; but of what worth is an immortality where individuality is lost, and each conscious atom drowned in the vast immensity? What a howling and screeching the wind makes in the rigging! If I were given to superstition, I could fancy that a legion from the nether world were bestriding the ropes, yelping in grand jubilation at the sight of—"

Here his thoughts were abruptly cut short. A combing wave struck the vessel. She lurched with violence, and a shower of foam flew over her side. Vinal lost his balance. His feet slipped from under him. He fell, and slid quickly across the wet and tossing deck. Instinctively he braced his feet to stop himself against the bulwark on the lee side. But at the point where they touched it was the large port before mentioned. Though closed to all appearance, the bolt was still unfastened. It flew open at his touch. Vinal clutched to save himself. His fingers slipped on the wet timbers, and with a cry of horror, he was shot into the bubbling surges. There was a blinding in his eyes, a ringing in his ears; then, for an instant, he saw the light, and the black hulk of the vessel fled past like a shadow. Then a wave swept over him: all was darkness and convulsion, and a maddened sense of being flung high aloft, as the wave rolled him towards its crest like a drift sea weed. Here again light broke upon him; and flying above the merciless chaos, he saw something like the white wing of a huge bird. It was the reefed main-topsail of the receding vessel. He shrieked wildly. A torrent of brine dashed back the cry, and foaming over his head, plunged him down into darkness again. Again he rose, gasping and half senseless; and again the ravenous breakers beat him down. A moment of struggle and of agony; and then a long nightmare of dreamy horror, while, slowly settling downward, he sank below the turmoil of the storm; slowly and more slowly still, till the denser water sustained his weight. Then with limbs outstretched, he hovered in mid ocean, lonely, void, and vast, like a hawk poised in mid-air, while his felon spirit, bubbling to the surface, winged its dreary flight through the whistling storm.

[THE ROMANCE OF TRAVEL]

[AN ADVENTURE IN THE MOUNTAINS]
(From his Diary)

This afternoon I achieved the most serious adventure it was ever my lot to encounter. I walked down the Notch to the Willey House, and out of curiosity began to ascend the pathway of the avalanche on the mountain directly behind. This pathway is a deep ravine channelled in the side of the mountain, which in this place is extremely steep. In the bottom of this gulf a little stream comes down from a spring above, and renders the precipitous rocks as slippery as clay. The sides of the ravine, which runs directly up and down the mountain, are a decaying granite, while the bottom is formed by a trap-dike. I ascended at first easily, but the way began to be steeper and the walls on each side more precipitous. Still I kept on until I came to a precipice about forty feet high and not far from perpendicular. I could see that this was followed by a similar one above. Professor Silliman, a year or two ago, ascended in this place until, as he says, "further progress was prevented by inaccessible precipices of the trap-rock." The exploit of the Professor occurred to me as I stood below, and I determined that the "inaccessible precipices" which had cooled his scientific ardor should prove no barriers to me. I began to climb, and with considerable difficulty and danger, and with the loss of my stick, which went rattling and bounding down the ravine many rods before it found a resting-place, I surmounted both precipices. I climbed on, but finding that I was becoming drenched by the scanty stream, and seeing, moreover, a huge cloud not far up, settling slowly towards me, I bethought me of retracing my steps. I knew that it would be impossible to descend by the way I had come, and accordingly, I tried to get out of the ravine to the side of the mountain which was covered with wood which I could grasp hold of to assist me. But I was inclosed between two walls of fifty feet high and so steep, and composed of such materials that an attempt to climb would only bring down the rotting granite upon my head. So I began to descend the ravine, nothing doubting that I could find some means of getting out before reaching the critical point. But it was impossible, and I found myself at the top of the precipice with no alternative but to slide down, or clamber the perpendicular and decaying walls to the surface of the mountain. The former was certain destruction, as I proved by suffering a rotten log to slide down. It glanced by the first descent like an arrow, struck at the bottom, bounded six feet into the air, and leaped down the mountain, splintering into twenty pieces as it went. The other method was scarcely less dangerous, but it was my only chance, and I braced my nerves and began to climb. Down went stones and pebbles, clattering hundreds of feet below and giving me a grateful indication of my inevitable fate in case my head should swim or my courage fail. I had got half way up and was climbing to the face of the precipice, when the two stones which supported my feet loosened and leaped down the ravine. My finger ends, among the rotten gravel were all which sustained me, and they, of course, would have failed had I not thought on the instant of lowering my body gradually, and so diminishing its weight, until my feet found new supporters. I sunk the length of my arms and then hung for the time, in tolerable safety, with one foot resting on a projecting stone. Loosening the hold of one hand, I took my large jack-knife from my pocket, opened it, with the assistance of my teeth, and dug with it a hollow among the decayed stones, large enough to receive and support one foot. Then thrusting the knife as far as possible into the wall to assist my hold, I grasped it, and the stones with the unoccupied hand, and raised my foot to the hollow prepared for it; thus, foot by foot, I made my way, and in ten minutes, as time seemed to me, I seized a projecting root at the top and drew myself up. During the whole time of climbing I felt perfectly cool, but when fairly up I confess I shuddered as I looked down at the gulf I had escaped. A large stone, weighing, perhaps, a hundred pounds, lay on the edge. I thrust it off with my foot, and down it went, struck the bottom of the ravine with a tremendous crash, and thundered down, leaping from side to side, until it lodged at last, far below against a projecting rock. I descended the mountain by means of the trees and bushes, cut a fishing-pole at the bottom, and having amused myself with an hour's fishing, went to the tavern and astonished the company with a recital of my adventure. Crawford expressed considerable astonishment at my escape, and the young lady in whose company I got my ducking on the stage transferred an account to her journal, but refused to let me see it, promising to send me a copy the moment her book was out of press.

[A VACATION TRIP]

July 15th, '42. Albany. Left Boston this morning at half-past six, for this place, where I am now happily arrived, it being the longest day's journey I ever made. For all that, I would rather have come thirty miles by stage than the whole distance by railroad, for of all methods of progressing, that by steam is incomparably the most disgusting. . . .

July 16th. Caldwell. This morning we left Albany—which I devoutly hope I may never see again—in the cars, for Saratoga. . . . After passing the inclined plane and riding a couple of hours, we reached the valley of the Mohawk and Schenectady. I was prepared for something filthy in the last mentioned venerable town, but for nothing quite so disgusting as the reality. Canal docks, full of stinking water, superannuated rotten canal-boats, and dirty children and pigs paddling about formed the foreground of the delicious picture, while in the rear was a mass of tumbling houses and sheds, bursting open in all directions, green with antiquity, dampness, and lack of paint. Each house had its peculiar dunghill, with the group of reposing hogs. In short, London itself could exhibit nothing much nastier. . . . Finally reached Saratoga, having traveled latterly at the astonishing rate of about seven miles an hour. "Caldwell stage ready." We got our baggage on board, and I found time to enter one or two of the huge hotels. After perambulating the entries filled with sleek waiters and sneaking fops, dashing through the columned porticoes and inclosures, drinking some of the water and spitting it out again in high disgust, I sprang onto the stage, cursing Saratoga and all New York. . . .

Dined at the tavern, and rode on. Country dreary as before; the driver one of the best of his genus I ever met. He regaled me as we rode on with stories of his adventures with deer, skunks, and passengers. A mountain heaved up against the sky some distance before us, with a number of small hills stretching away on each hand, all wood-crowned to the top. . . . But as we drew near, the mountain in front assumed a wilder and a loftier aspect. Crags started from its woody sides and leaned over a deep valley below. "What mountain is that?" "That 'ere is French Mounting,"—the scene of one of the most desperate and memorable battles in the old French War. As we passed down the valley, the mountain rose above the forest half a mile on our right, while a hill on the left, close to the road, formed the other side. The trees flanked the road on both sides. In a little opening in the woods, a cavity in the ground with a pile of stones at each end marked the spot where was buried that accomplished warrior and gentleman, Colonel Williams, whose bones, however, have since been removed. Farther on is the rock on the right where he was shot, having mounted it on the look-out—an event which decided the day; the Indians and English broke and fled at once. Still farther on is the scene of the third tragedy of that day, when the victorious French, having been in their turn, by a piece of good luck, beaten by the valorous Johnson at his intrenchment by the lake, were met at this place on their retreat by McGinnis, and almost cut to pieces. Bloody Pond, a little slimy dark sheet of stagnant water, covered with weeds and pond-lilies and shadowed by the gloomy forest around it, is the place where hundreds of dead bodies were flung after the battle, and where the bones still lie. A few miles farther, and Lake George lay before us, the mountains and water confused and indistinct in the mist. We rode into Caldwell, took supper—a boat—and then a bed.

July 17th. Caldwell. The tavern is full of fashionable New Yorkers—all of a piece. Henry and myself both look like the Old Nick, and are evidently looked upon in a manner corresponding. I went this morning to see William Henry. The old fort is much larger than I had thought; the earthen mounds cover many acres. It stood on the southwest extremity of the lake, close by the water. The enterprising genius of the inhabitants has made a road directly through the ruins, and turned bastion, moat, and glacis into a flourishing cornfield, so that the spot so celebrated in our colonial history is now scarcely to be distinguished. Large trees are growing on the untouched parts, especially on the embankment along the lake shore. In the rear, a hundred or two yards distant, is a gloomy wood of pines, where the lines of Montcalm can easily be traced. A little behind these lines is the burying place of the French who fell during that memorable siege. The marks of a thousand graves can be seen among the trees, which of course have sprung up since. . . . One of Montcalm's lines ran northwest of the tavern toward the mountains. Two or three years ago in digging for some purpose, a great quantity of deer, bear, and moose bones were found here, with arrows and hatchets, which the tavern keeper thinks mark the place of some Indian feast. The spikes and timbers of sunken vessels may be seen in strong sunlight, when the water is still, at the bottom of the lake, along the southern beach. Abercrombie sunk his boats here. There are remains of batteries on French Mt., and the mountain north of it, I suppose to command the road from Ft. Edward. This evening visited the French graves. I write this at camp, July 18th. Just turned over my ink bottle and spilt all the ink.

July 18th. Camp at Diamond Island. Set out this morning in an excellent boat, hired at Caldwell. . . . We landed occasionally, and fished as we went along. About ten o'clock stretched across Middle Bay and got bread, pork, and potatoes at a farmhouse, with which and our fish we regaled ourselves at a place half way down the Bay. Here I wrote my journal for yesterday; we slept an hour or two on the ground, bathed, and read Goldsmith, which Henry brought in his knapsack. At three we proceeded to explore the bay to its bottom, returned, made for Diamond Island, which is now uninhabited, prepared our camp and went to sleep.

July 19th. I woke this morning about as weak and spiritless as well could be. All enterprise and activity was fairly gone; how I cannot tell, but I cursed the weather as the most probable cause. Such has been the case with me, to a greater or less degree, for the last three or four weeks. Rowed to-day along the eastern shore. . . . But everything was obscured with mist. When the wind became less violent we rowed to an island in the middle, where we are now encamped.

Wednesday, July 20th. Entered the narrows this morning, and rowed among all the islands and along all the shores. . . . We passed under Black Mt., whose precipices and shaggy woods wore a very savage and impressive aspect in that peculiar weather, and kept down the lake seven miles to Sabbath Day Pt. High and steep mountains flanked the lake the whole way. In front, at some distance they seemed to slope gradually away, and a low green point, with an ancient dingy house upon it, closed the perspective. This was Sabbath Day Pt., the famous landing place of many a huge army. . . . We ran our boat on the beach of Sabbath Day Pt. and asked lodging at the house. An old woman, after a multitude of guesses and calculations, guessed as how she could accommodate us with a supper and a bed, though she couldn't say nohow how we should like it, seeing as how she warn't used to visitors. The house was an old, rickety, dingy shingle palace, with a potato garden in front, hogs perambulating the outhouses, and a group of old men and women engaged in earnest conversation in the tumble-down portico. The chief figure was an old gray-haired man, tall and spare as a skeleton, who was giving some advice to a chubby old lady about her corns.

"Well now," said the old lady, "I declare they hurt me mighty bad."

"I'll give you something to cure them right off."

"What is it? I hope it ain't snails. I always hated snails since I was a baby, but I've heerd say they are better for corns nor anything else at all," etc., etc.

The old man was a revolutionary pensioner, Captain Patchin by name, and stout-hearted, hale, and clever by nature. . . .

Thursday, 21st. Fished for bass. . . . We caught fish enough, landed, and with Myrtle Bailey, one of the young Brobdignagians, a simple, good-natured, strong-handed, grinning son of the plough, set out on a rattlesnake hunt on the mountain back of the Point. . . . We soon reached a still higher point, which commanded the noblest view of the lake I had yet seen. There would be no finer place for gentlemen's seats than this; but now, for the most part, it is occupied by a race of boors about as uncouth, mean, and stupid as the hogs they seem chiefly to delight in. The captain's household is an exception. . . . Afternoon: Fished again. Evening: Fished again, and caught a very large bass—all in company of Myrtle, whose luck not satisfying him, he cursed the "Darned cussed fish" in most fervent style.

Friday, 22nd. Left old Patchin's this morning. . . . We broke an oar when within about half a mile, and paddled to shore with great difficulty through a considerable surf which was dashing against the beach like the waves of the ocean. We found the post-office a neat little tavern kept by one Garfield, entitled the Judge. He referred us to a carpenter, who promised to make an oar forthwith, and worked six hours upon it, an interval which I spent chiefly in wandering through the country. . . . Returned to Garfield's, and found there Mr. Gibbs with his wife the "vocalist." Presently the man appeared with the oar finished. White undertook to pay him with a Naumkeag Bank bill—the only bills he had. "Don't know nothing about that money: wait till Garfield comes and he'll tell whether it's genuine or not." "There's the paper," said I; "look and see." He looked—all was right. "Well, are you satisfied?" "How do I know but what that ere bill is counterfeit. It has a sort of counterfeit look about it to my eyes. Deacon, what do you say to it?" The deacon put on his spectacles, held the bill to the light, turned it this way and that, tasted of it, and finally pronounced that according to his calculation it was good. But the carpenter was not contented. " 'Bijah, you're a judge of bills;

what do you think?" 'Bijah, after a long examination, gave as his opinion that it was counterfeit. All parties were beginning to wax wroth, when the judge entered and decided that the bill was good.

We pushed from the beach and steered down the lake, passed some islands, and beheld in front of us two grim mountains, standing guard over a narrow strait of dark water between. . . . One of these mountains was the noted Rogers Slide, the other, almost as famous, Anthony's Nose, Jr. Both had witnessed, in their day, the passage of twenty vast armies in the strait between; and there was not an echo on either but had answered to the crack of rifles and screams of dying men. We skirted the base of the Nose—for which sentimental designation I could find no manner of reason—till we arrived opposite the perpendicular front of his savage neighbor. About a mile of water was between. We ran the boat ashore on a shelving rock, and looked for a camping place among the precipices. We found, to our surprise, at the side of a steep rock, amid a growth of cedars and hemlocks, a little inclosure of logs, like a diminutive log cabin without a roof. We made beds in it of hemlock boughs—there was just space enough—brought up our baggage and guns, ate what supper we had, and essayed to go asleep. But we might as well have slept under a shower-bath of melted iron. In that deep sheltered spot, bugs, mosquitoes, and "no-see-ems" swarmed innumerable. . . . This morning was the most toilsome we have passed. The wind was dead against us; the waves ran with a violence I had never seen before except on the ocean. It required the full force of both arms to hold the boat on her course. If we slackened our efforts for a single moment, she would spin round and drive backwards. We had about twelve miles to row under these agreeable auspices.

"Well," said White, "you call this fun, do you? To be eaten by bugs all night and work against head winds all day isn't according to my taste, whatever you may think of it."

"Are you going to back out?" said I.

"Back out, yes; when I get into a bad scrape, I back out of it as quick as I can," and so he went on with marvelous volubility to recount his grievances. Lake George he called a "scrubby looking place,"—said there was no fishing in it—he hated camping, and would have no more of it,—he wouldn't live so for another week to save his life, etc., etc. Verily, what is one man's meat is another man's poison. What troubles me more than his treachery to our plans is his want of cash, which will make it absolutely necessary to abandon our plan of descending through Maine. His scruples I trust to overcome in time.

We reached Patchin's at last, and were welcomed by the noble old veteran as cordially as if we were his children. We dined, and sat in his portico, listening to his stories. He is eighty-six. . . .

We consigned our boat to the captain, to be carried back to Caldwell, and got on a stage we found at the wharf, which carried us to the village of Ty. [Ticonderoga]. It is a despicable manufacturing place, straggling and irregular,—mills, houses, and heaps of lumber,—situated in a broad valley with the outlet of Lake George running through the middle, a succession of fierce rapids, with each its saw-mill. I bespoke me here a pair of breeches of a paddy tailor who asked me if I did not work on board the steamboat, a question which aggravated me not a little. I asked a fellow the way to the fort. "Well," said he, "I've heerd of such a place, seems to me, but I never seen it, and couldn't tell ye where it be." "You must be an idiot," thought I; but I found his case by no means singular. At last I got the direction, and walked about two miles before I saw the remains of a high earthen parapet with a ditch running through a piece of woods for a great distance. This, I suppose, was the place where the French beat off Abercrombie's army. Farther on, in a great plain scantily covered with wood, were breast-works and ditches in abundance running in all directions, which I took for the work of Amherst's besieging army. Still farther were two or three square redoubts. At length, mounting a little hill, a cluster of gray ruined walls, like an old chateau, with mounds of earth and heaps of stone about them, appeared crowning an eminence in front. When I reached them, I was astonished at the extent of the ruins. Thousands of men might have encamped in the area. All around were ditches, of such depth that it would be death to jump down, with walls of masonry sixty feet high. Ty stands on a promontory, with Champlain on one side and the outlet of Lake George on the other; his cannon commanded the passage completely. At the very extremity is the oldest part of the fortress, a huge mass of masonry, with walls sinking sheer down to the two lakes. All kinds of weeds and vines are clambering over them. The senseless blockheads in the neighborhood have stolen tons upon tons of the stone to build their walls and houses of,—may they meet their reward.

Wednesday, 27th. In Yankee land again, thank heaven. Left Ty this noon—after going over the ruins again—in one of the great Champlain steamboats, and reached Burlington at night. Visited the college. It was term time and the students were lounging about the ugly buildings or making abortive attempts at revelry in their rooms. The air was full of their diabolical attempts at song. We decided that they were all green, and went back, drawing comparisons by the way between the University of Vermont and old Harvard.

Thursday, 28th. Left Burlington this morning, knapsack on back, for Canada. . . . We followed the road through a deep wood, and when we emerged from it the village of Cambridge lay before us, twenty-five miles from Burlington. We stopped here for the night.

Friday, 29th. From Cambridge we walked on to Johnson. . . . At Johnson we took the stage for Stanstead, in Canada. The "stage" was a broken down carryall, into which six passengers with luggage were stowed, and the thing set in motion —under the auspicious influences of two sick horses—over a road of diabolical roughness.

Saturday, July 30th. Stanstead, Canada. Resumed our journey this morning in the same "stage." . . . The place is large, with several handsome churches. There was nothing in particular to distinguish it from a flourishing Yankee town till we pulled up at the tavern, where were two or three British soldiers, in their undress, standing on the porch. There were thirteen of them, with a cornet, quartered at the house, as there now are in all the border villages. They were good-looking fellows, civil enough; natives of the provinces. They were gathered round a fire in the barroom, smoking and telling stories, or else indulging in a little blackguardism and knocking one another about the room. They invited us to drink with them, and the liquor being mead—the house being temperance—we consented. They have just clubbed to buy a barrel of cider.

Sunday, July 31st. Last night we were kept awake by the din of bugles and drums with which the soldiers were regaling themselves in the entry, singing and dancing meanwhile. This morning rainy and dismal. Soldiers and all gathered round the stove in the barroom. Their conversation was about as decent and their jokes as good as those of a convocation of Harvard students. . . .

We set out on foot for Canaan, which promised land some told us was twenty miles distant, while others reckoned it thirty. The road for a few miles was good, but we were soon compelled to leave it and take a path through the woods. A beautiful river—smooth and rapid—ran across the road under a bridge of logs, between forest-covered banks. Not far from Stanstead we had crossed a furious stream, answering to the sentimental designation of the Nigger River. We had walked but a few miles when the clouds settled on the hills and it began to rain. We went to a log cabin for shelter. The "old man" was frank and hospitable like all his genus I ever met, and the "old woman"—a damsel of twenty-two, who sat combing her hair in the corner—extremely sprightly and talkative. She seemed somewhat moved at heart by the doctrines of Miller, whose apostles are at work all along the Vermont frontier. We abused that holy man to our content, and, the rain ceasing, left the cabin. Soon after leaving this place we entered the afore-mentioned path through the woods. Now and then there would be a clearing with its charred stumps, its boundary of frowning wood, and its log cabin, but for the most part the forest was in its original state. The average depth of the mud in the path was one foot. . . . The day was showery, with occasional glimpses of the sun; so that we were alternately wet and dry. . . . Thence passing various dwellings, and holding various colloquies with the inmates, we reached Canaan, and a good tavern. The landlord has quartered [us] in his hall—large as a barn. Canaan is a microscopic village, the houses scattered through a valley among low mountains, all covered with forest. We saw here the Connecticut for the first time—rapid and full of rocks and foam. We follow its banks to-morrow.

Tuesday (2d). Weather still cold and blustering. Thick clouds all over the sky. Set out after breakfast for the Connecticut Lake, twenty miles distant. . . . White seems to have lost his apathy and is now quite ready to proceed. Reports of the Margalloway trout have inflamed him. The road was still hilly, narrow, and great part of the way flanked by woods. The valley of the river looked, as it always does, rich and fertile, but the hills and mountains around presented one broad unbroken expanse of forest, made the more sombre by the deep shadows of the clouds. In the afternoon we reached a hilltop and a vast panorama of mountains and forests lay before us. A glistening spot of water, some miles to the north, girt with mountains which sloped down to it from all sides with a smooth and gradual descent, was Lake Connecticut. As far as we could see, one mountain of peculiar form rose above the rest which we afterward learned was the Camel's Hump. Passing a river with rapids and a saw-mill, at the end of the day we reached the lake, where are two houses, Barns' and Abbot's. There are steep rapids at the outlet, with a mill, of course. We went to Abbot's house, and asked for lodging and a supper. . . . Abbot says that one of his relations, Kenfield by name, fought at William Henry, and, at the massacre, seeing an Indian about to strip a fallen officer, caught him, raised him in his arms, and dashed him to the ground with such violence as to make him senseless. Our host greatly exults in the bodily strength for which his family have been eminent—he himself noway dishonors his race in that respect.

Wednesday (3d). . . . We lived in backwoods style to-day—sugarless tea for dinner—water drunk from a mug common to all the company, etc. We liked it—I did, at least. Abbot sat cobbling his shoe against his projected expedition towards evening, but as I came up he turned round and remarked that he was not a disciple of St. Crispin but only an occasional follower. As I was marveling at this unexpected display of erudition, his wife thrust her head from the door, and exclaimed, "Here, supper's ready. Where's that other man gone to?" We accepted the elegant invitation and walked in, where Abbot astonished us still more by comparing the democrat levelers to Procrustes, who wished to reduce all men to the same dimensions by his iron bedstead. All this was while he was squatting on his home-made chair, one leg cocked into the air, shirt-sleeves rolled up to his elbows, bushy hair straggling over his eyes, and eating meanwhile as if his life depended on his efforts. I have since found that he has read a vast amount of history, ancient and modern, and various other things—all fact, however, for fiction, he says, he cannot bear. When twenty-five— he is now thirty-six—he defended himself against a good lawyer in a court, and won his case, his opponent confessing himself outmatched by Abbot's general knowledge and quick memory.

Thursday (4th). Started this morning to strike the Little Margalloway. We proceeded first towards the north, with a path for the first few miles. It soon failed us, and we had to force our way through tangled woods. . . . White had hurt his foot the day before and constantly lagged behind, so that we had to wait for him, every minute the prey of torturing flies. At length the ascent of the first mountain made the way still more laborious. When at length we reached the top we could see nothing on account of the thick growth of trees. We passed through a singular piece of boggy ground, of an oblong shape, inclosed in a fringe of cedars rising one above the other, all hung with tassels of white moss. There was another place, partially open, near the summit. As we passed it, a large buck sprang from the ground, and leaped with long bounds down the mountain, before my rifle was at my shoulder. We heard him crashing the boughs far below. In this spot were several springs of cold water, in broad cup-shaped hollows in the ground, which had probably attracted the deer. We went down the mountain and found a little stream flowing through the valley at the bottom. Both Abbot and myself were for proceeding, but White said he could not go on on account of his foot; so we found a convenient spot and encamped. It was by the stream, flowing half concealed beneath brushwood and fallen trees, in a thick growth of firs, spruces, and birches. We made a fire, and proceeded to cook our supper. We had brought with us seven pounds of bread, six and a half of rice, and a quantity of butter. We had beside about an ounce of tea, and salt, of course.

We made our fire in the middle of the grove, cut spruce boughs for a bed, lay down on our blankets, and with our knives speedily made way with a mess of rice placed on a broad piece of birch bark amongst us. Then we heaped new wood on the fire, and lay down again, cooled by a gentle rain which just now began to fall. The fire blazed up a column of bright flame, and flung its light deep into the recesses of the woods. In the morning we breakfasted on rice, bread, and tea without sugar and cream, and then—Friday—prepared to resume our course. . . . After journeying many hours in this painful style, we heard the plunging of waters in a valley below us, and joyfully turned towards the sound. We had struck a branch of the Little Margalloway. White's lameness seemed mysteriously to leave him; he seized his fishing tackle and rushed up and down the rocks, pulling a trout from every deep hole and the foot of every waterfall. I soon followed his example. Abbot built a fire by the bank and cooked our fish. We made a plentiful dinner, and then began to follow downward the course of the stream. . . .

Saturday, Aug. 5th. The morning opened with a grand council. How were we to get down the river? Abbot could make a raft, thought he could make a spruce canoe, and was certain that he could make a log one. I told him to make a log one. We roused White from the spruce boughs where he persisted in snoring, in spite of our momentous discussion, and

then prepared and ate our breakfast. White went to fishing.
Abbot shouldered his axe and he and I went off together for a
suitable pine-tree to make our canoe of. He found one to his
satisfaction on the other side of the stream, some distance down.
I built him a fire to "smudge" the flies, waded back across the
stream, and as I ascended the farther bank heard the thundering
crash of the falling pine behind me, bellowing over the wilderness, and rolling in echoes far up the mountains. . . . As I went
back to camp, I found that Abbot was not at work on his canoe.
While I was marveling at this I stumbled upon a half finished
spruce canoe, which Abbot had set about making, having
found the pine-tree, which he had cut down for his log boat,
rotten. I was not much pleased at this change of plan; nevertheless, as the thing was begun I lent him assistance as I could,
so that by nightfall we had finished something which had the
semblance of a canoe, but, owing chiefly to haste and want of
tools, had such a precarious and doubtful aspect that White
christened it the Forlorn Hope. We put it into the water. It
leaked. We took it out and stuffed the seams with pounded
spruce bark, chewed spruce gum, and bits of cloth. It still
leaked, but we hoped it would do, with diligent baling; so, fas-
tening it to the bank, we cooked our supper, rolled ourselves in
our blankets, and went to sleep before the fire.

Sunday, Aug. 6th. We were obliged perforce to adopt the
sailor's maxim, "No Sunday off soundings," for our provisions
were in a fair way of failing, and starvation in the wilderness is
not a pleasant prospect to look forward to. . . . After breakfast
we packed our luggage, and proceeded to make the dubious
experiment of the canoe. All were embarked; White in the
middle to bale, Abbot at the stern, I in the prow. "Push off!"
the canoe glided with a quiet and gentle motion down the
swift stream, between the tall walls of forest on each side, but
soon the ripple and tumbling of a rapid appeared in front and
the hour of trial came. She quivered and shook as she entered
the disturbed waters; at last there was a little grating sound.
She had struck upon the stones at the bottom, but the peril was
past; the water grew smooth and deep again, and again we

floated quietly and prosperously down in the shadows of the woods. At last another rapid came. She entered it, grated heavily over the stones, and struck hard against a large one before her. The water spouted in like a stream from a pump. It would not do. The experiment was an utter failure. We left Abbot with the canoe to conduct that and the baggage as he could down to the basin, and waded to shore ourselves to walk there through the woods. We had not gone [a] quarter of a mile when "Hello, here," came from the river. "What's the matter now?" shouted we in return. "The canoe's burst all to pieces!" Sure enough, we found it so. Abbot stood in the middle of a rapid, up to the knees, holding our baggage aloft to keep it dry, while the miserable remnant of the demolished vessel was leisurely taking its way down the current. We pushed through the woods towards the basin, deliberating what to do next. Abbot was sure he could make a raft which would carry us down to the settlements, and yet draw so little water as to pass the "rips" in safety. The navigation would indeed be slow with such a machine, but it could be made in an hour or two, and this would more than counterbalance the want of speed. The river was high; the plan seemed eligible, and we proceeded to execute it. Meanwhile it began to rain furiously. We walked into the water to our waists and held the timbers in place while Abbot withed them together. Jerome's camp was demolished to furnish materials, his setting-poles and birch-bark vessels appropriated to our use. After about two hours of aquatic exertion, during which we were wet equally by the rain above and the river beneath, the raft was finished. Owing to the badness of the timber it drew twice as much water as we expected. We pushed from shore in a deluge of rain. Like its luckless predecessor, the raft passed the first rapid in safety, only venting a groan or two as its logs encountered the stones beneath. These rapids in the main river were of course much deeper than those of the Little Margalloway, above the basin, where the canoe had met its fate. When it came on the second rapid, the machine seemed to shiver in direful expectancy of its approaching destruction. Presently it grunted loud and dolefully. We set our poles and pushed it into the deepest part. For a while it bumped and blundered downward; at length there was a heavy shock, a crash, a boiling and rushing of many waters. The river spouted up between the logs. We were fixed irrecoverably aground. The water coursed savagely by us, and broke over the end of the raft, but it could not be moved. The result of this second experiment was more dismal than of the first. We were in the middle of the river; the trees on both shores loomed gloomily through rain and mist, and a volume of boiling and roaring waves rolled between. However, there being no remedy, we walked in, and, by dint of considerable struggling, waded safe to the western bank, where I directed Abbot to try no more experiments but to work on a log canoe till he had finished it. He accordingly felled another tree, while we were, with great difficulty on account of the rain, building a fire. Abbot worked with great perseverance and skill. Before night, his canoe was nearly hewed out. We plied him with tea to keep his spirits up, relieved him of the cooking and all his other duties, so that his task was accomplished in what seemed an incredibly short time. That afternoon I went back to the basin to get fish for the public benefit. At night the rain, which had ceased for a while, began to pour afresh. We put up White's blanket, which was wet, for a tent, and spreading mine on the ground beneath, made a great fire before it, ate our supper, and lay down. As soon as we were quiet, the continual dropping and splashing of rain through the forest had a sound singularly melancholy and impressive. White dropped asleep, after his established custom on all occasions, but Abbot and myself, both of us wet to the skin, chose to lie and talk before the fire till past midnight. Our guide is a remarkably intelligent fellow, has astonishing information for one of his condition, is resolute and as independent as the wind. Unluckily, he is rather too conscious of his superiority in these respects, and likes too well to talk of his own achievements. He is coarse and matter-of-fact to a hopeless extremity, self-willed, and self-confident as the devil; if any one would get respect or attention from him, he must meet him on his own ground in this matter. He is very talkative. I learned

more, from his conversation, about the manners and customs of
the semi-barbarians he lives among, than I could have done
from a month's living among them. That night in the rain,
leagues from the dwellings of men, was a very pleasant one. We
slept a few hours towards day, and rose before it was fairly light,
he to finish the canoe, we to prepare breakfast. We launched
the boat soon after, embarked, and paddled down stream. . . .
At length we saw, on the left bank, a camp built of logs for the
use of "loggers." We went ashore. The place was dry, the
roof being slant and thatched waterproof, with a hole at one
side to let out the smoke of the fire. . . . Fortunately, I had
secured my matches in a tin case, and this in my waterproof
knapsack, so that we were able to build a fire with the aid of
some dry birch bark we found in the hut. . . . Hanging our
superfluous clothing to dry, we laid down in the rest and slept
comfortably all night. . . .

Wednesday, Aug. 9th. Left Brag's this morning to walk to
Colebrook. I had to carry about thirty pounds weight, including my blanket, which having covered White's shoulders
through all the storms of yesterday, had become saturated with
moisture, and was about as heavy when rolled up as a log of
hard wood. Abbot carried his for him. The day was overcast
and showery. When we had got about six miles, we overtook
an old fellow in a wagon, who was jolting along over stones,
logs, gullies, and all other impediments, towards Colebrook.
White got in with him and rode the rest of the way, Abbot
and I going on together, first committing the baggage to
his care, except my knapsack, which I chose to keep with
me. . . .

Thursday, Aug. 10th. Stayed at Colebrook today, for want
of means to get off. In the villainous little hole of a tavern
there, there is never anything stirring to break the dismal
monotony. Every day is a Sunday. . . .

Friday, Aug. 11th. The stage came by this morning from
Canaan. It is called a stage, but is in reality a milk-cart. We
got in. At noon we reached Lancaster, where White stopped,
being reduced to his last quarter of a dollar, to see his uncle

and borrow the needful of him. I kept on to Littleton, where I now am.

Saturday, Aug. 12th. Started for home by way of Plymouth. . . . With an accommodating driver and a pleasant party of ladies and gentlemen—one of the former exceedingly handsome, romantic, and spirited—we rode on towards Plymouth, and got there late at night. There was a general on board,—a man of exalted character and vast political influence which he exercised on the righteous side of radical democracy, fiercely maintaining that ninepence was better than a million dollars, insomuch that the possessor of the first is invariably a good man and contented with his lot, while the owner of the last is always a grasping, avaricious child of the devil. When the general alighted at his own tavern he saluted the first loafer who met him at the door as "Major," the next but one was "Colonel," while our driver answered to the title of "Captain."

[A TRIP TO EUROPE]

[AN ATLANTIC CROSSING]

Barque Nautilus, November 16th, '43.
(Devil of a sea—cabin dark as Hades.)

Got under weigh from Central Wharf about 10 A.M. of Sunday, Dec. 12th [Nov. 12]—fine weather, and a noble west wind. . . . Before long we were pitched up and down on an execrable swell—the fruit of yesterday's east wind. The barque tossed about like a cork, snorted, spouted the spray all over her deck, and went rushing along like mad in a great caldron of foam she raised about her. At the same time it grew cloudy, and the wind became stronger. The sea rose and fell in great masses, green as grass, the wind driving the spray in clouds from their white tops. As I came from the cabin, I beheld to my great admiration a huge wall of water piled up in front, into which the vessel was apparently driving her bows; a moment more, and the case was reversed—her bowsprit and half her length rose straight from the waters and stood relieved against the sky. In consequence of which state of things, I, like a true greenhorn, grew seasick by the time we were fairly out of sight of land. Accordingly I got into my berth as soon as it was dark, and stayed there twelve hours.

When I came on deck in the morning, the weather had changed nowise for the better. I wrapped myself in my cloak, and sprawling on the poop-deck read the "Bible in Spain." A schooner, with only topsails set, went scouring past us, before the wind, homeward bound—also, in the afternoon, a brig, tossing so that her keel was almost visible. A troop of porpoises went tumbling about us, and I ransacked the vessel in vain for a musket to get a shot at them.

The next morning opened under direful auspices. I came on deck, disconsolate with seasickness, when I was straightway saluted by about two hogsheads of water which came dashing over the gunnel, accommodating me with a most unwelcome morning shower-bath. . . . I spent most of the morning in my berth, reasonably miserable with seasickness—cogitating, meanwhile, on things human and divine, past, present, and to come. When dinner-time came, I heard the captain's invitation to dinner, and staggered to the cabin door, determined to accept it, in spite of fate, when lo! the ship gave a lurch, the plates and the rack which should have secured them slid together from the table, in a general ruin, to the floor. . . . We have a singular company on board—the three officers, "the passenger," the steward, and six men, viz: a Yankee, a Portuguese, a Dane, an Englishman, a Prussian, and an old gray-haired Dutchman, the best sailor in the ship. Of the officers, the captain is a sensible gentlemanly man; the mate has rather more individuality, being, as to his outer man, excessively tall, narrow-shouldered, spindle-shanked, and lantern-jawed, with a complexion like dirty parchment. Mr. Jonathan Snow is from Cape Cod, a man of the sea from his youth up. When I first came on board he was evidently inclined to regard me with some dislike, as being *rich* (!). He constantly sighs forth a wish that he had five thousand dollars "then ketch me going to sea again, that's all." He is rather given to polemic controversies, of which I have held several with him, on the tenets of sophists, Unitarians, Universalists, Christians, etc., etc. Of course, he imagines that men of his rank in life labor under all sorts of oppressions and injustice at the hands of the rich. Harvard College he regards with peculiar jealousy, as a nurse of aristocracy. "Ah! riches carry the day there, I guess. It's a hard thing to see merit crushed down, just for want of a thousand dollars."

Mr. Hansen, second mate, is the stoutest man on board, and has seen most service, but being, as Mr. Snow remarks, a man of no education, he has not risen very high in the service. He accompanied Wyeth's trapping party to the Rocky Mts., where he was more than once nearly starved and within a hair's breadth of being shot. He speaks with great contempt of Indians, but not with quite so much virulence as I have known from some others of his stamp. He plumes himself on having killed two or three. "Oh, damn it, I'd shoot an Indian quicker than I'd shoot a dog." He is now seated at supper, amusing me and himself with some such discourse as follows:—

"I've lost all my appetite,—and got a horse's. Here, steward, you nigger, where be yer—fetch along that beefsteak. What do you call this here? Well, never mind what it be; it goes down damned well, anyhow." Here he sat stuffing a minute or two in silence, with his grizzly whiskers close to the table, rolling his eyes, and puffing out his ruddy cheeks. At last pausing, and laying down his knife a moment:

"I've knowed the time when I could have ate a Blackfoot Indian, bones and all, and couldn't get a mouthful, noway you could fix it." Then resuming his labors—"I tell you what, this here agrees with me. It's better than doctor stuff. Some folks are always running after the doctors, and getting sick. *Eat!* that's the way I do. Well, doctoring is a good thing, just like religion—to them that likes it; but damn the doctors for all me; I shan't die," etc., etc.

By treating Mr. Hansen with brandy and water, I have got on very good terms with him, and made him very communicative on the subject of his Oregon experiences. Would that we had a consumptive minister, with his notions of peace, philanthropy, Christian forgiveness, and so forth, on board with us!

It would be sport of the first water to set Mr. Hansen talking at him, and see with what grace the holy man would listen to his backwoods ideas of retributive justice and a proper organization of society. "Shoot him over, and that damn quick, too," is Mr. Hansen's penalty for all serious offenses. . . . As soon as it was daybreak I went on deck. Two or three sails were set, the vessel scouring along, leaning over so that her lee gunnel scooped up the water; the water in a foam, and clouds of spray flying over us, frequently as high as the main yard. The spray was driven with such force that it pricked the cheek like needles. I stayed on deck two or three hours; when, being thoroughly salted, I went down, changed my clothes, and read Don Quixote till Mr. Snow appeared at the door with, "You're the man that wants to see a gale of wind, are ye? Now's your chance; only just come up on deck." Accordingly I went. The wind was yelling and howling in the rigging in a fashion that reminded me of a storm in a Canada forest. The ship was hove to. One small rag of a topsail set to keep her steady—all the rest was bare poles and black wet cordage. I got hold of a rope by the mizzen mast, and looked about on a scene that it would be perfect folly to attempt to describe—though nothing more, I suppose, than an ordinary gale of wind. . . .

Friday. As yesterday was Thanksgiving, I may as well record how we fared. Our breakfast was utterly demolished by the same catastrophe that overtook a former repast, that, namely, of being dashed in ruins upon the floor by an ill-timed lurch of the ship. We dined on a lump of ham, Cuffee being unable to purvey a more sumptuous banquet, because the seas put out the fire in his galley as fast as he kindled it. As for our supper, it was of bread, pork, and onions. Not that this is a fair sample of our bills of fare, which are usually quite as luxurious as any reasonable man need desire. . . .

Wednesday, Dec. 6th. We have been tormented for ten days past with a series of accursed head winds. Here we are, within thirty-six hours' sail of Gibraltar, standing alternately north and south, with no prospect of seeing land for many days. The captain is half mad, and walks about swearing to himself in an undertone. Mr. Snow's philosophy has given way—and I never had any. Hansen alone is perfectly indifferent. He sits on deck whistling and talking over his work, without troubling himself about our whereabouts, or caring whether we are in the North Sea or at Cape Horn.

Thursday, Dec. 7th.

> "Day after day, day after day,
>   We stuck, nor breath nor motion;
>   As idle as a painted ship
>   Upon a painted ocean."

This has been our enviable position to-day. A dead calm—a stupid flapping of sails and creaking of masts.

Saturday. Again a calm! The captain's signs and portents have come to nought. A turtle came up at the ship's side to sleep on the quiet surface, but prudently sunk back to the depths just as Mr. Hansen was lowering me by a rope to take him prisoner. A few bonitos splashed about the bow, some "rudder fish" played alongside; and a pair of "garfish" glided about in defiance of all attempts to capture them. Before noon a breeze—a favorable one—sprang up! It bore us on a hundred miles farther, but now has subsided into the old trebly accursed calm.

Tuesday. A light wind to-day but dead ahead. More porpoises and more fruitless attempts at harpooning, on the part of Mr. Snow. I am rapidly growing insane. My chief resource is the conversation of Mr. Hansen, who has humor, volubility, much good feeling, and too much coarse rough manhood in his nature to be often offensive in his speech. Moreover, one man may say a thing with a very good grace that would be insufferable from the mouth of another. Witticisms and stories which, uttered by Snow, would make me turn my back on the fellow with contempt and disgust, sound well enough in the frank and bold accents of Hansen.

Evening. We have beat up against the wind into full view of the Spanish coast. Right and left, from Trafalgar far beyond Cadiz, the line of rugged and steep bluffs reaches, with here

and there a tower just visible with the glass. But about noon
our evil genius becalmed us again!

Thirty days from Boston. Old Worthington promised that
I should see Gibraltar in eighteen, but he is a deacon.

[EUROPE]

Wednesday evening. We have not yet reached Tarifa.
Dozens of vessels come past us from Gibraltar, some of them
of a most outlandish aspect to my eye.

Thursday. More delay and vexation. The captain has not
slept for two nights, and is half worn out by fatigue and anxiety.
For myself, I was so exasperated by our continued ill fortune
that I could not stay below. We passed Tarifa light about midnight—then were driven back four miles by a rain squall. But
by nine in the morning we had fairly entered Gibraltar Bay!

[Gibraltar.] Saturday. Yesterday I came ashore in the
barque's boat, landed, got passport signed and established myself at the "King's Arms."

I dined at the consul's and spent the day in exploring this
singular city—the world in epitome. More of it in future. This
morning I set out, in company with a midshipman, the son of
Captain Newton of the Missouri, to ride around the Bay to the
Spanish town of Algeciras.

Sunday. . . . Sunday is the day to see the motley population
of Gibraltar at one glance. Just without the walls is a parade
large enough to hold the six regiments stationed here. This
evening, according to custom, everybody was thronging up
there. I established myself at the foot of a bronze statue of the
defender of Gibraltar—I forget his name, General Eliot—but
there he stands towering above the trees and aloes at the summit of a hill above the parade, with the emblematic key in his
hand, and with a huge cannon and a mortar on each side of him.
Here I had a specimen of every nation on earth, it seemed,
around me. A dozen Moors with white turbans and slippered
feet lolled one side; Jews by couples in their gaberdines; the
Spanish gentleman in his black cloak and sombrero—the Spanish laborer with his red cap hanging on one side of his head—

the Spanish blackguard in bespangled tights and embroidered jacket. On benches among the trees officers and soldiers
carried on successful love suits; on the parade below English
captains were showing forth good horsemanship to the best
advantage. The red coats of soldiers appeared everywhere
among the trees and in the crowd below. There were women
in cloaks of red and black, ladies with the mantilla and followed
by the duenna,—no needless precaution,—and ten thousand
more, soldier and civilian, bond and free, man and woman and
child. Not the least singular of the group were the little black
slaves belonging to the Moors, who were arrayed in a very
splendid and outlandish attire, following after their masters like
dogs. Bands were stationed on the parade and around a sum-
mer-house among the trees. The evening gun dissolved the
pageant—*God save the Queen* rose on the air; then the crowd
poured through the gates into the town.

I went to a diminutive theatre in the evening, to see a play
performed by the privates of an artillery company. . . .

A "rock scorpion" carried me off to the frigates in the harbor, English and American. The reptile in question was a mixture of Genoese and French blood—spoke both languages
fluently, besides English and half a score of others. . . .

Sunday, Dec. —. Got tired of Gibraltar—heard of a government steamer about to sail for Malta—embarked on her,
abandoning my previous design of penetrating Spain immediately. . . . I was prepared for no very agreeable passage,
knowing the hauteur approaching to insolence of a certain class
of English naval officers, and was surprised as well as gratified by
the polite attentions of Lt. Spark, the commander of the boat,
with whom I spent about half the night in conversation. Unfortunately I am the only passenger. Lt. Spark seems resolved
that my voyage shall be agreeable notwithstanding—certainly,
he spares no pains for my accommodation, opening his library
to me, producing an endless variety of wines, doing all he can,
in short, to promote my enjoyment.

We have passed Cape de Got and the Sierra Nevada, which
looks down on the city of Granada. The coast of Barbary is

now in full sight. To-day the old man mustered his sailors and marines in the cabin—a large and elegant one—and read the service of the Church, not forgetting a special prayer for the British Navy, and the success of the British arms. He knew Sir John Moore, Sir P. Parker, and other heroes of those days, has shaken hands with Blucher, has fought the French by sea and land. Beside his manifold experiences in active life, he has been a great reader, not only of English works but of all the eminent American authors. . . . Here in this old world I seem, thank Heaven, to be carried about half a century backwards in time. As far as religion is concerned, there are the ceremonies of the Catholic church and the English litany, with rough soldiers and sailors making the responses. A becoming horror of dissenters, especially Unitarians, prevails everywhere. No one cants here of the temperance reform, or of systems of diet— eat, drink, and be merry is the motto everywhere, and a stronger and hardier race of men than those round me now never laughed at the doctors. Above all, there is no canting of peace. A wholesome system of coercion is manifest in all directions— thirty-two pounders looking over the bows, piles of balls on deck, muskets and cutlasses hung up below, the red jackets of marines, and the honest prayer that success should crown all these warlike preparations, yesterday responded to by fifty voices. There was none of the new-fangled suspicion that such belligerent petition might be averse to the spirit of a religion that inculcates peace as its foundation. And I firmly believe that there was as much hearty faith and worship in many of those men as in any feeble consumptive wretch at home, who, when smitten on one cheek, literally turns the other likewise, instead of manfully kicking the offender into the gutter.

Thursday. After a passage of about five days we reached Malta.

Friday. Late last evening I made an attempt to see the Church of St. John. It was closed. My servant pommeled the oaken door in vain. He then proceeded to sundry coffee-houses in the neighborhood, hoping to find the man who had the doors in charge. Three or four Maltese, all jabbering their bastard

Arabic, soon aided in the search. At length the great bell began to roar from the church tower, an unequivocal evidence that somebody was there. "Gulielmo, Gulielmo!" roared my troop of assistants. After a lapse of five minutes Gulielmo descended and issued from a portal among the columns at one side, summoning me in. . . . [Here he describes the church.] Leaving reluctantly the church where so many brave men had kneeled to God for his blessing on their matchless enterprises, I got into a boat, and was put on board the Neapolitan steamer Francesco Primo, bound for Messina, where I lay for an hour or two on deck, listening to the distant music of the English drums and trumpets.

As I lounged about the deck in the morning, utterly unable to hold any intercourse with any one on board except by signs, a sleek-looking fellow came up and accosted me in English. We soon got deep into conversation. My new acquaintance proved to be Giuseppe Jackson, a Sicilian with an English grandfather, who had been a cook at the Albion, and at Murdoch's tavern, had frequently been to Fresh Pond, knew some of the Cambridge students, and was now on his way to Mr. Marston's in Palermo. I was right glad to see him, cook though he was. He made me a very good interpreter. In the course of our conversation he made some remark about "the Pope, that fool."

"What," said I, "do you speak so of the Pope. Are you not a Roman Catholic?"

"Ah! I was till I live in America. I was all in the dark—you understand what I say—till I come there. Then my eyes open; I say, dat for the Pope, and his old red cap. Ah! once I was afraid to think of him."

"You are no longer a Catholic; what religion do you believe in now?"

"Oh, no religion in particular."

I congratulated him on so happy a conversion from the error of his ways.

At breakfast—a Mediterranean breakfast of eggs, fruit, and nuts—an old man, of severe countenance and tremendous mustache, sat opposite me. We made various attempts at conversation; as neither understood the other, we had to be satisfied with reiterated bowings, and mutual attentions of various kinds, in which the old man showed himself exceedingly apt and polite. I afterwards found that he was no less a personage than il Principe Statelli, a general of the Sicilian army—but Sicilian "Principes" are apt to be humbugs.

Mount Ætna is smoking vigorously in front of us. We are skirting the shore of Sicily.

[SICILY]

We stopped at Syracuse. . . . In going ashore, a little square-built English-looking man, making a low congee, presented me with a bundle of papers, which proved to be certificates of his qualifications as a guide to the curiosities of the place. Accordingly Jack Robinson—for such was his name—and I got into a kind of ferry-boat and landed on the other side of the bay. . . .

Jack insisting on showing me his certificates of service in the American Navy, and I, being desirous of seeing how the Syracusans lived, went home with him, and enjoyed the exhibition of his numerous progeny, who were all piled together in bed. This done we took boat and went off to the steamer. Jack was so well satisfied with the dollar and a half I gave him for his day's services that he must needs salute me after the Sicilian style with a kiss on the cheek, which I submitted to. He then departed, kissing his hand as his head disappeared over the ship's side. The stubborn English temper was well nigh melted away with his long sojourn among the Gentiles. He had been pressed in early youth into the navy—had served both England and America (though the latter, I believe, in the capacity of a washerman). As far as I could see, Jack was an honest man, an exceedingly rara avis in these quarters.

Arriving at Messina in the morning, my acquaintance the cook—an experienced traveler—was of the greatest service to me. Indeed, without his assistance my inexperience and ignorance of the language would have put me to serious embarrassment. He showed me how to treat a Sicilian landlord, and to bribe a custom-house officer. I am indebted to him for very excellent accommodations at a very reasonable price.

Messina, Sunday. I took my station outside one of the gates in the rear of the city, to look at the scum of humanity that came pouring out. All was filth, and age, and ruin,—the walls, the tall gateway with its images and inscriptions, the hovels at the top of the wall and in the ancient suburb, all seemed crumbling to decay. The orange and lemon groves in the ditch of the fortification were dingy and dirty, but away in the distance appeared the summits of the mountains, almost as wild and beautiful as our mountains of New England. I thought of them, and, in the revival of old feelings, half wished myself at home. I soon forgot, however, all but what was before my eyes, in watching the motley array that passed by me. Men and women literally hung with rags, half hid in dirt, hideous with every imaginable species of deformity, and bearing on their persons a population as numerous as that of Messina itself,— these formed the bulk of the throng. Priests with their black broad-brimmed hats and their long robes,—fat and good-looking men,—were the next numerous class. They draw life and sustenance from these dregs of humanity, just as tall pig-weed flourishes on a dunghill. Then there were mustachioed soldiers, very different from the stately and sedate soldier of England. There were men bearing holy pictures and images; ladies in swarms, whose profession was stamped on their faces; musicians, with a troop of vagabonds in their rear. All around the gateway were the tables of butchers, fruiterers, confectioners, money-changers, boot-blackers, and a throng of dirty men, women, and children. Shouts, yells, and a universal hubbub.

Tuesday, Jan. 2nd. This morning I set out on an expedition to see a little of the country, in company with a Spanish gentleman, Don Mateo Lopez, who speaks good English. We hired a carriage together, and got outside the gates by eleven, after some trouble in procuring passports. At night we reached a little fishing town called Giardini, not far from Ætna. The weather was beautiful, the atmosphere clear and soft. As for the scenery on the road, it was noble beyond expression. For myself, I never imagined that so much pleasure could be conveyed through the eye. The road was a succession of beautiful scenes,—of mountains and valleys on one side and the sea on the other; but as to the people, they are a gang of ragamuffins. . . . These disgusting holes of villages only added zest to the pleasure of the scenery,—a pleasure not inferior and not unlike that of looking upon the face of a beautiful woman. In many respects our own scenery is far beyond it; but I cannot say that I have ever looked with more delight on any of our New England mountains and streams than upon these of Sicily. The novelty of the sight, and the ruined fortresses on the highest crags, add much to the effect. . . .

I went to the museum of Prince Boscari, a valuable collection of antiquities, etc. In the midst of a hall, surrounded by precious fragments of statues and broken pottery, lay the skeleton of a Chippeway birch canoe. I welcomed it as a countryman and an old friend.

I bought some specimens of lava and amber of a couple of rascals who asked twice their value, and abated it at once when I refused to buy.

I went to see an opera of Bellini—a native, I have heard, of Catania. . . . Lopez had a friend waiting for him here—a lighthearted and lively young Spaniard whose youthful eccentricities sat as easily and gracefully upon him as awkwardly upon old Mateo. When we set out on our return, *il mio amico*, as Lopez called him, was rattling away incessantly, and imitating every dog, hog, or jackass we met.

We had a sort of calêche. Besides the driver, a small boy ran along by our side, or clung behind, ready to do what offices might be required of him. A still smaller one was stowed away in a net, slung between the wheels where he kept a constant eye on the baggage. The larger one employed himself in tying knots in the horses' tails as he ran along—or he would dart along the road before us, clamber on a wall, and sit till we came by, when he would spring down with a shout and run on again. . . .

The women of this country are not handsome. You see groups of them about the stone doorways spinning twine, with their hair drawn back in the fashion represented in the portraits of our grandmothers.

We stopped at night at Giardini. The "padrone" showed us with great complacency the register of his house, which, he said, contained the recommendations of the guests who had honored him with their company. One man's "recommendation" warned all travelers that the padrone's beds were full of fleas; another's that nothing in the house was fit to eat, etc. The importunate padrone could not read English. . . .

The Church of the Benedictines is the noblest edifice I have seen. This and others not unlike it have impressed me with new ideas of the Catholic religion. Not exactly, for I reverenced it before as the religion of generations of brave and great men, but now I honor it for itself. They are mistaken who sneer at its ceremonies as a mere mechanical force; they have a powerful and salutary effect on the mind. Those who have witnessed the services in this Benedictine church, and deny what I say, must either be singularly stupid and insensible by nature, or rendered so by prejudice.

Saturday. I recall what I said of the beauty of the Sicilian women—so far, at least, as concerns those of high rank. This is a holyday. They are all abroad, in carriages and on foot. One passed me in the church of the Capuchin convent, with the black eye, the warm rich cheek, and the bright glance that belong to southern climates. They are beautiful beyond all else.

Sunday. Took leave of the hospitable family of Consul Payson with much regret, and went off to the steamer Palermo, bound for Palermo. I found her completely surrounded by boats, wedged close together; friends were kissing their adieus, and boatmen cursing. The delicacy of sentiment expressed in the Italian national oath is admirable—they rival the Spaniards in that matter,—"Arcades ambo; id est, blackguards both." At length visitors were warned off, the boats dispersed, scattering from a common centre, in all directions; a man screamed the names of the passengers, by way of roll-call; and among the rest the illustrious one of Signore Park-a-man; and we got under weigh. It was late at night. We passed the long array of bright lights from the fine buildings along the quay of Messina,—could just discern the mountains behind the town, indistinct in the darkness, like thunder-clouds,—left a long train of phosphoric light behind us, as we steered down between Scylla and Charybdis, and in half an hour were fairly out on the Sicilian Sea. The ghost of departed perils still lingers about the scene of Ulysses' submarine adventures; an apology for a whirlpool on one side—still bearing the name of Scylla—and an insignificant shoal on the other. I thought as we passed, and the moon made a long stream of light on the water, that it would be an adventure worth encountering, to be cast away in that place,—but my unwonted classical humor was of very short duration; for, going below, I found a cabin full of seasick wretches, which attractive spectacle banished all recollection of Virgil and Homer. I was doomed to lie all night a witness to their evolutions; a situation not many degrees more desirable than being yourself a sufferer. . . .

Wednesday. I have just arranged an expedition to Girgenti, at the southern point of the island. Traveling in Sicily is no joke, especially at this season. I engaged a man named Luigi to furnish three mules, supplies of provisions, cooking apparatus, an attendant, and thus to pilot me round the island, paying himself all tavern reckonings and *buona manos*. For this I am to give him four dollars a day. I thus avoid all hazard of being imposed upon, or robbed, for I shall have scarce any money with me. Luigi is perfectly familiar with the island; has, moreover, the reputation of an honest man, notwithstanding which I follow Mr. Marston's advice in making him sign a written agreement. I have laid it down as an inviolable rule to look on everybody here as a rascal of the first water, till he has shown himself by undeniable evidence to be an honest man.

Giuseppe has been with me as a servant of late. The chief fault with him was his continually stopping to kiss some of his acquaintances in the street. He seems to know everybody, understands perfectly how to cheat everybody, has astonishing promptness and readiness for all kinds of service. "It is 'trange, Mister Park-a-man," he modestly remarked the other day, "that I cannot go nowhere, but what all the people seem to like-a me, and be good friends with me." He is vain as a turkey-cock—dresses infinitely better than I ever did. He is a great coward, trembling continually with fear of robbers in all our rides. The Sicilian robbers, by the way, are a great humbug. When I engaged Giuseppe I offered him half a dollar a day for wages. "No, Mist'r Park-a-man, I no take-a wages at all. When you go away, you make-a me a present, just as much as you like; then I feel more better." So I told him I would make-a him a present of half a dollar a day; which I did, a mode of remuneration more suited to Giuseppe's self-importance.

Thursday, Jan. 18th. All this morning Luigi Rannesi was in a fever-heat of preparation. I told him to be ready at two; he came to me at twelve announcing that all was ready; that he had engaged mules at Marineo, and that the carriage was at the door to take us there. I was not prepared for such promptitude. After some delay, I got ready too, and we set out. Luigi, a diminutive Sicilian with a thin brown face and an air of alertness about every inch of him, began to jabber Italian with such volubility that I could not understand a word. He must needs exhibit every article of the provisions he had got ready for the journey, extolling the qualities of each,—and they deserved all his praises,—and always ended by pounding himself on the breast, rolling up his eyes, and exclaiming, "Do you think Luigi loves money? No! Luigi loves honor!" and then launching forth into interminable eulogies of the country we were going to see, and the adventures we should meet there. We stopped at night at Marineo, where Luigi provided a most sumptuous dinner; talked and gesticulated, half frenzied because he found I could not understand half he said; then seized my hand, which he dutifully kissed, and left me to my meditations. He reappeared, however, bringing a decanter of wine, and a large book of antiquities which he had brought for me to read. All this was at his own expense. The terms of his bargain bound him to nothing else than to keep me alive on the road.

(Castel Termini.) Luigi is a great antiquarian. He rakes up ancient money at every village as he goes along. His antiquarian skill is a passport to introduce him anywhere; to the nobles and princes, who are not always, however, such dignified personages as would appear from their titles. I went with him to-night to the house of a judge, who produced a bottle of rosolio and showed me a grotto in his garden which he had stuck all over with specimens of the Sicily minerals. I then went with him to a "conversazione," where some dozen people were playing cards. They looked at the "signore Americano," as the judge introduced me to them, with great curiosity, and at last left their game and clustered around me, very curious to know something of the place I came from. I talked to them for some time in a most original style of Italian; but getting tired of being lionized in such a manner, I bade them good-night and went back to the albergo.

I went to visit the famous sulphur works not far from these places. In the shaft I entered the rock was solid sulphur—scarce any mixture of foreign ingredients. As we rode away, a noble prospect of volcanic mountains lay off on our right. Soon after the mule-track became a good road. A carriage from Caltanisetta passed us, belonging to some English travelers who had made a wide détour for the sake of a road. We saw at last the battlements and church spires of Girgenti, crowning a high hill before us, and had occasional glimpses of the sea through the valleys. Approaching the hill, we found a deep and shadowed valley intervening. Luigi left the road and descended into it by a wretched mule-track. Flocks of goats passed on the road above us, mules and asses loaded with their panniers came down from the city. One of his fits of enthusiasm had taken possession of Luigi. He began to lash his mule and drive him along over sand and rocks at such a rate that I thought him mad, till he told me that it was necessary to get to Girgenti before the Englishmen. "Corragio! my brave mule! Corragio, signore," he shouted, "we shall be the victors!" At that he drove full speed up the steep hill toward the gate. Nothing would stop him. He leaped over ditches, scrambled through mud and stones, shouting "Corragio" at the top of his lungs. At last an insuperable gully brought him up short. He clapped his hand to his forehead, exclaiming, "Santissima Maria!" in a tone of wrath and despair, then recovered his spirits and dashed off in another direction. We succeeded. When we got to the top the carriage was [a] quarter of a mile off, and Luigi shouted "Vittoria!" as he rode into the gate, as much elated as if he had accomplished some great achievement. It was a festa day. All the people in the crowded streets and in the little square wore white caps. They were a hardy and athletic race—their faces, their strong short necks, their broad and prominent chests, were all burnt to a dark ruddy brown.

(Girgenti.) Luigi brings me pockets full of ancient money and seems greatly astonished at my indifference. As for himself he is rabid. He dodges into every house and shop, inquiring for "antica moneta," stops contadini at work with the same question; he has scraped together an enormous bagful for which he pays scarce anything, perfectly familiar as he is with its true value, and with the "costumi del paese," as he says, the customs of the country. His enthusiasm embraces every object, far and wide. He raves of love on the road—tells how he eloped with his wife—sings love songs, then falls into the martial vein, shouts "Corragio," defies the wind, rain, and torrents. He enters into all my plans with the most fervid zeal, leaving me nothing to do. Every night he comes upstairs bringing all kinds of dresses and utensils of the people for me to look at. Sometimes he comes in with a handful of old coins, telling me with a chuckle that he had bought them for "pochissimo," kissing them repeatedly in the exultation of a good bargain. I have lived most sumptuously ever since I have been with him. He puts the whole inn into a ferment, rakes the town to find the best of everything, and waits on table with an eulogium of every dish. "Ah! signore," he repeats, "do you think Luigi loves money? No, Luigi loves honor." He has something to give to every beggar he meets. In short, the fellow is a jewel, and shall be my particular friend henceforward.

At the English consul's I met a blind traveler, a Mr. Hole-man, who has been over Siberia, New Holland, and other re-mote regions, for the most part alone, and written seven volumes of his travels. Traveling, he told me, was a passion with him. He could not sit at home. I walked home with him through the streets, admiring his indomitable energy. I saw him the next morning sitting on his mule, with the guide he had hired, —his strong frame, his manly English face, his gray beard and mustaches, and his sightless eyeballs gave him a noble appear-ance in the crowd of wondering Sicilians about him.

From Girgenti our course lay westward to a village called Mont' Allegro. . . .

Luigi came up in the evening to hold "un discorso" with me, according to his custom. He was in his usual state of excitement. He takes a glass of wine in his hand, "Viva l'onore, signorino mio!" rolling up his eyes and flourishing his hands, "viva Bacco; viva Dio; viva il consolo Americano!" and so on, the finale being a seizure and kissing of my hand; after which he inquires if I shall want him, looks about to see that all is right, kisses my hand again, and goes off.

One of Luigi's dignified acquaintances in this place was the Marchese Giacomo, a nobleman of great wealth and a deter-mined virtuoso. Luigi called on him with an offering of coins, and returned with an invitation to his "signore" to visit the Marchese and see his pictures. He had a most admirable pic-ture-gallery—among the rest was an original of Guido. He kindly invited me to dine with him, but Luigi's care had sup-plied me a plentiful meal already. So much for one specimen of a Sicilian nobleman. I saw one or two more of nearly the same stamp at a conversazione. The next morning I found Luigi at the albergo, sitting over a bottle of wine with a large, fat, sleepy-looking man, in rather a dingy coat, whom on my enter-ing he slapped on the shoulder, "Ecco, signore, mio amico il barone; un brav' uomo," etc., running on with a long string of praises of his friend the baron, at which this extraordinary specimen of a noble kept shaking his large head in modest denial. . . .

The way was enlivened by the edifying singularities of the muleteer Michele, who walked along talking without intermission for an hour together, though no one listened or replied. He interrupted his discourse only to belabor his mule and curse him in Sicilian. When we came to a steep place, he would take a firm hold of the beast's tail with one hand, while he belabored him with a rope's end that he held in the other, and thus they would scramble up together. Where the mud was more than a foot deep Michele would place both hands on the mule's rump and vault, with a sort of grunt, upon his back; wriggle himself about for a while to find a comfortable seat, and then burst forth with some holy canticle in praise of a saint.

Just after leaving the ruins of Selinuntum we were struggling along in the mud of a lane between rows of cork-trees and aloes, when Michele suddenly set up a yowling like a tom-cat,— stopped in the midst of a note to expostulate with his mule,— and then proceeded in a more dismal tone than before. Luigi clapped his hands and shouted, "Bravo! compare Michele, bellisima!" at which the gratified Michele redoubled his exertions, and squalled at the top of his throat, putting his hand to the side of his mouth to increase the volume of sound. A young contadino who was wading along on an ass at a little distance behind was seized with a fit of emulation, and set up a counter howl to one of the airs peculiar to the contadini. I cried bravo to this new vocalist, while Luigi cried bella and bellissima to the exertions of Michele. Michele jogged along on his mule, the tassel of his woolen cap flapping; while Luigi twisted himself in his saddle to see how I relished the entertainment, remarking with a grin, "Canta Michele," Michele is singing.

Marsala, as everybody knows, is famous for its wine. For travelers there is little to see. . . .

[NAPLES AND ROME]

I have seen my last of Sicily. I bade adieu to Luigi, who insisted on my receiving a number of valuable ancient coins, and would have given me an hundred if I had let him have his own way—took leave of the Marstons and Gardiners—had my baggage carried on board the Palermo by three facchini, and followed it myself.

The next morning the famous Bay of Naples looked wretched and dismal enough under the influences of an easterly storm, through which Vesuvius was just visible. I went to the Hotel de Rome, an excellent house, with a restaurant beneath where you get and pay for precisely what you want, an arrangement far better than a table d'hôte.

I spent the first day at the Royal Museum, where I could not determine which I liked best, the Hercules Farnese or the Venus of Praxiteles.

I met, at the house of Mr. Rogers, Mr. Theodore Parker and Mr. Farnam from Philadelphia. I had already met Mr. Parker at the Hotel de Rome. Yesterday we went up Vesuvius together. . . . We got some of the famous *Lacrimæ Christi* wine at a house half way down. We reached Naples at three, where the outskirts of the town were deserted, with the exception of a few miserable old men and women sitting in the doorways. It was Sunday, the great day of the carnival. King Ferdinand, however, sets his face against the carnival, which for several years has been a mere nothing at Naples. This year, in consideration of the distress of tradesmen, he has consented, much against his inclination, to make a fool of himself. This was the day appointed for a grand masked procession, in which the king and his ministers were to pelt his subjects with sugar-plums, and be pelted in return. There was a great crowd as we entered the square upon the Toledo—the main street of Naples. While we were slowly driving through it, the head of the procession appeared. First came a dragon about fifty feet long, with his back just visible above the throng of heads, as if he was swimming in the water. He was drawn by a long train of horses. Five or six masked noblemen were on his back pelting the crowd and the people in the galleries of the houses on each side. Then came a sort of car, full of bears, cats, and monkeys, all flinging sugar-plums. The horses of this vehicle were appropriately ridden by jackasses. Then came a long train of carriages, which we joined. The crowd was enormous. The

Toledo was one wide river of heads, the procession slowly moving down on one side and returning on the other. Along the middle, a line of dragoons sat motionless, with drawn swords, on their horses. Mrs. P. was hit on the nose by a formidable sugar-plum flung by a vigorous hand from one of the balconies. She was in great trouble, but there was no such thing as retreat. We got our full share. Mr. Farnam's dignity was disturbed. Mr. Parker had a glass of his spectacles broken. I alone escaped uninjured. At length the royal carriage appeared. Ferdinand—a gigantic man, taller and heavier than any of his subjects—was flinging sugar-plums with hearty good-will, like all the rest. As they passed our carriage the royal family greeted us with a broadside, which completed Mrs. Parker's discomposure. They threw genuine sugar-plums— the others were quite uneatable. The king wore a black silk dress which covered him from head to foot. His face was protected by a wire mask. He carried a brass machine in his hand to fling sugar-plums with. His uncle, his mother, his wife, and all his chief noblemen soon appeared, all protected by masks.

The procession passed several times up and down the Toledo, with occasional stoppages. One of these happened when the king's carriage was not far before us, while directly over against it, on the other side of the street, was a triumphal car full of noblemen. Instantly there began a battle. Ferdinand and the princes sent volley after volley against their opponents, who returned it with interest. The crowd set up a roar, and made a rush for the spoils. There was a genuine battle for the sugar-plums that fell between the two carriages, pushing, scrambling, shouting, yelling, confusion worse confounded, till the dignified combatants thought proper to separate. . . .

The remoter and more obscure parts of this great city are quite as interesting. Here you may see an endless variety of costumes, of the women, almost all beautiful and neat. There is something particularly attractive about these women, who are seldom, however, handsome, properly speaking, but there is the devil in their bright faces and full rounded forms. Each town in the environs has its peculiar costume.

On Saturday I left Naples for Rome in the diligence, with Mr. and Mrs. Parker. . . .

At length we got a glimpse of St. Peter's. On every side of us were remains of temples, aqueducts, and tombs; Mr. Parker became inspired, and spouted Cicero and Virgil. Three young Romans followed us for a mile, running along in their rags, with their dingy peaked hats in their hands, constantly exclaiming in a wailing tone, "*Eccelenʒ, eccelenʒ! povero miserabile, molto di fame!*"—Your excellency, your excellency, I am a poor miserable devil, very hungry.

Monday. To-day is one of the great days. Mr. P. with his lady and myself went in a carriage to see the "show." The streets were crowded with maskers of all descriptions, in carriages and on foot. A blast of trumpets from the end of the Corso was the signal for all the carriages to draw up to one side and the crowd to divide, to make way for a column of the Pope's soldiers. First came the sappers, with beards and mustaches that fell over their chests, shaggy bearskin caps and leather aprons. Each carried a broad-axe over his shoulder, and his musket slung at his back. They were savage and martial-looking fellows. A long train of soldiers followed, with a body of cavalry bringing up the rear. So much for the Pope's summary measures for preserving order. After this the carnival began in earnest.

It was not the solemn sugar-plum foolery of Naples, but foolery entered into with right heartiness and good-will. There were devils of every description, from the imp of two feet high to a six foot monster with horns and hoofs and tail, and a female friend on each arm. There were harlequins with wooden swords, or with bladders tied to poles, which they beat over the heads of all they met; Pulcinellas, and an endless variety of nondescripts. Some of the carriages were triumphal cars gayly ornamented, full of maskers, men and girls, in spangled dresses. Instead of sugar-plums, they flung flowers at one another. Some of the women wore wire masks or little vizards, which left the lower part of the face bare; many, however, had no covering at all to their faces. Few had any regular beauty of features, but there was an expression of heart and spirit, and a loftiness, beside, which did not shame their birth. They flung their flowers at you with the freest and most graceful action imaginable. To battle with flowers against a laughing and conscious face—showering your ammunition thick as the carriage slowly passes the balcony—then straining your eyes to catch the last glance of the black-eyed witch and the last wave of her hand as the crowd closes around her,—all this is no contemptible amusement.

The inferior class of women walked in the street, very prettily dressed in a laced jacket and a white frock that came an inch below the knee. Some were disguised as boys, some wore fierce mustaches, which set off well enough their spirited faces. Hundreds of men were shouting round the carriages with flowers for sale. Thus it went on for hours, till the report of a cannon gave the signal for clearing the Corso for the horse-race. . . .

So much for my classic "first impressions" of Rome! Yesterday was the 22nd of February—the birthday of Washington. The Americans here must needs get up a dinner with speeches, toasts, etc. It was like a visit home. There they sat, slight, rather pale and thin men, not like beef-fed and ruddy Englishmen; very quiet and apparently timid; speaking low to the waiters instead of roaring in the imperative tone of John Bull. There was not a shadow of that boisterous and haughty confidence of manner that you see among Englishmen—in fact most of them seemed a little green. A General Dix presided and made a speech about the repudiation; the consul, Mr. Green, made another excellent speech, so did Dr. Howe. Mr. Conrade of Virginia gave us a most characteristic specimen of American eloquence, and toasted "Washington and Cincinnatus! Patrick Henry and Cicero!"

There are numbers of American artists here, some of them fine fellows. In fact, it is some consolation, after looking at the thin faces, narrow shoulders, and awkward attitudes of the "Yankees," to remember that in genius, enterprise, and courage—nay, in bodily strength—they are a full match for the sneering Englishmen. Would that they bore themselves more boldly and confidently. But a time will come when they may meet Europeans on an equal footing.

Feb. 27th. A weary week of lionizing. I would not give a damn for all the churches and ruins in Rome—at least, such are my sentiments at present. There is unbounded sublimity in the Coliseum by moonlight,—that cannot be denied,—St. Peter's, too, is a miracle in its way; but I would give them all for one ride on horseback among the Apennines.

A Virginian named St. Ives, lately converted to Catholicism, has been trying to convert me, along with some of the Jesuits here. He has abandoned the attempt in disgust, telling me that I have not logic enough in me to be convinced of anything, to which I replied by cursing logic and logicians.

I have now been three or four weeks in Rome, have been presented to his Holiness the Pope, have visited churches, convents, cemeteries, catacombs, common sewers, including the Cloaca Maxima, and ten thousand works of art. This will I say of Rome,—that a place on every account more interesting, and which has a more vivifying and quickening influence on the faculties, could not be found on the face of the earth, or, at least, I should not wish to go to it if it could. . . .

Rome, Friday. Yesterday I went to the Capuchins for permission to stay there, which was refused peremptorily; but the Passionists told me to come again at night, and they would tell me if I could be admitted. I came as directed, and was shown a room in the middle of the building, which contains hundreds of chambers connected by long and complicated passages, hung with pictures of saints and crucifixes. The monk told me that when the bell rang I must leave my hat, come out, and join the others, and then, displaying some lives of the saints and other holy works on the table, he left me to my meditations. The room has a hideous bleeding image of Christ, a vessel of holy water, and a number of holy pictures—a bed, a chair and a table. Also, hung against the wall was a "Notice to persons withdrawn from the world for spiritual exercises, to the end that they may derive all possible profit from their holy seclusion." The "Notice" prohibited going out of the chamber without necessity; prohibited also speaking at any time, or making any noise whatever, writing also, and looking out of the window. It enjoined the saying of three Ave Marias, at least, at night, also to make your own bed, etc.

The devil! thought I, here is an adventure. The secret of my getting in so easily was explained. There were about thirty Italians retired from the world, preparing for the General Confession,—and even while I was coming to this conclusion the bell clanged along the passage, and I went out to join the rest. After climbing several dark stairs, and descending others, pulling off their skull-caps to the great images of Christ on the landing places, they got into a little chapel, and after kneeling to the altar, seated themselves. The shutters were closed, and the curtains drawn immediately after; there was a prayer with the responses, and then a sermon of an hour and a half long, in which the monk kept felicitating himself and his hearers that they were of the genuine church—little thinking that there was a black sheep among his flock. The sermon over, we filed off to our rooms. In five minutes the bell rang again for supper, then we marched off to a conversazione in another part of the building, where the injunction of silence was taken off. I told the directing priest that I was a Protestant. He seemed a little startled at first, then insinuated a hope that I might be reclaimed from my damnable heresy, and said that an American had been there before, who had been converted—meaning my acquaintance St. Ives. He then opened a little battery of arguments upon me, after which he left me saying that a lay brother would make the rounds to wake us before sunrise.

The lay brother came in fact, but not before I had been waked by a howling procession of the Passionists themselves, who passed along about midnight. There was a mass, another prayer, and another endless sermon, soon after which we were summoned to coffee. I observed several of the Italians looking hard at me as I drank a glass of water instead of coffee, on account of my cursed neuralgia. Doubtless they were thinking within themselves, How that pious man is mortifying the flesh!

There was an hour's repose allowed, after which came another sermon in the chapel. This over, a bell rang for dinner, which was at eleven in the morning. The hall was on the lower floor—very long, high, and dark—with panels of oak, and ugly pictures on the walls—narrow oaken tables set all round the sides of the place. The monks were all there, in their black robes, with the emblem of their order on the breast. They had their scowling faces, as well they might, for their discipline is tremendously strict. Before each was placed an earthen bottle of wine and a piece of bread, on the bare board. Each drew a cup, a knife, fork, and wooden spoon from a drawer under the table; the attendant lay brothers placed a bowl of singular-looking soup before each, and they eat in lugubrious silence. The superior of the order sat at the upper end of the hall—a large and powerful man, who looked sterner, if possible, than his inferiors. We, who sat at another table, were differently served—with rice, eggs, fish, and fruit. No one spoke, but from a pulpit above a monk read at the top of his lungs from a book of religious precepts in that peculiar drawling tone which the Catholics employ in their exercises. There was, apparently, little fructification in the minds of his hearers. The monks eat and scowled; the laymen eat and smiled at each other, exchanging looks of meaning, though not a word passed between them. There were among them men of every age and of various conditions, from the field laborer to the gentleman of good birth. The meal concluded with a prayer and the growling responses of the Passionists, who then filed off through the galleries to their dens, looking like the living originals of the black pictures that hang along the whitewashed walls.

A monk has just been here, trying to convert me, but was not so good a hand at argument, or sophistry, as the Jesuits. I told him that he could do nothing with me, but he persisted, clapping his hand on my knee and exclaiming, "Ah, *figlio*, you will be a good Catholic, no doubt." There was a queer sort of joviality about him. He kept offering me his snuff-box, and when he thought he had made a good hit in argument, he would wink at me, with a most comical expression, as if to say, "you see you can't come round me with your heresy." He gave over at the ringing of a bell which summoned us to new readings and lecturings in the chapel, after which we were turned out into the garden of the convent, where we lounged along walks shaded with olives and oleanders. Padre Lucca, the directing priest, talked over matters of faith to me. He was an exception to the rest of the establishment—plump and well-fed, with a double chin like a bull-frog, and a most contented and good-humored countenance.

After supper to-night some of the Italians in the conversazione expressed great sympathy for my miserable state of heresy; one of them, with true charity, according to his light, said that he would pray to the Virgin, who could do all things, to show me the truth. The whole community assembled to vespers. The dark and crowded chapel fairly shook with the din of more than a hundred manly voices chanting the service.

There is nothing gloomy and morose in the religion of these Italians here, no camp-meeting long faces. They talk and laugh gayly in the intervals allowed them for conversation; but when the occasion calls it forth, they speak of religion with an earnestness, as well as a cheerfulness, that shows that it has a hold on their hearts.

Saturday. This morning, among the rest, they went through the Exercise of the Via Crucis, which consists in moving in a body around the chapel, where are suspended pictures, fourteen in number, representing different scenes in the passion of Christ. Before each of these they stop, the priest reads the appropriate prayer and expressions of contrition from the book, repeats a Pater Noster, etc., and so they make a circuit of the whole. I saw the same ceremony, on a larger scale, in the Coliseum, without knowing what it was.

A thin, hollow-eyed father tried to start my heresy this morning, but was horrified at the enormity of my disbelief; and when I told him that I belonged to a Unitarian family, he rolled up his bloodshot eyes in their black sockets, and stretched his skinny neck out of his cowl, like a turtle basking on a stone in summer. He gave me a little brass medal of the Virgin with a kind of prayer written on it. This medal he begged me to wear round my neck, and to repeat two or three Aves now and then. It was by this means, he said, that Ratisbon the Jew was converted, not long since; who, though he wore the medal and repeated the Aves merely to get rid of the importunities of a Catholic friend, yet nevertheless was favored with a miraculous vision of the Virgin, whereupon he fell on his knees and was joined to the number of the Faithful. I told the monk that I would wear the medal if he wished me to, but should not repeat the Aves; so I have it now round my neck, greatly to his satisfaction. Miracles, say all the Catholics here, happen frequently nowadays. The other day a man was raised to life who had just died in consumption, and now is walking the streets in complete health!

These Italians have come to the seclusion of this convent in order that their minds may not be distracted by contact with the world, and that the religious sentiments may grow up unimpeded and receive all possible nutriment from the constant exercises in which they are engaged. It is partly, also, with the intention of preparing them for the General Confession. It is only for a few days in the year that any are here. Their "exercises" are characteristic of the Church. The forms of prayer are all written down; they read, repeat, and sing. Very little time is allowed them for private examinations and meditations, and even in these they are directed by a printed card hung in each of the rooms, and containing a list of the subjects on which they ought to examine themselves, together with a form of contrition to be repeated by them. The sermons and readings are full of pictures of Christ's sufferings, exhortations to virtue, etc., but contain not a syllable of doctrine. One of the first in the printed list of questions which the self-examiner is to ask himself is, "Have I ever dared to inquire into the mysteries of the Faith?"

Sunday. This is Palm Sunday, the first day of the famous Settimana Santa,—the Holy Week. I determined to get out of the convent and see what was going on. The day and night previous I had worn the medal, but had no vision of the Virgin,

—at least of Santissima Maria. Padre Lucca was unfeignedly sorry to have me go with unimpaired prospects of damnation. He said he still had hopes of me; and taking the kindest leave of me, gave me a book of Catholic devotions, which I shall certainly keep in remembrance of a very excellent man. He looked at the book I had been reading the night before, and expressed his approbation,—it was a life of Blessed Paul of the Cross, detailing among other matters how the apostle hated women with a holy and religious hatred, justly regarding them as types of the devil, and fountains of unbounded evil to the sons of men; and how, when women were near, he never raised his eyes from the ground, but continually repeated Pater Nosters that the malign influence might be averted.

When I got into the fresh air I felt rather glad to be free of the gloomy galleries and cells, which, nevertheless, contain so much to be admired. . . .

[FROM FLORENCE TO EDINBURGH]

The next day I left Rome for Florence, in the diligence—and left it with much regret, and a hope to return. A young American named Marquand went with me. . . .

I went to the studio of Powers the sculptor, a noble-looking fellow and a wonderful artist. I have seen Florence—that is, I have had a glance at everything there, but one might stay with pleasure for months. Its peculiar architecture and its romantic situation make it striking enough at first sight, but the interest increases, instead of diminishing. It is impossible to have seen enough of its splendid picture galleries, gardens, and museums.

On Wednesday I left Florence, unsatisfied, but unable to stay longer. After all, I shall not see Granada—at least for some years, thanks to the cursed injury that brought me to Europe; for as I find no great improvement, I judge it best to see what a French doctor can do for me, instead of running about Spain.

At ten in the evening we left Parma. At five in the morning we were at Piacenza. Here we stopped an hour or two. Here again the striking difference between the towns of northern and southern Italy was manifested. The people looked as grave and solemn as the brick fronts of the palaces and churches. . . .

We crossed the Po, by a wretched bridge of boats, and entered Lombardy and the domains of Austria. The black eagle of Austria was painted above the guard-house, on the farther bank, where a dozen sullen-looking soldiers loitered about. There was a barrack of them near the custom-house, where we must stop an hour and a half to be searched, and to pay the fellows for doing it. After that we rode all day through a beautiful and fertile country, passing through Lodi, the scene of Bonaparte's victory, till at night we entered Milan, saturated with dust.

As for the city, it is well enough. The people are different in appearance, in manners, in language, and in habits, from the southern Italians. The women are all out sunning themselves; whole flights of them came out of the Cathedral, with little black veils flung over their heads, and mass books in their hands. Their faces and figures are round and rich—of the fiery black eye of Rome I have seen nothing; their eyes are blue and soft, and have rather a drowsy meek expression, and they *look* excessively modest.

This morning, when the whole city was quiet, the shops shut in honor of Sunday, the people issuing from the Cathedral, gentlemen walking listlessly about, and porters and contadini sitting idle at the edge of the sidewalks. There was a group of gentlemen taking their coffee under awnings in front of each of the caffès on the piazza before the Cathedral. This vagabond way of breakfasting and seeing the world at the same time is very agreeable. There is no place where you can be more independent than in one of these cities; when you are hungry there is always a restaurant and a dinner at a moment's notice, when you are thirsty there is always a caffè at hand. If you are sleepy, your room awaits you, a dozen sneaking waiters are ready at your bidding, and glide about like shadows to do what you may require, in hope of your shilling when you go away. But give me Ethan Crawford, or even Tom, in place of the whole race of waiters and garçons. I would ask their pardon for putting them in the same sentence, if they were here.

A funeral procession filed into the Cathedral, each priest, layman, woman, and child with an enormous wax candle in hand. The noble chapel, at the left extremity of the transept, was hung with black for the occasion—the coffin was placed in the midst, and the ceremonies were performed. The priests seemed not fairly awake. One fat bull-frog of a fellow would growl out of his throat his portion of the holy psalmody, interrupting himself in some interesting conversation with his neighbor, and resuming it again as soon as the religious office was performed. Another would gape and yawn in the midst of his musical performances, another would walk about looking at the people, or the coffin, or the kneeling women, singing meanwhile with the most supreme indifference and content on his fat countenance. I could imagine the subject of their conversation, as they walked out in a double file, leaving the coffin to the care of the proper officials, after they had grunted a concluding anthem over it. "Well, we've fixed this fellow's soul for him. It was a nasty job; but it's over now. Come! won't you take something to drink?"

[The foregoing quotation and some others that I shall make to indicate the ginger and spice of his character, must be read with the recollection that they are the hasty jottings of a young man who was writing in his private notebook, never expecting them to be seen. If we were to misinterpret these sallies unfairly even for a moment, we should do injustice to the reasonableness of his character. Had he spoken them, his smile would have dispelled any misunderstanding.—*Sedgwick's note.*]

I used to like priests, and take my hat off and make a low bow, half in sport and half in earnest, whenever I met them, but I have got to despise the fellows. Yet I have met admirable men among them; and have always been treated by them all with the utmost civility and attention.

I write on the Lake of Como, with three women, a boy, and four men looking over my shoulder, but they cannot read English.

I have seen nothing, at home or abroad, more beautiful than this lake. It reminds me of Lake George—the same extent, the same figure, the same crystal purity of waters, the same wild and beautiful mountains on either side. But the comparison will not go farther. Here are a hundred palaces and villages scattered along the water's edge and up the declivities. . . . All here is like a finished picture; even the wildest rocks seem softened in the air of Italy. Give me Lake George, and the smell of the pine and fir! . . .

When I got to London, I thought I had been there before. There, in flesh and blood, was the whole host of characters that figure in Pickwick. Every species of cockney was abroad in the dark and dingy looking streets, all walking with their heads stuck forward, their noses turned up, their chin pointing down, their knee-joints shaking, as they shuffled along with a gait perfectly ludicrous, but indescribable. The hackney coachmen and cabmen, with their peculiar phraseology, the walking advertisements in the shape of a boy completely hidden between two placards, and a hundred others seemed so many incarnations of Dickens' characters. A strange contrast to Paris! The cities are no more alike than the "dining room" of London and the elegant restaurant of Paris, the one being a quiet dingy establishment where each guest is put into a box and supplied with porter, beef, potatoes, and plum-pudding. Red-faced old gentlemen of three hundred weight mix their "brandy go" and read the "Times." In Paris the tables are set in elegant galleries and saloons, and among the trees and flowers of a garden, and here resort coats cut by the first tailors and bonnets of the latest mode, whose occupants regale their delicate tastes on the lightest and most delicious viands. The waiters spring from table to table as noiselessly as shadows, prompt at the slightest sign; a lady, elegantly attired, sits within an arbor to preside over the whole. Dine at these places, then go to a London "dining room"—swill porter and devour roast beef!

I went immediately to Catlin's Indian Gallery. It is in the Egyptian Hall, Piccadilly. There was a crowd around the door; servants in livery waiting; men with handbills of the exhibition for sale; cabmen, boys, and pickpockets. I was rejoicing in Mr. Catlin's success, when the true point of attraction caught my eye, in the shape of a full-length portrait of Major Tom Thumb, the celebrated American dwarf, who it seems occupies the Indian Gallery for the present. I paid my shilling and went in. The little wretch was singing Yankee Doodle with a voice like a smothered mouse, and prancing about on a table, à la Jeffrey Hudson, with a wooden sword in his hand; a great crowd of cockneys and gentlemen and ladies were contemplating his evolutions. But for the Indian Gallery, its glory had departed; it had evidently ceased to be a lion. The portraits of the chiefs, dusty and faded, hung round the walls, and above were a few hunting shirts and a bundle or two of arrows; but the rich and invaluable collection I had seen in Boston had disappeared, and no one thought of looking at the poor remains of that great collection that were hung about the walls. Catlin had done right. He would not suffer the fruits of his six years' labor and danger to rot in the dampness to gratify a few miserable cockneys, so has packed up the best part of his trophies. . . .

St. Paul's, which the English ridiculously compare to St. Peter's, is without exception the dirtiest and gloomiest church I have been in yet. I went up to the ball at the top of the cupola, whence the prospect is certainly a most wonderful one. . . .

Walk out in the evening, and keep a yard or two behind some wretched clerk, who with nose elevated in the air, elbows stuck out at right angles, and the pewter knob of his cane playing upon his under lip, is straddling his bow legs over the sidewalk with a most majestic air. Get behind him, and you see his dignity greatly disturbed. First he glances over one of his narrow shoulders, then over the other, then he edges off to the other side of the walk, and turns his vacant lobster eyes full upon you, then he passes his hand over his coat-tail, and finally he draws forth from his pocket the object of all this solicitude in the shape of a venerable and ragged cotton handkerchief, which he holds in his hand to keep it out of harm's way. I have been thus taken for a pickpocket more than a dozen times to-night, not the less so for being respectably dressed, for these gentry are the most dashy men on the Strand.

There is an interesting mixture of vulgarity and helplessness in the swarm of ugly faces you see in the streets—meagre, feeble, ill-proportioned, or not proportioned at all, the blockheads must needs put on a game air and affect the "man of the world" in their small way. I have not met one handsome woman yet, though I have certainly walked more than fifty miles since I have been here, and have kept my eyes open. To be sure, the weather has been raw and chill enough to keep beauty at home. Elsewhere Englishmen are tall, strong, and manly; here, the crowd that swarms through the streets are like the outcasts of a hospital. . . .

I spent seven or eight days in London. On the eighth day I went up the river to Richmond in a steamboat, with a true cockney pleasure party on board, whose evolutions were very entertaining. . . .

I got into the cars one night—having sent my trunks to Liverpool—and found myself in the morning at Darlington, nearly three hundred miles distant. Thence I took stage for Carlisle, famous in Border story.

I went away at four in the morning for Abbotsford. We were in the region where one thinks of nothing but of Scott, and of the themes which he has rendered so familiar to the whole world. The Cheviot was on our right—the Teviot hills before us. The wind came down from them raw and cold, and the whole sky was obscured with stormy clouds. I thought as we left the town of the burden of one of his ballads: "The sun shines fair on Carlisle wall." It was little applicable now. The ancient fortification looked sullen and cheerless as tottering battlements and black crumbling walls, beneath a sky as dark and cold as themselves, could make it. I was prepared for storms and a gloomy day, but soon the clouds parted and the sun broke out clear over the landscape. The dark heathery sides of Teviot—the numberless bright rapid streams that came from the different glens, and the woods of ash, larch, and birch that followed their course, and grew on the steeper declivities of the hills—never could have appeared to more advantage. Esk and Liddel, Yarrow, the Teviot, Minto Crag, Ettrick Forest, Branksome

Castle—these and more likewise we passed before we reached the Tweed and saw Abbotsford on its banks among the forests planted by Scott himself. I left my luggage at the inn at Galashiels, telling the landlord that I was going away, and might return at night, or might not. I visited Abbotsford, Melrose, and Dryburgh—and consider the day better spent than the whole four months I was in Sicily and Italy. I slept at Melrose, and returned to Galashiels in the morning.

I like the Scotch—I like the country and everything in it. The Liverpool packet will not wait, or I should stay long here, and take a trout from every "burnie" in the Cheviot. The scenery has been grossly belied by Irving and others. It is wild and beautiful. I have seen none more so. There is wood enough along the margins of the streams (which are as transparent as our own); the tops of the hills alone are bare. The country abounds in game, pheasants, moor-cock, curlew, and rabbits. . . .

I walked up Arthur's Seat, passing the spot where Jeanie Deans had her interview with her sister's seducer, and, when I arrived at the top, looking [*sic*] down on the site of her father's cottage. Under the crags here is the place where Scott and James Ballantyne used to sit when boys and read and make romances together. Edinburgh, half wrapped in smoke, lies many hundred feet below, seen beyond the ragged projecting edge of Salisbury Crag, the castle rising obscurely in the extreme distance. . . .

[INDIAN DOMESTIC LIFE]
(From *The Oregon Trail*, 1847–49)

Up went the lodges in a circle on the margin of the stream. For the sake of quiet we pitched our tent among some trees half a mile distant. In the afternoon we were in the village. The day was a glorious one, and the whole camp seemed lively and animated in sympathy. Groups of children and young girls were laughing gayly outside the lodges. The shields, the lances, and the bows were removed from the tall tripods on which they usually hung, before the dwellings of their owners. The warriors were mounting their horses, and one by one riding away over the prairie towards the neighboring hills.

Shaw and I sat on the grass near the lodge of Reynal. An old woman, with true Indian hospitality, brought a bowl of boiled venison and placed it before us. We amused ourselves with watching a few young squaws who were playing together and chasing each other in and out of one of the lodges. Suddenly the wild yell of the war-whoop came pealing from the hills. A crowd of horsemen appeared, rushing down their sides, and riding at full speed towards the village, each warrior's long hair flying behind him in the wind like a ship's streamer. As they approached, the confused throng assumed a regular order, and entering two by two, they circled round the area at full gallop, each warrior singing his war-song as he rode. Some of their dresses were superb. They wore crests of feathers, and close tunics of antelope skins, fringed with the scalp-locks of their enemies; many of their shields, too, fluttered with the war-eagle's feathers. All had bows and arrows at their backs; some carried long lances, and a few were armed with guns. The White Shield, their partisan, rode in gorgeous attire at their head, mounted on a black-and-white horse. Mahto-Tatonka and his brothers took no part in this parade, for they were in mourning for their sister, and were all sitting in their lodges, their bodies bedaubed from head to foot with white clay, and a lock of hair cut from the forehead of each.

The warriors rode three times round the village; and as each noted champion passed, the old women would scream out his name, to honor his bravery, and excite the emulation of the younger warriors. Little urchins, not two years old, followed the warlike pageant with glittering eyes, and gazed with eager admiration at the heroes of their tribe.

The procession rode out of the village as it had entered it, and in half an hour all the warriors had returned again, dropping quietly in, singly or in parties of two or three.

The parade over, we were entertained with an episode of Indian domestic life. A vicious-looking squaw, beside herself with rage, was berating her spouse, who, with a look of total unconcern, sat cross-legged in the middle of his lodge, smoking his pipe in silence. At length, maddened by his coolness, she made a rush at the lodge, seized the poles which supported it, and tugged at them, one after the other, till she brought down the whole structure, poles, hides, and all, clattering on his head, burying him in the wreck of his habitation. He pushed aside the hides with his hand, and presently his head emerged, like a turtle's from its shell. Still he sat smoking sedately as before, a wicked glitter in his eyes alone betraying the pent-up storm within. The squaw, scolding all the while, proceeded to saddle her horse, bestride him, and canter out of the camp, intending, as it seemed, to return to her father's lodge, wherever that might be. The warrior, who had not deigned even to look at her, now coolly arose, disengaged himself from the ruins, tied a cord of hair by way of bridle round the jaw of his buffalo-horse, broke a stout cudgel, about four feet long, from the butt-end of a lodge-pole, mounted, and galloped majestically over the prairie to discipline his offending helpmeet.

[A CLOSE VIEW OF INDIAN WARFARE]

When the first pipe was smoked out, I rose and withdrew to the lodge of my host. Here I was stooping, in the act of taking off my powder-horn and bullet-pouch, when suddenly, and close at hand, pealing loud and shrill, and in right good earnest, came the terrific yell of the war-whoop. Kongra-Tonga's squaw snatched up her youngest child, and ran out of the lodge. I followed, and found the whole village in confusion, resounding with cries and yells. The circle of old men in the centre had vanished. The warriors, with glittering eyes, came darting, weapons in hand, out of the low openings of the lodges, and running with wild yells towards the farther end of the village. Advancing a few rods in that direction, I saw a crowd in furious agitation. Just then I distinguished the voices of Raymond and Reynal, shouting to me from a distance, and looking back, I saw the latter with his rifle in his hand, standing on the farther bank of a little stream that ran along the outskirts of the camp.

He was calling to Raymond and me to come over and join him, and Raymond, with his usual deliberate gait and stolid countenance, was already moving in that direction.

This was clearly the wisest course, unless we wished to involve ourselves in the fray; so I turned to go, but just then a pair of eyes, gleaming like a snake's, and an aged familiar countenance was thrust from the opening of a neighboring lodge, and out bolted old Mene-Seela, full of fight, clutching his bow and arrows in one hand and his knife in the other. At that instant he tripped and fell sprawling on his face, while his weapons flew scattering in every direction. The women with loud screams were hurrying with their children in their arms to place them out of danger, and I observed some hastening to prevent mischief, by carrying away all the weapons they could lay hands on. On a rising ground close to the camp stood a line of old women singing a medicine-song to allay the tumult. As I approached the side of the brook, I heard gun-shots behind me, and turning back saw that the crowd had separated into two long lines of naked warriors confronting each other at a respectful distance, and yelling and jumping about to dodge the shot of their adversaries, while they discharged bullets and arrows against each other. At the same time certain sharp, humming sounds in the air over my head, like the flight of beetles on a summer evening, warned me that the danger was not wholly confined to the immediate scene of the fray. So wading through the brook, I joined Reynal and Raymond, and we sat down on the grass, in the posture of an armed neutrality, to watch the result.

Happily it may be for ourselves, though contrary to our expectation, the disturbance was quelled almost as soon as it began. When I looked again, the combatants were once more mingled together in a mass. Though yells sounded occasionally from the throng, the firing had entirely ceased, and I observed five or six persons moving busily about, as if acting the part of peace-makers. One of the village heralds or criers proclaimed in a loud voice something which my two companions were too much engrossed in their own observations to translate for me.

The crowd began to disperse, though many a deep-set black eye still glittered with an unnatural lustre, as the warriors slowly withdrew to their lodges. This fortunate suppression of the disturbance was owing to a few of the old men, less pugnacious than Mene-Seela, who boldly ran in between the combatants, and aided by some of the "soldiers," or Indian police, succeeded in effecting their object.

It seemed very strange to me that although many arrows and bullets were discharged, no one was mortally hurt, and I could only account for this by the fact that both the marksman and the object of his aim were leaping about incessantly. By far the greater part of the villagers had joined in the fray, for although there were not more than a dozen guns in the whole camp, I heard at least eight or ten shots fired.

In a quarter of an hour all was comparatively quiet. A group of warriors was again seated in the middle of the village, but this time I did not venture to join them, because I could see that the pipe, contrary to the usual order, was passing from the left hand to the right around the circle; a sure sign that a "medicine-smoke" of reconciliation was going forward, and that a white man would be an intruder. When I again entered the still agitated camp it was nearly dark, and mournful cries, howls, and wailings resounded from many female voices. Whether these had any connection with the late disturbance, or were merely lamentations for relatives slain in some former war expeditions, I could not distinctly ascertain.

To inquire too closely into the cause of the quarrel was by no means prudent, and it was not until some time after that I discovered what had given rise to it. Among the Dahcotah there are many associations or fraternities, superstitious, war-like, or social. Among them was one called "The Arrow-Breakers," now in great measure disbanded and dispersed. In the village there were, however, four men belonging to it, distinguished by the peculiar arrangement of their hair, which rose in a high bristling mass above their foreheads, adding greatly to their apparent height, and giving them a most ferocious appearance. The principal among them was the Mad

Wolf, a warrior of remarkable size and strength, great courage, and the fierceness of a demon. I had always looked upon him as the most dangerous man in the village; and though he often invited me to feasts, I never entered his lodge unarmed. The Mad Wolf had taken a fancy to a fine horse belonging to another Indian, called the Tall Bear; and anxious to get the animal into his possession, he made the owner a present of another horse nearly equal in value. According to the customs of the Dahcotah, the acceptance of this gift involved a sort of obligation to make a return; and the Tall Bear well understood that the other had his favorite buffalo-horse in view. He, however, accepted the present without a word of thanks, and having picketed the horse before his lodge, suffered day after day to pass without making the expected return. The Mad Wolf grew impatient; and at last, seeing that his bounty was not likely to produce the desired result, he resolved to reclaim it. So this evening, as soon as the village was encamped, he went to the lodge of the Tall Bear, seized upon the horse he had given him, and led him away. At this the Tall Bear broke into one of those fits of sullen rage not uncommon among Indians, ran up to the unfortunate horse, and gave him three mortal stabs with his knife. Quick as lightning, the Mad Wolf drew his bow to its utmost tension, and held the arrow quivering close to the breast of his adversary. The Tall Bear, as the Indians who were near him said, stood with his bloody knife in his hand, facing the assailant with the utmost calmness. Some of his friends and relatives, seeing his danger, ran hastily to his assistance. The remaining three Arrow-Breakers, on the other hand, came to the aid of their associate. Their friends joined them, the war-cry was raised, and the tumult became general.

The "soldiers," who lent their timely aid in putting it down, are the most important executive functionaries in an Indian village. The office is one of considerable honor, being confided only to men of courage and repute. They derive their authority from the old men and chief warriors of the village, who elect them in councils occasionally convened for the purpose, and thus can exercise a degree of authority which no one else in the village would dare to assume. While very few Ogillallah chiefs could venture without risk of their lives to strike or lay hands upon the meanest of their people, the "soldiers," in the discharge of their appropriate functions, have full license to make use of these and similar acts of coercion.

[HUNTING THE BUFFALO]

"Tongues and hump-ribs to-morrow," said Shaw, looking with contempt at the venison steaks which Deslauriers placed before us. Our meal finished, we lay down to sleep. A shout from Henry Chatillon aroused us, and we saw him standing on the cart-wheel, stretching his tall figure to its full height while he looked towards the prairie beyond the river. Following the direction of his eyes, we could clearly distinguish a large dark object, like the black shadow of a cloud, passing rapidly over swell after swell of the distant plain; behind it followed another of similar appearance, though smaller, moving more rapidly, and drawing closer and closer to the first. It was the hunters of the Arapahoe camp chasing a band of buffalo. Shaw and I caught and saddled our best horses, and went plunging through sand and water to the farther bank. We were too late. The hunters had already mingled with the herd, and the work of slaughter was nearly over. When we reached the ground we found it strewn far and near with numberless carcasses, while the remnants of the herd, scattered in all directions, were flying away in terror, and the Indians still rushing in pursuit. Many of the hunters, however, remained upon the spot, and among the rest was our yesterday's acquaintance, the chief of the village. He had alighted by the side of a cow, into which he had shot five or six arrows, and his squaw, who had followed him on horseback to the hunt, was giving him a draught of water from a canteen, purchased or plundered from some volunteer soldier. Recrossing the river, we overtook the party, who were already on their way.

We had gone scarcely a mile when we saw an imposing spectacle. From the river bank on the right, away over the swelling prairie on the left, and in front as far as the eye could reach, was one vast host of buffalo. The outskirts of the herd were within a quarter of a mile. In many parts they were crowded so densely together that in the distance their rounded backs presented a surface of uniform blackness; but elsewhere they were more scattered, and from amid the multitude rose little columns of dust where some of them were rolling on the ground. Here and there a battle was going forward among the bulls. We could distinctly see them rushing against each other, and hear the clattering of their horns and their hoarse bellowing. Shaw was riding at some distance in advance, with Henry Chatillon; I saw him stop and draw the leather covering from his gun. With such a sight before us, but one thing could be thought of. That morning I had used pistols in the chase. I had now a mind to try the virtue of a gun. Deslauriers had one, and I rode up to the side of the cart; there he sat under the white covering, biting his pipe between his teeth and grinning with excitement.

"Lend me your gun, Deslauriers."

"Oui, Monsieur, oui," said Deslauriers, tugging with might and main to stop the mule, which seemed obstinately bent on going forward. Then every thing but his moccasins disappeared as he crawled into the cart and pulled at the gun to extricate it.

"Is it loaded?" I asked.

"Oui, bien chargé; you'll kill, mon bourgeois; yes, you'll kill—c'est un bon fusil."

I handed him my rifle and rode forward to Shaw.

"Are you ready?" he asked.

"Come on," said I.

"Keep down that hollow," said Henry, "and then they won't see you till you get close to them."

The hollow was a kind of wide ravine; it ran obliquely towards the buffalo, and we rode at a canter along the bottom until it became too shallow; then we bent close to our horses' necks, and, at last, finding that it could no longer conceal us, came out of it and rode directly towards the herd. It was within gunshot; before its outskirts, numerous grizzly old bulls were scattered, holding guard over their females. They glared at us in anger and astonishment, walked towards us a few yards, and then turning slowly round, retreated at a trot which afterwards broke into a clumsy gallop. In an instant the main body caught the alarm. The buffalo began to crowd away from the point towards which we were approaching, and a gap was opened in the side of the herd. We entered it, still restraining our excited horses. Every instant the tumult was thickening. The buffalo, pressing together in large bodies, crowded away from us on every hand. In front and on either side we could see dark columns and masses, half hidden by clouds of dust, rushing along in terror and confusion, and hear the tramp and clattering of ten thousand hoofs. That countless multitude of powerful brutes, ignorant of their own strength, were flying in a panic from the approach of two feeble horsemen. To remain quiet longer was impossible.

"Take that band on the left," said Shaw; "I'll take these in front."

He sprang off, and I saw no more of him. A heavy Indian whip was fastened by a band to my wrist; I swung it into the air and lashed my horse's flank with all the strength of my arm. Away she darted, stretching close to the ground. I could see nothing but a cloud of dust before me, but I knew that it concealed a band of many hundreds of buffalo. In a moment I was in the midst of the cloud, half suffocated by the dust and stunned by the trampling of the flying herd; but I was drunk with the chase and cared for nothing but the buffalo. Very soon a long dark mass became visible, looming through the dust; then I could distinguish each bulky carcass, the hoofs flying out beneath, the short tails held rigidly erect. In a moment I was so close that I could have touched them with my gun. Suddenly, to my amazement, the hoofs were jerked upwards, the tails flourished in the air, and amid a cloud of dust the buffalo seemed to sink into the earth before me. One vivid impression of that instant remains upon my mind. I remember looking down upon the backs of several buffalo dimly visible through the dust. We had run unawares upon a ravine. At that moment I was not the most accurate judge of depth and width, but when I passed it on my return, I found it about twelve feet deep and not quite twice as wide at the bottom. It was impossible to stop; I would have done so gladly if I could; so, half sliding, half plunging, down went the little mare. She came down on her knees in the loose sand at the bottom; I was pitched forward against her neck and nearly thrown over her head among the buffalo, who amid dust and confusion came tumbling in all around. The mare was on her feet in an instant and scrambling like a cat up the opposite side. I thought for a moment that she would have fallen back and crushed me, but with a violent effort she clambered out and gained the hard prairie above. Glancing back, I saw the huge head of a bull clinging as it were by the forefeet at the edge of the dusty gulf. At length I was fairly among the buffalo. They were less densely crowded than before, and I could see nothing but bulls, who always run at the rear of a herd to protect their females. As I passed among them they would lower their heads, and turning as they ran, try to gore my horse; but as they were already at full speed there was no force in their onset, and as Pauline ran faster than they, they were always thrown behind her in the effort. I soon began to distinguish cows amid the throng. One just in front of me seemed to my liking, and I pushed close to her side. Dropping the reins, I fired, holding the muzzle of the gun within a foot of her shoulder. Quick as lightning she sprang at Pauline; the little mare dodged the attack, and I lost sight of the wounded animal amid the tumult. Immediately after, I selected another, and urging forward Pauline, shot into her both pistols in succession. For a while I kept her in view, but in attempting to load my gun, lost sight of her also in the confusion. Believing her to be mortally wounded and unable to keep up with the herd, I checked my horse. The crowd rushed onwards. The dust and tumult passed away, and on the prairie, far behind the rest, I saw a solitary buffalo galloping heavily. In a moment I and my victim were running side by side. My firearms were all empty, and I had in my pouch nothing but rifle bullets, too large for the pistols and too small for the gun. I loaded the gun, however, but as often as I levelled it to fire, the bullets would roll out of the muzzle and the gun returned only a report like a squib, as the powder harmlessly exploded. I rode in front of the buffalo and tried to turn her back; but her eyes glared, her mane bristled, and, lowering her head, she rushed at me with the utmost fierceness and activity. Again and again I rode before her, and again and again she repeated her furious charge. But little Pauline was in her element. She dodged her enemy at every rush, until at length the buffalo stood still, exhausted with her own efforts, her tongue lolling from her jaws.

Riding to a little distance, I dismounted, thinking to gather a handful of dry grass to serve the purpose of wadding, and load the gun at my leisure. No sooner were my feet on the ground than the buffalo came bounding in such a rage towards me that I jumped back again into the saddle with all possible despatch. After waiting a few minutes more, I made an attempt to ride up and stab her with my knife; but Pauline was near being gored in the attempt. At length, bethinking me of the fringes at the seams of my buckskin trousers, I jerked off a few of them, and, reloading the gun, forced them down the barrel to keep the bullet in its place; then approaching, I shot the wounded buffalo through the heart. Sinking to her knees, she rolled over lifeless on the prairie. To my astonishment, I found that, instead of a cow, I had been slaughtering a stout yearling bull. No longer wondering at his fierceness, I opened his throat, and cutting out his tongue, tied it at the back of my saddle. My mistake was one which a more experienced eye than mine might easily make in the dust and confusion of such a chase.

Then for the first time I had leisure to look at the scene around me. The prairie in front was darkened with the retreating multitude, and on either hand the buffalo came filing up in endless columns from the low plains upon the river. The Arkansas was three or four miles distant. I turned and moved slowly towards it. A long time passed before, far in the distance, I distinguished the white covering of the cart and the little black specks of horsemen before and behind it. Drawing near, I recognized Shaw's elegant tunic, the red flannel shirt, conspicuous far off. I overtook the party, and asked him what success he had had. He had assailed a fat cow, shot her with two bullets, and mortally wounded her. But neither of us was prepared for the chase that afternoon, and Shaw, like myself, had no spare bullets in his pouch; so he abandoned the disabled animal to Henry Chatillon, who followed, despatched her with his rifle, and loaded his horse with the meat.

We encamped close to the river. The night was dark, and as we lay down we could hear, mingled with the howlings of wolves, the hoarse bellowing of the buffalo, like the ocean beating upon a distant coast.

[WESTWARD OVER THE OREGON TRAIL]

We were now at the end of our solitary journeyings along the St. Joseph trail. On the evening of the twenty-third of May we encamped near its junction with the old legitimate trail of the Oregon emigrants. We had ridden long that afternoon, trying in vain to find wood and water, until at length we saw the sunset sky reflected from a pool encircled by bushes and rocks. The water lay in the bottom of a hollow, the smooth prairie gracefully rising in ocean-like swells on every side. We pitched our tents by it; not, however, before the keen eye of Henry Chatillon had discerned some unusual object upon the faintly-defined outline of the distant swell. But in the moist, hazy atmosphere of the evening, nothing could be clearly distinguished. As we lay around the fire after supper, a low and distant sound, strange enough amid the loneliness of the prairie, reached our ears—peals of laughter, and the faint voices of men and women. For eight days we had not encountered a human being, and this singular warning of their vicinity had an effect extremely impressive.

About dark a sallow-faced fellow descended the hill on horseback, and splashing through the pool, rode up to the tents. He was enveloped in a huge cloak, and his broad felt hat was weeping about his ears with the drizzling moisture of the evening. Another followed, a stout, square-built, intelligent-looking man, who announced himself as leader of an emigrant party, encamped a mile in advance of us. About twenty wagons, he said, were with him; the rest of his party were on the other side of the Big Blue, waiting for a woman who was in the pains of childbirth, and quarrelling meanwhile among themselves.

These were the first emigrants that we had overtaken, although we had found abundant and melancholy traces of their progress throughout the course of the journey. Sometimes we passed the grave of one who had sickened and died on the way. The earth was usually torn up, and covered thickly with wolf-tracks. Some had escaped this violation. One morning, a piece of plank, standing upright on the summit of a grassy hill, attracted our notice, and riding up to it, we found the following words very roughly traced upon it, apparently with a red-hot piece of iron:—

MARY ELLIS
DIED MAY 7th, 1845
AGED TWO MONTHS

Such tokens were of common occurrence.

We were late in breaking up our camp on the following morning, and scarcely had we ridden a mile when we saw, far in advance of us, drawn against the horizon, a line of objects stretching at regular intervals along the level edge of the prairie. An intervening swell soon hid them from sight, until, ascending it a quarter of an hour after, we saw close before us the emigrant caravan, with its heavy white wagons creeping on in slow procession, and a large drove of cattle following behind. Half a dozen yellow-visaged Missourians, mounted on horseback, were cursing and shouting among them, their lank angular proportions enveloped in brown homespun, evidently cut and adjusted by the hands of a domestic female tailor. As we approached, they called out to us: "How are ye, boys? Are ye for Oregon or California?"

As we pushed rapidly by the wagons, children's faces were thrust out from the white coverings to look at us; while the care-worn, thin-featured matron, or the buxom girl, seated in front, suspended the knitting on which most of them were engaged to stare at us with wondering curiosity. By the side of each wagon stalked the proprietor, urging on his patient oxen, who shouldered heavily along, inch by inch, on their interminable journey. It was easy to see that fear and dissension prevailed among them; some of the men—but these, with one exception, were bachelors—looked wistfully upon us as we rode lightly and swiftly by, and then impatiently at their own lumbering wagons and heavy-gaited oxen. Others were unwilling to advance at all, until the party they had left behind should have rejoined them. Many were murmuring against the leader they had chosen, and wished to depose him; and this discontent was fomented by some ambitious spirits, who had hopes of succeeding in his place. The women were divided between regrets for the homes they had left and fear of the deserts and savages before them.

We soon left them far behind, and hoped that we had taken a final leave; but our companions' wagon stuck so long in a deep muddy ditch, that before it was extricated the van of the emigrant caravan appeared again, descending a ridge close at hand. Wagon after wagon plunged through the mud; and as it was nearly noon, and the place promised shade and water, we saw with satisfaction that they were resolved to encamp. Soon the wagons were wheeled into a circle: the cattle were grazing over the meadow, and the men, with sour, sullen faces, were looking about for wood and water. They seemed to meet but indifferent success. As we left the ground, I saw a tall, slouching fellow, with the nasal accent of "down east," contemplating the contents of his tin cup, which he had just filled with water.

"Look here, you," said he; "it's chock-full of animals!"

The cup, as he held it out, exhibited in fact an extraordinary variety and profusion of animal and vegetable life.

Riding up the little hill, and looking back on the meadow, we could easily see that all was not right in the camp of the emigrants. The men were crowded together, and an angry discussion seemed to be going forward. R—— was missing from his wonted place in the line, and the captain told us that he had remained behind to get his horse shod by a blacksmith attached to the emigrant party. Something whispered in our ears that mischief was on foot; we kept on, however, and coming soon to a stream of tolerable water, we stopped to rest and dine. Still the absentee lingered behind. At last, at the distance of a mile, he and his horse suddenly appeared, sharply defined against the sky on the summit of a hill; and close behind, a huge white object rose slowly into view.

"What is that blockhead bringing with him now?"

A moment dispelled the mystery. Slowly and solemnly, one behind the other, four long trains of oxen and four emigrant wagons rolled over the crest of the hill and gravely descended, while R—— rode in state in the van. It seems that, during the process of shoeing the horse, the smothered dissensions among the emigrants suddenly broke into open rupture. Some insisted on pushing forward, some on remaining where they were, and some on going back. Kearsley, their captain, threw up his command in disgust. "And now, boys," said he, "if any of you are for going ahead, just you come along with me."

Four wagons, with ten men, one woman, and one small child, made up the force of the "go-ahead" faction, and R——, with his usual proclivity toward mischief, invited them to join our party. Fear of the Indians—for I can conceive no other motive—must have induced him to court so burdensome an alliance. At all events, the proceeding was a cool one. The men who joined us, it is true, were all that could be desired; rude indeed in manners, but frank, manly, and intelligent. To tell them we could not travel with them was out of the question. I merely reminded Kearsley that if his oxen could not keep up with our mules he must expect to be left behind, as we could not consent to be farther delayed on the journey; but he immediately replied, that his oxen "*should* keep up; and if they couldn't, why, he allowed, he'd find out how to make 'em."

On the next day, as it chanced, our English companions broke the axle-tree of their wagon, and down came the whole cumbrous machine lumbering into the bed of a brook. Here was a day's work cut out for us. Meanwhile our emigrant associates kept on their way, and so vigorously did they urge forward their powerful oxen, that, what with the broken axle-tree and other mishaps, it was full a week before we overtook them; when at length we discovered them, one afternoon, crawling quietly along the sandy brink of the Platte. But meanwhile various incidents occurred to ourselves.

It was probable that at this stage of our journey the Pawnees would attempt to rob us. We began therefore to stand guard in turn, dividing the night into three watches, and appointing two men for each. Deslauriers and I held guard together. We did not march with military precision to and fro before the tents: our discipline was by no means so strict. We wrapped ourselves in our blankets, and sat down by the fire; and Deslauriers, combining his culinary functions with his duties as sentinel, employed himself in boiling the head of an antelope for our breakfast. Yet we were models of vigilance in comparison with some of the party; for the ordinary practice of the guard was to lay his rifle on the ground, and, enveloping his nose in his blanket, meditate on his mistress, or whatever subject best pleased him. This is all well enough when among Indians who do not habitually proceed further in their hostility than robbing travellers of their horses and mules, though, indeed, a Pawnee's forbearance is not always to be trusted; but in certain regions farther to the west, the guard must beware how he exposes his person to the light of the fire, lest some keen-eyed skulking marksman should let fly a bullet or an arrow from the darkness.

Among various tales that circulated around our camp-fire was one told by Boisverd, and not inappropriate here. He was trapping with several companions on the skirts of the Blackfoot country. The man on guard, knowing that it behooved him to put forth his utmost precaution, kept aloof from the fire-light, and sat watching intently on all sides. At length he was aware of a dark, crouching figure, stealing noiselessly into the circle of the light. He hastily cocked his rifle, but the sharp click of the lock caught the ear of the Blackfoot, whose senses were all on the alert. Raising his arrow, already fitted to the string, he shot it in the direction of the sound. So sure was his aim, that he drove it through the throat of the unfortunate guard, and then, with a loud yell, bounded from the camp.

As I looked at the partner of my watch, puffing and blowing over his fire, it occurred to me that he might not prove the most efficient auxiliary in time of trouble.

"Deslauriers," said I, "would you run away if the Pawnees should fire at us?"

"Ah! oui, oui, Monsieur!" he replied very decisively.

At this instant a whimsical variety of voices,—barks, howls, yelps, and whines,—all mingled together, sounded from the prairie, not far off, as if a conclave of wolves of every age and sex were assembled there. Deslauriers looked up from his work with a laugh, and began to imitate this medley of sounds with a ludicrous accuracy. At this they were repeated with redoubled emphasis, the musician being apparently indignant at the successful efforts of a rival. They all proceeded from the throat of one little wolf, not larger than a spaniel, seated by himself at some distance. He was of the species called the prairie-wolf: a grim-visaged, but harmless little brute, whose worst propensity is creeping among horses and gnawing the ropes of raw hide by which they are picketed around the camp. Other beasts roam the prairies, far more formidable in aspect and in character. These are the large white and gray wolves, whose deep howl we heard at intervals from far and near.

At last I fell into a doze, and awaking from it, found Deslauriers fast asleep. Scandalized by this breach of discipline, I was about to stimulate his vigilance by stirring him with the stock of my rifle; but, compassion prevailing, I determined to let him sleep a while, and then arouse him to administer a suitable reproof for such forgetfulness of duty. Now and then I walked the rounds among the silent horses, to see that all was right. The night was chill, damp, and dark, the dank grass bending under the icy dew-drops. At the distance of a rod or two the tents were invisible, and nothing could be seen but the obscure figures of the horses, deeply breathing, and restlessly starting as they slept, or still slowly champing the grass. Far off, beyond the black outline of the prairie, there was a ruddy light, gradually increasing, like the glow of a conflagration; until at length the broad disk of the moon, blood-red, and vastly magnified by the vapors, rose slowly upon the darkness, flecked by one or two little clouds, and as the light poured over the gloomy plain, a fierce and stern howl, close at hand, seemed to greet it as an unwelcome intruder. There was something impressive and awful in the place and the hour; for I and the beasts were all that had consciousness for many a league around.

Some days elapsed, and brought us near the Platte. Two men on horseback approached us one morning, and we watched them with the curiosity and interest that, upon the solitude of the plains, such an encounter always excites. They were evidently whites, from their mode of riding, though, contrary to the usage of that region, neither of them carried a rifle.

"Fools!" remarked Henry Chatillon, "to ride that way on the prairie; Pawnee find them—then they catch it."

Pawnee *had* found them, and they had come very near "catching it"; indeed, nothing saved them but the approach of our party. Shaw and I knew one of them,—a man named Turner, whom we had seen at Westport. He and his companion belonged to an emigrant party encamped a few miles in advance, and had returned to look for some stray oxen, leaving their rifles, with characteristic rashness or ignorance, behind them. Their neglect had nearly cost them dear; for, just before we came up, half-a-dozen Indians approached, and seeing them apparently defenceless, one of the rascals seized the bridle of Turner's horse and ordered him to dismount. Turner was wholly unarmed; but the other jerked a pistol out of his pocket, at which the Pawnee recoiled; and just then some of our men appearing in the distance, the whole party whipped their rugged little horses and made off. In no way daunted, Turner foolishly persisted in going forward.

Long after leaving him, and late that afternoon, in the midst of a gloomy and barren prairie, we came suddenly upon the great trail of the Pawnees, leading from their villages on the Platte to their war and hunting grounds to the southward. Here every summer passes the motley concourse: thousands of savages, men, women, and children, horses and mules, laden with their weapons and implements, and an innumerable multitude of unruly wolfish dogs, who have not acquired the civilized accomplishment of barking, but howl like their wild cousins of the prairie.

The permanent winter villages of the Pawnees stand on the lower Platte, but throughout the summer the greater part of the inhabitants are wandering over the plains,—a treacherous, cowardly banditti, who, by a thousand acts of pillage and murder, have deserved chastisement at the hands of government. Last year a Dahcotah warrior performed a notable exploit at one of these villages. He approached it alone, in the middle of a dark night, and clambering up the outside of one of the lodges, which are in the form of a half-sphere, looked in at the round hole made at the top for the escape of smoke. The dusky light from the embers showed him the forms of the sleeping inmates; and dropping lightly through the opening, he unsheathed his knife, and, stirring the fire, coolly selected his victims. One by one, he stabbed and scalped them; when a child suddenly awoke and screamed. He rushed from the lodge, yelled a Sioux warcry, shouted his name in triumph and defiance, and darted out upon the dark prairie, leaving the whole village behind him in a tumult, with the howling and baying of dogs, the screams of women, and the yells of the enraged warriors.

Our friend Kearsley, as we learned on rejoining him, signalized himself by a less bloody achievement. He and his men were good woodsmen, well skilled in the use of the rifle, but found themselves wholly out of their element on the prairie. None of them had ever seen a buffalo; and they had very vague conceptions of his nature and appearance. On the day after they reached the Platte, looking towards a distant swell, they beheld a multitude of little black specks in motion upon its surface.

"Take your rifles, boys," said Kearsley, "and we'll have fresh meat for supper." This inducement was quite sufficient. The ten men left their wagons, and set out in hot haste, some on horseback and some on foot, in pursuit of the supposed buffalo.

Meanwhile a high, grassy ridge shut the game from view; but mounting it after half an hour's running and riding, they found themselves suddenly confronted by about thirty mounted Pawnees. Amazement and consternation were mutual. Having nothing but their bows and arrows, the Indians thought their hour was come, and the fate that they were conscious of richly deserving about to overtake them. So they began, one and all, to shout forth the most cordial salutations, running up with extreme earnestness to shake hands with the Missourians, who were as much rejoiced as they were to escape the unexpected conflict.

A low, undulating line of sand-hills bounded the horizon before us. That day we rode ten hours, and it was dusk before we entered the hollows and gorges of these gloomy little hills. At length we gained the summit, and the long-expected valley of the Platte lay before us. We all drew rein, and sat joyfully looking down upon the prospect. It was right welcome; strange, too, and striking to the imagination, and yet it had not one picturesque or beautiful feature; nor had it any of the features of grandeur, other than its vast extent, its solitude, and its wildness. For league after league, a plain as level as a lake was outspread beneath us; here and there the Platte, divided into a dozen thread-like sluices, was traversing it, and an occasional clump of wood, rising in the midst like a shadowy island, relieved the monotony of the waste. No living thing was moving throughout the vast landscape, except the lizards that darted over the sand and through the rank grass and prickly pears at our feet.

We had passed the more tedious part of the journey; but four hundred miles still intervened between us and Fort Laramie; and to reach that point cost us the travel of three more weeks. During the whole of this time we were passing up the middle of a long, narrow, sandy plain, reaching like an outstretched belt nearly to the Rocky Mountains. Two lines of sand-hills, broken often into the wildest and most fantastic forms, flanked the valley at the distance of a mile or two on the right and left; while beyond them lay a barren, trackless waste, extending for hundreds of miles to the Arkansas on the one side, and the Missouri on the other. Before and behind us, the level monotony of the plain was unbroken as far as the eye could reach. Sometimes it glared in the sun, an expanse of hot, bare sand; sometimes it was veiled by long coarse grass. Skulls and whitening bones of buffalo were scattered everywhere; the ground was tracked by myriads of them, and often covered with the circular indentations where the bulls had wallowed in the hot weather. From every gorge and ravine, opening from the hills, descended deep, well-worn paths, where the buffalo issue twice a day in regular procession to drink in the Platte. The river itself runs through the midst, a thin sheet of rapid, turbid water, half a mile wide, and scarcely two feet deep. Its low banks, for the most part without a bush or a tree, are of loose sand, with which the stream is so charged that it grates on the teeth in drinking. The naked landscape is, of itself, dreary and monotonous enough; and yet the wild beasts and wild men that frequent the valley of the Platte make it a scene of interest and excitement to the traveller. Of those who have journeyed there, scarcely one, perhaps, fails to look back with fond regret to his horse and his rifle.

Early in the morning after we reached the Platte, a long procession of squalid savages approached our camp. Each was on foot, leading his horse by a rope of bull-hide. His attire consisted merely of a scanty cincture, and an old buffalo robe, tattered and begrimed by use, which hung over his shoulders. His head was close shaven, except a ridge of hair reaching over the crown from the middle of the forehead, very much like the long bristles on the back of a hyena, and he carried his bow and arrows in his hand, while his meagre little horse was laden with dried buffalo meat, the produce of his hunting. Such were the first specimens that we met—and very indifferent ones they were—of the genuine savages of the prairie.

They were the Pawnees whom Kearsley had encountered the day before, and belonged to a large hunting party, known to be ranging the prairie in the vicinity. They strode rapidly by, within a furlong of our tents, not pausing or looking towards us, after the manner of Indians when meditating mischief, or conscious of ill desert. I went out to meet them, and had an amicable conference with the chief, presenting him with half a pound of tobacco, at which unmerited bounty he expressed much gratification. These fellows, or some of their companions, had committed a dastardly outrage upon an emigrant party in advance of us. Two men, at a distance from the rest, were seized by them, but, lashing their horses, they broke away and fled. At this the Pawnees raised the yell and shot at them, transfixing the hindmost through the back with several arrows, while his companion galloped away and brought in the news to his party. The panic-stricken emigrants remained for several days in camp, not daring even to send out in quest of the dead body.

Our New-England climate is mild and equable compared with that of the Platte. This very morning, for instance, was close and sultry, the sun rising with a faint oppressive heat; when suddenly darkness gathered in the west, and a furious blast of sleet and hail drove full in our faces, icy cold, and urged with such demoniac vehemence that it felt like a storm of needles. It was curious to see the horses; they faced about in extreme displeasure, holding their tails like whipped dogs, and shivering as the angry gusts, howling louder than a concert of wolves, swept over us. Wright's long train of mules came sweeping round before the storm, like a flight of snow-birds driven by a winter tempest. Thus we all remained stationary for some minutes, crouching close to our horses' necks, much too surly to speak, though once the Captain looked up from between the collars of his coat, his face blood-red, and the muscles of his mouth contracted by the cold into a most ludicrous grin of agony. He grumbled something that sounded like a curse, directed, as we believed, against the unhappy hour when he had first thought of leaving home. The thing was too good to last long; and the instant the puffs of wind subsided we pitched our tents, and remained in camp for the rest of a gloomy and lowering day. The emigrants also encamped near at hand. We being first on the ground, had appropriated all the wood within reach; so that our fire alone blazed cheerily. Around it soon gathered a group of uncouth figures, shivering in the drizzling rain. Conspicuous among them were two or three of the half-savage men who spend their reckless lives in trapping among the Rocky Mountains, or in trading for the Fur Company in the Indian villages. They were all of Canadian extraction; their hard, weather-beaten faces and bushy moustaches looked out from beneath the hoods of their white capotes with a bad and brutish expression, as if their owners might be the willing agents of any villany. And such in fact is the character of many of these men.

On the day following we overtook Kearsley's wagons, and thenceforward, for a week or two, we were fellow-travellers. One good effect, at least, resulted from the alliance; it materially diminished the fatigues of standing guard; for the party being now more numerous, there were longer intervals between each man's turns of duty.

SCENES AT FORT LARAMIE

Looking back, after the expiration of a year, upon Fort Laramie and its inmates, they seem less like a reality than like some fanciful picture of the olden time; so different was the scene from any which this tamer side of the world can present. Tall Indians, enveloped in their white buffalo-robes, were striding across the area or reclining at full length on the low roofs of the buildings which enclosed it. Numerous squaws, gayly bedizened, sat grouped in front of the rooms they occupied; their mongrel offspring, restless and vociferous, rambled in every direction through the fort; and the trappers, traders, and *engagés* of the establishment were busy at their labor or their amusements.

We were met at the gate, but by no means cordially welcomed. Indeed, we seemed objects of some distrust and suspicion, until Henry Chatillon explained that we were not traders, and we, in confirmation, handed to the *bourgeois* a letter of introduction from his principals. He took it, turned it upside down, and tried hard to read it; but his literary attainments not being adequate to the task, he applied for relief to the clerk, a sleek, smiling Frenchman, named Monthalon. The letter read, Bordeaux (the *bourgeois*) seemed gradually to awaken to a sense of what was expected of him. Though not deficient in hospitable intentions, he was wholly unaccustomed to act as master of ceremonies. Discarding all formalities of reception, he did not honor us with a single word, but walked swiftly across the area, while we followed in some admiration to a railing and a flight of steps opposite the entrance. He signed to us that we had better fasten our horses to the railing; then he walked up the steps, tramped along a rude balcony, and, kicking open a door, displayed a large room, rather more elaborately furnished than a barn. For furniture it had a rough bedstead, but no bed; two chairs, a chest of drawers, a tin pail to hold water, and a board to cut tobacco upon. A brass crucifix hung on the wall, and close at hand a recent scalp, with hair full a yard long, was suspended from a nail. I shall again have occasion to mention this dismal trophy, its history being connected with that of our subsequent proceedings.

This apartment, the best in Fort Laramie, was that usually occupied by the legitimate *bourgeois*, Papin, in whose absence the command devolved upon Bordeaux. The latter, a stout, bluff little fellow, much inflated by a sense of his new authority, began to roar for buffalo-robes. These being brought and spread upon the floor, formed our beds; much better ones than we had of late been accustomed to. Our arrangements made, we stepped out to the balcony to take a more leisurely survey of the long-looked-for haven at which we had arrived at last. Beneath us was the square area surrounded by little rooms, or rather cells, which opened upon it. These were devoted to various purposes, but served chiefly for the accommodation of the men employed at the fort, or of the equally numerous squaws whom they were allowed to maintain in it. Opposite to us rose the blockhouse above the gateway; it was adorned with the figure of a horse at full speed, daubed upon the boards with red paint, and exhibiting a degree of skill which might rival that displayed by the Indians in executing similar designs upon their robes and lodges. A busy scene was enacting in the area. The wagons of Vaskiss, an old trader, were about to set out for a remote post in the mountains, and the Canadians were going through their preparations with all possible bustle, while here and there an Indian stood looking on with imperturbable gravity.

Fort Laramie is one of the posts established by the "American Fur Company," which well-nigh monopolizes the Indian trade of this region. Here its officials rule with an absolute sway; the arm of the United States has little force; for when we were there, the extreme outposts of her troops were about seven hundred miles to the eastward. The little fort is built of bricks dried in the sun, and externally is of an oblong form, with bastions of clay, in the form of ordinary blockhouses, at two of the corners. The walls are about fifteen feet high, and surmounted by a slender palisade. The roofs of the apartments within, which are built close against the walls, serve the purpose of a banquette. Within, the fort is divided by a partition: on one side is the square area, surrounded by the store-rooms, offices, and apartments of the inmates; on the other is the *corral*, a narrow place, encompassed by the high clay walls, where at night, or in presence of dangerous Indians, the horses and mules of the fort are crowded for safe keeping The main entrance has two gates, with an arched passage intervening. A little square window, high above the ground, opens laterally from an adjoining chamber into this passage; so that when the inner gate is closed and barred, a person without may still hold communication with those within, through this narrow aperture. This obviates the necessity of admitting suspicious Indians, for purposes of trading, into the body of the fort; for when danger is apprehended, the inner gate is shut fast, and all traffic is carried on by means of the window. This precaution, though necessary at some of the Company's posts, is seldom resorted to at Fort Laramie; where, though men are frequently killed in the neighborhood, no apprehensions are felt of any general designs of hostility from the Indians.

We did not long enjoy our new quarters undisturbed. The door was silently pushed open, and two eyeballs and a visage as black as night looked in upon us; then a red arm and shoulder intruded themselves, and a tall Indian, gliding in, shook us by the hand, grunted his salutation, and sat down on the floor. Others followed, with faces of the natural hue, and letting fall their heavy robes from their shoulders, took their seats, quite at ease, in a semi-circle before us. The pipe was now to be lighted and passed from one to another; and this was the only entertainment that at present they expected from us. These visitors were fathers, brothers, or other relatives of the squaws in the fort, where they were permitted to remain, loitering about in perfect idleness. All those who smoked with us were men of standing and repute. Two or three others dropped in also; young fellows who neither by their years nor their exploits were entitled to rank with the old men and warriors, and who, abashed in the presence of their superiors, stood aloof, never withdrawing their eyes from us. Their cheeks were adorned with vermilion, their ears with pendants of shell, and their necks with beads. Never yet having signalized themselves as hunters, or performed the honorable exploit of killing a man, they were held in slight esteem, and were diffident and bashful in proportion. Certain formidable inconveniences attended this influx of visitors. They were bent on inspecting every thing in the room; our equipments and our dress alike underwent their scrutiny; for though the contrary has been asserted, few beings have more curiosity than Indians in regard to subjects within their ordinary range of thought. As to other matters, indeed, they seem utterly indifferent. They will not trouble themselves to inquire into what they cannot comprehend, but are quite contented to place their hands over their mouths in token of wonder, and exclaim that it is "great medicine." With this comprehensive solution, an Indian never is at a loss. He never launches into speculation and conjecture; his reason moves in its beaten track. His soul is dormant; and no exertions of the missionaries, Jesuit or Puritan, of the old world or of the new, have as yet availed to arouse it.

As we were looking, at sunset, from the wall, upon the desolate plains that surround the fort, we observed a cluster of strange objects, like scaffolds, rising in the distance against the red western sky. They bore aloft some singular-looking burdens; and at their foot glimmered something white, like bones. This was the place of sepulture of some Dahcotah chiefs, whose remains their people are fond of placing in the vicinity of the fort, in the hope that they may thus be protected from violation at the hands of their enemies. Yet it has happened more than once, and quite recently, that war-parties of the Crow Indians, ranging through the country, have thrown the bodies from the scaffolds, and broken them to pieces, amid the yells of the Dahcotah, who remained pent up in the fort, too few to defend the honored relics from insult. The white objects upon the ground were buffalo skulls, arranged in the mystic circle commonly seen at Indian places of sepulture upon the prairie.

We soon discovered, in the twilight, a band of fifty or sixty horses approaching the fort. These were the animals belonging to the establishment; who, having been sent out to feed, under the care of armed guards, in the meadows below, were now being driven into the *corral* for the night. A gate opened into this enclosure: by the side of it stood one of the guards, an old Canadian, with gray bushy eyebrows, and a dragoon-pistol stuck into his belt; while his comrade, mounted on horseback, his rifle laid across the saddle in front, and his long hair blowing before his swarthy face, rode at the rear of the disorderly troop, urging them up the ascent. In a moment the narrow *corral* was thronged with the half-wild horses, kicking, biting, and crowding restlessly together.

The discordant jingling of a bell, rung by a Canadian in the area, summoned us to supper. The repast was served on a rough table in one of the lower apartments of the fort, and consisted of cakes of bread and dried buffalo-meat,—an excellent thing for strengthening the teeth. At this meal were seated the *bourgeois* and superior dignitaries of the establishment, among whom Henry Chatillon was worthily included. No sooner was it finished, than the table was spread a second time (the luxury of bread being now, however, omitted), for the benefit of certain hunters and trappers of an inferior standing; while the ordinary Canadian *engagés* were regaled on dried meat in one of their lodging-rooms. By way of illustrating the domestic economy of Fort Laramie, it may not be amiss to introduce in this place a story current among the men when we were there.

There was an old man named Pierre, whose duty it was to bring the meat from the store-room for the men. Old Pierre, in the kindness of his heart, used to select the fattest and the best pieces for his companions. This did not long escape the keen-eyed *bourgeois*, who was greatly disturbed at such improvidence, and cast about for some means to stop it. At last he hit on a plan that exactly suited him. At the side of the meat-room, and separated from it by a clay partition, was another apartment, used for the storage of furs. It had no communication with the fort, except through a square hole in the partition; and of course it was perfectly dark. One evening the *bourgeois*, watching for a moment when no one observed him, dodged into the meat-room, clambered through the hole, and ensconced himself among the furs and buffalo-robes. Soon after, old Pierre came in with his lantern, and, muttering to himself, began to pull over the bales of meat, and select the best pieces, as usual. But suddenly a hollow and sepulchral voice proceeded from the inner room: "Pierre, Pierre! Let that fat meat alone. Take nothing but lean." Pierre dropped his lantern, and bolted out into the fort, screaming, in an agony of terror, that the devil was in the store-room; but tripping on the threshold, he pitched over upon the gravel, and lay senseless, stunned by the fall. The Canadians ran out to the rescue. Some lifted the unlucky Pierre; and others, making an extempore crucifix of two sticks, were proceeding to attack the devil in his stronghold, when the *bourgeois*, with a crestfallen countenance, appeared at the door. To add to his mortification, he was obliged to explain the whole stratagem to Pierre, in order to bring him to his senses.

We were sitting, on the following morning, in the passage-way between the gates, conversing with the traders Vaskiss and May. These two men, together with our sleek friend, the clerk Monthalon, were, I believe, the only persons then in the fort who could read and write. May was telling a curious story about the traveller Catlin, when an ugly, diminutive Indian, wretchedly mounted, came up at a gallop, and rode by us into the fort. On being questioned, he said that Smoke's village was close at hand. Accordingly only a few minutes elapsed before the hills beyond the river were covered with a disorderly swarm of savages, on horseback and on foot. May finished his story; and by that time the whole array had descended to Laramie Creek, and begun to cross it in a mass. I walked down to the bank. The stream is wide, and was then between three and four feet deep, with a very swift current. For several rods the water was alive with dogs, horses, and Indians. The long poles used in pitching the lodges are carried by the horses, fastened by the heavier end, two or three on each side, to a rude sort of pack-saddle, while the other end drags on the ground. About a foot behind the horse, a kind of large basket or pannier is suspended between the poles, and firmly lashed in its place. On the back of the horse are piled various articles of luggage; the basket also is well filled with domestic utensils, or, quite as often, with a litter of puppies, a brood of small children, or a superannuated old man. Numbers of these curious vehicles, *traineaux*, or, as the Canadians called them, *travaux*, were now splashing together through the stream. Among them swam countless dogs, often burdened with miniature *traineaux*; and dashing forward on horseback through the throng came the warriors, the slender figure of some lynx-eyed boy clinging fast behind them. The women sat perched on the pack-saddles, adding not a little to the load of the already overburdened horses. The confusion was prodigious. The dogs yelled and howled in chorus; the puppies in the *traineaux* set up a dismal whine as the water invaded their comfortable retreat; the little black-eyed children, from one year of age upward, clung fast with both hands to the edge of their basket, and looked over in alarm at the water rushing so near them, sputtering and making wry mouths as it splashed against their faces. Some of the dogs, encumbered by their load, were carried down by the current, yelping piteously; and the old squaws would rush into the water, seize their favorites by the neck, and drag them out. As each horse gained the bank, he scrambled up as he could. Stray horses and colts came among the rest, often breaking away at full speed through the crowd, followed by the old hags, screaming after their fashion on all occasions of excitement. Buxom young squaws, blooming in all the charms of vermilion, stood here and there on the bank, holding aloft their master's lance, as a signal to collect the scattered portions of his household. In a few moments the crowd melted away; each family, with its horses and equipage, filing off to the plain at the rear of the fort; and here, in the space of half an hour, arose sixty or seventy of their tapering lodges. Their horses were feeding by hundreds over the surrounding prairie, and their dogs were roaming everywhere. The fort was full of warriors, and the children were whooping and yelling incessantly under the walls.

These new-comers were scarcely arrived, when Bordeaux ran across the fort, shouting to his squaw to bring him his spyglass. The obedient Marie, the very model of a squaw, produced the instrument, and Bordeaux hurried with it to the wall. Pointing it eastward, he exclaimed, with an oath, that the families were coming. But a few moments elapsed before the heavy caravan of the emigrant wagons could be seen, steadily advancing from the hills. They gained the river, and, without turning or pausing, plunged in, passed through, and slowly ascending the opposing bank, kept directly on their way by the fort and the Indian village, until, gaining a spot a quarter of a mile distant, they wheeled into a circle. For some time our tranquillity was undisturbed. The emigrants were preparing their encampment; but no sooner was this accomplished, than Fort Laramie was taken by storm. A crowd of broad-brimmed hats, thin visages, and staring eyes, appeared suddenly at the gate. Tall, awkward men, in brown homespun; women, with cadaverous faces and long lank figures, came thronging in together, and, as if inspired by the very demon of curiosity, ransacked every nook and corner of the fort. Dismayed at this invasion, we withdrew in all speed to our chamber, vainly hoping that it might prove a sanctuary. The emigrants prosecuted their investigations with untiring vigor. They penetrated the rooms, or rather dens, inhabited by the astonished squaws. Resolved to search every mystery to the bottom, they explored the apartments of the men, and even that of Marie and the *bourgeois*. At last a numerous deputation appeared at our door, but found no encouragement to remain.

Having at length satisfied their curiosity, they next proceeded to business. The men occupied themselves in procuring supplies for their onward journey; either buying them, or giving in exchange superfluous articles of their own.

The emigrants felt a violent prejudice against the French Indians, as they called the trappers and traders. They thought, and with some reason, that these men bore them no good-will. Many of them were firmly persuaded that the French were instigating the Indians to attack and cut them off. On visiting the encampment we were at once struck with the extraordinary perplexity and indecision that prevailed among them. They seemed like men totally out of their element; bewildered and amazed, like a troop of schoolboys lost in the woods. It was impossible to be long among them without being conscious of the bold spirit with which most of them were animated. But the *forest* is the home of the backwoodsman. On the remote prairie he is totally at a loss. He differs as much from the genuine "mountain-man" as a Canadian *voyageur*, paddling his canoe on the rapids of the Ottawa, differs from an American sailor among the storms of Cape Horn. Still my companion and I were somewhat at a loss to account for this perturbed state of mind. It could not be cowardice: these men were of the same stock with the volunteers of Monterey and Buena Vista. Yet, for the most part, they were the rudest and most ignorant of the frontier population; they knew absolutely nothing of the country and its inhabitants; they had already experienced much misfortune, and apprehended more; they had seen nothing of mankind, and had never put their own resources to the test.

A full share of suspicion fell upon us. Being strangers, we were looked upon as enemies. Having occasion for a supply of lead and a few other necessary articles, we used to go over to the emigrant camps to obtain them. After some hesitation, some dubious glances, and fumbling of the hands in the pockets, the terms would be agreed upon, the price tendered, and the emigrant would go off to bring the article in question. After waiting until our patience gave out, we would go in search of him, and find him seated on the tongue of his wagon.

"Well, stranger," he would observe, as he saw us approach, "I reckon I won't trade."

Some friend of his had followed him from the scene of the bargain, and whispered in his ear that clearly we meant to cheat him, and he had better have nothing to do with us.

This timorous mood of the emigrants was doubly unfortunate, as it exposed them to real danger. Assume, in the presence of Indians, a bold bearing, self-confident yet vigilant, and you will find them tolerably safe neighbors. But your safety depends on the respect and fear you are able to inspire. If you betray timidity or indecision, you convert them from that moment into insidious and dangerous enemies. The Dahcotah saw clearly enough the perturbation of the emigrants, and instantly availed themselves of it. They became extremely insolent and exacting in their demands. It has become an established custom with them to go to the camp of every party, as it arrives in succession at the fort, and demand a feast. Smoke's village had come with this express design, having made several days' journey with no other object than that of enjoying a cup of coffee and two or three biscuit. So the "feast" was demanded, and the emigrants dared not refuse it.

One evening, about sunset, the village was deserted. We met old men, warriors, squaws, and children in gay attire, trooping off to the encampment, with faces of anticipation; and, arriving here, they seated themselves in a semicircle. Smoke occupied the centre, with his warriors on either hand;

the young men and boys came next, and the squaws and children formed the horns of the crescent. The biscuit and coffee
were promptly despatched, the emigrants staring open-mouthed
at their savage guests. With each emigrant party that arrived
at Fort Laramie this scene was renewed; and every day the
Indians grew more rapacious and presumptuous. One evening
they broke in pieces, out of mere wantonness, the cups from
which they had been feasted; and this so exasperated the emigrants that many of them seized their rifles and could scarcely
be restrained from firing on the insolent mob of Indians. Before
we left the country this dangerous spirit on the part of the
Dahcotah had mounted to a yet higher pitch. They began openly to threaten the emigrants with destruction, and actually fired
upon one or two parties of them. A military force and military
law are urgently called for in that perilous region; and unless
troops are speedily stationed at Fort Laramie, or elsewhere in
the neighborhood, both emigrants and other travellers will be
exposed to most imminent risks.

The Ogillallah, the Brulé, and the other western bands of the
Dahcotah or Sioux, are thorough savages, unchanged by any
contact with civilization. Not one of them can speak a European tongue, or has ever visited an American settlement. Until
within a year or two, when the emigrants began to pass through
their country on the way to Oregon, they had seen no whites,
except the few employed about the Fur Company's posts. They
thought them a wise people, inferior only to themselves, living
in leather lodges, like their own, and subsisting on buffalo. But
when the swarm of *Meneaska*, with their oxen and wagons,
began to invade them, their astonishment was unbounded.
They could scarcely believe that the earth contained such a
multitude of white men. Their wonder is now giving way to
indignation; and the result, unless vigilantly guarded against,
may be lamentable in the extreme.

But to glance at the interior of a lodge. Shaw and I used
often to visit them. Indeed we spent most of our evenings in
the Indian village, Shaw's assumption of the medical character
giving us a fair pretext. As a sample of the rest I will describe

one of these visits. The sun had just set, and the horses were driven into the *corral*. The Prairie Cock, a noted beau, came in at the gate with a bevy of young girls, with whom he began a dance in the area, leading them round and round in a circle, while he jerked up from his chest a succession of monotonous sounds, to which they kept time in a rueful chant. Outside the gate boys and young men were idly frolicking; and close by, looking grimly upon them, stood a warrior in his robe, with his face painted jet-black, in token that he had lately taken a Pawnee scalp. Passing these, the tall dark lodges rose between us and the red western sky. We repaired at once to the lodge of Old Smoke himself. It was by no means better than the others; indeed, it was rather shabby; for in this democratic community the chief never assumes superior state. Smoke sat cross-legged on a buffalo-robe, and his grunt of salutation as we entered was unusually cordial, out of respect no doubt to Shaw's medical character. Seated around the lodge were several squaws, and an abundance of children. The complaint of Shaw's patients was, for the most part, a severe inflammation of the eyes, occasioned by exposure to the sun, a species of disorder which he treated with some success. He had brought with him a homœopathic medicine-chest, and was, I presume, the first who introduced that harmless system of treatment among the Ogillallah. No sooner had a robe been spread at the head of the lodge for our accommodation, and we had seated ourselves upon it, than a patient made her appearance: the chief's daughter herself, who, to do her justice, was the best-looking girl in the village. Being on excellent terms with the physician, she placed herself readily under his hands, and submitted with a good grace to his applications, laughing in his face during the whole process, for a squaw hardly knows how to smile. This case despatched, another of a different kind succeeded. A hideous, emaciated old woman sat in the darkest corner of the lodge, rocking to and fro with pain, and hiding her eyes from the light by pressing the palms of both hands against her face. At Smoke's command she came forward, very unwillingly, and exhibited a pair of eyes that had nearly disappeared from excess of inflammation. No sooner had the doctor fastened his grip upon her, than she set up a dismal moaning, and writhed so in his grasp that he lost all patience; but being resolved to carry his point, he succeeded at last in applying his favorite remedies.

"It is strange," he said, when the operation was finished, "that I forgot to bring any Spanish flies with me; we must have something here to answer for a counter-irritant."

So, in the absence of better, he seized upon a red-hot brand from the fire, and clapped it against the temple of the old squaw, who set up an unearthly howl, at which the rest of the family broke into a laugh.

During these medical operations Smoke's eldest squaw entered the lodge, with a mallet in her hand, the stone head of which, precisely like those sometimes ploughed up in the fields of New England, was made fast to the handle by a covering of raw hide. I had observed some time before a litter of well-grown black puppies, comfortably nestled among some buffalo-robes at one side; but this new-comer speedily disturbed their enjoyment; for seizing one of them by the hind paw, she dragged him out, and carrying him to the entrance of the lodge, hammered him on the head till she killed him. Conscious to what this preparation tended, I looked through a hole in the back of the lodge to see the next steps of the process. The squaw, holding the puppy by the legs, was swinging him to and fro through the blaze of a fire, until the hair was singed off. This done, she unsheathed her knife and cut him into small pieces, which she dropped into a kettle to boil. In a few moments a large wooden dish was set before us, filled with this delicate preparation. A dog-feast is the greatest compliment a Dahcotah can offer to his guest; and, knowing that to refuse eating would be an affront, we attacked the little dog, and devoured him before the eyes of his unconscious parent. Smoke in the mean time was preparing his great pipe. It was lighted when we had finished our repast, and we passed it from one to another till the bowl was empty. This done, we took our leave without farther ceremony, knocked at the gate of the fort, and, after making ourselves known, were admitted.

[SCENES AT AN INDIAN CAMP]

Reynal heard guns fired one day, at the distance of a mile or two from the camp. He grew nervous instantly. Visions of Crow war-parties began to haunt his imagination; and when we returned (for we were all absent), he renewed his complaints about being left alone with the Canadians and the squaw. The day after, the cause of the alarm appeared. Four trappers, called Morin, Saraphin, Rouleau, and Gingras, came to our camp and joined us. They it was who fired the guns and disturbed the dreams of our confederate Reynal. They soon encamped by our side. Their rifles, dingy and battered with hard service, rested with ours against the old tree; their strong rude saddles, their buffalo-robes, their traps, and the few rough and simple articles of their travelling equipment were piled near our tent. Their mountain-horses were turned to graze in the meadow among our own; and the men themselves, no less rough and hardy, used to lie half the day in the shade of our tree, lolling on the grass, lazily smoking, and telling stories of their adventures; and I defy the annals of chivalry to furnish the record of a life more wild and perilous than that of a Rocky Mountain trapper.

With this efficient reinforcement the agitation of Reynal's nerves subsided. We began to conceive a sort of attachment to our old camping ground; yet it was time to change our quarters, since remaining too long on one spot must lead to unpleasant results, not to be borne unless in case of dire necessity. The grass no longer presented a smooth surface of turf; it was trampled into mud and clay. So we removed to another old tree, larger yet, that grew by the side of the river a furlong distant. Its trunk was full six feet in diameter; on one side it was marked by a party of Indians with various inexplicable hieroglyphics, commemorating some warlike enterprise, and aloft among the branches were the remains of a scaffold, where dead bodies had once been deposited, after the Indian manner.

"There comes Bull-Bear," said Henry Chatillon, as we sat on the grass at dinner. Looking up, we saw several horsemen coming over the neighboring hill, and in a moment four stately young men rode up and dismounted. One of them was Bull-Bear, or Mahto-Tatonka, a compound name which he inherited from his father, the principal chief in the Ogillallah band. One of his brothers and two other young men accompanied him. We shook hands with the visitors, and when we had finished our meal—for this is the approved manner of entertaining Indians, even the best of them—we handed to each a tin cup of coffee and a biscuit, at which they ejaculated from the bottom of their throats, "How! how!" a monosyllable by which an Indian contrives to express half the emotions of which he is susceptible. Then we lighted the pipe, and passed it to them as they squatted on the ground.

"Where is the village?"

"There," said Mahto-Tatonka, pointing southward; "it will come in two days."

"Will they go to the war?"

"Yes."

No man is a philanthropist on the prairie. We welcomed this news cordially, and congratulated ourselves that Bordeaux's interested efforts to divert The Whirlwind from his congenial vocation of bloodshed had failed of success, and that no further obstacles would interpose between us and our plan of repairing to the rendezvous at La Bonté's camp.

For that and several succeeding days, Mahto-Tatonka and his friends remained our guests. They devoured the relics of our meals; they filled the pipe for us, and also helped us to smoke it. Sometimes they stretched themselves side by side in the shade, indulging in raillery and equivocal jokes, ill becoming the dignity of brave and aspiring warriors, such as two of them in reality were.

Two days dragged away, and on the morning of the third we hoped confidently to see the Indian village. It did not come; so we rode out to look for it. In place of the eight hundred Indians we expected, we met one solitary savage riding towards us over the prairie, who told us that the Indians had changed their plan, and would not come within three days. Taking along with us this messenger of evil tidings, we retraced our footsteps to the camp, amusing ourselves by the way with execrating Indian inconstancy. When we came in sight of our little white tent under the big tree, we saw that it no longer stood alone. A huge old lodge was erected by its side, discolored by rain and storms, rotten with age, with the uncouth figures of horses and men and out-stretched hands that were painted upon it, well nigh obliterated. The long poles which supported this squalid habitation thrust themselves rakishly out from its pointed top, and over its entrance were suspended a "medicine-pipe" and various other implements of the magic art. While we were yet at a distance, we observed a greatly increased population of various colors and dimensions, swarming about our quiet encampment. Morin, the trapper, having been absent for a day or two, had returned, it seemed, bringing all his family with him. He had taken to himself a wife, for whom he had paid the established price of one horse. This looks cheap at first sight, but in truth the purchase of a squaw is a transaction which no man should enter into without mature deliberation, since it involves not only the payment of the price, but the burden of feeding and supporting a rapacious horde of the bride's relatives, who hold themselves entitled to feed upon the indiscreet white man. They gather about him like leeches, and drain him of all he has.

Morin had not made an aristocratic match. His bride's relatives occupied but a contemptible position in Ogillallah society; for among these democrats of the prairie, as among others more civilized, there are virtual distinctions of rank and place. Morin's partner was not the most beautiful of her sex, and he had the bad taste to array her in an old calico gown, bought from an emigrant woman, instead of the neat tunic of whitened deer-skin usually worn by the squaws. The moving spirit of the establishment was an old hag of eighty. Human imagination never conceived hobgoblin or witch more ugly than she. You could count all her ribs through the wrinkles of her leathery skin. Her withered face more resembled an old skull than the countenance of a living being, even to the hollow, darkened sockets, at the bottom of which glittered her little black eyes.

Her arms had dwindled into nothing but whip-cord and wire. Her hair, half black, half gray, hung in total neglect nearly to the ground, and her sole garment consisted of the remnant of a discarded buffalo-robe tied round her waist with a string of hide. Yet the old squaw's meagre anatomy was wonderfully strong. She pitched the lodge, packed the horses, and did the hardest labor of the camp. From morning till night she bustled about the lodge, screaming like a screech-owl when any thing displeased her. Her brother, a "medicine-man," or magician, was equally gaunt and sinewy with herself. His mouth spread from ear to ear, and his appetite, as we had occasion to learn, was ravenous in proportion. The other inmates of the lodge were a young bride and bridegroom, the latter one of those idle, good-for-nothing fellows who infest an Indian village as well as more civilized communities. He was fit neither for hunting nor war, as one might see from the stolid unmeaning expression of his face. The happy pair had just entered upon the honeymoon. They would stretch a buffalo-robe upon poles, to protect them from the rays of the sun, and spreading under it a couch of furs, would sit affectionately side by side for half the day, though I could not discover that much conversation passed between them. Probably they had nothing to say; for an Indian's supply of topics for conversation is far from being copious. There were half a dozen children, too, playing and whooping about the camp, shooting birds with little bows and arrows, or making miniature lodges of sticks, as children of a different complexion build houses of blocks.

A day passed, and Indians began rapidly to come in. Parties of two, three, or more would ride up and silently seat themselves on the grass. The fourth day came at last, when about noon horsemen appeared in view on the summit of the neighboring ridge. Behind followed a wild procession, hurrying in haste and disorder down the hill and over the plain below; horses, mules, and dogs; heavily-burdened *traineaux*, mounted warriors, squaws walking amid the throng, and a host of children. For a full half-hour they continued to pour down; and keeping directly to the bend of the stream, within a furlong of us, they soon assembled there, a dark and confused throng, until, as if by magic, a hundred and fifty tall lodges sprang up. The lonely plain was transformed into the site of a swarming encampment. Countless horses were soon grazing over the meadows around us, and the prairie was animated by restless figures careering on horseback, or sedately stalking in their long white robes. The Whirlwind was come at last. One question yet remained to be answered: "Will he go to the war in order that we, with so respectable an escort, may pass over to the somewhat perilous rendezvous at La Bonté's camp?"

This still remained in doubt. Characteristic indecision perplexed their councils. Indians cannot act in large bodies. Though their object be of the highest importance, they cannot combine to attain it by a series of connected efforts. King Philip, Pontiac, and Tecumseh, all felt this to their cost. The Ogillallah once had a war-chief who could control them; but he was dead, and now they were left to the sway of their own unsteady impulses.

As this Indian village and its inhabitants will hold a prominent place in the rest of the story, perhaps it may not be amiss to glance for an instant at the savage people of which they form a part. The Dahcotah or Sioux range over a vast territory, from the river St. Peter to the Rocky Mountains. They are divided into several independent bands, united under no central government, and acknowledging no common head. The same language, usages, and superstitions form the sole bond between them. They do not unite even in their wars. The bands of the east fight the Ojibwas on the Upper Lakes; those of the west make incessant war upon the Snake Indians in the Rocky Mountains. As the whole people is divided into bands, so each band is divided into villages. Each village has a chief, who is honored and obeyed only so far as his personal qualities may command respect and fear. Sometimes he is a mere nominal chief; sometimes his authority is little short of absolute, and his fame and influence reach beyond his own village, so that the whole band to which he belongs is ready to acknowledge him as their head. This was, a few years since, the case with the Ogillallah. Courage, address, and enterprise may raise any warrior to the highest honor, especially if he be the son of a former chief, or a member of a numerous family, to support him and avenge his quarrels; but when he has reached the dignity of chief, and the old men and warriors, by a peculiar ceremony, have formally installed him, let it not be imagined that he assumes any of the outward signs of rank and honor. He knows too well on how frail a tenure he holds his station. He must conciliate his uncertain subjects. Many a man in the village lives better, owns more squaws and more horses, and goes better clad than he. Like the Teutonic chiefs of old, he ingratiates himself with his young men by making them presents, thereby often impoverishing himself. If he fails to gain their favor, they will set his authority at naught, and may desert him at any moment; for the usages of his people have provided no means of enforcing his authority. Very seldom does it happen, at least among these western bands, that a chief attains to much power, unless he is the head of a numerous family. Frequently the village is principally made up of his relatives and descendants, and the wandering community assumes much of the patriarchal character.

The western Dahcotah have no fixed habitations. Hunting and fighting, they wander incessantly, through summer and winter. Some follow the herds of buffalo over the waste of prairie; others traverse the Black Hills, thronging, on horse-back and on foot, through the dark gulfs and sombre gorges, and emerging at last upon the "Parks," those beautiful but most perilous hunting-grounds. The buffalo supplies them with the necessaries of life; with habitations, food, clothing, beds, and fuel; strings for their bows, glue, thread, cordage, trail-ropes for their horses, coverings for their saddles, vessels to hold wa-ter, boats to cross streams, and the means of purchasing all that they want from the traders. When the buffalo are extinct, they too must dwindle away.

War is the breath of their nostrils. Against most of the neighboring tribes they cherish a rancorous hatred, transmitted from father to son, and inflamed by constant aggression and retaliation. Many times a year, in every village, the Great Spirit is called upon, fasts are made, the war-parade is celebrated, and the warriors go out by handfuls at a time against the enemy. This fierce spirit awakens their most eager aspirations, and calls forth their greatest energies. It is chiefly this that saves them from lethargy and utter abasement. Without its powerful stimulus they would be like the unwarlike tribes beyond the mountains, scattered among the caves and rocks like beasts, and living on roots and reptiles. These latter have little of humanity except the form; but the proud and ambitious Dahcotah warrior can sometimes boast heroic virtues. It is seldom that distinction and influence are attained among them by any other course than that of arms. Their superstition, however, sometimes gives great power to those among them who pretend to the character of magicians; and their orators, such as they are, have their share of honor.

But to return. Look into our tent, or enter, if you can bear the stifling smoke and the close air. There, wedged close together, you will see a circle of stout warriors, passing the pipe around, joking, telling stories, and making themselves merry after their fashion. We were also infested by little copper-colored naked boys and snake-eyed girls. They would come up to us, muttering certain words, which being interpreted conveyed the concise invitation, "Come and eat." Then we would rise, cursing the pertinacity of Dahcotah hospitality, which allowed scarcely an hour of rest between sun and sun, and to which we were bound to do honor, unless we would offend our entertainers. This necessity was particularly burdensome to me, as I was scarcely able to walk, from the effects of illness, and was poorly qualified to dispose of twenty meals a day. So bounteous an entertainment looks like an outgushing of good-will; but, doubtless, half at least of our kind hosts, had they met us alone and unarmed on the prairie, would have robbed us of our horses, and perhaps have bestowed an arrow upon us besides.

One morning we were summoned to the lodge of an old man, the Nestor of his tribe. We found him half sitting, half reclining, on a pile of buffalo-robes; his long hair, jet-black, though he had seen some eighty winters, hung on either side of his thin features. His gaunt but symmetrical frame did not more clearly exhibit the wreck of by-gone strength, than did his dark, wasted features, still prominent and commanding, bear the stamp of mental energies. Opposite the patriarch was his nephew, the young aspirant Mahto-Tatonka; and besides these, there were one or two women in the lodge.

The old man's story is peculiar, and illustrative of a superstition that prevails in full force among many of the Indian tribes. He was one of a powerful family, renowned for warlike exploits. When a very young man, he submitted to the singular rite to which most of the tribe subject themselves before entering upon life. He painted his face black; then seeking out a cavern in a sequestered part of the Black Hills, he lay for several days, fasting, and praying to the spirits. In the dreams and visions produced by his weakened and excited state, he fancied, like all Indians, that he saw supernatural revelations. Again and again the form of an antelope appeared before him. The antelope is the graceful peace spirit of the Ogillallah; but seldom is it that such a gentle visitor presents itself during the initiatory fasts of their young men. The terrible grizzly bear, the divinity of war, usually appears to fire them with martial ardor and thirst for renown. At length the antelope spoke. It told the young dreamer that he was not to follow the path of war; that a life of peace and tranquillity was marked out for him; that thenceforward he was to guide the people by his counsels, and protect them from the evils of their own feuds and dissensions. Others were to gain renown by fighting the enemy; but greatness of a different kind was in store for him.

The visions beheld during the period of this fast usually determine the whole course of the dreamer's life. From that time, Le Borgne, which was the only name by which we knew him, abandoned all thoughts of war, and devoted himself to the labors of peace. He told his vision to the people. They honored his commission and respected him in his novel capacity.

A far different man was his brother, Mahto-Tatonka, who had left his name, his features, and many of his qualities, to his son. He was the father of Henry Chatillon's squaw, a circumstance which proved of some advantage to us, as it secured the friendship of a family perhaps the most noted and influential in the whole Ogillallah band; Mahto-Tatonka, in his way, was a hero. No chief could vie with him in warlike renown, or in power over his people. He had a fearless spirit, and an impetuous and inflexible resolution. His will was law. He was politic and sagacious, and with true Indian craft, always befriended the whites, knowing that he might thus reap great advantages for himself and his adherents. When he had resolved on any course of conduct, he would pay to the warriors the compliment of calling them together to deliberate upon it, and when their debates were over, quietly state his own opinion, which no one ever disputed. It fared hard with those who incurred his displeasure. He would strike them or stab them on the spot; and this act, which if attempted by any other chief would have cost him his life, the awe inspired by his name enabled him to repeat again and again with impunity. In a community where, from immemorial time, no man has acknowledged any law but his own will, Mahto-Tatonka raised himself to power little short of despotic. His career came at last to an end. He had a host of enemies patiently biding their time; and our old friend Smoke in particular, together with all his kinsmen, hated him cordially. Smoke sat one day in his lodge, in the midst of his own village, when Mahto-Tatonka entered it alone, and approaching the dwelling of his enemy, challenged him in a loud voice to come out, and fight. Smoke would not move. At this, Mahto-Tatonka proclaimed him a coward and an old woman, and, striding to the entrance of the lodge, stabbed the chief's best horse, which was picketed there. Smoke was daunted, and even this insult failed to bring him out. Mahto-Tatonka moved haughtily away; all made way for him; but his hour of reckoning was near.

One hot day, five or six years ago, numerous lodges of Smoke's kinsmen were gathered about some of the Fur Company's men, who were trading in various articles with them, whiskey among the rest. Mahto-Tatonka was also there with a few of his people. As he lay in his own lodge, a fray arose between his adherents and the kinsmen of his enemy. The war-whoop was raised, bullets and arrows began to fly, and the camp was in confusion. The chief sprang up, and rushing in a fury from the lodge, shouted to the combatants on both sides to cease. Instantly—for the attack was preconcerted—came the reports of two or three guns, and the twanging of a dozen bows, and the savage hero, mortally wounded, pitched forward head-long to the ground. Rouleau was present, and told me the par-ticulars. The tumult became general, and was not quelled until several had fallen on both sides. When we were in the country the feud between the two families was still rankling.

Thus died Mahto-Tatonka; but he left behind him a goodly army of descendants, to perpetuate his renown and avenge his fate. Besides daughters, he had thirty sons, a number which need not stagger the credulity of those acquainted with Indian usages and practices. We saw many of them, all marked by the same dark complexion, and the same peculiar cast of features. Of these, our visitor, young Mahto-Tatonka, was the eldest, and some reported him as likely to succeed to his father's honors. Though he appeared not more than twenty-one years old, he had oftener struck the enemy, and stolen more horses and more squaws, than any young man in the village. Horse-stealing is well known as an avenue to distinction on the prairies, and the other kind of depredation is esteemed equally meritorious. Not that the act can confer fame from its own intrinsic merits. Any one can steal a squaw, and if he chooses afterwards to make an adequate present to her rightful proprietor, the easy husband for the most part rests content, his vengeance falls asleep, and all danger from that quarter is averted. Yet this is regarded as a pitiful and mean-spirited transaction. The danger is averted, but the glory of the achievement also is lost. Mahto-Tatonka proceeded after a more dashing fashion. Out of several dozen squaws whom he had stolen, he could boast that he had never paid for one, but snapping his fingers in the face of the injured husband, had defied the extremity of his indignation, and no one yet had dared to lay the finger of violence upon him. He was following close in the footsteps of his father. The young men and the young squaws, each in their way, admired him. The former would always follow him to war, and he was esteemed to have an unrivalled charm in the eyes of the latter. Perhaps his impunity may excite some wonder. An arrow-shot from a ravine, or a stab given in the dark, require no great valor, and are especially suited to the Indian genius; but Mahto-Tatonka had a strong protection. It was not alone his courage and audacious will that enabled him to career so dashingly among his compeers. His enemies did not forget that he was one of thirty warlike brethren, all growing up to manhood. Should they wreak their anger upon him, many keen eyes would be ever upon them, and many fierce hearts thirst for their blood. The avenger would dog their footsteps everywhere. To kill Mahto-Tatonka would be an act of suicide.

Though he found such favor in the eyes of the fair, he was no dandy. He was indifferent to the gaudy trappings and orna-ments of his companions, and was content to rest his chances of success upon his own warlike merits. He never arrayed himself in gaudy blanket and glittering necklaces, but left his statue-like form, limbed like an Apollo of bronze, to win its way to favor. His voice was singularly deep and strong, and sounded from his chest like the deep notes of an organ. Yet, after all, he was but an Indian. See him as he lies there in the sun before our tent, kicking his heels in the air and cracking jokes with his brother. Does he look like a hero? See him now in the hour of his glory, when at sunset the whole village empties itself to behold him, for to-morrow their favorite young partisan goes out against the enemy. His head-dress is adorned with a crest of the war-eagle's feathers, rising in a waving ridge above his brow, and sweeping far behind him. His round white shield hangs at his breast, with feathers radiating from the centre like a star. His quiver is at his back; his tall lance in his hand, the iron point flashing against the declining sun, while the long scalp-locks of his enemies flutter from the shaft. Thus, gor-geous as a champion in panoply, he rides round and round with-in the great circle of lodges, balancing with a graceful buoyancy to the free movements of his war-horse, while with a sedate

brow he sings his song to the Great Spirit. Young rival warriors look askance at him; vermilion-cheeked girls gaze in admiration; boys whoop and scream in a thrill of delight, and old
women yell forth his name and proclaim his praises from lodge
to lodge.

Mahto-Tatonka was the best of all our Indian friends. Hour
after hour, and day after day, when swarms of savages of every
age, sex, and degree beset our camp, he would lie in our tent, his
lynx-eye ever open to guard our property from pillage.

The Whirlwind invited us one day to his lodge. The feast
was finished and the pipe began to circulate. It was a remarkably large and fine one, and I expressed admiration of it.

"If the Meneaska likes the pipe," asked The Whirlwind,
"why does he not keep it?"

Such a pipe among the Ogillallah is valued at the price of a
horse. The gift seemed worthy of a chieftain and a warrior;
but The Whirlwind's generosity rose to no such pitch. He gave
me the pipe, confidently expecting that I in return would make
him a present of equal or superior value. This is the implied
condition of every gift among the Indians, and should it not
be complied with, the present is usually reclaimed. So I arranged
upon a gaudy calico handkerchief an assortment of vermilion,
tobacco, knives, and gunpowder, and summoning the chief to
camp, assured him of my friendship, and begged his acceptance
of a slight token of it. Ejaculating, "How! how!" he folded up
the offerings and withdrew to his lodge.

Late one afternoon a party of Indians on horseback came
suddenly in sight from behind some clumps of bushes that lined
the bank of the stream, leading with them a mule, on whose
back was a wretched negro, sustained in his seat by the high
pommel and cantle of the Indian saddle. His cheeks were
shrunken in the hollow of his jaws; his eyes were unnaturally
dilated, and his lips shrivelled and drawn back from his teeth
like those of a corpse. When they brought him before our
tent, and lifted him from the saddle, he could not walk or stand,
but crawled a short distance, and with a look of utter misery
sat down on the grass. All the children and women came pour-

ing out of the lodges, and with screams and cries made a circle about him, while he sat supporting himself with his hands, and looking from side to side with a vacant stare. The wretch was starving to death. For thirty-three days he had wandered alone on the prairie, without weapon of any kind; without shoes, moccasins, or any other clothing than an old jacket and trousers; without intelligence to guide his course, or any knowledge of the productions of the prairie. All this time he had subsisted on crickets and lizards, wild onions, and three eggs which he found in the nest of a prairie-dove. He had not seen a human being. Bewildered in the boundless, hopeless desert that stretched around him, he had walked on in despair, till he could walk no longer, and then crawled on his knees, till the bone was laid bare. He chose the night for travelling, lying down by day to sleep in the glaring sun, always dreaming, as he said, of the broth and corn-cake he used to eat under his old master's shed in Missouri. Every man in the camp, both white and red, was astonished at his escape not only from starvation, but from the grizzly bears, which abound in that neighborhood, and the wolves which howled around him every night.

Reynal recognized him the moment the Indians brought him in. He had run away from his master about a year before and joined the party of Richard, who was then leaving the frontier for the mountains. He had lived with Richard until, at the end of May, he with Reynal and several other men went out in search of some stray horses, when he was separated from the rest in a storm, and had never been heard of to this time. Knowing his inexperience and helplessness, no one dreamed that he could still be living. The Indians had found him lying exhausted on the ground.

As he sat there, with the Indians gazing silently on him, his haggard face and glazed eye were disgusting to look upon. Deslauriers made him a bowl of gruel, but he suffered it to remain untasted before him. At length he languidly raised the spoon to his lips; again he did so, and again; and then his appetite seemed suddenly inflamed into madness, for he seized the bowl, swallowed all its contents in a few seconds, and eagerly demanded meat. This we refused, telling him to wait until morning; but he begged so eagerly that we gave him a small piece, which he devoured, tearing it like a dog. He said he must have more. We told him that his life was in danger if he ate so immoderately at first. He assented, and said he knew he was a fool to do so, but he must have meat. This we absolutely refused, to the great indignation of the senseless squaws, who, when we were not watching him, would slyly bring dried meat and *pommes blanches*, and place them on the ground by his side. Still this was not enough for him. When it grew dark he contrived to creep away between the legs of the horses and crawl over to the Indian camp. Here he fed to his heart's content, and was brought back again in the morning, when Gingras, the trapper, put him on horseback and carried him to the fort. He managed to survive the effects of his greediness. Though slightly deranged when we left this part of the country, he was otherwise in tolerable health, and expressed his firm conviction that nothing could ever kill him.

When the sun was yet an hour high, it was a gay scene in the village. The warriors stalked sedately among the lodges, or along the margin of the stream, or walked out to visit the bands of horses that were feeding over the prairie. Half the population deserted the close and heated lodges and betook themselves to the water; and here you might see boys and girls, and young squaws, splashing, swimming, and diving, beneath the afternoon sun, with merry screams and laughter. But when the sun was resting above the broken peaks, and the purple mountains threw their shadows for miles over the prairie; when our old tree basked peacefully in the horizontal rays, and the swelling plains and scattered groves were softened into a tranquil beauty, —then the scene around our tent was worthy of a Salvator. Savage figures, with quivers at their backs, and guns, lances, or tomahawks in their hands, sat on horseback, motionless as statues, their arms crossed on their breasts and their eyes fixed in a steady unwavering gaze upon us. Others stood erect, wrapped from head to foot in their long white robes of buffalo-hide. Others sat together on the grass, holding their shaggy horses by a rope, with their dark busts exposed to view as they suffered their robes to fall from their shoulders. Others again stood carelessly among the throng, with nothing to conceal the matchless symmetry of their forms. There was one in particular, a ferocious fellow, named The Mad Wolf, who, with the bow in his hand and the quiver at his back, might have seemed, but for his face, the Pythian Apollo himself. Such a figure rose before the imagination of West, when, on first seeing the Belvedere in the Vatican, he exclaimed, "By God, a Mohawk!"

When the prairie grew dark, the horses were driven in and secured near the camp, and the crowd began to melt away. Fires gleamed around, duskily revealing the rough trappers and the graceful Indians. One of the families near us was always gathered about a bright fire that lighted up the interior of their lodge. Withered, witch-like hags flitted around the blaze; and here for hour after hour sat a circle of children and young girls, laughing and talking, their round merry faces glowing in the ruddy light. We could hear the monotonous notes of the drum from the Indian camp, with the chant of the war-song, deadened in the distance, and the long chorus of quavering yells, where the war-dance was going on in the largest lodge. For several nights, too, we heard wild and mournful cries, rising and dying away like the melancholy voice of a wolf. They came from the sisters and female relatives of Mahto-Tatonka, who were gashing their limbs with knives, and bewailing the death of Henry Chatillon's squaw. The hour would grow late before all went to rest in our camp. Then, while the embers of the fires glowed dimly, the men lay stretched in their blankets on the ground, and nothing could be heard but the restless motions of the crowded horses.

I recall these scenes with a mixed feeling of pleasure and pain. At this time, I was so reduced by illness that I could seldom walk without reeling like a drunken man, and when I rose from my seat upon the ground, the landscape suddenly grew dim before my eyes, the trees and lodges seemed to sway to and fro, and the prairie to rise and fall like the swells of the ocean. Such a state of things is not enviable anywhere. In a country where a man's life may at any moment depend on the strength of his arm, or it may be on the activity of his legs, it is more particularly inconvenient. Nor is sleeping on damp ground, with an occasional drenching from a shower, very beneficial in such cases. I sometimes suffered the extremity of exhaustion, and was in a tolerably fair way of atoning for my love of the prairie by resting there for ever.

I tried repose and a very sparing diet. For a long time, with exemplary patience, I lounged about the camp, or at the utmost staggered over to the Indian village, and walked faint and dizzy among the lodges. It would not do; and I bethought me of starvation. During five days I sustained life on one small biscuit a day. At the end of that time I was weaker than before, but the disorder seemed shaken in its stronghold, and very gradually I began to resume a less rigid diet.

I used to lie languid and dreamy before our tent, musing on the past and the future, and when most overcome with lassitude, my eyes turned always towards the distant Black Hills. There is a spirit of energy in mountains, and they impart it to all who approach them. At that time I did not know how many dark superstitions and gloomy legends are associated with the Black Hills in the minds of the Indians, but I felt an eager desire to penetrate their hidden recesses, and explore the chasms and precipices, black torrents and silent forests, that I fancied were concealed there.

[A BOOK ON ONE'S HOBBY]

[THE ROSE]

(From *The Book of Roses*, 1866)

Like all things living, in the world of mind or of matter, the rose is beautified, enlarged, and strengthened by a course of judicious and persevering culture, continued through successive generations. The art of horticulture is no leveller. Its triumphs are achieved by rigid systems of selection and rejection, founded always on the broad basis of intrinsic worth. The good cultivator propagates no plants but the best. He carefully chooses those marked out by conspicuous merit; protects them from the pollen of inferior sorts; intermarries them, perhaps, with other varieties of equal vigor and beauty; saves their seed, and raises from it another generation. From the new plants thus obtained he again chooses the best, and repeats with them the same process. Thus the rose and other plants are brought slowly to their perfect development. It is in vain to look for much improvement by merely cultivating one individual. Culture alone will not make a single rose double, or a dull rose brilliant. We cultivate the parent, and look for our reward in the offspring.

The village maiden has a beauty and a charm of her own; and so has her counterpart in the floral world,—the wild rose that grows by the roadside. Transplanted to the garden, and, with its offspring after it to the fourth and fifth generation, made an object of skilful culture, it reaches at last a wonderful development. The flowers which in the ancestress were single and small become double in the offspring, and expand their countless petals to the sun in all the majesty of the Queen of Flowers. The village maid has risen to regal state. She has lost her native virgin charm; but she sits throned and crowned in imperial beauty.

Now, all the roses of our gardens have some wild ancestress of the woods and meadows, from whom, in the process of suc-

cessive generations, their beauties have been developed, sometimes by happy accidents, but oftener by design. Thus have
arisen families of roses, each marked with traces of its parentage. These are the patricians of the floral commonwealth,
gifted at once with fame, beauty, and rank.

The various wild roses differ greatly in their capacity of
improvement and development. In some cases, the offspring
grow rapidly, in color, fulness, and size, with every successive
generation. In other cases, they will not improve at all; and the
rose remains a wild rose still, good only for the roadside. With
others yet, there seems to be a fixed limit, which is soon reached,
and where improvement stops. It requires, even with the best,
good culture and selection through several generations before
the highest result appears. In horticulture, an element of
stability is essential to progress. When the florist sees in any
rose a quality which he wishes to develop and perfect, he does
not look for success to the plant before him, but to the offspring
which he produces from this plant. But this production and
culture must be conducted wisely and skilfully, or the offspring
will degenerate instead of improving.

There are different kinds of culture, with different effects.
That which is founded in the laws of Nature, and aims at a universal development, produces for its result not only increased
beauty, but increased symmetry, strength, and vitality. On the
other hand, it is in the power of the skilful florist to develop or
to repress whatever quality he may please. By artificial processes
of culture, roses have been produced, beautiful in form and
color, but so small, that the whole plant, it is said, might be
covered with an egg-shell. These are results of the ingenious
florists of China and Japan. The culture that refines without invigorating, belongs, it seems, to a partial or perverted
civilization.

[ADVENTURES IN POLITICS AND EDUCATION]

THE TALE OF THE "RIPE SCHOLAR"

(From the *Nation*, December 23, 1869)

Not many years ago, a certain traditional prestige, independent of all considerations of practical utility, attached to the scholastic character, at least in New England, where the clergy long held a monopoly of what passed for learning. New England colleges were once little more than schools for making ministers. As the clergyman has lost in influence, so the scholar has lost in repute, and the reasons are not hard to find. The really good scholars were exceptions, and very rare ones. In the matter of theology some notable results were produced, but secular scholarship was simply an exotic and a sickly one. It never recovered from its transplantation and drew no vital juices from the soil. The climate was hostile to it. All the vigor of the country drifted into practical pursuits, and the New England man of letters, when he happened not to be a minister, was usually some person whom constitutional defects, bodily or mental, had unsuited for politics or business. He was apt to be a recluse, ignorant of the world, bleached by a close room and an iron stove, never breathing the outer air when he could help it, and resembling a mediæval monk in his scorn of the body, or rather in his utter disregard of it. Sometimes he was reputed a scholar merely because he was nothing else. The products of his mind were as pallid as the hue of his face, and, like their parent, void of blood, bone, sinew, muscle, and marrow. That he should be provincial was, for a long time, inevitable, but that he was emasculate was chiefly his own fault. As his scholarship was not fruitful of any very valuable results, as it did not make itself felt in the living world that ranged around it, as, in short, it showed no vital force, it began at length to be regarded as a superfluous excrescence. Nevertheless, like the monkish learning of the middle ages, it served a good purpose in keeping alive the tradition of liberal culture against a future renaissance. We shall be told that we exaggerate, and, in one sense, this is true, for we describe not an individual, but a type, from which, however, the reality was rarely very remote, and with which it was sometimes identified. The most finished and altogether favorable example of this devitalized scholarship, with many graceful additions, was Edward Everett, and its echoes may still be heard in the halls of Congress, perplexing Western members with Latin quotations, profuse, if not always correct.

As the nation grew in importance and in sensitiveness, the want of intellectual productiveness began to trouble the popular pride, and an impatient public called on its authors to be "original." Spasmodic efforts were made to respond, and the results were such as may be supposed. The mountain went into convulsions of labor and produced a mouse, or something as ridiculous. After an analogous fashion some of the successors of our pallid, clerical scholars raise the cry, "Let us be strong," and fall into the moral and physical gymnastics of muscular Christianity. This, certainly, is no bad sign, in so far as it indicates the consciousness of a want; but neither originality nor force can be got up to order. They must spring from a deeper root and grow by laws of their own. Happily our soil has begun to put forth such a growth, promising in quality, but as yet, in quantity and in maturity, wholly inadequate to the exigent need.

In times of agitation, alive with engrossing questions of pressing moment, when all is astir with pursuit and controversy, when some are mad for gold, and some are earnest and some rabid for this cause or for that, the scholarship of the past is naturally pronounced not up with the times. Despite his manifold failings, "the self-made man," with his palatial mansion, his exploits in the gold-room, in the caucus, on the stump, in Congress, and in the presidential chair, flatters popular self-love and fills the public eye. Only a slight reason is wanted for depreciating the scholar, and a strong one is offered. Because the culture which our colleges supplied, and which too many of them still supply, was weak, thin, and unsuitable, it was easy to depreciate all culture. By culture we mean development, not polish or adornment, though these are its natural and by no means useless belongings. Using the word, then, in this sense, culture is with us a supreme necessity, not for the profit of a few but of all. The presence of minds highly and vigorously developed is the most powerful aid to popular education, and the necessary condition of its best success. In a country where the ruling power is public opinion, it is above all things necessary that the best and maturest thought should have a fair share in forming it. Such thought cannot exist in any force in the community without propagating its own image, and a class of strong thinkers is the palladium of democracy. They are the natural enemies of ignorant, ostentatious, and aggressive wealth, and the natural friends of all that is best in the popular heart. They are sure of the hatred of charlatans, demagogues, and political sharpers. They are the only hope of our civilization; without them it is a failure, a mere platitude of mediocrity, stagnant or turbid, as the case may be. The vastest aggregate of average intelligences can do nothing to supply their place, and even material growth is impeded by an ignorance of its conditions and laws. If we may be forgiven the metaphor, our civilization is at present a creature with a small and feeble head, a large, muscular, and active body, and a tail growing at such a rate that it threatens to become unmanageable and shake the balance of the vital powers.

The tendency of a partial education, such as the best popular education must of necessity be, is to produce an excess of self-confidence; and one of its results in this country is a prodigious number of persons who think, and persuade others to think, that they know everything necessary to be known, and are fully competent to form opinions and make speeches upon all questions whatever. As these are precisely the persons who make the most noise on the most momentous questions of the day, who have the most listeners and admirers, and who hold each other up as shining examples for imitation, their incompetency becomes a public evil of the first magnitude. If rash and ignorant theorizing, impulsive outcries, and social and political charlatanry of all sorts are to have the guiding of our craft, then farewell to the hope that her voyage will be a success. The remedy is to infuse into the disordered system the sedative and tonic of a broad knowledge and a vigorous reason. This means to invigorate and extend the higher education; to substitute for the effete and futile scholasticism which the popular mind justly holds in slight account, an energetic and manly development, trained to grapple with the vast questions of the present, and strong enough in numbers as well as quality to temper with its mature thought the rashness of popular speculation. Our best colleges are moving hopefully in this direction; none of them with more life and vigor than the oldest of them all. The present generation will see an increase in the number of our really efficient thinkers, but it is a positive, not a relative increase, and is far behind the fast increasing need. Powerful causes are at work against it, and we will try to explain what, to our thinking, some of these causes are.

Perhaps the most obvious of them is the ascendency of material interests among us. To the great mass of our population, the clearing of lands, the acquiring of new territory, the building of cities, the multiplication of railroads, steamboats, and telegraph lines, the growth of trade and manufactures, the opening of mines, with the resulting fine houses, fine clothes, and sumptuous fare, constitute the real sum and substance of progress and civilization. Art, literature, philosophy, and science—so far as science has no direct bearing on material interests—are regarded as decorations, agreeable and creditable, but not essential. In other words, the material basis of civilization is accepted for the entire structure. A prodigious number of persons think that money-making is the only serious business of life, and there is no corresponding number who hold a different faith. There are not a few among us who would "improve" our colleges into schools of technology, where young men may be trained with a view mainly to the production of more steamboats, railroads, and telegraphs; more breadstuffs; more iron, copper, silver, and gold; more cottons and woollens; and, consequently, more fine houses and fine clothes. All this is very well, but it does not answer the great and crying need of the time. The truth is, our material growth so greatly exceeds our other growth that the body politic suffers from diseases of repletion. A patient bloated with generous living, and marked already with the eruptions of a perverted, diseased blood, is not to be cured solely by providing him with more food.

The drift towards material activity is so powerful among us that it is very difficult for a young man to resist it; and the difficulty increases in proportion as his nature is active and energetic. Patient and devoted study is rarely long continued in the vortex of American life. The dusty arena of competition and strife has fascinations almost irresistible to one conscious of his own vigor. Intellectual tastes may, however, make a compromise. Journalism and the lecture-room offer them a field midway between the solitude of the study and the bustle of the world of business; but the journal and the lecture-room have influences powerfully adverse to solid, mature, and independent thinking. There, too, is the pulpit, for those who have a vocation that way; but in this, also, a mighty and increasing temptation besets the conscientious student. As for politics, they have fallen to such a pass that the men are rare who can mingle in them without deteriorating.

Paradoxical as it may seem, the diffusion of education and intelligence is at present acting against the free development of the highest education and intelligence. Many have hoped and still hope that by giving a partial teaching to great numbers of persons, a stimulus would be applied to the best minds among them, and a thirst for knowledge awakened which would lead to high results; but thus far these results have not equalled the expectation. There has been a vast expenditure of brick and mortar for educational purposes, and, what is more to the purpose, many excellent and faithful teachers of both sexes have labored diligently in their vocation; but the system of competitive cramming in our public schools has not borne fruits on which we have much cause to congratulate ourselves. It has produced an immense number of readers; but what thinkers are to be found may be said to exist in spite of it. The public school has put money in abundance into the pockets of the dealers in sensation stories, sensation illustrated papers, and all the swarm of trivial, sickly, and rascally literature. From this and cheap newspapers thousands—nay, millions—draw all their mental improvement, and pamper their mental stomachs with adulterated, not to say poisoned, sweetmeats, till they have neither desire nor digestion for strong and wholesome food. But we would speak rather of that truly intelligent and respectable public which forms the auditories of popular preachers and popular lecturers, which is the lavish patron of popular periodical literature, which interests itself in the questions of the day, and has keen mental appetites of a certain kind. This public is strong in numbers and very strong in collective wealth. Its voice can confer celebrity, if not reputation; and it can enrich those who win its favor. In truth, it is the American people. Now, what does this great public want? It is, in the main, busied with the active work of life, and though it thinks a little and feels a great deal on matters which ought to engage the attention of every self-governing people, yet it is impatient of continuous and cool attention to anything but its daily business, and sometimes even to that. Indeed, the exciting events of the last ten years, joined to the morbid stimulus applied to all departments of business, have greatly increased this tendency; and to-day there are fewer serious and thoughtful readers than in the last decade. More than ever before, the public demands elocution rather than reason of those who address it; something to excite the feelings and captivate the fancy rather than something to instruct the understanding. It rejoices in sweeping statements, confident assertions, bright lights and black shadows alternating with something funny. Neither does it care much for a terse, idiomatic, and pointed diction, but generally prefers the flatulent periods of the ready writers. On matters of the greatest interest it craves to be excited or amused. Lectures professing to instruct are turned to a tissue of jokes, and the pulpit itself is sometimes enlivened after a similar fashion. The pill must be sugared and the food highly seasoned, for the public mind is in a state of laxity and needs a tonic. But the public taste is very exacting, and it offers great and tempting rewards to those who please it.

That which pleases it pays so much better in money and notoriety, and is so much cheaper of production, than the better article which does not please it, that the temptation to accept light work and high wages in place of hard work and low wages is difficult to resist. Nothing but a deep love of truth or of art can stand unmoved against it. In our literary markets, educated tastes are completely outridden by uneducated or half-educated tastes, and the commodity is debased accordingly. Thus, the editor of a magazine may be a man of taste and talents; but his interests as a man of letters and his interests as a man of business are not the same. "Why don't you make your magazine what it ought to be?" we once asked of a well-known editor. "Because," he replied, "if we did, we should lose four-fifths of our circulation." A noted preacher not long ago confessed to us that the temptation to give his audience the sort of preaching which they liked to hear, instead of that which it was best that they should hear, was almost irresistible.

The amount of what we have been saying is, that the public which demands a second-rate article is so enormously large in comparison with the public which demands a first-rate article that it impairs the quality of literary production, and exercises an influence adverse to the growth of intellectual eminence. Now, what is the remedy? It seems to us to be twofold. First, to direct popular education, not to stuffing the mind with crude aggregations of imperfect knowledge, but rather to the development of its powers of observation, comparison, analysis, and reasoning; to strengthening and instructing its moral sense, and leading it to self-knowledge and consequent modesty. All this, no doubt, is vastly more difficult and far less showy in its results than the present system of competitive cramming, and requires in its teachers a high degree of good sense and sound instruction. The other remedy consists in a powerful re-enforcement of the higher education, and the consequent development of a class of persons, whether rich or poor, so well instructed and so numerous as to hold their ground against charlatanry, and propagate sound and healthy thought through the community. He who gives or bequeaths money to a well-established and wisely-conducted university confers a blessing which radiates through all the ranks of society. He does a service eminently practical, and constitutes himself the patron of the highest and best utilitarianism.

THE FAILURE OF UNIVERSAL SUFFRAGE

(From the *North American Review*, July–August, 1878)

In different times and countries, patriotism has different work to do. For the last two or three centuries its business has usually been the bridling of tyrants, the dethroning of arbitrary kings and the setting up of constitutional ones, or the getting rid of kings altogether; in short, the extension of popular liberties at the expense of the wearers of crowns and bearers of sceptres. Going farther back, we see another state of things. Toward the end of the middle ages we find the relations of kings and peoples the reverse of what they afterward became. We find oppression divided and diffused in the persons of a multitude of feudal tryants, and the masses looking to their sovereign as a protector. The feudal oppressor was both his enemy and theirs, and the progress of monarchical centralization was in the interest both of prince and peasant. It was not until feudalism was prostrate that the masses ceased to bless their sovereign as a friend, and began to curse him as a tyrant.

Still farther back in the centuries we find feudalism itself acting a part which could not have been spared in the reorganization of society. The foe of one generation is the friend of another, and there is scarcely a form of government so bad that it has not, at some time, prevented a worse or prepared for a better.

It is but lately, then, that crowns and sceptres have been denounced as enemies of the rights of man; but the war against them has been waged so hotly, and has left such vigorous traditions behind it, that the same battle-cry is still raised in quarters where the foe has been driven off the field and utterly annihilated; where the present danger is not above but beneath, and where the real tyrant is organized ignorance, led by unscrupulous craft, and marching, amid the applause of fools, under the flag of equal rights. One might be better employed than in hooting and throwing stones at the ghost of dead and buried privilege. But the amusement is safe and popular. Habit has made it second nature, and it gives excellent occasion for the display of oratorical fireworks. The transfer of sovereignty to the people, and the whole people, is proclaimed the panacea of political and social ills, and we are but rarely reminded that popular sovereignty has evils of its own, against which patriotism may exercise itself to better purpose. Here and there one hears a whisper that perhaps the masses have not learned how to use their power; but the whisper is greeted with obloquy.

We speak, of course, of our own country, where no royalty is left to fear, except the many-headed one that bears the name of Demos, with its portentous concourse of courtiers, sycophants, and panders. Those who live on its favors, and pretend most devotion to it, have been heard of late warning us to beware, and telling us that Demos is a "dangerous beast," whose caprices it behooves us to humor, lest he should turn and rend us. Far be it from us to echo this treason. Let others call him beast: we are his subject, and will but touch with reverence a few flaws in his armor.

Once he was a reasonable and sensible monarch, who had a notion of good government, and ruled himself and his realm with wisdom and moderation; but prosperity has a little turned his head, and hordes of native and foreign barbarians, all armed with the ballot, have so bewildered him that he begins to lose his wits and forget his kingcraft.

When a king makes himself oppressive to any considerable part of his subjects, it is not worth while to consider whether he wears one head or millions; whether he sits enthroned in the palace of his ancestors, or smokes his pipe in a filthy wardroom among blackguards like himself. Nevertheless, if we are to be oppressed, we would rather the oppressor were clean, and, if we are to be robbed, we like to be robbed with civility.

Demos is a Protean monarch, and can put on many shapes. He can be benign, imposing, or terrible; but of late we have oftener seen him under his baser manifestations, keeping vile company, and doing his best to shake our loyalty by strange, unkingly pranks. The worst things about him are his courtiers, who in great part are a disreputable crew, abject flatterers, vicious counselors, and greedy plunderers; behind their master in morals, and in most things else but cunning. If the politicians would let him alone, Demos would be the exact embodiment of the average intelligence and worth of a great people; but, deluded and perverted as he is, he falls below this mark, and passes for worse than his real self. Yet, supposing that his evil counselors were all exterminated as they deserve, it would avail us little, for he would soon choose others like them, under the influence of notions which, of late, have got the better of his former good sense. He is the master, and can do what he will. He is answerable for all, and, if he is ill-served, he has nobody to blame but himself. In fact, he is jealous of his nobles, and, like certain other kings before him, loves to raise his barber, his butcher, and his scullion, to places of power. They yield him divine honor, proclaim him infallible as the pope, and call his voice the voice of God; yet they befool and cheat him not the less. He is the type of collective folly as well as wisdom, collective ignorance as well as knowledge, and collective frailty as well as strength. In short, he is utterly mortal, and must rise or fall as he is faithful or false to the great laws that regulate the destinies of men.

A generation or more ago, a cry of "Eureka!" rose over all the land, or rather over all the northern part of it. It was the triumphant acclaim of a nation hailing its king. The enthusiasm had its focus in New England, at that time, perhaps, the most successful democracy on earth—a fact which, however, was mainly to be ascribed to wholesome traditions, which had become part of the popular life. These the jubilants overlooked, and saw the fountain of all political and social blessings in the beneficent sway of an absolute Demos; that is to say, in the uncurbed exercise of the "inalienable right" of man to govern himself. A little cloud, no bigger than a man's hand, rose presently above the sea, the herald of an invasion of peasants. With this in-pouring of labor came railroads, factories, and a thousand prolific industries, which heads without hands could not have awakened or sustained. Population increased, wealth grew apace; men became rabid in making money, and women frivolous in spending it. The same influences were at work through all the Northern States. A vast industrial development, an immense prosperity, rested safely for a while on the old national traditions, love of country, respect for law, and the habit of self-government. Then began the inevitable strain. Crowded cities, where the irresponsible and ignorant were numerically equal, or more than equal, to the rest, and where the weakest and most worthless was a match, by his vote, for the wisest and best; bloated wealth and envious poverty; a tinseled civilization above, and a discontented proletariat beneath—all these have broken rudely upon the dreams of equal brotherhood once cherished by those who made their wish the father of their thought, and fancied that this favored land formed an exception to the universal laws of human nature. They cried out for elevating the masses, but the masses have sunk lower. They called for the diffusion of wealth, but wealth has gathered into more numerous and portentous accumulations. Two enemies, unknown before, have risen like spirits of darkness on our social and political horizon—an ignorant proletariat and a half-taught plutocracy. Between lie the classes, happily still numerous and strong, in whom rests our salvation.

To these we must look for the sterling ability and worth of the nation, sometimes in wealth, now and then in poverty; but for the most part in neither the one nor the other. They are the natural enemies of the vulgar plutocrat, and the natural friends of all that is best in the popular heart; but, as they neither flatter, lie, nor bribe, they have little power over these barbarians of civilization that form the substratum of great industrial communities.

Liberty was the watchword of our fathers, and so it is of ourselves. But, in their hearts, the masses of the nation cherish desires not only different from it, but inconsistent with it. They want equality more than they want liberty. Now, there is a factitious inequality and a real and intrinsic one. Rank, titles, privileges, and wealth, make up the first; and character, ability, and culture, the second. Excepting only the distinctions of wealth, we have abolished the artificial inequality, and now we are doing what we can to abolish the real one. Vaguely and half unconsciously, but every day more and more, the masses hug the flattering illusion that one man is essentially about as good as another. They will not deny that there is great difference in the quality of horses or dogs, but they refuse to see it in their own genus. A jockey may be a democrat in the street, but he is sure to be an aristocrat in the stable. And yet the essential difference between man and man is incomparably greater than that between horse and horse, or dog and dog; though, being chiefly below the surface, the general eye can hardly see it.

Mountains and mole-hills, deserts and fertile valleys, and all the universal inequality of Nature, are but types of inequality in men. To level the outward world would turn it into barrenness, and to level human minds to one stature would make them barren as well. The history of the progress of mankind is the history of its leading minds. The masses, left to themselves, are hardly capable of progress, except material progress, and even that imperfectly. Through the long course of history, a few men, to be counted by scores or by tens, have planted in the world the germs of a growth whose beneficent vitality has extended itself through all succeeding ages; and any one of these men outweighs in value to mankind myriads of nobles, citizens, and peasants, who have fought or toiled in their generation, and then rotted into oblivion. Condé used to say that a thousand frogs were not worth one salmon. The saying, as he meant it, was false, but there is a sense in which it is true, though it tells the truth but feebly and imperfectly.

The highest man may comprehend the lowest, but the lowest can no more comprehend the highest than if he belonged to another order of beings, as for some purposes he practically does. A single human mind may engender thoughts which the combined efforts of millions of lower intelligences cannot conceive. This is not the faith of Demos. In his vague way, he fancies that aggregated ignorance and weakness will bear the fruits of wisdom. He begins to think that science, thought, and study, are old-time illusions; that everybody has a right to form his own opinion as to whether the world is round or flat, and that the votes of the majority ought to settle the question.

We have said that intrinsic equality is inconsistent with liberty. It is so because, in order to produce it, very unequal opportunities of development must be granted to different kinds of mind and character, and an even distributive justice refused to human nature. The highest must be repressed and the lowest stimulated in order to produce a level average. In such an attempt no political or social system can completely succeed; but in so far as it tends this way it is false and pernicious. If it could succeed, or approach to success, it would be an outrage upon humanity. Asiatic despotisms have done so as nearly, perhaps, as is possible; but the Amuraths and Bajazets will hardly be thought fit examples for emulation. Democracy can no more succeed in producing a level than they did, but it can do prodigious mischief by trying to produce one. It may pretend that it is only "leveling upward," but this phrase of pleasing sound means leveling downward also; for, if the lower strata of humanity are raised as high as their nature and the inexorable conditions of human life will permit, there will still be no equality till the upper strata are pushed down to meet them.

A society where liberty was complete, and where all men had equal opportunities of development, according to their several qualities, would show immense diversities of all kinds; like the vegetable world, where the tallest trees and the humblest shrubs, plants climbing and crawling, poisonous and wholesome, all grow out of the same soil and are formed of the same essential elements. So the essential elements of human nature are the same, but mixed in such different proportion, and controlled by such different tendencies, that they often result less in resemblances than in contrasts.

Shall we look for an ideal society in that which tends to a barren average and a weary uniformity, treats men like cattle, counts them by the head, and gives them a vote apiece without asking whether or not they have the sense to use it; or in that which recognizes the inherent differences between man and man, gives the preponderance of power to character and intelligence, yet removes artificial barriers, keeps circulation free through all its parts, and rewards merit wherever it appears with added influence? This, of course, is a mere idea, never to be fully realized; but it makes vast difference at what a republic aims, and whether it builds on numbers or on worth. The methods by which it tries to reach its mark may be more or less effective, but it is all-important that the mark should be a true one.

The success of an experiment of indiscriminate suffrage hangs on the question whether the better part of the community is able to outweigh the worse. There are certain social conditions, rarely to be found except in small communities and a civilization not the most advanced, in which this question may be answered confidently in the affirmative; but, as numbers, wealth, and luxury increase, the difficulty grows with them. It is aggravated by the fact, generally acknowledged by those most competent to judge of it, that intellectual development and high civilization are not favorable to fecundity, so that the unintelligent classes, except when in actual destitution, multiply faster than those above them. Thus the power of ignorance tends to increase, or rather the power of the knaves who are always at hand to use it.

A New England village of the olden time—that is to say, of some forty years ago—would have been safely and well governed by the votes of every man in it; but, now that the village has grown into a populous city, with its factories and workshops, its acres of tenement-houses, and thousands and ten thousands of restless workmen, foreigners for the most part, to whom liberty means license and politics means plunder, to whom the public good is nothing and their own most trivial interests everything, who love the country for what they can get out of it, and whose ears are open to the promptings of every rascally agitator, the case is completely changed, and universal suffrage becomes a questionable blessing. Still we are told it is an inalienable right. Suppose for an instant that it were so, wild as the supposition is. The community has rights as well as the individual, and it has also duties. It is both its right and its duty to provide good government for itself, and, the moment the vote of any person or class of persons becomes an obstacle to its doing so, this person or class forfeits the right to vote; for, where the rights of a part clash with the rights of the whole, the former must give way.

When a man has not sense to comprehend the questions at issue, know a bad candidate from a good one, or see his own true interests—when he cares not a farthing for the general good, and will sell his vote for a dollar—when, by a native instinct, he throws up his cap at the claptrap declamation of some lying knave, and turns with indifference or dislike from the voice of honesty and reason—then his vote becomes a public pest. Somebody uses him, and profits by him. Probably it is a demagogue, possibly a priest, or possibly both. In any case, it is folly to call him a free agent. His inalienable right may perhaps be valuable to him for the bribe he gets out of it; but it makes him a nuisance and a danger to the state. It causes pulpit, platform, and press, to condone his vices, and debauch the moral sense of the people by discovering objects of sympathy in vagabonds, thieves, and ruffians. It gives power to the communistic attack on property, and makes it difficult to deal with outbreaks of brutal violence against which even humanity itself demands measures of the most stern and exemplary repression.

Universal suffrage, imposed upon the country by the rivalries of contending parties bidding against each other for votes, has since been promoted into a "principle," regarded by many persons as almost sacred. This so-called principle, however, is by no means of universal application, and, when applied in the wrong place, at once reduces itself to absurdity. Distribute ballot-boxes among the subjects of King John of Abyssinia or those of the Khan of Kelat, and set them to govern themselves by the full exercise of their inalienable rights, and our panacea would result in anarchy. Universal suffrage is applicable only to those peoples, if such there are, who by character and training are prepared for it; and the only rational question is as to the degree of preparation that will serve the purpose. In any case, preparation must be the work of time. There must be hereditary traditions of self-government. Universal suffrage exists in some European nations, and exists along with a high degree of civilization and prosperity; but in these the traditions and material forces of a centralized government are extremely strong, and the evils of an ignorant or vicious vote are held in check by powers of resistance which are unknown here. Yet even in these countries the final results of the experiment are, and well may be, the objects of deep anxiety.

We are told that, to make a bad voter a good one, we have only to educate him. His defect, however, is not merely intellectual. It consists also in the want of the feeling that his own interests are connected with those of the community, and in the weakness or absence of the sense of moral and political duty. The evil is not to be cured by reading, writing, and arithmetic. The public school may cram his brain with all it is capable of containing, and he will be no whit the better citizen for the process. It might train instead of cramming him, lay the foundation of a sound morality, and teach him something of political and social duty; but such education is more difficult than that now in vogue, and demands more judgment and ability in those who conduct it. To teach the teacher must be the first step; and here, as in everything else connected with public education, we find ourselves moving in a vicious circle. To whom have we intrusted these high and delicate interests? They demand the best intelligence and the best conscience of the community; and yet their control rests, in the last resort, with legislatures and municipal bodies representing in part that very public which needs education the most—wretched, wire-pulling demagogues, ignorant as the constituencies that chose them, reckless of public duty, and without the faintest notion of what true education is. In such education rests the only hope of democracies; but it is vain to look for it unless the wiser half of the public can regain its virtual control.

The results thus far of our present style of popular education are not flattering. That portion of young America which has sprung from humble and ignorant parentage ought to show its effects most conspicuously; but it may be doubted whether, as a general rule, the young Irish-American is a better or safer citizen than his parent from Cork. He can read; but he reads nothing but sensation stories and scandalous picture-papers, which fill him with preposterous notions, and would enfeeble a stronger brain than his and debauch a sounder conscience. He is generally less industrious than his sire, and equally careless of the public good.

Those who bray loudest for inalienable rights extol the ballot as an education in itself, capable of making good citizens out of the poorest material. Under certain conditions, there is a measure of truth in this. An untaught and reckless voter, enveloped by honest and rational ones, is apt to change greatly for the better; but, to this end, it is essential that those whom the ballot is to educate should be segregated and surrounded by healthy influences. When extensive districts and, notably, large portions of populous cities are filled by masses of imported ignorance and hereditary ineptitude, the whole ferments together till the evil grows insufferable. The ballot then educates only to mischief. If the voter has a conscience, he votes it away. His teacher is a demagogue who plays on his prejudices or his greed, and out of a bad citizen makes him a worse. Witness the municipal corruptions of New York, and the monstrosities of negro rule in South Carolina.

It is said that vigilance is the price of liberty; but it has another condition no less essenial. It demands moderation. It must stand on the firm ground, avoid rash theorizing and sweeping generalization, and follow the laws of development that reason and experience point out. It must build its future on its past. When it rushes deliriously after dazzling abstractions, it is rushing toward its ruin. In short, it must be practical, not in the vile sense in which that word is used by political sharpers, but in the sense in which it is used by thoughtful and high-minded men.

There is an illusion, or a superstition, among us respecting the ballot. The means are confounded with the end. Good government is the end, and the ballot is worthless except so far as it helps to reach this end. Any reasonable man would willingly renounce his privilege of dropping a piece of paper into a box, provided that good government were assured to him and his descendants.

The champions of indiscriminate suffrage—such of them, that is, as deign to give reasons for their faith—point in triumph to the prosperity which the country has enjoyed till within the last few years, and proclaim it a result of the unlimited power of the masses. This prosperity, however, had been founded and half built up before the muddy tide of ignorance rolled in upon us. It rests on the institutions and habits bequeathed to us by our fathers; and, if until lately the superstructure has continued to rise, it is in spite of a debased suffrage, and not in consequence of it. With still more confidence, and more apparent reason, we are told to look at the great popular uprising of the civil war. Here, indeed, democracy revealed itself in its grandest aspect. The degrading elements had not then reached the volume and force that they have reached to-day. The issue was definite and distinct. The Union was to be saved, and popular government vindicated. There were no doubts and no complications. Victory meant national integrity, and defeat meant national disintegration. Above all, the cause had its visible emblem—the national flag; and thousands and hundreds of thousands of eyes were turned upon it in ardent and loving devotion. We heard a great deal at that time about "thinking bayonets." The bayonets did not think, nor did those who carried them. They did what was more to the purpose—they felt. The emergency did not call for thought, but for faith and courage, and both were there in abundance. The political reptiles hid away, or pretended to change their nature, and for a time the malarious air was purged as by a thunderstorm. Peace brought a change. Questions intricate and difficult, demanding brains more than hearts, and discretion more than valor, took the place of the simple alternative, to be or not to be. The lion had had his turn, and now the fox, the jackal, and the wolf, took theirs. Every sly political trickster, whom the storm had awed into obscurity, now found his opportunity. The reptiles crawled out again, multiplied, and infested caucuses, conventions, and Congress. But the people were the saddest spectacle; the same people that had shown itself so heroic in the hour of military trial were now perplexed, bewildered, tossed between sense and folly, right and wrong, taking advice of mountebanks, and swallowing their filthy nostrums. The head of Demos was as giddy as his heart had been strong.

But why descant on evils past cure? Indiscriminate suffrage is an accomplished fact, and cannot be undone. Then why not accept it, look on the bright side, and hope that, "somehow or other," all will be well in the end? Because the recognition of an evil must go before its cure, and because there is too much already of the futile optimism that turns wishes into beliefs, and discourses in every tone of sickly commonplace about popular rights and universal brotherhood. Beneath it all lies an anxious sense of present and approaching evil. Still the case is not yet desperate. The country is full of recuperative force, latent just now, and kept so by the easy and apathetic good-nature which so strangely marks our people. This is not the quality by which liberty is won and kept, and yet popular orators and preachers do their best to perpetuate it. Prominent among obstacles to reform is this weary twaddle of the optimists.

It is well to be reminded how far we have sundered ourselves from the only true foundation of republics—intelligence and worth. The evil is not to be cured by hiding it, turning away our eyes from it, or pretending that it is a blessing. If it is to be overcome, it must be first looked in the face. All nations have in them some element of decay. Systems and peoples have perished, and not one was ever saved by shutting the eyes and murmuring that all was for the best. Faith without reason will only beguile us to destruction, and Liberty may elope while we are bragging most of her favors. We believe that our present evils are not past cure, and that, if the sound and rational part of the people can be made to feel that the public wounds need surgery, they will find means of applying it.

Under what shape shall we look for deliverance? It is easy to say where we need not look for it. To dream of a king would be ridiculous. We might set up an oligarchy, or rather an oligarchy might set up itself; but it would be one made up of the "boss," the "railroad king," and the bonanza Crœsus—a tyranny detestable and degrading as that of the rankest democracy, with which it would be in league. The low politician is the accomplice of the low plutocrat, and the low voter is the ready tool of both. There are those who call on imperialism to help us; but, supposing this heroic cure to be possible, we should rue the day that brought us to it. Our emperor would be nothing but a demagogue on a throne, forced to conciliate the masses by giving efficacy to their worst desires.

There is no hope but in purging and strengthening the republic. The remedy must be slow, not rash and revolutionary. A debased and irresponsible suffrage is at the bottom of the evil, but the state is sick of diseases that do not directly and immediately spring from this source. Something is due to the detestable maxim that to the victor belong the spoils, and the fatuity that makes office the reward of party service, demands incessant rotation, dismisses the servant of the public as soon as he has learned to serve it well, prefers the interests of needy politicians to the interests of the whole people, sets a premium on trickery and discourages faithful industry. When the scraps and marrow-bones of office are flung down to be scrambled for, the dogs are sure to get the lion's share.

Never was there a more damning allegation against popular government than was made unwittingly by the popularity-loving Governor of a certain State, who, talking for reform in one breath and against it in the next, said in substance that good administration might be expected in monarchies, but that with us the conduct of public affairs is in the hands of the people, and that to complain of bad civil service is to arraign democracy itself. Let us emulate this worthy gentleman: sit in smiling and serene despair, banish reflection, and drift placidly down the tide, fishing as we go. It is thus that republics are brought to their ruin. What the times need are convictions, and the courage to enforce them. The hope lies in an organized and determined effort to rouse the better half of the people to a sense that honest and trained capacity, in our public service, is essential to our well-being, and that the present odious and contemptible system is kept up in the interest of the few, and not of the whole. There is much, too, in the organization of legislative and municipal bodies which might be changed in the interest of honesty against knavery, and of ability against artifice, without involving any attack against "inalienable rights." Yet, so long as a debased suffrage retains its present power for mischief, the snake is scotched, not killed. When a majority of the people become convinced that no aggregate of folly can produce sense, and no aggregate of worthlessness can produce honesty, and when they return to the ancient faith that sense and honesty are essential to good government, then it will become possible—not, perhaps, peaceably to abolish a debased suffrage—but to counteract and so far neutralize it that it may serve as a safety-valve and cease to be a danger.

There are prophets of evil who see in the disorders that involve us the precursors of speedy ruin; but complete disruption and anarchy are, we may hope, still far off, thanks to an immense vitality and an inherited conservative strength. The immediate question is this: Is the nation in the way of keeping its lofty promise, realizing its sublime possibilities, advancing the best interests of humanity, and helping to ennoble and not vulgarize the world? Who dares answer that it is?

Great fault is found with men of education and social position, because they withdraw from public life and abandon the field to men half taught and *sans aveu*. Tried by the standard of ideal perfection they ought, for the good of the country, to sacrifice inclination, peace, and emolument, go down into the arena, and jostle with the rest in the scrub-race of American politics, even if victory brings them no prize which they greatly care to win. Such men we have. Those who to-day save our politics from absolute discredit do so, in one degree or another, at a personal sacrifice. If the conflicts and the rewards of public life have something to attract them, they have also a great deal to repel. They enter a career where the arts of political management are of more avail than knowledge, training, and real ability; or, in other words, where the politician carries the day and not the statesman; where fitness for a high place is not the essential condition of reaching it, and where success must often be bought by compliances repugnant to them. The public service is paid neither by profit nor by honor, except such profit and honor as those best fitted to serve the public hold in slight account. It is only in the highest walks of political life that honor is to be found at all. For the rest, it might almost be said that he who enters them throws on himself the burden of proof to show that he is an honest man. More and more, we drift into the condition of those unhappy countries where "the post of honor is a private station"; and perhaps at this moment there is no civilized nation on earth of which this saying holds more true.

Out of this springs a double evil: bad government first, and then an increasing difficulty in regaining a good one. Good government cannot be maintained or restored unless the instructed and developed intellect of the country is in good degree united with political habits and experience. The present tendency is to divorce it from them; and this process of separation, begun long ago, is moving on now more rapidly than ever. Within a generation the quality of public men has sunk conspicuously. The masses have grown impatient of personal eminence, and look for leaders as nearly as may be like themselves. Young men of the best promise have almost ceased to regard politics as a career. This is not from want of patriotism. When the Union was in danger there were none who hastened to its defense with more ardent and devoted gallantry, rejoicing to serve their country in a field where it was to be served by manhood and not by trickery. Peace came, they sheathed their swords, and were private citizens again. They would die in the public service, but they would not live in it.

In fact, the people did not want them there. The qualities of the most highly gifted and highly cultivated are discarded for cheaper qualities, which are easier of popular comprehension, and which do not excite jealousy. Therefore the strongest incentive to youthful ambition, the hope of political fame, is felt least by those who, for the good of the country, ought to feel it most. The natural results follow. A century ago three millions of people produced the wise, considerate, and temperate statesmanship on which our nationality is built. Now we are forty millions, and what sort of statesmanship these forty millions produce let the records of Congress show. The germs of good statesmanship are among us in abundance, but they are not developed, and, under our present system and in the present temper of our people, they cannot be developed. The conditions of human greatness are difficult to trace, but one thing is reasonably sure: it will not grow where it is not wanted. It may be found in a republic that demands the service of its best and ablest, but not in one that prefers indifferent service of indifferent men, and pleases itself with the notion that this is democratic equality.

The irrepressible optimist, who discovers in every disease of the state a blessing in disguise, will say that eminent abilities are unnecessary in democracies. We commend him to a short study of the recent doings of Congress, and, if this cannot dispel his illusion, his case is beyond hope. This same illusion, in one shape or another, is wide-spread through all the realm of Demos, where we sometimes hear the value of personal eminence of any kind openly called in question, on the ground that the object of popular government is the good of the many and not of the few. This is true, but it remains to ask what the good of the many requires. It does not require that the qualities most essential to the conduct of national affairs should be dwarfed and weakened; but that they should be developed to the utmost, not merely as a condition of good government, but because they are an education to the whole people. To admire a brazen demagogue sinks the masses, and to admire a patriot statesman elevates them. Example is better than schooling; and, if average humanity is encouraged in the belief that there is nobody essentially much above itself, it will not rise above its own level. A low standard means low achievement. In every one of the strata into which civilized society must of necessity be divided there are men capable of a higher place, and it is injustice to those whom Nature has so favored not to show them the heights to which they may aspire. What they do see clearly enough are the factitious heights of wealth and office; what they need also to see are those of human nature in its loftiest growth.

A nation is judged by its best products. To stand in the foremost rank, it must give to the human race great types of manhood, and add new thought to the treasury of the world. No extent of territory, no growth of population, no material prosperity, no average of intelligence, will ever be accepted as substitutes. They may excite fear, wonder, or even a kind of admiration, but they will never win or deserve the highest place.

Our civilization is weak in the head, though the body is robust and full of life. With all the practical vigor and diffused intelligence of the American people, our cultivated class is inferior to that of the leading countries of Europe; for not only does the sovereign Demos think he can do without it, but he is totally unable to distinguish the sham education from the real one. The favorite of his heart is that deplorable political failure, the "self-made man," whom he delights to honor, and to whom he confides the most perplexed and delicate interests, in full faith that, if he cannot unravel them, then nobody else can. He thinks that he must needs be a person of peculiar merit and unequaled vigor. His idea of what constitutes him is somewhat singular. He commends as self-made the man who picks up a half education at hap-hazard; but if, no matter with what exertion, he makes use of systematic and effective methods of training and instructing himself, then, in the view of Demos, he is self-made no longer.

The truth is, liberal education is at a prodigious disadvantage among us. In its nature it is only the beginning of a process that should continue through life; of a growth that will bear its fruit only in the fullness of time. Of what avail to nurse and enrich the young tree, if its after-years are to be spent in a soil and climate hostile or at least unfavorable to it? We do not say this in despondency, but simply to illustrate the position and its necessities. Amid the morbid leveling of the times, few signs are so hopeful as the growing strength of the higher education; but it is well to recognize with what it has to contend. In the platitudes of democratic society two counter-influences are apparent—the one a curse, and the other a blessing: First, those sudden upheavals of accumulated wealth which break with sinister portent that broad distribution of property which once formed our safety; and, secondly, this recent reënforcement of trained intelligence. Each confronts the other; for culture is no friend of vulgar wealth, and most of the mountains of gold and silver we have lately seen are in the keeping of those who are very ill fitted to turn them to the profit of civilization.

But culture—to use that inadequate word for want of a better—has, as we have said, to contend with formidable difficulties. The lower forms of ambition among us are stimulated to the utmost. The prizes held before them are enormous. The faculties that lead to money-making, and those that lead to political notoriety as distinguished from political eminence, have every opportunity and every incentive. Ability, poor and obscure, may hope to win untold wealth, rule over mines, railroads, and cities, and mount to all the glories of official station. As a consequence, we have an abundance of rich men and an abundance of clever politicians. Again, we would not be misunderstood. We have no wish to declaim against self-made men. There are those among them who deserve the highest respect and the warmest gratitude. If rarely themselves on the highest pinnacle of civilization, they are generally the sources, immediate or remote, from which our best civilization springs. Yet there are achievements to which they are equal only in exceptional cases. We have had but one Franklin; and even that great man had failings from which different influences would have delivered him. Nor was Franklin a product of democracy full-fledged.

While the faculties that win material success are spurred to the utmost, and urged to their strongest development, those that find their exercise in the higher fields of thought and action are far from being so. For the minds that mere wealth and mere notoriety cannot satisfy, the inducements are weak and the difficulties great. The slow but ominous transfer of power from superior to inferior types of men, as shown in city councils, legislatures, and Congress, has told with withering effect on the growth of true political ability. Debased as our politics are, they do not invite, and hardly even admit, the higher and stronger faculties to a part in them. Liberal education is robbed of its best continuance and consummation, in so far as it is shut out from that noblest field of human effort, the direction of affairs of state; that career of combined thought and action where all the forces of the mind are called forth, and of which the objects and results are to those of the average American politician what the discoveries and inventions of applied science are to the legerdemain of a street juggler. The professions still remain open, and in these comparatively limited fields the results are good. Literature offers another field; but here the temptation is powerful to write or speak down to the level of that vast average of education which makes the largest returns in profit and celebrity. The best literature we have has followed the natural law and sprung up in two or three places where educated intelligence had reached a point high enough to promise it a favorable hearing. For the rest, our writers address themselves to an audience so much accustomed to light food that they have no stomach for the strong. The public demand has its effect, too, on the pulpit. It is pleasanter to tell the hearer what he likes to hear than to tell him what he needs; and the love of popularity is not confined to the laity.

From one point of view, the higher education is of no great use among us. It is not necessary to make a millionaire, a party leader, such as our party leaders are, or a popular preacher or writer. So little is it needed for such purposes, that the country is full of so-called "practical men," who cry out against it in scorn. Yet, from a true point of view, it is of supreme use and necessity, and a deep responsibility rests on those who direct it. What shall be its aims? Literature, scholarship, and physical science, are all of importance; but, considered in themselves, their place is subordinate, for they cannot alone meet the requirements of the times. It has been said that liberal culture tends to separate men from the nation at large, and form them into a class apart; and, without doubt, this is to a certain degree true of the merely æsthetic, literary, or scholastic culture. What we most need is a broad and masculine education, bearing on questions of society and government; not repelling from active life, but preparing for it and impelling toward it. The discipline of the university should be a training for the arena; and, within the past few years, no little progress has been made in this direction.

Some half a century ago, a few devoted men began what seemed a desperate crusade against a tremendous national evil. American slavery has now passed into history. It died a death of violence, to our shame be it said; for the nation had not virtue, temperance, and wisdom enough, to abolish it peacefully and harmlessly; but it is dead. We would not compare the agitation against it to the far more complex and less animating movement by which alone our present evils can be met and checked. Conviction and enthusiasm, with very little besides, served the purpose of the abolition agitators. Their appeal was to sentiment and conscience, not to reason; and their work demanded a kind of men very different from those demanded by the work of political regeneration. The champion of the new reform will need no whit less enthusiasm, but it must be tempered with judgment and armed with knowledge. One idea will not serve him. He must have many, all tending to one end; an integrity that can neither be tempted nor ensnared, and a courage that nothing can shake.

Here, then, is a career worthy of the best, and demanding the best, for none but they can grapple with the complicated mischiefs of our politics. Those gallant youths, and others such as they, who were so ready to lay down life for their country, may here find a strife more difficult, and not less honorable. If there is virtue in them for an effort so arduous, then it is folly to despair. If a depraved political system sets them aside in favor of meaner men, and denies them the career to which the best interests of the nation call them, then let them attack this depraved system, and, in so doing, make a career of their own. The low politician is not a noble foe, but he is strong and dangerous enough to make it manly to fight him; and the cause of his adversary is the cause of the people, did they but know it; or at least of that part of the people that is worth the name. No doubt, the strife is strangely unequal; for on one side are ranged all the forces of self-interest, always present and always active; and on the other only duty and patriotism. But if the virtue and reason of the nation can be as well organized as its folly and knavery are organized to-day, a new hope will rise upon us, and they who can achieve such a result will not lack their reward. The "literary feller" may yet make himself a practical force, and, in presence of the public opinion which he has evoked, the scurvy crew who delight to give at him may be compelled to disguise themselves in garments of unwonted decency.

It is in the cities that the diseases of the body politic are gathered to a head, and it is here that the need of attacking them is most urgent. Here the dangerous classes are most numerous and strong, and the effects of flinging the suffrage to the mob are most disastrous. Here the barbarism that we have armed and organized stands ready to overwhelm us. Our cities have become a prey. Where the carcass is, the vultures gather together. The industrious are taxed to feed the idle, and offices are distributed to perpetuate abuses and keep knaves in power. Some of our city councils, where every ward sends its representatives, each according to its nature, offer a curious and instructive spectacle; for here one sees men of mind and character striving for honest government under vast and ever-increasing difficulties, mingled with vicious boors in whose faces brute, knave, and fool, contend which shall write his mark most vilely.

The theory of inalienable rights becomes an outrage to justice and common-sense, when it hands over great municipal corporations, the property of those who hold stock in them, to the keeping of greedy and irresponsible crowds controlled by adventurers as reckless as themselves, whose object is nothing but plunder. But the question is not one of politics; it is one of business, and political rights, inalienable or otherwise, are not in any true sense involved in it. The city which can so reorganize itself that those who supply the means of supporting it shall have the chief control over their expenditure, will lead the way in abolishing an anomaly as ridiculous as it is odious, and give an impulse to its own prosperity which will impel other cities to follow its example. That better class of citizens who have abandoned civic affairs in disgust, will gradually return and acquire in municipal administration a training which may avail them afterward in wider fields. The reform of cities would be a long and hopeful step toward the reform of the States and the nation.

THE WOMAN QUESTION

(From the *North American Review*, October, 1879)

The nineteenth century will be the riddle of history. With its universal activity and universal restlessness, currents and counter-currents, progress and reaction; now assailing old faiths, and now patching their venerable battlements to make itself a den there; now proclaiming the religion of science, now prone before the Vatican, and now groveling in prehistoric superstition; attacking the foundations of modern society; denouncing mediævalism and borrowing its rusty tools to build a new order of things—this nineteenth century, among its heterogeneous progeny has brought one to light that the world has not seen for many a day. The demand that women shall take an active part in politics is not quite new. That marvelous people of antiquity, the richness of whose political experience matched the power and splendor of their intellectual and æsthetic achievement, were not strangers to this supposed product of modern democracy. It appeared at Athens in the time of Aristophanes, who mocks it with not over-delicate satire. Much has been talked and written about it; yet we beg to add a few words more. It involves the whole question of the relations of men and women.

One would think that the subject to which men have given their chief attention since the world began would by this time be tolerably well understood, and that little doubt would remain as to the nature, capacities, and position of women. Varieties of race, modes of life, degrees of barbarism or civilization, have modified their relations to the other sex and changed the estimate set upon them. But, while shading and coloring differ, the outlines remain the same, answering in the human race to those that rudely but plainly mark the relations of sex through all the orders of animated nature. Nevertheless, when one sees the vast changes for the better which have already taken place in the position of women, it is impossible not to hope that the future has still others in store. In what direction are we to look for them, and through what influences? These are questions on which those who have at heart the welfare of women, in other words of all humanity, have differed and will no doubt continue for a long time to differ. Let us hope that, in discussing them, the airs of benign mastery which naturally annoy women will be avoided on one side, and postures of antagonism on both. The two sexes are one, and their interests are the same.

The order of Nature is marked by a prevailing consistency. Over all her great fields of action, she is at one with herself, though irregularities and contradictions appear in special cases. Individual men and women are often inharmonious in physical or mental structure, but it is not so with men as a whole, or women as a whole. The typical man or woman is perfectly self-consistent. The one is made for conflict—whether the physical conflict of actual war, or that sometimes no less bitter and cruel, of the competitions of business and ambition. His greater stature and firmer muscles are matched with a sterner spirit, less tender sensibilities, and susceptible nerves, a ruder hardihood, and, in nearly all strongly masculine natures, with a certain remnant of primitive ferocity, which lies latent in the bosom of the highest civilizations and impels their male offspring to adventures of war, the chase, and travel in savage and perilous lands. In short, this fighting animal is well appointed for his work, whether to confront his enemy in deadly strife, or to battle in the interest of a purpose or an idea against cold, hunger, fatigue, want, obloquy, or hope deferred. And to these qualities of achievement, he joins, at least relatively, a mind governed rather by reason than emotion, and a deliberate and logical adaptation of means to ends.

There is equal harmony on the other side. Here, the whole nature corresponds to the rounded outlines and softer muscles of the physical frame. There is the same universal fitness to a purpose, but a widely different one. The susceptibilities that unfit the typical woman for rude conflict are joined to high and priceless qualities, without which life would be a curse. Not that men are incapable of equal moral elevation. In this respect we believe that men and women stand, in different attitudes, on about the same level. Nor, because, under the inspiration of passion, men have drawn ideal portraits of women in prose and verse, does it follow that women are superior to the other sex. Women have admired men as much as men have admired women; but their admiration has not found the same expression, by reason of that principle of universal nature which makes the man the wooer, and not the woman. The ideal woman is a very noble creature, and so is the ideal man; and this is not the less true because the ideal is not often realized in either case.

It has been pretended that the distinctive mental qualities of women are inherited from ages of oppression. Never was there a shallower fallacy. Whatever qualities of a woman are transmissible by inheritance, may descend to all her offspring alike. The male infant would be as apt to receive them as the female.

The mental qualities of the latter are no more results of hereditary oppression than her bodily qualities. The supreme law of
sex has decreed that the boys shall be boys and that the girls
shall be girls. The natures of the two sexes are like the two
electricities of the magnet. Each needs the other, and is drawn
to the other; and as each is emphatically masculine or emphatically feminine, so is the strength of this mutual need.

The reciprocity between the two separate halves of human
nature extends over a wide field, not only in passions and emotions, but in the regions of moral and intellectual life. Most intelligent men have felt the stimulus and refreshment of the
faculties that spring from the companionship of an intelligent
and congenial woman, and which is unlike anything resulting
from the contact of a male mind. It is a fructifying power, with
which neither the world of thought nor the world of action
could well dispense. Many men of the higher sort recall as an
epoch in their lives that wonderful awakening of energies, ambitions, and aspirations which comes with the first consciousness of the influence of the other sex. Sometimes the change
amounts to revolution in character, and the young man can
hardly recognize himself in the boy of two or three years before.
The influence that begins the awakening is powerful to maintain
it. Hunger, thirst, the instinct of self-preservation, avarice,
malice, envy, and other of the lower motive forces, are self-
sustaining. But, excepting those that belong to the province
of religion, the nobler desires and energies draw impulse and
aliment from the principle of sex. Truth itself would seem
hardly worth the pursuit if women were not in the world.

This principle of sexual reciprocity, reigning through all
organized nature, except its lowest forms, widening and
strengthening as the scale of being rises, and culminating at
last in man, more intense and more comprehensive in him as he
is more highly and variously endowed than the creatures beneath him—this principle is the most pervading among the
forces of human life. Its degrees of power over individuals are
almost infinitely various, but the whole race is more or less in
subjection to it, or to the influences that rise out of it. Other

forces may outrival it in different persons at different times, but none of them has the same character of universality, and none is so prolific in results of all kinds, for evil and for good. It is the spring of the chief pleasures and the chief pains of life. It fires the noblest ambitions, and, misplaced or abused, becomes the source of unspeakable degradation.

What we are to observe is, that this imperial and all-essential power is founded not on resemblances but on differences of nature and function. These differences are so great that it may be doubted if men and women can ever quite understand each other. Women have a nice perception of male psychology in certain phases of life and character; but there are regions of masculine nature in which their perception is exceedingly faint and dim, because there is nothing that answers to them in their own consciousness; and no doubt the same holds good of men in their comprehension of women. It is true that the differences between the sexes are not uniform in degree. There are masculine women and feminine men. But when the two thus resemble each other, it is, for the most part, rather through defects than positive qualities. A woman is called masculine oftener because she lacks womanliness than because she possesses manliness; and a man is called feminine oftener because he lacks manliness than because he possesses womanliness. There are men who, through defects of nature, are indifferent to the society of women; and there are women equally so to the society of men. But the ocean rolls and surges, though in lazy nooks and quiet bays the waters lie unruffled, unconscious and incredulous of the turmoil without.

It has been said that question of the rights and employment of women should be treated without regard to sex. Mr. Wendell Phillips tells us that all those who so treat it are "high-minded," and all the others "low-minded." It should rather be said that those who consider it regardless of sex do not consider it at all. It will not do to exclude from the problem the chief factor in it, and deal with women only as if they were smaller and weaker men. Yet these have been the tactics of the agitators for female suffrage, and to them they mainly owe what little success they have had. Hence their extreme sensitiveness whenever the subject is approached on its most essential side. If it could be treated like other subjects, and discussed fully and freely, the cause of the self-styled reformers would have been hopeless from the first. It is happy for them that the relations of women to society can not be so discussed without giving just offense. Their most important considerations can be touched but slightly; and even then offense will be taken. It is only for us to see that it be not taken reasonably.

The immense disadvantages under which women are placed; the cruel hardship and injustice to which many of them are often subjected; the terrible and crushing penalties, sometimes grievously disproportioned to the real fault, to which they are liable; the misery and degradation of a numerous class, resulting in many cases more from circumstance than from intrinsic viciousness—all these taken together form the most perplexing and painful problem in human life. A remedy is looked for in a change of public opinion which shall visit the breach of chastity with equal condemnation in men and women. This remedy has long been urged, and probably at this moment there is in the world at large as little disposition to accept it as ever. There is nothing in the case of men in the slightest degree answering to these penalties imposed on women, except the contempt and disgrace with which every spirited people visits a display of cowardice. Fear, or the yielding to it, is great shame in a man, and none at all in a woman. But the cases are not parallel, for a man can retrieve lost honor, and a woman can not. Whence arise the different values attached to the same virtue in men and women, and why has every attempt to make them equal signally failed? The difference is due to the structure of civilized society, which, on both its political and its social side, is built on the family. Women, and not men, are of necessity the guardians of the integrity of the family and the truth of succession, with all the interests of affection, of maintenance, and of inheritance involved in them. Hence the virtue in question is far more important in them than in men. Some savage or barbarous peoples have evaded the difficulty by refusing to recognize the father at all in the question of kinship. When the whole system of lineage is traced through the woman alone, the reason for imposing special penalties upon her ceases, for her children must always be legitimate. This remedy, which exempts the father from any obligation to support his children if he does not choose to do so, can belong only to a low state of barbarism, though a practical adoption of it has lately been proposed, professedly in the interest of women. Nations less barbarous have tried to secure the object by constant watching and restriction, sometimes amounting to actual slavery. European civilization uses better and more effective means. It establishes a standard of honor, and trusts women to conform to it. In this they are generally aided by more delicate sensibilities, by passivity of temperament, and by being protected from the countless temptations that beset every man who mingles much with the world. Nor to him is the temptation from within less than those from without. To impose the same penalties on him that are imposed on a woman would not only be without the same necessity, but would be a far greater hardship.

Whatever liberty the best civilization may accord to women, they must always be subject to restrictions unknown to the other sex, and they can never dispense with the protecting influences which society throws about them. A man, in lonely places, has nothing to lose but life and property; and he has nerve and muscles to defend them. He is free to go whither he pleases, and run what risks he pleases. Without a radical change in human nature, of which the world has never given the faintest sign, women can not be equally emancipated. It is not a question of custom, habit, or public opinion; but of an all-pervading force, always formidable in the vast number of men in whom it is not controlled by higher forces. A woman is subject, also, to many other restrictions, more or less stringent, necessary to the maintenance of self-respect and the respect of others, and yet placing her at a disadvantage, as compared to men, in the active work of the world. All this is mere truism, but the plainest truism may be ignored in the interest of a theory or a "cause."

Again, everybody knows that the physical and mental constitution of woman is more delicate than in the other sex; and, we may add, the relations between mind and body more intimate and subtile. It is true that they are abundantly so in men; but their harder organism is neither so sensitive to disturbing influences nor subject to so many of them.

It is these and other inherent conditions, joined to the engrossing nature of a woman's special functions, that have determined through all time her relative position. What we have just said—and we might have said much more—is meant as a reminder that her greatest limitations are not of human origin. Men did not make them, and they can not unmake them. Through them, God and Nature have ordained that those subject to them shall not be forced to join in the harsh conflicts of the world militant. It is folly to ignore them, or try to counteract them by political and social quackery. They set at naught legislatures and peoples.

Notwithstanding limitations on one side and comparative freedom on the other, it would not be safe to say that the allotment of happiness to the two sexes is unequal. The life of men, like that of women, has its own hardships—the deadly strain of fierce competition, exhaustion without possibility of rest, heavy responsibilities, agonies of suspense and ruin. Aside from the low state of health of women in some civilized countries, and in America above all, it is likely that, on the whole, they have about the same share as men in the enjoyment of life. It is among those who have no part in the occupations and duties of the rest of their sex that one is most apt to find that morbid introversion, those restless cravings, that vague but torturing sense of destinies unfulfilled, and activities without an object, which rarely receive much pity, but perhaps deserve it as much as any of the more positive woes. There is no misery like the misery of vacuum. But among all the causes of female unhappiness, and involving and aggravating all the rest, there is none more fruitful of tribulation than ill health, which, in American women, brings with it disabilities equal, probably, to all the rest together. If our women are to rise to the height of their capacities, the first and indispensable requisite is physical regeneration.

It is the interest of men in general that women should reach their best development, just as it is the interest of individual men that those with whom they associate should be refined, instructed, intelligent, and high-minded. The question is only of means.

There is a universal law of growth and achievement. The man who knows himself, understands his own powers and aptitudes, forms purposes in accord with them, and pursues these purposes steadily, is the man of success. He who takes no account of his own nature, makes his will the father of his thought, shuts his eyes to unwelcome truths, places himself in false positions, and turns from the good within his reach to strain after the unattainable, is predestined to vexation and failure. Every one has his place in the world, and the wise and fortunate find it. As it is with men, so, in a measure, it is with women; and as it is with men and women as individuals, so it is with men as a whole, and women as a whole. One must make Nature an ally and not an enemy, for the strife is unequal. The palm will not grow in the soil and climate of the pine.

Most metaphors express more or less than the truth; and so does this. Between the life for which men alone are fit and that for which women alone are fit there lies a region where both may prosper. They may pursue the same objects, though seldom in precisely the same way, or with exactly the same results. In some employments women, with equal application and persistency, would certainly have an advantage. We do not mean to consider the relative intellectual power of the sexes. It is enough for our purpose to remember that the faculties of the two are exercised under different physical and moral conditions, which modify their action.

It is often and most justly said that the intellectual growth of the country bears no proportion to its material progress. The drift toward pursuits called practical is so strong that it carries with it nearly all the best male talent. The rush and whirl of business catches the men as in a maelstrom, and, if it sharpens and invigorates some of their powers, it dwarfs others, and narrows the mental horizon. Women are free from these disadvantages. Many of them have abundant leisure and opportunities of culture better than the best within the reach of men on this continent forty years ago. Their sex is itself a power if they use it rightly. They can, if they will, create and maintain higher standards of thought and purpose, raise the whole tone of national life, and give our civilization the fullness that it lacks; for, if they raise themselves, they will infallibly raise the men with them. But they will not do it by frothy declamation on platforms, or flooding the bookstalls with sensation stories, any more than by those other trivialities which professional female reformers denounce. Nor will they do it by trying to forget that they are women.

There is a strange want of dignity in the attitude of some of these reformers toward the question of the relations of their sex to society. Instead of claiming for them what is theirs, a nature of their own, with laws of its own, and a high capacity of independent development, they propose, as the aim of their ambition, the imitation of men. The position in which they try to place women may be said to answer to that of a colony to its metropolis; a provincialism which can not disappear till the colony learns the nature of its own worth, and accepts the conditions of its own vitality. Till then, its attitude is a continual admission of inferiority.

There is no country in which women enjoy such large and various liberty as with us; but it would be bold to say that American women, as a whole, are superior to those of other leading nations. In spite of their advantages, a vast proportion of them fall immeasurably short of the influence and consideration that ought to belong to them. We would by no means be understood to intimate that this is a consequence of liberty. It proceeds from a variety of causes, some of which act injuriously on men also; and foremost among them is an overstrained and morbid activity, an incessant tension of nerves, bred partly by climate, but incomparably more by the peculiar social conditions of a country where all kinds of competition, spurred by all kinds of stimulus, keep mind and body always on the stretch. The men feel them in the struggles of active life; the women in the ambitions, anxieties, and worries of a social existence, where emulation prevails from the highest to the lowest. And they, as the more susceptible and more easily deranged, suffer more than the men.

To reach the best results there must be a harmony and balance between body and mind, which can only come by giving its due exercise to each. In an athlete, who devotes his life to nothing but athletics, the muscles and sinews thrive at the expense of the mental faculties; but, in a man or women whose brain is overwrought, whether by important matters or by trifles, the body suffers without profit to the mind; for the abused physical nature quickly reacts on the mental, and both are impaired together. Worn as so many of our women are by this morbid action and reaction of body and mind, it is impossible for them to reach that full womanhood than which the world has nothing more beneficent or more noble.

In this condition of things, what do certain women demand for the good of their sex? To add to the excitements that are wasting them other and greater excitements, and to cares too much for their strength other and greater cares. Because they can not do their own work, to require them to add to it the work of men, and launch them into the turmoil where the most robust sometimes fail. It is much as if a man in a state of nervous exhaustion were told by his physician to enter at once for a foot-race or a boxing-match.

This brings us to our object, the consideration of the movement for female suffrage. It has been claimed as a right that women should vote. It is no right, but a wrong, that a small number of women should impose on all the rest political duties which there is no call for their assuming, which they do not want to assume, and which, if duly discharged, would be a cruel and intolerable burden. This pretense of the female suffragists was reduced to an absurdity when some of them gravely affirmed that, if a single woman wanted to vote, all the others ought to be required to do so.

Government by doctrines of abstract right, of which the French Revolution set the example and bore the fruits, involves enormous danger and injustice. No political right is absolute and of universal application. Each has its conditions, qualifications, and limitations. If these are disregarded, one right collides with another, or with many others. Even a man's right to liberty is subject to the condition that he does not use it to infringe the rights of his neighbors. It is in the concrete, and not in the abstract, that rights prevail in every sound and wholesome society. They are applied where they are applicable. A government of glittering generalities quickly destroys itself. The object of government is the accomplishment of a certain result, the greatest good of the governed; and the ways of reaching it vary in different countries and different social conditions. Neither liberty nor the suffrage are the end; they are nothing but means to reach it; and each should be used to the extent in which it is best adapted to its purpose. If the voting of women conduces to the greatest good of the community, then they ought to vote, and otherwise they ought not. The question of female suffrage thus becomes a practical question, and not one of declamation.

High civilization, ancient or modern, has hitherto rested on the family. The family, and not the individual, has been the political unit, and the head of the family, *in esse* or *in posse*, actual or prospective, has been the political representative of the rest. To give the suffrage to women would be to reject the principle that has thus far formed the basis of civilized government.

It is said, and incessantly repeated, that the influence of women has kept even pace with the growth of civilization. As respects direct political influence, this is certainly untrue. In former times, and under low social conditions, women have occasionally had a degree of power in public affairs unknown in the foremost nations of the modern world. The most savage tribe on this continent listened, in solemn assembly, to the counsels of its matrons, with a deference that has no parallel among its civilized successors. The people of ancient Lycia, at a time when they were semi-barbarians, gave such power to their women that they were reported to live under a gynecocracy, or female government. The word gynecocracy, by the way, belongs to antiquity. It has no application in modern life; and, in the past, its applications were found, not in the higher developments of ancient society, but in the lower. In the splendid civilization of Athens, women held a very subordinate place. In the France of two centuries and more ago, they had a share of political power greater than at any time since, though France had not then mounted to her full height.

A certain benign influence, indefinite and almost mystical in character, has been ascribed to "woman," which, it is proclaimed, will purify our politics. That, in some relations of life, the instincts of women are preëminently delicate and true; that in them the moral nature and the better emotions are more apt to rule than in the other sex; that their conscience is more sensitive, and their religious susceptibilities quicker and more controlling—is, happily, not to be denied; but they are no whit less human than men. Like them, they have "the defects of their qualities," and the very delicacy and impressibility of their mental and moral structure give efficacy to these defects. There are circumstances under which they rarely appear to advantage, or avail much for good.

There are some means of judging from experience whether they are likely to exert, in public life, the beneficent power ascribed to them. Many countries of Europe have been governed by queens, and this at a time when to wear a crown meant to hold a dominant power. According to the theory, these female reigns ought to have shown more virtuous and benign government than is generally found under the rule of men. The facts do not answer to the expectation. Isabella of Castile was full of amiable qualities, but she permitted herself to be made the instrument of diabolical religious persecution. Catharine II. of Russia was one of the ablest women who ever held a scepter, and one of the most profligate. Maria Theresa of Austria was in many respects far above the common level; but she was a sharer in what has been called the greatest of political crimes—the partition of Poland. That outrage was the work of three accomplices, two women and a man—the Empress of Russia, the Archduchess of Austria, and the King of Prussia. The reign of Henry IV. of France was one of the most beneficent in history. His first queen was a profligate and his second a virago, gravely suspected of having procured his assassination in collusion with her lover. The last wife of Louis XIV. was discreet and devout, but she favored the dragonnades, and called her brother to share the spoils of those atrocious persecutions. A throng of matchless statesmen, soldiers, philosophers, and poets made the reign of Elizabeth of England brilliant and great. It was adorned by the high and courageous spirit of the Queen, and sullied by her meanness, jealousy, and inordinate vanity. Mary of England lives in the memory of her bloody persecutions. Mary of Scotland was the thorn of her kingdom. Her fascinations have outlived three centuries, and so have her tumults of unbridled love and the dark suspicion of crime that rests upon her. The queen-mother of Charles IX. of France fomented, if she did not cause, the frightful massacre of St. Bartholomew, and surrounded herself with a band of beautiful and unscrupulous girls, whose charms she used systematically as means of political influence. There have been many bad kings, many indifferent ones, and a few who have earned the gratitude of all time. Many women have worn crowns, but we look among them in vain for one of those royal benefactors of the race. Not that women have less power for good than men. In some circumstances they have more. Their desire of good is often intense; but this desire has not been best fulfilled in the field of politics.

Besides queens, women in less eminent stations have sometimes had great political influence. This was never more true than in France at the middle of the seventeenth century, when the wives and daughters of the high nobility played a remarkable part in the politics of the day. The sagacious and able De Retz, who lived in the midst of these events, and took an important part in them, had unrivaled opportunities of studying women in their political character. His judgment is that they were very adroit in managing the strings of a party intrigue, but failed on great questions of policy. Two other points are prominent at this time: First, the action of these political ladies always had a personal bearing, and turned about some man or men from motives of love, predilection, jealousy, or schemes of alliance; secondly, with a few exceptions, they used their own charms, or those of other women, as means of gaining political advantages, and this without scruple, and sometimes without shame. Instead of purifying politics, they corrupted them.

Finally—and this instance, if it yields an argument to only half the country, yields it to the half that alone has need of it—the women of the South were more ardent for secession and slavery than the men; and, when the men knew that the cause was lost, their weaker partners refused to yield. Fighting was useless: but fair lips still cried, "Fight on!" It was the action of those two very different qualities—a woman's will and a man's resolution. The one can be argued with, and the other can not. The one is subject to reason; the other sees nothing but the object on which its heart is set, and strains after it in the teeth of ruin. Not that one does not continually meet women entirely reasonable in their aims, and in their pursuit of them; but this intractable element of "a woman's will" will have to be accounted with whenever the sex enters the lists of active politics.

Shakespeare gives a superb illustration of these two qualities, or rather of one of them. An intense desire possesses Lady Macbeth, and masters her whole being. A crown glitters before her eyes, and, as she gazes on it, fear, conscience, loyalty, the sacred law of hospitality, are all forgotten. The vehemence of her longing bears her on like a fate. Her husband hesitates, divided between duty and ambition. She taunts him with fear, and his admirable answer—

> "I dare do all that may become a man;
> Who dares do more is none"—

is wholly lost upon her. He yields; the deed is done, and the prize seized. Then come the avenging furies. She pines and dies under the tortures of the mind, while the sterner nature lives on, to perish at last by the sword, fighting with fierce desperation against the retributive doom.

This impetuous property of feminine nature, no doubt, may have its use at times. When a people is afflicted by some overwhelming evil, to be thrown off at any risk or sacrifice, then a one-idea vehemence of attack is not out of place. Such modes of attack are not confined to women. Ardent philanthropic reformers have commonly shown feminine characteristics, and assumed corresponding attitudes toward the objects of their zeal. But, useful as men of this stamp are in exceptional emergencies of a certain kind, the habitual reformer is generally a nuisance when he tries to deal with the broad and many-sided questions involved in the government of nations. These demand qualities widely different from his; and, as the foundation of them all, the essentially masculine one of justice.

One of the chief dangers of popular government is that of inconsiderate and rash legislation. In impatience to be rid of one evil, ulterior consequences are apt to be forgotten. In the haste to redress one wrong, a door may be opened to many. This danger would be increased immeasurably if the most impulsive and excitable half of humanity had an equal voice in the making of laws. And, in the administration of them, abstract right would then be made to prevail after a fashion somewhat startling. A lady of intelligence and admirable intentions, an ardent partisan on principles of pure humanitarianism, confessed that, in the last Presidential election, Florida had given a majority for the Democrats; but insisted that it was right to count it for Hayes, because other States had been counted wrongfully for Tilden. It was impossible to make her comprehend that government conducted on such principles would end in anarchy. In politics, the virtues of women would sometimes be as dangerous as their faults.

But it is not their virtues that we should see in the dust and scramble of the political arena. As, when white sand is mingled with black, the black is drawn to the magnet and the white is left behind, so the coarse and contentious among women would be drawn to politics by a sort of elective affinity. Those of finer sensibilities and more delicate scruples would remain in more congenial climates, and the law of natural selection would rule in all its force. The great majority of the sex would employ themselves in the duties which must be discharged so long as the world goes on, and distract themselves as little as might be with primary meetings, canvasses, conventions, and election campaigns. It has been said, and too truly, that the best men shun politics. Their endless complication, the innumerable wires that guide their machinery, and the dexterity required to work it, give to the practiced trickster who has made them his trade an advantage over far abler men who have not. The system of spoils draws hungry and rapacious crowds to choke incessantly the highways and by-ways of the public service, and the brevity and uncertainty of the tenure of office make it certain that those most fit for it will least care to accept it. If these and other causes have deterred the best men from taking part in active politics, they would deter the best women far more. All that is repulsive to the one would be incomparably more so to the other. If politics are to be purified by artfulness, effrontery, insensibility, a pushing self-assertion, and a glib tongue, then we may look for regeneration; for the typical female politician will be richly endowed with all these gifts.

Thus accoutered for the conflict, she may fairly hope to have the better of her masculine antagonist. A woman has the inalienable right of attacking without being attacked in turn. She may strike but must not be struck, either literally or figuratively. Most women refrain from abusing their privilege of non-combatants; but there are those in whom the sense of impunity breeds the cowardly courage of the virago, and makes the tongue more terrible than the sword. A man's tongue is strong only as the organ of reason or eloquence; but a woman's is a power in itself. During some angry party debate, the future House of Representatives will present an animated scene when, in or out of order, the female members take the floor.

In reckoning the resources of the female politicians, there is one which can by no means be left out. None know better than women the potency of feminine charms aided by feminine arts.

The woman "inside politics" will not fail to make use of an influence so subtle and strong, and of which the management is peculiarly suited to her talents. If—and the contingency is in the highest degree probable—she is not gifted with charms of her own, she will have no difficulty in finding and using others of her sex who are. If report is to be trusted, Delilah has already spread her snares for the Congressional Samson; and the power before which the wise fail and the mighty fall has been invoked against the sages and heroes of the Capitol. When "woman" is fairly "inside politics," the sensation press will reap a harvest of scandals more lucrative to itself than profitable to public morals. And, as the zeal of one class of female reformers has been, and no doubt will be, largely directed to their grievances in matters of sex, we shall have shrill-tongued discussions of subjects which had far better be let alone.

It may be said that the advocates of female suffrage do not look to political women for the purifying of politics, but to the votes of the sex at large. The two, however, can not be separated. It should be remembered that the question is not of a limited and select female suffrage, but of a universal one. To limit would be impossible. It would seek the broadest areas and the lowest depths, and spread itself through the marshes and malarious pools of society. Those instincts that dart to their goal while the reason of man gropes and wanders; that love of the good and the beautiful which is to soothe the raging waters, and guide their currents in ways of peace and right—these belong to the chosen of their sex alone; and, even in them, it may be doubted whether they would find profitable exercise in American politics. Faith is indispensable to all achievement; but it must not quarrel with common sense, nor walk with eyes shut. If it does, it will lead not to success, but to disaster. Now, the most ardent faith, if joined with common sense and the faintest knowledge of human nature, will fail to discern in the great mass of the female sex any promise of purer and wiser government. Women, as a whole, have less sense of political responsibility than men. For this there are various reasons, but one will suffice. They have shared very imperfectly in the traditions, and not at all in the practice of self-government. The men of free countries have been trained to a sense of political responsibility by long striving for political rights, the memory of which has acted as a continual education, special to one sex because the other has had neither the will nor the opportunity to share it. By slow progress in the acquisition of these rights, they have acquired a consciousness of their value, some knowledge of the conditions on which they rest, and the skill to use them. In the freest countries, and our own among the rest, there are large numbers of men who have not received this training, have never learned the art of self-government, and can not share in it without injury and danger to the state. Women as a whole may be said to be in the condition of persons devoid of this training, and of the sense of political responsibility that grows out of it, excepting a minority composed of the more thoughtful, who have acquired it by education, conscientiousness, and association with the better sort of men. But the vast majority have little or none of it; and hence, if they are to be admitted at all to a share in public affairs, they should be admitted very gradually. We say nothing here of those differences of nature that have hitherto in all ages, countries, and races, made men the governing half of the race. What we urge is, that now and for generations to come, woman as a whole must of necessity come into politics far less prepared for them than men as a whole. Large masses now vote who are unprepared to vote. The unprepared women are incomparably more numerous, and in many of them the want of preparation is complete and absolute. This is the condition of nearly all those in the lower strata of society. We shall of course be told that they must go into the water before they can learn to swim; but what is proposed is not to teach them to swim: it is to throw them all at once into a fathomless ocean, where they will drown themselves, and pull down those who were swimming there, or trying to swim before them.

A French statesman once said that, against a mob of women, the Government is entirely helpless. There are no means of repression. Bullets, bayonets, sabers, and grapeshot are out of the question. And yet, in the French Revolution, female mobs were fiercer and more destructive than those of men. To give women the suffrage is to expose the most excitable part of the human race to the influence of political passions with no means of defense against possible consequences. A body of legislators coerced by a female mob would be in a position as pitiable as ridiculous. There are those who think that the suffrage would act as a safety-valve to political passions; but it has not so acted in the case of men. Dissatisfied masses, foiled of their purpose at the polls, are more apt to resort to force than if they had not already tried lawful means without success. The bloody riots of 1877 were the work of men in full enjoyment of the suffrage. It is to the dread of lead and steel that the friends of order must look in the last resort; and, when this does not exist, political frenzy will have its way.

If the better class of women flatter themselves that they can control the others, they are doomed to disappointment. They will be outvoted in their own kitchens, without reckoning the agglomerations of poverty, ineptitude, and vice that form a startling proportion of our city populations. It is here that the male vote alone threatens our system with its darkest perils. The female vote would enormously increase the evil, for it is often more numerous, always more impulsive, and less subject to reason; and, through causes which we gave above, almost devoid of the sense of responsibility. Here the bad politician would find his richest resources. He could not reach the better class of female voters, but the rest would be ready to his hand. Many women will sell themselves; many more would sell their votes. Three fourths of them, when not urged by some pressing need or contagious passion, would be moved, not by principles, but by personal predilections. These, even with the best of their sex, do not always lean to the soundest and most stable wisdom, either for public or private life. We deprecate any interpretation of disrespect. We have known a gracious and noble example of cultured womanhood who could by no means be persuaded that one of the worst of our politicians, reputed also one of the most agreeable, was not all that he appeared; and who would infallibly have given him her vote, if she had had one to give. The female cohorts of crowded cities would espouse the cause of their favorites with a vehemence unknown to men; but it would be fatuity to believe that they would choose them in the interest of good government. We say nothing of the outcasts of society; though they, too, would have their watchword and their chief.

The evils of universal female, as of universal male suffrage, would be greatest in dense industrial populations. In the country, they would be less felt, and least of all in the rough and simple life of the thinly-settled borders, or the far West. Like other political evils, they would reach their climax in great cities. The government of these is difficult enough already. To make it impossible would be madness.

If it is urged that tax-paying women ought to vote in virtue of their tax-paying, it should be remembered that men have no such right. With us, the beggar and the millionaire vote alike. No political power is granted to the rich that is not granted to the poor; or, in other words, property is not acknowledged as a basis of representation. It is taxed, not because it confers a franchise, but because the Government protects or is presumed to protect it. The same measure of protection is given to the property of a woman as to that of a man. If female tax-payers were allowed to vote, one of two things would happen: a principle of government which was repudiated in the interest of democracy would be restored in the interest of wealth; or else all women, rich or poor, would receive the franchise together. The first alternative is hardly possible; under the second, the female property-holder would have her own vote to defend her property along with several needy female votes to imperil it; for the poor women outnumber the rich.

Those who wish the Roman Catholic Church to subvert our school system, control legislation, and become a mighty political force, can not do better than labor day and night for female suffrage. This, it is true, is opposed to every principle and tradition of that great Church, which, nevertheless, would reap from it immense benefits. The priests have little influence over a considerable part of their male flock; but their power is great over the women, who would repair to the polls at the word of command with edifying docility and zeal.

The right of voting and the duty of fighting should never be divorced. Women, though non-combatant, are abundantly combative when excited. It is conceivable that they might discover a *casus belli* when the men could not see it; and, with or without the help of sympathizing male zealots, might vote in majority that the men should fight. This they would probably refuse to do against their wishes and convictions, and the women, with law clearly on their side, could not help themselves. Law with no power to enforce it is futile and sometimes ridiculous. The above contingency is not likely to occur; but that it is simply possible shows the false position of a government subject to female suffrage.

Neither Congress, nor the States, nor the united voice of the whole people could permanently change the essential relations of the sexes. Universal female suffrage, even if decreed, would undo itself in time; but the attempt to establish it would work deplorable mischief. The question is, whether the persistency of a few agitators shall plunge us blindfold into the most reckless of all experiments; whether we shall adopt this supreme device for developing the defects of women, and demolish their real power to build an ugly mockery instead. For the sake of womanhood, let us hope not. In spite of the effect on the popular mind of the incessant repetition of a few trite fallacies, and in spite of the squeamishness that prevents the vast majority averse to the movement from uttering a word against it, let us trust that the good sense of the American people will vindicate itself against this most unnatural and pestilent revolution. In the full and normal development of womanhood lie the best interests of the world. Let us labor earnestly for it, and, that we may not labor in vain, let us save women from the barren perturbations of American politics. Let us respect them, and, that we may do so, let us pray for deliverance from female suffrage.

[LITERARY CRITICISM]

THE WORKS OF JAMES FENIMORE COOPER

(From the *North American Review*, January, 1852)

The Works of James Fenimore Cooper. Author's Revised Edition. New York: G. P. Putnam. 1851. 12mo.

No American writer has been so extensively read as James Fenimore Cooper. His novels have been translated into nearly every European tongue. Nay, we are told—but hardly know how to believe it—that they may be had duly rendered into Persian at the bazaars of Ispahan. We have seen some of them, well thumbed and worn, at a little village in a remote mountainous district of Sicily; and in Naples and Milan, the bookstalls bear witness that "*L'Ultimo dei Mohecanni*" is still a popular work. In England, these American novels have been eagerly read and transformed into popular dramas; while cheap and often stupidly mutilated editions of them have been circulated through all her colonies, garrisons, and naval stations, from New Zealand to Canada.

Nor is this widely spread popularity undeserved. Of all American writers, Cooper is the most original, the most thoroughly national. His genius drew aliment from the soil where God had planted it, and rose to a vigorous growth, rough and gnarled, but strong as a mountain cedar. His volumes are a faithful mirror of that rude transatlantic nature, which to European eyes appears so strange and new. The sea and the forest have been the scenes of his countrymen's most conspicuous achievements; and it is on the sea and in the forest that Cooper is most at home. Their spirit inspired him, their images were graven on his heart; and the men whom their embrace has nurtured, the sailor, the hunter, the pioneer, move and act upon his pages with all the truth and energy of real life.

There is one great writer with whom Cooper has been often compared, and the comparison is not void of justice; for though, on the whole, far inferior, there are certain high points of literary excellence in regard to which he may contest the palm with Sir Walter Scott. It is true, that he has no claim to share the humor and pathos, the fine perception of beauty and delicacy in character, which adds such charms to the romances of Scott. Nor can he boast that compass and variety of power, which could deal alike with forms of humanity so diverse; which could portray with equal mastery the Templar Bois Guilbert, and the Jewess Rebecca; the manly heart of Henry Morton, and the gentle heroism of Jeanie Deans. But notwithstanding this unquestioned inferiority on the part of Cooper, there were marked affinities between him and his great contemporary. Both were practical men, able and willing to grapple with the hard realities of the world. Either might have learned with ease to lead a regiment, or command a line-of-battle ship. Their conceptions of character were no mere abstract ideas, or unsubstantial images, but solid embodiments in living flesh and blood. Bulwer and Hawthorne—the conjunction may excite a smile—are writers of a different stamp. Their conceptions are often exhibited with consummate skill, and, in one of these examples at least, with admirable truthfulness; but they never cheat us into a belief of their reality. We may marvel at the skill of the artist, but we are prone to regard his creations rather as figments of art than as reproductions of nature,—as a series of vivified and animate pictures, rather than as breathing men and women. With Scott and with Cooper it is far otherwise. Dominie Sampson and the Antiquary are as distinct and familiar to our minds as some eccentric acquaintance of our childhood. If we met Long Tom Coffin on the wharf at New Bedford, we should wonder where we had before seen that familiar face and figure. The tall, gaunt form of Leatherstocking, the weather-beaten face, the bony hand, the cap of foxskin, and the old hunting frock, polished with long service, seem so palpable and real, that, in some moods of mind, one may easily confound them with the memories of his own experiences. Others have been gifted to conceive the elements of far loftier character, and even to combine these elements in a manner equally truthful; but few have rivalled Cooper in the power of breathing into his creations the breath of life, and turning the phantoms of his brain into seeming realities. It is to this, in no small measure, that he owes his widely spread popularity. His most successful portraitures are drawn, it is true, from humble walks and rude associations; yet they are instinct with life, and stamped with the impress of a masculine and original genius.

The descriptions of external nature with which Cooper's works abound bear a certain analogy to his portraitures of character. There is no glow upon his pictures, no warm and varied coloring, no studied contrast of light and shade. Their virtue consists in their fidelity, in the strength with which they impress themselves upon the mind, and the strange tenacity with which they cling to the memory. For our own part, it was many years since we had turned the pages of Cooper, but still we were haunted by the images which his spell had evoked;—the dark gleaming of hill-embosomed lakes, the tracery of forest boughs against the red evening sky, and the raven flapping his black wings above the carnage field near the Horican. These descriptions have often, it must be confessed, the great fault of being overloaded with detail; but they are utterly mistaken who affirm, as some have done, that they are but a catalogue of commonplaces,—mountains and woods, rivers and torrents, thrown together as a matter of course. A genuine love of nature inspired the artist's pen; and they who cannot feel the efficacy of its strong picturing have neither heart nor mind for the grandeur of the outer world.

Before proceeding, however, we must observe that, in speaking of Cooper's writings, we have reference only to those happier offspring of his genius which form the basis of his reputation; for, of that numerous progeny which of late years have swarmed from his pen, we have never read one, and therefore, notwithstanding the ancient usage of reviewers, do not think ourselves entitled to comment upon them.

The style of Cooper is, as style must always be, in no small measure the exponent of the author's mind. It is not elastic or varied, and is certainly far from elegant. Its best characteristics are a manly directness, and a freedom from those prettinesses, studied turns of expression, and petty tricks of rhetoric, which are the pride of less masculine writers. Cooper is no favorite with *dilettanti* critics. In truth, such criticism does not suit his case. He should be measured on deeper principles, not by his manner, but by his pith and substance. A rough diamond, and he is one of the roughest, is worth more than a jewel of paste, though its facets may not shine so clearly.

And yet, try Cooper by what test we may, we shall discover in him grave defects. The field of his success is, after all, a narrow one, and even in his best works he often oversteps its limits. His attempts at sentiment are notoriously unsuccessful. Above all, when he aspires to portray a heroine, no words can express the remarkable character of the product. With simple country girls he succeeds somewhat better; but when he essays a higher flight, his failure is calamitous. The most rabid asserter of the rights of woman is scarcely more ignorant of woman's true power and dignity. This is the more singular, as his novels are very far from being void of feeling. They seldom, however —and who can wonder at it?—find much favor with women, who for the most part can see little in them but ghastly stories of shipwrecks, ambuscades, and bush fights, mingled with prolix descriptions and stupid dialogues. Their most appreciating readers may perhaps be found, not among persons of sedentary and studious habits, but among those of a more active turn, military officers and the like, whose tastes have not been trained into fastidiousness, and who are often better qualified than literary men to feel the freshness and truth of the author's descriptions.

The merit of a novelist is usually measured less by his mere power of description than by his skill in delineating character. The permanency of Cooper's reputation must, as it seems to us, rest upon three or four finely conceived and admirably executed portraits. We do not allude to his Indian characters, which it must be granted, are for the most part either superficially or falsely drawn; while the long conversations which he puts into their mouths, are as truthless as they are tiresome. Such as they are, however, they have been eagerly copied by a legion of the smaller poets and novel writers; so that, jointly with Thomas Campbell, Cooper is responsible for the fathering of those aboriginal heroes, lovers, and sages, who have long formed a petty nuisance in our literature. The portraits of which we have spoken are all those of white men, from humble ranks of society, yet not of a mean or vulgar stamp. Conspicuous before them all stands the well known figure of Leatherstocking. The life and character of this personage are contained in a series of five independent novels, entitled, in honor of him, The Leatherstocking Tales. Cooper has been censured, and even ridiculed, for this frequent reproduction of his favorite hero, which, it is affirmed, argues poverty of invention; and yet there is not one of the tales in question with which we would willingly part. To have drawn such a character is in itself sufficient honor; and had Cooper achieved nothing else, this alone must have insured him a wide and merited renown. There is something admirably felicitous in the conception of this hybrid offspring of civilization and barbarism, in whom uprightness, kindliness, innate philosophy, and the truest moral perceptions are joined with the wandering instincts and hatred of restraint which stamp the Indian or the Bedouin. Nor is the character in the least unnatural. The white denizens of the forest and the prairie are often among the worst, though never among the meanest, of mankind; but it is equally true, that where the moral instincts are originally strong, they may find nutriment and growth among the rude scenes and grand associations of the wilderness. Men as true, generous, and kindly as Leatherstocking may still be found among the perilous solitudes of the West. The quiet, unostentatious courage of Cooper's hero had its counterpart in the character of Daniel Boone; and the latter had the same unaffected love of nature which forms so pleasing a feature in the mind of Leatherstocking.

Civilization has a destroying as well as a creating power. It is exterminating the buffalo and the Indian, over whose fate too many lamentations, real or affected, have been sounded for us to renew them here. It must, moreover, eventually sweep from before it a class of men, its own precursors and pioneers, so remarkable both in their virtues and their faults, that few will see their extinction without regret. Of these men Leatherstocking is the representative; and though in him the traits of the individual are quite as prominent as those of the class, yet his character is not on this account less interesting, or less worthy of permanent remembrance. His life conveys in some sort an epitome of American history, during one of its most busy and decisive periods. At first, we find him a lonely young hunter in what was then the wilderness of New York. Ten or twelve years later, he is playing his part manfully in the Old French War. After the close of the Revolution, we meet him again on the same spot where he was first introduced to us; but now every thing is changed. The solitary margin of the Otsego lake is transformed into the seat of a growing settlement, and the hunter, oppressed by the restraints of society, turns his aged footsteps westward in search of his congenial solitudes. At length, we discover him for the last time, an octogenarian trapper, far out on the prairies of the West. It is clear that the successive stages of his retreat from society could not well be presented in a single story, and that the repetition which has been charged against Cooper as a fault was indispensable to the development of his design.

The Deerslayer, the first novel in the series of the Leatherstocking Tales, seems to us one of the most interesting of Cooper's productions. He has chosen for the scene of his story the Otsego lake, on whose banks he lived and died, and whose scenery he has introduced into three, if not more, of his novels. The Deerslayer, or Leatherstocking, here makes his first appearance as a young man, in fact scarcely emerged from boyhood, yet with all the simplicity, candor, feeling, and penetration, which mark his riper years. The old buccaneer in his aquatic habitation, and the contrasted characters of his two daughters, add a human interest to the scene, for the want of which the highest skill in mere landscape painting cannot compensate. The character of Judith seems to us the best drawn, and by far the most interesting, female portrait in any of Cooper's novels with which we are acquainted. The story, however, is not free from the characteristic faults of its author. Above all, it contains, in one instance at least, a glaring exhibition of his aptitude for describing horrors. When he compels his marvellously graphic pen to depict scenes which would disgrace the shambles or the dissecting table, none can wonder that ladies and young clergymen regard his pages with abhorrence. These, however, are but casual defects in a work which bears the unmistakable impress of genius.

The Pathfinder forms the second volume of the series, and is remarkable, even among its companions, for the force and distinctness of its pictures. For ourselves—though we diligently perused the despatches—the battle of Palo Alto and the storming of Monterey are not more real and present to our mind than some of the scenes and characters of The Pathfinder, though we have not read it for nine years;—the little fort on the margin of Lake Ontario, the surrounding woods and waters, the veteran major in command, the treacherous Scotchman, the dogmatic old sailor, and the Pathfinder himself. Several of these scenes are borrowed in part from Mrs. Grant's Memoirs of an American Lady; but in borrowing, Cooper has transmuted shadows into substance. Mrs. Grant's facts—for as such we are to take them—have an air of fiction; while Cooper's fiction wears the aspect of solid fact. His peculiar powers could not be better illustrated than by a comparison of the passages alluded to in the two books.

One of the most widely known of Cooper's novels is The Last of the Mohicans, which forms the third volume of the series, and which, with all the elements of a vulgar popularity, combines excellences of a far higher order. It has, nevertheless, its great and obstrusive faults. It takes needless liberties with history; and though it would be folly to demand that an historical novelist should always conform to received authorities, yet it is certainly desirable that he should not unnecessarily set them at defiance; since the incidents of the novel are apt to remain longer in the memory than those of the less palatable history. But whatever may be the extent of the novelist's license, it is, at all events, essential that his story should have some semblance of probability, and not run counter to nature and common sense. In The Last of the Mohicans, the machinery of the plot falls little short of absurdity. Why a veteran officer, pent up in a little fort, and hourly expecting to be beleaguered by a vastly superior force, consisting in great part of bloodthirsty savages, should at that particular time desire or permit a visit from his two daughters, is a question not easy to answer. Nor is the difficulty lessened when it is remembered, that the young ladies are to make the journey through a wilderness full of Indian scalping parties. It is equally difficult to see why the lover of Alice should choose, merely for the sake of a romantic ride, to conduct her and her sister by a circuitous and most perilous by-path through the forests, when they might more easily have gone by a good road under the safe escort of a column of troops who marched for the fort that very morning. The story founded on these gross inventions is sustained by various minor improbabilities, which cannot escape the reader unless his attention is absorbed by the powerful interest of the narrative.

It seems to us a defect in a novel or a poem, when the heroine is compelled to undergo bodily hardship, to sleep out at night in the woods, drenched by rain, stung by mosquitos and scratched by briars,—to forego all appliances of the toilet, and above all, to lodge in an Indian wigwam. Women have sometimes endured such privation, and endured it with fortitude; but it may be safely affirmed, that for the time, all grace and romance were banished from their presence. We read Longfellow's Evangeline with much sympathy in the fortunes of the errant heroine, until, as we approached the end of the poem, every other sentiment was lost in admiration at the unparalleled extent of her wanderings, at the dexterity with which she contrived to elude at least a dozen tribes of savages at that time in a state of war, at the strength of her constitution, and at her marvellous proficiency in woodcraft. When, however, we had

followed her for about two thousand miles on her forest pilgrimage, and reflected on the figure she must have made, so
tattered and bepatched, bedrenched and bedraggled, we could
not but esteem it a happy circumstance that she failed, as she
did, to meet her lover; since, had he seen her in such plight,
every spark of sentiment must have vanished from his breast,
and all the romance of the poem have been ingloriously extinguished. With Cooper's heroines, Cora and Alice, the case is
not so hard. Yet, as it does not appear that, on a journey of
several weeks, they were permitted to carry so much as a valise
or a carpet bag, and as we are expressly told, that on several
occasions, they dropped by the wayside their gloves, veils, and
other useful articles of apparel, it is certain, that at the journey's end, they must have presented an appearance more adapted
to call forth a Christian sympathy than any emotion of a more
romantic nature.

In respect to the delineation of character, The Last of the
Mohicans is surpassed by several other works of the author. Its
distinguishing merit lies in its descriptions of scenery and action.
Of the personages who figure in it, one of the most interesting
is the young Mohican, Uncas, who, however, does not at all
resemble a genuine Indian. Magua, the villain of the story, is a
less untruthful portrait. Cooper has been criticized for having
represented him as falling in love with Cora; and the criticism
is based on the alleged ground that passions of this kind are
not characteristic of the Indian. This may, in some qualified
sense, be true; but it is well known that Indians, in real life as
well as in novels, display a peculiar partiality for white women,
on the same principle by which Italians are prone to admire a
light complexion, while Swedes regard a brunette with highest
esteem. Cora was the very person to fascinate an Indian. The
coldest warrior would gladly have received her into his lodge,
and promoted her to be his favorite wife, wholly dispensing, in
honor of her charms, with flagellation or any of the severer
marks of conjugal displeasure.

The character of Hawkeye or Leatherstocking is, in the Mohicans as elsewhere, clearly and admirably drawn. He often

displays, however, a weakness which excites the impatience of the reader,—an excessive and ill-timed loquacity. When, for example, in the fight at Glenn's Falls, he and Major Heywood are crouching in the thicket, watching the motions of four Indians, whose heads are visible above a log at a little distance, and who, in the expression of Hawkeye himself, are gathering for a rush, the scout employs the time in dilating upon the properties of the "long-barrelled, soft-metalled rifle." The design is, no doubt, to convey an impression of his coolness in moments of extreme danger; but under such circumstances, the bravest man would judge it the part of good sense to use his eyes rather than his tongue. Men of Hawkeye's class, however talkative they may be at the camp-fire, are remarkable for preserving a close silence while engaged in the active labors of their calling.

It is easy to find fault with The Last of the Mohicans; but it is far from easy to rival or even approach its excellences. The book has the genuine game flavor; it exhales the odors of the pine woods and the freshness of the mountain wind. Its dark and rugged scenery rises as distinctly on the eye as the images of the painter's canvas, or rather as the reflection of nature herself. But it is not as the mere rendering of material forms, that these wood paintings are most highly to be esteemed. They are instinct with life, with the very spirit of the wilderness; they breathe the sombre poetry of solitude and danger. In these achievements of his art, Cooper, we think, has no equal, unless it may be the author of that striking romance, Wacousta or the Prophecy, whose fine powers of imagination are, however, even less under the guidance of a just taste than those of the American novelist.

The most obvious merit of The Last of the Mohicans consists in its descriptions of action, in the power with which the author absorbs the reader's sympathies, and leads him, as it were, to play a part in the scene. One reads the accounts of a great battle—aside from any cause or principle at issue—with the same kind of interest with which he beholds the grand destructive phenomena of nature, a tempest at sea, or a tornado in the tropics; yet with a feeling far more intense, since the conflict is not a mere striving of insensate elements, but of living tides of human wrath and valor. With descriptions of petty skirmishes or single combats, the feeling is of a different kind. The reader is enlisted in the fray, a partaker, as it were, in every thought and movement of the combatants, in the alternations of fear and triumph, the prompt expedient, the desperate resort, the palpitations of human weakness, or the courage that faces death. Of this species of description, the scene of the conflict at Glenn's Falls is an admirable example, unsurpassed, we think, even by the combat of Balfour and Bothwell, or by any other passage of the kind in the novels of Scott. The scenery of the fight, the foaming cataract, the little islet with its stout-hearted defenders, the precipices and the dark pine woods, add greatly to the effect. The scene is conjured before the reader's eye, not as a vision or a picture, but like the tangible presence of rock, river, and forest. His very senses seem conspiring to deceive him. He seems to feel against his cheek the wind and spray of the cataract, and hear its sullen roar, amid the yells of the assailants and the sharp crack of the answering rifle. The scene of the strife is pointed out to travellers as if this fictitious combat were a real event of history. Mills, factories, and bridges have marred the native wildness of the spot, and a village has usurped the domain of the forest; yet still those foaming waters and black sheets of limestone rock are clothed with all the interest of an historic memory; and the cicerone of the place can show the caves where the affrighted sisters took refuge, the point where the Indians landed, and the rock whence the despairing Huron was flung into the abyss. Nay, if the lapse of a few years has not enlightened his understanding, the guide would as soon doubt the reality of the battle of Saratoga, as that of Hawkeye's fight with the Mingoes.

The Pioneers, the fourth volume of the series, is, in several respects, the best of Cooper's works. Unlike some of its companions, it bears every mark of having been written from the results of personal experience; and indeed, Cooper is well known to have drawn largely on the recollections of his earlier years in the composition of this novel. The characters are full of vitality and truth, though, on one or two instances, the excellence of delineation is impaired by a certain taint of vulgarity. Leatherstocking, as he appears in The Pioneers, must certainly have had his living original in some gaunt, gray-haired old woodsman, to whose stories of hunts and Indian fights the author may perhaps have listened in his boyhood with rapt ears, unconsciously garnering up in memory the germs which time was to develop into a rich harvest. The scenes of the Christmas turkey-shooting, the fish-spearing by firelight on Otsego lake, the rescue from the panther, and the burning of the woods, are all inimitable in their way. Of all Cooper's works, The Pioneers seems to us most likely to hold a permanent place in literature, for it preserves a vivid reflection of scenes and characters which will soon have passed away.

The Prairie, the last of the Leatherstocking Tales, is a novel of far inferior merit. The story is very improbable, and not very interesting. The pictures of scenery are less true to nature than in the previous volumes, and seem to indicate that Cooper had little or no personal acquaintance with the remoter parts of the West. The book, however, has several passages of much interest, one of the best of which is the scene in which the aged trapper discovers, in the person of a young officer, the grandson of Duncan Heywood and Alice Munro, whom, half a century before, he had protected when in such imminent jeopardy on the rocks of Glenn's Falls and among the mountains of Lake George. The death of Abiram White is very striking, though reminding the reader too much of a similar scene in The Spy. The grand deformity of the story is the wretched attempt at humor in the person of Dr. Obed Battius. David Gamut, in The Mohicans, is bad enough; but Battius outherods Herod, and great must be the merit of the book which one such incubus would not sink beyond redemption.

The novel, which first brought the name of Cooper into distinguished notice, was The Spy; and this book, which gave him his earliest reputation, will contribute largely to preserve it. The story is full of interest, and the character of Harvey Birch is drawn with singular skill.

The Pilot is usually considered the best of Cooper's sea tales. It is in truth a masterpiece of his genius; and although the reader is apt to pass with impatience over the long conversations among the ladies at St. Ruth's, and between Alice Dunscombe and the disguised Paul Jones, yet he is amply repaid when he follows the author to his congenial element. The description of the wreck of the Ariel, and the death of Long Tom Coffin, can scarcely be spoken of in terms of too much admiration. Long Tom is to Cooper's sea tales what Leatherstocking is to the novels of the forest,—a conception so original and forcible, that posterity will hardly suffer it to escape from remembrance. The Red Rover, The Water-Witch, and the remainder of the sea tales, are marked with the same excellences and defects with the novels already mentioned, and further comments would therefore be useless.

The recent death of the man who had achieved so much in the cause of American literature has called forth, as it should have done, a general expression of regret; and the outcries, not unprovoked, which of late have been raised against him, are drowned in the voice of sorrow. The most marked and original of American writers has passed from among us. It was an auspicious moment when his earlier works first saw the light; for there was promise in their rude vigor,—a good hope that from such rough beginnings the country might develop a literary progeny which, taking lessons in the graces, and refining with the lapse of years, might one day do honor to its parentage; and when the chastened genius of Bryant arose, it seemed that the fulfilment of such a hope was not far remote. But this fair promise has failed, and to this hour the purpose, the energy, the passion of America have never found their adequate expression on the printed page. The number of good writers truly American, by which we mean all those who are not imitators of foreign modes, might be counted on the fingers of the two hands; nor are the writers of this small class, not excepting even Bryant himself, in any eminent degree the favorites of those among their countrymen who make pretensions to taste and refinement. As in life and manners the American people seem bent on aping the polished luxury of another hemisphere, so likewise they reserve their enthusiasm and their purses for the honeyed verse and the sugared prose of an emasculate and supposititious literature.

Some French writer,—Chateaubriand, we believe,—observes that the only portion of the American people who exhibit any distinctive national character are the backwoodsmen of the West. The remark is not strictly true. The whole merchant marine, from captains to cabin-boys, the lumbermen of Maine, the farmers of New England, and indeed all the laboring population of the country, not of foreign origin, are marked with strong and peculiar traits. But when we ascend into the educated and polished classes, these peculiarities are smoothed away, until, in many cases, they are invisible. An educated Englishman is an Englishman still; an educated Frenchman is often intensely French; but an educated American is apt to have no national character at all. The condition of the literature of the country is, as might be expected, in close accordance with these peculiarities of its society. With but few exceptions, the only books which reflect the national mind are those which emanate from, or are adapted to, the unschooled classes of the people; such, for example, as Dr. Bird's Nick of the Woods, The Life of David Crockett, The Big Bear of Arkansas, with its kindred legends, and, we may add, the earlier novels of Cooper. In the politer walks of literature, we find much grace of style, but very little originality of thought,—productions which might as readily be taken for the work of an Englishman as of an American.

This lack of originality has been loudly complained of, but it seems to us inevitable under the circumstances. The healthful growth of the intellect, whether national or individual, like healthful growth of every other kind, must proceed from the action of internal energies, and not from foreign aid. Too much assistance, too many stimulants, weaken instead of increasing it. The cravings of the American mind, eager as they are, are amply supplied by the copious stream of English current literature. Thousands, nay, millions of readers and writers drink from this bounteous source, and feed on this foreign aliment, till the whole complexion of their thoughts is tinged with it, and by a sort of necessity they think and write at second hand. If this transatlantic supply were completely cut off, and the nation abandoned to its own resources, it would eventually promote, in a high degree, the development of the national intellect. The vitality and force, which are abundantly displayed in every department of active life, would soon find their way into a higher channel, to meet the new and clamorous necessity for mental food; and in the space of a generation, the oft-repeated demand for an original literature would be fully satisfied.

In respect to every department of active life, the United States are fully emancipated from their ancient colonial subjection. They can plan, invent, and achieve for themselves, and this, too, with a commanding success. But in all the finer functions of thought, in all matters of literature and taste, we are still essentially provincial. England once held us in a state of political dependency. That day is past; but she still holds us in an intellectual dependency far more complete. Her thoughts become our thoughts, by a process unconscious, but inevitable. She caters for our mind and fancy with a liberal hand. We are spared the labor of self-support; but by the universal law, applicable to nations no less than individuals, we are weakened by the want of independent exercise. It is a matter of common remark, that the most highly educated classes among us are far from being the most efficient either in thought or action. The vigorous life of the nation springs from the deep rich soil at the bottom of society. Its men of greatest influence are those who have studied men before they studied books, and who, by hard battling with the world, and boldly following out the bent of their native genius, have hewn their own way to wealth, station, or knowledge, from the ploughshare or the forecastle. The comparative shortcomings of the best educated among us may be traced to several causes; but, as we are constrained to think, they are mainly owing to the fact that the highest civilization of America is communicated from without instead of being developed from within, and is therefore nerveless and unproductive.

[CHARLEVOIX'S HISTORY OF NEW FRANCE]

(From the *Atlantic Monthly*, July, 1867)

History and General Description of New France. By the Rev. P. F. de Charlevoix, S. J. Translated, with Notes, by John Gilmary Shea. New York: J. G. Shea. Vol. I.

Charlevoix's "History of New France" is very well known to all who study American history in its sources. It is a well-written, scholarlike, and readable book, treating of a subject which the author perfectly understood, and of which he may be said to have been a part. Tried by the measure of his times, his research was thorough and tolerably exact. The work, in short, has always been justly regarded as a "standard," and very few later writers have thought it necessary to go beyond or behind it. Appended to it is a journal of the author's travels in America, in the form of a series of letters to the Duchesse de Lesdiguières, full of interest, and a storehouse of trustworthy information.

Charlevoix had been largely quoted and extensively read. Not to know him, indeed, was to be ignorant of some of the most memorable passages in the history of this continent; but, what is certainly remarkable, he had never found an English translator. At the time of the Old French War, when the public curiosity was strongly interested in everything relating to America, the journal appended to the history was "done into English" and eagerly read; but the history itself had remained to this time in the language in which it was originally written. This is not to be regretted, if it has been the occasion of giving us the truly admirable work which is the subject of this notice.

The spirit and the manner in which Mr. Shea has entered upon his task are above all praise. It is with him a "labor of love." In these days of literary "jobs," when bad translating and careless editing are palmed off upon the amateurs of choice books in all the finery of broad margins and faultless typography, it is refreshing to meet with a book of which the mechanical excellence is fully equalled by the substantial value of its contents, and by the thorough, conscientious, and scholarlike character of the literary execution. The labor and the knowledge bestowed on this translation would have sufficed to produce an original history of high merit. Charlevoix rarely gives his authorities. Mr. Shea has more than supplied this deficiency. Not only has he traced out the sources of his author's statements and exhibited them in notes, but he has had recourse to sources of which Charlevoix knew nothing. He is thus enabled to substantiate, correct, or amplify the original narrative. He translates it, indeed, with literal precision, but in his copious notes he sheds such a flood of new light upon it that this translation is of far more value to the student than the original work. Since Charlevoix's time, many documents, unknown to him, though bearing on his subject, have been discovered, and Mr. Shea has diligently availed himself of them. The tastes and studies of many years have made him familiar with this field of research, and prepared him to accomplish an undertaking which would otherwise have been impracticable.

The first volume is illustrated by facsimiles of Charlevoix's maps, together with his portrait and those of Cartier and Menendez. It forms a large octavo of about three hundred pages, and as a specimen of the typographical art is scarcely to be surpassed. We learn that the second volume is about to appear.

[CASGRAIN'S BOOK ON ACADIA]

(From the *Nation*, March 14, 1889)

Un Pèlerinage au pays d'Évangeline. Par l'Abbé H. R. Casgrain. Deuxième edition. Quebec. 1888. 8vo, 544 pp.

There is more in this book than its fanciful title imports. The author seems to have been thrown into a state of intense chronic excitement by the two chapters on the Acadians in Mr. Parkman's "Montcalm and Wolfe." At least, ever since their publication in 1884, he has been writing books and articles against them. He has chosen to make the question a national and religious one, and hence the remarkable heat with which he has pursued his task; a difficult one, in view of the awkward circumstance that Mr. Parkman not only stated unwelcome truths, but proved them by unanswerable French and Catholic evidence. Moreover, in 1886 Sir Adams Archibald, late Governor of Nova Scotia, read before the Nova Scotia Historical Society, of which he is the President, a paper on the same subject, written in a spirit equally just and humane, in which he expressed the same conclusions as those of Mr. Parkman, and gave his reasons for them.

Here was an added stimulus to the active pen of Abbé Casgrain, who had already published a series of articles in a French Canadian journal, and printed them in a volume under the title given above. Then followed two or more papers which he read before the Royal Society of Canada; then another series of articles running for a year through the numbers of a Canadian review; then the same articles with some changes and additions, printed in a second and enlarged edition of the "Pèlerinage"— that goodly octavo of 544 pages which is the subject of this notice—the whole forming a vast and heterogeneous monograph, backed by a prodigious quantity of documents gathered in Canada, Nova Scotia, France, England, and the United States. These documents have also been printed, along with a profusion of notes and comments; and the whole amazing array of letter-press is set in motion to overwhelm the two chapters which are the head and front of the offending. Clearly, the sense of humor is wanting in the mind of the fervent author. If every subject of American history were treated on the same scale in proportion to its importance, some of them would fill whole libraries, and the world could not contain the books that would be written.

It is curious that after all this immense preparation Abbé Casgrain has not ventured to attack the allegations that have so distressed him, but has only railed at them from a distance. The position of Mr. Parkman and Sir Adams Archibald is this: They declare that the removal of the Acadians was an act too harsh and indiscriminate to be justified, and they do not attempt to conceal the cruelties that attended it. At the same time they show that the story has two sides; that the sufferers were victims as much of Frenchmen and Catholics as of Englishmen and Protestants, and that the government of Louis XV., through agents civil, military, and ecclesiastical, intrigued to stir up the Acadian subjects of the British crown to revolt against it in time of peace; that these intrigues were attended with terrorism and cruelty to the Acadians themselves, and treachery, outrage, and murder to the English settlers, and that they produced at last in the Acadian population a state of things which, in the words of Mr. Parkman, "made some act of force on the part of the English a necessity"; that, in short, without these intrigues the removal of this unfortunate people would have had neither reason nor pretext, and therefore would not have taken place. Mr. Parkman proves his statements by the correspondence of the intriguers themselves, still preserved in the archives of France.

Abbé Casgrain has been more than once reminded that he must meet these statements squarely or lose his case. He has not accepted the challenge. What he has done is to scour archives and libraries for everything that could tell against the hated "Anglais" and the yet more hated "Yankee," and to record the results with a passionate prolixity, matchless in its way. As for the ugly truths which he was invited to attack, he lets them severely alone, and follows, or tries to follow, the advice of *Dogberry* to the constables when they had fallen foul of a culprit too muscular to handle, "Let him go, and thank God you are rid of a knave." But the ugly truth will not go. Once or twice only he fancies that he sees an opportunity to make a fierce demonstration against some small point of no bearing on the main issue; as when, in the memorable row raised by Sam Weller upon Mr. Pickwick's being carried before the magistrate at Ipswich, his friend Mr. Winkle shunned all collision with the myrmidons of the law, and sparred valiantly against a little boy by the roadside.

Abbé Casgrain possesses in a supreme degree the comfortable gift of finding in his inquiries nothing but what he wants to find. On the other hand, the sense of historical proportion has been denied him. The removal of the Acadians, which few persons in Canada or the United States ever heard of before Longfellow made a poem out of it, looms on his sight like a hideous black cloud, darkening the whole field of American history. He has pursued his protracted labors with an amazing singleness of purpose, snatching with delighted avidity at anything that might serve as a stone to cast at the abominable Yankee. He calls it impartiality to see one side of the story, and obstinate prejudice, if not moral obliquity, to see both.

Yet he has not toiled four years for nothing. It is true that he has dodged the facts which have so exercised his soul, and tried to bury them under a foaming torrent of recrimination, seeking comfort in the prophecy that he who has dared to make them public will be punished with speedy and deserved oblivion. It is also true that, all ablaze as he is with zeal and passion, he is anything but a safe guide; that his wish is father to his thought; that when he is met by a dangerous truth he shuns it by shutting his eyes and hiding his head in a bush; and, moreover, that he is not only highly imaginative, but agile beyond belief in jumping at conclusions. Hence he must be followed with the most watchful caution.

So much labor, however, concentred on so narrow a space, must needs produce its effect. He has utterly failed to show that the Acadian story has not another side, fully as dark and repulsive as that which, till lately, has been the only known one. The following are the chief points he makes: That the removal of the Acadians was not the work of the British Government, but of its servants in America—a fact, however, which everybody knew who had looked into the matter at all. Next, that the Englishman Lawrence, chief actor in the tragedy of removal, and already known as harsh and violent, was also a bad governor and a corrupt man. Next, that the New Englander Morris is chargeable with duplicity and cruelty. The most important documents which Abbé Casgrain has printed do not, however, relate to the removal of the Acadians, but to a period from thirty to forty years earlier—a period, by the way, with which

Mr. Parkman has not yet had occasion to deal except in the way of brief reference. These papers show that when the country was passed over to the British crown, the English governors used inexcusable means to prevent the Acadians from emigrating, being apparently as anxious to keep them in the province as later governors were to get them out of it. Finally, Abbé Casgrain produces the first real evidence we have seen in support of the oft-repeated charge that New Englanders coveted Acadian lands. These points should be fully and fairly considered in recounting the miserable story; but, while they add to the burden of one party, they do not lighten that of the other.

If Abbé Casgrain means to confute Mr. Parkman and Sir Adams Archibald, he must fall to and write another book, for all his multifarious productions of the last four or five years have done nothing towards dislodging the adversary. Yet he has the claim to our gratitude of giving us all that can be said by the most eager and industrious of advocates on one side of a mooted question. That after all his labors he has not answered the allegations he so detests, is good proof that they are unanswerable. The truth is, that the treatment of the Acadians was a scandal on both sides.

[THE FIRST HISTORY]

[THE INDIAN CHARACTER]

(From *The Conspiracy of Pontiac*, 1851)

Of the Indian character, much has been written foolishly, and credulously believed. By the rhapsodies of poets, the cant of sentimentalists, and the extravagance of some who should have known better, a counterfeit image has been tricked out, which might seek in vain for its likeness through every corner of the habitable earth; an image bearing no more resemblance to its original, than the monarch of the tragedy and the hero of the epic poem bear to their living prototypes in the palace and the camp. The shadows of his wilderness home, and the darker mantle of his own inscrutable reserve, have made the Indian warrior a wonder and a mystery. Yet to the eye of rational observation there is nothing unintelligible in him. He is full, it is true, of contradiction. He deems himself the centre of greatness and renown; his pride is proof against the fiercest torments of fire and steel; and yet the same man would beg for a dram of whiskey, or pick up a crust of bread thrown to him like a dog, from the tent door of the traveller. At one moment, he is wary and cautious to the verge of cowardice; at the next, he abandons himself to a very insanity of recklessness; and the habitual self-restraint which throws an impenetrable veil over emotion is joined to the unbridled passions of a madman or a beast.

Such inconsistencies, strange as they seem in our eyes, when viewed under a novel aspect, are but the ordinary incidents of humanity. The qualities of the mind are not uniform in their action through all the relations of life. With different men, and different races of men, pride, valor, prudence, have different forms of manifestation, and where in one instance they lie dormant, in another they are keenly awake. The conjunction of greatness and littleness, meanness and pride, is older than the days of the patriarchs; and such antiquated phenomena, displayed under a new form in the unreflecting, undisciplined mind of a savage, call for no special wonder, but should rather be classed with the other enigmas of the fathomless human heart. The dissecting knife of a Rochefoucault might lay bare matters of no less curious observation in the breast of every man.

Nature has stamped the Indian with a hard and stern physiognomy. Ambition, revenge, envy, jealousy, are his ruling passions; and his cold temperament is little exposed to those effeminate vices which are the bane of milder races. With him revenge is an overpowering instinct; nay, more, it is a point of honor and a duty. His pride sets all language at defiance. He loathes the thought of coercion; and few of his race have ever stooped to discharge a menial office. A wild love of liberty, an utter intolerance of control, lie at the basis of his character, and fire his whole existence. Yet, in spite of this haughty independence, he is a devout hero-worshipper; and high achievement in war or policy touches a chord to which his nature never fails to respond. He looks up with admiring reverence to the sages and heroes of his tribe; and it is this principle, joined to the respect for age springing from the patriarchal element in his social system, which, beyond all others, contributes union and harmony to the erratic members of an Indian community. With him the love of glory kindles into a burning passion; and to allay its cravings, he will dare cold and famine, fire, tempest, torture, and death itself.

These generous traits are overcast by much that is dark, cold, and sinister, by sleepless distrust, and rankling jealousy. Treacherous himself, he is always suspicious of treachery in others. Brave as he is,—and few of mankind are braver,—he will vent his passion by a secret stab rather than an open blow. His warfare is full of ambuscade and stratagem; and he never rushes into battle with that joyous self-abandonment with which the warriors of the Gothic races flung themselves into the ranks of their enemies. In his feasts and his drinking bouts we find none of that robust and full-toned mirth which reigned at the rude carousals of our barbaric ancestry. He is never jovial in his cups, and maudlin sorrow or maniacal rage is the sole result of his potations.

Over all emotion he throws the veil of an iron self-control, originating in a peculiar form of pride, and fostered by rigorous discipline from childhood upward. He is trained to conceal passion, and not to subdue it. The inscrutable warrior is aptly imaged by the hackneyed figure of a volcano covered with snow; and no man can say when or where the wild-fire will burst forth. This shallow self-mastery serves to give dignity to public deliberation, and harmony to social life. Wrangling and quarrel are strangers to an Indian dwelling; and while an assembly of the ancient Gauls was garrulous as a convocation of magpies, a Roman senate might have taken a lesson from the grave solemnity of an Indian council. In the midst of his family and friends, he hides affections, by nature none of the most tender, under a mask of icy coldness; and in the torturing fires of his enemy, the haughty sufferer maintains to the last his look of grim defiance.

His intellect is as peculiar as his moral organization. Among all savages, the powers of perception preponderate over those of reason and analysis; but this is more especially the case with the Indian. An acute judge of character, at least of such parts of it as his experience enables him to comprehend; keen to a proverb in all exercises of war and the chase, he seldom traces effects to their causes, or follows out actions to their remote results. Though a close observer of external nature, he no sooner attempts to account for her phenomena than he involves himself in the most ridiculous absurdities; and quite content with these puerilities, he has not the least desire to push his inquiries further. His curiosity, abundantly active within its own narrow circle, is dead to all things else; and to attempt rousing it from its torpor is but a bootless task. He seldom takes cognizance of general or abstract ideas; and his language has scarcely the power to express them, except through the medium of figures drawn from the external world, and often highly picturesque and forcible. The absence of reflection makes him grossly improvident, and unfits him for pursuing any complicated scheme of war or policy.

Some races of men seem moulded in wax, soft and melting, at once plastic and feeble. Some races, like some metals, combine the greatest flexibility with the greatest strength. But the Indian is hewn out of a rock. You can rarely change the form without destruction of the substance. Races of inferior energy have possessed a power of expansion and assimilation to which he is a stranger; and it is this fixed and rigid quality which has proved his ruin. He will not learn the arts of civilization, and he and his forest must perish together. The stern, unchanging features of his mind excite our admiration from their very immutability; and we look with deep interest on the fate of this irreclaimable son of the wilderness, the child who will not be weaned from the breast of his rugged mother. And our interest increases when we discern in the unhappy wanderer the germs of heroic virtues mingled among his vices,—a hand bountiful to bestow as it is rapacious to seize, and even in extremest famine, imparting its last morsel to a fellow-sufferer; a heart which, strong in friendship as in hate, thinks it not too much to lay down life for its chosen comrade; a soul true to its own idea of honor, and burning with an unquenchable thirst for greatness and renown.

The imprisoned lion in the showman's cage differs not more widely from the lord of the desert than the beggarly frequenter of frontier garrisons and dramshops differs from the proud denizen of the woods. It is in his native wilds alone that the Indian must be seen and studied. Thus to depict him is the aim of the ensuing History; and if, from the shades of rock and forest, the savage features should look too grimly forth, it is because the clouds of a tempestuous war have cast upon the picture their murky shadows and lurid fires.

[THE INDIANS PREPARE FOR WAR]

We have seen how, when the tide of affairs changed, the subtle and ambitious chief trimmed his bark to the current, and gave the hand of friendship to the English. That he was disappointed in their treatment of him, and in all the hopes that he had formed from their alliance, is sufficiently evident from one of his speeches. A new light soon began to dawn upon his untaught but powerful mind, and he saw the altered posture of affairs under its true aspect.

It was a momentous and gloomy crisis for the Indian race, for never before had they been exposed to such imminent and pressing danger. With the downfall of Canada, the tribes had sunk at once from their position of importance. Hitherto the two rival European nations had kept each other in check upon the American continent, and the Indians had, in some measure, held the balance of power between them. To conciliate their good will and gain their alliance, to avoid offending them by injustice and encroachment, was the policy both of the French and English. But now the face of affairs was changed. The English had gained an undisputed ascendency, and the Indians, no longer important as allies, were treated as mere barbarians, who might be trampled upon with impunity. Abandoned to their own feeble resources and divided strength, they must fast recede, and dwindle away before the steady progress of the colonial power. Already their best hunting-grounds were invaded, and from the eastern ridges of the Alleghanies they might see, from far and near, the smoke of the settlers' clearings, rising in tall columns from the dark-green bosom of the forest. The doom of the race was sealed, and no human power could avert it; but they, in their ignorance, believed otherwise, and vainly thought that, by a desperate effort, they might yet uproot and overthrow the growing strength of their destroyers.

It would be idle to suppose that the great mass of the Indians understood, in its full extent, the danger which threatened their race. With them, the war was a mere outbreak of fury, and they turned against their enemies with as little reason or forecast as a panther when he leaps at the throat of the hunter. Goaded by wrongs and indignities, they struck for revenge, and for relief from the evil of the moment. But the mind of Pontiac could embrace a wider and deeper view. The peril of the times was unfolded in its full extent before him, and he resolved to unite the tribes in one grand effort to avert it. He did not, like many of his people, entertain the absurd idea that the Indians, by their unaided strength, could drive the English into the sea. He adopted the only plan consistent with reason, that of restoring the French ascendency in the west, and once more opposing a check to British encroachment. With views like these, he lent a greedy ear to the plausible falsehoods of the Canadians, who assured him that the armies of King Louis were already advancing to recover Canada, and that the French and their red brethren, fighting side by side, would drive the English dogs back within their own narrow limits.

Revolving these thoughts, and remembering that his own ambitious views might be advanced by the hostilities he meditated, Pontiac no longer hesitated. Revenge, ambition, and patriotism wrought upon him alike, and he resolved on war. At the close of the year 1762, he sent ambassadors to the different nations. They visited the country of the Ohio and its tributaries, passed northward to the region of the upper lakes, and the borders of the river Ottawa; and far southward towards the mouth of the Mississippi. Bearing with them the war-belt of wampum, broad and long, as the importance of the message demanded, and the tomahawk stained red, in token of war, they went from camp to camp, and village to village. Wherever they appeared, the sachems and old men assembled, to hear the words of the great Pontiac. Then the chief of the embassy flung down the tomahawk on the ground before them, and holding the war-belt in his hand, delivered, with vehement gesture, word for word, the speech with which he was charged. It was heard everywhere with approval; the belt was accepted, the hatchet snatched up, and the assembled chiefs stood pledged to take part in the war. The blow was to be struck at a certain time in the month of May following, to be indicated by the changes of the moon. The tribes were to rise together, each destroying the English garrison in its neighborhood, and then, with a general rush, the whole were to turn against the settlements of the frontier.

The tribes, thus banded together against the English, comprised, with a few unimportant exceptions, the whole Algonquin stock, to whom were united the Wyandots, the Senecas, and several tribes of the lower Mississippi. The Senecas were the only members of the Iroquois confederacy who joined in the league, the rest being kept quiet by the influence of Sir William Johnson, whose utmost exertions, however, were barely sufficient to allay their irritation.

While thus on the very eve of an outbreak, the Indians concealed their designs with the dissimulation of their race. The warriors still lounged about the forts, with calm, impenetrable faces, begging, as usual, for tobacco, gunpowder, and whiskey. Now and then, some slight intimation of danger would startle the garrisons from their security. An English trader, coming in from the Indian villages, would report that, from their manner and behavior, he suspected them of brooding mischief; or some scoundrel half-breed would be heard boasting in his cups that before next summer he would have English hair to fringe his hunting-frock. On one occasion, the plot was nearly discovered. Early in March, 1763, Ensign Holmes, commanding at Fort Miami, was told by a friendly Indian that the warriors in the neighboring village had lately received a war-belt, with a message urging them to destroy him and his garrison, and that this they were preparing to do. Holmes called the Indians together, and boldly charged them with their design. They did as Indians on such occasions have often done, confessed their fault with much apparent contrition, laid the blame on a neighboring tribe, and professed eternal friendship to their brethren, the English. Holmes writes to report his discovery to Major Gladwyn, who, in his turn, sends the information to Sir Jeffrey Amherst, expressing his opinion that there has been a general irritation among the Indians, but that the affair will soon blow over, and that, in the neighborhood of his own post, the savages were perfectly tranquil. Within cannon-shot of the deluded officer's palisades, was the village of Pontiac himself, the arch enemy of the English, and prime mover in the plot.

With the approach of spring, the Indians, coming in from their wintering grounds, began to appear in small parties about the various forts; but now they seldom entered them, encamping at a little distance in the woods. They were fast pushing their preparations for the meditated blow, and waiting with stifled eagerness for the appointed hour.

I interrupt the progress of the narrative to glance for a moment at the Indians in their military capacity, and observe how far they were qualified to prosecute the formidable war into which they were about to plunge.

A people living chiefly by the chase, and therefore, of necessity, thinly and widely scattered; divided into numerous tribes, held together by no strong principle of cohesion, and with no central government to combine their strength, could act with little efficiency against such an enemy as was now opposed to them. Loose and disjointed as a whole, the government even of individual tribes, and of their smallest separate communities, was too feeble to deserve the name. There were, it is true, chiefs whose office was in a manner hereditary; but their authority was wholly of a moral nature, and enforced by no compulsory law. Their province was to advise, and not to command. Their influence, such as it was, is chiefly to be ascribed to the principle of hero-worship, natural to the Indian character, and to the reverence for age, which belongs to a state of society where a patriarchal element largely prevails. It was their office to declare war and make peace; but when war was declared, they had no power to carry the declaration into effect. The warriors fought if they chose to do so; but if, on the contrary, they preferred to remain quiet, no man could force them to raise the hatchet. The war-chief, whose part it was to lead them to battle, was a mere partisan, whom his bravery and exploits had led to distinction. If he thought proper, he sang his war-song and danced his war-dance; and as many of the young men as were disposed to follow him gathered around and enlisted themselves under him. Over these volunteers he had no legal authority, and they could desert him at any moment, with no other penalty than disgrace. When several war parties, of different bands or tribes, were united in a common enterprise, their chiefs elected a leader, who was nominally to command the whole; but unless this leader was a man of uncommon reputation and ability, his commands were disregarded, and his authority was a cipher. Among his followers, every latent element of discord, pride, jealousy, and ancient half-smothered feuds, were ready at any moment to break out, and tear the whole asunder. His warriors would often desert in bodies; and many an Indian army, before reaching the enemy's country, has been known to dwindle away until it was reduced to a mere scalping party.

To twist a rope of sand would be as easy a task as to form a permanent and effective army of such materials. The wild love of freedom, and impatience of all control, which mark the Indian race, render them utterly intolerant of military discipline. Partly from their individual character, and partly from this absence of subordination, spring results highly unfavorable to continued and extended military operations. Indian warriors, when acting in large masses, are to the last degree wayward, capricious, and unstable; infirm of purpose as a mob of children, and devoid of providence and foresight. To provide supplies for a campaign forms no part of their system. Hence the blow must be struck at once, or not struck at all; and to postpone victory is to insure defeat. It is when acting in small, detached parties that the Indian warrior puts forth his energies, and displays his admirable address, endurance, and intrepidity. It is then that he becomes a truly formidable enemy. Fired with the hope of winning scalps, he is stanch as a bloodhound. No hardship can divert him from his purpose, and no danger subdue his patient and cautious courage.

From their inveterate passion for war, the Indians are always prompt enough to engage in it; and on the present occasion, the prevailing irritation gave ample assurance that they would not remain idle. While there was little risk that they would capture any strong and well-defended fort, or carry any important position, there was, on the other hand, every reason to apprehend wide-spread havoc, and a destructive war of detail. That the war might be carried on with effect, it was the part of the Indian leaders to work upon the passions of their people, and keep alive their irritation; to whet their native appetite for blood and glory, and cheer them on to the attack; to guard against all that might quench their ardor, or cool their fierceness; to avoid pitched battles; never to fight except under advantage; and to avail themselves of all the aid which craft and treachery could afford. The very circumstances which unfitted the Indians for continued and concentrated attack were, in another view, highly advantageous, by preventing the enemy from assailing them with vital effect. It was no easy task to penetrate tangled woods in search of a foe, alert and active as a lynx, who would seldom stand and fight, whose deadly shot and triumphant whoop were the first and often the last tokens of his presence, and who, at the approach of a hostile force, would vanish into the black recesses of forests and pine swamps, only to renew his attacks with unabated ardor. There were no forts to capture, no magazines to destroy, and little property to seize upon. No warfare could be more perilous and harassing in its prosecution, or less satisfactory in its results.

The English colonies at this time were but ill fitted to bear the brunt of the impending war. The army which had conquered Canada was broken up and dissolved; the provincials were disbanded, and most of the regulars sent home. A few fragments of regiments, miserably wasted by war and sickness, had just arrived from the West Indies; and of these, several were already ordered to England, to be disbanded. There remained barely troops enough to furnish feeble garrisons for the various forts on the frontier and in the Indian country. At the head of this dilapidated army was Sir Jeffrey Amherst, who had achieved the reduction of Canada, and clinched the nail which Wolfe had driven. In some respects he was well fitted for the emergency; but, on the other hand, he held the Indians in supreme contempt, and his arbitrary treatment of them and total want of every quality of conciliation where they were concerned, had had no little share in exciting them to war.

While the war was on the eve of breaking out, an event occurred which had afterwards an important effect upon its progress,—the signing of the treaty of peace at Paris, on the tenth of February, 1763. By this treaty France resigned her claims to the territories east of the Mississippi, and that great river now became the western boundary of the British colonial possessions. In portioning out her new acquisitions into separate governments, England left the valley of the Ohio and the adjacent regions as an Indian domain, and by the proclamation of the seventh of October following, the intrusion of settlers upon these lands was strictly prohibited. Could these just and necessary measures have been sooner adopted, it is probable that the Indian war might have been prevented, or, at all events, rendered less general and violent, for the treaty would have made it apparent that the French could never repossess themselves of Canada, and would have proved the futility of every hope which the Indians entertained of assistance from that quarter, while, at the same time, the royal proclamation would have tended to tranquillize their minds, by removing the chief cause of irritation. But the remedy came too late, and served only to inflame the evil. While the sovereigns of France, England, and Spain, were signing the treaty at Paris, countless Indian warriors in the American forests were singing the war-song, and whetting their scalping-knives.

Throughout the western wilderness, in a hundred camps and villages, were celebrated the savage rites of war. Warriors, women, and children were alike eager and excited; magicians consulted their oracles, and prepared charms to insure success; while the war-chief, his body painted black from head to foot, concealed himself in the solitude of rocks and caverns, or the dark recesses of the forest. Here, fasting and praying, he calls day and night upon the Great Spirit, consulting his dreams, to draw from them auguries of good or evil; and if, perchance, a vision of the great war-eagle seems to hover over him with expanded wings, he exults in the full conviction of triumph. When a few days have elapsed, he emerges from his retreat, and the people discover him descending from the woods, and approaching their camp, black as a demon of war, and shrunken with fasting and vigil. They flock around and listen to his wild harangue. He calls on them to avenge the blood of their slaughtered relatives; he assures them that the Great Spirit is on their side, and that victory is certain. With exulting cries they dis-

perse to their wigwams, to array themselves in the savage decorations of the war-dress. An old man now passes through the
camp, and invites the warriors to a feast in the name of the chief.
They gather from all quarters to his wigwam, where they find
him seated, no longer covered with black, but adorned with
the startling and fantastic blazonry of the war-paint. Those
who join in the feast pledge themselves, by so doing, to follow
him against the enemy. The guests seat themselves on the
ground, in a circle around the wigwam, and the flesh of dogs is
placed in wooden dishes before them, while the chief, though
goaded by the pangs of his long, unbroken fast, sits smoking
his pipe with unmoved countenance, and takes no part in the
feast.

Night has now closed in; and the rough clearing is illumined
by the blaze of fires and burning pine-knots, casting their deep
red glare upon the dusky boughs of the surrounding forest, and
upon the wild multitude who, fluttering with feathers and bedaubed with paint, have gathered for the celebration of the war-
dance. A painted post is driven into the ground, and the crowd
form a wide circle around it. The chief leaps into the vacant
space, brandishing his hatchet as if rushing upon an enemy, and,
in a loud, vehement tone, chants his own exploits and those of
his ancestors, enacting the deeds which he describes, yelling the
war-whoop, throwing himself into all the postures of actual
fight, striking the post as if it were an enemy, and tearing the
scalp from the head of the imaginary victim. Warrior after
warrior follows his example, until the whole assembly, as if
fired with sudden frenzy, rush together into the ring, leaping,
stamping, and whooping, brandishing knives and hatchets in
the fire-light, hacking and stabbing the air, and breaking at
intervals into a burst of ferocious yells, which sounds for miles
away over the lonely, midnight forest.

In the morning, the warriors prepare to depart. They leave
the camp in single file, still decorated with all their finery of
paint, feathers, and scalp-locks; and, as they enter the woods,
the chief fires his gun, the warrior behind follows his example,
and the discharges pass in slow succession from front to rear,

the salute concluding with a general whoop. They encamp at no great distance from the village, and divest themselves of their much-prized ornaments, which are carried back by the women, who have followed them for this purpose. The warriors pursue their journey, clad in the rough attire of hard service, and move silently and stealthily through the forest towards the hapless garrison, or defenceless settlement, which they have marked as their prey.

The woods were now filled with war-parties such as this, and soon the first tokens of the approaching tempest began to alarm the unhappy settlers of the frontier. At first, some trader or hunter, weak and emaciated, would come in from the forest, and relate that his companions had been butchered in the Indian villages, and that he alone had escaped. Next succeeded vague and uncertain rumors of forts attacked and garrisons slaughtered; and soon after, a report gained ground that every post throughout the Indian country had been taken, and every soldier killed. Close upon these tidings came the enemy himself. The Indian war-parties broke out of the woods like gangs of wolves, murdering, burning, and laying waste; while hundreds of terror-stricken families, abandoning their homes, fled for refuge towards the older settlements, and all was misery and ruin.

Passing over, for the present, this portion of the war, we will penetrate at once into the heart of the Indian country, and observe those passages of the conflict which took place under the auspices of Pontiac himself,—the siege of Detroit, and the capture of the interior posts and garrisons.

THE COUNCIL AT THE RIVER ECORCES

To begin the war was reserved by Pontiac as his own peculiar privilege. With the first opening of spring his preparations were complete. His light-footed messengers, with their wampum belts and gifts of tobacco, visited many a lonely hunting camp in the gloom of the northern woods, and called chiefs and warriors to attend the general meeting. The appointed spot

was on the banks of the little River Ecorces, not far from Detroit.
Thither went Pontiac himself, with his squaws and his children.
Band after band came straggling in from every side, until the
meadow was thickly dotted with their frail wigwams. Here
were idle warriors smoking and laughing in groups, or beguiling the lazy hours with gambling, feasting, or doubtful stories
of their own martial exploits. Here were youthful gallants, bedizened with all the foppery of beads, feathers, and hawks'
bells, but held as yet in light esteem, since they had slain no
enemy, and taken no scalp. Here too were young damsels, ra-
diant with bears' oil, ruddy with vermilion, and versed in all the
arts of forest coquetry; shrivelled hags, with limbs of wire and
the voices of screech-owls; and troops of naked children, with
small, black, mischievous eyes, roaming along the outskirts of
the woods.

The great Roman historian observes of the ancient Germans
that when summoned to a public meeting, they would lag behind the appointed time in order to show their independence.
The remark holds true, and perhaps with greater emphasis, of
the American Indians; and thus it happened that several days
elapsed before the assembly was complete. In such a motley
concourse of barbarians, where different bands and different
tribes were mustered on one common camp ground, it would
need all the art of a prudent leader to prevent their dormant
jealousies from starting into open strife. No people are more
prompt to quarrel, and none more prone, in the fierce excitement of the present, to forget the purpose of the future; yet,
through good fortune, or the wisdom of Pontiac, no rupture
occurred; and at length the last loiterer appeared, and farther
delay was needless.

The council took place on the twenty-seventh of April. On
that morning, several old men, the heralds of the camp, passed
to and fro among the lodges, calling the warriors, in a loud
voice, to attend the meeting.

In accordance with the summons, they issued from their
cabins: the tall, naked figures of the wild Ojibwas, with quivers
slung at their backs, and light war-clubs resting in the hollow of

their arms; Ottawas, wrapped close in their gaudy blankets; Wyandots, fluttering in painted shirts, their heads adorned with feathers, and their leggins garnished with bells. All were soon seated in a wide circle upon the grass, row within row, a grave and silent assembly. Each savage countenance seemed carved in wood, and none could have detected the ferocious passions hidden beneath that immovable mask. Pipes with ornamented stems were lighted, and passed from hand to hand.

Then Pontiac rose, and walked forward into the midst of the council. According to Canadian tradition, he was not above the middle height, though his muscular figure was cast in a mould of remarkable symmetry and vigor. His complexion was darker than is usual with his race, and his features, though by no means regular, had a bold and stern expression; while his habitual bearing was imperious and peremptory, like that of a man accustomed to sweep away all opposition by the force of his impetuous will. His ordinary attire was that of the primitive savage,— a scanty cincture girt about his loins, and his long, black hair flowing loosely at his back; but on occasions like this he was wont to appear as befitted his power and character, and he stood doubtless before the council plumed and painted in the full costume of war.

Looking round upon his wild auditors he began to speak, with fierce gesture, and a loud, impassioned voice; and at every pause, deep, guttural ejaculations of assent and approval responded to his words. He inveighed against the arrogance, rapacity, and injustice of the English, and contrasted them with the French, whom they had driven from the soil. He declared that the British commandant had treated him with neglect and contempt; that the soldiers of the garrison had abused the Indians; and that one of them had struck a follower of his own. He represented the danger that would arise from the supremacy of the English. They had expelled the French, and now they only waited for a pretext to turn upon the Indians and destroy them. Then, holding out a broad belt of wampum, he told the council that he had received it from their great father the King of France, in token that he had heard the voice of his red children; that his sleep was at an end; and that his great war canoes would soon sail up the St. Lawrence, to win back Canada, and wreak vengeance on his enemies. The Indians and their French brethren would fight once more side by side, as they had always fought; they would strike the English as they had struck them many moons ago, when their great army marched down the Monongahela, and they had shot them from their ambush, like a flock of pigeons in the woods.

Having roused in his warlike listeners their native thirst for blood and vengeance, he next addressed himself to their superstition, and told the following tale. Its precise origin is not easy to determine. It is possible that the Delaware prophet, mentioned in a former chapter, may have had some part in it; or it might have been the offspring of Pontiac's heated imagination, during his period of fasting and dreaming. That he deliberately invented it for the sake of the effect it would produce, is the least probable conclusion of all; for it evidently proceeds from the superstitious mind of an Indian, brooding upon the evil days in which his lot was cast, and turning for relief to the mysterious Author of his being. It is, at all events, a characteristic specimen of the Indian legendary tales, and, like many of them, bears an allegoric significancy. Yet he who endeavors to interpret an Indian allegory through all its erratic windings and puerile inconsistencies, has undertaken no enviable task.

"A Delaware Indian," said Pontiac, "conceived an eager desire to learn wisdom from the Master of Life; but, being ignorant where to find him, he had recourse to fasting, dreaming, and magical incantations. By these means it was revealed to him, that, by moving forward in a straight, undeviating course, he would reach the abode of the Great Spirit. He told his purpose to no one, and having provided the equipments of a hunter,—gun, powder-horn, ammunition, and a kettle for preparing his food,—he set out on his errand. For some time he journeyed on in high hope and confidence. On the evening of the eighth day, he stopped by the side of a brook at the edge of a meadow, where he began to make ready his evening meal, when, looking up, he saw three large openings in the woods before him, and three well-beaten paths which entered them. He was much surprised; but his wonder increased, when, after it had grown dark, the three paths were more clearly visible than ever. Remembering the important object of his journey, he could neither rest nor sleep; and, leaving his fire, he crossed the meadow, and entered the largest of the three openings. He had advanced but a short distance into the forest, when a bright flame sprang out of the ground before him, and arrested his steps. In great amazement, he turned back, and entered the second path, where the same wonderful phenomenon again encountered him; and now, in terror and bewilderment, yet still resolved to persevere, he took the last of the three paths. On this he journeyed a whole day without interruption, when at length, emerging from the forest, he saw before him a vast mountain, of dazzling whiteness. So precipitous was the ascent that the Indian thought it hopeless to go farther, and looked around him in despair: at that moment, he saw, seated at some distance above, the figure of a beautiful woman arrayed in white, who arose as he looked upon her, and thus accosted him: 'How can you hope, encumbered as you are, to succeed in your design? Go down to the foot of the mountain, throw away your gun, your ammunition, your provisions, and your clothing; wash yourself in the stream which flows there, and you will then be prepared to stand before the Master of Life.' The Indian obeyed, and again began to ascend among the rocks, while the woman, seeing him still discouraged, laughed at his faintness of heart, and told him that, if he wished for success, he must climb by the aid of one hand and one foot only. After great toil and suffering, he at length found himself at the summit. The woman had disappeared, and he was left alone. A rich and beautiful plain lay before him, and at a little distance he saw three great villages, far superior to the squalid wigwams of the Delawares. As he approached the largest, and stood hesitating whether he should enter, a man gorgeously attired stepped forth, and, taking him by the hand, welcomed him to the celestial abode. He then conducted him into the presence of the

Great Spirit, where the Indian stood confounded at the unspeakable splendor which surrounded him. The Great Spirit bade him be seated, and thus addressed him:—

"'I am the Maker of heaven and earth, the trees, lakes, rivers, and all things else. I am the Maker of mankind; and because I love you, you must do my will. The land on which you live I have made for you, and not for others. Why do you suffer the white men to dwell among you? My children, you have forgotten the customs and traditions of your forefathers. Why do you not clothe yourselves in skins, as they did, and use the bows and arrows, and the stone-pointed lances, which they used? You have bought guns, knives, kettles, and blankets, from the white men, until you can no longer do without them; and, what is worse, you have drunk the poison fire-water, which turns you into fools. Fling all these things away; live as your wise forefathers lived before you. And as for these English,—these dogs dressed in red, who have come to rob you of your hunting-grounds, and drive away the game,—you must lift the hatchet against them. Wipe them from the face of the earth, and then you will win my favor back again, and once more be happy and prosperous. The children of your great father, the King of France, are not like the English. Never forget that they are your brethren. They are very dear to me, for they love the red men, and understand the true mode of worshipping me.'"

The Great Spirit next gave his hearer various precepts of morality and religion, such as the prohibition to marry more than one wife; and a warning against the practice of magic, which is worshipping the devil. A prayer, embodying the substance of all that he had heard, was then presented to the Delaware. It was cut in hieroglyphics upon a wooden stick, after the custom of his people; and he was directed to send copies of it to all the Indian villages.

The adventurer now departed, and, returning to the earth, reported all the wonders he had seen in the celestial regions.

Such was the tale told by Pontiac to the council; and it is worthy of notice, that not he alone, but many of the most notable men who have arisen among the Indians have been opponents of civilization, and stanch advocates of primitive barbarism. Red Jacket and Tecumseh would gladly have brought back their people to the rude simplicity of their original condition. There is nothing progressive in the rigid, inflexible nature of an Indian. He will not open his mind to the idea of improvement; and nearly every change that has been forced upon him has been a change for the worse.

Many other speeches were doubtless made in the council, but no record of them has been preserved. All present were eager to attack the British fort; and Pontiac told them, in conclusion, that on the second of May he would gain admittance, with a party of his warriors, on pretence of dancing the calumet dance before the garrison; that they would take note of the strength of the fortification; and that he would then summon another council to determine the mode of attack.

The assembly now dissolved, and all the evening the women were employed in loading the canoes, which were drawn up on the bank of the stream. The encampments broke up at so early an hour, that when the sun rose, the savage swarm had melted away; the secluded scene was restored to its wonted silence and solitude, and nothing remained but the slender framework of several hundred cabins, with fragments of broken utensils, pieces of cloth, and scraps of hide, scattered over the trampled grass; while the smouldering embers of numberless fires mingled their dark smoke with the white mist which rose from the little river.

Every spring, after the winter hunt was over, the Indians were accustomed to return to their villages, or permanent encampments, in the vicinity of Detroit; and, accordingly, after the council had broken up, they made their appearance as usual about the fort. On the first of May, Pontiac came to the gate with forty men of the Ottawa tribe, and asked permission to enter and dance the calumet dance, before the officers of the garrison. After some hesitation, he was admitted; and proceeding to the corner of the street, where stood the house of the commandant, Major Gladwyn, he and thirty of his warriors began their dance, each recounting his own exploits, and boasting himself the bravest of mankind. The officers and men gathered around them; while, in the mean time, the remaining ten of the Ottawas strolled about the fort, observing every thing it contained. When the dance was over, they all quietly withdrew, not a suspicion of their designs having arisen in the minds of the English.

After a few days had elapsed, Pontiac's messengers again passed among the Indian cabins, calling the principal chiefs to another council, in the Pottawattamie village. Here there was a large structure of bark, erected for the public use on occasions like the present. A hundred chiefs were seated around this dusky council-house, the fire in the centre shedding its fitful light upon their dark, naked forms, while the pipe passed from hand to hand. To prevent interruption, Pontiac had stationed young men as sentinels, near the house. He once more addressed the chiefs; inciting them to hostility against the English, and concluding by the proposal of his plan for destroying Detroit. It was as follows: Pontiac would demand a council with the commandant concerning matters of great importance; and on this pretext he flattered himself that he and his principal chiefs would gain ready admittance within the fort. They were all to carry weapons concealed beneath their blankets. While in the act of addressing the commandant in the council-room, Pontiac was to make a certain signal, upon which the chiefs were to raise the war-whoop, rush upon the officers present, and strike them down. The other Indians, waiting meanwhile at the gate, or loitering among the houses, on hearing the yells and firing within the building, were to assail the astonished and half-armed soldiers; and thus Detroit would fall an easy prey.

In opening this plan of treachery, Pontiac spoke rather as a counsellor than as a commander. Haughty as he was, he had too much sagacity to wound the pride of a body of men over whom he had no other control than that derived from his personal character and influence. No one was hardy enough to venture opposition to the proposal of their great leader. His plan was eagerly adopted. Hoarse ejaculations of applause echoed his speech; and, gathering their blankets around them, the chiefs withdrew to their respective villages, to prepare for the destruction of the unsuspecting garrison.

[THE ATTACK ON DETROIT]

In the Pottawattamie village, if there be truth in tradition, lived an Ojibwa girl, who could boast a larger share of beauty than is common in the wigwam. She had attracted the eye of Gladwyn. He had formed a connection with her, and she had become much attached to him. On the afternoon of the sixth, Catharine—for so the officers called her—came to the fort, and repaired to Gladwyn's quarters, bringing with her a pair of elk-skin moccasons, ornamented with porcupine work, which he had requested her to make. There was something unusual in her look and manner. Her face was sad and downcast. She said little, and soon left the room; but the sentinel at the door saw her still lingering at the street corner, though the hour for closing the gates was nearly come. At length she attracted the notice of Gladwyn himself; and calling her to him, he pressed her to declare what was weighing upon her mind. Still she remained for a long time silent, and it was only after much urgency and many promises not to betray her, that she revealed her momentous secret.

To-morrow, she said, Pontiac will come to the fort with sixty of his chiefs. Each will be armed with a gun, cut short, and hidden under his blanket. Pontiac will demand to hold a council; and after he has delivered his speech, he will offer a peace-belt of wampum, holding it in a reversed position. This will be the signal of attack. The chiefs will spring up and fire upon the officers, and the Indians in the street will fall upon the garrison. Every Englishman will be killed, but not the scalp of a single Frenchman will be touched.

Such is the story told in 1768 to the traveller Carver at Detroit, and preserved in local tradition, but not sustained by contemporary letters or diaries. What is certain is, that Gladwyn received secret information, on the night of the sixth of

May, that an attempt would be made on the morrow to capture the fort by treachery. He called some of his officers, and told them what he had heard. The defences of the place were feeble and extensive, and the garrison by far too weak to repel a general assault. The force of the Indians at this time is variously estimated at from six hundred to two thousand; and the commandant greatly feared that some wild impulse might precipitate their plan, and that they would storm the fort before the morning. Every preparation was made to meet the sudden emergency. Half the garrison were ordered under arms, and all the officers prepared to spend the night upon the ramparts.

The day closed, and the hues of sunset faded. Only a dusky redness lingered in the west, and the darkening earth seemed her dull self again. Then night descended, heavy and black, on the fierce Indians and the sleepless English. From sunset till dawn, an anxious watch was kept from the slender palisades of Detroit. The soldiers were still ignorant of the danger; and the sentinels did not know why their numbers were doubled, or why, with such unwonted vigilance, their officers repeatedly visited their posts. Again and again Gladwyn mounted his wooden ramparts, and looked forth into the gloom. There seemed nothing but repose and peace in the soft, moist air of the warm spring evening, with the piping of frogs along the river-bank, just roused from their torpor by the genial influence of May. But, at intervals, as the night wind swept across the bastion, it bore sounds of fearful portent to the ear, the sullen booming of the Indian drum and the wild chorus of quavering yells, as the warriors, around their distant camp-fires, danced the war-dance, in preparation for the morrow's work.

The night passed without alarm. The sun rose upon fresh fields and newly budding woods, and scarcely had the morning mists dissolved, when the garrison could see a fleet of birch canoes crossing the river from the eastern shore, within range of cannon-shot above the fort. Only two or three warriors appeared in each, but all moved slowly, and seemed deeply laden. In truth, they were full of savages, lying flat on their faces, that their numbers might not excite the suspicion of the English.

At an early hour the open common behind the fort was thronged with squaws, children, and warriors, some naked, and others fantastically arrayed in their barbarous finery. All seemed restless and uneasy, moving hither and thither, in apparent preparation for a general game of ball. Many tall warriors, wrapped in their blankets, were seen stalking towards the fort, and casting malignant furtive glances upward at the palisades. Then, with an air of assumed indifference, they would move towards the gate. They were all admitted; for Gladwyn who, in this instance at least, showed some knowledge of Indian character, chose to convince his crafty foe that, though their plot was detected, their hostility was despised.

The whole garrison was ordered under arms. Sterling, and the other English fur-traders, closed their storehouses and armed their men, and all in cool confidence stood waiting the result.

Meanwhile, Pontiac, who had crossed with the canoes from the eastern shore, was approaching along the river road, at the head of his sixty chiefs, all gravely marching in Indian file. A Canadian settler, named Beaufait, had been that morning to the fort. He was now returning homewards, and as he reached the bridge which led over the stream then called Parent's Creek, he saw the chiefs in the act of crossing from the farther bank. He stood aside to give them room. As the last Indian passed, Beaufait recognized him as an old friend and associate. The savage greeted him with the usual ejaculation, opened for an instant the folds of his blanket, disclosed the hidden gun, and, with an emphatic gesture towards the fort, indicated the purpose to which he meant to apply it.

At ten o'clock, the great war-chief, with his treacherous followers, reached the fort, and the gateway was thronged with their savage faces. All were wrapped to the throat in colored blankets. Some were crested with hawk, eagle, or raven plumes; others had shaved their heads, leaving only the fluttering scalp-lock on the crown; while others, again, wore their long, black hair flowing loosely at their backs, or wildly hanging about their brows like a lion's mane. Their bold yet crafty features, their cheeks besmeared with ochre and vermilion, white lead and soot, their keen, deep-set eyes gleaming in their sockets, like those of rattlesnakes, gave them an aspect grim, uncouth, and horrible. For the most part, they were tall, strong men, and all had a gait and bearing of peculiar stateliness.

As Pontiac entered, it is said that he started, and that a deep ejaculation half escaped from his breast. Well might his stoicism fail, for at a glance he read the ruin of his plot. On either hand, within the gateway, stood ranks of soldiers and hedges of glittering steel. The swarthy *engagés* of the fur-traders, armed to the teeth, stood in groups at the street corners, and the measured tap of a drum fell ominously on the ear. Soon regaining his composure, Pontiac strode forward into the narrow street; and his chiefs filed after him in silence, while the scared faces of women and children looked out from the windows as they passed. Their rigid muscles betrayed no sign of emotion; yet, looking closely, one might have seen their small eyes glance from side to side with restless scrutiny.

Traversing the entire width of the little town, they reached the door of the council-house, a large building standing near the margin of the river. On entering, they saw Gladwyn, with several of his officers, seated in readiness to receive them, and the observant chiefs did not fail to remark that every English-man wore a sword at his side, and a pair of pistols in his belt. The conspirators eyed each other with uneasy glances. "Why," demanded Pontiac, "do I see so many of my father's young men standing in the street with their guns?" Gladwyn replied through his interpreter, La Butte, that he had ordered the soldiers under arms for the sake of exercise and discipline. With much delay and many signs of distrust, the chiefs at length sat down on the mats prepared for them; and, after the customary pause, Pontiac rose to speak. Holding in his hand the wampum belt which was to have given the fatal signal, he addressed the commandant, professing strong attachment to the English, and declaring, in Indian phrase, that he had come to smoke the pipe of peace, and brighten the chain of friendship. The officers watched him keenly as he uttered these hollow words, fearing lest, though conscious that his designs were suspected, he might still attempt to accomplish them. And once, it is said, he raised the wampum belt as if about to give the signal of attack. But at that instant Gladwyn signed slightly with his hand. The sudden clash of arms sounded from the passage without, and a drum rolling the charge filled the council-room with its stunning din. At this, Pontiac stood like one confounded. Some writers will have it, that Gladwyn, rising from his seat, drew the chief's blanket aside, exposed the hidden gun, and sternly rebuked him for his treachery. But the commandant wished only to prevent the consummation of the plot, without bringing on an open rupture. His own letters affirm that he and his officers remained seated as before. Pontiac, seeing his unruffled brow and his calm eye fixed steadfastly upon him, knew not what to think, and soon sat down in amazement and perplexity. Another pause ensued, and Gladwyn commenced a brief reply. He assured the chiefs that friendship and protection should be extended towards them as long as they continued to deserve it, but threatened ample vengeance for the first act of aggression. The council then broke up; but, before leaving the room, Pontiac told the officers that he would return in a few days, with his squaws and children, for he wished that they should all shake hands with their fathers, the English. To this new piece of treachery Gladwyn deigned no reply. The gates of the fort, which had been closed during the conference, were again flung open, and the baffled savages were suffered to depart, rejoiced, no doubt, to breathe once more the free air of the open fields.

Gladwyn has been censured, and perhaps with justice, for not detaining the chiefs as hostages for the good conduct of their followers. An entrapped wolf meets no quarter from the huntsman; and a savage, caught in his treachery, has no claim to forbearance. Perhaps the commandant feared lest, should he arrest the chiefs when gathered at a public council, and guiltless as yet of open violence, the act might be interpreted as cowardly and dishonorable. He was ignorant, moreover, of the true nature of the plot. In his view, the whole affair was one of those impulsive outbreaks so common among Indians; and he trusted that, could an immediate rupture be averted, the threatening clouds would soon blow over.

Here, and elsewhere, the conduct of Pontiac is marked with the blackest treachery; and one cannot but lament that a commanding and magnanimous nature should be stained with the odious vice of cowards and traitors. He could govern, with almost despotic sway, a race unruly as the winds. In generous thought and deed, he rivalled the heroes of ancient story; and craft and cunning might well seem alien to a mind like his. Yet Pontiac was a thorough savage, and in him stand forth, in strongest light and shadow, the native faults and virtues of the Indian race. All children, says Sir Walter Scott, are naturally liars; and truth and honor are developments of later education. Barbarism is to civilization what childhood is to maturity; and all savages, whatever may be their country, their color, or their lineage, are prone to treachery and deceit. The barbarous ancestors of our own frank and manly race are no less obnoxious to the charge than those of the cat-like Bengalee; for in this childhood of society brave men and cowards are treacherous alike.

The Indian differs widely from the European in his notion of military virtue. In his view, artifice is wisdom; and he honors the skill that can circumvent, no less than the valor that can subdue, an adversary. The object of war, he argues, is to destroy the enemy. To accomplish this end, all means are honorable; and it is folly, not bravery, to incur a needless risk. Had Pontiac ordered his followers to storm the palisades of Detroit, not one of them would have obeyed him. They might, indeed, after their strange superstition, have reverenced him as a madman; but, from that hour, his fame as a war-chief would have sunk forever.

Balked in his treachery, the great chief withdrew to his village, enraged and mortified, yet still resolved to persevere. That Gladwyn had suffered him to escape, was to his mind an ample proof either of cowardice or ignorance. The latter supposition seemed the more probable; and he resolved to visit the

English once more, and convince them, if possible, that their suspicions against him were unfounded. Early on the following morning, he repaired to the fort with three of his chiefs, bearing in his hand the sacred calumet, or pipe of peace, its bowl carved in stone, and its stem adorned with feathers. Offering it to the commandant, he addressed him and his officers to the following effect: "My fathers, evil birds have sung lies in your ear. We that stand before you are friends of the English. We love them as our brothers; and, to prove our love, we have come this day to smoke the pipe of peace." At his departure, he gave the pipe to Captain Campbell, second in command, as a farther pledge of his sincerity.

That afternoon, the better to cover his designs, Pontiac called the young men of all the tribes to a game of ball, which took place, with great noise and shouting, on the neighboring fields. At nightfall, the garrison were startled by a burst of loud, shrill yells. The drums beat to arms, and the troops were ordered to their posts; but the alarm was caused only by the victors in the ball play, who were announcing their success by these discordant outcries. Meanwhile, Pontiac was in the Pottawattamie village, consulting with the chiefs of that tribe, and with the Wyandots, by what means they might compass the ruin of the English.

Early on the following morning, Monday, the ninth of May, the French inhabitants went in procession to the principal church of the settlement, which stood near the river bank, about half a mile above the fort. Having heard mass, they all returned before eleven o'clock, without discovering any signs that the Indians meditated an immediate act of hostility. Scarcely, however, had they done so, when the common behind the fort was once more thronged with Indians of all the four tribes; and Pontiac, advancing from among the multitude, approached the gate. It was closed and barred against him. He shouted to the sentinels, and demanded why he was refused admittance. Gladwyn himself replied, that the great chief might enter, if he chose, but that the crowd he had brought with him must remain outside. Pontiac rejoined, that he wished all his warriors to enjoy the fragrance of the friendly calumet. Gladwyn's answer was more concise than courteous, and imported that he would have none of his rabble in the fort. Thus repulsed, Pontiac threw off the mask which he had worn so long. With a grin of hate and rage, he turned abruptly from the gate, and strode towards his followers, who, in great multitudes, lay flat upon the ground, just beyond reach of gunshot. At his approach, they all leaped up and ran off, "yelping," in the words of an eye-witness, "like so many devils."

Looking out from the loopholes, the garrison could see them running in a body towards the house of an old English woman, who lived, with her family, on a distant part of the common. They beat down the doors, and rushed tumultuously in. A moment more, and the mournful scalp-yell told the fate of the wretched inmates. Another large body ran, yelling, to the river bank, and, leaping into their canoes, paddled with all speed to the Isle-au-Cochon, where dwelt an Englishman, named Fisher, formerly a sergeant of the regulars.

They soon dragged him from the hiding-place where he had sought refuge, murdered him on the spot, took his scalp, and made great rejoicings over this miserable trophy of brutal malice. On the following day, several Canadians crossed over to the island to inter the body, which they accomplished, as they thought, very effectually. Tradition, however, relates, as undoubted truth, that when, a few days after, some of the party returned to the spot, they beheld the pale hands of the dead man thrust above the ground, in an attitude of eager entreaty. Having once more covered the refractory members with earth, they departed, in great wonder and awe; but what was their amazement, when, on returning a second time, they saw the hands protruding as before. At this, they repaired in horror to the priest, who hastened to the spot, sprinkled the grave with holy water, and performed over it the neglected rites of burial. Thenceforth, says the tradition, the corpse of the murdered soldier slept in peace.

Pontiac had borne no part in the wolfish deeds of his followers. When he saw his plan defeated, he turned towards the shore; and no man durst approach him, for he was terrible in his rage. Pushing a canoe from the bank, he urged it with vigorous strokes, against the current, towards the Ottawa village, on the farther side. As he drew near, he shouted to the inmates. None remained in the lodges but women, children, and old men, who all came flocking out at the sound of his imperious voice. Pointing across the water, he ordered that all should prepare to move the camp to the western shore, that the river might no longer interpose a barrier between his followers and the English. The squaws labored with eager alacrity to obey him. Provisions, utensils, weapons, and even the bark covering to the lodges, were carried to the shore; and before evening all was ready for embarkation. Meantime, the warriors had come dropping in from their bloody work, until, at nightfall, nearly all had returned. Then Pontiac, hideous in his war-paint, leaped into the central area of the village. Brandishing his tomahawk, and stamping on the ground, he recounted his former exploits, and denounced vengeance on the English. The Indians flocked about him. Warrior after warrior caught the fierce contagion, and soon the ring was filled with dancers, circling round and round with frantic gesture, and startling the distant garrison with unearthly yells.

The war-dance over, the work of embarkation was commenced, and long before morning the transfer was complete. The whole Ottawa population crossed the river, and pitched their wigwams on the western side, just above the mouth of the little stream then known as Parent's Creek, but since named Bloody Run, from the scenes of terror which it witnessed.

During the evening, fresh tidings of disaster reached the fort. A Canadian, named Desnoyers, came down the river in a birch canoe, and, landing at the water gate, brought news that two English officers, Sir Robert Davers and Captain Robertson, had been waylaid and murdered by the Indians, above Lake St. Clair. The Canadian declared, moreover, that Pontiac had just been joined by a formidable band of Ojibwas, from the Bay of Saginaw. These were a peculiarly ferocious horde, and their wretched descendants still retain the character.

Every Englishman in the fort, whether trader or soldier, was now ordered under arms. No man lay down to sleep, and Gladwyn himself walked the ramparts throughout the night.

All was quiet till the approach of dawn. But as the first dim redness tinged the east, and fields and woods grew visible in the morning twilight, suddenly the war-whoop rose on every side at once. As wolves assail the wounded bison, howling their gathering cries across the wintry prairie, so the fierce Indians, pealing their terrific yells, came bounding naked to the assault. The men hastened to their posts. And truly it was time; for not the Ottawas alone, but the whole barbarian swarm —Wyandots, Pottawattamies, and Ojibwas—were upon them, and bullets rapped hard and fast against the palisades. The soldiers looked from the loopholes, thinking to see their assailants gathering for a rush against the feeble barrier. But, though their clamors filled the air, and their guns blazed thick and hot, yet very few were visible. Some were ensconced behind barns and fences, some skulked among bushes, and some lay flat in hollows of the ground; while those who could find no shelter were leaping about with the agility of monkeys, to dodge the shot of the fort. Each had filled his mouth with bullets, for the convenience of loading, and each was charging and firing without suspending these agile gymnastics for a moment. There was one low hill, at no great distance from the fort, behind which countless black heads of Indians alternately appeared and vanished; while, all along the ridge, their guns emitted incessant white puffs of smoke. Every loophole was a target for their bullets; but the fire was returned with steadiness, and not without effect. The Canadian *engagés* of the fur-traders retorted the Indian war-whoops with outcries not less discordant, while the British and provincials paid back the clamor of the enemy with musket and rifle balls. Within half gunshot of the palisades was a cluster of outbuildings, behind which a host of Indians found shelter. A cannon was brought to bear upon them, loaded with red-hot spikes. They were soon wrapped in flames, upon which the disconcerted savages broke away in a body, and ran off yelping, followed by a shout of laughter from the soldiers.

For six hours, the attack was unabated; but as the day advanced, the assailants grew weary of their futile efforts. Their fire slackened, their clamors died away, and the garrison was left once more in peace, though from time to time a solitary shot, or lonely whoop, still showed the presence of some lingering savage, loath to be balked of his revenge. Among the garrison, only five men had been wounded, while the cautious enemy had suffered but trifling loss.

[CAPTIVES OF THE INDIANS]

Among the records of that day's sufferings and disasters, none are more striking than the narratives of those whose lives were spared that they might be borne captive to the Indian villages. Exposed to the extremity of hardship, they were urged forward with the assurance of being tomahawked or burnt in case their strength should fail them. Some made their escape from the clutches of their tormentors; but of these not a few found reason to repent their success, lost in a trackless wilderness, and perishing miserably from hunger and exposure. Such attempts could seldom be made in the neighborhood of the settlements. It was only when the party had penetrated deep into the forest that their vigilance began to relax, and their captives were bound and guarded with less rigorous severity. Then, perhaps, when encamped by the side of some mountain brook, and when the warriors lay lost in sleep around their fire, the prisoner would cut or burn asunder the cords that bound his wrists and ankles, and glide stealthily into the woods. With noiseless celerity he pursues his flight over the fallen trunks, through the dense undergrowth, and the thousand pitfalls and impediments of the forest; now striking the rough, hard trunk of a tree, now tripping among the insidious network of vines and brambles. All is darkness around him, and through the black masses of foliage above he can catch but dubious and uncertain glimpses of the dull sky. At length, he can hear the gurgle of a neighboring brook; and, turning towards it, he wades along its pebbly channel, fearing lest the

soft mould and rotten wood of the forest might retain traces
enough to direct the bloodhound instinct of his pursuers. With
the dawn of the misty and cloudy morning, he is still pushing
on his way, when his attention is caught by the spectral figure
of an ancient birch-tree, which, with its white bark hanging
about it in tatters, seems wofully familiar to his eye. Among the
neighboring bushes, a blue smoke curls faintly upward; and, to
his horror and amazement, he recognizes the very fire from
which he had fled a few hours before, and the piles of spruce-
boughs upon which the warriors had slept. They have gone,
however, and are ranging the forest, in keen pursuit of the
fugitive, who, in his blind flight amid the darkness, had circled
round to the very point whence he set out; a mistake not uncommon with careless or inexperienced travellers in the woods.
Almost in despair, he leaves the ill-omened spot, and directs
his course eastward with greater care; the bark of the trees,
rougher and thicker on the northern side, furnishing a precarious clew for his guidance. Around and above him nothing
can be seen but the same endless monotony of brown trunks
and green leaves, closing him in with an impervious screen. He
reaches the foot of a mountain, and toils upwards against the
rugged declivity; but when he stands on the summit, the view
is still shut out by impenetrable thickets. High above them all
shoots up the tall, gaunt stem of a blasted pine-tree; and, in his
eager longing for a view of the surrounding objects, he strains
every muscle to ascend. Dark, wild, and lonely, the wilderness
stretches around him, half hidden in clouds, half open to the
sight, mountain and valley, crag and glistening stream; but
nowhere can he discern the trace of human hand or any hope
of rest and harborage. Before he can look for relief, league
upon league must be passed, without food to sustain or weapon
to defend him. He descends the mountain, forcing his way
through the undergrowth of laurel-bushes; while the clouds
sink lower, and a storm of sleet and rain descends upon the
waste. Through such scenes, and under such exposures, he
presses onward, sustaining life with the aid of roots and berries
or the flesh of reptiles. Perhaps, in the last extremity, some

party of Rangers find him, and bring him to a place of refuge; perhaps, by his own efforts, he reaches some frontier post, where rough lodging and rough fare seem to him unheard-of luxury; or perhaps, spent with fatigue and famine, he perishes in despair, a meagre banquet for the wolves.

[THE DEATH OF PONTIAC]

The winter passed quietly away. Already the Indians began to feel the blessings of returning peace in the partial reopening of the fur-trade; and the famine and nakedness, the misery and death, which through the previous season had been rife in their encampments, were exchanged for comparative comfort and abundance. With many precautions, and in meagre allowances, the traders had been permitted to throw their goods into the Indian markets; and the starving hunters were no longer left, as many of them had been, to gain precarious sustenance by the bow, the arrow, and the lance,—the half-forgotten weapons of their fathers. Some troubles arose along the frontiers of Pennsylvania and Virginia. The reckless borderers, in contempt of common humanity and prudence, murdered several straggling Indians, and enraged others by abuse and insult; but these outrages could not obliterate the remembrance of recent chastisement, and, for the present at least, the injured warriors forbore to draw down the fresh vengeance of their destroyers.

Spring returned, and Pontiac remembered the promise he had made to visit Sir William Johnson at Oswego. He left his encampment on the Maumee, accompanied by his chiefs, and by an Englishman named Crawford, a man of vigor and resolution, who had been appointed, by the superintendent, to the troublesome office of attending the Indian deputation, and supplying their wants.

We may well imagine with what bitterness of mood the defeated war-chief urged his canoe along the margin of Lake Erie, and gazed upon the horizon-bounded waters, and the lofty shores, green with primeval verdure. Little could he have dreamed, and little could the wisest of that day have imagined, that, within the space of a single human life, that lonely lake would be studded with the sails of commerce; that cities and villages would rise upon the ruins of the forest; and that the poor mementoes of his lost race—the wampum beads, the rusty tomahawk, and the arrowhead of stone, turned up by the ploughshare—would become the wonder of school-boys, and the prized relics of the antiquary's cabinet. Yet it needed no prophetic eye to foresee that, sooner or later, the doom must come. The star of his people's destiny was fading from the sky; and, to a mind like his, the black and withering future must have stood revealed in all its desolation.

The birchen flotilla gained the outlet of Lake Erie, and, shooting downwards with the stream, landed beneath the palisades of Fort Schlosser. The chiefs passed the portage, and, once more embarking, pushed out upon Lake Ontario. Soon their goal was reached, and the cannon boomed hollow salutation from the batteries of Oswego.

Here they found Sir William Johnson waiting to receive them, attended by the chief sachems of the Iroquois, whom he had invited to the spot, that their presence might give additional weight and solemnity to the meeting. As there was no building large enough to receive so numerous a concourse, a canopy of green boughs was erected to shade the assembly from the sun; and thither, on the twenty-third of July, repaired the chiefs and warriors of the several nations. Here stood the tall figure of Sir William Johnson, surrounded by civil and military officers, clerks, and interpreters; while before him reclined the painted sachems of the Iroquois, and the great Ottawa war-chief, with his dejected followers.

Johnson opened the meeting with the usual formalities, presenting his auditors with a belt of wampum to wipe the tears from their eyes, with another to cover the bones of their relatives, another to open their ears that they might hear, and another to clear their throats that they might speak with ease. Then, amid solemn silence, Pontiac's great peace-pipe was lighted and passed round the assembly, each man present inhaling a whiff of the sacred smoke. These tedious forms, together with a few speeches of compliment, consumed the whole morning; for this savage people, on whose supposed simplicity poets and rhetoricians have lavished their praises, may challenge the world to outmatch their bigoted adherence to usage and ceremonial.

On the following day, the council began in earnest, and Sir William Johnson addressed Pontiac and his attendant chiefs:—

"Children, I bid you heartily welcome to this place; and I trust that the Great Spirit will permit us often to meet together in friendship, for I have now opened the door and cleared the road, that all nations may come hither from the sunsetting. This belt of wampum confirms my words.

"Children, it gave me much pleasure to find that you who are present behaved so well last year, and treated in so friendly a manner Mr. Croghan, one of my deputies; and that you expressed such concern for the bad behavior of those, who, in order to obstruct the good work of peace, assaulted and wounded him, and killed some of his party, both whites and Indians; a thing before unknown, and contrary to the laws and customs of all nations. This would have drawn down our strongest resentment upon those who were guilty of so heinous a crime, were it not for the great lenity and kindness of your English father, who does not delight in punishing those who repent sincerely of their faults.

"Children, I have now, with the approbation of General Gage (your father's chief warrior in this country), invited you here in order to confirm and strengthen your proceedings with Mr. Croghan last year. I hope that you will remember all that then passed, and I desire that you will often repeat it to your young people, and keep it fresh in your minds.

"Children, you begin already to see the fruits of peace, from the number of traders and plenty of goods at all the garrisoned posts; and our enjoying the peaceable possession of the Illinois will be found of great advantage to the Indians in that country. You likewise see that proper officers, men of honor and probity, are appointed to reside at the posts, to prevent abuses in trade, to hear your complaints, and to lay before me such of them as they cannot redress. Interpreters are likewise sent for the assistance of each of them; and smiths are sent to the posts to repair your arms and implements. All this, which is attended with a great expense, is now done by the great King, your father, as a proof of his regard; so that, casting from you all jealousy and apprehension, you should now strive with each other who should show the most gratitude to this best of princes. I do now, therefore, confirm the assurances which I give you of his Majesty's good will, and do insist on your casting away all evil thoughts, and shutting your ears against all flying idle reports of bad people."

The rest of Johnson's speech was occupied in explaining to his hearers the new arrangements for the regulation of the fur-trade; in exhorting them to forbear from retaliating the injuries they might receive from reckless white men, who would meet with due punishment from their own countrymen; and in urging them to deliver up to justice those of their people who might be guilty of crimes against the English. "Children," he concluded, "I now, by this belt, turn your eyes to the sun-rising, where you will always find me your sincere friend. From me you will always hear what is true and good; and I charge you never more to listen to those evil birds, who come, with lying tongues, to lead you astray and to make you break the solemn engagements which you have entered into, in presence of the Great Spirit, with the King your father and the English people. Be strong, then, and keep fast hold of the chain of friendship, that your children, following your example, may live happy and prosperous lives."

Pontiac made a brief reply, and promised to return on the morrow an answer in full. The meeting then broke up.

The council of the next day was opened by the Wyandot chief, Teata, in a short and formal address; at the conclusion of which Pontiac himself arose, and addressed the superintendent in words, of which the following is a translation:—

"Father, we thank the Great Spirit for giving us so fine a day to meet upon such great affairs. I speak in the name of all the nations to the westward, of whom I am the master. It is the will of the Great Spirit that we should meet here to-day; and before him I now take you by the hand. I call him to witness that I speak from my heart; for since I took Colonel Croghan by the hand last year, I have never let go my hold, for I see that the Great Spirit will have us friends.

"Father, when our great father of France was in this country, I held him fast by the hand. Now that he is gone, I take you, my English father, by the hand, in the name of all the nations, and promise to keep this covenant as long as I shall live."

Here he delivered a large belt of wampum.

"Father, when you address me, it is the same as if you addressed all the nations of the west. Father, this belt is to cover and strengthen our chain of friendship and to show you that, if any nation shall lift the hatchet against our English brethren, we shall be the first to feel it and resent it."

Pontiac next took up in succession the various points touched upon in the speech of the superintendent, expressing in all things a full compliance with his wishes. The succeeding days of the conference were occupied with matters of detail relating chiefly to the fur-trade, all of which were adjusted to the apparent satisfaction of the Indians, who, on their part, made reiterated professions of friendship. Pontiac promised to recall the war-belts which had been sent to the north and west, though, as he alleged, many of them had proceeded from the Senecas, and not from him; adding that, when all were gathered together, they would be more than a man could carry. The Iroquois sachems then addressed the western nations, exhorting them to stand true to their engagements, and hold fast the chain of friendship; and the councils closed on the thirty-first, with a bountiful distribution of presents to Pontiac and his followers.

Thus ended this memorable meeting, in which Pontiac sealed his submission to the English, and renounced forever the bold design by which he had trusted to avert or retard the ruin of his race. His hope of seeing the empire of France restored in America was scattered to the winds, and with it vanished every rational scheme of resistance to English encroachment. Nothing now remained but to stand an idle spectator, while, in the north and in the south, the tide of British power rolled westward in resistless might; while the fragments of the rival empire, which he would fain have set up as a barrier against the flood, lay scattered a miserable wreck; and while the remnant of his people melted away or fled for refuge to remoter deserts. For them the prospects of the future were as clear as they were calamitous. Destruction or civilization—between these lay their choice; and few who knew them could doubt which alternative they would embrace.

Pontiac, his canoe laden with the gifts of his enemy, steered homeward for the Maumee; and in this vicinity he spent the following winter, pitching his lodge in the forest with his wives and children, and hunting like an ordinary warrior. With the succeeding spring, 1767, fresh murmurings of discontent arose among the Indian tribes, from the lakes to the Potomac, the first precursors of the disorders which, a few years later, ripened into a brief but bloody war along the borders of Virginia. These threatening symptoms might easily be traced to their source. The incorrigible frontiersmen had again let loose their murdering propensities; and a multitude of squatters had built their cabins on Indian lands beyond the limits of Pennsylvania, adding insult to aggression, and sparing neither oaths, curses, nor any form of abuse and maltreatment against the rightful owners of the soil. The new regulations of the fur-trade could not prevent disorders among the reckless men engaged in it. This was particularly the case in the region of the Illinois, where the evil was aggravated by the renewed intrigues of the French, and especially of those who had fled from the English side of the Mississippi, and made their abode around the new settlement of St. Louis. It is difficult to say how far Pontiac was involved in this agitation. It is certain that some of the English traders regarded him with jealousy and fear, as prime mover of the whole, and eagerly watched an opportunity to destroy him.

The discontent among the tribes did not diminish with the lapse of time; yet for many months we can discern no trace of Pontiac. Records and traditions are silent concerning him.

It is not until April, 1769, that he appears once more distinctly on the scene. At about that time he came to the Illinois, with what design does not appear, though his movements excited much uneasiness among the few English in that quarter. Soon after his arrival, he repaired to St. Louis, to visit his former acquaintance, St. Ange, who was then in command at that post, having offered his services to the Spaniards after the cession of Louisiana. After leaving the fort, Pontiac proceeded to the house of which young Pierre Chouteau was an inmate; and to the last days of his protracted life, the latter could vividly recall the circumstances of the interview. The savage chief was arrayed in the full uniform of a French officer, which had been presented to him as a special mark of respect and favor by the Marquis of Montcalm, towards the close of the French war, and which Pontiac never had the bad taste to wear, except on occasions when he wished to appear with unusual dignity. St. Ange, Chouteau, and the other principal inhabitants of the infant settlement, whom he visited in turn, all received him cordially, and did their best to entertain him and his attendant chiefs. He remained at St. Louis for two or three days, when, hearing that a large number of Indians were assembled at Cahokia, on the opposite side of the river, and that some drinking bout or other social gathering was in progress, he told St. Ange that he would cross over to see what was going forward. St. Ange tried to dissuade him, and urged the risk to which he would expose himself; but Pontiac persisted, boasting that he was a match for the English, and had no fear for his life. He entered a canoe with some of his followers, and Chouteau never saw him again.

He who, at the present day, crosses from the city of St. Louis to the opposite shore of the Mississippi, and passes southward through a forest festooned with grapevines, and fragrant with the scent of flowers, will soon emerge upon the ancient hamlet of Cahokia. To one fresh from the busy suburbs of the American city, the small French houses, scattered in picturesque disorder, the light-hearted, thriftless look of their inmates, and the woods which form the background of the picture, seem like the remnants of an earlier and simpler world. Strange changes have passed around that spot. Forests have fallen, cities have sprung up, and the lonely wilderness is thronged with human life. Nature herself has taken part in the general transformation; and the Mississippi has made a fearful inroad, robbing from the luckless Creoles a mile of rich meadow and woodland. Yet, in the midst of all, this relic of the lost empire of France has preserved its essential features through the lapse of a century, and offers at this day an aspect not widely different from that which met the eye of Pontiac, when he and his chiefs landed on its shore.

The place was full of Illinois Indians; such a scene as in our own time may often be met with in some squalid settlement of the border, where the vagabond guests, bedizened with dirty finery, tie their small horses in rows along the fences, and stroll idly among the houses, or lounge about the dramshops. A chief so renowned as Pontiac could not remain long among the friendly Creoles of Cahokia without being summoned to a feast; and at such primitive entertainment the whiskey-bottle would not fail to play its part. This was in truth the case. Pontiac drank deeply, and, when the carousal was over, strode down the village street to the adjacent woods, where he was heard to sing the medicine songs, in whose magic power he trusted as the warrant of success in all his undertakings.

An English trader, named Williamson, was then in the village. He had looked on the movements of Pontiac with a jealousy probably not diminished by the visit of the chief to the French at St. Louis; and he now resolved not to lose so favorable an opportunity to despatch him. With this view, he gained the ear of a strolling Indian, belonging to the Kaskaskia tribe of the Illinois, bribed him with a barrel of liquor, and promised him a farther reward if he would kill the chief. The bargain was quickly made. When Pontiac entered the forest, the assassin stole close upon his track; and, watching his moment, glided behind him, and buried a tomahawk in his brain.

The dead body was soon discovered, and startled cries and wild howlings announced the event. The word was caught up from mouth to mouth, and the place resounded with infernal yells. The warriors snatched their weapons. The Illinois took part with their guilty countryman; and the few followers of Pontiac, driven from the village, fled to spread the tidings and call the nations to revenge. Meanwhile the murdered chief lay on the spot where he had fallen, until St. Ange, mindful of former friendship, sent to claim the body, and buried it with warlike honors, near his fort of St. Louis.

Thus basely perished this champion of a ruined race. But could his shade have revisited the scene of murder, his savage spirit would have exulted in the vengeance which overwhelmed the abettors of the crime. Whole tribes were rooted out to expiate it. Chiefs and sachems, whose veins had thrilled with his eloquence; young warriors, whose aspiring hearts had caught the inspiration of his greatness, mustered to revenge his fate; and, from the north and the east, their united bands descended on the villages of the Illinois. Tradition has but faintly preserved the memory of the event; and its only annalists, men who held the intestine feuds of the savage tribes in no more account than the quarrels of panthers or wildcats, have left but a meagre record. Yet enough remains to tell us that over the grave of Pontiac more blood was poured out in atonement, than flowed from the veins of the slaughtered heroes on the corpse of Patroclus; and the remnant of the Illinois who survived the carnage remained for ever after sunk in utter insignificance.

Neither mound nor tablet marked the burial-place of Pontiac. For a mausoleum, a city has risen above the forest hero; and the race whom he hated with such burning rancor trample with unceasing footsteps over his forgotten grave.

[THE GREAT HISTORY]

[FRANCE AND ENGLAND IN NORTH AMERICA]

(From *Pioneers of France in the New World*, 1865)

. . . The springs of American civilization, unlike those of the elder world, lie revealed in the clear light of History. In appearance they are feeble; in reality, copious and full of force. Acting at the sources of life, instruments otherwise weak become mighty for good and evil, and men, lost elsewhere in the crowd, stand forth as agents of Destiny. In their toils, their sufferings, their conflicts, momentous questions were at stake, and issues vital to the future world,—the prevalence of races, the triumph of principles, health or disease, a blessing or a curse. On the obscure strife where men died by tens or by scores hung questions of as deep import for posterity as on those mighty contests of national adolescence where carnage is reckoned by thousands. . . .

The subject to which the earlier narratives of the proposed series will be devoted is that of "France in the New World,"— the attempt of Feudalism, Monarchy, and Rome to master a continent where, at this hour, half a million of bayonets are vindicating the ascendency of a regulated freedom;—Feudalism still strong in life, though enveloped and overborne by new-born Centralization; Monarchy in the flush of triumphant power; Rome, nerved by disaster, springing with renewed vitality from ashes and corruption, and ranging the earth to reconquer abroad what she had lost at home. These banded powers, pushing into the wilderness their indomitable soldiers and devoted priests, unveiled the secrets of the barbarous continent, pierced the forests, traced and mapped out the streams, planted their emblems, built their forts, and claimed all as their own. New France was all head. Under King, Noble, and Jesuit, the lank, lean body would not thrive. Even Commerce wore the sword, decked itself with badges of nobility, aspired to forest seigniories and hordes of savage retainers.

Along the borders of the sea, an adverse power was strengthening and widening with slow, but steadfast growth, full of blood and muscle,—a body without a head. Each had its strength, each its weakness, each its own modes of vigorous life: but the one was fruitful, the other barren; the one instinct with hope, the other darkening with shadows of despair.

By name, local position, and character, one of these communities of freemen stands forth as the most conspicuous representative of this antagonism;—Liberty and Absolutism, New England and New France. The one was the offspring of a triumphant government; the other, of an oppressed and fugitive people: the one, an unflinching champion of the Roman Catholic reaction; the other, a vanguard of the Reform. Each followed its natural laws of growth, and each came to its natural result. Vitalized by the principles of its foundation, the Puritan commonwealth grew apace. New England was preeminently the land of material progress. Here the prize was within every man's reach; patient industry need never doubt its reward; nay, in defiance of the four Gospels, assiduity in pursuit of gain was promoted to the rank of a duty, and thrift and godliness were linked in equivocal wedlock. Politically, she was free; socially, she suffered from that subtile and searching oppression which the dominant opinion of a free community may exercise over the members who compose it. As a whole, she grew upon the gaze of the world, a signal example of expansive energy; but she has not been fruitful in those salient and striking forms of character which often give a dramatic life to the annals of nations far less prosperous.

We turn to New France, and all is reversed. Here was a bold attempt to crush under the exactions of a grasping hierarchy, to stifle under the curbs and trappings of a feudal monarchy, a people compassed by influences of the wildest freedom, —whose schools were the forest and the sea, whose trade was an armed barter with savages, and whose daily life a lesson of lawless independence. But this fierce spirit had its vent. The story of New France is, from the first, a story of war: of war— for so her founders believed—with the adversary of mankind

himself; war with savage tribes and potent forest common-
wealths; war with the encroaching powers of Heresy and of
England. Her brave, unthinking people were stamped with
the soldier's virtues and the soldier's faults; and in their leaders
were displayed, on a grand and novel stage, the energies, aspirations, and passions which belong to hopes vast and vague,
ill-restricted powers, and stations of command.

The growth of New England was a result of the aggregate
efforts of a busy multitude, each in his narrow circle toiling for
himself, to gather competence or wealth. The expansion of
New France was the achievement of a gigantic ambition striving
to grasp a continent. It was a vain attempt. Long and valiantly
her chiefs upheld their cause, leading to battle a vassal population, warlike as themselves. Borne down by numbers from
without, wasted by corruption from within, New France fell
at last; and out of her fall grew revolutions whose influence,
to this hour, is felt through every nation of the civilized
world.

The French dominion is a memory of the past; and, when we
evoke its departed shades, they rise upon us from their graves
in strange romantic guise. Again their ghostly camp-fires
seem to burn, and the fitful light is cast around on lord and
vassal and black-robed priest, mingled with wild forms of
savage warriors, knit in close fellowship on the same stern
errand. A boundless vision grows upon us: an untamed continent; vast wastes of forest verdure; mountains silent in
primeval sleep; river, lake, and glimmering pool; wilderness
oceans mingling with the sky. Such was the domain which
France conquered for Civilization. Plumed helmets gleamed
in the shade of its forests, priestly vestments in its dens and
fastnesses of ancient barbarism. Men steeped in antique learning, pale with the close breath of the cloister, here spent the
noon and evening of their lives, ruled savage hordes with a
mild, parental sway, and stood serene before the direst shapes
of death. Men of courtly nurture, heirs to the polish of a far-
reaching ancestry, here, with their dauntless hardihood, put to
shame the boldest sons of toil. . . .

EARLY SPANISH ADVENTURE

Towards the close of the fifteenth century, Spain achieved her final triumph over the infidels of Granada, and made her name glorious through all generations by the discovery of America. The religious zeal and romantic daring which a long course of Moorish wars had called forth were now exalted to redoubled fervor. Every ship from the New World came freighted with marvels which put the fictions of chivalry to shame; and to the Spaniard of that day America was a region of wonder and mystery, of vague and magnificent promise. Thither adventurers hastened, thirsting for glory and for gold, and often mingling the enthusiasm of the crusader and the valor of the knight-errant with the bigotry of inquisitors and the rapacity of pirates. They roamed over land and sea; they climbed unknown mountains, surveyed unknown oceans, pierced the sultry intricacies of tropical forests; while from year to year and from day to day new wonders were unfolded, new islands and archipelagoes, new regions of gold and pearl, and barbaric empires of more than Oriental wealth. The extravagance of hope and the fever of adventure knew no bounds. Nor is it surprising that amid such waking marvels the imagination should run wild in romantic dreams; that between the possible and the impossible the line of distinction should be but faintly drawn, and that men should be found ready to stake life and honor in pursuit of the most insane fantasies.

Such a man was Juan Ponce de Leon, a veteran cavalier, whose restless spirit age could not tame. Still greedy of honors and of riches, he embarked at Porto Rico with three brigantines, bent on schemes of discovery. But that which gave the chief stimulus to his enterprise was a story, current among the Indians of Cuba and Hispaniola, that on the island of Bimini, one of the Lucayos [Bahamas], there was a fountain of such virtue, that, bathing in its waters, old men resumed their youth. It was said, moreover, that on a neighboring shore might be found a river gifted with the same beneficent property, and believed by some to be no other than the Jordan. Ponce de Leon found the island of Bimini, but not the fountain. Farther westward, in the latitude of thirty degrees and eight minutes, he approached an unknown land which he named Florida, and steering southward, explored its coast as far as the extreme point of the peninsula, when, after some farther explorations, he retraced his course to Porto Rico.

Ponce de Leon had not regained his youth, but his active spirit was unsubdued.

Nine years later he attempted to plant a colony in Florida; but the Indians attacked him fiercely; he was mortally wounded, and died soon afterwards in Cuba.

The voyages of Garay and Vasquez de Ayllon threw new light on the discoveries of Ponce, and the general outline of the coasts of Florida became known to the Spaniards. Meanwhile, Cortés had conquered Mexico, and the fame of that iniquitous but magnificent exploit rang through all Spain. Many an impatient cavalier burned to achieve a kindred fortune. To the excited fancy of the Spaniards the unknown land of Florida seemed the seat of surpassing wealth, and Pamphilo de Narvaez essayed to possess himself of its fancied treasures. Landing on its shores, and proclaiming destruction to the Indians unless they acknowledged the sovereignty of the Pope and the Emperor, he advanced into the forests with three hundred men. Nothing could exceed their sufferings. Nowhere could they find the gold they came to seek. The village of Appalache, where they hoped to gain a rich booty, offered nothing but a few mean wigwams. The horses gave out, and the famished soldiers fed upon their flesh. The men sickened, and the Indians unceasingly harassed their march. At length, after two hundred and eighty leagues of wandering, they found themselves on the northern shore of the Gulf of Mexico, and desperately put to sea in such crazy boats as their skill and means could construct. Cold, disease, famine, thirst, and the fury of the waves, melted them away. Narvaez himself perished, and of his wretched followers no more than four escaped, reaching by land, after years of vicissitude, the Christian settlements of New Spain.

The interior of the vast country then comprehended under the name of Florida still remained unexplored. The Spanish voyager, as his caravel ploughed the adjacent seas, might give full scope to his imagination, and dream that beyond the long, low margin of forest which bounded his horizon lay hid a rich harvest for some future conqueror; perhaps a second Mexico with its royal palace and sacred pyramids, or another Cuzco with its temple of the Sun, encircled with a frieze of gold. Haunted by such visions, the ocean chivalry of Spain could not long stand idle.

Hernando de Soto was the companion of Pizarro in the conquest of Peru. He had come to America a needy adventurer, with no other fortune than his sword and target. But his exploits had given him fame and fortune, and he appeared at court with the retinue of a nobleman. Still his active energies could not endure repose, and his avarice and ambition goaded him to fresh enterprises. He asked and obtained permission to conquer Florida. While this design was in agitation, Cabeça de Vaca, one of those who had survived the expedition of Narvaez, appeared in Spain, and for purposes of his own spread abroad the mischievous falsehood, that Florida was the richest country yet discovered. De Soto's plans were embraced with enthusiasm. Nobles and gentlemen contended for the privilege of joining his standard; and, setting sail with an ample armament, he landed at the Bay of Espiritu Santo, now Tampa Bay, in Florida, with six hundred and twenty chosen men, a band as gallant and well appointed, as eager in purpose and audacious in hope, as ever trod the shores of the New World. The clangor of trumpets, the neighing of horses, the fluttering of pennons, the glittering of helmet and lance, startled the ancient forest with unwonted greeting. Amid this pomp of chivalry, religion was not forgotten. The sacred vessels and vestments with bread and wine for the Eucharist were carefully provided; and De Soto himself declared that the enterprise was undertaken for God alone, and seemed to be the object of His especial care. These devout marauders could not neglect the spiritual welfare of the Indians whom they had come to plunder; and besides fetters to bind, and bloodhounds to hunt them, they brought priests and monks for the saving of their souls.

The adventurers began their march. Their story has been often told. For month after month and year after year, the procession of priests and cavaliers, crossbowmen, arquebusiers, and Indian captives laden with the baggage, still wandered on through wild and boundless wastes, lured hither and thither by the *ignis-fatuus* of their hopes. They traversed great portions of Georgia, Alabama, and Mississippi, everywhere inflicting and enduring misery, but never approaching their phantom El Dorado. At length, in the third year of their journeying, they reached the banks of the Mississippi, a hundred and thirty-two years before its second discovery by Marquette. One of their number describes the great river as almost half a league wide, deep, rapid, and constantly rolling down trees and drift-wood on its turbid current.

The Spaniards crossed over at a point above the mouth of the Arkansas. They advanced westward, but found no treasures,—nothing indeed but hardships, and an Indian enemy, furious, writes one of their officers, "as mad dogs." They heard of a country towards the north where maize could not be cultivated because the vast herds of wild cattle devoured it. They penetrated so far that they entered the range of the roving prairie tribes; for, one day, as they pushed their way with difficulty across great plains covered with tall, rank grass, they met a band of savages who dwelt in lodges of skins sewed together, subsisting on game alone, and wandering perpetually from place to place. Finding neither gold nor the South Sea, for both of which they had hoped, they returned to the banks of the Mississippi.

De Soto, says one of those who accompanied him, was a "stern man, and of few words." Even in the midst of reverses, his will had been law to his followers, and he had sustained himself through the depths of disappointment with the energy of a stubborn pride. But his hour was come. He fell into deep dejection, followed by an attack of fever, and soon after died miserably. To preserve his body from the Indians, his followers sank it at midnight in the river, and the sullen waters of the Mississippi buried his ambition and his hopes.

The adventurers were now, with few exceptions, disgusted with the enterprise, and longed only to escape from the scene of their miseries. After a vain attempt to reach Mexico by land, they again turned back to the Mississippi, and labored, with all the resources which their desperate necessity could suggest, to construct vessels in which they might make their way to some Christian settlement. Their condition was most forlorn. Few of their horses remained alive; their baggage had been destroyed at the burning of the Indian town of Mavila, and many of the soldiers were without armor and without weapons. In place of the gallant array which, more than three years before, had left the harbor of Espiritu Santo, a company of sickly and starving men were laboring among the swampy forests of the Mississippi, some clad in skins, and some in mats woven from a kind of wild vine.

Seven brigantines were finished and launched; and, trusting their lives on board these frail vessels, they descended the Mississippi, running the gantlet between hostile tribes who fiercely attacked them. Reaching the Gulf, though not without the loss of eleven of their number, they made sail for the Spanish settlement on the River Panuco, where they arrived safely, and where the inhabitants met them with a cordial welcome. Three hundred and eleven men thus escaped with life, leaving behind them the bones of their comrades strewn broadcast through the wilderness.

De Soto's fate proved an insufficient warning, for those were still found who begged a fresh commission for the conquest of Florida; but the Emperor would not hear them. A more pacific enterprise was undertaken by Cancello, a Dominican monk, who with several brother-ecclesiastics undertook to convert the natives to the true faith, but was murdered in the attempt. Nine years later a plan was formed for the colonization of Florida, and Guido de las Bazares sailed to explore the coasts, and find a spot suitable for the establishment. After his return, a squadron, commanded by Angel de Villafañe, and freighted with supplies and men, put to sea from San Juan d'Ulloa; but the elements were adverse, and the result was a total failure. Not a Spaniard had yet gained foothold in Florida.

That name, as the Spaniards of that day understood it, comprehended the whole country extending from the Atlantic on the east to the longitude of New Mexico on the west, and from the Gulf of Mexico and the River of Palms indefinitely northward towards the polar sea. This vast territory was claimed by Spain in right of the discoveries of Columbus, the grant of the Pope, and the various expeditions mentioned above. England claimed it in right of the discoveries of Cabot; while France could advance no better title than might be derived from the voyage of Verazzano.

With restless jealousy Spain watched the domain which she could not occupy, and on France, especially, she kept an eye of deep distrust. When, in 1541, Cartier and Roberval essayed to plant a colony in the part of ancient Spanish Florida now called Canada, she sent spies and fitted out caravels to watch that abortive enterprise. Her fears proved just. Canada, indeed, was long to remain a solitude; but, despite the Papal bounty gifting Spain with exclusive ownership of a hemisphere, France and Heresy at length took root in the sultry forests of modern Florida.

MENENDEZ

The monk, the inquisitor, the Jesuit, these were the lords of Spain,—sovereigns of her sovereign, for they had formed the dark and narrow mind of that tyrannical recluse. They had formed the minds of her people, quenched in blood every spark of rising heresy, and given over a noble nation to a bigotry blind and inexorable as the doom of fate. Linked with pride, ambition, avarice, every passion of a rich, strong nature, potent for good and ill, it made the Spaniard of that day a scourge as dire as ever fell on man.

Day was breaking on the world. Light, hope, freedom, pierced with vitalizing ray the clouds and the miasma that hung so thick over the prostrate Middle Age, once noble and mighty, now a foul image of decay and death. Kindled with new life, the nations gave birth to a progeny of heroes, and the stormy glories of the sixteenth century rose on awakened Europe. But Spain was the citadel of darkness,—a monastic cell, an inquisitorial dungeon, where no ray could pierce. She was the bulwark of the Church, against whose adamantine wall the waves of innovation beat in vain. In every country of Europe the party of freedom and reform was the national party, the party of reaction and absolutism was the Spanish party, leaning on Spain, looking to her for help. Above all, it was so in France; and, while within her bounds there was a semblance of peace, the national and religious rage burst forth on a wilder theatre. Thither it is for us to follow it, where, on the shores of Florida, the Spaniard and the Frenchman, the bigot and the Huguenot, met in the grapple of death.

In a corridor of his palace, Philip the Second was met by a man who had long stood waiting his approach, and who with proud reverence placed a petition in the hand of the pale and sombre King. The petitioner was Pedro Menendez de Avilés, one of the ablest and most distinguished officers of the Spanish marine. He was born of an ancient Asturian family. His boyhood had been wayward, ungovernable, and fierce. He ran off at eight years of age, and when, after a search of six months, he was found and brought back, he ran off again. This time he was more successful, escaping on board a fleet bound against the Barbary corsairs, when his precocious appetite for blood and blows had reasonable contentment. A few years later, he found means to build a small vessel, in which he cruised against the corsairs and the French, and, though still hardly more than a boy, displayed a singular address and daring. The wonders of the New World now seized his imagination. He made a voyage thither, and the ships under his charge came back freighted with wealth. The war with France was then at its height. As captain-general of the fleet, he was sent with troops to Flanders; and to their prompt arrival was due, it is said, the victory of St. Quentin. Two years later, he commanded the luckless armada which bore back Philip to his native shore.

On the way, the King narrowly escaped drowning in a storm off the port of Laredo. This mischance, or his own violence and insubordination, wrought to the prejudice of Menendez. He complained that his services were ill repaid. Philip lent him a favoring ear, and despatched him to the Indies as general of the fleet and army. Here he found means to amass vast riches; and, in 1561, on his return to Spain, charges were brought against him of a nature which his too friendly biographer does not explain. The Council of the Indies arrested him. He was imprisoned and sentenced to a heavy fine, but, gaining his release, hastened to court to throw himself on the royal clemency. His petition was most graciously received. Philip restored his command, but remitted only half his fine, a strong presumption of his guilt.

Menendez kissed the royal hand; he had still a petition in reserve. His son had been wrecked near the Bermudas, and he would fain go thither to find tidings of his fate. The pious King bade him trust in God, and promised that he should be despatched without delay to the Bermudas and to Florida with a commission to make an exact survey of those perilous seas for the profit of future voyagers; but Menendez was ill content with such an errand. He knew, he said, nothing of greater moment to His Majesty than the conquest and settlement of Florida. The climate was healthful, the soil fertile; and, worldly advantages aside, it was peopled by a race sunk in the thickest shades of infidelity. "Such grief," he pursued, "seizes me, when I behold this multitude of wretched Indians, that I should choose the conquest and settling of Florida above all commands, offices, and dignities which your Majesty might bestow." Those who think this to be hypocrisy do not know the Spaniard of the sixteenth century.

The King was edified by his zeal. An enterprise of such spiritual and temporal promise was not to be slighted, and Menendez was empowered to conquer and convert Florida at his own cost. The conquest was to be effected within three years. Menendez was to take with him five hundred men, and supply them with five hundred slaves, besides horses, cattle, sheep, and hogs. Villages were to be built, with forts to defend them, and sixteen ecclesiastics, of whom four should be Jesuits, were to form the nucleus of a Floridan church. The King, on his part, granted Menendez free trade with Hispaniola, Porto Rico, Cuba, and Spain, the office of Adelantado of Florida for life with the right of naming his successor, and large emoluments to be drawn from the expected conquest.

The compact struck, Menendez hastened to his native Asturias to raise money among his relatives. Scarcely was he gone, when tidings reached Madrid that Florida was already occupied by a colony of French Protestants, and that a reinforcement, under Ribaut, was on the point of sailing thither. A French historian of high authority declares that these advices came from the Catholic party at the French court, in whom every instinct of patriotism was lost in their hatred of Coligny and the Huguenots. Of this there can be little doubt, though information also came about this time from the buccaneer Frenchmen captured in the West Indies.

Foreigners had invaded the territory of Spain. The trespassers, too, were heretics, foes of God, and liegemen of the Devil. Their doom was fixed. But how would France endure an assault, in time of peace, on subjects who had gone forth on an enterprise sanctioned by the Crown, and undertaken in its name and under its commission?

The throne of France, where the corruption of the nation seemed gathered to a head, was trembling between the two parties of the Catholics and the Huguenots, whose chiefs aimed at royalty. Flattering both, caressing both, playing one against the other, and betraying both, Catherine de Medicis, by a thousand crafty arts and expedients of the moment, sought to retain the crown on the head of her weak and vicious son. Of late her crooked policy had led her towards the Catholic party, in other words, the party of Spain; and already she had given ear to the savage Duke of Alva, urging her to the course which, seven years later, led to the carnage of St. Bartholomew. In short, the Spanish policy was in the ascendant, and no thought of the national interest or honor could restrain that basest of courts from consigning by hundreds to the national enemy those whom it was itself meditating to immolate by thousands.

Menendez was summoned back in haste to the Spanish court. There was counsel, deep and ominous, in the palace of Madrid. His force must be strengthened. Three hundred and ninety-four men were added at the royal charge, and a corresponding number of transport and supply ships. It was a holy war, a crusade, and as such was preached by priest and monk along the western coasts of Spain. All the Biscayan ports flamed with zeal, and adventurers crowded to enroll themselves; since to plunder heretics is good for the soul as well as the purse, and broil and massacre have double attraction when promoted into a means of salvation: a fervor, deep and hot, but not of celestial kindling; nor yet that buoyant and inspiring zeal, which, when the Middle Age was in its youth and prime, glowed in the souls of Tancred, Godfrey, and St. Louis, and which, when its day was long since past, could still find its home in the great heart of Columbus. A darker spirit urged the new crusade,— born, not of hope, but of fear, slavish in its nature, the creature and the tool of despotism. For the typical Spaniard of the sixteenth century was not in strictness a fanatic; he was bigotry incarnate.

Heresy was a plague-spot, an ulcer to be eradicated with fire and the knife, and this foul abomination was infecting the shores which the Vicegerent of Christ had given to the King of Spain, and which the Most Catholic King had given to the Adelantado. Thus would countless heathen tribes be doomed to an eternity of flame, and the Prince of Darkness hold his ancient sway unbroken. And, for the Adelantado himself, should the vast outlays, the vast debts, of his bold Floridian venture be all in vain? Should his fortunes be wrecked past redemption through these tools of Satan? As a Catholic, as a Spaniard, as an adventurer, his course was clear.

But what was the scope of this enterprise, and what were the limits of the Adelantado's authority? He was invested with power almost absolute, not merely over the peninsula which now retains the name of Florida, but over all North America, from Labrador to Mexico, for this was the Florida of the old Spanish geographers, and the Florida designated in the commission of Menendez. It was a continent which he was to conquer and occupy out of his own purse. The impoverished King contracted with his daring and ambitious subject to win and hold for him the territory of the future United States and British Provinces. His plan, as subsequently exposed at length in his letters to Philip the Second, was, first, to plant a garrison at Port Royal, and next to fortify strongly on Chesapeake Bay, called by him St. Mary's. He believed that this bay was an arm of the sea, running northward and eastward, and communicating with the Gulf of St. Lawrence, thus making New England, with adjacent districts, an island. His proposed fort on the Chesapeake, securing access, by this imaginary passage, to the seas of Newfoundland, would enable the Spaniards to command the fisheries, on which both the French and the English had long encroached, to the great prejudice of Spanish rights. Doubtless, too, these inland waters gave access to the South Sea, and their occupation was necessary to prevent the French from penetrating thither; for that ambitious people, since the time of Cartier, had never abandoned their schemes of seizing this portion of the dominions of the King of Spain. Five hundred soldiers and one hundred sailors must, he urges, take possession, without delay, of Port Royal and the Chesapeake.

Preparation for his enterprise was pushed with a furious energy. His whole force amounted to two thousand six hundred and forty-six persons, in thirty-four vessels, one of which, the San Pelayo, bearing Menendez himself, was of nine hundred and ninety-six tons' burden, and is described as one of the finest ships afloat. There were twelve Franciscans and eight Jesuits, besides other ecclesiastics; and many knights of Galicia, Biscay, and the Asturias took part in the expedition. With a slight exception, the whole was at the Adelantado's charge. Within the first fourteen months, according to his admirer, Barcia, the adventure cost him a million ducats.

Before the close of the year, Sancho de Arciniega was commissioned to join Menendez with an additional force of fifteen hundred men.

Red-hot with a determined purpose, the Adelantado would brook no delay. To him, says the chronicler, every day seemed a year. He was eager to anticipate Ribaut, of whose designs and whose force he seems to have been informed to the minutest particular, but whom he hoped to thwart and ruin by gaining Fort Caroline before him. With eleven ships, therefore, he sailed from Cadiz on the twenty-ninth of June, 1565, leaving the smaller vessels of his fleet to follow with what speed they might. He touched first at the Canaries, and on the eighth of July left them, steering for Dominica. A minute account of the voyage has come down to us, written by Mendoza, chaplain of the expedition, a somewhat dull and illiterate person, who busily jots down the incidents of each passing day, and is constantly betraying, with a certain awkward simplicity, how the cares of this world and of the next jostle each other in his thoughts.

On Friday, the twentieth of July, a storm fell upon them with appalling fury. The pilots lost their wits, the sailors gave themselves up to their terrors. Throughout the night, they beset Mendoza for confession and absolution, a boon not easily granted, for the seas swept the crowded decks with cataracts of foam, and the shriekings of the gale in the rigging overpowered the exhortations of the half-drowned priest. Cannon, cables, spars, water-casks, were thrown overboard, and the chests of the sailors would have followed, had not the latter, in spite of their fright, raised such a howl of remonstrance that the order was revoked. At length day dawned. Plunging, reeling, half submerged, quivering under the shock of the seas, whose mountain ridges rolled down upon her before the gale, the ship lay in deadly peril from Friday till Monday noon. Then the storm abated; the sun broke forth; and again she held her course.

They reached Dominica on Sunday, the fifth of August. The chaplain tells us how he went on shore to refresh himself,—

how, while his Italian servant washed his linen at a brook, he strolled along the beach and picked up shells,—and how he was scared, first, by a prodigious turtle, and next by a vision of the cannibal natives, which caused his prompt retreat to the boats.

On the tenth, they anchored in the harbor of Porto Rico, where they found two ships of their squadron, from which they had parted in the storm. One of them was the San Pelayo, with Menendez on board. Mendoza informs us, that in the evening the officers came on board the ship to which he was attached, when he, the chaplain, regaled them with sweetmeats, and that Menendez invited him not only to supper that night, but to dinner the next day, "for the which I thanked him, as reason was," says the gratified churchman.

Here thirty men deserted, and three priests also ran off, of which Mendoza bitterly complains, as increasing his own work. The motives of the clerical truants may perhaps be inferred from a worldly temptation to which the chaplain himself was subjected. "I was offered the service of a chapel where I should have got a *peso* for every mass I said, the whole year round; but I did not accept it, for fear that what I hear said of the other three would be said of me. Besides, it is not a place where one can hope for any great advancement, and I wished to try whether, in refusing a benefice for the love of the Lord, He will not repay me with some other stroke of fortune before the end of the voyage; for it is my aim to serve God and His blessed Mother."

The original design had been to rendezvous at Havana, but, with the Adelantado, the advantages of despatch outweighed every other consideration. He resolved to push directly for Florida. Five of his scattered ships had by this time rejoined company, comprising, exclusive of officers, a force of about five hundred soldiers, two hundred sailors, and one hundred colonists. Bearing northward, he advanced by an unknown and dangerous course along the coast of Hayti and through the intricate passes of the Bahamas. On the night of the twenty-sixth, the San Pelayo struck three times on the shoals; "but," says the chaplain, "inasmuch as our enterprise was undertaken for the sake of Christ and His blessed Mother, two heavy seas struck her abaft, and set her afloat again."

At length the ships lay becalmed in the Bahama Channel, slumbering on the glassy sea, torpid with the heats of a West-Indian August. Menendez called a council of the commanders. There was doubt and indecision. Perhaps Ribaut had already reached the French fort, and then to attack the united force would be an act of desperation. Far better to await their lagging comrades. But the Adelantado was of another mind; and, even had his enemy arrived, he was resolved that he should have no time to fortify himself.

"It is God's will," he said, "that our victory should be due, not to our numbers, but to His all-powerful aid. Therefore has He stricken us with tempests, and scattered our ships." And he gave his voice for instant advance.

There was much dispute; even the chaplain remonstrated; but nothing could bend the iron will of Menendez. Nor was a sign of celestial approval wanting. At nine in the evening, a great meteor burst forth in mid-heaven, and, blazing like the sun, rolled westward towards the coast of Florida. The fainting spirits of the crusaders were revived. Diligent preparation was begun. Prayers and masses were said; and, that the temporal arm might not fail, the men were daily practised on deck in shooting at marks, in order, says the chronicle, that the recruits might learn not to be afraid of their guns.

The dead calm continued. "We were all very tired," says the chaplain, "and I above all, with praying to God for a fair wind. To-day, at about two in the afternoon, He took pity on us, and sent us a breeze." Before night they saw land,—the faint line of forest, traced along the watery horizon, that marked the coast of Florida. But where, in all this vast monotony, was the lurking-place of the French? Menendez anchored, and sent fifty men ashore, who presently found a band of Indians in the woods, and gained from them the needed information. He stood northward, till, on the afternoon of Tuesday, the fourth of September, he descried four ships anchored near the mouth of a river. It was the River St. John's, and the ships were four of Ribaut's squadron. The prey was in sight. The Spaniards prepared for battle, and bore down upon the Lutherans; for, with them, all Protestants alike were branded with the name of the arch-heretic. Slowly, before the faint breeze, the ships glided on their way; but while, excited and impatient, the fierce crews watched the decreasing space, and when they were still three leagues from their prize, the air ceased to stir, the sails flapped against the mast, a black cloud with thunder rose above the coast, and the warm rain of the South descended on the breathless sea. It was dark before the wind moved again and the ships resumed their course. At half-past eleven they reached the French. The San Pelayo slowly moved to windward of Ribaut's flag-ship, the Trinity, and anchored very near her. The other ships took similar stations. While these preparations were making, a work of two hours, the men labored in silence, and the French, thronging their gangways, looked on in equal silence. "Never, since I came into the world," writes the chaplain, "did I know such a stillness."

It was broken, at length, by a trumpet from the deck of the San Pelayo. A French trumpet answered. Then Menendez, "with much courtesy," says his Spanish eulogist, inquired, "Gentlemen, whence does this fleet come?"

"From France," was the reply.

"What are you doing here?" pursued the Adelantado.

"Bringing soldiers and supplies for a fort which the King of France has in this country, and for many others which he soon will have."

"Are you Catholics or Lutherans?"

Many voices cried out together, "Lutherans, of the new religion"; then, in their turn, they demanded who Menendez was, and whence he came. He answered,—

"I am Pedro Menendez, General of the fleet of the King of Spain, Don Philip the Second, who have come to this country to hang and behead all Lutherans whom I shall find by land or sea, according to instructions from my King, so precise that I have power to pardon none; and these commands I shall fulfil, as you will see. At daybreak I shall board your ships, and if I find there any Catholic, he shall be well treated; but every heretic shall die."

The French with one voice raised a cry of wrath and defiance.

"If you are a brave man, don't wait till day. Come on now, and see what you will get!"

And they assailed the Adelantado with a shower of scoffs and insults.

Menendez broke into a rage, and gave the order to board. The men slipped the cables, and the sullen black hulk of the San Pelayo drifted down upon the Trinity. The French by no means made good their defiance. Indeed, they were incapable of resistance, Ribaut with his soldiers being ashore at Fort Caroline. They cut their cables, left their anchors, made sail, and fled. The Spaniards fired, the French replied. The other Spanish ships had imitated the movement of the San Pelayo; "but," writes the chaplain, Mendoza, "these devils run mad are such adroit sailors, and manœuvred so well, that we did not catch one of them." Pursuers and pursued ran out to sea, firing useless volleys at each other.

In the morning Menendez gave over the chase, turned, and, with the San Pelayo alone, ran back for the St. John's. But here a welcome was prepared for him. He saw bands of armed men drawn up on the beach, and the smaller vessels of Ribaut's squadron, which had crossed the bar several days before, anchored behind it to oppose his landing. He would not venture an attack, but, steering southward, sailed along the coast till he came to an inlet which he named San Agustin.

Here he found three of his ships already debarking their troops, guns, and stores. Two officers, Patiño and Vicente, had taken possession of the dwelling of the Indian chief Seloy, a huge barn-like structure, strongly framed of entire trunks of trees, and thatched with palmetto-leaves. Around it they were throwing up intrenchments of fascines and sand. Gangs of negroes, with pick, shovel, and spade, were toiling at the work. Such was the birth of St. Augustine, the oldest town of the United States, and such the introduction of slave-labor upon their soil.

On the eighth, Menendez took formal possession of his domain. Cannon were fired, trumpets sounded, and banners displayed, as, at the head of his officers and nobles, he landed in state. Mendoza, crucifix in hand, came to meet him, chanting "*Te Deum laudamus*," while the Adelantado and all his company, kneeling, kissed the crucifix, and the assembled Indians gazed in silent wonder.

Meanwhile the tenants of Fort Caroline were not idle. Two or three soldiers, strolling along the beach in the afternoon, had first seen the Spanish ships and hastily summoned Ribaut. He came down to the mouth of the river, followed by an anxious and excited crowd; but, as they strained their eyes through the darkness, they could see nothing but the flashes of the distant guns. At length, the returning light showed, far out at sea, the Adelantado in hot chase of their flying comrades. Pursuers and pursued were soon out of sight. The drums beat to arms. After many hours of suspense, the San Pelayo reappeared, hovering about the mouth of the river, then bearing away towards the south. More anxious hours ensued, when three other sail came in sight, and they recognized three of their own returning ships. Communication was opened, a boat's crew landed, and they learned from Cosette, one of the French captains, that, confiding in the speed of his ship, he had followed the Spaniards to St. Augustine, reconnoitred their position, and seen them land their negroes and intrench themselves.

In his chamber at Fort Caroline, Laudonnière lay sick in bed, when Ribaut entered, and with him La Grange, Sainte Marie, Ottigny, Yonville, and other officers. At the bedside of the displaced commandant, they held their council of war. Three plans were proposed: first, to remain where they were and fortify; next, to push overland for St. Augustine, and attack the invaders in their intrenchments; and, finally, to embark, and assail them by sea. The first plan would leave their ships a prey to the Spaniards; and so too, in all likelihood, would the second, besides the uncertainties of an overland march through an unknown wilderness. By sea, the distance was short and the route explored. By a sudden blow they could capture or destroy the Spanish ships, and master the troops on shore before reinforcements could arrive, and before they had time to complete their defences.

Such were the views of Ribaut, with which, not unnaturally, Laudonnière finds fault, and Le Moyne echoes the censures of his chief. And yet the plan seems as well conceived as it was bold, lacking nothing but success. The Spaniards, stricken with terror, owed their safety to the elements, or, as they affirm, to the special interposition of the Holy Virgin. Let us be just to Menendez. He was a leader fit to stand with Cortés and Pizarro; but he was matched with a man as cool, skilful, prompt, and daring as himself. The traces that have come down to us indicate, in Ribaut, one far above the common stamp: "a distinguished man, of many high qualities," as even the faultfinding Le Moyne calls him; devout after the best spirit of the Reform; and with a human heart under his steel breastplate.

La Grange and other officers took part with Laudonnière, and opposed the plan of an attack by sea; but Ribaut's conviction was unshaken, and the order was given. All his own soldiers fit for duty embarked in haste, and with them went La Caille, Arlac, and, as it seems, Ottigny, with the best of Laudonnière's men. Even Le Moyne, though wounded in the fight with Outina's warriors, went on board to bear his part in the fray, and would have sailed with the rest, had not Ottigny, seeing his disabled condition, ordered him back to the fort.

On the tenth, the ships, crowded with troops, set sail. Ribaut was gone, and with him the bone and sinew of the colony. The miserable remnant watched his receding sails with dreary foreboding, a foreboding which seemed but too just, when, on the next day, a storm, more violent than the Indians had ever known, howled through the forest and lashed the ocean into fury. Most forlorn was the plight of these exiles, left, it might be, the prey of a band of ferocious bigots more terrible than the fiercest hordes of the wilderness. And, when night closed on the stormy river and the gloomy waste of pines, what dreams of terror may not have haunted the helpless women who crouched under the hovels of Fort Caroline!

The fort was in a ruinous state, with the palisade on the water side broken down, and three breaches in the rampart. In the driving rain, urged by the sick Laudonnière, the men, bedrenched and disheartened, labored as they might to strengthen their defences. Their muster-roll shows but a beggarly array. "Now," says Laudonnière, "let them which have bene bold to say that I had men ynough left me, so that I had meanes to defend my selfe, give eare a little now vnto mee, and if they have eyes in their heads, let them see what men I had." Of Ribaut's followers left at the fort, only nine or ten had weapons, while only two or three knew how to use them. Four of them were boys, who kept Ribaut's dogs, and another was his cook. Besides these, he had left a brewer, an old crossbow-maker, two shoemakers, a player on the spinet, four valets, a carpenter of threescore,—Challeux, no doubt, who has left us the story of his woes,—with a crowd of women, children, and eighty-six camp-followers. To these were added the remnant of Laudonnière's men, of whom seventeen could bear arms, the rest being sick or disabled by wounds received in the fight with Outina.

Laudonnière divided his force, such as it was, into two watches, over which he placed two officers, Saint Cler and La Vigne, gave them lanterns for going the rounds, and an hour-glass for setting the time; while he himself, giddy with weakness and fever, was every night at the guard-room.

It was the night of the nineteenth of September; floods of rain drenched the sentries on the rampart, and, as day dawned on the dripping barracks and deluged parade, the storm increased in violence. What enemy could venture forth on such a night? La Vigne, who had the watch, took pity on the sentries and on himself, dismissed them, and went to his quarters. He little knew what human energies, urged by ambition, avarice, bigotry, and desperation, will dare and do.

To return to the Spaniards at St. Augustine. On the morning of the eleventh, the crew of one of their smaller vessels, lying outside the bar, saw through the twilight of early dawn two of Ribaut's ships close upon them. Not a breath of air was stirring. There was no escape, and the Spaniards fell on their knees in supplication to Our Lady of Utrera, explaining to her that the heretics were upon them, and begging her to send them a little wind. "Forthwith," says Mendoza, "one would have said that Our Lady herself came down upon the vessel." A wind sprang up, and the Spaniards found refuge behind the bar. The returning day showed to their astonished eyes all the ships of Ribaut, their decks black with men, hovering off the entrance of the port; but Heaven had them in its charge, and again they experienced its protecting care. The breeze sent by Our Lady of Utrera rose to a gale, then to a furious tempest; and the grateful Adelantado saw through rack and mist the ships of his enemy tossed wildly among the raging waters as they struggled to gain an offing. With exultation in his heart the skilful seaman read their danger, and saw them in his mind's eye dashed to utter wreck among the sand-bars and breakers of the lee shore.

A bold thought seized him. He would march overland with five hundred men, and attack Fort Caroline while its defenders were absent. First, he ordered a mass; then he called a council. Doubtless it was in that great Indian lodge of Seloy, where he had made his head-quarters; and here, in this dim and smoky abode, nobles, officers, and priests gathered at his summons. There were fears and doubts and murmurings, but Menendez was desperate; not with the mad desperation that strikes wildly and at random, but the still white heat that melts and burns and seethes with a steady, unquenchable fierceness. "Comrades," he said, "the time has come to show our courage and our zeal. This is God's war, and we must not flinch. It is a war with Lutherans, and we must wage it with blood and fire."

But his hearers would not respond. They had not a million of ducats at stake, and were no wise ready for a cast so desperate. A clamor of remonstrance rose from the circle. Many voices, that of Mendoza among the rest, urged waiting till their main forces should arrive. The excitement spread to the men without, and the swarthy, black-bearded crowd broke into tumults mounting almost to mutiny, while an officer was heard to say that he would not go on such a hare-brained errand to be butchered like a beast. But nothing could move the Adelantado. His appeals or his threats did their work at last; the confusion was quelled, and preparation was made for the march.

On the morning of the seventeenth, five hundred arquebusiers and pikemen were drawn up before the camp. To each was given a sack of bread and a flask of wine. Two Indians and a renegade Frenchman, called François Jean, were to guide them, and twenty Biscayan axe-men moved to the front to clear the way. Through floods of driving rain, a hoarse voice shouted the word of command, and the sullen march began.

With dismal misgiving, Mendoza watched the last files as they vanished in the tempestuous forest. Two days of suspense ensued, when a messenger came back with a letter from the Adelantado, announcing that he had nearly reached the French fort, and that on the morrow, September the twentieth, at sunrise, he hoped to assault it. "May the Divine Majesty deign to protect us, for He knows that we have need of it," writes the scared chaplain; "the Adelantado's great zeal and courage make us hope he will succeed, but, for the good of his Majesty's service, he ought to be a little less ardent in pursuing his schemes."

Meanwhile the five hundred had pushed their march through forest and quagmire, through swollen streams and inundated savannas, toiling knee-deep through mud, rushes, and the rank, tangled grass,—hacking their way through thickets of the yucca, or Spanish bayonet, with its clumps of dagger-like leaves, or defiling in gloomy procession through the drenched forest, to the moan and roar of the storm-racked pines. As they bent before the tempest, the water trickling from the rusty head-piece crept clammy and cold betwixt the armor and the skin; and when they made their wretched bivouac, their bed was the spongy soil, and the exhaustless clouds their tent.

The night of Wednesday, the nineteenth, found their vanguard in a deep forest of pines, less than a mile from Fort Caroline, and near the low hills which extended in its rear, and formed a continuation of St. John's Bluff. All around was one great morass. In pitchy darkness, knee-deep in weeds and water, half starved, worn with toil and lack of sleep, drenched to the skin, their provision spoiled, their ammunition wet, and their spirit chilled out of them, they stood in shivering groups, cursing the enterprise and the author of it. Menendez heard an ensign say aloud to his comrades,—"This Asturian *Corito*, who knows no more of war on shore than an ass, has betrayed us all. By ——, if my advice had been followed, he would have had his deserts the day he set out on this cursed journey!"

The Adelantado pretended not to hear.

Two hours before dawn he called his officers about him. All night, he said, he had been praying to God and the Virgin.

"Señores, what shall we resolve on? Our ammunition and provisions are gone. Our case is desperate." And he urged a bold rush on the fort.

But men and officers alike were disheartened and disgusted. They listened coldly and sullenly; many were for returning at every risk; none were in the mood for fight. Menendez put forth all his eloquence, till at length the dashed spirits of his followers were so far revived that they consented to follow him.

All fell on their knees in the marsh; then, rising, they formed their ranks and began to advance, guided by the renegade Frenchman, whose hands, to make sure of him, were tied behind his back. Groping and stumbling in the dark among trees, roots, and underbrush, buffeted by wind and rain, and lashed in the face by the recoiling boughs which they could not see, they soon lost their way, fell into confusion, and came to a stand, in a mood more savagely desponding than before. But soon a glimmer of returning day came to their aid, and showed them the dusky sky, and the dark columns of the surrounding pines. Menendez ordered the men forward on pain of death. They obeyed, and presently, emerging from the forest, could dimly discern the ridge of a low hill, behind which, the Frenchman told them, was the fort. Menendez, with a few officers and men, cautiously mounted to the top. Beneath lay Fort Caroline, three bowshots distant; but the rain, the imperfect light, and a cluster of intervening houses prevented his seeing clearly, and he sent two officers to reconnoitre. As they descended, they met a solitary Frenchman. They knocked him down with a sheathed sword, wounded him, took him prisoner, kept him for a time, and then stabbed him as they returned towards the top of the hill. Here, clutching their weapons, all the gang stood in fierce expectancy.

"Santiago!" cried Menendez. "At them! God is with us! Victory!"

And, shouting their hoarse war-cries, the Spaniards rushed down the slope like starved wolves.

Not a sentry was on the rampart. La Vigne, the officer of the guard, had just gone to his quarters; but a trumpeter, who chanced to remain, saw, through sheets of rain, the swarm of assailants sweeping down the hill. He blew the alarm, and at the summons a few half-naked soldiers ran wildly out of the barracks. It was too late. Through the breaches and over the ramparts, the Spaniards came pouring in.

"Santiago! Santiago!"

Sick men leaped from their beds. Women and children, blind with fright, darted shrieking from the houses. A fierce, gaunt visage, the thrust of a pike, or blow of a rusty halberd,— such was the greeting that met all alike. Laudonnière snatched his sword and target, and ran towards the principal breach, calling to his soldiers. A rush of Spaniards met him; his men were cut down around him; and he, with a soldier named Bartholomew, was forced back into the court-yard of his house. Here stood a tent, and as the pursuers stumbled among the cords, he escaped behind Ottigny's house, sprang through the breach in the western rampart, and fled for the woods.

Le Moyne had been one of the guard. Scarcely had he thrown himself into a hammock which was slung in his room, when a savage shout, and a wild uproar of shrieks, outcries, and the clash of weapons, brought him to his feet. He rushed by two Spaniards in the door-way, ran behind the guard-house, leaped through an embrasure into the ditch, and escaped to the forest.

Challeux, the carpenter, was going betimes to his work, a chisel in his hand. He was old, but pike and partisan brandished at his back gave wings to his flight. In the ecstasy of his terror, he leaped upward, clutched the top of the palisade, and threw himself over with the agility of a boy. He ran up the hill, no one pursuing, and, as he neared the edge of the forest, turned and looked back. From the high ground where he stood he could see the butchery, the fury of the conquerors, the agonizing gestures of the victims. He turned again in horror, and plunged into the woods. As he tore his way through the briers and thickets, he met several fugitives, escaped like himself. Others presently came up, haggard and wild, like men broke loose from the jaws of death. They gathered together and consulted. One of them, in great repute for his knowledge of the Bible, was for returning and surrendering to the Spaniards. "They are men," he said; "perhaps, when their fury is over, they will spare our lives; and, even if they kill us, it will only be a few moments' pain. Better so, than to starve here in the woods, or be torn to pieces by wild beasts."

The greater part of the naked and despairing company assented, but Challeux was of a different mind. The old Huguenot quoted Scripture, and called the names of prophets and apostles to witness, that, in the direst extremity, God would not abandon those who rested their faith in Him. Six of the fugitives, however, still held to their desperate purpose. Issuing from the woods, they descended towards the fort, and, as with beating hearts their comrades watched the result, a troop of Spaniards rushed out, hewed them down with swords and halberds, and dragged their bodies to the brink of the river, where the victims of the massacre were already flung in heaps.

Le Moyne, with a soldier named Grandchemin, whom he had met in his flight, toiled all day through the woods, in the hope of reaching the small vessels anchored behind the bar. Night found them in a morass. No vessel could be seen, and the soldier, in despair, broke into angry upbraidings against his companion,—saying that he would go back and give himself up. Le Moyne at first opposed him, then yielded. But when they drew near the fort, and heard the uproar of savage revelry that rose from within, the artist's heart failed him. He embraced his companion, and the soldier advanced alone. A party of Spaniards came out to meet him. He kneeled, and begged for his life. He was answered by a death-blow; and the horrified Le Moyne, from his hiding-place in the thicket, saw his limbs hacked apart, stuck on pikes, and borne off in triumph.

Meanwhile, Menendez, mustering his followers, had offered thanks to God for their victory; and this pious butcher wept with emotion as he recounted the favors which Heaven had showered upon their enterprise. His admiring historian gives it in proof of his humanity, that, after the rage of the assault was spent, he ordered that women, infants, and boys under fifteen should thenceforth be spared. Of these, by his own account, there were about fifty. Writing in October to the King, he says that they cause him great anxiety, since he fears the anger of God, should he now put them to death, while, on the other hand, he is in dread lest the venom of their heresy should infect his men.

A hundred and forty-two persons were slain in and around the fort, and their bodies lay heaped together on the bank of the river. Nearly opposite was anchored a small vessel, called the Pearl, commanded by Jacques Ribaut, son of the Admiral. The ferocious soldiery, maddened with victory and drunk with blood, crowded to the water's edge, shouting insults to those on board, mangling the corpses, tearing out their eyes, and throwing them towards the vessel from the points of their daggers. Thus did the Most Catholic Philip champion the cause of Heaven in the New World.

It was currently believed in France, and, though no eyewitness attests it, there is reason to think it true, that among those murdered at Fort Caroline there were some who died a death of peculiar ignominy. Menendez, it is affirmed, hanged his prisoners on trees, and placed over them the inscription, "I do this, not as to Frenchmen, but as to Lutherans."

The Spaniards gained a great booty: armor, clothing, and provisions. "Nevertheless," says the devout Mendoza, after closing his inventory of the plunder, "the greatest profit of this victory is the triumph which our Lord has granted us, whereby His holy Gospel will be introduced into this country, a thing so needful for saving so many souls from perdition." Again, he writes in his journal,—"We owe to God and His Mother, more than to human strength, this victory over the adversaries of the holy Catholic religion."

To whatever influence, celestial or other, the exploit may best be ascribed, the victors were not yet quite content with their success. Two small French vessels, besides that of Jacques Ribaut, still lay within range of the fort. When the storm had a little abated, the cannon were turned on them. One of them was sunk, but Ribaut, with the others, escaped down the river, at the mouth of which several light craft, including that bought from the English, had been anchored since the arrival of his father's squadron.

While this was passing, the wretched fugitives were flying from the scene of massacre through a tempest, of whose persistent violence all the narratives speak with wonder. Exhausted, starved, half clothed,—for most of them had escaped in their shirts,—they pushed their toilsome way amid the ceaseless wrath of the elements. A few sought refuge in Indian villages; but these, it is said, were afterwards killed by the Spaniards. The greater number attempted to reach the vessels at the mouth of the river. Among the latter was Le Moyne, who, despite his former failure, was toiling through the mazes of tangled forests, when he met a Belgian soldier with the woman described as Laudonnière's maid-servant, the latter wounded in the breast; and, urging their flight towards the vessels, they fell in with other fugitives, and among them with Laudonnière himself. As they struggled through the salt-marsh, the rank sedge cut their naked limbs, and the tide rose to their waists. Presently they descried others, toiling like themselves through the matted vegetation, and recognized Challeux and his companions, also in quest of the vessels. The old man still, as he tells us, held fast to his chisel, which had done good service in cutting poles to aid the party to cross the deep creeks that channelled the morass. The united band, twenty-six in all, were cheered at length by the sight of a moving sail. It was the vessel of Captain Mallard, who, informed of the massacre, was standing along-shore in the hope of picking up some of the fugitives. He saw their signals, and sent boats to their rescue; but such was their exhaustion, that, had not the sailors, wading to their armpits among the rushes, borne them out on their shoulders, few could have escaped. Laudonnière was so feeble that nothing but the support of a soldier, who held him upright in his arms, had saved him from drowning in the marsh.

On gaining the friendly decks, the fugitives counselled together. One and all, they sickened for the sight of France.

After waiting a few days, and saving a few more stragglers from the marsh, they prepared to sail. Young Ribaut, though ignorant of his father's fate, assented with something more than willingness; indeed, his behavior throughout had been stamped with weakness and poltroonery. On the twenty-fifth of September they put to sea in two vessels; and, after a voyage whose privations were fatal to many of them, they arrived, one party at Rochelle, the other at Swansea, in Wales.

[CARTIER AND THE ST. LAWRENCE]

. . . The ancient town of St. Malo, thrust out like a buttress into the sea, strange and grim of aspect, breathing war from its walls and battlements of ragged stone,—a stronghold of privateers, the home of a race whose intractable and defiant independence neither time nor change has subdued,—has been for centuries a nursery of hardy mariners. Among the earliest and most eminent on its list stands the name of Jacques Cartier. St. Malo still preserves his portrait,—bold, keen features, bespeaking a spirit not apt to quail before the wrath of man or of the elements. In him Chabot found a fit agent of his design, if, indeed, its suggestion is not due to the Breton navigator.

Sailing from St. Malo on the twentieth of April, 1534, Cartier steered for Newfoundland, passed through the Straits of

Belle Isle, crossed to the main, entered the Gulf of Chaleurs, planted a cross at Gaspé, and, never doubting that he was on the high road to Cathay, advanced up the St. Lawrence till he saw the shores of Anticosti. But autumnal storms were gathering. The voyagers took counsel together, turned their prows eastward, and bore away for France, carrying thither, as a sample of the natural products of the New World, two young Indians, lured into their clutches by an act of villanous treachery. The voyage was a mere reconnoissance.

The spirit of discovery was awakened. A passage to India could be found, and a new France built up beyond the Atlantic. Mingled with such views of interest and ambition was another motive scarcely less potent. The heresy of Luther was convulsing Germany, and the deeper heresy of Calvin infecting France. Devout Catholics, kindling with redoubled zeal, would fain requite the Church for her losses in the Old World by winning to her fold the infidels of the New. But, in pursuing an end at once so pious and so politic, Francis the First was setting at nought the supreme Pontiff himself, since, by the preposterous bull of Alexander the Sixth, all America had been given to the Spaniards.

[In October, 1534,] Cartier was commissioned afresh. Three vessels, the largest not above a hundred and twenty tons, were placed at his disposal, and Claude de Pontbriand, Charles de la Pommeraye, and other gentlemen of birth enrolled themselves for the voyage. On the sixteenth of May, 1535, officers and sailors assembled in the Cathedral of St. Malo, where, after confession and hearing mass, they received the parting blessing of the bishop. Three days later they set sail. The dingy walls of the rude old seaport, and the white rocks that line the neighboring shores of Brittany, faded from their sight, and soon they were tossing in a furious tempest. But the scattered ships escaped the danger, and, reuniting at the Straits of Belle Isle, steered westward along the coast of Labrador, till they reached a small bay opposite the Island of Anticosti. Cartier called it the Bay of St. Lawrence, a name afterwards extended to the entire gulf, and to the great river above.

To ascend this great river, and tempt the hazards of its intricate navigation, with no better pilots than the two young Indians kidnapped the year before, was a venture of no light risk. But skill or fortune prevailed; and, on the first of September, the voyagers reached in safety the gorge of the gloomy Saguenay, with its towering cliffs and sullen depth of waters. Passing the Isle des Coudres, and the lofty promontory of Cape Tourmente, they came to anchor in a quiet channel between the northern shore and the margin of a richly wooded island, where the trees were so thickly hung with grapes that Cartier named it the Island of Bacchus.

Indians came swarming from the shores, paddled their birch canoes about the ships, and clambered to the decks to gaze in bewilderment at the novel scene, and listen to the story of their travelled countrymen, marvellous in their ears as a visit to another planet. Cartier received them kindly, listened to the long harangue of the great chief Donnacona, regaled him with bread and wine; and, when relieved at length of his guests, set forth in a boat to explore the river above.

As he drew near the opening of the channel, the Hochelaga again spread before him the broad expanse of its waters. A mighty promontory, rugged and bare, thrust its scarped front into the surging current. Here, clothed in the majesty of solitude, breathing the stern poetry of the wilderness, rose the cliffs now rich with heroic memories, where the fiery Count Frontenac cast defiance at his foes, where Wolfe, Montcalm, and Montgomery fell. As yet, all was a nameless barbarism, and a cluster of wigwams held the site of the rock-built city of Quebec. Its name was Stadaconé, and it owned the sway of the royal Donnacona.

Cartier set forth to visit this greasy potentate, ascended the River St. Charles, by him called the St. Croix, landed, crossed the meadows, climbed the rocks, threaded the forest, and emerged upon a squalid hamlet of bark cabins. When, their curiosity satisfied, he and his party were rowing for the ships, a friendly interruption met them at the mouth of the St. Charles. An old chief harangued them from the bank, men, boys, and children screeched welcome from the meadow, and a troop of hilarious squaws danced knee-deep in the water. The gift of a few strings of beads completed their delight and redoubled their agility; and, from the distance of a mile, their shrill songs of jubilation still reached the ears of the receding Frenchmen.

The hamlet of Stadaconé, with its king, Donnacona, and its naked lords and princes, was not the metropolis of this forest State, since a town far greater—so the Indians averred—stood by the brink of the river, many days' journey above. It was called Hochelaga, and the great river itself, with a wide reach of adjacent country, had borrowed its name. Thither, with his two young Indians as guides, Cartier resolved to go; but misgivings seized the guides, as the time drew near, while Donnacona and his tribesmen, jealous of the plan, set themselves to thwart it. The Breton captain turned a deaf ear to their dissuasions; whereat, failing to touch his reason, they appealed to his fears.

One morning, as the ships still lay at anchor, the French beheld three Indian devils descending in a canoe towards them, dressed in black and white dog-skins, with faces black as ink, and horns long as a man's arm. Thus arrayed, they drifted by, while the principal fiend, with fixed eyes, as of one piercing the secrets of futurity, uttered in a loud voice a long harangue. Then they paddled for the shore; and no sooner did they reach it than each fell flat like a dead man in the bottom of the canoe. Aid, however, was at hand; for Donnacona and his tribesmen, rushing pell-mell from the adjacent woods, raised the swooning masqueraders, and, with shrill clamors, bore them in their arms within the sheltering thickets. Here, for a full half-hour, the French could hear them haranguing in solemn conclave. Then the two young Indians whom Cartier had brought back from France came out of the bushes, enacting a pantomime of amazement and terror, clasping their hands, and calling on Christ and the Virgin; whereupon Cartier, shouting from the vessel, asked what was the matter. They replied, that the god Coudouagny had sent to warn the French against all attempts to ascend the great river, since, should they persist, snows, tempests, and drifting ice would requite their rashness with inevitable ruin. The French replied that Coudouagny was a fool; that he could not hurt those who believed in Christ; and that they might tell this to his three messengers. The assembled Indians, with little reverence for their deity, pretended great contentment at this assurance, and danced for joy along the beach.

Cartier now made ready to depart. And, first, he caused the two larger vessels to be towed for safe harborage within the mouth of the St. Charles. With the smallest, a galleon of forty tons, and two open boats, carrying in all fifty sailors, besides Pontbriand, La Pommeraye, and other gentlemen, he set forth for Hochelaga.

Slowly gliding on their way, by walls of verdure, brightened in the autumnal sun, they saw forests festooned with grapevines, and waters alive with wild-fowl; they heard the song of the blackbird, the thrush, and, as they fondly thought, the nightingale. The galleon grounded; they left her, and, advancing with the boats alone, on the second of October neared the goal of their hopes, the mysterious Hochelaga.

Where now are seen the quays and storehouses of Montreal, a thousand Indians thronged the shore, wild with delight, dancing, singing, crowding about the strangers, and showering into the boats their gifts of fish and maize; and, as it grew dark, fires lighted up the night, while, far and near, the French could see the excited savages leaping and rejoicing by the blaze.

At dawn of day, marshalled and accoutred, they set forth for Hochelaga. An Indian path led them through the forest which covered the site of Montreal. The morning air was chill and sharp, the leaves were changing hue, and beneath the oaks the ground was thickly strewn with acorns. They soon met an Indian chief with a party of tribesmen, or, as the old narrative has it, "one of the principal lords of the said city," attended with a numerous retinue. Greeting them after the concise courtesy of the forest, he led them to a fire kindled by the side of the path for their comfort and refreshment, seated them on the earth, and made them a long harangue, receiving in requital

of his eloquence two hatchets, two knives, and a crucifix, the
last of which he was invited to kiss. This done, they resumed
their march, and presently issued forth upon open fields,
covered far and near with the ripened maize, its leaves rustling, its yellow grains gleaming between the parting husks.
Before them, wrapped in forests painted by the early frosts,
rose the ridgy back of the Mountain of Montreal, and below,
encompassed with its cornfields, lay the Indian town. Nothing
was visible but its encircling palisades. They were of trunks of
trees, set in a triple row. The outer and inner ranges inclined
till they met and crossed near the summit, while the upright row
between them, aided by transverse braces, gave to the whole
an abundant strength. Within were galleries for the defenders,
rude ladders to mount them, and magazines of stones to throw
down on the heads of assailants. It was a mode of fortification
practised by all the tribes speaking dialects of the Iroquois.

The voyagers entered the narrow portal. Within, they saw
some fifty of those large oblong dwellings so familiar in after
years to the eyes of the Jesuit apostles in Iroquois and Huron
forests. They were fifty yards or more in length, and twelve or
fifteen wide, framed of sapling poles closely covered with
sheets of bark, and each containing many fires and many
families. In the midst of the town was an open area, or public
square, a stone's-throw in width. Here Cartier and his followers
stopped, while the surrounding houses of bark disgorged their
inmates,—swarms of children, and young women and old,
their infants in their arms. They crowded about the visitors,
crying for delight, touching their beards, feeling their faces,
and holding up the screeching infants to be touched in turn.
Strange in hue, strange in attire, with moustached lip and
bearded chin, with arquebuse and glittering halberd, helmet,
and cuirass,—were the marvellous strangers demigods or men?

Due time allowed for this exuberance of feminine rapture,
the warriors interposed, banished the women and children
to a distance, and squatted on the ground around the French,
row within row of swarthy forms and eager faces, "as if,"
says Cartier, "we were going to act a play." Then appeared a

troop of women, each bringing a mat, with which they carpeted the bare earth for the behoof of their guests. The latter being seated, the chief of the nation was borne before them on a deer-skin by a number of his tribesmen, a bedridden old savage, paralyzed and helpless, squalid as the rest in his attire, and distinguished only by a red fillet, inwrought with the dyed quills of the Canada porcupine, encircling his lank, black hair. They placed him on the ground at Cartier's feet and made signs of welcome for him, while he pointed feebly to his powerless limbs, and implored the healing touch from the hand of the French chief. Cartier complied, and received in acknowledgment the red fillet of his grateful patient. And now from surrounding dwellings appeared a woful throng, the sick, the lame, the blind, the maimed, the decrepit, brought or led forth and placed on the earth before the perplexed commander, "as if," he says, "a God had come down to cure them." His skill in medicine being far behind the emergency, he pronounced over his petitioners a portion of the Gospel of St. John, of infallible efficacy on such occasions, made the sign of the cross, and uttered a prayer, not for their bodies only, but for their miserable souls. Next he read the passion of the Saviour, to which, though comprehending not a word, his audience listened with grave attention. Then came a distribution of presents. The squaws and children were recalled, and, with the warriors, placed in separate groups. Knives and hatchets were given to the men, beads to the women, and pewter rings and images of the *Agnus Dei* were flung among the troop of children, whence ensued a vigorous scramble in the square of Hochelaga. Now the French trumpeters pressed their trumpets to their lips, and blew a blast that filled the air with warlike din and the hearts of the hearers with amazement and delight. Bidding their hosts farewell, the visitors formed their ranks and defiled through the gate once more, despite the efforts of a crowd of women, who, with clamorous hospitality, beset them with gifts of fish, beans, corn, and other viands of strangely uninviting aspect, which the Frenchmen courteously declined.

A troop of Indians followed, and guided them to the top of the neighboring mountain. Cartier called it *Mont Royal*, Montreal; and hence the name of the busy city which now holds the site of the vanished Hochelaga. Stadaconé and Hochelaga, Quebec and Montreal, in the sixteenth century as in the nineteenth, were the centres of Canadian population.

From the summit, that noble prospect met his eye which at this day is the delight of tourists, but strangely changed, since, first of white men, the Breton voyager gazed upon it. Tower and dome and spire, congregated roofs, white sail, and gliding steamer, animate its vast expanse with varied life. Cartier saw a different scene. East, west, and south, the mantling forest was over all, and the broad blue ribbon of the great river glistened amid a realm of verdure. Beyond, to the bounds of Mexico, stretched a leafy desert, and the vast hive of industry, the mighty battle-ground of later centuries, lay sunk in savage torpor, wrapped in illimitable woods.

The French re-embarked, bade farewell to Hochelaga, retraced their lonely course down the St. Lawrence, and reached Stadaconé in safety. On the bank of the St. Charles, their companions had built in their absence a fort of palisades, and the ships, hauled up the little stream, lay moored before it. Here the self-exiled company were soon besieged by the rigors of the Canadian winter. The rocks, shores, pine-trees, the solid floor of the frozen river, all alike were blanketed in snow beneath the keen cold rays of the dazzling sun. The drifts rose above the sides of their ships; masts, spars, cordage, were thick with glittering incrustations and sparkling rows of icicles; a frosty armor, four inches thick, encased the bulwarks. Yet, in the bitterest weather, the neighboring Indians, "hardy," says the journal, "as so many beasts," came daily to the fort, wading, half naked, waist-deep through the snow. At length, their friendship began to abate; their visits grew less frequent, and, during December, had wholly ceased, when an appalling calamity fell upon the French.

A malignant scurvy broke out among them. Man after man went down before the hideous disease, till twenty-five were dead, and only three or four were left in health. The sound were too few to attend the sick, and the wretched sufferers lay in helpless despair, dreaming of the sun and the vines of France. The ground, hard as flint, defied their feeble efforts, and, unable to bury their dead, they hid them in snow-drifts. Cartier appealed to the Saints; but they turned a deaf ear. Then he nailed against a tree an image of the Virgin, and on a Sunday summoned forth his woe-begone followers, who, haggard, reeling, bloated with their maladies, moved in procession to the spot, and, kneeling in the snow, sang litanies and psalms of David. That day died Philippe Rougemont, of Amboise, aged twenty-two years. The Holy Virgin deigned no other response.

There was fear that the Indians, learning their misery, might finish the work the scurvy had begun. None of them, therefore, were allowed to approach the fort; and when, perchance, a party of savages lingered within hearing, Cartier forced his invalid garrison to beat with sticks and stones against the walls, that their dangerous neighbors, deluded by the clatter, might think them vigorously engaged in hard labor. These objects of their fear proved, however, the instruments of their salvation. Cartier, walking one day near the river, met an Indian, who not long before had been prostrate like many of his fellows with the scurvy, but who now, to all appearances, was in high health and spirits. What agency had wrought this marvellous recovery? According to the Indian, it was a certain evergreen, called by him *ameda*, a decoction of the leaves of which was sovereign against the disease. The experiment was tried. The sick men drank copiously of the healing draught,—so copiously indeed that in six days they drank a tree as large as a French oak. Thus vigorously assailed, the distemper relaxed its hold, and health and hope began to revisit the hapless company.

When this winter of misery had worn away, when spring appeared, and the ships were thawed from their icy fetters, Cartier prepared to return. He had made notable discoveries, but these were as nothing to the tales of wonder that had reached his ear,—of a land of gold and rubies, of a nation white like the French, of men who lived without food, and of others to whom

Nature had granted but one leg. Should he stake his credit on these marvels? Far better that they who had recounted them to him should, with their own lips, recount them also to the King. To this end, he resolved that Donnacona and his chiefs should go with him to court. He lured them therefore to the fort, and led them into an ambuscade of sailors, who, seizing the astonished guests, hurried them on board the ships. This treachery accomplished, the voyagers proceeded to plant the emblem of Christianity. The cross was raised, the fleur-de-lis hung upon it, and, spreading their sails, they steered for home. It was the sixteenth of July, 1536, when Cartier again cast anchor under the walls of St. Malo.

CHAMPLAIN AT QUEBEC

A lonely ship sailed up the St. Lawrence. The white whales floundering in the Bay of Tadoussac, and the wild duck diving as the foaming prow drew near,—there was no life but these in all that watery solitude, twenty miles from shore to shore. The ship was from Honfleur, and was commanded by Samuel de Champlain. He was the Æneas of a destined people, and in her womb lay the embryo life of Canada.

De Monts, after his exclusive privilege of trade was revoked and his Acadian enterprise ruined, had abandoned it, as we have seen, to Poutrincourt. Well, perhaps, would it have been for him, had he abandoned with it all Transatlantic enterprises; but the passion for discovery, the noble ambition of founding colonies, had taken possession of his mind. Nor does it appear that he was actuated by hopes of gain. Yet the profits of the fur-trade were vital to the new designs he was meditating, to meet the heavy outlay they demanded; and he solicited and obtained a fresh monopoly of the traffic for one year.

Champlain was, at the time, in Paris; but his unquiet thoughts turned westward. He was enamoured of the New World, whose rugged charms had seized his fancy and his heart; and as explorers of Arctic seas have pined in their repose for polar ice and snow, so did he, with restless longing, revert to the fog-wrapped coasts, the piny odors of forests, the noise of waters, the sharp and piercing sunlight, so dear to his remembrance. Fain would he unveil the mystery of that boundless wilderness, and plant the Catholic faith and the power of France amid its ancient barbarism.

Five years before, he had explored the St. Lawrence as far as the rapids above Montreal. On its banks, as he thought, was the true site for a settlement, a fortified post, whence, as from a secure basis, the waters of the vast interior might be traced back toward their sources, and a western route discovered to China and the East. For the fur-trade, too, the innumerable streams that descended to the great river might all be closed against foreign intrusion by a single fort at some commanding point, and made tributary to a rich and permanent commerce; while—and this was nearer to his heart, for he had often been heard to say that the saving of a soul was worth more than the conquest of an empire—countless savage tribes, in the bondage of Satan, might by the same avenues be reached and redeemed.

De Monts embraced his views; and, fitting out two ships, gave command of one to the elder Pontgravé, of the other to Champlain. The former was to trade with the Indians and bring back the cargo of furs which, it was hoped, would meet the expense of the voyage. To the latter fell the harder task of settlement and exploration.

Pontgravé, laden with goods for the Indian trade of Tadoussac, sailed from Honfleur on the fifth of April, 1608. Champlain, with men, arms, and stores for the colony, followed, eight days later. On the fifteenth of May he was on the Grand Bank; on the thirtieth he passed Gaspé, and on the third of June neared Tadoussac. No life was to be seen. Had Pontgravé yet arrived? He anchored, lowered a boat, and rowed into the port, round the rocky point at the southeast, then, from the fury of its winds and currents, called La Pointe de Tous les Diables. There was life enough within, and more than he cared to find. In the still anchorage under the cliffs lay Pontgravé's vessel, and at her side another ship. The latter was a Basque fur-trader.

Pontgravé, arriving a few days before, had found himself anticipated by the Basques, who were busied in a brisk trade with bands of Indians cabined along the borders of the cove. In all haste he displayed the royal letters, and commanded a cessation of the prohibited traffic; but the Basques proved refractory, declared that they would trade in spite of the King, fired on Pontgravé with cannon and musketry, wounded him and two of his men, and killed a third. They then boarded his vessel, and carried away all his cannon, small arms, and ammunition, saying that they would restore them when they had finished their trade and were ready to return home.

Champlain found his comrade on shore, in a disabled condition. The Basques, though still strong enough to make fight, were alarmed for the consequences of their procedure, and anxious to come to terms. A peace, therefore, was signed on board their vessel; all differences were referred to the judgment of the French courts, harmony was restored, and the choleric strangers betook themselves to catching whales.

This port of Tadoussac was long the centre of the Canadian fur-trade. A desolation of barren mountains closes around it, betwixt whose ribs of rugged granite, bristling with savins, birches, and firs, the Saguenay rolls its gloomy waters from the northern wilderness. Centuries of civilization have not tamed the wildness of the place; and still, in grim repose, the mountains hold their guard around the waveless lake that glistens in their shadow, and doubles, in its sullen mirror, crag, precipice, and forest.

Near the brink of the cove or harbor where the vessels lay, and a little below the mouth of a brook which formed one of the outlets of this small lake, stood the remains of the wooden barrack built by Chauvin eight years before. Above the brook were the lodges of an Indian camp,—stacks of poles covered with birch-bark. They belonged to an Algonquin horde, called *Montagnais*, denizens of surrounding wilds, and gatherers of their only harvest,—skins of the moose, caribou, and bear; fur of the beaver, marten, otter, fox, wild-cat, and lynx. Nor was this all, for there were intermediate traders betwixt the French and the shivering bands who roamed the weary stretch of stunted forest between the head waters of the Saguenay and Hudson's Bay. Indefatigable canoe-men, in their birchen vessels, light as egg-shells, they threaded the devious tracks of countless rippling streams, shady by-ways of the forest, where the wild duck scarcely finds depth to swim; then descended to their mart along those scenes of picturesque yet dreary grandeur which steam has made familiar to modern tourists. With slowly moving paddles, they glided beneath the cliff whose shaggy brows frown across the zenith, and whose base the deep waves wash with a hoarse and hollow cadence; and they passed the sepulchral Bay of the Trinity, dark as the tide of Acheron,—a sanctuary of solitude and silence, where the soul of the wilderness dwells embodied in voiceless rock: depths which, as the fable runs, no sounding line can fathom, and heights at whose dizzy verge the wheeling eagle seems a speck.

And now, peace being established with the Basques, and the wounded Pontgravé busied, as far as might be, in transferring to the hold of his ship the rich lading of the Indian canoes, Champlain spread his sails, and once more held his course up the St. Lawrence. Far to the south, in sun and shadow, slumbered the woody mountains whence fell the countless springs of the St. John, behind tenantless shores, now white with glimmering villages,—La Chenaie, Granville, Kamouraska, St. Roche, St. Jean, Vincelot, Berthier. But on the north, the jealous wilderness still asserts its sway, crowding to the river's verge its rocky walls, its domes, and towers of granite; and, to this hour, its solitude is scarcely broken.

Above the point of the Island of Orleans, a constriction of the vast channel narrows it to a mile; on one hand, the green heights of Point Levi; on the other, the cliffs of Quebec. Here, a small stream, the St. Charles, enters the St. Lawrence, and in the angle betwixt them rises the promontory, on two sides a natural fortress. Land among the walnut-trees that formed a belt between the cliffs and the St. Lawrence. Climb the steep height, now bearing aloft its ponderous load of churches, convents, dwellings, ramparts, and batteries,—there was an accessible point, a rough passage, gullied downward where Prescott Gate now opens on the Lower Town. Mount to the highest summit, Cape Diamond, now zigzagged with warlike masonry. Then the fierce sun fell on the bald, baking rock, with its crisped mosses and parched lichens. Two centuries and a half have quickened the solitude with swarming life, covered the deep bosom of the river with barge and steamer and gliding sail, and reared cities and villages on the site of forests; but nothing can destroy the surpassing grandeur of the scene.

Grasp the savin anchored in the fissure, lean over the brink of the precipice, and look downward, a little to the left, on the belt of woods which covers the strand between the water and the base of the cliffs. Here a gang of axe-men are at work, and Points Levi and Orleans echo the crash of falling trees.

These axe-men were pioneers of an advancing host,—advancing, it is true, with feeble and uncertain progress: priests, soldiers, peasants, feudal scutcheons, royal insignia. Not the Middle Age, but engendered of it by the stronger life of modern centralization, sharply stamped with a parental likeness, heir to parental weakness and parental force.

A few weeks passed, and a pile of wooden buildings rose on the brink of the St. Lawrence, on or near the site of the market-place of the Lower Town of Quebec. The pencil of Champlain, always regardless of proportion and perspective, has preserved its likeness. A strong wooden wall, surmounted by a gallery loop-holed for musketry, enclosed three buildings, containing quarters for himself and his men, together with a courtyard, from one side of which rose a tall dove-cot, like a belfry. A moat surrounded the whole, and two or three small cannon were planted on salient platforms towards the river. There was a large magazine near at hand, and a part of the adjacent ground was laid out as a garden.

In this garden Champlain was one morning directing his laborers, when the pilot of the ship approached him with an anxious countenance, and muttered a request to speak with him in private. Champlain assenting, they withdrew to the neighboring woods, when the pilot disburdened himself of his secret. One Antoine Natel, a locksmith, smitten by conscience or fear, had revealed to him a conspiracy to murder his commander and deliver Quebec into the hands of the Basques and of certain Spaniards lately arrived at Tadoussac. Another locksmith, named Duval, was the author of the plot, and, with the aid of three accomplices, had befooled or frightened nearly all the company into bearing a part in it. Each was assured that he should make his fortune, and all were mutually pledged to poniard the first betrayer of the secret. The critical point of their enterprise was the killing of Champlain. Some were for strangling him, some for raising a false alarm in the night and shooting him as he came out from his quarters.

Having heard the pilot's story, Champlain, remaining in the woods, desired his informant to find Antoine Natel, and bring him to the spot. Natel soon appeared, trembling with excitement and fear, and a close examination left no doubt of the truth of his statement. A small vessel, built by Pontgravé at Tadoussac, had lately arrived, and orders were now given that it should anchor close at hand. On board was a young man in whom confidence could be placed. Champlain sent him two bottles of wine, with a direction to tell the four ringleaders that they had been given him by his Basque friends at Tadoussac, and to invite them to share the good cheer. They came aboard in the evening, and were seized and secured. *"Voyla donc mes galants bien estonnez,"* writes Champlain.

It was ten o'clock, and most of the men on shore were asleep. They were wakened suddenly, and told of the discovery of the plot and the arrest of the ringleaders. Pardon was then promised them, and they were dismissed again to their beds, greatly relieved, for they had lived in trepidation, each fearing the other. Duval's body, swinging from a gibbet, gave wholesome warning to those he had seduced; and his head was displayed on a pike, from the highest roof of the buildings, food for birds and a lesson to sedition. His three accomplices were carried by Pontgravé to France, where they made their atonement in the galleys.

It was on the eighteenth of September that Pontgravé set sail, leaving Champlain with twenty-eight men to hold Quebec through the winter. Three weeks later, and shores and hills glowed with gay prognostics of approaching desolation,—the yellow and scarlet of the maples, the deep purple of the ash, the garnet hue of young oaks, the crimson of the tupelo at the water's edge, and the golden plumage of birch saplings in the fissure of the cliff. It was a short-lived beauty. The forest dropped its festal robes. Shrivelled and faded, they rustled to the earth. The crystal air and laughing sun of October passed away, and November sank upon the shivering waste, chill and sombre as the tomb.

A roving band of Montagnais had built their huts near the buildings, and were busying themselves with their autumn eel-fishery, on which they greatly relied to sustain their miserable lives through the winter. Their slimy harvest being gathered, and duly smoked and dried, they gave it for safe-keeping to Champlain, and set out to hunt beavers. It was deep in the winter before they came back, reclaimed their eels, built their birch cabins again, and disposed themselves for a life of ease, until famine or their enemies should put an end to their enjoyments. These were by no means without alloy. While, gorged with food, they lay dozing on piles of branches in their smoky huts, where, through the crevices of the thin birch bark, streamed in a cold capable at times of congealing mercury, their slumbers were beset with nightmare visions of Iroquois forays, scalping, butcherings, and burnings. As dreams were their oracles, the camp was wild with fright. They sent out no scouts and placed no guard; but, with each repetition of these nocturnal terrors, they came flocking in a body to beg admission within the fort. The women and children were allowed to enter the yard and remain during the night, while anxious fathers and jealous husbands shivered in the darkness without.

On one occasion, a group of wretched beings was seen on the farther bank of the St. Lawrence, like wild animals driven by famine to the borders of the settler's clearing. The river was full of drifting ice; none could cross without risk of life.

The Indians, in their desperation, made the attempt; and midway their canoes were ground to atoms among the tossing masses. Agile as wild-cats, they all leaped upon a huge raft of ice, the squaws carrying their children on their shoulders, a feat at which Champlain marvelled when he saw their starved and emaciated condition. Here they began a wail of despair; when happily the pressure of other masses thrust the sheet of ice against the northern shore. They landed and soon made their appearance at the fort, worn to skeletons and horrible to look upon. The French gave them food, which they devoured with a frenzied avidity, and, unappeased, fell upon a dead dog left on the snow by Champlain for two months past as a bait for foxes. They broke this carrion into fragments, and thawed and devoured it, to the disgust of the spectators, who tried vainly to prevent them.

This was but a severe access of that periodical famine which, during winter, was a normal condition of the Algonquin tribes of Acadia and the Lower St. Lawrence, who, unlike the cognate tribes of New England, never tilled the soil or made any reasonable provision against the time of need.

One would gladly know how the founders of Quebec spent the long hours of their first winter; but on this point the only man among them, perhaps, who could write, has not thought it necessary to enlarge. He himself beguiled his leisure with trapping foxes, or hanging a dead dog from a tree and watching the hungry martens in their efforts to reach it. Towards the close of winter, all found abundant employment in nursing themselves or their neighbors, for the inevitable scurvy broke out with virulence. At the middle of May, only eight men of the twenty-eight were alive, and of these half were suffering from disease.

This wintry purgatory wore away; the icy stalactites that hung from the cliffs fell crashing to the earth; the clamor of the wild geese was heard; the bluebirds appeared in the naked woods; the water-willows were covered with their soft caterpillar-like blossoms; the twigs of the swamp maple were flushed with ruddy bloom; the ash hung out its black-tufted flowers; the shadbush seemed a wreath of snow; the white stars of the blood-root gleamed among the dank, fallen leaves; and in the young grass of the wet meadows, the marsh-marigolds shone like spots of gold.

Great was the joy of Champlain when he saw a sail-boat rounding the Point of Orleans, betokening that the spring had brought with it the longed-for succors. A son-in-law of Pontgravé, named Marais, was on board, and he reported that Pontgravé was then at Tadoussac, where he had lately arrived. Thither Champlain hastened, to take counsel with his comrade. His constitution or his courage had defied the scurvy. They met, and it was determined betwixt them, that, while Pontgravé remained in charge of Quebec, Champlain should enter at once on his long-meditated explorations, by which, like La Salle seventy years later, he had good hope of finding a way to China.

But there was a lion in the path. The Indian tribes, war-hawks of the wilderness, to whom peace was unknown, infested with their scalping parties the streams and pathways of the forest, increasing tenfold its inseparable risks. That to all these hazards Champlain was more than indifferent, his after-career bears abundant witness; yet now an expedient for evading them offered itself, so consonant with his instincts that he was fain to accept it.

During the last autumn, a young chief from the banks of the then unknown Ottawa had been at Quebec; and, amazed at what he saw, he had begged Champlain to join him in the spring against his enemies. These enemies were a formidable race of savages, the Iroquois, or Five Confederate Nations, dwellers in fortified villages within limits now embraced by the State of New York, to whom was afterwards given the fanciful name of "Romans of the New World," and who even then were a terror to all the surrounding forests. Conspicuous among their enemies were their kindred, the tribes of the Hurons, dwellers on the lake which bears their name, and allies of Algonquin bands on the Ottawa. All alike were tillers of the soil, living at ease when compared to the famished Algonquins of the Lower St. Lawrence.

What was Champlain's plan, or had he a plan? To influence Indian counsels, to hold the balance of power between adverse tribes, to envelop in the network of her power and diplomacy the remotest hordes of the wilderness,—such, from first to last, was the policy of France in America. Of this policy the Father of New France may perhaps be held to have set a rash and premature example. Yet while he was apparently following the dictates of his own adventurous spirit, it became evident, a few years later, that, under his thirst for discovery and spirit of knight-errantry lay a consistent and deliberate purpose. . . . That it had already assumed a definite shape is not likely; but his after course makes it plain that, in embroiling himself and his colony with the most formidable savages on the continent, he was by no means acting so recklessly as at first sight would appear.

LAKE CHAMPLAIN

The canoes advanced, the river widening as they went. Great islands appeared, leagues in extent: Isle à la Motte, Long Island, Grande Isle. Channels where ships might float and broad reaches of expanding water stretched between them, and Champlain entered the lake which preserves his name to posterity. Cumberland Head was passed, and from the opening of the great channel between Grande Isle and the main he could look forth on the wilderness sea. Edged with woods, the tranquil flood spread southward beyond the sight. Far on the left, the forest ridges of the Green Mountains were heaved against the sun, patches of snow still glistening on their tops; and on the right the Adirondacks, haunts in these later years of amateur sportsmen from counting-rooms or college halls, nay, of adventurous beauty, with sketch-book and pencil. Then the Iroquois made them their hunting-ground; and beyond, in the valleys of the Mohawk, the Onondaga, and the Genesee, stretched the long line of their five cantons and palisaded towns.

At night, they were encamped again. The scene is a familiar one to tourist and sportsman; and, perhaps, standing at sunset on the peaceful strand, Champlain saw what a roving student of this generation has seen on those same shores, at that same hour, —the glow of the vanished sun behind the western mountains, darkly piled in mist and shadow along the sky; near at hand, the dead pine, mighty in decay, stretching its ragged arms athwart the burning heaven, the crow perched on its top like an image carved in jet; and aloft, the night-hawk, circling in his flight, and, with a strange whirring sound, diving through the air each moment for the insects he makes his prey.

The progress of the party was becoming dangerous. They changed their mode of advance, and moved only in the night. All day, they lay close in the depth of the forest, sleeping, lounging, smoking tobacco of their own raising, and beguiling the hours, no doubt, with the shallow banter and obscene jesting with which knots of Indians are wont to amuse their leisure. At twilight they embarked again, paddling their cautious way till the eastern sky began to redden. Their goal was the rocky promontory where Fort Ticonderoga was long afterward built. Thence, they would pass the outlet of Lake George, and launch their canoes again on that Como of the wilderness, whose waters, limpid as a fountain-head, stretched far southward between their flanking mountains. Landing at the future site of Fort William Henry, they would carry their canoes through the forest to the river Hudson, and descending it, attack, perhaps, some outlying town of the Mohawks. In the next century this chain of lakes and rivers became the grand highway of savage and civilized war, a bloody, debatable ground linked to memories of momentous conflicts.

The allies were spared so long a progress. On the morning of the twenty-ninth of July, after paddling all night, they hid as usual in the forest on the western shore, not far from Crown Point. The warriors stretched themselves to their slumbers, and Champlain, after walking for a time through the surrounding woods, returned to take his repose on a pile of spruce-boughs. Sleeping, he dreamed a dream, wherein he beheld the Iroquois drowning in the lake; and, essaying to rescue them, he was told by his Algonquin friends that they were good for nothing, and had better be left to their fate. Now, he had been daily beset, on awakening, by his superstitious allies, eager to learn about his dreams; and, to this moment, his unbroken slumbers had failed to furnish the desired prognostics. The announcement of this auspicious vision filled the crowd with joy, and at nightfall they embarked, flushed with anticipated victories.

It was ten o'clock in the evening, when they descried dark objects in motion on the lake before them. These were a flotilla of Iroquois canoes, heavier and slower than theirs, for they were made of oak-bark. Each party saw the other, and the mingled war-cries pealed over the darkened water. The Iroquois, who were near the shore, having no stomach for an aquatic battle, landed, and, making night hideous with their clamors, began to barricade themselves. Champlain could see them in the woods, laboring like beavers, hacking down trees with iron axes taken from the Canadian tribes in war, and with stone hatchets of their own making. The allies remained on the lake, a bowshot from the hostile barricade, their canoes made fast together by poles lashed across. All night they danced with as much vigor as the frailty of their vessels would permit, their throats making amends for the enforced restraint of their limbs. It was agreed on both sides that the fight should be deferred till daybreak; but meanwhile a commerce of abuse, sarcasm, menace, and boasting gave unceasing exercise to the lungs and fancy of the combatants,—"much," says Champlain, "like the besiegers and besieged in a beleaguered town."

As day approached, he and his two followers put on the light armor of the time. Champlain wore the doublet and long hose then in vogue. Over the doublet he buckled on a breastplate, and probably a back-piece, while his thighs were protected by cuisses of steel, and his head by a plumed casque. Across his shoulder hung the strap of his bandoleer, or ammunition-box; at his side was his sword, and in his hand his arquebuse, which he had loaded with four balls. Such was the equipment of this ancient Indian-fighter, whose exploits date eleven years before the landing of the Puritans at Plymouth, and sixty-six years before King Philip's War.

Each of the three Frenchmen was in a separate canoe, and, as it grew light, they kept themselves hidden, either by lying at the bottom, or covering themselves with an Indian robe. The canoes approached the shore, and all landed without opposition at some distance from the Iroquois, whom they presently could see filing out of their barricade, tall, strong men, some two hundred in number, the boldest and fiercest warriors of North America. They advanced through the forest with a steadiness which excited the admiration of Champlain. Among them could be seen several chiefs, made conspicuous by their tall plumes. Some bore shields of wood and hide, and some were covered with a kind of armor made of tough twigs interlaced with a vegetable fibre supposed by Champlain to be cotton.

The allies, growing anxious, called with loud cries for their champion, and opened their ranks that he might pass to the front. He did so, and, advancing before his red companions-in-arms, stood revealed to the astonished gaze of the Iroquois, who, beholding the warlike apparition in their path, stared in mute amazement. "I looked at them," says Champlain, "and they looked at me. When I saw them getting ready to shoot their arrows at us, I levelled my arquebuse, which I had loaded with four balls, and aimed straight at one of the three chiefs. The shot brought down two, and wounded another. On this, our Indians set up such a yelling that one could not have heard a thunder-clap, and all the while the arrows flew thick on both sides. The Iroquois were greatly astonished and frightened to see two of their men killed so quickly, in spite of their arrow-proof armor. As I was reloading, one of my companions fired a shot from the woods, which so increased their astonishment that, seeing their chiefs dead, they abandoned the field and fled into the depth of the forest." The allies dashed after them. Some of the Iroquois were killed; more were taken. Camp, canoes, provisions, all were abandoned, and many weapons flung down in the panic flight. The arquebuse had done its work. The victory was complete. . . .

Thus did New France rush into collision with the redoubted warriors of the Five Nations. Here was the beginning, and in some measure doubtless the cause, of a long suite of murderous conflicts, bearing havoc and flame to generations yet unborn. Champlain had invaded the tiger's den; and now, in smothered fury, the patient savage would lie biding his day of blood.

[DAILY LIFE OF THE MISSIONARY PRIESTS]

(From *The Jesuits in North America*, 1867)

. . . In respect to the commodities of life, the Jesuits were but a step in advance of the Indians. Their house, though well ventilated by numberless crevices in its bark walls, always smelt of smoke, and, when the wind was in certain quarters, was filled with it to suffocation. At their meals, the Fathers sat on logs around the fire, over which their kettle was slung in the Indian fashion. Each had his wooden platter, which, from the difficulty of transportation, was valued, in the Huron country, at the price of a robe of beaver-skin, or a hundred francs. Their food consisted of sagamite, or "mush," made of pounded Indian-corn, boiled with scraps of smoked fish. Chaumonot compares it to the paste used for papering the walls of houses. The repast was occasionally varied by a pumpkin or squash baked in the ashes, or, in the season, by Indian corn roasted in the ear. They used no salt whatever. They could bring their cumbrous pictures, ornaments, and vestments through the savage journey of the Ottawa; but they could not bring the common necessaries of life. By day, they read and studied by the light that streamed in through the large smoke-holes in the roof,—at night, by the blaze of the fire. Their only candles were a few of wax, for the altar. They cultivated a patch of ground, but raised nothing on it except wheat for making the sacramental bread. Their food was supplied by the Indians, to whom they gave, in return, cloth, knives, awls, needles, and various trinkets. Their supply of wine for the Eucharist was so scanty, that they limited themselves to four or five drops for each mass.

Their life was regulated with a conventual strictness. At four in the morning, a bell roused them from the sheets of bark on which they slept. Masses, private devotions, reading religious books, and breakfasting, filled the time until eight, when they opened their door and admitted the Indians. As many of these proved intolerable nuisances, they took what Lalemant calls the *honnête* liberty of turning out the most intrusive and impracticable,—an act performed with all tact and courtesy, and rarely taken in dudgeon. Having thus winnowed their company, they catechized those that remained, as opportunity offered. In the intervals, the guests squatted by the fire and smoked their pipes.

As among the Spartan virtues of the Hurons that of thieving was especially conspicuous, it was necessary that one or more of the Fathers should remain on guard at the house all day. The rest went forth on their missionary labors, baptizing and instructing, as we have seen. To each priest who could speak Huron was assigned a certain number of houses,—in some instances, as many as forty; and as these often had five or six fires, with two families to each, his spiritual flock was as numerous as it was intractable. It was his care to see that none of the number died without baptism, and by every means in his power to commend the doctrines of his faith to the acceptance of those in health.

At dinner, which was at two o'clock, grace was said in Huron,—for the benefit of the Indians present,—and a chapter of the Bible was read aloud during the meal. At four or five, according to the season, the Indians were dismissed, the door closed, and the evening spent in writing, reading, studying the language, devotion, and conversation on the affairs of the mission.

The local missions here referred to embraced Ossossané and the villages of the neighborhood; but the priests by no means confined themselves within these limits. They made distant excursions, two in company, until every house in every Huron town had heard the annunciation of the new doctrine. On these journeys, they carried blankets or large mantles at their backs, for sleeping in at night, besides a supply of needles, awls, beads, and other small articles, to pay for their lodging and entertainment; for the Hurons, hospitable without stint to each other, expected full compensation from the Jesuits.

At Ossossané, the house of the Jesuits no longer served the double purpose of dwelling and chapel. In 1638, they had in their pay twelve artisans and laborers, sent up from Quebec, who had built, before the close of the year, a chapel of wood. Hither they removed their pictures and ornaments; and here, in winter, several fires were kept burning, for the comfort of the half-naked converts. Of these they now had at Ossossané about sixty,—a large, though evidently not a very solid nucleus for the Huron church,—and they labored hard and anxiously to confirm and multiply them. Of a Sunday morning in winter, one could have seen them coming to mass, often from a considerable distance, "as naked," says Lalemant, "as your hand, except a skin over their backs like a mantle, and, in the coldest weather, a few skins around their feet and legs." They knelt, mingled with the French mechanics, before the altar,—very awkwardly at first, for the posture was new to them,—and all received the sacrament together: a spectacle which, as the missionary chronicler declares, repaid a hundred times all the labor of their conversion.

Some of the principal methods of conversion are curiously illustrated in a letter written by Garnier to a friend in France. "Send me," he says, "a picture of Christ without a beard." Several Virgins are also requested, together with a variety of souls in perdition—*âmes damnées*—most of them to be mounted in a portable form. Particular directions are given with respect to the demons, dragons, flames, and other essentials of these works of art. Of souls in bliss—*âmes bienheureuses*—he thinks that one will be enough. All the pictures must be in full face, not in profile; and they must look directly at the beholder, with open eyes. The colors should be bright; and there must be no flowers or animals, as these distract the attention of the Indians.

The first point with the priests was of course to bring the objects of their zeal to an acceptance of the fundamental doctrines of the Roman Church; but, as the mind of the savage was by no means that beautiful blank which some have represented it, there was much to be erased as well as to be written. They must renounce a host of superstitions, to which they were attached with a strange tenacity, or which may rather be said to have been ingrained in their very natures. Certain points of Christian morality were also strongly urged by the missionaries, who insisted that the convert should take but one wife, and not cast her off without grave cause, and that he should renounce the gross license almost universal among the Hurons. Murder, cannibalism, and several other offences, were also forbidden. Yet, while laboring at the work of conversion with an energy never surpassed, and battling against the powers of darkness with the mettle of paladins, the Jesuits never had the folly to assume towards the Indians a dictatorial or overbearing tone. Gentleness, kindness, and patience were the rule of their intercourse. They studied the nature of the savage, and conformed themselves to it with an admirable tact. Far from treating the Indian as an alien and barbarian, they would fain have adopted him as a countryman; and they proposed to the Hurons that a number of young Frenchmen should settle among them, and marry their daughters in solemn form. The listeners were gratified at an overture so flattering. "But what is the use," they demanded, "of so much ceremony? If the Frenchmen want our women, they are welcome to come and take them whenever they please, as they always used to do."

The Fathers are well agreed that their difficulties did not arise from any natural defect of understanding on the part of the Indians, who, according to Chaumonot, were more intelligent than the French peasantry, and who, in some instances, showed in their way a marked capacity. It was the inert mass of pride, sensuality, indolence, and superstition that opposed the march of the Faith, and in which the Devil lay intrenched as behind impregnable breastworks.

It soon became evident that it was easier to make a convert than to keep him. Many of the Indians clung to the idea that baptism was a safeguard against pestilence and misfortune; and when the fallacy of this notion was made apparent, their zeal cooled. Their only amusements consisted of feasts, dances, and games, many of which were, to a greater or less degree, of a superstitious character; and as the Fathers could rarely prove to their own satisfaction the absence of the diabolic element in any one of them, they proscribed the whole indiscriminately, to the extreme disgust of the neophyte. His countrymen, too, beset him with dismal prognostics: as, "You will kill no more game,—" "All your hair will come out before spring," and so forth. Various doubts also assailed him with regard to the substantial advantages of his new profession; and several converts were filled with anxiety in view of the probable want of tobacco in Heaven, saying that they could not do without it. Nor was it pleasant to these incipient Christians, as they sat in class listening to the instructions of their teacher, to find themselves and him suddenly made the targets of a shower of sticks, snowballs, corn-cobs, and other rubbish, flung at them by a screeching rabble of vagabond boys.

Yet, while most of the neophytes demanded an anxious and diligent cultivation, there were a few of excellent promise; and of one or two especially, the Fathers, in the fulness of their satisfaction, assure us again and again "that they were savage only in name."

As the town of Ihonatiria, where the Jesuits had made their first abode, was ruined by the pestilence, the mission established there, and known by the name of St. Joseph, was removed, in the summer of 1638, to Teanaustayé, a large town at the foot of a range of hills near the southern borders of the Huron territory. The Hurons, this year, had had unwonted successes in their war with the Iroquois, and had taken, at various times, nearly a hundred prisoners. Many of these were brought to the seat of the new mission of St. Joseph, and put to death with frightful tortures, though not before several had been converted and baptized. The torture was followed, in spite of the remonstrances of the priests, by those cannibal feasts customary with the Hurons on such occasions. Once, when the Fathers had been strenuous in their denunciations, a hand of the victim, duly prepared, was flung in at their door, as an invitation to

join in the festivity. As the owner of the severed member had
been baptized, they dug a hole in their chapel, and buried it
with solemn rites of sepulture.

BRÉBEUF AND HIS ASSOCIATES

Where should the Fathers make their abode? Their first
thought had been to establish themselves at a place called by
the French *Rochelle*, the largest and most important town of
the Huron confederacy; but Brébeuf now resolved to remain
at Ihonatiria. Here he was well known; and here, too, he
flattered himself, seeds of the Faith had been planted, which,
with good nurture, would in time yield fruit.

By the ancient Huron custom, when a man or a family
wanted a house, the whole village joined in building one. In
the present case, not Ihonatiria only, but the neighboring town
of Wenrio also, took part in the work,—though not without
the expectation of such gifts as the priests had to bestow. Before October, the task was finished. The house was constructed after the Huron model. It was thirty-six feet long and
about twenty feet wide, framed with strong sapling poles
planted in the earth to form the sides, with the ends bent into
an arch for the roof,—the whole lashed firmly together, braced
with cross-poles, and closely covered with overlapping sheets
of bark. Without, the structure was strictly Indian; but within,
the priests, with the aid of their tools, made innovations which
were the astonishment of all the country. They divided their
dwelling by transverse partitions into three apartments, each
with its wooden door,—a wondrous novelty in the eyes of
their visitors. The first served as a hall, an ante-room, and a
place of storage for corn, beans, and dried fish. The second—
the largest of the three—was at once kitchen, workshop, dining-
room, drawing-room, school-room, and bed-chamber. The
third was the chapel. Here they made their altar, and here
were their images, pictures, and sacred vessels. Their fire was
on the ground, in the middle of the second apartment, the smoke
escaping by a hole in the roof. At the sides were placed two

wide platforms, after the Huron fashion, four feet from the earthen floor. On these were chests in which they kept their clothing and vestments, and beneath them they slept, reclining on sheets of bark, and covered with skins and the garments they wore by day. Rude stools, a hand-mill, a large Indian mortar of wood for crushing corn, and a clock, completed the furniture of the room.

There was no lack of visitors, for the house of the black-robes contained marvels the fame of which was noised abroad to the uttermost confines of the Huron nation. Chief among them was the clock. The guests would sit in expectant silence by the hour, squatted on the ground, waiting to hear it strike. They thought it was alive, and asked what it ate. As the last stroke sounded, one of the Frenchmen would cry "Stop!"— and, to the admiration of the company, the obedient clock was silent. The mill was another wonder, and they were never tired of turning it. Besides these, there was a prism and a magnet; also a magnifying-glass, wherein a flea was transformed to a frightful monster, and a multiplying lens, which showed them the same object eleven times repeated. "All this," says Brébeuf, "serves to gain their affection, and make them more docile in respect to the admirable and incomprehensible mysteries of our Faith; for the opinion they have of our genius and capacity makes them believe whatever we tell them."

"What does the Captain say?" was the frequent question; for by this title of honor they designated the clock.

"When he strikes twelve times, he says, 'Hang on the kettle'; and when he strikes four times, he says, 'Get up, and go home.'"

Both interpretations were well remembered. At noon, visitors were never wanting, to share the Fathers' sagamite; but at the stroke of four, all rose and departed, leaving the missionaries for a time in peace. Now the door was barred, and, gathering around the fire, they discussed the prospects of the mission, compared their several experiences, and took counsel for the future. But the standing topic of their evening talk was the Huron language. Concerning this each had some new discovery to relate, some new suggestion to offer; and in the task of analyzing its construction and deducing its hidden laws, these intelligent and highly cultivated minds found a congenial employment.

But while zealously laboring to perfect their knowledge of the language, they spared no pains to turn their present acquirements to account. Was man, woman, or child sick or suffering, they were always at hand with assistance and relief,—adding, as they saw opportunity, explanations of Christian doctrine, pictures of Heaven and Hell, and exhortations to embrace the Faith. Their friendly offices did not cease here, but included matters widely different. The Hurons lived in constant fear of the Iroquois. At times the whole village population would fly to the woods for concealment, or take refuge in one of the neighboring fortified towns, on the rumor of an approaching war-party. The Jesuits promised them the aid of the four Frenchmen armed with arquebuses, who had come with them from Three Rivers. They advised the Hurons to make their palisade forts, not, as hitherto, in a circular form, but rectangular, with small flanking towers at the corners for the arquebuse-men. The Indians at once saw the value of the advice, and soon after began to act on it in the case of their great town of Ossossané, or Rochelle.

At every opportunity, the missionaries gathered together the children of the village at their house. On these occasions, Brébeuf, for greater solemnity, put on a surplice, and the close, angular cap worn by Jesuits in their convents. First he chanted the *Pater Noster*, translated by Father Daniel into Huron rhymes,—the children chanting in their turn. Next he taught them the sign of the cross; made them repeat the *Ave*, the *Credo*, and the Commandments; questioned them as to past instructions; gave them briefly a few new ones; and dismissed them with a present of two or three beads, raisins, or prunes. A great emulation was kindled among this small fry of heathendom. The priests, with amusement and delight, saw them gathered in groups about the village, vying with each other in making the sign of the cross, or in repeating the rhymes they had learned.

At times, the elders of the people, the repositories of its ancient traditions, were induced to assemble at the house of the Jesuits, who explained to them the principal points of their doctrine, and invited them to a discussion. The auditors proved pliant to a fault, responding, "Good," or "That is true," to every proposition; but, when urged to adopt the faith which so readily met their approval, they had always the same reply: "It is good for the French; but we are another people, with different customs." On one occasion, Brébeuf appeared before the chiefs and elders at a solemn national council, described Heaven and Hell with images suited to their comprehension, asked to which they preferred to go after death, and then, in accordance with the invariable Huron custom in affairs of importance, presented a large and valuable belt of wampum, as an invitation to take the path to Paradise.

Notwithstanding all their exhortations, the Jesuits, for the present, baptized but few. Indeed, during the first year or more, they baptized no adults except those apparently at the point of death; for, with excellent reason, they feared backsliding and recantation. They found especial pleasure in the baptism of dying infants, rescuing them from the flames of perdition, and changing them, to borrow Le Jeune's phrase, "from little Indians into little angels."

The Fathers' slumbers were brief and broken. Winter was the season of Huron festivity; and, as they lay stretched on their hard couch, suffocating with smoke and tormented by an inevitable multitude of fleas, the thumping of the drum resounded all night long from a neighboring house, mingled with the sound of the tortoise-shell rattle, the stamping of moccasined feet, and the cadence of voices keeping time with the dancers. Again, some ambitious villager would give a feast, and invite all the warriors of the neighboring towns; or some grand wager of gambling, with its attendant drumming, singing, and outcries, filled the night with discord.

But these were light annoyances, compared with the insane rites to cure the sick, prescribed by the "medicine-men," or ordained by the eccentric inspiration of dreams. In one case, a young sorcerer, by alternate gorging and fasting,—both in the interest of his profession,—joined with excessive exertion in singing to the spirits, contracted a disorder of the brain, which caused him, in mid-winter, to run naked about the village, howling like a wolf. The whole population bestirred itself to effect a cure. The patient had, or pretended to have, a dream, in which the conditions of his recovery were revealed to him. These were equally ridiculous and difficult; but the elders met in council, and all the villagers lent their aid, till every requisition was fulfilled, and the incongruous mass of gifts which the madman's dream had demanded were all bestowed upon him. This cure failing, a "medicine-feast" was tried; then several dances in succession. As the patient remained as crazy as before, preparations were begun for a grand dance, more potent than all the rest. Brébeuf says, that, except the masquerades of the Carnival among Christians, he never saw a folly equal to it. "Some," he adds, "had sacks over their heads, with two holes for the eyes. Some were as naked as your hand, with horns or feathers on their heads, their bodies painted white, and their faces black as devils. Others were daubed with red, black, and white. In short, every one decked himself as extravagantly as he could, to dance in this ballet, and contribute something to-wards the health of the sick man." This remedy also failing, a crowning effort of the medical art was essayed. Brébeuf does not describe it, for fear, as he says, of being tedious; but, for the time, the village was a pandemonium. This, with other ceremonies, was supposed to be ordered by a certain image like a doll, which a sorcerer placed in his tobacco-pouch, whence it uttered its oracles, at the same time moving as if alive. "Truly," writes Brébeuf, "here is nonsense enough: but I greatly fear there is something more dark and myste-rious in it."

But all these ceremonies were outdone by the grand festival of the *Ononhara*, or Dream Feast,—esteemed the most powerful remedy in cases of sickness, or when a village was infested with evil spirits. The time and manner of holding it were determined at a solemn council. This scene of madness began at night. Men, women, and children, all pretending to have lost their senses, rushed shrieking and howling from house to house, upsetting everything in their way, throwing fire-brands, beating those they met or drenching them with water, and availing themselves of this time of license to take a safe revenge on any who had ever offended them. This scene of frenzy continued till daybreak. No corner of the village was secure from the maniac crew. In the morning there was a change. They ran from house to house, accosting the inmates by name, and demanding of each the satisfaction of some secret want, revealed to the pretended madman in a dream, but of the nature of which he gave no hint whatever. The person addressed thereupon threw to him at random any article at hand, as a hatchet, a kettle, or a pipe; and the applicant continued his rounds till the desired gift was hit upon, when he gave an outcry of delight, echoed by gratulatory cries from all present. If, after all his efforts, he failed in obtaining the object of his dream, he fell into a deep dejection, convinced that some disaster was in store for him.

The approach of summer brought with it a comparative peace. Many of the villagers dispersed,—some to their fishing, some to expeditions of trade, and some to distant lodges by their detached corn-fields. The priests availed themselves of the respite to engage in those exercises of private devotion which the rule of St. Ignatius enjoins. About midsummer, however, their quiet was suddenly broken. The crops were withering under a severe drought, a calamity which the sandy nature of the soil made doubly serious. The sorcerers put forth their utmost power, and, from the tops of the houses, yelled incessant invocations to the spirits. All was in vain; the pitiless sky was cloudless. There was thunder in the east and thunder in the west; but over Ihonatiria all was serene. A renowned "rain-maker," seeing his reputation tottering under his repeated failures, bethought him of accusing the Jesuits, and gave out that the red color of the cross which stood before their house scared the bird of thunder, and caused him to fly another way. On this a clamor arose. The popular ire turned against the priests, and the obnoxious cross was condemned to be hewn down. Aghast at the threatened sacrilege, they attempted to reason away the storm, assuring the crowd that the lightning was not a bird, but certain hot and fiery exhalations, which, being imprisoned, darted this way and that, trying to escape. As this philosophy failed to convince the hearers, the missionaries changed their line of defence.

"You say that the red color of the cross frightens the bird of thunder. Then paint the cross white, and see if the thunder will come."

This was accordingly done; but the clouds still kept aloof. The Jesuits followed up their advantage.

"Your spirits cannot help you, and your sorcerers have deceived you with lies. Now ask the aid of Him who made the world, and perhaps He will listen to your prayers." And they added, that, if the Indians would renounce their sins and obey the true God, they would make a procession daily to implore His favor towards them.

There was no want of promises. The processions were begun, as were also nine masses to St. Joseph; and, as heavy rains occurred soon after, the Indians conceived a high idea of the efficacy of the French "medicine."

In spite of the hostility of the sorcerers, and the transient commotion raised by the red cross, the Jesuits had gained the confidence and good-will of the Huron population. Their patience, their kindness, their intrepidity, their manifest disinterestedness, the blamelessness of their lives, and the tact which, in the utmost fervors of their zeal, never failed them, had won the hearts of these wayward savages; and chiefs of distant villages came to urge that they would make their abode with them. As yet, the results of the mission had been faint and few; but the priests toiled on courageously, high in hope that an abundant harvest of souls would one day reward their labors.

[THE FOUNDING OF MONTREAL]

It was the eighth of May when Maisonneuve and his followers embarked at St. Michel; and as the boats, deep-laden with men, arms, and stores, moved slowly on their way, the forest, with leaves just opening in the warmth of spring, lay on their right hand and on their left, in a flattering semblance of tranquillity and peace. But behind woody islets, in tangled thickets and damp ravines, and in the shade and stillness of the columned woods, lurked everywhere a danger and a terror.

What shall we say of these adventurers of Montreal,—of these who bestowed their wealth, and, far more, of these who sacrificed their peace and risked their lives, on an enterprise at once so romantic and so devout? Surrounded as they were with illusions, false lights, and false shadows,—breathing an atmosphere of miracle,—compassed about with angels and devils,— urged with stimulants most powerful, though unreal,—their minds drugged, as it were, to preternatural excitement,—it is very difficult to judge of them. High merit, without doubt, there was in some of their number; but one may beg to be spared the attempt to measure or define it. To estimate a virtue involved in conditions so anomalous demands, perhaps, a judgment more than human.

The Roman Church, sunk in disease and corruption when the Reformation began, was roused by that fierce trumpet-blast to purge and brace herself anew. Unable to advance, she drew back to the fresher and comparatively purer life of the past; and the fervors of mediæval Christianity were renewed in the sixteenth century. In many of its aspects, this enterprise of Montreal belonged to the time of the first Crusades. The spirit of Godfrey de Bouillon lived again in Chomedey de Maisonneuve; and in Marguerite Bourgeoys was realized that fair ideal of Christian womanhood, a flower of Earth expanding in the rays of Heaven, which soothed with gentle influence the wildness of a barbarous age.

On the seventeeth of May, 1642, Maisonneuve's little flotilla —a pinnace, a flat-bottomed craft moved by sails, and two rowboats—approached Montreal; and all on board raised in unison a hymn of praise. Montmagny was with them, to deliver the island, in behalf of the Company of the Hundred Associates, to Maisonneuve, representative of the Associates of Montreal. And here, too, was Father Vimont, Superior of the missions; for the Jesuits had been prudently invited to accept the spiritual charge of the young colony. On the following day, they glided along the green and solitary shores now thronged with the life of a busy city, and landed on the spot which Champlain, thirty-one years before, had chosen as the fit site of a settlement. It was a tongue or triangle of land, formed by the junction of a rivulet with the St. Lawrence, and known afterwards as Point Callière. The rivulet was bordered by a meadow, and beyond rose the forest with its vanguard of scattered trees. Early spring flowers were blooming in the young grass, and birds of varied plumage flitted among the boughs.

Maisonneuve sprang ashore, and fell on his knees. His followers imitated his example; and all joined their voices in enthusiastic songs of thanksgiving. Tents, baggage, arms, and stores were landed. An altar was raised on a pleasant spot near at hand; and Mademoiselle Mance, with Madame de la Peltrie, aided by her servant, Charlotte Barré, decorated it with a taste which was the admiration of the beholders. Now all the company gathered before the shrine. Here stood Vimont, in the rich vestments of his office. Here were the two ladies, with their servant; Montmagny, no very willing spectator; and Maisonneuve, a warlike figure, erect and tall, his men clustering around him,—soldiers, sailors, artisans, and laborers,—all alike soldiers at need. They kneeled in reverent silence as the Host was raised aloft; and when the rite was over, the priest turned and addressed them:—

"You are a grain of mustard-seed, that shall rise and grow till its branches overshadow the earth. You are few, but your work is the work of God. His smile is on you, and your children shall fill the land."

The afternoon waned; the sun sank behind the western forest, and twilight came on. Fireflies were twinkling over the darkened meadow. They caught them, tied them with threads into shining festoons, and hung them before the altar, where the Host remained exposed. Then they pitched their tents, lighted their bivouac fires, stationed their guards, and lay down to rest. Such was the birth-night of Montreal.

Is this true history, or a romance of Christian chivalry? It is both.

[THE RUIN OF THE HURONS]

More than eight months had passed since the catastrophe of St. Joseph. The winter was over, and that dreariest of seasons had come, the churlish forerunner of spring. Around Sainte Marie the forests were gray and bare, and, in the cornfields, the oozy, half-thawed soil, studded with the sodden stalks of the last autumn's harvest, showed itself in patches through the melting snow.

At nine o'clock on the morning of the sixteenth of March, the priests saw a heavy smoke rising over the naked forest towards the south-east, about three miles distant. They looked at each other in dismay. "The Iroquois! They are burning St. Louis!" Flames mingled with the smoke; and, as they stood gazing, two Christian Hurons came, breathless and aghast, from the burning town. Their worst fear was realized. The Iroquois were there; but where were the priests of the mission, Brébeuf and Lalemant?

Late in the autumn, a thousand Iroquois, chiefly Senecas and Mohawks, had taken the war-path for the Hurons. They had been all winter in the forests, hunting for subsistence, and moving at their leisure towards their prey. The destruction of the two towns of the mission of St. Joseph had left a wide gap, and in the middle of March they entered the heart of the Huron country, undiscovered. Common vigilance and common sense would have averted the calamities that followed; but the Hurons were like a doomed people, stupefied, sunk in dejection, fearing everything, yet taking no measures for defence. They could easily have met the invaders with double their force, but the besotted warriors lay idle in their towns, or hunted at leisure in distant forests; nor could the Jesuits, by counsel or exhortation, rouse them to face the danger.

Before daylight of the sixteenth, the invaders approached St. Ignace, which, with St. Louis and three other towns, formed the mission of the same name. They reconnoitred the place in the darkness. It was defended on three sides by a deep ravine, and further strengthened by palisades fifteen or sixteen feet high, planted under the direction of the Jesuits. On the fourth side it was protected by palisades alone; and these were left, as usual, unguarded. This was not from a sense of security; for the greater part of the population had abandoned the town, thinking it too much exposed to the enemy, and there remained only about four hundred, chiefly women, children, and old men, whose infatuated defenders were absent hunting, or on futile scalping-parties against the Iroquois. It was just before dawn, when a yell, as of a legion of devils, startled the wretched inhabitants from their sleep; and the Iroquois, bursting in upon them, cut them down with knives and hatchets, killing many, and reserving the rest for a worse fate. They had entered by the weakest side; on the other sides there was no exit, and only three Hurons escaped. The whole was the work of a few minutes. The Iroquois left a guard to hold the town, and secure the retreat of the main body in case of a reverse; then, smearing their faces with blood, after their ghastly custom, they rushed, in the dim light of the early dawn, towards St. Louis, about a league distant.

The three fugitives had fled, half naked, through the forest, for the same point, which they reached about sunrise, yelling the alarm. The number of inhabitants here was less, at this time, than seven hundred; and, of these, all who had strength to escape, excepting about eighty warriors, made in wild terror for a place of safety. Many of the old, sick, and decrepit were left perforce in the lodges. The warriors, ignorant of the strength of the assailants, sang their war-songs, and resolved to hold the place to the last. It had not the natural strength of St. Ignace, but, like it, was surrounded by palisades.

Here were the two Jesuits, Brébeuf and Lalemant. Brébeuf's converts entreated him to escape with them; but the Norman zealot, bold scion of a warlike stock, had no thought of flight. His post was in the teeth of danger, to cheer on those who fought, and open heaven to those who fell. His colleague, slight of frame and frail of constitution, trembled despite himself; but deep enthusiasm mastered the weakness of Nature, and he, too, refused to fly.

Scarcely had the sun risen, and scarcely were the fugitives gone, when, like a troop of tigers, the Iroquois rushed to the assault. Yell echoed yell, and shot answered shot. The Hurons, brought to bay, fought with the utmost desperation, and with arrows, stones, and the few guns they had, killed thirty of their assailants, and wounded many more. Twice the Iroquois recoiled, and twice renewed the attack with unabated ferocity. They swarmed at the foot of the palisades, and hacked at them with their hatchets, till they had cut them through at several different points. For a time there was a deadly fight at these breaches. Here were the two priests, promising Heaven to those who died for their faith,—one giving baptism, and the other absolution. At length the Iroquois broke in, and captured all the surviving defenders, the Jesuits among the rest. They set the town on fire; and the helpless wretches who had remained, unable to fly, were consumed in their burning dwellings. Next they fell upon Brébeuf and Lalemant, stripped them, bound them fast, and led them with the other prisoners back to St. Ignace, where all turned out to wreak their fury on the two priests, beating them savagely with sticks and clubs as they drove them into the town. At present, there was no time for further torture, for there was work in hand.

The victors divided themselves into several bands, to burn the neighboring villages and hunt their flying inhabitants. In the flush of their triumph, they meditated a bolder enterprise; and, in the afternoon, their chiefs sent small parties to reconnoitre Sainte Marie, with a view to attacking it on the next day.

Meanwhile the fugitives of St. Louis, joined by other bands as terrified and as helpless as they, were struggling through the soft snow which clogged the forests towards Lake Huron, where the treacherous ice of spring was still unmelted. One fear expelled another. They ventured upon it, and pushed forward all that day and all the following night, shivering and famished, to find refuge in the towns of the Tobacco Nation. Here, when they arrived, they spread a universal panic.

Ragueneau, Bressani, and their companions waited in suspense at Sainte Marie. On the one hand, they trembled for Brébeuf and Lalemant; on the other, they looked hourly for an attack: and when at evening they saw the Iroquois scouts prowling along the edge of the bordering forest, their fears were confirmed. They had with them about forty Frenchmen, well armed; but their palisades and wooden buildings were not fire-proof, and they had learned from fugitives the number and ferocity of the invaders. They stood guard all night, praying to the Saints, and above all to their great patron, Saint Joseph, whose festival was close at hand.

In the morning they were somewhat relieved by the arrival of about three hundred Huron warriors, chiefly converts from La Conception and Sainte Madeleine, tolerably well armed, and full of fight. They were expecting others to join them; and meanwhile, dividing into several bands, they took post by the passes of the neighboring forest, hoping to waylay parties of the enemy. Their expectation was fulfilled; for, at this time, two hundred of the Iroquois were making their way from St. Ignace, in advance of the main body, to begin the attack on Sainte Marie. They fell in with a band of the Hurons, set upon them, killed many, drove the rest to headlong flight, and, as they plunged in terror through the snow, chased them within sight of Sainte Marie. The other Hurons, hearing the yells and firing, ran to the rescue, and attacked so fiercely, that the Iroquois in turn were routed, and ran for shelter to St. Louis, followed closely by the victors. The houses of the town had been burned, but the palisade around them was still standing, though breached and broken. The Iroquois rushed in; but the Hurons were at their heels. Many of the fugitives were captured, the rest killed or put to utter rout, and the triumphant Hurons remained masters of the place.

The Iroquois who escaped fled to St. Ignace. Here, or on

the way thither, they found the main body of the invaders; and when they heard of the disaster, the whole swarm, beside themselves with rage, turned towards St. Louis to take their revenge. Now ensued one of the most furious Indian battles on record. The Hurons within the palisade did not much exceed a hundred and fifty; for many had been killed or disabled, and many, perhaps, had straggled away. Most of their enemies had guns, while they had but few. Their weapons were bows and arrows, war-clubs, hatchets, and knives; and of these they made good use, sallying repeatedly, fighting like devils, and driving back their assailants again and again. There are times when the Indian warrior forgets his cautious maxims, and throws himself into battle with a mad and reckless ferocity. The desperation of one party, and the fierce courage of both, kept up the fight after the day had closed; and the scout from Sainte Marie, as he bent listening under the gloom of the pines, heard, far into the night, the howl of battle rising from the darkened forest. The principal chief of the Iroquois was severely wounded, and nearly a hundred of their warriors were killed on the spot. When, at length, their numbers and persistent fury prevailed, their only prize was some twenty Huron warriors, spent with fatigue and faint with loss of blood. The rest lay dead around the shattered palisades which they had so valiantly defended. Fatuity, not cowardice, was the ruin of the Huron nation.

The lamps burned all night at Sainte Marie, and its defenders stood watching till daylight, musket in hand. The Jesuits prayed without ceasing, and Saint Joseph was besieged with invocations. "Those of us who were priests," writes Ragueneau, "each made a vow to say a mass in his honor every month, for the space of a year; and all the rest bound themselves by vows to divers penances." The expected onslaught did not take place. Not an Iroquois appeared. Their victory had been bought too dear, and they had no stomach for more fighting. All the next day, the eighteenth, a stillness, like the dead lull of a tempest, followed the turmoil of yesterday,—as if, says the Father Superior, "the country were waiting, palsied with fright, for some new disaster."

On the following day,—the journalist fails not to mention that it was the festival of Saint Joseph,—Indians came in with tidings that a panic had seized the Iroquois camp, that the chiefs could not control it, and that the whole body of invaders was retreating in disorder, possessed with a vague terror that the Hurons were upon them in force. They had found time, however, for an act of atrocious cruelty. They planted stakes in the bark houses of St. Ignace, and bound to them those of their prisoners whom they meant to sacrifice, male and female, from old age to infancy, husbands, mothers, and children, side by side. Then, as they retreated, they set the town on fire, and laughed with savage glee at the shrieks of anguish that rose from the blazing dwellings.

They loaded the rest of their prisoners with their baggage and plunder, and drove them through the forest southward, braining with their hatchets any who gave out on the march. An old woman, who had escaped out of the midst of the flames of St. Ignace, made her way to St. Michel, a large town not far from the desolate site of St. Joseph. Here she found about seven hundred Huron warriors, hastily mustered. She set them on the track of the retreating Iroquois, and they took up the chase,— but evidently with no great eagerness to overtake their dangerous enemy, well armed as he was with Dutch guns, while they had little beside their bows and arrows. They found, as they advanced, the dead bodies of prisoners tomahawked on the march, and others bound fast to trees and half burned by the fagots piled hastily around them. The Iroquois pushed forward with such headlong speed, that the pursuers could not, or would not, overtake them; and, after two days, they gave over the attempt.

[THE FAILURE OF THE MISSIONARIES]

With the fall of the Hurons, fell the best hope of the Canadian mission. They, and the stable and populous communities around them, had been the rude material from which the Jesuit would have formed his Christian empire in the wilderness; but, one by one, these kindred peoples were uprooted and swept away, while the neighboring Algonquins, to whom they had been a bulwark, were involved with them in a common ruin. The land of promise was turned to a solitude and a desolation. There was still work in hand, it is true,—vast regions to explore, and countless heathens to snatch from perdition; but these, for the most part, were remote and scattered hordes, from whose conversion it was vain to look for the same solid and decisive results.

In a measure, the occupation of the Jesuits was gone. Some of them went home, "well resolved," writes the Father Superior, "to return to the combat at the first sound of the trumpet"; while of those who remained, about twenty in number, several soon fell victims to famine, hardship, and the Iroquois. A few years more, and Canada ceased to be a mission; political and commercial interests gradually became ascendant, and the story of Jesuit propagandism was interwoven with her civil and military annals.

Here, then, closes this wild and bloody act of the great drama of New France; and now let the curtain fall, while we ponder its meaning.

The cause of the failure of the Jesuits is obvious. The guns and tomahawks of the Iroquois were the ruin of their hopes. Could they have curbed or converted those ferocious bands, it is little less than certain that their dream would have become a reality. Savages tamed—not civilized, for that was scarcely possible—would have been distributed in communities through the valleys of the Great Lakes and the Mississippi, ruled by priests in the interest of Catholicity and of France. Their habits of agriculture would have been developed, and their instincts of mutual slaughter repressed. The swift decline of the Indian population would have been arrested; and it would have been made, through the fur-trade, a source of prosperity to New France. Unmolested by Indian enemies, and fed by a rich commerce, she would have put forth a vigorous growth. True to her far-reaching and adventurous genius, she would have occupied the West with traders, settlers, and garrisons, and cut up the virgin wilderness into fiefs, while as yet the colonies of England were but a weak and broken line along the shore of the Atlantic; and when at last the great conflict came, England and Liberty would have been confronted, not by a depleted antagonist, still feeble from the exhaustion of a starved and persecuted infancy, but by an athletic champion of the principles of Richelieu and of Loyola.

Liberty may thank the Iroquois, that, by their insensate fury, the plans of her adversary were brought to nought, and a peril and a woe averted from her future. They ruined the trade which was the life-blood of New France; they stopped the current of her arteries, and made all her early years a misery and a terror. Not that they changed her destinies. The contest on this continent between Liberty and Absolutism was never doubtful; but the triumph of the one would have been dearly bought, and the downfall of the other incomplete. Populations formed in the ideas and habits of a feudal monarchy, and controlled by a hierarchy profoundly hostile to freedom of thought, would have remained a hindrance and a stumbling-block in the way of that majestic experiment of which America is the field.

The Jesuits saw their hopes struck down; and their faith, though not shaken, was sorely tried. The Providence of God seemed in their eyes dark and inexplicable; but, from the standpoint of Liberty, that Providence is clear as the sun at noon. Meanwhile let those who have prevailed yield due honor to the defeated. Their virtues shine amidst the rubbish of error, like diamonds and gold in the gravel of the torrent.

THE DISCOVERY OF THE MISSISSIPPI

(From *La Salle and the Discovery of the Great West*, 1869–79)

Before sailing for France, Talon recommended Joliet as a suitable agent for the discovery of the Mississippi, and the governor accepted his counsel.

Louis Joliet was the son of a wagon-maker in the service of the Company of the Hundred Associates, then owners of Canada. He was born at Quebec in 1645, and was educated by the Jesuits. When still very young, he resolved to be a priest. He received the tonsure and the minor orders at the age of seventeen. Four years after, he is mentioned with especial honor for the part he bore in the disputes in philosophy, at which the dignitaries of the colony were present, and in which the intendant himself took part. Not long after, he renounced his clerical vocation, and turned fur-trader. Talon sent him, with one Péré, to explore the copper-mines of Lake Superior; and it was on his return from this expedition that he met La Salle and the Sulpitians near the head of Lake Ontario.

In what we know of Joliet, there is nothing that reveals any salient or distinctive trait of character, any especial breadth of view or boldness of design. He appears to have been simply a merchant, intelligent, well educated, courageous, hardy, and enterprising. Though he had renounced the priesthood, he retained his partiality for the Jesuits; and it is more than probable that their influence had aided not a little to determine Talon's choice. One of their number, Jacques Marquette, was chosen to accompany him.

He passed up the lakes to Michillimackinac, and found his destined companion at Point St. Ignace, on the north side of the strait, where, in his palisaded mission-house and chapel, he had labored for two years past to instruct the Huron refugees from St. Esprit, and a band of Ottawas who had joined them. Marquette was born in 1637, of an old and honorable family at Laon, in the north of France, and was now thirty-five years of age. When about seventeen, he had joined the Jesuits, evidently from motives purely religious; and in 1666 he was sent to the missions of Canada. At first, he was destined to the station of Tadoussac; and to prepare himself for it, he studied the Montagnais language under Gabriel Druilletes. But his destination was changed, and he was sent to the Upper Lakes in 1668, where he had since remained. His talents as a linguist must have been great; for, within a few years, he learned to speak with ease six Indian languages. The traits of his character are unmistakable. He was of the brotherhood of the early Canadian missionaries, and the true counterpart of Garnier or Jogues. He was a devout votary of the Virgin Mary, who, imaged to his mind in shapes of the most transcendent loveliness with which the pencil of human genius has ever informed the canvas, was to him the object of an adoration not unmingled with a sentiment of chivalrous devotion. The longings of a sensitive heart, divorced from earth, sought solace in the skies. A subtile element of romance was blended with the fervor of his worship, and hung like an illumined cloud over the harsh and hard realities of his daily lot. Kindled by the smile of his celestial mistress, his gentle and noble nature knew no fear. For her he burned to dare and to suffer, discover new lands and conquer new realms to her sway.

He begins the journal of his voyage thus: "The day of the Immaculate Conception of the Holy Virgin; whom I had continually invoked, since I came to this country of the Ottawas, to obtain from God the favor of being enabled to visit the nations on the river Mississippi,—this very day was precisely that on which M. Joliet arrived with orders from Count Frontenac, our governor, and from M. Talon, our intendant, to go with me on this discovery. I was all the more delighted at this good news, because I saw my plans about to be accomplished, and found myself in the happy necessity of exposing my life for the salvation of all these tribes; and especially of the Illinois, who, when I was at Point St. Esprit, had begged me very earnestly to bring the word of God among them."

The outfit of the travellers was very simple. They provided themselves with two birch canoes, and a supply of smoked meat and Indian corn; embarked with five men; and began their voyage on the seventeenth of May. They had obtained all possible information from the Indians, and had made, by means of it, a species of map of their intended route. "Above all," writes Marquette, "I placed our voyage under the protection of the Holy Virgin Immaculate, promising that, if she granted us the favor of discovering the great river, I would give it the name of the Conception." Their course was westward; and, plying their paddles, they passed the Straits of Michillimackinac, and coasted the northern shores of Lake Michigan, landing at evening to build their camp-fire at the edge of the forest, and draw up their canoes on the strand. They soon reached the river Menomonie, and ascended it to the village of the Menomonies, or Wild-rice Indians. When they told them the object of their voyage, they were filled with astonishment, and used their best ingenuity to dissuade them. The banks of the Mississippi, they said, were inhabited by ferocious tribes, who put every stranger to death, tomahawking all new-comers without cause or provocation. They added that there was a demon in a certain part of the river, whose roar could be heard at a great distance, and who would engulf them in the abyss where he dwelt; that its waters were full of frightful monsters, who would devour them and their canoe; and, finally, that the heat was so great that they would perish inevitably. Marquette set their counsel at naught, gave them a few words of instruction in the mysteries of the Faith, taught them a prayer, and bade them farewell.

The travellers next reached the mission at the head of Green Bay; entered Fox River; with difficulty and labor dragged their canoes up the long and tumultuous rapids; crossed Lake Winnebago; and followed the quiet windings of the river beyond, where they glided through an endless growth of wild rice, and scared the innumerable birds that fed upon it. On either hand rolled the prairie, dotted with groves and trees, browsing elk and deer. On the seventh of June, they reached the Mascoutins and Miamis, who, since the visit of Dablon and Allouez, had been joined by the Kickapoos. Marquette, who had an eye for natural beauty, was delighted with the situation of the town, which he describes as standing on the crown of a hill; while, all around, the prairie stretched beyond the sight, interspersed with groves and belts of tall forest. But he was still more delighted when he saw a cross planted in the midst of the place. The Indians had decorated it with a number of dressed deer-skins, red girdles, and bows and arrows, which they had hung upon it as an offering to the Great Manitou of the French; a sight by which Marquette says he was "extremely consoled."

The travellers had no sooner reached the town than they called the chiefs and elders to a council. Joliet told them that the governor of Canada had sent him to discover new countries, and that God had sent his companion to teach the true faith to the inhabitants; and he prayed for guides to show them the way to the waters of the Wisconsin. The council readily consented; and on the tenth of June the Frenchmen embarked again, with two Indians to conduct them. All the town came down to the shore to see their departure. Here were the Miamis, with long locks of hair dangling over each ear, after a fashion which Marquette thought very becoming; and here, too, the Mascoutins and the Kickapoos, whom he describes as mere boors in comparison with their Miami townsmen. All stared alike at the seven adventurers, marvelling that men could be found to risk an enterprise so hazardous.

The river twisted among lakes and marshes choked with wild rice; and, but for their guides, they could scarcely have followed the perplexed and narrow channel. It brought them at last to the portage, where, after carrying their canoes a mile and a half over the prairie and through the marsh, they launched them on the Wisconsin, bade farewell to the waters that flowed to the St. Lawrence, and committed themselves to the current that was to bear them they knew not whither,—perhaps to the Gulf of Mexico, perhaps to the South Sea or the Gulf of California. They glided calmly down the tranquil stream, by islands choked with trees and matted with entangling grape-vines; by forests, groves, and prairies, the parks and pleasure-grounds of a prodigal nature; by thickets and marshes and broad bare sand-bars; under the shadowing trees, between whose tops looked down from afar the bold brow of some woody bluff. At night, the bivouac,—the canoes inverted on the bank, the flickering fire, the meal of bison-flesh or venison, the evening pipes, and slumber beneath the stars; and when in the morning they embarked again, the mist hung on the river like a bridal veil, then melted before the sun, till the glassy water and the languid woods basked breathless in the sultry glare.

On the 17th of June, they saw on their right the broad meadows, bounded in the distance by rugged hills, where now stand the town and fort of Prairie du Chien. Before them a wide and rapid current coursed athwart their way, by the foot of lofty heights wrapped thick in forests. They had found what they sought, and "with a joy," writes Marquette, "which I cannot express," they steered forth their canoes on the eddies of the Mississippi.

Turning southward, they paddled down the stream, through a solitude unrelieved by the faintest trace of man. A large fish, apparently one of the huge cat-fish of the Mississippi, blundered against Marquette's canoe, with a force which seems to have startled him; and once, as they drew in their net, they caught a "spade-fish," whose eccentric appearance greatly astonished them. At length, the buffalo began to appear, grazing in herds on the great prairies which then bordered the river; and Marquette describes the fierce and stupid look of the old bulls, as they stared at the intruders through the tangled mane which nearly blinded them.

They advanced with extreme caution, landed at night, and made a fire to cook their evening meal; then extinguished it, embarked again, paddled some way farther, and anchored in the stream, keeping a man on the watch till morning. They had journeyed more than a fortnight without meeting a human being, when, on the twenty-fifth, they discovered footprints of men in the mud of the western bank, and a well-trodden path that led to the adjacent prairie. Joliet and Marquette resolved to follow it; and, leaving the canoes in charge of their men, they set out on their hazardous adventure. The day was fair, and they walked two leagues in silence, following the path through the forest and across the sunny prairie, till they discovered an Indian village on the banks of a river, and two others on a hill half a league distant. Now, with beating hearts, they invoked the aid of Heaven, and, again advancing, came so near, without being seen, that they could hear the voices of the Indians among the wigwams. Then they stood forth in full view, and shouted to attract attention. There was great commotion in the village. The inmates swarmed out of their huts, and four of their chief men presently came forward to meet the strangers, advancing very deliberately, and holding up toward the sun two calumets, or peace-pipes, decorated with feathers. They stopped abruptly before the two Frenchmen, and stood gazing at them without speaking a word. Marquette was much relieved on seeing that they wore French cloth, whence he judged that they must be friends and allies. He broke the silence, and asked them who they were; whereupon they answered that they were Illinois, and offered the pipe; which having been duly smoked, they all went together to the village. Here the chief received the travellers after a singular fashion, meant to do them honor. He stood stark naked at the door of a large wigwam, holding up both hands as if to shield his eyes. "Frenchmen, how bright the sun shines when you come to visit us! All our village awaits you; and you shall enter our wigwams in peace." So saying, he led them into his own, which was crowded to suffocation with savages, staring at their guests in silence. Having smoked with the chiefs and old men, they were invited to visit the great chief of all the Illinois, at one of the villages they had seen in the distance; and thither they proceeded, followed by a throng of warriors, squaws, and children. On arriving, they were forced to smoke again, and listen to a speech of welcome from the great chief, who delivered it standing between two old men, naked like himself. His lodge was crowded with the dignitaries of the tribe, whom Marquette addressed in Algonquin, announcing himself as a messenger sent by the God who had made them, and whom it behooves them to recognize and obey. He added a few words touching the power and glory of Count Frontenac, and concluded by asking information concerning the Mississippi, and the tribes along its banks, whom he was on his way to visit. The chief replied with a speech of compliment; assuring his guests that their presence added flavor to his tobacco, made the river more calm, the sky more serene, and the earth more beautiful. In conclusion, he gave them a young slave and a calumet, begging them at the same time to abandon their purpose of descending the Mississippi.

A feast of four courses now followed. First, a wooden bowl full of a porridge of Indian meal boiled with grease was set before the guests; and the master of ceremonies fed them in turn, like infants, with a large spoon. Then appeared a platter of fish; and the same functionary, carefully removing the bones with his fingers, and blowing on the morsels to cool them, placed them in the mouths of the two Frenchmen. A large dog, killed and cooked for the occasion, was next placed before them; but, failing to tempt their fastidious appetites, was supplanted by a dish of fat buffalo-meat, which concluded the entertainment. The crowd having dispersed, buffalo-robes were spread on the ground, and Marquette and Joliet spent the night on the scene of the late festivity. In the morning, the chief, with some six hundred of his tribesmen, escorted them to their canoes, and bade them, after their stolid fashion, a friendly farewell.

Again they were on their way, slowly drifting down the great river. They passed the mouth of the Illinois, and glided beneath that line of rocks on the eastern side, cut into fantastic forms by the elements, and marked as "The Ruined Castles" on some of the early French maps. Presently they beheld a sight which reminded them that the Devil was still lord paramount of this wilderness. On the flat face of a high rock were painted, in red, black, and green, a pair of monsters, each "as large as a calf, with horns like a deer, red eyes, a beard like a tiger, and a frightful expression of countenance. The face is something like that of a man, the body covered with scales; and the tail so long that it passes entirely round the body, over the head and between the legs, ending like that of a fish." Such is the account which the worthy Jesuit gives of these manitous, or Indian gods. He confesses that at first they frightened him; and his imagination and that of his credulous companions were so wrought upon by these unhallowed efforts of Indian art, that they continued for a long time to talk of them as they plied their paddles. They were thus engaged, when they were suddenly aroused by a real danger. A torrent of yellow mud rushed furiously athwart the calm blue current of the Mississippi, boiling and surging, and sweeping in its course logs, branches, and uprooted trees. They had reached the mouth of the Missouri, where that savage river, descending from its mad career through a vast unknown of barbarism, poured its turbid floods into the bosom of its gentler sister. Their light canoes whirled on the miry vortex like dry leaves on an angry brook. "I never," writes Marquette, "saw any thing more terrific"; but they escaped with their fright, and held their way down the turbulent and swollen current of the now united rivers. They passed the lonely forest that covered the site of the destined city of St. Louis, and, a few days later, saw on their left the mouth of the stream to which the Iroquois had given the well-merited name of Ohio, or the Beautiful River. Soon they began to see the marshy shores buried in a dense growth of the cane, with its tall straight stems and feathery light-green foliage. The sun glowed through the hazy air with a languid stifling heat, and by day and night mosquitoes in myriads left them no peace. They floated slowly down the current, crouched in the shade of the sails which they had spread as awnings, when suddenly they saw Indians on the east bank. The surprise was mutual, and each party was as much frightened as the other. Marquette hastened to display the calumet which the Illinois had given him by way of passport; and the Indians, recognizing the pacific symbol, replied with an invitation to land. Evidently, they were in communication with Europeans, for they were armed with guns, knives, and hatchets, wore garments of cloth, and carried their gunpowder in small bottles of thick glass. They feasted the Frenchmen with buffalo-meat, bear's oil, and white plums; and gave them a variety of doubtful information, including the agreeable but delusive assurance that they would reach the mouth of the river in ten days. It was, in fact, more than a thousand miles distant.

They resumed their course, and again floated down the interminable monotony of river, marsh, and forest. Day after day passed on in solitude, and they had paddled some three hundred miles since their meeting with the Indians, when, as they neared the mouth of the Arkansas, they saw a cluster of wigwams on the west bank. Their inmates were all astir, yelling the war-whoop, snatching their weapons, and running to the shore to meet the strangers, who, on their part, called for succor to the Virgin. In truth, they had need of her aid; for several large wooden canoes, filled with savages, were putting out from the shore, above and below them, to cut off their retreat, while a swarm of headlong young warriors waded into the water to attack them. The current proved too strong; and, failing to reach the canoes of the Frenchmen, one of them threw his war-club, which flew over the heads of the startled travellers. Meanwhile, Marquette had not ceased to hold up his calumet, to which the excited crowd gave no heed, but strung their bows and notched their arrows for immediate action; when at length the elders of the village arrived, saw the peace-pipe, restrained the ardor of the youth, and urged the Frenchmen to come ashore. Marquette and his companions complied, trembling, and found a better reception than they had reason to expect. One of the Indians spoke a little Illinois, and served as interpreter; a friendly conference was followed by a feast of sagamite and fish; and the travellers, not without sore misgivings, spent the night in the lodges of their entertainers.

Early in the morning, they embarked again, and proceeded to a village of the Arkansas tribe, about eight leagues below. Notice of their coming was sent before them by their late hosts; and, as they drew near, they were met by a canoe, in the prow of which stood a naked personage, holding a calumet, singing, and making gestures of friendship. On reaching the village, which was on the east side, opposite the mouth of the river Arkansas, they were conducted to a sort of scaffold, before the lodge of the war-chief. The space beneath had been prepared for their reception, the ground being neatly covered with rush mats. On these they were seated; the warriors sat around them in a semi-circle; then the elders of the tribe; and then the promiscuous crowd of villagers, standing, and staring over the heads of the more dignified members of the assembly. All the men were naked; but, to compensate for the lack of clothing, they wore strings of beads in their noses and ears. The women were clothed in shabby skins, and wore their hair clumped in a mass behind each ear. By good luck, there was a young Indian in the village, who had an excellent knowledge of Illinois; and through him Marquette endeavored to explain the mysteries of Christianity, and to gain information concerning the river below.

To this end he gave his auditors the presents indispensable on such occasions, but received very little in return. They told him that the Mississippi was infested by hostile Indians, armed with guns procured from white men; and that they, the Arkansas, stood in such fear of them that they dared not hunt the buffalo, but were forced to live on Indian corn, of which they raised three crops a year.

During the speeches on either side, food was brought in without ceasing: sometimes a platter of sagamite or mush; sometimes of corn boiled whole; sometimes a roasted dog. The villagers had large earthen pots and platters, made by themselves with tolerable skill, as well as hatchets, knives, and beads, gained by traffic with the Illinois and other tribes in contact with the French or Spaniards. All day there was feasting without respite, after the merciless practice of Indian hospitality; but at night some of their entertainers proposed to kill and plunder them, a scheme which was defeated by the vigilance of the chief, who visited their quarters, and danced the calumet dance to reassure his guests.

The travellers now held counsel as to what course they should take. They had gone far enough, as they thought, to establish one important point: that the Mississippi discharged its waters, not into the Atlantic or sea of Virginia, nor into the Gulf of California or Vermilion Sea, but into the Gulf of Mexico. They thought themselves nearer to its mouth than they actually were, the distance being still about seven hundred miles; and they feared that, if they went farther, they might be killed by Indians or captured by Spaniards, whereby the results of their discovery would be lost. Therefore they resolved to return to Canada, and report what they had seen.

They left the Arkansas village, and began their homeward voyage on the seventeenth of July. It was no easy task to urge their way upward, in the heat of midsummer, against the current of the dark and gloomy stream, toiling all day under the parching sun, and sleeping at night in the exhalations of the unwholesome shore, or in the narrow confines of their birchen vessels, anchored on the river. Marquette was attacked with dysentery. Languid and well-nigh spent, he invoked his celestial mistress, as day after day, and week after week, they won their slow way northward. At length, they reached the Illinois, and, entering its mouth, followed its course, charmed, as they went, with its placid waters, its shady forests, and its rich plains, grazed by the bison and the deer. They stopped at a spot soon to be made famous in the annals of western discovery. This was a village of the Illinois, then called Kaskaskia; a name afterwards transferred to another locality. A chief, with a band of young warriors, offered to guide them to the Lake of the Illinois; that is to say, Lake Michigan. Thither they repaired; and, coasting its shores, reached Green Bay at the end of September, after an absence of about four months, during which they had paddled their canoes somewhat more than two thousand five hundred miles.

Marquette remained to recruit his exhausted strength; but Joliet descended to Quebec, to bear the report of his discovery to Count Frontenac. Fortune had wonderfully favored him on his long and perilous journey; but now she abandoned him on the very threshold of home. At the foot of the rapids of La Chine, and immediately above Montreal, his canoe was overset, two of his men and an Indian boy were drowned, all his papers were lost, and he himself narrowly escaped. In a letter to Frontenac, he speaks of the accident as follows: "I had escaped every peril from the Indians; I had passed forty-two rapids; and was on the point of disembarking, full of joy at the success of so long and difficult an enterprise, when my canoe capsized, after all the danger seemed over. I lost two men and my box of papers, within sight of the first French settlements, which I had left almost two years before. Nothing remains to me but my life, and the ardent desire to employ it on any service which you may please to direct."

[AN ILLINOIS VILLAGE]

Go to the banks of the Illinois where it flows by the village of Utica, and stand on the meadow that borders it on the north. In front glides the river, a musket-shot in width; and from the farther bank rises, with gradual slope, a range of wooded hills that hide from sight the vast prairie behind them. A mile or more on your left these gentle acclivities end abruptly in the lofty front of the great cliff, called by the French the Rock of St. Louis, looking boldly out from the forests that environ it; and, three miles distant on your right, you discern a gap in the steep bluffs that here bound the valley, marking the mouth of the river Vermilion, called Aramoni by the French. Now stand in fancy on this same spot in the early autumn of the year 1680. You are in the midst of the great town of the Illinois,—hundreds of mat-covered lodges, and thousands of congregated savages. Enter one of their dwellings: they will not think you an intruder. Some friendly squaw will lay a mat for you by the fire; you may seat yourself upon it, smoke your pipe, and study the lodge and its inmates by the light that streams through the holes at the top. Three or four fires smoke and smoulder on the ground down the middle of the long arched structure; and, as to each fire there are two families, the place is somewhat crowded when all are present. But now there is breathing room, for many are in the fields. A squaw sits weaving a mat of rushes; a warrior, naked except his moccasins, and tattooed with fantastic devices, binds a stone arrow-head to its shaft, with the fresh sinews of a buffalo. Some lie asleep, some sit staring in vacancy, some are eating, some are squatted in lazy chat around a fire. The smoke brings water to your eyes; the fleas annoy you; small unkempt children, naked as young puppies, crawl about your knees and will not be repelled. You have seen enough. You rise and go out again into the sunlight. It is, if not a peaceful, at least a languid scene. A few voices break the stillness, mingled with the joyous chirping of crickets from the grass. Young men lie flat on their faces, basking in the sun; a group of their elders are smoking around a buffalo-skin on which they have just been playing a game of chance with cherry-stones. A lover and his mistress, perhaps, sit together under a shed of bark, without uttering a word. Not far off is the grave-yard, where lie the dead of the village, some buried in the earth, some wrapped in skins and laid aloft on scaffolds, above the reach of wolves. In the cornfields around, you see squaws at their labor, and children driving off intruding birds; and your eye ranges over the meadows beyond, spangled with the yellow blossoms of the resin-weed and the Rudbeckia, or over the bordering hills still green with the foliage of summer.

This, or something like it, one may safely affirm, was the aspect of the Illinois village. . . .

[LA SALLE REACHES THE MOUTH OF THE MISSISSIPPI]

The season was far advanced. On the bare limbs of the forest hung a few withered remnants of its gay autumnal livery; and the smoke crept upward through the sullen November air from the squalid wigwams of La Salle's Abenaki and Mohegan allies. These, his new friends, were savages whose midnight yells had startled the border hamlets of New England; who had danced around Puritan scalps, and whom Puritan imaginations painted as incarnate fiends. La Salle chose eighteen of them, whom he added to the twenty-three Frenchmen who remained with him, some of the rest having deserted and others lagged behind. The Indians insisted on taking their squaws with them. These were ten in number, besides three children; and thus the expedition included fifty-four persons, of whom some were useless, and others a burden.

On the 21st of December, Tonty and Membré set out from Fort Miami with some of the party in six canoes, and crossed to the little river Chicago. La Salle, with the rest of the men, joined them a few days later. It was the dead of winter, and the streams were frozen. They made sledges, placed on them the canoes, the baggage, and a disabled Frenchman; crossed from the Chicago to the northern branch of the Illinois, and filed in a long procession down its frozen course. They reached the site of the great Illinois village, found it tenantless, and continued their journey, still dragging their canoes, till at length they reached open water below Lake Peoria.

La Salle had abandoned for a time his original plan of building a vessel for the navigation of the Mississippi. Bitter experience had taught him the difficulty of the attempt, and he resolved to trust to his canoes alone. They embarked again, floating prosperously down between the leafless forests that flanked the tranquil river; till, on the sixth of February, they issued upon the majestic bosom of the Mississippi. Here, for the time, their progress was stopped; for the river was full of floating ice. La Salle's Indians, too, had lagged behind; but, within a week, all had arrived, the navigation was once more free, and they resumed their course. Towards evening, they saw on their right the mouth of a great river; and the clear current was invaded by the headlong torrent of the Missouri, opaque with mud. They built their camp-fires in the neighboring forest; and at daylight, embarking anew on the dark and mighty stream, drifted swiftly down towards unknown destinies. They passed a deserted town of the Tamaroas; saw, three days after, the mouth of the Ohio; and, gliding by the wastes of bordering swamp, landed on the twenty-fourth of February near the Third Chickasaw Bluffs. They encamped, and the hunters went out for game. All returned, excepting Pierre Prudhomme; and, as the others had seen fresh tracks of Indians, La Salle feared that he was killed. While some of his followers built a small stockade fort on a high bluff by the river, others ranged the woods in pursuit of the missing hunter. After six days of ceaseless and fruitless search, they met two Chickasaw Indians in the forest; and, through them, La Salle sent presents and peace-messages to that warlike people, whose villages were a few days' journey distant. Several days later, Prudhomme was found, and brought in to the camp, half-dead. He had lost his way while hunting; and, to console him for his woes, La Salle christened the newly built fort with his name, and left him, with a few others, in charge of it.

Again they embarked; and, with every stage of their adventurous progress, the mystery of this vast New World was more and more unveiled. More and more they entered the realms of spring. The hazy sunlight, the warm and drowsy air, the tender foliage, the opening flowers, betokened the reviving life of Nature. For several days more they followed the writhings of the great river, on its tortuous course through wastes of swamp and canebrake, till on the thirteenth of March they found themselves wrapped in a thick fog. Neither shore was visible; but they heard on the right the booming of an Indian drum and the shrill outcries of the war-dance. La Salle at once crossed to the opposite side, where, in less than an hour, his men threw up a rude fort of felled trees. Meanwhile, the fog cleared; and, from the farther bank, the astonished Indians saw the strange visitors at their work. Some of the French advanced to the edge of the water, and beckoned them to come over. Several of them approached, in a wooden canoe, to within the distance of a gun-shot. La Salle displayed the calumet, and sent a Frenchman to meet them. He was well received; and, the friendly mood of the Indians being now apparent, the whole party crossed the river.

On landing, they found themselves at a town of the Kappa band of the Arkansas, a people dwelling near the mouth of the river which bears their name. "The whole village," writes Membré to his superior, "came down to the shore to meet us, except the women, who had run off. I cannot tell you the civility and kindness we received from these barbarians, who brought us poles to make huts, supplied us with firewood during the three days we were among them, and took turns in feasting us. But, my Reverend Father, this gives no idea of the good qualities of these savages, who are gay, civil, and free-hearted. The young men, though the most alert and spirited we had seen, are nevertheless so modest that not one of them would take the liberty to enter our hut, but all stood quietly at the door. They are so well formed that we were in admiration at their beauty. We did not lose the value of a pin while we were among them."

Various were the dances and ceremonies with which they entertained the strangers, who, on their part, responded with a solemnity which their hosts would have liked less, if they had understood it better. La Salle and Tonty, at the head of their followers, marched to the open area in the midst of the village. Here, to the admiration of the gazing crowd of warriors, women, and children, a cross was raised bearing the arms of

France. Membré, in canonicals, sang a hymn; the men shouted *Vive le Roi;* and La Salle, in the king's name, took formal possession of the country. The friar, not, he flatters himself, without success, labored to expound by signs the mysteries of the Faith; while La Salle, by methods equally satisfactory, drew from the chief an acknowledgment of fealty to Louis XIV.

After touching at several other towns of this people, the voyagers resumed their course, guided by two of the Arkansas; passed the sites, since become historic, of Vicksburg and Grand Gulf; and, about three hundred miles below the Arkansas, stopped by the edge of a swamp on the western side of the river. Here, as their two guides told them, was the path to the great town of the Taensas. Tonty and Membré were sent to visit it. They and their men shouldered their birch canoe through the swamp, and launched it on a lake which had once formed a portion of the channel of the river. In two hours, they reached the town; and Tonty gazed at it with astonishment. He had seen nothing like it in America: large square dwellings, built of sun-baked mud mixed with straw, arched over with a dome-shaped roof of canes, and placed in regular order around an open area. Two of them were larger and better than the rest. One was the lodge of the chief; the other was the temple, or house of the sun. They entered the former, and found a single room, forty feet square, where, in the dim light, —for there was no opening but the door,—the chief sat awaiting them on a sort of bedstead, three of his wives at his side, while sixty old men, wrapped in white cloaks woven of mulberry-bark, formed his divan. When he spoke, his wives howled to do him honor; and the assembled councillors listened with the reverence due to a potentate for whom, at his death, a hundred victims were to be sacrificed. He received the visitors graciously, and joyfully accepted the gifts which Tonty laid before him. This interview over, the Frenchmen repaired to the temple, wherein were kept the bones of the departed chiefs. In construction, it was much like the royal dwelling. Over it were rude wooden figures, representing three eagles turned towards the east. A strong mud wall surrounded it, planted with stakes, on which were stuck the skulls of enemies sacrificed to the sun; while before the door was a block of wood, on which lay a large shell surrounded with the braided hair of the victims. The interior was rude as a barn, dimly lighted from the doorway, and full of smoke. There was a structure in the middle which Membré thinks was a kind of altar; and before it burned a perpetual fire, fed with three logs laid end to end, and watched by two old men devoted to this sacred office. There was a mysterious recess, too, which the strangers were forbidden to explore, but which, as Tonty was told, contained the riches of the nation, consisting of pearls from the Gulf, and trinkets obtained, probably through other tribes, from the Spaniards and other Europeans.

The chief condescended to visit La Salle at his camp; a favor which he would by no means have granted, had the visitors been Indians. A master of ceremonies and six attendants preceded him, to clear the path and prepare the place of meeting. When all was ready, he was seen advancing, clothed in a white robe, and preceded by two men bearing white fans, while a third displayed a disk of burnished copper,—doubtless to represent the sun, his ancestor, or, as others will have it, his elder brother. His aspect was marvellously grave, and he and La Salle met with gestures of ceremonious courtesy. The interview was very friendly; and the chief returned well pleased with the gifts which his entertainer bestowed on him, and which, indeed, had been the principal motive of his visit.

On the next morning, as they descended the river, they saw a wooden canoe full of Indians; and Tonty gave chase. He had nearly overtaken it, when more than a hundred men appeared suddenly on the shore, with bows bent to defend their countrymen. La Salle called out to Tonty to withdraw. He obeyed; and the whole party encamped on the opposite bank. Tonty offered to cross the river with a peace-pipe, and set out accordingly with a small party of men. When he landed, the Indians made signs of friendship by joining their hands,—a proceeding by which Tonty, having but one hand, was somewhat embarrassed; but he directed his men to respond in his stead. La Salle and Membré now joined him, and went with the Indians to their village, three leagues distant. Here they spent the night. "The Sieur de la Salle," writes Membré, "whose very air, engaging manners, tact, and address attract love and respect alike, produced such an effect on the hearts of these people that they did not know how to treat us well enough."

The Indians of this village were the Natchez; and their chief was brother of the great chief, or Sun, of the whole nation. His town was several leagues distant, near the site of the city of Natchez; and thither the French repaired to visit him. They saw what they had already seen among the Taensas,—a religious and political despotism, a privileged caste descended from the sun, a temple, and a sacred fire. La Salle planted a large cross, with the arms of France attached, in the midst of the town; while the inhabitants looked on with a satisfaction which they would hardly have displayed, had they understood the meaning of the act.

The French next visited the Coroas, at their village, two leagues below; and here they found a reception no less auspicious. On the thirty-first of March, as they approached Red River, they passed in the fog a town of the Oumas, and, three days later, discovered a party of fishermen, in wooden canoes, among the canes along the margin of the water. They fled at sight of the Frenchmen. La Salle sent men to reconnoitre, who, as they struggled through the marsh, were greeted with a shower of arrows; while, from the neighboring village of the Quinipissas, invisible behind the canebrake, they heard the sound of an Indian drum and the whoops of the mustering warriors. La Salle, anxious to keep the peace with all the tribes along the river, recalled his men, and pursued his voyage. A few leagues below, they saw a cluster of Indian lodges on the left bank, apparently void of inhabitants. They landed, and found three of them filled with corpses. It was a village of the Tangibao, sacked by their enemies only a few days before.

And now they neared their journey's end. On the sixth of April the river divided itself into three broad channels. La Salle followed that of the west, and Dautray that of the east; while

Tonty took the middle passage. As he drifted down the turbid current, between the low and marshy shores, the brackish water changed to brine, and the breeze grew fresh with the salt breath of the sea. Then the broad bosom of the great Gulf opened on his sight, tossing its restless billows, limitless, voiceless, lonely as when born of chaos, without a sail, without a sign of life.

La Salle, in a canoe, coasted the marshy borders of the sea; and then the reunited parties assembled on a spot of dry ground, a short distance above the mouth of the river. Here a column was made ready, bearing the arms of France, and inscribed with the words,—

LOUIS LE GRAND, ROY DE FRANCE ET DE NAVARRE,
RÈGNE; LE NEUVIÈME AVRIL, 1682.

The Frenchmen were mustered under arms; and, while the New England Indians and their squaws looked on in wondering silence, they chanted the *Te Deum*, the *Exaudiat*, and the *Domine salvum fac Regem*. Then, amid volleys of musketry and shouts of *Vive le Roi*, La Salle planted the column in its place, and, standing near it, proclaimed in a loud voice,—

"In the name of the most high, mighty, invincible, and victorious Prince, Louis the Great, by the grace of God King of France and of Navarre, Fourteenth of that name, I, this ninth day of April, one thousand six hundred and eighty-two, in virtue of the commission of his Majesty, which I hold in my hand, and which may be seen by all whom it may concern, have taken, and do now take, in the name of his Majesty and of his successors to the crown, possession of this country of Louisiana, the seas, harbors, ports, bays, adjacent straits, and all the nations, peoples, provinces, cities, towns, villages, mines, minerals, fisheries, streams, and rivers, within the extent of the said Louisiana, from the mouth of the great river St. Louis, otherwise called the Ohio, . . . as also along the river Colbert, or Mississippi, and the rivers which discharge themselves thereinto, from its source beyond the country of the Nadouessioux . . . as far as its mouth at the sea, or Gulf of Mexico, and also to the mouth of the River of Palms, upon the assurance we have had from the natives of these countries, that we are the first Europeans who have descended or ascended the said river Colbert; hereby protesting against all who may hereafter undertake to invade any or all of these aforesaid countries, peoples, or lands, to the prejudice of the rights of his Majesty, acquired by the consent of the nations dwelling herein. Of which, and of all else that is needful, I hereby take to witness those who hear me, and demand an act of the notary here present."

Shouts of *Vive le Roi* and volleys of musketry responded to his words. Then a cross was planted beside the column, and a leaden plate buried near it, bearing the arms of France, with a Latin inscription, *Ludovicus Magnus regnat.* The weather-beaten voyagers joined their voices in the grand hymn of the *Vexilla Regis:*—

> "The banners of Heaven's King advance,
> The mystery of the Cross shines forth";

and renewed shouts of *Vive le Roi* closed the ceremony.

On that day, the realm of France received on parchment a stupendous accession. The fertile plains of Texas; the vast basin of the Mississippi, from its frozen northern springs to the sultry borders of the Gulf; from the woody ridges of the Alleghanies to the bare peaks of the Rocky Mountains,—a region of savannas and forests, sun-cracked deserts, and grassy prairies, watered by a thousand rivers, ranged by a thousand warlike tribes, passed beneath the sceptre of the Sultan of Versailles; and all by virtue of a feeble human voice, inaudible at half a mile.

[BISHOP LAVAL]

(From *The Old Régime in Canada*, 1874)

We are touching delicate ground. To many excellent Catholics of our own day Laval is an object of veneration. The Catholic university of Quebec glories in bearing his name, and certain modern ecclesiastical writers rarely mention him in terms less reverent than "the virtuous prelate," or "the holy prelate." Nor are some of his contemporaries less emphatic in eulogy.

Mother Juchereau de Saint-Denis, Superior of the Hôtel Dieu, wrote immediately after his death: "He began in his tenderest years the study of perfection, and we have reason to think that he reached it, since every virtue which Saint Paul demands in a bishop was seen and admired in him"; and on his first arrival in Canada, Mother Marie de l'Incarnation, Superior of the Ursulines, wrote to her son that the choice of such a prelate was not of man, but of God. "I will not," she adds, "say that he is a saint; but I may say with truth that he lives like a saint and an apostle." And she describes his austerity of life; how he had but two servants, a gardener—whom he lent on occasion to his needy neighbors—and a valet; how he lived in a small hired house, saying that he would not have one of his own if he could build it for only five sous; and how, in his table, furniture, and bed, he showed the spirit of poverty, even, as she thinks, to excess. His servant, a lay brother named Houssart, testified, after his death, that he slept on a hard bed, and would not suffer it to be changed even when it became full of fleas; and, what is more to the purpose, that he gave fifteen hundred or two thousand francs to the poor every year. Houssart also gives the following specimen of his austerities: "I have seen him keep cooked meat five, six, seven, or eight days in the heat of summer; and when it was all mouldy and wormy he washed it in warm water and ate it, and told me that it was very good." The old servant was so impressed by these and other proofs of his master's sanctity, that "I determined," he says, "to keep everything I could that had belonged to his holy person, and after his death to soak bits of linen in his blood when his body was opened, and take a few bones and cartilages from his breast, cut off his hair, and keep his clothes, and such things, to serve as most precious relics." These pious cares were not in vain, for the relics proved greatly in demand.

Several portraits of Laval are extant. A drooping nose of portentous size; a well-formed forehead; a brow strongly arched; a bright, clear eye; scanty hair, half hidden by a black skullcap; thin lips, compressed and rigid, betraying a spirit not easy to move or convince; features of that indescribable cast which marks the priestly type: such is Laval, as he looks grimly down on us from the dingy canvas of two centuries ago.

He is one of those concerning whom Protestants and Catholics, at least ultramontane Catholics, will never agree in judgment. The task of eulogizing him may safely be left to those of his own way of thinking. It is for us to regard him from the standpoint of secular history. And, first, let us credit him with sincerity. He believed firmly that the princes and rulers of this world ought to be subject to guidance and control at the hands of the Pope, the vicar of Christ on earth. But he himself was the Pope's vicar, and, so far as the bounds of Canada extended, the Holy Father had clothed him with his own authority. The glory of God demanded that this authority should suffer no abatement, and he, Laval, would be guilty before Heaven if he did not uphold the supremacy of the Church over the powers both of earth and of hell.

Of the faults which he owed to nature, the principal seems to have been an arbitrary and domineering temper. He was one of those who by nature lean always to the side of authority; and in the English Revolution he would inevitably have stood for the Stuarts; or, in the American Revolution, for the Crown. But being above all things a Catholic and a priest, he was drawn by a constitutional necessity to the ultramontane party, or the party of centralization. He fought lustily, in his way, against the natural man; and humility was the virtue to the culture of which he gave his chief attention, but soil and climate were not favorable. His life was one long assertion of the authority of the church, and this authority was lodged in himself. In his stubborn fight for ecclesiastical ascendancy, he was aided by the impulses of a nature that loved to rule, and could not endure to yield. His principles and his instinct of domination were acting in perfect unison, and his conscience was the handmaid of his fault. Austerities and mortifications, playing at beggar, sleeping in beds full of fleas, or performing prodigies of gratuitous dirtiness in hospitals, however fatal to self-respect, could avail little against influences working so powerfully and so insidiously to stimulate the most subtle of human vices. The history of the Roman church is full of Lavals.

The Jesuits, adepts in human nature, had made a sagacious choice when they put forward this conscientious, zealous, dogged, and pugnacious priest to fight their battles. Nor were they ill pleased that, for the present, he was not Bishop of Canada, but only vicar apostolic; for, such being the case, they could have him recalled if, on trial, they did not like him, while an unacceptable bishop would be an evil past remedy.

Canada was entering a state of transition. Hitherto ecclesiastical influence had been all in all. The Jesuits, by far the most educated and able body of men in the colony, had controlled it, not alone in things spiritual, but virtually in things temporal also; and the governor may be said to have been little else than a chief of police, under the direction of the missionaries. The early governors were themselves deeply imbued with the missionary spirit. Champlain was earnest above all things for converting the Indians; Montmagny was half-monk, for he was a Knight of Malta; Aillebout was so insanely pious, that he lived with his wife like monk and nun. A change was at hand. From a mission and a trading station, Canada was soon to become, in the true sense, a colony; and civil government had begun to assert itself on the banks of the St. Lawrence. The epoch of the martyrs and apostles was passing away, and the man of the sword and the man of the gown—the soldier and the legist—were threatening to supplant the paternal sway of priests: or, as Laval might have said, the hosts of this world were beleaguering the sanctuary, and he was called of Heaven to defend it. His true antagonist, though three thousand miles away, was the great minister Colbert, as purely a statesman as the vicar apostolic was purely a priest. Laval, no doubt, could see behind the statesman's back another adversary, the devil.

[HEROES OF THE LONG SAUT]

Canada had writhed for twenty years, with little respite, under the scourge of Iroquois war. During a great part of this dark period the entire French population was less than three thousand. What, then, saved them from destruction? In the first place, the settlements were grouped around three fortified posts, Quebec, Three Rivers, and Montreal, which in time of danger gave asylum to the fugitive inhabitants. Again, their assailants were continually distracted by other wars, and never, except at a few spasmodic intervals, were fully in earnest to destroy the French colony. Canada was indispensable to them. The four upper nations of the league soon became dependent on her for supplies; and all the nations alike appear, at a very early period, to have conceived the policy on which they afterwards distinctly acted, of balancing the rival settlements of the Hudson and the St. Lawrence, the one against the other. They would torture, but not kill. It was but rarely that, in fits of fury, they struck their hatchets at the brain; and thus the bleeding and gasping colony lingered on in torment.

The seneschal of New France, son of the governor Lauson, was surprised and killed on the island of Orleans, along with seven companions. About the same time, the same fate befell the son of Godefroy, one of the chief inhabitants of Quebec. Outside the fortifications there was no safety for a moment. A universal terror seized the people. A comet appeared above Quebec, and they saw in it a herald of destruction. Their excited imaginations turned natural phenomena into portents and prodigies. A blazing canoe sailed across the sky; confused cries and lamentations were heard in the air; and a voice of thunder sounded from mid-heaven. The Jesuits despaired for their scattered and persecuted flocks. "Everywhere," writes their superior, "we see infants to be saved for heaven, sick and dying to be baptized, adults to be instructed, but everywhere we see the Iroquois. They haunt us like persecuting goblins. They kill our new-made Christians in our arms. If they meet us on the river, they kill us. If they find us in the huts of our Indians, they burn us and them together." And he appeals urgently for troops to destroy them, as a holy work inspired by God, and needful for his service.

Canada was still a mission, and the influence of the Church was paramount and pervading. At Quebec, as at Montreal, the war with the Iroquois was regarded as a war with the hosts of

Satan. Of the settlers' cabins scattered along the shores above and below Quebec, many were provided with small iron cannon, made probably by blacksmiths in the colony; but they had also other protectors. In each was an image of the Virgin or some patron saint; and every morning the pious settler knelt before the shrine to beg the protection of a celestial hand in his perilous labors of the forest or the farm.

When, in the summer of 1658, the young Vicomte d'Argenson came to assume the thankless task of governing the colony, the Iroquois war was at its height. On the day after his arrival, he was washing his hands before seating himself at dinner in the hall of the Château St. Louis, when cries of alarm were heard, and he was told that the Iroquois were close at hand. In fact, they were so near that their war-whoops and the screams of their victims could plainly be heard. Argenson left his guests, and, with such a following as he could muster at the moment, hastened to the rescue; but the assailants were too nimble for him. The forests, which grew at that time around Quebec, favored them both in attack and in retreat. After a year or two of experience, he wrote urgently to the court for troops. He adds that, what with the demands of the harvest and the unmilitary character of many of the settlers, the colony could not furnish more than a hundred men for offensive operations. A vigorous, aggressive war, he insists, is absolutely necessary, and this not only to save the colony, but to save the only true faith; "for," to borrow his own words, "it is this colony alone which has the honor to be in the communion of the Holy Church. Everywhere else reigns the doctrine of England or Holland, to which I can give no other name, because there are as many creeds as there are subjects who embrace them. They do not care in the least whether the Iroquois and the other savages of this country have or have not a knowledge of the true God, or else they are so malicious as to inject the venom of their errors into souls incapable of distinguishing the truth of the gospel from the falsehoods of heresy; and hence it is plain that religion has its sole support in the French colony, and that, if this colony is in danger, religion is equally in danger."

Among the most interesting memorials of the time are two letters written by François Hertel, a youth of eighteen, captured at Three Rivers, and carried to the Mohawk towns in the summer of 1661. He belonged to one of the best families of Canada, and was the favorite child of his mother, to whom the second of the two letters is addressed. The first is to the Jesuit Le Moyne, who had gone to Onondaga, in July of that year, to effect the release of French prisoners in accordance with the terms of a truce. Both letters were written on birch bark:—

My Reverend Father:—The very day when you left Three Rivers I was captured, at about three in the afternoon, by four Iroquois of the Mohawk tribe. I would not have been taken alive, if, to my sorrow, I had not feared that I was not in a fit state to die. If you came here, my Father, I could have the happiness of confessing to you; and I do not think they would do you any harm; and I think that I could return home with you. I pray you to pity my poor mother, who is in great trouble. You know, my Father, how fond she is of me. I have heard from a Frenchman, who was taken at Three Rivers on the 1st of August, that she is well, and comforts herself with the hope that I shall see you. There are three of us Frenchmen alive here. I commend myself to your good prayers, and particularly to the Holy Sacrifice of the Mass. I pray you, my Father, to say a mass for me. I pray you give my dutiful love to my poor mother, and console her, if it pleases you.

My Father, I beg your blessing on the hand that writes to you, which has one of the fingers burned in the bowl of an Indian pipe, to satisfy the Majesty of God which I have offended. The thumb of the other hand is cut off; but do not tell my mother of it.

My Father, I pray you to honor me with a word from your hand in reply, and tell me if you shall come here before winter.

Your most humble and most obedient servant,

FRANÇOIS HERTEL.

The following is the letter to his mother, sent probably, with the other, to the charge of Le Moyne:—

My most dear and honored Mother:—I know very well that my capture must have distressed you very much. I ask you to forgive my disobedience. It is my sins that have placed me where I am. I owe my life to your prayers, and those of M. de Saint-Quentin, and of my sisters. I hope to see you again before winter. I pray you to tell the good brethren of Notre Dame to pray to God and the Holy Virgin for me, my dear mother, and for you and all my sisters.

Your poor
FANCHON.

This, no doubt, was the name by which she had called him familiarly when a child. And who was this "Fanchon," this devout and tender son of a fond mother? New England can answer to her cost. When, twenty-nine years later, a band of French and Indians issued from the forest and fell upon the fort and settlement of Salmon Falls, it was François Hertel who led the attack; and when the retiring victors were hard pressed by an overwhelming force, it was he who, sword in hand, held the pursuers in check at the bridge of Wooster River, and covered the retreat of his men. He was ennobled for his services, and died at the age of eighty, the founder of one of the most distinguished families of Canada. To the New England of old he was the abhorred chief of Popish malignants and murdering savages. The New England of to-day will be more just to the brave defender of his country and his faith.

In May, 1660, a party of French Algonquins captured a Wolf, or Mohegan, Indian, naturalized among the Iroquois, brought him to Quebec, and burned him there with their usual atrocity of torture. A modern Catholic writer says that the Jesuits could not save him; but this is not so. Their influence over the consciences of the colonists was at that time unbounded, and their direct political power was very great. A protest on their part, and that of the newly arrived bishop, who was in their interest, could not have failed of effect. The truth was, they did not care to prevent the torture of prisoners of war, not solely out of that spirit of compliance with the savage humor of Indian allies which stains so often the pages of French American history, but also, and perhaps chiefly, from motives purely religious. Torture, in their eyes, seems to have been a blessing in disguise. They thought it good for the soul, and in case of obduracy the surest way of salvation. "We have very rarely indeed," writes one of them, "seen the burning of an Iroquois without feeling sure that he was on the path to Paradise; and we never knew one of them to be surely on the path to Paradise without seeing him pass through this fiery punishment." So they let the Wolf burn; but first, having instructed him after their fashion, they baptized him, and his savage soul flew to heaven out of the fire. "Is it not," pursues the same writer, "a marvel to see a wolf changed at one stroke into a lamb, and enter into the fold of Christ, which he came to ravage?"

Before he died he requited their spiritual cares with a startling secret. He told them that eight hundred Iroquois warriors were encamped below Montreal; that four hundred more, who had wintered on the Ottawa, were on the point of joining them; and that the united force would swoop upon Quebec, kill the governor, lay waste the town, and then attack Three Rivers and Montreal. This time, at least, the Iroquois were in deadly earnest. Quebec was wild with terror. The Ursulines and the nuns of the Hôtel Dieu took refuge in the strong and extensive building which the Jesuits had just finished, opposite the Parish Church. Its walls and palisades made it easy of defence; and in its yards and court were lodged the terrified Hurons, as well as the fugitive inhabitants of the neighboring settlements. Others found asylum in the fort, and others in the convent of the Ursulines, which, in place of nuns, was occupied by twenty-four soldiers, who fortified it with redoubts, and barricaded the doors and windows. Similar measures of defence were taken at the Hôtel Dieu, and the streets of the Lower Town were strongly barricaded. Everybody was in arms, and the *Qui vive* of the sentries and patrols resounded all night.

Several days passed, and no Iroquois appeared. The refugees took heart, and began to return to their deserted farms and dwellings. Among the rest was a family consisting of an old woman, her daughter, her son-in-law, and four small children, living near St. Anne, some twenty miles below Quebec. On reaching home the old woman and the man went to their work in the fields, while the mother and children remained in the house. Here they were pounced upon and captured by eight renegade Hurons, Iroquois by adoption, who placed them in their large canoe, and paddled up the river with their prize. It was Saturday, a day dedicated to the Virgin; and the captive mother prayed to her for aid, "feeling," writes a Jesuit, "a full conviction that, in passing before Quebec on a Saturday, she would be delivered by the power of this Queen of Heaven." In fact, as the marauders and their captives glided in the darkness of night by Point Levi, under the shadow of the shore, they were greeted with a volley of musketry from the bushes, and a band of French and Algonquins dashed into the water to seize them. Five of the eight were taken, and the rest shot or drowned. The governor had heard of the descent at St. Anne, and despatched a party to lie in ambush for the authors of it. The Jesuits, it is needless to say, saw a miracle in the result. The Virgin had answered the prayer of her votary. "Though it is true," observes the father who records the marvel, "that, in the volley, she received a mortal wound." The same shot struck the infant in her arms. The prisoners were taken to Quebec, where four of them were tortured with even more ferocity than had been shown in the case of the unfortunate Wolf. Being questioned, they confirmed his story, and expressed great surprise that the Iroquois had not come, adding that they must have stopped to attack Montreal or Three Rivers. Again all was terror, and again days passed and no enemy appeared. Had the dying converts, so charitably despatched to heaven through fire, sought an unhallowed consolation in scaring the abettors of their torture with a lie? Not at all. Bating a slight exaggeration, they had told the truth. Where, then, were the Iroquois? As one small point of steel disarms the lightning of its terrors, so did the heroism of a few intrepid youths divert this storm of war and save Canada from a possible ruin.

In the preceding April, before the designs of the Iroquois were known, a young officer named Daulac, commandant of the garrison of Montreal, asked leave of Maisonneuve, the governor, to lead a party of volunteers against the enemy. His plan was bold to desperation. It was known that Iroquois warriors in great numbers had wintered among the forests of the Ottawa. Daulac proposed to waylay them on their descent of the river, and fight them without regard to disparity of force. The settlers of Montreal had hitherto acted solely on the defensive, for their numbers had been too small for aggressive war. Of late their strength had been somewhat increased, and Maisonneuve, judging that a display of enterprise and boldness might act as a check on the audacity of the enemy, at length gave his consent.

Adam Daulac, or Dollard, Sieur des Ormeaux, was a young man of good family, who had come to the colony three years before, at the age of twenty-two. He had held some military command in France, though in what rank does not appear. It was said that he had been involved in some affair which made him anxious to wipe out the memory of the past by a noteworthy exploit; and he had been busy for some time among the young men of Montreal, inviting them to join him in the enterprise he meditated. Sixteen of them caught his spirit, struck hands with him, and pledged their word. They bound themselves by oath to accept no quarter; and, having gained Maisonneuve's consent, they made their wills, confessed, and received the sacraments. As they knelt for the last time before the altar in the chapel of the Hôtel Dieu, that sturdy little population of pious Indian-fighters gazed on them with enthusiasm, not unmixed with an envy which had in it nothing ignoble. Some of the chief men of Montreal, with the brave Charles Le Moyne at their head, begged them to wait till the spring sowing was over, that they might join them; but Daulac refused. He was jealous of the glory and the danger, and he wished to command, which he could not have done had Le Moyne been present.

The spirit of the enterprise was purely mediæval. The enthusiasm of honor, the enthusiasm of adventure, and the enthusiasm of faith were its motive forces. Daulac was a knight of the early crusades among the forests and savages of the New World. Yet the incidents of this exotic heroism are definite and clear as a tale of yesterday. The names, ages, and occupations of the seventeen young men may still be read on the ancient register of the parish of Montreal; and the notarial acts of that year, preserved in the records of the city, contain minute accounts of such property as each of them possessed. The three eldest were of twenty-eight, thirty, and thirty-one years respectively. The age of the rest varied from twenty-one to twenty-seven. They were of various callings,—soldiers, armorers, locksmiths, lime-burners, or settlers without trades. The greater number had come to the colony as part of the reinforcement brought by Maisonneuve in 1653.

After a solemn farewell they embarked in several canoes well supplied with arms and ammunition. They were very indifferent canoe-men; and it is said that they lost a week in vain attempts to pass the swift current of St. Anne, at the head of the island of Montreal. At length they were more successful, and entering the mouth of the Ottawa, crossed the Lake of Two Mountains, and slowly advanced against the current.

Meanwhile, forty warriors of that remnant of the Hurons who, in spite of Iroquois persecutions, still lingered at Quebec, had set out on a war-party, led by the brave and wily Etienne Annahotaha, their most noted chief. They stopped by the way at Three Rivers, where they found a band of Christian Algonquins under a chief named Mituvemeg. Annahotaha challenged him to a trial of courage, and it was agreed that they should meet at Montreal, where they were likely to find a speedy opportunity of putting their mettle to the test. Thither, accordingly, they repaired, the Algonquin with three followers, and the Huron with thirty-nine.

It was not long before they learned the departure of Daulac and his companions. "For," observes the honest Dollier de Casson, "the principal fault of our Frenchmen is to talk too much." The wish seized them to share the adventure, and to that end the Huron chief asked the governor for a letter to Daulac, to serve as credentials. Maisonneuve hesitated. His faith in Huron valor was not great, and he feared the proposed alliance. Nevertheless, he at length yielded so far as to give Annahotaha a letter, in which Daulac was told to accept or reject the proffered reinforcement as he should see fit. The Hurons and Algonquins now embarked and paddled in pursuit of the seventeen Frenchmen.

They meanwhile had passed with difficulty the swift current at Carillon, and about the first of May reached the foot of the more formidable rapid called the Long Saut, where a tumult of waters, foaming among ledges and boulders, barred the onward way. It was needless to go farther. The Iroquois were sure to pass the Saut, and could be fought here as well as elsewhere. Just below the rapid, where the forests sloped gently to the shore, among the bushes and stumps of the rough clearing made in constructing it, stood a palisade fort, the work of an Algonquin war-party in the past autumn. It was a mere enclosure of trunks of small trees planted in a circle, and was already ruinous. Such as it was, the Frenchmen took possession of it. Their first care, one would think, should have been to repair and strengthen it; but this they seem not to have done: possibly, in the exaltation of their minds, they scorned such precaution. They made their fires, and slung their kettles on the neighboring shore; and here they were soon joined by the Hurons and Algonquins. Daulac, it seems, made no objection to their company, and they all bivouacked together. Morning and noon and night they prayed in three different tongues; and when at sunset the long reach of forests on the farther shore basked peacefully in the level rays, the rapids joined their hoarse music to the notes of their evening hymn.

In a day or two their scouts came in with tidings that two Iroquois canoes were coming down the Saut. Daulac had time to set his men in ambush among the bushes at a point where he thought the strangers likely to land. He judged aright. The canoes, bearing five Iroquois, approached, and were met by a volley fired with such precipitation that one or more of them escaped the shot, fled into the forest, and told their mischance to their main body, two hundred in number, on the river above. A fleet of canoes suddenly appeared, bounding down the rapids, filled with warriors eager for revenge. The allies had barely time to escape to their fort, leaving their kettles still slung over the fires. The Iroquois made a hasty and desultory attack, and were quickly repulsed. They next opened a parley, hoping, no doubt, to gain some advantage by surprise. Failing in this, they set themselves, after their custom on such occasions, to building a rude fort of their own in the neighboring forest.

This gave the French a breathing-time, and they used it for strengthening their defences. Being provided with tools, they planted a row of stakes within their palisade, to form a double fence, and filled the intervening space with earth and stones to the height of a man, leaving some twenty loop-holes, at each of which three marksmen were stationed. Their work was still unfinished when the Iroquois were upon them again. They had broken to pieces the birch canoes of the French and their allies, and, kindling the bark, rushed up to pile it blazing against the palisade; but so brisk and steady a fire met them that they recoiled, and at last gave way. They came on again, and again were driven back, leaving many of their number on the ground, —among them the principal chief of the Senecas. Some of the French dashed out, and, covered by the fire of their comrades, hacked off his head, and stuck it on the palisade, while the Iroquois howled in a frenzy of helpless rage. They tried another attack, and were beaten off a third time.

This dashed their spirits, and they sent a canoe to call to their aid five hundred of their warriors who were mustered near the mouth of the Richelieu. These were the allies whom, but for this untoward check, they were on their way to join for a combined attack on Quebec, Three Rivers, and Montreal. It was maddening to see their grand project thwarted by a few French and Indians ensconced in a paltry redoubt, scarcely better than a cattle-pen; but they were forced to digest the affront as best they might.

Meanwhile, crouched behind trees and logs, they beset the fort, harassing its defenders day and night with a spattering fire and a constant menace of attack. Thus five days passed. Hunger, thirst, and want of sleep wrought fatally on the strength of the French and their allies, who, pent up together in their narrow prison, fought and prayed by turns. Deprived as they were of water, they could not swallow the crushed Indian corn, or "hominy," which was their only food. Some of them, under cover of a brisk fire, ran down to the river and filled such small vessels as they had; but this pittance only tantalized their thirst. They dug a hole in the fort, and were rewarded at last by a little muddy water oozing through the clay.

Among the assailants were a number of Hurons, adopted by the Iroquois and fighting on their side. These renegades now shouted to their countrymen in the fort, telling them that a fresh army was close at hand; that they would soon be attacked by seven or eight hundred warriors; and that their only hope was in joining the Iroquois, who would receive them as friends. Annahotaha's followers, half dead with thirst and famine, listened to their seducers, took the bait, and, one, two, or three at a time, climbed the palisade and ran over to the enemy, amid the hootings and execrations of those whom they deserted. Their chief stood firm; and when he saw his nephew, La Mouche, join the other fugitives, he fired his pistol at him in a rage. The four Algonquins, who had no mercy to hope for, stood fast, with the courage of despair.

On the fifth day an uproar of unearthly yells from seven hundred savage throats, mingled with a clattering salute of musketry, told the Frenchmen that the expected reinforcement had come; and soon, in the forest and on the clearing, a crowd of warriors mustered for the attack. Knowing from the Huron deserters the weakness of their enemy, they had no doubt of an easy victory. They advanced cautiously, as was usual with the Iroquois before their blood was up, screeching, leaping from side to side, and firing as they came on; but the French were at their posts, and every loophole darted its tongue of fire. Besides muskets, they had heavy musketoons of large calibre, which, scattering scraps of lead and iron among the throng of savages, often maimed several of them at one discharge. The Iroquois, astonished at the persistent vigor of the defence, fell back discomfited. The fire of the French, who were themselves completely under cover, had told upon them with deadly effect. Three days more wore away in a series of futile attacks, made with little concert or vigor; and during all this time Daulac and his men, reeling with exhaustion, fought and prayed as before, sure of a martyr's reward.

The uncertain, vacillating temper common to all Indians now began to declare itself. Some of the Iroquois were for going home. Others revolted at the thought, and declared that it would be an eternal disgrace to lose so many men at the hands of so paltry an enemy, and yet fail to take revenge. It was resolved to make a general assault, and volunteers were called for to lead the attack. After the custom on such occasions, bundles of small sticks were thrown upon the ground, and those picked them up who dared, thus accepting the gage of battle, and enrolling themselves in the forlorn hope. No precaution was neglected. Large and heavy shields four or five feet high were made by lashing together three split logs with the aid of crossbars. Covering themselves with these mantelets, the chosen band advanced, followed by the motley throng of warriors. In spite of a brisk fire, they reached the palisade, and, crouching below the range of shot, hewed furiously with their hatchets to cut their way through. The rest followed close, and swarmed like angry hornets around the little fort, hacking and tearing to get in.

Daulac had crammed a large musketoon with powder, and plugged up the muzzle. Lighting the fuse inserted in it, he tried to throw it over the barrier, to burst like a grenade among the crowd of savages without; but it struck the ragged top of one of the palisades, fell back among the Frenchmen and exploded, killing and wounding several of them, and nearly blinding others. In the confusion that followed, the Iroquois got possession of the loopholes, and, thrusting in their guns, fired on those within. In a moment more they had torn a breach in the palisade; but, nerved with the energy of desperation, Daulac and his followers sprang to defend it. Another breach was made, and then another. Daulac was struck dead, but the survivors kept up the fight. With a sword or a hatchet in one hand and a knife in the other, they threw themselves against the throng of enemies, striking and stabbing with the fury of madmen; till the Iroquois, despairing of taking them alive, fired volley after volley and shot them down. All was over, and a burst of triumphant yells proclaimed the dear-bought victory.

Searching the pile of corpses, the victors found four Frenchmen still breathing. Three had scarcely a spark of life, and, as no time was to be lost, they burned them on the spot. The fourth, less fortunate, seemed likely to survive, and they reserved him for future torments. As for the Huron deserters, their cowardice profited them little. The Iroquois, regardless of their promises, fell upon them, burned some at once, and carried the rest to their villages for a similar fate. Five of the number had the good fortune to escape; and it was from them, aided by admissions made long afterwards by the Iroquois themselves, that the French of Canada derived all their knowledge of this glorious disaster.

To the colony it proved a salvation. The Iroquois had had fighting enough. If seventeen Frenchmen, four Algonquins, and one Huron, behind a picket fence, could hold seven hundred warriors at bay so long, what might they expect from many such, fighting behind walls of stone? For that year they thought no more of capturing Quebec and Montreal, but went home dejected and amazed, to howl over their losses, and nurse their dashed courage for a day of vengeance.

[THE CANADIAN FRONTIER]

We have seen the settler landed and married; let us follow him to his new home. At the end of Talon's administration, the head of the colony, that is to say the island of Montreal and the borders of the Richelieu, was the seat of a peculiar colonization, the chief object of which was to protect the rest of Canada against Iroquois incursions. The lands along the Richelieu, from its mouth to a point above Chambly, were divided in large seigniorial grants among several officers of the regiment of Carignan, who in their turn granted out the land to the soldiers, reserving a sufficient portion as their own. The officer thus became a kind of feudal chief, and the whole settlement a permanent military cantonment admirably suited to the object in view. The disbanded soldier was practically a soldier still, but he was also a farmer and a landholder.

Talon had recommended this plan as being in accordance with the example of the Romans. "The practice of that politic and martial people," he wrote, "may, in my opinion, be wisely adopted in a country a thousand leagues distant from its monarch. And as the peace and harmony of peoples depend above all things on their fidelity to their sovereign, our first kings, better statesmen than is commonly supposed, introduced into newly conquered countries men of war, of approved trust, in order at once to hold the inhabitants to their duty within, and repel the enemy from without."

The troops were accordingly discharged, and settled not alone on the Richelieu, but also along the St. Lawrence, between Lake St. Peter and Montreal, as well as at some other points. The Sulpitians, feudal owners of Montreal, adopted a similar policy, and surrounded their island with a border of fiefs large and small, granted partly to officers and partly to humbler settlers, bold, hardy, and practised in bush-fighting. Thus a line of sentinels was posted around their entire shore, ready to give the alarm whenever an enemy appeared. About Quebec the settlements, covered as they were by those above, were for the most part of a more pacific character.

To return to the Richelieu. The towns and villages which have since grown upon its banks and along the adjacent shores of the St. Lawrence owe their names to these officers of Carignan, ancient lords of the soil: Sorel, Chambly, Saint Ours, Contrecœur, Varennes, Verchères. Yet let it not be supposed that villages sprang up at once. The military seignior, valiant and poor as Walter the Penniless, was in no condition to work such magic. His personal possessions usually consisted of little but his sword and the money which the king had paid him for marrying a wife. A domain varying from half a league to six leagues in front on the river, and from half a league to two leagues in depth, had been freely given him. When he had distributed a part of it in allotments to the soldiers, a variety of tasks awaited him: to clear and cultivate his land; to build his seigniorial mansion, often a log hut; to build a fort; to build a chapel; and to build a mill. To do all this at once was impossible. Chambly, the chief proprietor on the Richelieu, was better able than the others to meet the exigency. He built himself a good house, where, with cattle and sheep furnished by the king, he lived in reasonable comfort. The king's fort, close at hand, spared him and his tenants the necessity of building one for themselves, and furnished, no doubt, a mill, a chapel, and a chaplain. His brother officers, Sorel excepted, were less fortunate. They and their tenants were forced to provide defence as well as shelter. Their houses were all built together, and surrounded by a palisade, so as to form a little fortified village. The ever-active benevolence of the king had aided them in the task, for the soldiers were still maintained by him while clearing the lands and building the houses destined to be their own; nor was it till this work was done that the provident government despatched them to Quebec with orders to bring back wives. The settler, thus lodged and wedded, was required on his part to aid in clearing lands for those who should come after him.

It was chiefly in the more exposed parts of the colony, that the houses were gathered together in palisaded villages, thus forcing the settler to walk or paddle some distance to his farm. He naturally preferred to build when he could on the front of his farm itself, near the river, which supplied the place of a road. As the grants of land were very narrow, his house was not far from that of his next neighbor, and thus a line of dwellings was ranged along the shore, forming what in local language was called a *côte*, a use of the word peculiar to Canada, where it still prevails.

The impoverished seignior rarely built a chapel. Most of the early Canadian churches were built with funds furnished by the seminaries of Quebec or of Montreal, aided by contributions of material and labor from the parishioners. Meanwhile mass was said in some house of the neighborhood by a missionary priest, paddling his canoe from village to village, or from *côte* to *côte*.

The mill was an object of the last importance. It was built of stone and pierced with loopholes, to serve as a blockhouse in case of attack. The great mill at Montreal was one of the chief defences of the place. It was at once the duty and the right of the seignior to supply his tenants, or rather vassals, with this essential requisite, and they on their part were required to grind their grain at his mill, leaving the fourteenth part in payment. But for many years there was not a seigniory in Canada, where this fraction would pay the wages of a miller; and, except the ecclesiastical corporations, there were few seigniors who could pay the cost of building. The first settlers were usually forced to grind for themselves after the tedious fashion of the Indians.

Talon, in his capacity of counsellor, friend, and father to all Canada, arranged the new settlements near Quebec in the manner which he judged best, and which he meant to serve as an example to the rest of the colony. It was his aim to concentrate population around this point, so that, should an enemy appear, the sound of a cannon-shot from the Château St. Louis might summon a numerous body of defenders to this the common point of rendezvous. He bought a tract of land near Quebec, laid it out, and settled it as a model seigniory, hoping, as he says, to kindle a spirit of emulation among the new-made seigniors to whom he had granted lands from the king. He also laid out at the royal cost three villages in the immediate neighborhood, planning them with great care, and peopling them partly with families newly arrived, partly with soldiers, and partly with old settlers, in order that the new-comers might take lessons from the experience of these veterans. That each village might be complete in itself, he furnished it as well as he could with the needful carpenter, mason, blacksmith, and shoemaker. These inland villages, called respectively Bourg Royal, Bourg la Reine, and Bourg Talon, did not prove very thrifty. Wherever the settlers were allowed to choose for themselves, they ranged their dwellings along the watercourses. With the exception of Talon's villages, one could have seen nearly every house in Canada, by paddling a canoe up the St. Lawrence and the Richelieu. The settlements formed long thin lines on the edges of the rivers; a convenient arrangement, but one very unfavorable to defence, to ecclesiastical control, and to strong government. The king soon discovered this; and repeated orders were sent to concentrate the inhabitants and form Canada into villages, instead of *côtes*. To do so would have involved a general revocation of grants and abandonment of houses and clearings, a measure too arbitrary and too wasteful, even for Louis XIV., and one extremely difficult to enforce. Canada persisted in attenuating herself, and the royal will was foiled.

As you ascended the St. Lawrence, the first harboring place of civilization was Tadoussac, at the mouth of the Saguenay, where the company had its trading station, where its agents ruled supreme, and where, in early summer, all was alive with canoes and wigwams, and troops of Montagnais savages, bringing their furs to market. Leave Tadoussac behind, and, embarked in a sail-boat or a canoe, follow the northern coast. Far on the left, twenty miles away, the southern shore lies pale and dim, and mountain ranges wave their faint outline along the sky. You pass the beetling rocks of Mal Bay, a solitude but for the bark hut of some wandering Indian beneath the cliff; the Eboulements with their wild romantic gorge, and foaming waterfalls; and the Bay of St. Paul with its broad valley and its woody mountains, rich with hidden stores of iron. Vast piles of savage verdure border the mighty stream, till at length the mountain of Cape Tourmente upheaves its huge bulk from the bosom of the water, shadowed by lowering clouds, and dark with forests. Just beyond, begin the settlements of Laval's vast seigniory of Beaupré, which had not been forgotten in the distribution of emigrants, and which, in 1667, contained more inhabitants than Quebec itself. The ribbon of rich meadow land that borders that beautiful shore, was yellow with wheat in harvest time, and on the woody slopes behind, the frequent clearings and the solid little dwellings of logs continued for a long distance to relieve the sameness of the forest. After passing the cataract of Montmorenci, there was another settlement, much smaller, at Beauport, the seigniory of the ex-physician Giffard, one of the earliest proprietors in Canada. The neighboring shores of the island of Orleans were also edged with houses and clearings. The promontory of Quebec now towered full in sight, crowned with church, fort, château, convents, and seminary. There was little else on the rock. Priests, nuns, government officials, and soldiers were the denizens of the Upper Town; while commerce and the trades were cabined along the strand beneath. From the gallery of the château, you might toss a pebble far down on their shingled roofs. In the midst of them was the magazine of the company, with its two round towers and two projecting wings. It was here that all the beaver-skins of the colony were collected, assorted, and shipped for France. The so-called Château St. Louis was an indifferent wooden structure planted on a site truly superb; above the Lower Town, above the river, above the ships, gazing abroad on a majestic panorama of waters, forests, and mountains. Behind it was the area of the fort, of which it formed one side. The governor lived in the château, and soldiers were on guard night and day in the fort. At some little distance was the convent of the Ursulines, ugly but substantial, where Mother Mary of the Incarnation ruled her pupils and her nuns; and a little further on, towards the right, was the Hôtel Dieu. Between them were the massive buildings of the Jesuits, then as now facing the principal square. At one side was their church, newly finished; and opposite, across the square, stood and still stands the great church of Notre Dame. Behind the church was Laval's seminary, with the extensive enclosures belonging to it. The *séné-chaussée* or court-house, the tavern of one Jacques Boisdon on the square near the church, and a few houses along the line of what is now St. Louis Street comprised nearly all the civil part of the Upper Town. The ecclesiastical buildings were of stone, and the church of Notre Dame and the Jesuit College were marvels of size and solidity in view of the poverty and weakness of the colony.

Proceeding upward along the north shore of the St. Lawrence, one found a cluster of houses at Cap Rouge, and, further on, the frequent rude beginnings of a seigniory. The settlements thickened on approaching Three Rivers, a fur-trading hamlet enclosed with a square palisade. Above this place, a line of incipient seigniories bordered the river, most of them granted to officers: Laubia, a captain; Labadie, a sergeant; Moras, an ensign; Berthier, a captain; Raudin, an ensign; La Valterie, a lieutenant. Under their auspices, settlers, military and civilian, were ranging themselves along the shore, and ugly gaps in the forest thickly set with stumps bore witness to their toils. These settlements rapidly extended, till in a few years a chain of houses and clearings reached with little interruption from Quebec to Montreal. Such was the fruit of Tracy's chastisement of the Mohawks, and the influx of immigrants that followed.

As you approached Montreal, the fortified mill built by the Sulpitians at Point aux Trembles towered above the woods; and soon after the newly built chapel of the Infant Jesus. More settlements followed, till at length the great fortified mill of Montreal rose in sight; then the long row of compact wooden houses, the Hôtel Dieu, and the rough masonry of the Seminary of St. Sulpice. Beyond the town, the clearings continued at intervals till you reached Lake St. Louis, where young Cavelier de la Salle had laid out his seigniory of La Chine, and abandoned it to begin his hard career of western exploration. Above the island of Montreal, the wilderness was broken only by a solitary trading station on the neighboring Isle Pérot.

Now cross Lake St. Louis, shoot the rapids of La Chine, and follow the southern shore downward. Here the seigniories of Longueuil, Boucherville, Varennes, Verchères, and Contrecœur were already begun. From the fort of Sorel one could visit the military seigniories along the Richelieu or descend towards Quebec, passing on the way those of Lussaudière, Becancour, Lotbinière, and others still in a shapeless infancy. Even far below Quebec, at St. Anne de la Pocatière, River Ouelle, and other points, cabins and clearings greeted the eye of the passing canoeman.

For a year or two, the settler's initiation was a rough one; but when he had a few acres under tillage he could support himself and his family on the produce, aided by hunting, if he knew how to use a gun, and by the bountiful profusion of eels which the St. Lawrence never failed to yield in their season, and which, smoked or salted, supplied his larder for months. In winter he hewed timber, sawed planks, or split shingles for the market of Quebec, obtaining in return such necessaries as he required. With thrift and hard work he was sure of comfort at last; but the former habits of the military settlers and of many of the others were not favorable to a routine of dogged industry. The same- ness and solitude of their new life often became insufferable; nor, married as they had been, was the domestic hearth likely to supply much consolation. Yet, thrifty or not, they multiplied apace. "A poor man," says Mother Mary, "will have eight children and more, who run about in winter with bare heads and bare feet, and a little jacket on their backs, live on nothing but bread and eels, and on that grow fat and stout." With such treatment the weaker sort died; but the strong survived, and out of this rugged nursing sprang the hardy Canadian race of bush-rangers and bush-fighters.

[THE IMPORTANCE OF ABSOLUTISM IN CANADA]

Not institutions alone, but geographical position, climate, and many other conditions unite to form the educational in- fluences that, acting through successive generations, shape the character of nations and communities.

It is easy to see the nature of the education, past and present, which wrought on the Canadians and made them what they were. An ignorant population, sprung from a brave and active race, but trained to subjection and dependence through cen- turies of feudal and monarchical despotism, was planted in the wilderness by the hand of authority, and told to grow and flour- ish. Artificial stimulants were applied, but freedom was with- held. Perpetual intervention of government, regulations, re- strictions, encouragements sometimes more mischievous than restrictions, a constant uncertainty what the authorities would do next, the fate of each man resting less with himself than with another, volition enfeebled, self-reliance paralyzed,—the con- dition, in short, of a child held always under the rule of a father,

in the main well-meaning and kind, sometimes generous, sometimes neglectful, often capricious, and rarely very wise,—such
were the influences under which Canada grew up. If she had
prospered, it would have been sheer miracle. A man, to be a
man, must feel that he holds his fate, in some good measure, in
his own hands.

But this was not all. Against absolute authority there was a
counter influence, rudely and wildly antagonistic. Canada was
at the very portal of the great interior wilderness. The St.
Lawrence and the Lakes were the highway to that domain of
savage freedom; and thither the disfranchised, half-starved
seignior, and the discouraged *habitant* who could find no market for his produce, naturally enough betook themselves. Their
lesson of savagery was well learned, and for many a year a
boundless license and a stiff-handed authority battled for the
control of Canada. Nor, to the last, were church and state
fairly masters of the field. The French rule was drawing towards
its close when the intendant complained that though twenty-
eight companies of regular troops were quartered in the colony,
there were not soldiers enough to keep the people in order.
One cannot but remember that in a neighboring colony, far
more populous, perfect order prevailed, with no other guardians than a few constables chosen by the people themselves.

Whence arose this difference, and other differences equally
striking, between the rival colonies? It is easy to ascribe them
to a difference of political and religious institutions; but the explanation does not cover the ground. The institutions of New
England were utterly inapplicable to the population of New
France, and the attempt to apply them would have wrought
nothing but mischief. There are no political panaceas, except
in the imagination of political quacks. To each degree and
each variety of public development there are corresponding institutions, best answering the public needs; and what is meat
to one is poison to another. Freedom is for those who are fit
for it. The rest will lose it, or turn it to corruption. Church and
state were right in exercising authority over a people which
had not learned the first rudiments of self-government. Their

fault was not that they exercised authority, but that they exercised too much of it, and, instead of weaning the child to go alone, kept him in perpetual leading-strings, making him, if possible, more and more dependent, and less and less fit for freedom.

In the building up of colonies, England succeeded and France failed. The cause lies chiefly in the vast advantage drawn by England from the historical training of her people in habits of reflection, forecast, industry, and self-reliance,—a training which enabled them to adopt and maintain an invigorating system of self-rule, totally inapplicable to their rivals.

The New England colonists were far less fugitives from oppression than voluntary exiles seeking the realization of an idea. They were neither peasants nor soldiers, but a substantial Puritan yeomanry, led by Puritan gentlemen and divines in thorough sympathy with them. They were neither sent out by the king, governed by him, nor helped by him. They grew up in utter neglect, and continued neglect was the only boon they asked. Till their increasing strength roused the jealousy of the Crown, they were virtually independent; a republic, but by no means a democracy. They chose their governor and all their rulers from among themselves, made their own government and paid for it, supported their own clergy, defended themselves, and educated themselves. Under the hard and repellent surface of New England society lay the true foundations of a stable freedom,—conscience, reflection, faith, patience, and public spirit. The cement of common interests, hopes, and duties compacted the whole people like a rock of conglomerate; while the people of New France remained in a state of political segregation, like a basket of pebbles held together by the enclosure that surrounds them.

It may be that the difference of historical antecedents would alone explain the difference of character between the rival colonies; but there are deeper causes, the influence of which went far to determine the antecedents themselves. The Germanic race, and especially the Anglo-Saxon branch of it, is peculiarly masculine, and, therefore, peculiarly fitted for self-government. It submits its action habitually to the guidance of reason, and has the judicial faculty of seeing both sides of a question. The French Celt is cast in a different mould. He sees the end distinctly, and reasons about it with an admirable clearness; but his own impulses and passions continually turn him away from it. Opposition excites him; he is impatient of delay, is impelled always to extremes, and does not readily sacrifice a present inclination to an ultimate good. He delights in abstractions and generalizations, cuts loose from unpleasing facts, and roams through an ocean of desires and theories.

While New England prospered and Canada did not prosper, the French system had at least one great advantage. It favored military efficiency. The Canadian population sprang in great part from soldiers, and was to the last systematically reinforced by disbanded soldiers. Its chief occupation was a continual training for forest war; it had little or nothing to lose, and little to do but fight and range the woods. This was not all. The Canadian government was essentially military. At its head was a soldier nobleman, often an old and able commander, and those beneath him caught his spirit and emulated his example. In spite of its political nothingness, in spite of poverty and hardship, and in spite even of trade, the upper stratum of Canadian society was animated by the pride and fire of that gallant *noblesse* which held war as its only worthy calling, and prized honor more than life. As for the *habitant*, the forest, lake, and river were his true school; and here, at least, he was an apt scholar. A skilful woodsman, a bold and adroit canoe-man, a willing fighter in time of need, often serving without pay, and receiving from government only his provisions and his canoe, he was more than ready at any time for any hardy enterprise; and in the forest warfare of skirmish and surprise there were few to match him. An absolute government used him at will, and experienced leaders guided his rugged valor to the best account.

The New England man was precisely the same material with that of which Cromwell formed his invincible "Ironsides"; but he had very little forest experience. His geographical position cut him off completely from the great wilderness of the interior. The sea was his field of action. Without the aid of government, and in spite of its restrictions, he built up a prosperous commerce, and enriched himself by distant fisheries, neglected by the rivals before whose doors they lay. He knew every ocean from Greenland to Cape Horn, and the whales of the north and of the south had no more dangerous foe. But he was too busy to fight without good cause, and when he turned his hand to soldiering it was only to meet some pressing need of the hour. The New England troops in the early wars were bands of raw fishermen and farmers, led by civilians decorated with military titles, and subject to the slow and uncertain action of legislative bodies. The officers had not learned to command, nor the men to obey. The remarkable exploit of the capture of Louisburg, the strongest fortress in America, was the result of mere audacity and hardihood, backed by the rarest good luck.

One great fact stands out conspicuous in Canadian history,—the Church of Rome. More even than the royal power she shaped the character and the destinies of the colony. She was its nurse and almost its mother; and, wayward and headstrong as it was, it never broke the ties of faith that held it to her. It was these ties which, in the absence of political franchises, formed under the old régime the only vital coherence in the population. The royal government was transient; the church was permanent. The English conquest shattered the whole apparatus of civil administration at a blow, but it left her untouched. Governors, intendants, councils, and commandants, all were gone; the principal seigniors fled the colony; and a people who had never learned to control themselves or help themselves were suddenly left to their own devices. Confusion, if not anarchy, would have followed but for the parish priests, who in a character of double paternity, half spiritual and half temporal, became more than ever the guardians of order throughout Canada.

This English conquest was the grand crisis of Canadian history. It was the beginning of a new life. With England came Protestantism, and the Canadian church grew purer and better in the presence of an adverse faith. Material growth, an increased mental activity, an education real though fenced and guarded, a warm and genuine patriotism, all date from the peace of 1763. England imposed by the sword on reluctant Canada the boon of rational and ordered liberty. Through centuries of striving she had advanced from stage to stage of progress, deliberate and calm,—never breaking with her past, but making each fresh gain the base of a new success, enlarging popular liberties while bating nothing of that height and force of individual development which is the brain and heart of civilization; and now, through a hard-earned victory, she taught the conquered colony to share the blessings she had won. A happier calamity never befell a people than the conquest of Canada by the British arms.

[FRONTENAC AND PHIPS: A PURITAN
CRUSADE AGAINST QUEBEC]

(From *Frontenac and New France under Louis XIV*)

When he [Phips] returned from Port Royal, he found Boston alive with martial preparation. A bold enterprise was afoot. Massachusetts of her own motion had resolved to attempt the conquest of Quebec. She and her sister colonies had not yet recovered from the exhaustion of Philip's war, and still less from the disorders that attended the expulsion of the royal governor and his adherents. The public treasury was empty, and the recent expeditions against the eastern Indians had been supported by private subscription. Worse yet, New England had no competent military commander. The Puritan gentlemen of the original emigration, some of whom were as well fitted for military as for civil leadership, had passed from the stage; and, by a tendency which circumstances made inevitable, they had left none behind them equally qualified. The great Indian conflict of fifteen years before had, it is true, formed good partisan chiefs, and proved that the New England yeoman, defending his family and his hearth, was not to be surpassed in stubborn fighting; but, since Andros and his soldiers had been driven out, there was scarcely a single man in the colony of the slightest training or experience in regular war. Up to this moment, New England had never asked help of the mother country. When thousands of savages burst on her defenceless settlements, she had conquered safety and peace with her own blood and her own slender resources; but now, as the proposed capture of Quebec would inure to the profit of the British Crown, Bradstreet and his council thought it not unfitting to ask for a supply of arms and ammunition, of which they were in great need. The request was refused, and no aid of any kind came from the English government, whose resources were engrossed by the Irish war.

While waiting for the reply, the colonial authorities urged on their preparations, in the hope that the plunder of Quebec would pay the expenses of its conquest. Humility was not among the New England virtues, and it was thought a sin to doubt that God would give his chosen people the victory over papists and idolaters; yet no pains were spared to ensure the divine favor. A proclamation was issued, calling the people to repentance; a day of fasting was ordained; and, as Mather expresses it, "the wheel of prayer was kept in continual motion." The chief difficulty was to provide funds. An attempt was made to collect a part of the money by private subscription; but, as this plan failed, the provisional government, already in debt, strained its credit yet farther, and borrowed the needful sums. Thirty-two trading and fishing vessels, great and small, were impressed for the service. The largest was a ship called the "Six Friends," engaged in the dangerous West India trade, and carrying forty-four guns. A call was made for volunteers, and many enrolled themselves; but, as more were wanted, a press was ordered to complete the number. So rigorously was it applied that, what with voluntary and enforced enlistment, one town, that of Gloucester, was deprived of two-thirds of its fencible men. There was not a moment of doubt as to the choice of a commander, for Phips was imagined to be the very man for the work. One John Walley, a respectable citizen of Barnstable, was made second in command with the modest rank of major;

and a sufficient number of ship-masters, merchants, master mechanics, and substantial farmers, were commissioned as subordinate officers. About the middle of July, the committee charged with the preparations reported that all was ready. Still there was a long delay. The vessel sent early in spring to ask aid from England had not returned. Phips waited for her as long as he dared, and the best of the season was over when he resolved to put to sea. The rustic warriors, duly formed into companies, were sent on board; and the fleet sailed from Nantasket on the ninth of August. Including sailors, it carried twenty-two hundred men, with provisions for four months, but insufficient ammunition and no pilot for the St. Lawrence.

While Massachusetts was making ready to conquer Quebec by sea, the militia of the land expedition against Montreal had mustered at Albany. Their strength was even less than was at first proposed; for, after the disaster at Casco, Massachusetts and Plymouth had recalled their contingents to defend their frontiers. The rest, decimated by dysentery and small-pox, began their march to Lake Champlain, with bands of Mohawk, Oneida, and Mohegan allies. The western Iroquois were to join them at the lake, and the combined force was then to attack the head of the colony, while Phips struck at its heart.

Frontenac was at Quebec during most of the winter and the early spring. When he had despatched the three war-parties, whose hardy but murderous exploits were to bring this double storm upon him, he had an interval of leisure, of which he made a characteristic use. The English and the Iroquois were not his only enemies. He had opponents within as well as without, and he counted as among them most of the members of the supreme council. Here was the bishop, representing that clerical power which had clashed so often with the civil rule; here was that ally of the Jesuits, the intendant Champigny, who, when Frontenac arrived, had written mournfully to Versailles that he would do his best to live at peace with him; here were Villeray and Auteuil, whom the governor had once banished, Damours, whom he had imprisoned, and others scarcely more agreeable to him. They and their clerical friends had conspired for his recall seven or eight years before; they had clung to Denonville, that faithful son of the Church, in spite of all his failures; and they had seen with troubled minds the return of King Stork in the person of the haughty and irascible count. He on his part felt his power. The country was in deadly need of him, and looked to him for salvation; while the king had shown him such marks of favor, that, for the moment at least, his enemies must hold their peace. Now, therefore, was the time to teach them that he was their master. Whether trivial or important the occasion mattered little. What he wanted was a conflict and a victory, or submission without a conflict.

The supreme council had held its usual weekly meetings since Frontenac's arrival; but as yet he had not taken his place at the board, though his presence was needed. Auteuil, the attorney-general, was thereupon deputed to invite him. He visited the count at his apartment in the château, but could get from him no answer, except that the council was able to manage its own business, and that he would come when the king's service should require it. The councillors divined that he was waiting for some assurance that they would receive him with befitting ceremony; and, after debating the question, they voted to send four of their number to repeat the invitation, and beg the governor to say what form of reception would be agreeable to him. Frontenac answered that it was for them to propose the form, and that, when they did so, he would take the subject into consideration. The deputies returned, and there was another debate. A ceremony was devised, which it was thought must needs be acceptable to the count; and the first councillor, Villeray, repaired to the château to submit it to him. After making him an harangue of compliment, and protesting the anxiety of himself and his colleagues to receive him with all possible honor, he explained the plan, and assured Frontenac that, if not wholly satisfactory, it should be changed to suit his pleasure. "To which," says the record, "Monsieur the governor only answered that the council could consult the bishop and other persons acquainted with such matters." The bishop was consulted, but pleaded ignorance. Another debate followed; and the first councillor was again despatched to the château, with proposals still more deferential than the last, and full power to yield, in addition, whatever the governor might desire. Frontenac replied that, though they had made proposals for his reception when he should present himself at the council for the first time, they had not informed him what ceremony they meant to observe when he should come to the subsequent sessions. This point also having been thoroughly debated, Villeray went again to the count, and with great deference laid before him the following plan: That, whenever it should be his pleasure to make his first visit to the council, four of its number should repair to the château, and accompany him, with every mark of honor, to the palace of the intendant, where the sessions were held; and that, on his subsequent visits, two councillors should meet him at the head of the stairs, and conduct him to his seat. The envoy further protested that, if this failed to meet his approval, the council would conform itself to all his wishes on the subject.

Frontenac now demanded to see the register in which the proceedings on the question at issue were recorded. Villeray was directed to carry it to him. The records had been cautiously made; and, after studying them carefully, he could find nothing at which to cavil. He received the next deputation with great affability, told them that he was glad to find that the council had not forgotten the consideration due to his office and his person, and assured them, with urbane irony, that, had they offered to accord him marks of distinction greater than they felt were due, he would not have permitted them thus to compromise their dignity, having too much regard for the honor of a body of which he himself was the head. Then, after thanking them collectively and severally, he graciously dismissed them, saying that he would come to the council after Easter, or in about two months. During four successive Mondays, he had forced the chief dignitaries of the colony to march in deputations up and down the rugged road from the intendant's palace to the chamber of the château where he sat in solitary state. A disinterested spectator might see the humor of the situation; but the council felt only its vexations. Frontenac had gained his point: the enemy had surrendered unconditionally.

Having settled this important matter to his satisfaction, he again addressed himself to saving the country. During the winter, he had employed gangs of men in cutting timber in the forests, hewing it into palisades, and dragging it to Quebec. Nature had fortified the Upper Town on two sides by cliffs almost inaccessible, but it was open to attack in the rear; and Frontenac, with a happy prevision of approaching danger, gave his first thoughts to strengthening this, its only weak side. The work began as soon as the frost was out of the ground, and before midsummer it was well advanced. At the same time, he took every precaution for the safety of the settlements in the upper parts of the colony, stationed detachments of regulars at the stockade forts, which Denonville had built in all the parishes above Three Rivers, and kept strong scouting parties in continual movement in all the quarters most exposed to attack. Troops were detailed to guard the settlers at their work in the fields, and officers and men were enjoined to use the utmost vigilance. Nevertheless, the Iroquois war-parties broke in at various points, burning and butchering, and spreading such terror that in some districts the fields were left untilled and the prospects of the harvest ruined.

Towards the end of July, Frontenac left Major Prévost to finish the fortifications, and, with the intendant Champigny, went up to Montreal, the chief point of danger. Here he arrived on the thirty-first; and, a few days after, the officer commanding the fort at La Chine sent him a messenger in hot haste with the startling news that Lake St. Louis was "all covered with canoes." Nobody doubted that the Iroquois were upon them again. Cannon were fired to call in the troops from the detached posts; when alarm was suddenly turned to joy by the arrival of other messengers to announce that the new comers were not enemies, but friends. They were the Indians of the upper lakes descending from Michillimackinac to trade at Montreal. Nothing so auspicious had happened since Frontenac's return. The messages he had sent them in the spring by Louvigny and Perrot, reinforced by the news of the victory on the Ottawa and the capture of Schenectady, had had the desired effect; and the Iroquois prisoner whom their missionary had persuaded them to torture had not been sacrificed in vain. Despairing of an English market for their beaver skins, they had come as of old to seek one from the French.

On the next day, they all came down the rapids, and landed near the town. There were fully five hundred of them,—Hurons, Ottawas, Ojibwas, Pottawatamies, Crees, and Nipissings,—with a hundred and ten canoes laden with beaver skins to the value of nearly a hundred thousand crowns. Nor was this all; for, a few days after, La Durantaye, late commander at Michillimackinac, arrived with fifty-five more canoes, manned by French traders, and filled with valuable furs. The stream of wealth dammed back so long was flowing upon the colony at the moment when it was most needed. Never had Canada known a more prosperous trade than now in the midst of her danger and tribulation. It was a triumph for Frontenac. If his policy had failed with the Iroquois, it had found a crowning success among the tribes of the lakes.

Having painted, greased, and befeathered themselves, the Indians mustered for the grand council which always preceded the opening of the market. The Ottawa orator spoke of nothing but trade, and, with a regretful memory of the cheapness of English goods, begged that the French would sell them at the same rate. The Huron touched upon politics and war, declaring that he and his people had come to visit their old father and listen to his voice, being well assured that he would never abandon them, as others had done, nor fool away his time, like Denonville, in shameful negotiations for peace; and he exhorted Frontenac to fight, not the English only, but the Iroquois also, till they were brought to reason. "If this is not done," he said, "my father and I shall both perish; but, come what may, we will perish together." "I answered," writes Frontenac, "that I would fight the Iroquois till they came to beg for peace, and that I would grant them no peace that did not include all my children, both white and red, for I was the father of both alike."

Now ensued a curious scene. Frontenac took a hatchet, brandished it in the air, and sang the war-song. The principal Frenchmen present followed his example. The Christian Iroquois of the two neighboring missions rose and joined them, and so also did the Hurons and the Algonquins of Lake Nipissing, stamping and screeching like a troop of madmen; while the governor led the dance, whooping like the rest. His predecessor would have perished rather than play such a part in such company; but the punctilious old courtier was himself half Indian at heart, as much at home in a wigwam as in the halls of princes. Another man would have lost respect in Indian eyes by such a performance. In Frontenac, it roused his audience to enthusiasm. They snatched the proffered hatchet and promised war to the death.

Then came a solemn war-feast. Two oxen and six large dogs had been chopped to pieces for the occasion, and boiled with a quantity of prunes. Two barrels of wine with abundant tobacco were also served out to the guests, who devoured the meal in a species of frenzy. All seemed eager for war except the Ottawas, who had not forgotten their late dalliance with the Iroquois. A Christian Mohawk of the Saut St. Louis called them to another council, and demanded that they should explain clearly their position. Thus pushed to the wall, they no longer hesitated, but promised like the rest to do all that their father should ask.

Their sincerity was soon put to the test. An Iroquois convert called La Plaque, a notorious reprobate though a good warrior, had gone out as a scout in the direction of Albany. On the day when the market opened and trade was in full activity, the buyers and sellers were suddenly startled by the sound of the death-yell. They snatched their weapons, and for a moment all was confusion; when La Plaque, who had probably meant to amuse himself at their expense, made his appearance, and explained that the yells proceeded from him. The news that he brought was, however, sufficiently alarming. He declared that he had been at Lake St. Sacrement, or Lake George, and had seen there a great number of men making canoes as if about to advance on Montreal. Frontenac, thereupon, sent the Chevalier de Clermont to scout as far as Lake Champlain. Clermont soon sent back one of his followers to announce that he had discovered a party of the enemy, and that they were already on their way down the Richelieu. Frontenac ordered cannon to be fired to call in the troops, crossed the St. Lawrence followed by all the Indians, and encamped with twelve hundred men at La Prairie to meet the expected attack. He waited in vain. All was quiet, and the Ottawa scouts reported that they could find no enemy. Three days passed. The Indians grew impatient, and wished to go home. Neither English nor Iroquois had shown themselves; and Frontenac, satisfied that their strength had been exaggerated, left a small force at La Prairie, recrossed the river, and distributed the troops again among the neighboring parishes to protect the harvesters. He now gave ample presents to his departing allies, whose chiefs he had entertained at his own table, and to whom, says Charlevoix, he bade farewell "with those engaging manners which he knew so well how to assume when he wanted to gain anybody to his interest." Scarcely were they gone, when the distant cannon of La Prairie boomed a sudden alarm.

The men whom La Plaque had seen near Lake George were a part of the combined force of Connecticut and New York, destined to attack Montreal. They had made their way along Wood Creek to the point where it widens into Lake Champlain, and here they had stopped. Disputes between the men of the two colonies, intestine quarrels in the New York militia, who were divided between the two factions engendered by the late revolution, the want of provisions, the want of canoes, and the ravages of small-pox, had ruined an enterprise which had been mismanaged from the first. There was no birch bark to make more canoes, and owing to the lateness of the season the bark of the elms would not peel. Such of the Iroquois as had joined them were cold and sullen; and news came that the three western tribes of the confederacy, terrified by the small-pox, had refused to move. It was impossible to advance; and Winthrop, the commander, gave orders to return to Albany, leaving Phips to conquer Canada alone.

But, first, that the campaign might not seem wholly futile, he permitted Captain John Schuyler to make a raid into Canada with a band of volunteers. Schuyler left the camp at Wood Creek with twenty-nine whites and a hundred and twenty Indians, passed Lake Champlain, descended the Richelieu to Chambly, and fell suddenly on the settlement of La Prairie, whence Frontenac had just withdrawn with his forces. Soldiers and inhabitants were reaping in the wheat-fields. Schuyler and his followers killed or captured twenty-five, including several women. He wished to attack the neighboring fort, but his Indians refused; and after burning houses, barns, and hay-ricks, and killing a great number of cattle, he seated himself with his party at dinner in the adjacent woods, while cannon answered cannon from Chambly, La Prairie, and Montreal, and the whole country was astir. "We thanked the Governor of Canada," writes Schuyler, "for his salute of heavy artillery during our meal."

The English had little to boast in this affair, the paltry termination of an enterprise from which great things had been expected. Nor was it for their honor to adopt the savage and cowardly mode of warfare in which their enemies had led the way. The blow that had been struck was less an injury to the French than an insult; but, as such, it galled Frontenac excessively, and he made no mention of it in his despatches to the court. A few more Iroquois attacks and a few more murders kept Montreal in alarm till the tenth of October, when matters of deeper import engaged the governor's thoughts.

A messenger arrived in haste at three o'clock in the afternoon, and gave him a letter from Prévost, town major of Quebec. It was to the effect that an Abenaki Indian had just come over land from Acadia, with news that some of his tribe had captured an English woman near Portsmouth, who told them that a great fleet had sailed from Boston to attack Quebec.

Frontenac, not easily alarmed, doubted the report. Nevertheless, he embarked at once with the intendant in a small vessel,
which proved to be leaky, and was near foundering with all on
board. He then took a canoe, and towards evening set out
again for Quebec, ordering some two hundred men to follow
him. On the next day he met another canoe, bearing a fresh
message from Prévost, who announced that the English fleet
had been seen in the river, and that it was already above Tadoussac. Frontenac now sent back Captain de Ramsay with
orders to Callières, governor of Montreal, to descend immediately to Quebec with all the force at his disposal, and to muster
the inhabitants on the way. Then he pushed on with the utmost
speed. The autumnal storms had begun, and the rain pelted
him without ceasing; but on the morning of the fourteenth he
neared the town. The rocks of Cape Diamond towered before
him; the St. Lawrence lay beneath them, lonely and still; and the
Basin of Quebec outspread its broad bosom, a solitude without
a sail.

Frontenac had arrived in time. He landed at the Lower
Town, and the troops and the armed inhabitants came crowding to meet him. He was delighted at their ardor. Shouts,
cheers, and the waving of hats greeted the old man as he
climbed the steep ascent of Mountain Street. Fear and doubt
seemed banished by his presence. Even those who hated him
rejoiced at his coming, and hailed him as a deliverer. He went
at once to inspect the fortifications. Since the alarm a week before, Prévost had accomplished wonders, and not only completed the works begun in the spring, but added others to secure
a place which was a natural fortress in itself. On two sides, the
Upper Town scarcely needed defence. The cliffs along the
St. Lawrence and those along the tributary river St. Charles
had three accessible points, guarded at the present day by the
Prescott Gate, the Hope Gate, and the Palace Gate. Prévost
had secured them by barricades of heavy beams and casks filled
with earth. A continuous line of palisades ran along the strand
of the St. Charles, from the great cliff called the Saut au Matelot
to the palace of the intendant. At this latter point began the

line of works constructed by Frontenac to protect the rear of the town. They consisted of palisades, strengthened by a ditch and an embankment, and flanked at frequent intervals by square towers of stone. Passing behind the garden of the Ursulines, they extended to a windmill on a hillock called Mt. Carmel, and thence to the brink of the cliffs in front. Here there was a battery of eight guns near the present Public Garden; two more, each of three guns, were planted at the top of the Saut au Matelot; another at the barricade of the Palace Gate; and another near the windmill of Mt. Carmel; while a number of light pieces were held in reserve for such use as occasion might require. The Lower Town had no defensive works; but two batteries, each of three guns, eighteen and twenty-four pounders, were placed here at the edge of the river.

Two days passed in completing these defences under the eye of the governor. Men were flocking in from the parishes far and near; and on the evening of the fifteenth about twenty-seven hundred, regulars and militia, were gathered within the fortifications, besides the armed peasantry of Beauport and Beaupré, who were ordered to watch the river below the town, and resist the English, should they attempt to land.

At length, before dawn on the morning of the sixteenth, the sentinels on the Saut au Matelot could descry the slowly moving lights of distant vessels. At daybreak the fleet was in sight. Sail after sail passed the Point of Orleans and glided into the Basin of Quebec. The excited spectators on the rock counted thirty-four of them. Four were large ships, several others were of considerable size, and the rest were brigs, schooners, and fishing craft, all thronged with men.

The delay at Boston, waiting aid from England that never came, was not propitious to Phips; nor were the wind and the waves. The voyage to the St. Lawrence was a long one; and when he began, without a pilot, to grope his way up the unknown river, the weather seemed in league with his enemies. He appears, moreover, to have wasted time. What was most vital to his success was rapidity of movement; yet, whether by his fault or his misfortune, he remained three weeks within three days' sail of Quebec. While anchored off Tadoussac, with the wind ahead, he passed the idle hours in holding councils of war and framing rules for the government of his men; and, when at length the wind veered to the east, it is doubtful if he made the best use of his opportunity.

He presently captured a small vessel, commanded by Granville, an officer whom Prévost had sent to watch his movements. He had already captured, near Tadoussac, another vessel, having on board Madame Lalande and Madame Joliet, the wife and the mother-in-law of the discoverer of the Mississippi. When questioned as to the condition of Quebec, they told him that it was imperfectly fortified, that its cannon were dismounted, and that it had not two hundred men to defend it. Phips was greatly elated, thinking that, like Port Royal, the capital of Canada would fall without a blow. The statement of the two prisoners was true, for the most part, when it was made; but the energy of Prévost soon wrought a change.

Phips imagined that the Canadians would offer little resistance to the Puritan invasion; for some of the Acadians had felt the influence of their New England neighbors, and shown an inclination to them. It was far otherwise in Canada, where the English heretics were regarded with abhorrence. Whenever the invaders tried to land at the settlements along the shore, they were met by a rebuff. At the river Ouelle, Francheville, the curé put on a cap and capote, took a musket, led his parishioners to the river, and hid with them in the bushes. As the English boats approached their ambuscade, they gave the foremost a volley, which killed nearly every man on board; upon which the rest sheared off. It was the same when the fleet neared Quebec. Bands of militia, vigilant, agile, and well commanded, followed it along the shore, and repelled with showers of bullets every attempt of the enemy to touch Canadian soil.

When, after his protracted voyage, Phips sailed into the Basin of Quebec, one of the grandest scenes on the western continent opened upon his sight: the wide expanse of waters, the lofty promontory beyond, and the opposing heights of Levi; the cataract of Montmorenci, the distant range of the

Laurentian Mountains, the warlike rock with its diadem of walls and towers, the roofs of the Lower Town clustering on the strand beneath, the Château St. Louis perched at the brink of the cliff, and over it the white banner, spangled with *fleurs-de-lis*, flaunting defiance in the clear autumnal air. Perhaps, as he gazed, a suspicion seized him that the task he had undertaken was less easy than he had thought; but he had conquered once by a simple summons to surrender, and he resolved to try its virtue again.

The fleet anchored a little below Quebec; and towards ten o'clock the French saw a boat put out from the admiral's ship, bearing a flag of truce. Four canoes went from the Lower Town, and met it midway. It brought a subaltern officer, who announced himself as the bearer of a letter from Sir William Phips to the French commander. He was taken into one of the canoes and paddled to the quay, after being completely blind-folded by a bandage which covered half his face. Prévost received him as he landed, and ordered two sergeants to take him by the arms and lead him to the governor. His progress was neither rapid nor direct. They drew him hither and thither, delighting to make him clamber in the dark over every possible obstruction; while a noisy crowd hustled him, and laughing women called him Colin Maillard, the name of the chief player in blindman's buff. Amid a prodigious hubbub, intended to bewilder him and impress him with a sense of immense warlike preparation, they dragged him over the three barricades of Mountain Street, and brought him at last into a large room of the château. Here they took the bandage from his eyes. He stood for a moment with an air of astonishment and some confusion. The governor stood before him, haughty and stern, surrounded by French and Canadian officers, Maricourt, Sainte-Hélène, Longueuil, Villebon, Valrenne, Bienville, and many more, bedecked with gold lace and silver lace, perukes and powder, plumes and ribbons, and all the martial foppery in which they took delight, and regarding the envoy with keen, defiant eyes. After a moment, he recovered his breath and his composure, saluted Frontenac, and, expressing a wish that the duty assigned him had been of a more agreeable nature, handed him the letter of Phips. Frontenac gave it to an interpreter, who read it aloud in French that all might hear. It ran thus:—

"Sir William Phips, Knight, General and Commander-in-chief in and over their Majesties' Forces of New England, by Sea and Land, to Count Frontenac, Lieutenant-General and Governour for the French King at Canada; or, in his absence, to his Deputy, or him or them in chief command at Quebeck:

"The war between the crowns of England and France doth not only sufficiently warrant, but the destruction made by the French and Indians, under your command and encouragement, upon the persons and estates of their Majesties' subjects of New England, without provocation on their part, hath put them under the necessity of this expedition for their own security and satisfaction. And although the cruelties and barbarities used against them by the French and Indians might, upon the present opportunity, prompt unto a severe revenge, yet, being desirous to avoid all inhumane and unchristian-like actions, and to prevent shedding of blood as much as may be,—

"I, the aforesaid William Phips, Knight, do hereby, in the name and in the behalf of their most excellent Majesties, William and Mary, King and Queen of England, Scotland, France, and Ireland, Defenders of the Faith, and by order of their said Majesties' government of the Massachuset-colony in New England, demand a present surrender of your forts and castles, undemolished, and the King's and other stores, unimbezzled, with a seasonable delivery of all captives; together with a surrender of all your persons and estates to my dispose: upon the doing whereof, you may expect mercy from me, as a Christian, according to what shall be found for their Majesties' service and the subjects' security. Which, if you refuse forthwith to do, I am come provided, and am resolved, by the help of God, in whom I trust, by force of arms to revenge all wrongs and injuries offered, and bring you under subjection to the Crown of England, and, when too late, make you wish you had accepted of the favour tendered.

"Your answer positive in an hour, returned by your own trumpet, with the return of mine, is required upon the peril that will ensue."

When the reading was finished, the Englishman pulled his watch from his pocket, and handed it to the governor. Frontenac could not, or pretended that he could not, see the hour. The messenger thereupon told him that it was ten o'clock, and that he must have his answer before eleven. A general cry of indignation arose; and Valrenne called out that Phips was nothing but a pirate, and that his man ought to be hanged. Frontenac contained himself for a moment, and then said to the envoy:—

"I will not keep you waiting so long. Tell your general that I do not recognize King William; and that the Prince of Orange, who so styles himself, is a usurper, who has violated the most sacred laws of blood in attempting to dethrone his father-in-law. I know no king of England but King James. Your general ought not to be surprised at the hostilities which he says that the French have carried on in the colony of Massachusetts; for, as the king my master has taken the king of England under his protection, and is about to replace him on his throne by force of arms, he might have expected that his Majesty would order me to make war on a people who have rebelled against their lawful prince." Then, turning with a smile to the officers about him: "Even if your general offered me conditions a little more gracious, and if I had a mind to accept them, does he suppose that these brave gentlemen would give their consent, and advise me to trust a man who broke his agreement with the governor of Port Royal, or a rebel who has failed in his duty to his king, and forgotten all the favors he had received from him, to follow a prince who pretends to be the liberator of England and the defender of the faith, and yet destroys the laws and privileges of the kingdom and overthrows its religion? The divine justice which your general invokes in his letter will not fail to punish such acts severely."

The messenger seemed astonished and startled; but he presently asked if the governor would give him his answer in writing.

"No," returned Frontenac, "I will answer your general only by the mouths of my cannon, that he may learn that a man like me is not to be summoned after this fashion. Let him do his best, and I will do mine"; and he dismissed the Englishman abruptly. He was again blindfolded, led over the barricades, and sent back to the fleet by the boat that brought him.

Phips had often given proof of personal courage, but for the past three weeks his conduct seems that of a man conscious that he is charged with a work too large for his capacity. He had spent a good part of his time in holding councils of war; and now, when he heard the answer of Frontenac, he called another to consider what should be done. A plan of attack was at length arranged. The militia were to be landed on the shore of Beauport, which was just below Quebec, though separated from it by the St. Charles. They were then to cross this river by a ford practicable at low water, climb the heights of St. Geneviève, and gain the rear of the town. The small vessels of the fleet were to aid the movement by ascending the St. Charles as far as the ford, holding the enemy in check by their fire, and carrying provisions, ammunition, and intrenching tools, for the use of the land troops. When these had crossed and were ready to attack Quebec in the rear, Phips was to cannonade it in front, and land two hundred men under cover of his guns to effect a diversion by storming the barricades. Some of the French prisoners, from whom their captors appear to have received a great deal of correct information, told the admiral that there was a place a mile or two above the town where the heights might be scaled and the rear of the fortifications reached from a direction opposite to that proposed. This was precisely the movement by which Wolfe afterwards gained his memorable victory; but Phips chose to abide by the original plan.

While the plan was debated, the opportunity for accomplishing it ebbed away. It was still early when the messenger returned from Quebec; but, before Phips was ready to act, the day was on the wane and the tide was against him. He lay quietly at his moorings when, in the evening, a great shouting, mingled with the roll of drums and the sound of fifes, was heard from the Upper Town. The English officers asked their prisoner, Granville, what it meant. "Ma foi, Messieurs," he replied, "you have lost the game. It is the governor of Montreal with the people from the country above. There is nothing for you now but to pack and go home." In fact, Callières had arrived with seven or eight hundred men, many of them regulars. With these were bands of *coureurs de bois* and other young Canadians, all full of fight, singing and whooping with martial glee as they passed the western gate and trooped down St. Louis Street.

The next day was gusty and blustering; and still Phips lay quiet, waiting on the winds and the waves. A small vessel, with sixty men on board, under Captain Ephraim Savage, ran in towards the shore of Beauport to examine the landing, and stuck fast in the mud. The Canadians plied her with bullets, and brought a cannon to bear on her. They might have waded out and boarded her, but Savage and his men kept up so hot a fire that they forbore the attempt; and, when the tide rose, she floated again.

There was another night of tranquillity; but at about eleven on Wednesday morning the French heard the English fifes and drums in full action, while repeated shouts of "God save King William!" rose from all the vessels. This lasted an hour or more; after which a great number of boats, loaded with men, put out from the fleet and rowed rapidly towards the shore of Beauport. The tide was low, and the boats grounded before reaching the landing-place. The French on the rock could see the troops through telescopes, looking in the distance like a swarm of black ants, as they waded through mud and water, and formed in companies along the strand. They were some thirteen hundred in number, and were commanded by Major Walley. Frontenac had sent three hundred sharpshooters, under Sainte-Hélène, to meet them and hold them in check. A battalion of troops followed; but long before they could reach the spot, Sainte-Hélène's men, with a few militia from the neighboring parishes, and a band of Huron warriors from Lorette, threw themselves into the thickets along the front of the English, and opened a distant but galling fire upon the compact bodies of the enemy. Walley ordered a charge. The New England men rushed, in a disorderly manner, but with great impetuosity, up the rising ground; received two volleys, which failed to check them; and drove back the assailants in some confusion. They turned, however, and fought in Indian fashion with courage and address, leaping and dodging among trees, rocks, and bushes, firing as they retreated, and inflicting more harm than they received. Towards evening they disappeared; and Walley, whose men had been much scattered in the desultory fight, drew them together as well as he could, and advanced towards the St. Charles, in order to meet the vessels which were to aid him in passing the ford. Here he posted sentinels, and encamped for the night. He had lost four killed and about sixty wounded, and imagined that he had killed twenty or thirty of the enemy. In fact, however, their loss was much less, though among the killed was a valuable officer, the Chevalier de Clermont, and among the wounded the veteran captain of Beauport, Juchereau de Saint-Denis, more than sixty-four years of age. In the evening, a deserter came to the English camp, and brought the unwelcome intelligence that there were three thousand armed men in Quebec.

Meanwhile, Phips, whose fault hitherto had not been an excess of promptitude, grew impatient, and made a premature movement inconsistent with the preconcerted plan. He left his moorings, anchored his largest ships before the town, and prepared to cannonade it; but the fiery veteran, who watched him from the Château St. Louis, anticipated him, and gave him the first shot. Phips replied furiously, opening fire with every gun that he could bring to bear; while the rock paid him back in kind, and belched flame and smoke from all its batteries. So fierce and rapid was the firing, that La Hontan compares it to volleys of musketry; and old officers, who had seen many sieges, declared that they had never known the like. The din was prodigious, reverberated from the surrounding heights, and rolled back from the distant mountains in one continuous roar. On the part of the English, however, surprisingly little was accomplished beside noise and smoke. The practice of their gunners was so bad that many of their shot struck harmlessly against the face of the cliff. Their guns, too, were very light, and appear to have been charged with a view to the most rigid economy of gunpowder; for the balls failed to pierce the stone walls of the buildings, and did so little damage that, as the French boasted, twenty crowns would have repaired it all. Night came at length, and the turmoil ceased.

Phips lay quiet till daybreak, when Frontenac sent a shot to waken him, and the cannonade began again. Sainte-Hélène had returned from Beauport; and he, with his brother Maricourt, took charge of the two batteries of the Lower Town, aiming the guns in person, and throwing balls of eighteen and twenty-four pounds with excellent precision against the four largest ships of the fleet. One of their shots cut the flagstaff of the admiral, and the cross of St. George fell into the river. It drifted with the tide towards the north shore; whereupon several Canadians paddled out in a birch canoe, secured it, and brought it back in triumph. On the spire of the cathedral in the Upper Town had been hung a picture of the Holy Family, as an invocation of divine aid. The Puritan gunners wasted their ammunition in vain attempts to knock it down. That it escaped their malice was ascribed to miracle, but the miracle would have been greater if they had hit it.

At length, one of the ships, which had suffered most, hauled off and abandoned the fight. That of the admiral had fared little better, and now her condition grew desperate. With her rigging torn, her mainmast half cut through, her mizzen-mast splintered, her cabin pierced, and her hull riddled with shot, another volley seemed likely to sink her, when Phips ordered her to be cut loose from her moorings, and she drifted out of fire, leaving cable and anchor behind. The remaining ships soon gave over the conflict, and withdrew to stations where they could neither do harm nor suffer it.

Phips had thrown away nearly all his ammunition in this futile and disastrous attack, which should have been deferred till the moment when Walley, with his land force, had gained the rear of the town. Walley lay in his camp, his men wet, shivering with cold, famished, and sickening with the small-pox. Food, and all other supplies, were to have been brought him by the small vessels, which should have entered the mouth of the St. Charles and aided him to cross it. But he waited for them in vain. Every vessel that carried a gun had busied itself in cannonading, and the rest did not move. There appears to have been insubordination among the masters of these small craft, some of whom, being owners or part-owners of the vessels they commanded, were probably unwilling to run them into danger. Walley was no soldier; but he saw that to attempt the passage of the river without aid, under the batteries of the town and in the face of forces twice as numerous as his own, was not an easy task. Frontenac, on his part, says that he wished him to do so, knowing that the attempt would ruin him. The New England men were eager to push on; but the night of Thursday, the day of Phips's repulse, was so cold that ice formed more than an inch in thickness, and the half-starved militia suffered intensely. Six field-pieces, with their ammunition, had been sent ashore; but they were nearly useless, as there were no means of moving them. Half a barrel of musket powder, and one biscuit for each man, were also landed; and with this meagre aid Walley was left to capture Quebec. He might, had he dared, have made a dash across the ford on the morning of Thursday, and assaulted the town in the rear while Phips was cannonading it in front; but his courage was not equal to so desperate a venture. The firing ceased, and the possible opportunity was lost.

The citizen soldier despaired of success; and, on the morning of Friday, he went on board the admiral's ship to explain his situation. While he was gone, his men put themselves in motion, and advanced along the borders of the St. Charles towards the ford. Frontenac, with three battalions of regular troops, went to receive them at the crossing; while Sainte-Hélène, with his brother Longueuil, passed the ford with a body of Canadians, and opened fire on them from the neighboring thickets. Their advance parties were driven in, and there was a hot skirmish, the chief loss falling on the New England men, who were fully exposed. On the side of the French, Sainte-Hélène was mortally wounded, and his brother was hurt by a spent ball.

Towards evening, the Canadians withdrew, and the English encamped for the night. Their commander presently rejoined them. The admiral had given him leave to withdraw them to the fleet, and boats were accordingly sent to bring them off; but, as these did not arrive till about daybreak, it was necessary to defer the embarkation till the next night.

At dawn, Quebec was all astir with the beating of drums and the ringing of bells. The New England drums replied; and Walley drew up his men under arms, expecting an attack, for the town was so near that the hubbub of voices from within could plainly be heard. The noise gradually died away; and, except a few shots from the ramparts, the invaders were left undisturbed. Walley sent two or three companies to beat up the neighboring thickets, where he suspected that the enemy was lurking. On the way, they had the good luck to find and kill a number of cattle, which they cooked and ate on the spot; whereupon, being greatly refreshed and invigorated, they dashed forward in complete disorder, and were soon met by the fire of the ambushed Canadians. Several more companies were sent to their support, and the skirmishing became lively. Three detachments from Quebec had crossed the river; and the militia of Beauport and Beaupré had hastened to join them. They fought like Indians, hiding behind trees or throwing themselves flat among the bushes, and laying repeated ambuscades as they slowly fell back. At length, they all made a stand on a hill behind the buildings and fences of a farm; and here they held their ground till night, while the New England men taunted them as cowards who would never fight except under cover.

Walley, who with his main body had stood in arms all day, now called in the skirmishers, and fell back to the landing-place, where, as soon as it grew dark, the boats arrived from the fleet. The sick men, of whom there were many, were sent on board, and then, amid floods of rain, the whole force embarked in noisy confusion, leaving behind them in the mud five of their cannon. Hasty as was their parting, their conduct on the whole had been creditable; and La Hontan, who was in Quebec at the time, says of them, "They fought vigorously, though as ill-disciplined as men gathered together at random could be; for they did not lack courage, and, if they failed, it was by reason of their entire ignorance of discipline, and because they were exhausted by the fatigues of the voyage." Of Phips he speaks with contempt, and says that he could not have served the French better if they had bribed him to stand all the while with his arms folded. Some allowance should, nevertheless, be made him for the unmanageable character of the force under his command, the constitution of which was fatal to military subordination.

On Sunday, the morning after the re-embarkation, Phips called a council of officers, and it was resolved that the men should rest for a day or two, that there should be a meeting for prayer, and that if ammunition enough could be found, another landing should be attempted; but the rough weather prevented the prayer-meeting, and the plan of a new attack was fortunately abandoned.

Quebec remained in agitation and alarm till Tuesday, when Phips weighed anchor and disappeared, with all his fleet, behind the Island of Orleans. He did not go far, as indeed he could not, but stopped four leagues below to mend rigging, fortify wounded masts, and stop shot-holes. Subercase had gone with a detachment to watch the retiring enemy; and Phips was repeatedly seen among his men, on a scaffold at the side of his ship, exercising his old trade of carpenter. This delay was turned to good use by an exchange of prisoners. Chief among those in the hands of the French was Captain Davis, late commander at Casco Bay; and there were also two young daughters of Lieutenant Clark, who had been killed at the same place. Frontenac himself had humanely ransomed these children from the Indians; and Madame de Champigny, wife of the intendant, had, with equal kindness, bought from them a little girl named Sarah Gerrish, and placed her in charge of the nuns at the Hôtel-Dieu, who had become greatly attached to her, while she, on her part, left them with reluctance. The French had the better in these exchanges, receiving able-bodied men, and returning, with the exception of Davis, only women and children.

The heretics were gone, and Quebec breathed freely again. Her escape had been a narrow one; not that three thousand men, in part regular troops, defending one of the strongest positions on the continent, and commanded by Frontenac, could not defy the attacks of two thousand raw fishermen and farmers, led by an ignorant civilian, but the numbers which were a source of strength were at the same time a source of weakness. Nearly all the adult males of Canada were gathered at Quebec, and there was imminent danger of starvation. Cattle from the neighboring parishes had been hastily driven into the town; but there was little other provision, and before Phips retreated the pinch of famine had begun. Had he come a week earlier or stayed a week later, the French themselves believed that Quebec would have fallen, in the one case for want of men, and in the other for want of food.

The Lower Town had been abandoned by its inhabitants, who bestowed their families and their furniture within the solid walls of the seminary. The cellars of the Ursuline convent were filled with women and children, and many more took refuge at the Hôtel-Dieu. The beans and cabbages in the garden of the nuns were all stolen by the soldiers; and their wood-pile was turned into bivouac fires. "We were more dead than alive when we heard the cannon," writes Mother Juchereau; but the Jesuit Fremin came to console them, and their prayers and their labors never ceased. On the day when the firing was heaviest, twenty-six balls fell into their yard and garden, and were sent to the gunners at the batteries, who returned them to their English owners. At the convent of the Ursulines, the corner of a nun's apron was carried off by a cannon-shot as she passed through her chamber. The sisterhood began a *novena*, or nine days' devotion, to St. Joseph, St. Ann, the angels, and the souls in purgatory; and one of their number remained day and night in prayer before the images of the Holy Family. The bishop came to encourage them; and his prayers and his chants were so fervent that they thought their last hour was come.

The Superior of the Jesuits, with some of the elder members of the Order, remained at their college during the attack, ready, should the heretics prevail, to repair to their chapel, and die before the altar. Rumor exaggerated the numbers of the enemy, and a general alarm pervaded the town. It was still greater at Lorette, nine miles distant. The warriors of that mission were in the first skirmish at Beauport; and two of them, running off in a fright, reported at the village that the enemy were carrying every thing before them. On this, the villagers fled to the woods, followed by Father Germain, their missionary, to whom this hasty exodus suggested the flight of the Holy Family into Egypt. The Jesuits were thought to have special reason to fear the Puritan soldiery, who, it was reported, meant to kill them all, after cutting off their ears to make necklaces.

When news first came of the approach of Phips, the bishop was absent on a pastoral tour. Hastening back, he entered Quebec at night, by torchlight, to the great joy of its inmates, who felt that his presence brought a benediction. He issued a pastoral address, exhorting his flock to frequent and full confession and constant attendance at mass, as the means of insuring the success of their arms. Laval, the former bishop, aided his efforts. "We appealed," he writes, "to God, his Holy Mother, to all the Angels, and to all the Saints." Nor was the appeal in vain: for each day seemed to bring some new token of celestial favor; and it is not surprising that the head-winds which delayed the approach of the enemy, the cold and the storms which hastened his departure, and, above all, his singularly innocent cannonade, which killed but two or three persons, should have been accepted as proof of divine intervention. It was to the Holy Virgin that Quebec had been most lavish of its vows, and to her the victory was ascribed.

One great anxiety still troubled the minds of the victors. Three ships, bringing large sums of money and the yearly supplies for the colony, were on their way to Quebec; and nothing was more likely than that the retiring fleet would meet and capture them. Messengers had been sent down the river, who passed the English in the dark, found the ships at St. Paul's

Bay, and warned them of the danger. They turned back, and hid themselves within the mouth of the Saguenay, but not soon enough to prevent Phips from discovering their retreat. He tried to follow them; but thick fogs arose, with a persistent tempest of snow, which completely baffled him, and, after waiting five days, he gave over the attempt. When he was gone, the three ships emerged from their hiding-place, and sailed again for Quebec, where they were greeted with a universal jubilee. Their deliverance was ascribed to Saint Ann, the mother of the Virgin, and also to St. Francis Xavier, whose name one of them bore.

Quebec was divided between thanksgiving and rejoicing. The captured flag of Phips's ship was borne to the cathedral in triumph; the bishop sang *Te Deum;* and, amid the firing of cannon, the image of the Virgin was carried to each church and chapel in the place by a procession, in which priests, people, and troops all took part. The day closed with a grand bonfire in honor of Frontenac.

One of the three ships carried back the news of the victory, which was hailed with joy at Versailles; and a medal was struck to commemorate it. The ship carried also a despatch from Frontenac. "Now that the king has triumphed by land and sea," wrote the old soldier, "will he think that a few squadrons of his navy would be ill employed in punishing the insolence of these genuine old parliamentarians of Boston, and crushing them in their den and the English of New York as well? By mastering these two towns, we shall secure the whole sea-coast, besides the fisheries of the Grand Bank, which is no slight matter; and this would be the true, and perhaps the only, way of bringing the wars of Canada to an end; for, when the English are conquered, we can easily reduce the Iroquois to complete submission."

Phips returned crestfallen to Boston late in November; and one by one the rest of the fleet came straggling after him, battered and weather-beaten. Some did not appear till February, and three or four never came at all. The autumn and early winter were unusually stormy. Captain Rainsford, with sixty men, was wrecked on the Island of Anticosti, where more than half their number died of cold and misery. In the other vessels, some were drowned, some frost-bitten, and above two hundred killed by small-pox and fever.

At Boston, all was dismay and gloom. The Puritan bowed before "this awful frown of God," and searched his conscience for the sin that had brought upon him so stern a chastisement. Massachusetts, already impoverished, found herself in extremity. The war, instead of paying for itself, had burdened her with an additional debt of fifty thousand pounds. The sailors and soldiers were clamorous for their pay; and, to satisfy them, the colony was forced for the first time in its history to issue a paper currency. It was made receivable at a premium for all public debts, and was also fortified by a provision for its early redemption by taxation; a provision which was carried into effect in spite of poverty and distress.

Massachusetts had made her usual mistake. She had confidently believed that ignorance and inexperience could match the skill of a tried veteran, and that the rude courage of her fishermen and farmers could triumph without discipline or leadership. The conditions of her material prosperity were adverse to efficiency in war. A trading republic, without trained officers, may win victories; but it wins them either by accident or by an extravagant outlay in money and life.

THE COMBATANTS

(From *Montcalm and Wolfe*, 1884)

The latter half of the reign of George II. was one of the most prosaic periods in English history. The civil wars and the Restoration had had their enthusiasms, religion and liberty on one side, and loyalty on the other; but the old fires declined when William III. came to the throne, and died to ashes under the House of Hanover. Loyalty lost half its inspiration when it lost the tenet of the divine right of kings; and nobody could now hold that tenet with any consistency except the defeated and despairing Jacobites. Nor had anybody as yet proclaimed the rival dogma of the divine right of the people. The reigning monarch held his crown neither of God nor of the nation, but of a parliament controlled by a ruling class. The Whig aristocracy had done a priceless service to English liberty. It was full of political capacity, and by no means void of patriotism; but it was only a part of the national life. Nor was it at present moved by political emotions in any high sense. It had done its great work when it expelled the Stuarts and placed William of Orange on the throne; its ascendency was now complete. The Stuarts had received their death-blow at Culloden; and nothing was left to the dominant party but to dispute on subordinate questions, and contend for office among themselves. The Tory squires sulked in their country-houses, hunted foxes, and grumbled against the reigning dynasty, yet hardly wished to see the nation convulsed by a counter-revolution and another return of the Stuarts.

If politics had run to commonplace, so had morals; and so too had religion. Despondent writers of the day even complained that British courage had died out. There was little sign to the common eye that, under a dull and languid surface, forces were at work preparing a new life, material, moral, and intellectual. As yet, Whitefield and Wesley had not wakened the drowsy conscience of the nation, nor the voice of William Pitt roused it like a trumpet-peal.

It was the unwashed and unsavory England of Hogarth, Fielding, Smollett, and Sterne; of Tom Jones, Squire Western, Lady Bellaston, and Parson Adams; of the "Rake's Progress" and "Marriage à la Mode"; of the lords and ladies who yet live in the undying gossip of Horace Walpole, be-powdered, be-patched, and be-rouged, flirting at masked balls, playing cards till daylight, retailing scandal, and exchanging double meanings. Beau Nash reigned king over the gaming-tables of Bath; the ostrich-plumes of great ladies mingled with the peacock-feathers of courtesans in the rotunda at Ranelagh Gardens; and young lords in velvet suits and embroidered ruffles played away their patrimony at White's Chocolate-House or Arthur's Club. Vice was bolder than to-day, and manners more courtly, perhaps, but far more coarse.

The humbler clergy were thought—sometimes with reason—
to be no fit company for gentlemen, and country parsons drank
their ale in the squire's kitchen. The passenger-wagon spent
the better part of a fortnight in creeping from London to York.
Travellers carried pistols against footpads and mounted high-
waymen. Dick Turpin and Jack Sheppard were popular heroes.
Tyburn counted its victims by scores; and as yet no Howard
had appeared to reform the inhuman abominations of the
prisons.

The middle class, though fast rising in importance, was
feebly and imperfectly represented in Parliament. The bor-
oughs were controlled by the nobility and gentry, or by
corporations open to influence or bribery. Parliamentary corruption had been reduced to a system; and offices, sinecures, pen-
sions, and gifts of money were freely used to keep ministers in
power. The great offices of State were held by men sometimes
of high ability, but of whom not a few divided their lives
among politics, cards, wine, horse-racing, and women, till time
and the gout sent them to the waters of Bath. The dull, pompous, and irascible old King had two ruling passions,—money,
and his Continental dominions of Hanover. His elder son, the
Prince of Wales, was a centre of opposition to him. His younger
son, the Duke of Cumberland, a character far more pronounced
and vigorous, had won the day at Culloden, and lost it at Fontenoy; but whether victor or vanquished, had shown the same
vehement bull-headed courage, of late a little subdued by fast-
growing corpulency. The Duke of Newcastle, the head of the
government, had gained power and kept it by his rank and connections, his wealth, his county influence, his control of bor-
oughs, and the extraordinary assiduity and devotion with
which he practised the arts of corruption. Henry Fox, grasping, unscrupulous, with powerful talents, a warm friend after
his fashion, and a most indulgent father; Carteret, with his
strong, versatile intellect and jovial intrepidity; the two Town-
shends, Mansfield, Halifax, and Chesterfield,—were conspicuous
figures in the politics of the time. One man towered above
them all. Pitt had many enemies and many critics. They called

him ambitious, audacious, arrogant, theatrical, pompous, domineering; but what he has left for posterity is a loftiness of soul, undaunted courage, fiery and passionate eloquence, proud incorruptibility, domestic virtues rare in his day, unbounded faith in the cause for which he stood, and abilities which without wealth or strong connections were destined to place him on the height of power. The middle class, as yet almost voiceless, looked to him as its champion; but he was not the champion of a class. His patriotism was as comprehensive as it was haughty and unbending. He lived for England, loved her with intense devotion, knew her, believed in her, and made her greatness his own; or rather, he was himself England incarnate.

The nation was not then in fighting equipment. After the peace of Aix-la-Chapelle, the army within the three kingdoms had been reduced to about eighteen thousand men. Added to these were the garrisons of Minorca and Gibraltar, and six or seven independent companies in the American colonies. Of sailors, less than seventeen thousand were left in the Royal Navy. Such was the condition of England on the eve of one of the most formidable wars in which she was ever engaged.

Her rival across the Channel was drifting slowly and unconsciously towards the cataclysm of the Revolution; yet the old monarchy, full of the germs of decay, was still imposing and formidable. The House of Bourbon held the three thrones of France, Spain, and Naples; and their threatened union in a family compact was the terror of European diplomacy. At home France was the foremost of the Continental nations; and she boasted herself second only to Spain as a colonial power. She disputed with England the mastery of India, owned the islands of Bourbon and Mauritius, held important possessions in the West Indies, and claimed all North America except Mexico and a strip of sea-coast. Her navy was powerful, her army numerous and well appointed; but she lacked the great commanders of the last reign. Soubise, Maillebois, Contades, Broglie, and Clermont were but weak successors of Condé,

Turenne, Vendôme, and Villars. Marshal Richelieu was supreme in the arts of gallantry, and more famous for conquests of love than of war. The best generals of Louis XV. were foreigners. Lowendal sprang from the royal house of Denmark; and Saxe, the best of all, was one of the three hundred and fifty-four bastards of Augustus the Strong, Elector of Saxony and King of Poland. He was now, 1750, dying at Chambord, his iron constitution ruined by debaucheries.

The triumph of the Bourbon monarchy was complete. The government had become one great machine of centralized administration, with a king for its head; though a king who neither could nor would direct it. All strife was over between the Crown and the nobles; feudalism was robbed of its vitality, and left the mere image of its former self, with nothing alive but its abuses, its caste privileges, its exactions, its pride and vanity, its power to vex and oppress. In England, the nobility were a living part of the nation, and if they had privileges, they paid for them by constant service to the State; in France, they had no political life, and were separated from the people by sharp lines of demarcation. From warrior chiefs, they had changed to courtiers. Those of them who could afford it, and many who could not, left their estates to the mercy of stewards, and gathered at Versailles to revolve about the throne as glittering satellites, paid in pomp, empty distinctions, or rich sinecures, for the power they had lost. They ruined their vassals to support the extravagance by which they ruined themselves. Such as stayed at home were objects of pity and scorn. "Out of your Majesty's presence," said one of them, "we are not only wretched, but ridiculous."

Versailles was like a vast and gorgeous theatre, where all were actors and spectators at once; and all played their parts to perfection. Here swarmed by thousands this silken nobility, whose ancestors rode cased in iron. Pageant followed pageant. A picture of the time preserves for us an evening in the great hall of the Château, where the King, with piles of louis d'or before him, sits at a large oval green table, throwing the dice, among princes and princesses, dukes and duchesses, ambassadors, marshals of France, and a vast throng of courtiers, like an animated bed of tulips; for men and women alike wear bright and varied colors. Above are the frescoes of Le Brun; around are walls of sculptured and inlaid marbles, with mirrors that reflect the restless splendors of the scene and the blaze of chandeliers, sparkling with crystal pendants. Pomp, magnificence, profusion, were a business and a duty at the Court. Versailles was a gulf into which the labor of France poured its earnings; and it was never full.

Here the graces and charms were a political power. Women had prodigious influence, and the two sexes were never more alike. Men not only dressed in colors, but they wore patches and carried muffs. The robust qualities of the old nobility still lingered among the exiles of the provinces, while at Court they had melted into refinements tainted with corruption. Yet if the butterflies of Versailles had lost virility, they had not lost courage. They fought as gayly as they danced. In the halls which they haunted of yore, turned now into a historical picture-gallery, one sees them still, on the canvas of Lenfant, Lepaon, or Vernet, facing death with careless gallantry, in their small three-cornered hats, powdered perukes, embroidered coats, and lace ruffles. Their valets served them with ices in the trenches, under the cannon of besieged towns. A troop of actors formed part of the army-train of Marshal Saxe. At night there was a comedy, a ballet, or a ball, and in the morning a battle. Saxe, however, himself a sturdy German, while he recognized their fighting value, and knew well how to make the best of it, sometimes complained that they were volatile, excitable, and difficult to manage.

The weight of the Court, with its pomps, luxuries, and wars, bore on the classes least able to support it. The poorest were taxed most; the richest not at all. The nobles, in the main, were free from imposts. The clergy, who had vast possessions, were wholly free, though they consented to make voluntary gifts to the Crown; and when, in a time of emergency, the minister Machault required them, in common with all others hitherto exempt, to contribute a twentieth of their revenues to the charges of government, they passionately refused, declaring that they would obey God rather than the King. The cultivators of the soil were ground to the earth by a threefold extortion,—the seigniorial dues, the tithes of the Church, and the multiplied exactions of the Crown, enforced with merciless rigor by the farmers of the revenue, who enriched themselves by wringing the peasant on the one hand, and cheating the King on the other. A few great cities shone with all that is most brilliant in society, intellect, and concentred wealth; while the country that paid the costs lay in ignorance and penury, crushed and despairing. On the inhabitants of towns, too, the demands of the tax-gatherer were extreme; but here the immense vitality of the French people bore up the burden. While agriculture languished, and intolerable oppression turned peasants into beggars or desperadoes; while the clergy were sapped by corruption, and the nobles enervated by luxury and ruined by extravagance,—the middle class was growing in thrift and strength. Arts and commerce prospered, and the seaports were alive with foreign trade. Wealth tended from all sides towards the centre. The King did not love his capital; but he and his favorites amused themselves with adorning it. Some of the chief embellishments that make Paris what it is to-day—the Place de la Concorde, the Champs Élysées, and many of the palaces of the Faubourg St. Germain—date from this reign.

One of the vicious conditions of the time was the separation in sympathies and interests of the four great classes of the nation, —clergy, nobles, burghers, and peasants; and each of these, again, divided itself into incoherent fragments. France was an aggregate of disjointed parts, held together by a meshwork of arbitrary power, itself touched with decay. A disastrous blow was struck at the national welfare when the government of Louis XV. revived the odious persecution of the Huguenots. The attempt to scour heresy out of France cost her the most industrious and virtuous part of her population, and robbed her of those most fit to resist the mocking scepticism and turbid passions that burst out like a deluge with the Revolution.

Her manifold ills were summed up in the King. Since the Valois, she had had no monarch so worthless. He did not want understanding, still less the graces of person. In his youth the people called him the "Well-beloved"; but by the middle of the century they so detested him that he dared not pass through Paris, lest the mob should execrate him. He had not the vigor of the true tyrant; but his languor, his hatred of all effort, his profound selfishness, his listless disregard of public duty, and his effeminate libertinism, mixed with superstitious devotion, made him no less a national curse. Louis XIII. was equally unfit to govern; but he gave the reins to the Great Cardinal. Louis XV. abandoned them to a frivolous mistress, content that she should rule on condition of amusing him. It was a hard task; yet Madame de Pompadour accomplished it by methods infamous to him and to her. She gained and long kept the power that she coveted: filled the Bastille with her enemies; made and unmade ministers; appointed and removed generals. Great questions of policy were at the mercy of her caprices. Through her frivolous vanity, her personal likes and dislikes, all the great departments of government—army, navy, war, foreign affairs, justice, finance—changed from hand to hand incessantly, and this at a time of crisis when the kingdom needed the steadiest and surest guidance. Few of the officers of State, except, perhaps, D'Argenson, could venture to disregard her. She turned out Orry, the comptroller-general, put her favorite, Machault, into his place, then made him keeper of the seals, and at last minister of marine. The Marquis de Puysieux, in the ministry of foreign affairs, and the Comte de Saint-Florentin, charged with the affairs of the clergy, took their cue from her. The King stinted her in nothing. First and last, she is reckoned to have cost him thirty-six million francs,—answering now to more than as many dollars.

The prestige of the monarchy was declining with the ideas that had given it life and strength. A growing disrespect for king, ministry, and clergy was beginning to prepare the catastrophe that was still some forty years in the future. While the valleys and low places of the kingdom were dark with misery and squalor, its heights were bright with a gay society,—elegant, fastidious, witty,—craving the pleasures of the mind as well as of the senses, criticising everything, analyzing everything, believing nothing. Voltaire was in the midst of it, hating, with all his vehement soul, the abuses that swarmed about him, and assailing them with the inexhaustible shafts of his restless and piercing intellect. Montesquieu was showing to a despot-ridden age the principles of political freedom. Diderot and D'Alembert were beginning their revolutionary Encyclopædia. Rousseau was sounding the first notes of his mad eloquence,—the wild revolt of a passionate and diseased genius against a world of falsities and wrongs. The *salons* of Paris, cloyed with other pleasures, alive to all that was racy and new, welcomed the pungent doctrines, and played with them as children play with fire, thinking no danger; as time went on, even embraced them in a genuine spirit of hope and good-will for humanity. The Revolution began at the top,—in the world of fashion, birth, and intellect,—and propagated itself downwards. "We walked on a carpet of flowers," Count Ségur afterwards said, "unconscious that it covered an abyss"; till the gulf yawned at last, and swallowed them.

Eastward, beyond the Rhine, lay the heterogeneous patchwork of the Holy Roman, or Germanic, Empire. The sacred bonds that throughout the Middle Ages had held together its innumerable fragments had lost their strength. The empire decayed as a whole; but not so the parts that composed it. In the south the House of Austria reigned over a formidable assemblage of States; and in the north the House of Brandenburg, promoted to royalty half a century before, had raised Prussia into an importance far beyond her extent and population. In her dissevered rags of territory lay the destinies of Germany. It was the late King, that honest, thrifty, dogged, headstrong despot, Frederic William, who had made his kingdom what it was, trained it to the perfection of drill, and left it to his son, Frederic II., the best engine of war in Europe. Frederic himself had passed between the upper and nether millstones of paternal discipline. Never did prince undergo such an apprenticeship. His father set him to the work of an overseer, or steward, flung plates at his head in the family circle, thrashed him with his rattan in public, bullied him for submitting to such treatment, and imprisoned him for trying to run away from it. He came at last out of purgatory; and Europe felt him to her farthest bounds. This bookish, philosophizing, verse-making cynic and profligate was soon to approve himself the first warrior of his time, and one of the first of all time.

Another power had lately risen on the European world. Peter the Great, half hero, half savage, had roused the inert barbarism of Russia into a titanic life. His daughter Elizabeth had succeeded to his throne,—heiress of his sensuality, if not of his talents.

Over all the continent the aspect of the times was the same. Power had everywhere left the plains and the lower slopes, and gathered at the summits. Popular life was at a stand. No great idea stirred the nations to their depths. The religious convulsions of the sixteenth and seventeenth centuries were over, and the earthquake of the French Revolution had not begun. At the middle of the eighteenth century the history of Europe turned on the balance of power; the observance of treaties; inheritance and succession; rivalries of sovereign houses struggling to win power or keep it, encroach on neighbors, or prevent neighbors from encroaching; bargains, intrigue, force, diplomacy, and the musket, in the interest not of peoples but of rulers. Princes, great and small, brooded over some real or fancied wrong, nursed some dubious claim born of a marriage, a will, or an ancient covenant fished out of the abyss of time, and watched their moment to make it good. The general opportunity came when, in 1740, the Emperor Charles VI. died and bequeathed his personal dominions of the House of Austria to his daughter, Maria Theresa. The chief Powers of Europe had been pledged in advance to sustain the will; and pending the event, the veteran Prince Eugene had said that two hundred thousand soldiers would be worth all their guaranties together. The two hundred thousand were not there, and not a sovereign kept his word. They flocked to share the spoil, and parcel out the motley heritage of the young Queen. Frederic of Prussia led the way, invaded her province of Silesia, seized it, and kept it. The Elector of Bavaria and the King of Spain claimed their share, and the Elector of Saxony and the King of Sardinia prepared to follow the example. France took part with Bavaria, and intrigued to set the imperial crown on the head of the Elector, thinking to ruin her old enemy, the House of Austria, and rule Germany through an emperor too weak to dispense with her support. England, jealous of her designs, trembling for the balance of power, and anxious for the Hanoverian possessions of her King, threw herself into the strife on the side of Austria. It was now that, in the Diet at Presburg, the beautiful and distressed Queen, her infant in her arms, made her memorable appeal to the wild chivalry of her Hungarian nobles; and, clashing their swords, they shouted with one voice: "Let us die for our king, Maria Theresa"; *Moriamur pro rege nostro, Mariâ Theresiâ,*— one of the most dramatic scenes in history; not quite true, perhaps, but near the truth. Then came that confusion worse confounded called the war of the Austrian Succession, with its Mollwitz, its Dettingen, its Fontenoy, and its Scotch episode of Culloden. The peace of Aix-la-Chapelle closed the strife in 1748. Europe had time to breathe; but the germs of discord remained alive.

THE AMERICAN COMBATANTS

The French claimed all America, from the Alleghanies to the Rocky Mountains, and from Mexico and Florida to the North Pole, except only the ill-defined possessions of the English on the borders of Hudson Bay; and to these vast regions, with adjacent islands, they gave the general name of New France. They controlled the highways of the continent, for they held its two great rivers. First, they had seized the St. Lawrence, and then planted themselves at the mouth of the Mississippi. Canada at the north, and Louisiana at the south, were the keys of a boundless interior, rich with incalculable possibilities. The English colonies, ranged along the Atlantic coast, had no royal road to the great inland, and were, in a manner, shut between the mountains and the sea. At the middle of the century they numbered in all, from Georgia to Maine, about eleven hundred and sixty thousand white inhabitants. By the census of 1754 Canada had but fifty-five thousand. Add those of Louisiana and Acadia, and the whole white population under the French flag might be something more than eighty thousand. Here is an enormous disparity; and hence it has been argued that the success of the English colonies and the failure of the French was not due to difference of religious and political systems, but simply to numerical preponderance. But this preponderance itself grew out of a difference of systems. We have said before, and it cannot be said too often, that in making Canada a citadel of the State religion,—a holy of holies of exclusive Roman Catholic orthodoxy,—the clerical monitors of the Crown robbed their country of a transatlantic empire. New France could not grow with a priest on guard at the gate to let in none but such as pleased him. One of the ablest of Canadian governors, La Galissonière, seeing the feebleness of the colony compared with the vastness of its claims, advised the King to send ten thousand peasants to occupy the valley of the Ohio, and hold back the British swarm that was just then pushing its advance-guard over the Alleghanies. It needed no effort of the King to people his waste domain, not with ten thousand peasants, but with twenty times ten thousand Frenchmen of every station,—the most industrious, most instructed, most disciplined by adversity and capable of self-rule, that the country could boast. While La Galissonière was asking for colonists, the agents of the Crown, set on by priestly fanaticism, or designing selfishness masked with fanaticism, were pouring volleys of musketry into Huguenot congregations, imprisoning for life those innocent of all but their faith,—the men in the galleys, the women in the pestiferous dungeons of Aigues Mortes,—hanging their ministers, kidnapping their children, and reviving, in short, the dragonnades. Now, as in the past century, many of the victims escaped to the British colonies, and became a part of them. The Huguenots would have hailed as a boon the permission to emigrate under the fleur-de-lis, and build up a Protestant France in the valleys of the West. It would have been a bane of absolutism, but a national glory; would have set bounds to English colonization, and changed the face of the continent. The opportunity was spurned. The dominant Church clung to its policy of rule and ruin. France built its best colony on a principle of exclusion, and failed; England reversed the system, and succeeded.

I have shown elsewhere the aspects of Canada, where a rigid scion of the old European tree was set to grow in the wilderness. The military governor, holding his miniature court on the rock of Quebec; the feudal proprietors, whose domains lined the shores of the St. Lawrence; the peasant; the roving bushranger; the half-tamed savage, with crucifix and scalping-knife; priests; friars; nuns; and soldiers,—mingled to form a society the most picturesque on the continent. What distinguished it from the France that produced it was a total absence of revolt against the laws of its being,—an absolute conservatism, an unquestioning acceptance of Church and King. The Canadian, ignorant of everything but what the priest saw fit to teach him, had never heard of Voltaire; and if he had known him, would have thought him a devil. He had, it is true, a spirit of insubordination born of the freedom of the forest; but if his instincts rebelled, his mind and soul were passively submissive. The unchecked control of a hierarchy robbed him of the independence of intellect and character, without which, under the conditions of modern life, a people must resign itself to a position of inferiority. Yet Canada had a vigor of her own. It was not in spiritual deference only that she differed from the country of her birth. Whatever she had caught of its corruptions, she had caught nothing of its effeminacy. The mass of her people lived in a rude poverty,—not abject, like the peasant of old France, nor ground down by the tax-gatherer; while those of the higher ranks—all more or less engaged in pursuits of war or adventure, and inured to rough journeyings and forest exposures—were rugged as their climate. Even the French regular troops, sent out to defend the colony, caught its hardy spirit, and set an example of stubborn fighting which their comrades at home did not always emulate.

Canada lay ensconced behind rocks and forests. All along her southern boundaries, between her and her English foes, lay a broad tract of wilderness, shaggy with primeval woods. Innumerable streams gurgled beneath their shadows; innumerable lakes gleamed in the fiery sunsets; innumerable mountains bared their rocky foreheads to the wind. These wastes were ranged by her savage allies,—Micmacs, Etechémins, Abenakis, Caughnawagas; and no enemy could steal upon her unawares. Through the midst of them stretched Lake Champlain, pointing straight to the heart of the British settlements,—a watery thoroughfare of mutual attack, and the only approach by which, without a long *détour* by wilderness or sea, a hostile army could come within striking distance of the colony. The French advanced post of Fort Frederic, called Crown Point by the English, barred the narrows of the lake, which thence spread northward to the portals of Canada guarded by Fort St. Jean. Southwestward, some fourteen hundred miles as a bird flies, and twice as far by the practicable routes of travel, was Louisiana, the second of the two heads of New France; while between lay the realms of solitude where the Mississippi rolled its sullen tide, and the Ohio wound its belt of silver through the verdant woodlands.

To whom belonged this world of prairies and forests? France claimed it by right of discovery and occupation. It was her explorers who, after De Soto, first set foot on it. The question of right, it is true, mattered little; for, right or wrong, neither claimant would yield her pretensions so long as she had strength to uphold them; yet one point is worth a moment's notice. The French had established an excellent system in the distribution of their American lands. Whoever received a grant from the Crown was required to improve it, and this within reasonable time. If he did not, the land ceased to be his, and was given to another more able or industrious. An international extension of her own principle would have destroyed the pretensions of France to all the countries of the West. She had called them hers for three-fourths of a century, and they were still a howling waste, yielding nothing to civilization but beaver-skins, with here and there a fort, trading-post, or mission, and three or four puny hamlets by the Mississippi and the Detroit. We have seen how she might have made for herself an indisputable title, and peopled the solitudes with a host to maintain it. She would not; others were at hand who both would and could; and the late claimant, disinherited and forlorn, would soon be left to count the cost of her bigotry.

The thirteen British colonies were alike, insomuch as they all had representative governments, and a basis of English law. But the differences among them were great. Some were purely English; others were made up of various races, though the Anglo-Saxon was always predominant. Some had one prevailing religious creed; others had many creeds. Some had charters, and some had not. In most cases the governor was appointed by the Crown; in Pennsylvania and Maryland he was appointed by a feudal proprietor, and in Connecticut and Rhode Island he was chosen by the people. The differences of disposition and character were still greater than those of form.

The four northern colonies, known collectively as New England, were an exception to the general rule of diversity. The smallest, Rhode Island, had features all its own; but the rest were substantially one in nature and origin. The principal among them, Massachusetts, may serve as the type of all. It was a mosaic of little village republics, firmly cemented together, and formed into a single body politic through representatives sent to the "General Court" at Boston. Its government, originally theocratic, now tended to democracy, ballasted as yet by strong traditions of respect for established worth and ability, as well as by the influence of certain families prominent in affairs for generations. Yet there were no distinct class-lines, and popular power, like popular education, was widely diffused.

Practically Massachusetts was almost independent of the mother-country. Its people were purely English, of sound yeoman stock, with an abundant leaven drawn from the best of the Puritan gentry; but their original character had been somewhat modified by changed conditions of life. A harsh and exacting creed, with its stiff formalism and its prohibition of wholesome recreation; excess in the pursuit of gain,—the only resource left to energies robbed of their natural play; the struggle for existence on a hard and barren soil; and the isolation of a narrow village life,—joined to produce, in the meaner sort, qualities which were unpleasant, and sometimes repulsive. Puritanism was not an unmixed blessing. Its view of human nature was dark, and its attitude towards it one of repression. It strove to crush out not only what is evil, but much that is innocent and salutary. Human nature so treated will take its revenge, and for every vice that it loses find another instead. Nevertheless, while New England Puritanism bore its peculiar crop of faults, it produced also many good and sound fruits. An uncommon vigor, joined to the hardy virtues of a masculine race, marked the New England type. The sinews, it is true, were hardened at the expense of blood and flesh,—and this literally as well as figuratively; but the staple of character was a sturdy conscientiousness, an undespairing courage, patriotism, public spirit, sagacity, and a strong good sense. A great change, both for better and for worse, has since come over it, due largely to reaction against the unnatural rigors of the past. That mixture, which is now too common, of cool emotions with excitable brains, was then rarely seen. The New England colonies abounded in high examples of public and private virtue, though not always under the most prepossessing forms. They were conspicuous, moreover, for intellectual activity, and were by no means without intellectual eminence. Massachusetts had produced at least two men whose fame had crossed the sea,— Edwards, who out of the grim theology of Calvin mounted to sublime heights of mystical speculation; and Franklin, famous already by his discoveries in electricity. On the other hand, there were few genuine New Englanders who, however personally modest, could divest themselves of the notion that they belonged to a people in an especial manner the object of divine approval; and this self-righteousness, along with certain other traits, failed to commend the Puritan colonies to the favor of their fellows. Then, as now, New England was best known to her neighbors by her worst side.

In one point, however, she found general applause. She was regarded as the most military among the British colonies. This reputation was well founded, and is easily explained. More than all the rest, she lay open to attack. The long waving line of the New England border, with its lonely hamlets and scattered farms, extended from the Kennebec to beyond the Connecticut, and was everywhere vulnerable to the guns and tomahawks of the neighboring French and their savage allies. The colonies towards the south had thus far been safe from danger. New York alone was within striking distance of the Canadian war-parties. That province then consisted of a line of settlements up the Hudson and the Mohawk, and was little exposed to attack except at its northern end, which was guarded by the fortified town of Albany, with its outlying posts, and by the friendly and warlike Mohawks, whose "castles" were close at hand. Thus New England had borne the heaviest brunt of the preceding wars, not only by the forest, but also by the sea; for the French of Acadia and Cape Breton confronted her coast, and she was often at blows with them. Fighting had been a necessity with her, and she had met the emergency after a method extremely defective, but the best that circumstances would permit. Having no trained officers and no disciplined soldiers, and being too poor to maintain either, she borrowed her warriors from the workshop and the plough, and officered them with lawyers, merchants, mechanics, or farmers. To compare them with good regular troops would be folly; but they did, on the whole, better than could have been expected, and in the last war achieved the brilliant success of the capture of Louisbourg. This exploit, due partly to native hardihood and partly to good luck, greatly enhanced the military repute of New England, or rather was one of the chief sources of it.

The great colony of Virginia stood in strong contrast to New England. In both the population was English; but the one was Puritan with Roundhead traditions, and the other, so far as concerned its governing class, Anglican, with Cavalier traditions. In the one, every man, woman, and child could read and write; in the other, Sir William Berkeley once thanked God that there were no free schools, and no prospect of any for a century. The hope had found fruition. The lower classes of Virginia were as untaught as the warmest friend of popular ignorance could wish. New England had a native literature more than respectable under the circumstances, while Virginia had none; numerous industries, while Virginia was all agriculture, with but a single crop; a homogeneous society and a democratic spirit, while her rival was an aristocracy. Virginian society was distinctly stratified. On the lowest level were the negro slaves, nearly as numerous as all the rest together; next, the indented servants and the poor whites, of low origin, good-humored, but boisterous, and sometimes vicious; next, the small and despised class of tradesmen and mechanics; next, the farmers and lesser planters, who were mainly of good English stock, and who merged insensibly into the ruling class of the great landowners. It was these last who represented the colony and made the laws. They may be described as English country squires transplanted to a warm climate and turned slave-masters. They sustained their position by entails, and constantly undermined it by the reckless profusion which ruined them at last. Many of them were well born, with an immense pride of descent, increased by the habit of domination. Indolent and energetic by turns; rich in natural gifts and often poor in book-learning, though some, in the lack of good teaching at home, had been bred in the English universities; high-spirited, generous to a fault; keeping open house in their capacious mansions, among vast tobacco-fields and toiling negroes, and living in a rude pomp where the fashions of St. James were somewhat oddly grafted on the roughness of the plantation,—what they wanted in schooling was supplied by an education which books alone would have been impotent to give, the education which came with the possession and exercise of political power, and the sense of a position to maintain, joined to a bold spirit of independence and a patriotic attachment to the Old Dominion. They were few in number; they raced, gambled, drank, and swore; they did everything that in Puritan eyes was most reprehensible; and in the day of need they gave the United Colonies a body of statesmen and orators which had no equal on the continent. A vigorous aristocracy favors the growth of personal eminence, even in those who are not of it, but only near it.

The essential antagonism of Virginia and New England was afterwards to become, and to remain for a century, an element of the first influence in American history. Each might have learned much from the other; but neither did so till, at last, the strife of their contending principles shook the continent. Pennsylvania differed widely from both. She was a conglomerate of creeds and races,—English, Irish, Germans, Dutch, and Swedes; Quakers, Lutherans, Presbyterians, Romanists, Moravians, and a variety of nondescript sects. The Quakers prevailed in the eastern districts; quiet, industrious, virtuous, and serenely obstinate. The Germans were strongest towards the centre of the colony, and were chiefly peasants; successful farmers, but dull, ignorant, and superstitious. Towards the west were the Irish, of whom some were Celts, always quarrelling with their German neighbors, who detested them; but the greater part were Protestants of Scotch descent, from Ulster; a vigorous border population. Virginia and New England had each a strong distinctive character. Pennsylvania, with her heterogeneous population, had none but that which she owed to the sober neutral tints of Quaker existence. A more thriving colony there was not on the continent. Life, if monotonous, was smooth and contented. Trade and the arts grew. Philadelphia, next to Boston, was the largest town in British America; and was, moreover, the intellectual centre of the middle and southern colonies. Unfortunately, for her credit in the approaching war, the Quaker influence made Pennsylvania non-combatant. Politically, too, she was an anomaly; for, though utterly unfeudal in disposition and character, she was under feudal superiors in the persons of the representatives of William Penn, the original grantee.

New York had not as yet reached the relative prominence which her geographical position and inherent strength afterwards gave her. The English, joined to the Dutch, the original settlers, were the dominant population; but a half-score of other languages were spoken in the province, the chief among them being that of the Huguenot French in the southern parts, and that of the Germans on the Mohawk. In religion, the province was divided between the Anglican Church, with government support and popular dislike, and numerous dissenting sects, chiefly Lutherans, Independents, Presbyterians, and members of the Dutch Reformed Church. The little city of New York, like its great successor, was the most cosmopolitan place on the continent, and probably the gayest. It had, in abundance, balls, concerts, theatricals, and evening clubs, with plentiful dances and other amusements for the poorer classes. Thither in the winter months came the great hereditary proprietors on the Hudson; for the old Dutch feudality still held its own, and the manors of Van Rensselaer, Cortland, and Livingston, with their seigniorial privileges, and the great estates and numerous tenantry of the Schuylers and other leading families, formed the basis of an aristocracy, some of whose members had done good service to the province, and were destined to do more. Pennsylvania was feudal in form, and not in spirit; Virginia in spirit, and not in form; New England in neither; and New York largely in both. This social crystallization had, it is true, many opponents. In politics, as in religion, there were sharp antagonisms and frequent quarrels. They centred in the city; for in the well-stocked dwellings of the Dutch farmers along the Hudson there reigned a tranquil and prosperous routine; and the Dutch border town of Albany had not its like in America for unruffled conservatism and quaint picturesqueness.

Of the other colonies, the briefest mention will suffice: New Jersey, with its wholesome population of farmers; tobacco-growing Maryland, which, but for its proprietary government and numerous Roman Catholics, might pass for another

Virginia, inferior in growth, and less decisive in features; Delaware, a modest appendage of Pennsylvania; wild and rude North Carolina; and, farther on, South Carolina and Georgia, too remote from the seat of war to take a noteworthy part in it. The attitude of these various colonies towards each other is hardly conceivable to an American of the present time. They had no political tie except a common allegiance to the British Crown. Communication between them was difficult and slow, by rough roads traced often through primeval forests. Between some of them there was less of sympathy than of jealousy kindled by conflicting interests or perpetual disputes concerning boundaries. The patriotism of the colonist was bounded by the lines of his government, except in the compact and kindred colonies of New England, which were socially united, though politically distinct. The country of the New Yorker was New York, and the country of the Virginian was Virginia. The New England colonies had once confederated; but, kindred as they were, they had long ago dropped apart. William Penn proposed a plan of colonial union wholly fruitless. James II. tried to unite all the northern colonies under one government; but the attempt came to naught. Each stood aloof, jealously independent. At rare intervals, under the pressure of an emergency, some of them would try to act in concert; and, except in New England, the results had been most discouraging. Nor was it this segregation only that unfitted them for war. They were all subject to popular legislatures, through whom alone money and men could be raised; and these elective bodies were sometimes factious and selfish, and not always either far-sighted or reasonable. Moreover, they were in a state of ceaseless friction with their governors, who represented the King, or, what was worse, the feudal proprietary. These disputes, though varying in intensity, were found everywhere except in the two small colonies which chose their own governors; and they were premonitions of the movement towards independence which ended in the war of Revolution. The occasion of difference mattered little. Active or latent, the quarrel was always present. In New York it turned on a question of the governor's salary; in Pennsylvania on the taxation of the proprietary estates; in Virginia on a fee exacted for the issue of land patents. It was sure to arise whenever some public crisis gave the representatives of the people an opportunity of extorting concessions from the representative of the Crown, or gave the representative of the Crown an opportunity to gain a point for prerogative. That is to say, the time when action was most needed was the time chosen for obstructing it.

In Canada there was no popular legislature to embarrass the central power. The people, like an army, obeyed the word of command,—a military advantage beyond all price.

Divided in government; divided in origin, feelings, and principles; jealous of each other, jealous of the Crown; the people at war with the executive, and, by the fermentation of internal politics, blinded to an outward danger that seemed remote and vague,—such were the conditions under which the British colonies drifted into a war that was to decide the fate of the continent.

This war was the strife of a united and concentred few against a divided and discordant many. It was the strife, too, of the past against the future; of the old against the new; of moral and intellectual torpor against moral and intellectual life; of barren absolutism against a liberty, crude, incoherent, and chaotic, yet full of prolific vitality.

[WOLFE BEFORE QUEBEC]

In early spring the chiefs of Canada met at Montreal to settle a plan of defence. What at first they most dreaded was an advance of the enemy by way of Lake Champlain. Bourlamaque, with three battalions, was ordered to take post at Ticonderoga, hold it if he could, or, if overborne by numbers, fall back to Isle-aux-Noix, at the outlet of the lake. La Corne was sent with a strong detachment to intrench himself at the head of the rapids of the St. Lawrence, and oppose any hostile movement from Lake Ontario. Every able-bodied man in the colony, and every boy who could fire a gun, was to be called to the field.

Vaudreuil sent a circular letter to the militia captains of all the parishes, with orders to read it to the parishioners. It exhorted them to defend their religion, their wives, their children, and their goods from the fury of the heretics; declared that he, the governor, would never yield up Canada on any terms whatever; and ordered them to join the army at once, leaving none behind but the old, the sick, the women, and the children. The bishop issued a pastoral mandate: "On every side, dearest brethren, the enemy is making immense preparations. His forces, at least six times more numerous than ours, are already in motion. Never was Canada in a state so critical and full of peril. Never were we so destitute, or threatened with an attack so fierce, so general, and so obstinate. Now, in truth, we may say, more than ever before, that our only resource is in the powerful succor of our Lord. Then, dearest brethren, make every effort to deserve it. 'Seek first the kingdom of God; and all these things shall be added unto you.'" And he reproves their sins, exhorts them to repentance, and ordains processions, masses, and prayers.

Vaudreuil bustled and boasted. In May he wrote to the minister: "The zeal with which I am animated for the service of the King will always make me surmount the greatest obstacles. I am taking the most proper measures to give the enemy a good reception whenever he may attack us. I keep in view the defence of Quebec. I have given orders in the parishes below to muster the inhabitants who are able to bear arms, and place women, children, cattle, and even hay and grain, in places of safety. Permit me, Monseigneur, to beg you to have the goodness to assure His Majesty that, to whatever hard extremity I may be reduced, my zeal will be equally ardent and indefatigable, and that I shall do the impossible to prevent our enemies from making progress in any direction, or, at least, to make them pay extremely dear for it." Then he writes again to say that Amherst with a great army will, as he learns, attack Ticonderoga; that Bradstreet, with six thousand men, will advance to Lake Ontario; and that six thousand more will march to the Ohio. "Whatever progress they may make," he adds, "I am resolved to yield them nothing, but hold my ground even to annihilation." He promises to do his best to keep on good terms with Montcalm, and ends with a warm eulogy of Bigot.

It was in the midst of all these preparations that Bougainville arrived from France with news that a great fleet was on its way to attack Quebec. The town was filled with consternation mixed with surprise, for the Canadians had believed that the dangerous navigation of the St. Lawrence would deter their enemies from the attempt. "Everybody," writes one of them, "was stupefied at an enterprise that seemed so bold." In a few days a crowd of sails was seen approaching. They were not enemies, but friends. It was the fleet of the contractor Cadet, commanded by an officer named Kanon, and loaded with supplies for the colony. They anchored in the harbor, eighteen sail in all, and their arrival spread universal joy. Admiral Durell had come too late to intercept them, catching but three stragglers that had lagged behind the rest. Still others succeeded in eluding him, and before the first of June five more ships had come safely into port.

When the news brought by Bougainville reached Montreal, nearly the whole force of the colony, except the detachments of Bourlamaque and La Corne, was ordered to Quebec. Montcalm hastened thither, and Vaudreuil followed. The governor-general wrote to the minister in his usual strain, as if all the hope of Canada rested in him. Such, he says, was his activity, that, though very busy, he reached Quebec only a day and a half after Montcalm; and, on arriving, learned from his scouts that English ships-of-war had already appeared at Isle-aux-Coudres. These were the squadron of Durell. "I expect," Vaudreuil goes on, "to be sharply attacked, and that our enemies will make their most powerful efforts to conquer this colony; but there is no ruse, no resource, no means which my zeal does not suggest to lay snares for them, and finally, when the exigency demands it, to fight them with an ardor, and even a fury, which exceeds the range of their ambitious designs. The troops, the Canadians, and the Indians are not ignorant of the resolution I have taken, and from which I shall not recoil under any circumstance whatever. The burghers of this city have already put their goods and furniture in places of safety. The old men, women, and children hold themselves ready to leave town. My firmness is generally applauded. It has penetrated every heart; and each man says aloud: 'Canada, our native land, shall bury us under its ruins before we surrender to the English!' This is decidedly my own determination, and I shall hold to it inviolably." He launches into high praise of the contractor Cadet, whose zeal for the service of the King and the defence of the colony he declares to be triumphant over every difficulty. It is necessary, he adds, that ample supplies of all kinds should be sent out in the autumn, with the distribution of which Cadet offers to charge himself, and to account for them at their first cost; but he does not say what prices his disinterested friend will compel the destitute Canadians to pay for them.

Five battalions from France, nearly all the colony troops, and the militia from every part of Canada poured into Quebec, along with a thousand or more Indians, who, at the call of Vaudreuil, came to lend their scalping-knives to the defence. Such was the ardor of the people that boys of fifteen and men of eighty were to be seen in the camp. Isle-aux-Coudres and Isle d'Orléans were ordered to be evacuated, and an excited crowd on the rock of Quebec watched hourly for the approaching fleet. Days passed and weeks passed, yet it did not appear. Meanwhile Vaudreuil held council after council to settle a plan of defence. They were strange scenes: a crowd of officers of every rank, mixed pell-mell in a small room, pushing, shouting, elbowing each other, interrupting each other; till Montcalm, in despair, took each aside after the meeting was over, and made him give his opinion in writing.

He himself had at first proposed to encamp the army on the plains of Abraham and the meadows of the St. Charles, making that river his line of defence; but he changed his plan, and, with the concurrence of Vaudreuil, resolved to post his whole force on the St. Lawrence below the city, with his right resting on the St. Charles, and his left on the Montmorenci. Here, accordingly, the troops and militia were stationed as they arrived. Early in

June, standing at the northeastern brink of the rock of Quebec, one could have seen the whole position at a glance. On the curving shore from the St. Charles to the rocky gorge of the Montmorenci, a distance of seven or eight miles, the whitewashed dwellings of the parish of Beauport stretched down the road in a double chain, and the fields on both sides were studded with tents, huts, and Indian wigwams. Along the borders of the St. Lawrence, as far as the eye could distinguish them, gangs of men were throwing up redoubts, batteries, and lines of intrenchment. About midway between the two extremities of the encampment ran the little river of Beauport; and on the rising ground just beyond it stood a large stone house, round which the tents were thickly clustered; for here Montcalm had made his headquarters.

A boom of logs chained together was drawn across the mouth of the St. Charles, which was further guarded by two hulks mounted with cannon. The bridge of boats that crossed the stream nearly a mile above formed the chief communication between the city and the camp. Its head towards Beauport was protected by a strong and extensive earthwork; and the banks of the stream on the Quebec side were also intrenched, to form a second line of defence in case the position at Beauport should be forced.

In the city itself every gate, except the Palace Gate, which gave access to the bridge, was closed and barricaded. A hundred and six cannon were mounted on the walls. A floating battery of twelve heavy pieces, a number of gunboats, eight fireships, and several firerafts formed the river defences. The largest merchantmen of Kanon's fleet were sacrificed to make the fireships; and the rest, along with the frigates that came with them, were sent for safety up the St. Lawrence beyond the river Richelieu, whence about a thousand of their sailors returned to man the batteries and gunboats.

In the camps along the Beauport shore were about fourteen thousand men, besides Indians. The regulars held the centre; the militia of Quebec and Three Rivers were on the right, and those of Montreal on the left. In Quebec itself there was a garrison of between one and two thousand men under the Chevalier de Ramesay. Thus the whole number, including Indians, amounted to more than sixteen thousand; and though the Canadians who formed the greater part of it were of little use in the open field, they could be trusted to fight well behind intrenchments. Against this force, posted behind defensive works, on positions almost impregnable by nature, Wolfe brought less than nine thousand men available for operations on land. The steep and lofty heights that lined the river made the cannon of the ships for the most part useless, while the exigencies of the naval service forbade employing the sailors on shore. In two or three instances only, throughout the siege, small squads of them landed to aid in moving and working cannon; and the actual fighting fell to the troops alone.

Vaudreuil and Bigot took up their quarters with the army. The governor-general had delegated the command of the land-forces to Montcalm, whom, in his own words, he authorized "to give orders everywhere, provisionally." His relations with him were more than ever anomalous and critical; for while Vaudreuil, in virtue of his office, had a right to supreme command, Montcalm, now a lieutenant-general, held a military grade far above him; and the governor, while always writing himself down in his despatches as the head and front of every movement, had too little self-confidence not to leave the actual command in the hands of his rival.

Days and weeks wore on, and the first excitement gave way to restless impatience. Why did not the English come? Many of the Canadians thought that Heaven would interpose and wreck the English fleet, as it had wrecked that of Admiral Walker half a century before. There were processions, prayers, and vows towards this happy consummation. Food was scarce. Bigot and Cadet lived in luxury; fowls by thousands were fattened with wheat for their tables, while the people were put on rations of two ounces of bread a day. Durell and his ships were reported to be still at Isle-aux-Coudres. Vaudreuil sent thither a party of Canadians, and they captured three midshipmen, who, says Montcalm, had gone ashore *pour polissonner,* that is, on a lark. These youths were brought to Quebec, where they increased the general anxiety by grossly exaggerating the English force.

At length it became known that eight English vessels were anchored in the north channel of Orleans, and on the twenty-first of June the masts of three of them could plainly be seen. One of the fireships was consumed in a vain attempt to burn them, and several firerafts and a sort of infernal machine were tried with no better success; the unwelcome visitors still held their posts.

Meanwhile the whole English fleet had slowly advanced, piloted by Denis de Vitré, a Canadian of good birth, captured at sea some time before, and now compelled to serve, under a threat of being hanged if he refused. Nor was he alone; for when Durell reached the place where the river pilots were usually taken on board, he raised a French flag to his mast-head, causing great rejoicings among the Canadians on shore, who thought that a fleet was come to their rescue, and that their country was saved. The pilots launched their canoes and came out to the ships, where they were all made prisoners; then the French flag was lowered, and the red cross displayed in its stead. The spectators on shore turned from joy to despair; and a priest who stood watching the squadron with a telescope is said to have dropped dead with the revulsion of feeling.

Towards the end of June the main fleet was near the mountain of Cape Tourmente. The passage called the Traverse, between the Cape and the lower end of the Island of Orleans, was reputed one of the most dangerous parts of the St. Lawrence; and as the ships successively came up, the captive pilots were put on board to carry them safely through, on pain of death. One of these men was assigned to the transport "Goodwill," in which was Captain Knox, who spoke French, and who reports thus in his Diary: "He gasconaded at a most extravagant rate, and gave us to understand that it was much against his will that he was become an English pilot. The poor fellow assumed great latitude in his conversation, and said 'he made no doubt that some of the fleet would return to England, but they should have a dismal tale to carry with them; for Canada should be the grave of the whole army, and he expected in a short time to see the walls of Quebec ornamented with English scalps.' Had it not been in obedience to the Admiral, who gave orders that he should not be ill-used, he would certainly have been thrown overboard." The master of the transport was an old sailor named Killick, who despised the whole Gallic race, and had no mind to see his ship in charge of a Frenchman. "He would not let the pilot speak," continues Knox, "but fixed his mate at the helm, charged him not to take orders from any person but himself, and going forward with his trumpet to the forecastle, gave the necessary instructions. All that could be said by the commanding officer and the other gentlemen on board was to no purpose; the pilot declared we should be lost, for that no French ship ever presumed to pass there without a pilot. 'Ay, ay, my dear,' replied our son of Neptune, 'but, damn me, I'll convince you that an Englishman shall go where a Frenchman dare not show his nose.' The 'Richmond' frigate being close astern of us, the commanding officer called out to the captain and told him our case; he inquired who the master was, and was answered from the forecastle by the man himself, who told him 'he was old Killick, and that was enough.' I went forward with this experienced mariner, who pointed out the channel to me as we passed; showing me by the ripple and color of the water where there was any danger, and distinguishing the places where there were ledges of rocks (to me invisible) from banks of sand, mud, or gravel. He gave his orders with great unconcern, joked with the sounding-boats which lay off on each side with different colored flags for our guidance; and when any of them called to him and pointed to the deepest water, he answered: 'Ay, ay, my dear, chalk it down, a damned dangerous navigation, eh! If you don't make a sputter about it you'll get no credit in England.' After we had cleared this remarkable place, where the channel forms a complete zigzag, the master called to his mate to give the helm to somebody else, saying, 'Damn me if there are not a thousand places in the Thames fifty times more hazardous than this; I am ashamed

that Englishmen should make such a rout about it.' The Frenchman asked me if the captain had not been there before. I assured him in the negative; upon which he viewed him with
great attention, lifting at the same time his hands and eyes to
heaven with astonishment and fervency."

Vaudreuil was blamed for not planting cannon at a certain
plateau on the side of the mountain of Cape Tourmente, where
the gunners would have been inaccessible, and whence they
could have battered every passing ship with a plunging fire.
As it was, the whole fleet sailed safely through. On the twenty-
sixth they were all anchored off the south shore of the Island of
Orleans, a few miles from Quebec; and, writes Knox, "here we
are entertained with a most agreeable prospect of a delightful
country on every side; windmills, watermills, churches, chapels,
and compact farmhouses, all built with stone, and covered,
some with wood, and others with straw. The lands appear to
be everywhere well cultivated; and with the help of my glass I
can discern that they are sowed with flax, wheat, barley, peas,
etc., and the grounds are enclosed with wooden pales. The
weather to-day is agreeably warm. A light fog sometimes
hangs over the highlands, but in the river we have a fine clear
air. In the curve of the river, while we were under sail, we had
a transient view of a stupendous natural curiosity called the
waterfall of Montmorenci."

That night Lieutenant Meech, with forty New England
rangers, landed on the Island of Orleans, and found a body of
armed inhabitants, who tried to surround him. He beat them
off, and took possession of a neighboring farmhouse, where he
remained till daylight; then pursued the enemy, and found that
they had crossed to the north shore. The whole army now
landed, and were drawn up on the beach. As they were kept
there for some time, Knox and several brother officers went to
visit the neighboring church of St. Laurent, where they found
a letter from the parish priest, directed to "The Worthy Officers
of the British Army," praying that they would protect the
sacred edifice, and also his own adjoining house, and adding,
with somewhat needless civility, that he wished they had come

sooner, that they might have enjoyed the asparagus and radishes
of his garden, now unhappily going to seed. The letter concluded with many compliments and good wishes, in which the
Britons to whom they were addressed saw only "the frothy
politeness so peculiar to the French." The army marched westward and encamped. Wolfe, with his chief engineer, Major
Mackellar, and an escort of light infantry, advanced to the
extreme point of the island.

Here he could see, in part, the desperate nature of the task he
had undertaken. Before him, three or four miles away, Quebec
sat perched upon her rock, a congregation of stone houses,
churches, palaces, convents, and hospitals; the green trees of
the Seminary garden and the spires of the Cathedral, the Ursulines, the Récollets, and the Jesuits. Beyond rose the loftier
height of Cape Diamond, edged with palisades and capped
with redoubt and parapet. Batteries frowned everywhere; the
Château battery, the Clergy battery, the Hospital battery, on
the rock above, and the Royal, Dauphin's, and Queen's batteries on the strand, where the dwellings and warehouses of the
lower town clustered beneath the cliff.

Full in sight lay the far-extended camp of Montcalm, stretching from the St. Charles, beneath the city walls, to the chasm
and cataract of the Montmorenci. From the cataract to the river
of Beauport, its front was covered by earthworks along the
brink of abrupt and lofty heights; and from the river of Beauport to the St. Charles, by broad flats of mud swept by the fire
of redoubts, intrenchments, a floating battery, and the city
itself. Above the city, Cape Diamond hid the view; but could
Wolfe have looked beyond it, he would have beheld a prospect
still more disheartening. Here, mile after mile, the St. Lawrence
was walled by a range of steeps, often inaccessible, and always
so difficult that a few men at the top could hold an army in
check; while at Cap-Rouge, about eight miles distant, the high
plateau was cleft by the channel of a stream which formed a
line of defence as strong as that of the Montmorenci. Quebec
was a natural fortress. Bougainville had long before examined
the position, and reported that "by the help of intrenchments,

easily and quickly made, and defended by three or four thousand men, I think the city would be safe. I do not believe that the English will make any attempt against it; but they may have the madness to do so, and it is well to be prepared against surprise."

Not four thousand men, but four times four thousand, now stood in its defence; and their chiefs wisely resolved not to throw away the advantages of their position. Nothing more was heard of Vaudreuil's bold plan of attacking the invaders at their landing; and Montcalm had declared that he would play the part, not of Hannibal, but of Fabius. His plan was to avoid a general battle, run no risks, and protract the defence till the resources of the enemy were exhausted, or till approaching winter forced them to withdraw. Success was almost certain but for one contingency. Amherst, with a force larger than that of Wolfe, was moving against Ticonderoga. If he should capture it, and advance into the colony, Montcalm would be forced to weaken his army by sending strong detachments to oppose him. Here was Wolfe's best hope. This failing, his only chance was in audacity. The game was desperate; but, intrepid gamester as he was in war, he was a man, in the last resort, to stake everything on the cast of the dice.

The elements declared for France. On the afternoon of the day when Wolfe's army landed, a violent squall swept over the St. Lawrence, dashed the ships together, drove several ashore, and destroyed many of the flat-boats from which the troops had just disembarked. "I never saw so much distress among shipping in my whole life," writes an officer to a friend in Boston. Fortunately the storm subsided as quickly as it rose. Vaudreuil saw that the hoped-for deliverance had failed; and as the tempest had not destroyed the British fleet, he resolved to try the virtue of his fireships. "I am afraid," says Montcalm, "that they have cost us a million, and will be good for nothing after all." This remained to be seen. Vaudreuil gave the chief command of them to a naval officer named Delouche; and on the evening of the twenty-eighth, after long consultation and much debate among their respective captains, they set sail together at ten o'clock. The night was moonless and dark. In less than an hour they were at the entrance of the north channel. Delouche had been all enthusiasm; but as he neared the danger his nerves failed, and he set fire to his ship half an hour too soon, the rest following his example.

There was an English outpost at the Point of Orleans; and, about eleven o'clock, the sentries descried through the gloom the ghostly outlines of the approaching ships. As they gazed, these mysterious strangers began to dart tongues of flame; fire ran like lightning up their masts and sails, and then they burst out like volcanoes. Filled as they were with pitch, tar, and every manner of combustible, mixed with fireworks, bombs, grenades, and old cannon, swivels, and muskets loaded to the throat, the effect was terrific. The troops at the Point, amazed at the sudden eruption, the din of the explosions, and the showers of grapeshot that rattled among the trees, lost their wits and fled. The blazing dragons hissed and roared, spouted sheets of fire, vomited smoke in black, pitchy volumes and vast illumined clouds, and shed their infernal glare on the distant city, the tents of Montcalm, and the long red lines of the British army, drawn up in array of battle, lest the French should cross from their encampments to attack them in the confusion. Knox calls the display "the grandest fireworks that can possibly be conceived." Yet the fireships did no other harm than burning alive one of their own captains and six or seven of his sailors who failed to escape in their boats. Some of them ran ashore before reaching the fleet; the others were seized by the intrepid English sailors, who, approaching in their boats, threw grappling-irons upon them and towed them towards land, till they swung round and stranded. Here, after venting their fury for a while, they subsided into quiet conflagration, which lasted till morning. Vaudreuil watched the result of his experiment from the steeple of the church at Beauport; then returned, dejected, to Quebec.

Wolfe longed to fight his enemy; but his sagacious enemy would not gratify him. From the heights of Beauport, the rock of Quebec, or the summit of Cape Diamond, Montcalm could look down on the river and its shores as on a map, and watch each movement of the invaders. He was hopeful, perhaps confident; and for a month or more he wrote almost daily to Bourlamaque at Ticonderoga, in a cheerful, and often a jocose vein, mingling orders and instructions with pleasantries and bits of news. Yet his vigilance was unceasing. "We pass every night in bivouac, or else sleep in our clothes. Perhaps you are doing as much, my dear Bourlamaque."

Of the two commanders, Vaudreuil was the more sanguine, and professed full faith that all would go well. He too corresponded with Bourlamaque, to whom he gave his opinion, founded on the reports of deserters, that Wolfe had no chance of success unless Amherst should come to his aid. This he pronounced impossible; and he expressed a strong desire that the English would attack him, "so that we may rid ourselves of them at once." He was courageous, except in the immediate presence of danger, and failed only when the crisis came.

Wolfe, held in check at every other point, had one movement in his power. He could seize the heights of Point Levi, opposite the city; and this, along with his occupation of the Island of Orleans, would give him command of the Basin of Quebec. Thence also he could fire on the place across the St. Lawrence, which is here less than a mile wide. The movement was begun on the afternoon of the twenty-ninth, when, shivering in a north wind and a sharp frost, a part of Monckton's brigade was ferried over to Beaumont, on the south shore, and the rest followed in the morning. The rangers had a brush with a party of Canadians, whom they drove off, and the regulars then landed unopposed. Monckton ordered a proclamation, signed by Wolfe, to be posted on the door of the parish church. It called on the Canadians, in peremptory terms, to stand neutral in the contest, promised them, if they did so, full protection in property and religion, and threatened that, if they presumed to resist the invaders, their houses, goods, and harvests should be destroyed, and their churches despoiled. As soon as the troops were out of sight the inhabitants took down the placard and carried it to Vaudreuil.

The brigade marched along the river road to Point Levi, drove off a body of French and Indians posted in the church, and took possession of the houses and the surrounding heights. In the morning they were intrenching themselves, when they were greeted by a brisk fire from the edge of the woods. It came from a party of Indians, whom the rangers presently put to flight, and, imitating their own ferocity, scalped nine of them. Wolfe came over to the camp on the next day, went with an escort to the heights opposite Quebec, examined it with a spyglass, and chose a position from which to bombard it. Cannon and mortars were brought ashore, fascines and gabions made, intrenchments thrown up, and batteries planted. Knox came over from the main camp, and says that he had "a most agreeable view of the city of Quebec. It is a very fair object for our artillery, particularly the lower town." But why did Wolfe wish to bombard it? Its fortifications were but little exposed to his fire, and to knock its houses, convents, and churches to pieces would bring him no nearer to his object. His guns at Point Levi could destroy the city, but could not capture it; yet doubtless they would have good moral effect, discourage the French, and cheer his own soldiers with the flattering belief that they were achieving something.

The guns of Quebec showered balls and bombs upon his workmen; but they still toiled on, and the French saw the fatal batteries fast growing to completion. The citizens, alarmed at the threatened destruction, begged the governor for leave to cross the river and dislodge their assailants. At length he consented. A party of twelve or fifteen hundred was made up of armed burghers, Canadians from the camp, a few Indians, some pupils of the Seminary, and about a hundred volunteers from the regulars. Dumas, an experienced officer, took command of them; and, going up to Sillery, they crossed the river on the night of the twelfth of July. They had hardly climbed the heights of the south shore when they grew exceedingly nervous, though the enemy was still three miles off. The Seminary scholars fired on some of their own party, whom they mistook for English; and the same mishap was repeated a second and a third time. A panic seized the whole body, and Dumas could not control them. They turned and made for their canoes, rolling over each other as they rushed down the heights, and reappeared at Quebec at six in the morning, overwhelmed with despair and shame.

The presentiment of the unhappy burghers proved too true. The English batteries fell to their work, and the families of the town fled to the country for safety. In a single day eighteen houses and the cathedral were burned by exploding shells; and fiercer and fiercer the storm of fire and iron hailed upon Quebec.

Wolfe did not rest content with distressing his enemy. With an ardor and a daring that no difficulties could cool, he sought means to strike an effective blow. It was nothing to lay Quebec in ruins if he could not defeat the army that protected it. To land from boats and attack Montcalm in front, through the mud of the Beauport flats or up the heights along the neighboring shore, was an enterprise too rash even for his temerity. It might, however, be possible to land below the cataract of Montmorenci, cross that stream higher up, and strike the French army in flank or rear; and he had no sooner secured his positions at the points of Levi and Orleans, than he addressed himself to this attempt.

On the eighth several frigates and a bomb-ketch took their stations before the camp of the Chevalier de Lévis, who, with his division of Canadian militia, occupied the heights along the St. Lawrence just above the cataract. Here they shelled and cannonaded him all day; though, from his elevated position, with very little effect. Towards evening the troops on the Point of Orleans broke up their camp. Major Hardy, with a detachment of marines, was left to hold that post, while the rest embarked at night in the boats of the fleet. They were the brigades of Townshend and Murray, consisting of five battalions, with a body of grenadiers, light infantry, and rangers,—in all three thousand men. They landed before daybreak in front of the parish of L'Ange Gardien, a little below the cataract. The only opposition was from a troop of Canadians and Indians, whom they routed, after some loss, climbed the heights, gained the plateau above, and began to intrench themselves. A company of rangers, supported by detachments of regulars, was sent into the neighboring forest to protect the parties who were cutting fascines, and apparently, also, to look for a fording-place.

Lévis, with his Scotch-Jacobite aide-de-camp, Johnstone, had watched the movements of Wolfe from the heights across the cataract. Johnstone says that he asked his commander if he was sure there was no ford higher up on the Montmorenci, by which the English could cross. Lévis averred that there was none, and that he himself had examined the stream to its source; on which a Canadian who stood by whispered to the aide-de-camp: "The general is mistaken; there is a ford." Johnstone told this to Lévis, who would not believe it, and so browbeat the Canadian that he dared not repeat what he had said. Johnstone, taking him aside, told him to go and find somebody who had lately crossed the ford, and bring him at once to the general's quarters; whereupon he soon reappeared with a man who affirmed that he had crossed it the night before with a sack of wheat on his back. A detachment was immediately sent to the place, with orders to intrench itself, and Repentigny, lieutenant of Lévis, was posted not far off with eleven hundred Canadians.

Four hundred Indians passed the ford under the partisan Langlade, discovered Wolfe's detachment, hid themselves, and sent their commander to tell Repentigny that there was a body of English in the forest, who might all be destroyed if he would come over at once with his Canadians. Repentigny sent for orders to Lévis, and Lévis sent for orders to Vaudreuil, whose quarters were three or four miles distant. Vaudreuil answered that no risk should be run, and that he would come and see to the matter himself. It was about two hours before he arrived; and meanwhile the Indians grew impatient, rose from their hiding-place, fired on the rangers, and drove them back with heavy loss upon the regulars, who stood their ground, and at last repulsed the assailants. The Indians recrossed the ford with thirty-six scalps. If Repentigny had advanced, and Lévis had followed with his main body, the consequences to the English might have been serious; for, as Johnstone remarks, "a Canadian in the woods is worth three disciplined soldiers, as a soldier in a plain is worth three Canadians." Vaudreuil called a council of war. The question was whether an effort should be made to dislodge Wolfe's main force. Montcalm and the governor were this time of one mind, and both thought it inexpedient to attack, with militia, a body of regular troops whose numbers and position were imperfectly known. Bigot gave his voice for the attack. He was overruled, and Wolfe was left to fortify himself in peace.

His occupation of the heights of Montmorenci exposed him to great risks. The left wing of his army at Point Levi was six miles from its right wing at the cataract, and Major Hardy's detachment on the Point of Orleans was between them, separated from each by a wide arm of the St. Lawrence. Any one of the three camps might be overpowered before the others could support it; and Hardy with his small force was above all in danger of being cut to pieces. But the French kept persistently on the defensive; and after the failure of Dumas to dislodge the English from Point Levi, Vaudreuil would not hear of another such attempt. Wolfe was soon well intrenched; but it was easier to defend himself than to strike at his enemy. Montcalm, when urged to attack him, is said to have answered: "Let him amuse himself where he is. If we drive him off, he may go to some place where he can do us harm." His late movement, however, had a discouraging effect on the Canadians, who now for the first time began to desert. His batteries, too, played across the chasm of Montmorenci upon the left wing of the French army with an effect extremely annoying.

The position of the hostile forces was a remarkable one. They were separated by the vast gorge that opens upon the St. Lawrence; an amphitheatre of lofty precipices, their brows crested with forests, and their steep brown sides scantily feathered with stunted birch and fir. Into this abyss leaps the Montmorenci with one headlong plunge of nearly two hundred and fifty feet, a living column of snowy white, with its spray, its foam, its mists, and its rainbows; then spreads itself in broad, thin sheets over a floor of rock and gravel, and creeps tamely to the St. Lawrence. It was but a gunshot across the gulf, and the sentinels on each side watched each other over the roar and turmoil of the cataract. Captain Knox, coming one day from Point Levi to receive orders from Wolfe, improved a spare hour to visit this marvel of nature. "I had very nigh paid dear for my inquisitiveness; for while I stood on the eminence I was hastily called to by one of our sentinels, when, throwing my eyes about, I saw a Frenchman creeping under the eastern extremity of their breastwork to fire at me. This obliged me to retire as fast as I could out of his reach, and, making up to the sentry to thank him for his attention, he told me the fellow had snapped his piece twice, and the second time it flashed in the pan at the instant I turned away from the Fall." Another officer, less fortunate, had a leg broken by a shot from the opposite cliffs.

Day after day went by, and the invaders made no progress. Flags of truce passed often between the hostile camps. "You will demolish the town, no doubt," said the bearer of one of them, "but you shall never get inside of it." To which Wolfe replied: "I will have Quebec if I stay here till the end of November." Sometimes the heat was intense, and sometimes there were floods of summer rain that inundated the tents. Along the river, from the Montmorenci to Point Levi, there were ceaseless artillery fights between gunboats, frigates, and batteries on shore. Bands of Indians infested the outskirts of the camps, killing sentries and patrols. The rangers chased them through the woods; there were brisk skirmishes, and scalps lost and won. Sometimes the regulars took part in these forest battles; and once it was announced, in orders of the day, that "the General has ordered two sheep and some rum to Captain Cosnan's company of grenadiers for the spirit they showed this morning in pushing those scoundrels of Indians." The Indians complained that the British soldiers were learning how to fight, and no longer stood still in a mass to be shot at, as in Braddock's time. The Canadian *coureurs de bois* mixed with their red allies and wore their livery. One of them was caught on the eighteenth. He was naked, daubed red and blue, and adorned with a bunch of painted feathers dangling from the top of his head. He and his companions used the scalping-knife as freely as the Indians themselves; nor were the New England rangers much behind them in this respect, till an order came from Wolfe forbidding "the inhuman practice of scalping, except when the enemy are Indians, or Canadians dressed like Indians."

A part of the fleet worked up into the Basin, beyond the Point of Orleans; and here, on the warm summer nights, officers and men watched the cannon flashing and thundering from the heights of Montmorenci on one side, and those of Point Levi on the other, and the bombs sailing through the air in fiery semi-circles. Often the gloom was lighted up by the blaze of the burning houses of Quebec, kindled by incendiary shells. Both the lower and the upper town were nearly deserted by the inhabitants, some retreating into the country, and some into the suburb of St. Roch; while the Ursulines and Hospital nuns abandoned their convents to seek harborage beyond the range of shot. The city was a prey to robbers, who pillaged the empty houses, till an order came from headquarters promising the gallows to all who should be caught. News reached the French that Niagara was attacked, and that the army of Amherst was moving against Ticonderoga. The Canadians deserted more and more. They were disheartened by the defensive attitude in which both Vaudreuil and Montcalm steadily persisted; and accustomed as they were to rapid raids, sudden strokes, and a quick return to their homes, they tired of long weeks of inaction. The English patrols caught one of them as he was passing the time in fishing. "He seemed to be a subtle old rogue," says Knox, "of seventy years of age, as he told us. We plied him well with port wine, and then his heart was more open; and seeing that we laughed at the exaggerated accounts he had given us, he said he 'wished the affair was well over, one way or the other; that his countrymen were all discontented, and would either surrender, or disperse and act a neutral part, if it were not for the persuasions of their priests and the fear of being maltreated by the savages, with whom they are threatened on all occasions.'" A deserter reported on the nineteenth of July that nothing but dread of the Indians kept the Canadians in the camp.

Wolfe's proclamation, at first unavailing, was now taking effect. A large number of Canadian prisoners, brought in on the twenty-fifth, declared that their countrymen would gladly accept his offers but for the threats of their commanders that if they did so the Indians should be set upon them. The prisoners said further that "they had been under apprehension for several days past of having a body of four hundred barbarians sent to rifle their parish and habitations." Such threats were not wholly effectual. A French chronicler of the time says: "The Canadians showed their disgust every day, and deserted at every opportunity, in spite of the means taken to prevent them." "The people were intimidated, seeing all our army kept in one body and solely on the defensive; while the English, though far less numerous, divided their forces, and undertook various bold enterprises without meeting resistance."

On the eighteenth the English accomplished a feat which promised important results. The French commanders had thought it impossible for any hostile ship to pass the batteries of Quebec; but about eleven o'clock at night, favored by the wind, and covered by a furious cannonade from Point Levi, the ship "Sutherland," with a frigate and several small vessels, sailed safely by and reached the river above the town. Here they at once attacked and destroyed a fireship and some small craft that they found there. Now, for the first time, it became necessary for Montcalm to weaken his army at Beauport by sending six hundred men, under Dumas, to defend the accessible points in the line of precipices between Quebec and Cap-Rouge. Several hundred more were sent on the next day, when it became known that the English had dragged a fleet of boats over Point Levi, launched them above the town, and despatched troops to embark in them. Thus a new feature was introduced into the siege operations, and danger had risen on a side where the French thought themselves safe. On the other hand, Wolfe had become more vulnerable than ever. His army was now divided, not into three parts, but into four, each so far from the rest that, in case of sudden attack, it must defend itself alone. That Montcalm did not improve his opportunity was apparently due to want of confidence in his militia.

The force above the town did not lie idle. On the night of the twentieth, Colonel Carleton, with six hundred men, rowed eighteen miles up the river, and landed at Pointe-aux-Trembles, on the north shore. Here some of the families of Quebec had sought asylum; and Wolfe had been told by prisoners that not only were stores in great quantity to be found here, but also letters and papers throwing light on the French plans. Carleton and his men drove off a band of Indians who fired on them, and spent a quiet day around the parish church; but found few papers, and still fewer stores. They withdrew towards evening, carrying with them nearly a hundred women, children, and old men; and they were no sooner gone than the Indians returned to plunder the empty houses of their unfortunate allies. The prisoners were treated with great kindness. The ladies among them were entertained at supper by Wolfe, who jested with them on the caution of the French generals, saying: "I have given good chances to attack me, and am surprised that they have not profited by them." On the next day the prisoners were all sent to Quebec under a flag of truce.

Thus far Wolfe had refrained from executing the threats he had affixed the month before to the church of Beaumont. But now he issued another proclamation. It declared that the Canadians had shown themselves unworthy of the offers he had made them, and that he had therefore ordered his light troops to ravage their country and bring them prisoners to his camp. Such of the Canadian militia as belonged to the parishes near Quebec were now in a sad dilemma; for Montcalm threatened them on one side, and Wolfe on the other. They might desert to their homes, or they might stand by their colors; in the one case their houses were to be burned by French savages, and in the other by British light infantry.

Wolfe at once gave orders in accord with his late proclamation; but he commanded that no church should be profaned, and no woman or child injured. The first effects of his stern policy are thus recorded by Knox: "Major Dalling's light infantry brought in this afternoon to our camp two hundred and fifty male and female prisoners. Among this number was a very respectable looking priest, and about forty men fit to bear arms. There was almost an equal number of black cattle, with about seventy sheep and lambs, and a few horses. Brigadier Monckton entertained the reverend father and some other fashionable personages in his tent, and most humanely ordered refreshments to all the rest of the captives; which noble example was followed by the soldiery, who generously crowded about those unhappy people, sharing their provisions, rum, and tobacco with them. They were sent in the evening on board of transports in the river." Again, two days later: "Colonel Fraser's detachment returned this morning, and presented us with more scenes of distress and the dismal consequences of war, by a great number of wretched families, whom they brought in prisoners, with some of their effects, and near three hundred black cattle, sheep, hogs, and horses."

On the next night the attention of the excellent journalist was otherwise engaged. Vaudreuil tried again to burn the English fleet. "Late last night," writes Knox, under date of the twenty-eighth, "the enemy sent down a most formidable fire-raft, which consisted of a parcel of schooners, shallops, and stages chained together. It could not be less than a hundred fathoms in length, and was covered with grenades, old swivels, gun and pistol barrels loaded up to their muzzles, and various other inventions and combustible matters. This seemed to be their last attempt against our fleet, which happily miscarried, as before; for our gallant seamen, with their usual expertness, grappled them before they got down above a third part of the Basin, towed them safe to shore, and left them at anchor, continually repeating, *All's well*. A remarkable expression from some of these intrepid souls to their comrades on this occasion I must not omit, on account of its singular uncouthness; namely: 'Damme, Jack, didst thee ever take hell in tow before?'"

According to a French account, this aquatic infernal machine consisted of seventy rafts, boats, and schooners. Its failure was due to no shortcoming on the part of its conductors; who, under a brave Canadian named Courval, acted with coolness and resolution. Nothing saved the fleet but the courage of the sailors, swarming out in their boats to fight the approaching conflagration.

It was now the end of July. More than half the summer was gone, and Quebec seemed as far as ever beyond the grasp of Wolfe. Its buildings were in ruins, and the neighboring parishes were burned and ravaged; but its living rampart, the army of Montcalm, still lay in patient defiance along the shores of Beauport, while above the city every point where a wildcat could climb the precipices was watched and guarded, and Dumas with a thousand men held the impregnable heights of Cap-Rouge. Montcalm persisted in doing nothing that his enemy wished him to do. He would not fight on Wolfe's terms, and Wolfe resolved at last to fight him on his own; that is, to attack his camp in front.

The plan was desperate; for, after leaving troops enough to hold Point Levi and the heights of Montmorenci, less than five thousand men would be left to attack a position of commanding strength, where Montcalm at an hour's notice could collect twice as many to oppose them. But Wolfe had a boundless trust in the disciplined valor of his soldiers, and an utter scorn of the militia who made the greater part of his enemy's force.

Towards the Montmorenci the borders of the St. Lawrence are, as we have seen, extremely high and steep. At a mile from the gorge of the cataract there is, at high tide, a strand, about the eighth of a mile wide, between the foot of these heights and the river; and beyond this strand the receding tide lays bare a tract of mud nearly half a mile wide. At the edge of the dry ground the French had built a redoubt mounted with cannon, and there were other similar works on the strand a quarter of a mile nearer the cataract. Wolfe could not see from the river that these redoubts were commanded by the musketry of the intrenchments along the brink of the heights above. These intrenchments were so constructed that they swept with cross-fires the whole face of the declivity, which was covered with grass, and was very steep. Wolfe hoped that, if he attacked one of the redoubts, the French would come down to defend it, and so bring on a general engagement; or, if they did not, that he should gain an opportunity of reconnoitring the heights to find some point where they could be stormed with a chance of success.

In front of the gorge of the Montmorenci there was a ford during several hours of low tide, so that troops from the adjoining English camp might cross to co-operate with their comrades landing in boats from Point Levi and the Island of Orleans. On the morning of the thirty-first of July, the tide then being at the flood, the French saw the ship "Centurion," of sixty-four guns, anchor near the Montmorenci and open fire on the redoubts. Then two armed transports, each of fourteen guns, stood in as close as possible to the first redoubt and fired upon it, stranding as the tide went out, till in the afternoon they lay bare upon the mud. At the same time a battery of more than forty heavy pieces, planted on the lofty promontory beyond the Montmorenci, began a furious cannonade upon the flank of the French intrenchments. It did no great harm, however, for the works were protected by a great number of traverses, which stopped the shot; and the Canadians, who manned this part of the lines, held their ground with excellent steadiness.

About eleven o'clock a fleet of boats filled with troops, chiefly from Point Levi, appeared in the river and hovered off the shore west of the parish church of Beauport, as if meaning to land there. Montcalm was perplexed, doubting whether the real attack was to be made here, or toward the Montmorenci. Hour after hour the boats moved to and fro, to increase his doubts and hide the real design; but he soon became convinced that the camp of Lévis at the Montmorenci was the true object of his enemy; and about two o'clock he went thither, greeted as he rode along the lines by shouts of *Vive notre Général!* Lévis had already made preparations for defence with his usual skill. His Canadians were reinforced by the battalions of Béarn, Guienne, and Royal Roussillon; and, as the intentions of Wolfe became certain, the right of the camp was nearly abandoned, the main strength of the army being gathered between the river of Beauport and the Montmorenci, where, according to a French writer, there were, towards the end of the afternoon, about twelve thousand men.

At half-past five o'clock the tide was out, and the crisis came. The batteries across the Montmorenci, the distant batteries of Point Levi, the cannon of the "Centurion," and those of the two stranded ships, all opened together with redoubled fury. The French batteries replied; and, amid this deafening roar of artillery, the English boats set their troops ashore at the edge of the broad tract of sedgy mud that the receding river had left bare. At the same time a column of two thousand men was seen, a mile away, moving in perfect order across the Montmorenci ford. The first troops that landed from the boats were thirteen companies of grenadiers and a detachment of Royal Americans. They dashed swiftly forward; while at some distance behind came Monckton's brigade, composed of the fifteenth, or Amherst's regiment, and the seventy-eighth, or Fraser's Highlanders. The day had been fair and warm; but the sky was now thick with clouds, and large raindrops began to fall, the precursors of a summer storm.

With the utmost precipitation, without orders, and without waiting for Monckton's brigade to come up, the grenadiers in front made a rush for the redoubt near the foot of the hill. The French abandoned it; but the assailants had no sooner gained their prize than the thronged heights above blazed with musketry, and a tempest of bullets fell among them. Nothing daunted, they dashed forward again, reserving their fire, and struggling to climb the steep ascent; while, with yells and shouts of *Vive le Roi!* the troops and Canadians at the top poured upon them a hailstorm of musket-balls and buck-shot, and dead and wounded in numbers rolled together down the slope. At that instant the clouds burst, and the rain fell in torrents. "We could not see halfway down the hill," says the Chevalier Johnstone, who was at this part of the line. Ammunition was wet on both sides, and the grassy steeps became so slippery that it was impossible to climb them. The English say that the storm saved the French; the French, with as much reason, that it saved the English.

The baffled grenadiers drew back into the redoubt. Wolfe saw the madness of persisting, and ordered a retreat. The rain ceased, and troops of Indians came down the heights to scalp the fallen. Some of them ran towards Lieutenant Peyton, of the Royal Americans, as he lay disabled by a musket-shot. With his double-barrelled gun he brought down two of his assailants, when a Highland sergeant snatched him in his arms, dragged him half a mile over the mud-flats, and placed him in one of the boats. A friend of Peyton, Captain Ochterlony, had received a mortal wound, and an Indian would have scalped him but for the generous intrepidity of a soldier of the battalion of Guienne; who, seizing the enraged savage, held him back till several French officers interposed, and had the dying man carried to a place of safety.

The English retreated in good order, after setting fire to the two stranded vessels. Those of the grenadiers and Royal Americans who were left alive rowed for the Point of Orleans; the fifteenth regiment rowed for Point Levi; and the Highlanders, led by Wolfe himself, joined the column from beyond the Montmorenci, placing themselves in its rear as it slowly retired along the flats and across the ford, the Indians yelling and the French shouting from the heights, while the British waved their hats, daring them to come down and fight.

The grenadiers and the Royal Americans, who had borne the brunt of the fray, bore also nearly all the loss; which, in proportion to their numbers, was enormous. Knox reports it at four hundred and forty-three, killed, wounded, and missing, including one colonel, eight captains, twenty-one lieutenants, and three ensigns.

Vaudreuil, delighted, wrote to Bourlamaque an account of the affair. "I have no more anxiety about Quebec. M. Wolfe, I can assure you, will make no progress. Luckily for him, his prudence saved him from the consequences of his mad enterprise, and he contented himself with losing about five hundred of his best soldiers. Deserters say that he will try us again in a few days. That is what we want; he'll find somebody to talk to (*il trouvera à qui parler*)."

[THE BATTLE ON THE PLAINS OF ABRAHAM]

Wolfe was deeply moved by the disaster at the heights of Montmorenci, and in a General Order on the next day he rebuked the grenadiers for their precipitation. "Such impetuous, irregular, and unsoldierlike proceedings destroy all order, make it impossible for the commanders to form any disposition for an attack, and put it out of the general's power to execute his plans. The grenadiers could not suppose that they could beat the French alone."

The French were elated by their success. "Everybody," says the commissary Berniers, "thought that the campaign was as good as ended, gloriously for us." They had been sufficiently confident even before their victory; and the bearer of a flag of truce told the English officers that he had never imagined they were such fools as to attack Quebec with so small a force. Wolfe, on the other hand, had every reason to despond. At the outset, before he had seen Quebec and learned the nature of the ground, he had meant to begin the campaign by taking post on the Plains of Abraham, and thence laying siege to the town; but he soon discovered that the Plains of Abraham were hardly more within his reach than was Quebec itself. Such hope as was left him lay in the composition of Montcalm's army. He respected the French commander, and thought his disciplined soldiers not unworthy of the British steel; but he held his militia in high scorn, and could he but face them in the open field, he never doubted the result. But Montcalm also distrusted them, and persisted in refusing the coveted battle.

Wolfe, therefore, was forced to the conviction that his chances were of the smallest. It is said that, despairing of any decisive stroke, he conceived the idea of fortifying Isle-aux-Coudres, and leaving a part of his troops there when he sailed for home, against another attempt in the spring. The more to weaken the enemy and prepare his future conquest, he began at the same time a course of action which for his credit one would gladly wipe from the record; for, though far from inhuman, he threw himself with extraordinary intensity into whatever work he had in hand, and, to accomplish it, spared others scarcely more than he spared himself. About the middle of August he issued a third proclamation to the Canadians, declaring that as they had refused his offers of protection and "had made such ungrateful returns in practising the most unchristian barbarities against his troops on all occasions, he could no longer refrain in justice to himself and his army from chastising them as they deserved." The barbarities in question consisted in the frequent scalping and mutilating of sentinels and men on outpost duty, perpetrated no less by Canadians than by Indians. Wolfe's object was twofold: first, to cause the militia to desert, and, secondly, to exhaust the colony. Rangers, light infantry, and Highlanders were sent to waste the settlements far and wide. Wherever resistance was offered, farmhouses and villages were laid in ashes, though churches were generally spared. St. Paul, far below Quebec, was sacked and burned, and the settlements of the opposite shore were partially destroyed. The parishes of L'Ange Gardien, Château Richer, and St. Joachim were wasted with fire and sword. Night after night the garrison of Quebec could see the light of burning houses as far down as the mountain of Cape Tourmente. Near St. Joachim there was a severe skirmish, followed by atrocious cruelties. Captain Alexander Montgomery, of the forty-third regiment, who commanded the detachment, and who has been most unjustly confounded with the revolutionary general, Richard Montgomery, ordered the prisoners to be shot in cold blood, to the indignation of his own officers. Robineau de Portneuf, curé of St. Joachim, placed himself at the head of thirty parishioners and took possession of a large stone house in the adjacent parish of Château Richer, where for a time he held the English at bay. At length he and his followers were drawn out into an ambush, where they were surrounded and killed; and, being disguised as Indians, the rangers scalped them all.

Most of the French writers of the time mention these barbarities without much comment, while Vaudreuil loudly denounces them. Yet he himself was answerable for atrocities incomparably worse, and on a far larger scale. He had turned loose his savages, red and white, along a frontier of six hundred miles, to waste, burn, and murder at will. "Women and children," such were the orders of Wolfe, "are to be treated with humanity; if any violence is offered to a woman, the offender shall be punished with death." These orders were generally obeyed. The English, with the single exception of Montgomery, killed none but armed men in the act of resistance or attack; Vaudreuil's war-parties spared neither age nor sex.

Montcalm let the parishes burn, and still lay fast intrenched in his lines of Beauport. He would not imperil all Canada to save a few hundred farmhouses; and Wolfe was as far as ever from the battle that he coveted. Hitherto, his attacks had been made chiefly below the town; but, these having failed, he now changed his plan and renewed on a larger scale the movements begun above it in July. With every fair wind, ships and transports passed the batteries of Quebec, favored by a hot fire from Point Levi, and generally succeeded, with more or less damage, in gaining the upper river. A fleet of flatboats was also sent thither, and twelve hundred troops marched overland to embark in them, under Brigadier Murray. Admiral Holmes took command of the little fleet now gathered above the town, and operations in that quarter were systematically resumed.

To oppose them, Bougainville was sent from the camp at Beauport with fifteen hundred men. His was a most arduous and exhausting duty. He must watch the shores for fifteen or twenty miles, divide his force into detachments, and subject himself and his followers to the strain of incessant vigilance and incessant marching. Murray made a descent at Pointe-aux-Trembles, and was repulsed with loss. He tried a second time at another place, was met before landing by a body of ambushed Canadians, and was again driven back, his foremost boats full of dead and wounded. A third time he succeeded, landed at Deschambault, and burned a large building filled with stores and all the spare baggage of the French regular officers. The blow was so alarming that Montcalm hastened from Beauport to take command in person; but when he arrived the English were gone.

Vaudreuil now saw his mistake in sending the French frigates up the river out of harm's way, and withdrawing their crews to serve the batteries of Quebec. Had these ships been there, they might have overpowered those of the English in detail as they passed the town. An attempt was made to retrieve the blunder. The sailors were sent to man the frigates anew and attack the squadron of Holmes. It was too late. Holmes was already too strong for them, and they were recalled. Yet the difficulties of the English still seemed insurmountable. Dysentery and fever broke out in their camps, the number of their effective men was greatly reduced, and the advancing season told them that their work must be done quickly, or not done at all.

On the other side, the distress of the French grew greater every day. Their army was on short rations. The operations of the English above the town filled the camp of Beauport with dismay, for troops and Canadians alike dreaded the cutting off of their supplies. These were all drawn from the districts of Three Rivers and Montreal; and, at best, they were in great danger, since when brought down in boats at night they were apt to be intercepted, while the difficulty of bringing them by land was extreme, through the scarcity of cattle and horses. Discipline was relaxed, disorder and pillage were rife, and the Canadians deserted so fast, that towards the end of August two hundred of them, it is said, would sometimes go off in one night. Early in the month the disheartening news came of the loss of Ticonderoga and Crown Point, the retreat of Bourlamaque, the fall of Niagara, and the expected advance of Amherst on Montreal. It was then that Lévis was despatched to the scene of danger; and Quebec was deplorably weakened by his absence. About this time the Lower Town was again set on fire by the English batteries, and a hundred and sixty-seven houses were burned in a night. In the front of the Upper Town nearly every building was a ruin. At the General Hospital, which was remote enough to be safe from the bombardment, every barn, shed, and garret, and even the chapel itself, were crowded with sick and wounded, with women and children from the town, and the nuns of the Ursulines and the Hôtel-Dieu, driven thither for refuge. Bishop Pontbriand, though suffering from a mortal disease, came almost daily to visit and console them from his lodging in the house of the curé at Charlesbourg.

Towards the end of August the sky brightened again. It became known that Amherst was not moving on Montreal, and Bourlamaque wrote that his position at Isle-aux-Noix was impregnable. On the twenty-seventh a deserter from Wolfe's army brought the welcome assurance that the invaders despaired of success, and would soon sail for home; while there were movements in the English camps and fleet that seemed to confirm what he said. Vaudreuil breathed more freely, and renewed hope and confidence visited the army of Beauport.

Meanwhile a deep cloud fell on the English. Since the siege began, Wolfe had passed with ceaseless energy from camp to camp, animating the troops, observing everything, and directing everything; but now the pale face and tall lean form were seen no more, and the rumor spread that the general was dangerously ill. He had in fact been seized by an access of the disease that had tortured him for some time past; and fever had followed. His quarters were at a French farmhouse in the camp at Montmorenci; and here, as he lay in an upper chamber, helpless in bed, his singular and most unmilitary features haggard with disease and drawn with pain, no man could less have looked the hero. But as the needle, though quivering, points always to the pole, so, through torment and languor and the heats of fever, the mind of Wolfe dwelt on the capture of Quebec. His illness, which began before the twentieth of August, had so far subsided on the twenty-fifth that Knox wrote in his Diary of that day: "His Excellency General Wolfe is on the recovery, to the inconceivable joy of the whole army." On the twenty-ninth he was able to write or dictate a letter to the three brigadiers, Monckton, Townshend, and Murray: "That the public service may not suffer by the General's indisposition, he begs the brigadiers will meet and consult together for the public utility and advantage, and consider of the best method to attack the enemy." The letter then proposes three plans, all bold to audacity. The first was to send a part of the army to ford the Montmorenci eight or nine miles above its mouth, march through the forest, and fall on the rear of the French at Beauport, while the rest landed and attacked them in front. The second was to cross the ford at the mouth of the Montmorenci and march along the strand, under the French intrenchments, till a place could be found where the troops might climb the heights. The third was to make a general attack from boats at the Beauport flats. Wolfe had before entertained two other plans, one of which was to scale the heights at St. Michel, about a league above Quebec; but this he had abandoned on learning that the French were there in force to receive him. The other was to storm the Lower Town; but this also he had abandoned, because the Upper Town, which commanded it, would still remain inaccessible.

The brigadiers met in consultation, rejected the three plans proposed in the letter, and advised that an attempt should be made to gain a footing on the north shore above the town, place the army between Montcalm and his base of supply, and so force him to fight or surrender. The scheme was similar to that of the heights of St. Michel. It seemed desperate, but so did all the rest; and if by chance it should succeed, the gain was far greater than could follow any success below the town. Wolfe embraced it at once.

Not that he saw much hope in it. He knew that every chance was against him. Disappointment in the past and gloom in the future, the pain and exhaustion of disease, toils, and anxieties "too great," in the words of Burke, "to be supported by a delicate constitution, and a body unequal to the vigorous and enterprising soul that it lodged," threw him at times into deep dejection. By those intimate with him he was heard to say that he would not go back defeated, "to be exposed to the censure and reproach of an ignorant populace." In other moods he felt that he ought not to sacrifice what was left of his diminished army in vain conflict with hopeless obstacles. But his final resolve once taken, he would not swerve from it. His fear was that he might not be able to lead his troops in person. "I know perfectly well you cannot cure me," he said to his physician; "but pray make me up so that I may be without pain for a few days, and able to do my duty: that is all I want."

In a despatch which Wolfe had written to Pitt, Admiral Saunders conceived that he had ascribed to the fleet more than its just share in the disaster at Montmorenci; and he sent him a letter on the subject. Major Barré kept it from the invalid till the fever had abated. Wolfe then wrote a long answer, which reveals his mixed dejection and resolve. He affirms the justice of what Saunders had said, but adds: "I shall leave out that part of my letter to Mr. Pitt which you object to. I am sensible of my own errors in the course of the campaign, see clearly wherein I have been deficient, and think a little more or less blame to a man that must necessarily be ruined, of little or no consequence. I take the blame of that unlucky day entirely upon my own shoulders, and I expect to suffer for it." Then, speaking of the new project of an attack above Quebec, he says despondingly: "My ill state of health prevents me from executing my own plan; it is of too desperate a nature to order others to execute." He proceeds, however, to give directions for it. "It will be necessary to run as many small craft as possible above the town, with provisions for six weeks, for about five thousand, which is all I intend to take. My letters, I hope, will be ready to-morrow, and I hope I shall have strength to lead these men to wherever we can find the enemy."

On the next day, the last of August, he was able for the first time to leave the house. It was on this same day that he wrote his last letter to his mother: "My writing to you will convince you that no personal evils worse than defeats and disappointments have fallen upon me. The enemy puts nothing to risk, and I can't in conscience put the whole army to risk. My antagonist has wisely shut himself up in inaccessible intrenchments, so that I can't get at him without spilling a torrent of blood, and that perhaps to little purpose. The Marquis de Montcalm is at the head of a great number of bad soldiers, and I am at the head of a small number of good ones, that wish for nothing so much as to fight him; but the wary old fellow avoids an action, doubtful of the behavior of his army. People must be of the profession to understand the disadvantages and difficulties we labor under, arising from the uncommon natural strength of the country."

On the second of September a vessel was sent to England with his last despatch to Pitt. It begins thus: "The obstacles we have met with in the operations of the campaign are much greater than we had reason to expect or could foresee; not so much from the number of the enemy (though superior to us) as from the natural strength of the country, which the Marquis of Montcalm seems wisely to depend upon. When I learned that succors of all kinds had been thrown into Quebec; that five battalions of regular troops, completed from the best inhabitants of the country, some of the troops of the colony, and every Canadian that was able to bear arms, besides several nations of savages, had taken the field in a very advantageous situation,—I could not flatter myself that I should be able to reduce the place. I sought, however, an occasion to attack their army, knowing well that with these troops I was able to fight, and hoping that a victory might disperse them." Then, after recounting the events of the campaign with admirable clearness, he continues: "I found myself so ill, and am still so weak, that I begged the general officers to consult together for the general utility. They are all of opinion that, as more ships and provisions are now got above the town, they should try, by conveying up a corps of four or five thousand men (which is nearly the whole strength of the army after the Points of Levi and Orleans are left in a proper state of defence), to draw the enemy from their present situation and bring them to an action. I have acquiesced in the proposal, and we are preparing to put it into execution." The letter ends thus: "By the list of disabled officers, many of whom are of rank, you may perceive that the army is much weakened. By the nature of the river, the most formidable part of this armament is deprived of the power of acting; yet we have almost the whole force of Canada to oppose. In this situation there is such a choice of difficulties that I own myself at a loss how to determine. The affairs of Great Britain, I know, require the most vigorous measures; but the courage of a handful of brave troops should be exerted only when there is some hope of a favorable event; however, you may be assured that the small part of the campaign which remains shall be employed, as far as I am able, for the honor of His Majesty and the interest of the nation, in which I am sure of being well seconded by the Admiral and by the generals; happy if our efforts here can contribute to the success of His Majesty's arms in any other parts of America."

Some days later, he wrote to the Earl of Holdernesse: "The Marquis of Montcalm has a numerous body of armed men (I cannot call it an army), and the strongest country perhaps in the world. Our fleet blocks up the river above and below the town, but can give no manner of aid in an attack upon the Canadian army. We are now here [*off Cap-Rouge*] with about thirty-six hundred men, waiting to attack them when and wherever they can best be got at. I am so far recovered as to do business; but my constitution is entirely ruined, without the consolation of doing any considerable service to the state, and without any prospect of it." He had just learned, through the letter brought from Amherst by Ensign Hutchins, that he could expect no help from that quarter.

Perhaps he was as near despair as his undaunted nature was capable of being. In his present state of body and mind he was a hero without the light and cheer of heroism. He flattered himself with no illusions, but saw the worst and faced it all. He seems to have been entirely without excitement. The languor of disease, the desperation of the chances, and the greatness of the stake may have wrought to tranquillize him. His energy was doubly tasked: to bear up his own sinking frame, and to achieve an almost hopeless feat of arms.

Audacious as it was, his plan cannot be called rash if we may accept the statement of two well-informed writers on the

French side. They say that on the tenth of September the English naval commanders held a council on board the flagship, in which it was resolved that the lateness of the season required the fleet to leave Quebec without delay. They say further that Wolfe then went to the admiral, told him that he had found a place where the heights could be scaled, that he would send up a hundred and fifty picked men to feel the way, and that if they gained a lodgement at the top, the other troops should follow; if, on the other hand, the French were there in force to oppose them, he would not sacrifice the army in a hopeless attempt, but embark them for home, consoled by the thought that all had been done that man could do. On this, concludes the story, the admiral and his officers consented to wait the result.

As Wolfe had informed Pitt, his army was greatly weakened. Since the end of June his loss in killed and wounded was more than eight hundred and fifty, including two colonels, two majors, nineteen captains, and thirty-four subalterns; and to these were to be added a greater number disabled by disease.

The squadron of Admiral Holmes above Quebec had now increased to twenty-two vessels, great and small. One of the last that went up was a diminutive schooner, armed with a few swivels, and jocosely named the "Terror of France." She sailed by the town in broad daylight, the French, incensed at her impudence, blazing at her from all their batteries; but she passed unharmed, anchored by the admiral's ship, and saluted him triumphantly with her swivels.

Wolfe's first move towards executing his plan was the critical one of evacuating the camp at Montmorenci. This was accomplished on the third of September. Montcalm sent a strong force to fall on the rear of the retiring English. Monckton saw the movement from Point Levi, embarked two battalions in the boats of the fleet, and made a feint of landing at Beauport. Montcalm recalled his troops to repulse the threatened attack; and the English withdrew from Montmorenci unmolested, some to the Point of Orleans, other to Point Levi. On the night of the fourth a fleet of flatboats passed above the town with the baggage and stores. On the fifth, Murray, with four battalions, marched up the river Etechemin, and forded it under a hot fire from the French batteries at Sillery. Monckton and Townshend followed with three more battalions, and the united force, of about thirty-six hundred men, was embarked on board the ships of Holmes, where Wolfe joined them on the same evening.

These movements of the English filled the French commanders with mingled perplexity, anxiety, and hope. A deserter told them that Admiral Saunders was impatient to be gone. Vaudreuil grew confident. "The breaking up of the camp at Montmorenci," he says, "and the abandonment of the intrenchments there, the re-embarkation on board the vessels above Quebec of the troops who had encamped on the south bank, the movements of these vessels, the removal of the heaviest pieces of artillery from the batteries of Point Levi,— these and the lateness of the season all combined to announce the speedy departure of the fleet, several vessels of which had even sailed down the river already. The prisoners and the deserters who daily came in told us that this was the common report in their army." He wrote to Bourlamaque on the first of September: "Everything proves that the grand design of the English has failed."

Yet he was ceaselessly watchful. So was Montcalm; and he, too, on the night of the second, snatched a moment to write to Bourlamaque from his headquarters in the stone house, by the river of Beauport: "The night is dark; it rains; our troops are in their tents, with clothes on, ready for an alarm; I in my boots; my horses saddled. In fact, this is my usual way. I wish you were here; for I cannot be everywhere, though I multiply myself, and have not taken off my clothes since the twenty-third of June." On the eleventh of September he wrote his last letter to Bourlamaque, and probably the last that his pen ever traced. "I am overwhelmed with work, and should often lose temper, like you, if I did not remember that I am paid by Europe for not losing it. Nothing new since my last. I give the enemy another month, or something less, to stay here." The more sanguine Vaudreuil would hardly give them a week.

Meanwhile, no precaution was spared. The force under Bougainville above Quebec was raised to three thousand men. He was ordered to watch the shore as far as Jacques-Cartier, and follow with his main body every movement of Holmes's squadron. There was little fear for the heights near the town; they were thought inaccessible. Even Montcalm believed them safe, and had expressed himself to that effect some time before. "We need not suppose," he wrote to Vaudreuil, "that the enemy have wings"; and again, speaking of the very place where Wolfe afterwards landed, "I swear to you that a hundred men posted there would stop their whole army." He was right. A hundred watchful and determined men could have held the position long enough for reinforcements to come up.

The hundred men were there. Captain de Vergor, of the colony troops, commanded them, and reinforcements were within his call; for the battalion of Guienne had been ordered to encamp close at hand on the Plains of Abraham. Vergor's post, called Anse du Foulon, was a mile and a half from Quebec. A little beyond it, by the brink of the cliffs, was another post, called Samos, held by seventy men with four cannon; and, beyond this again, the heights of Sillery were guarded by a hundred and thirty men, also with cannon. These were outposts of Bougainville, whose headquarters were at Cap-Rouge, six miles above Sillery, and whose troops were in continual movement along the intervening shore. Thus all was vigilance; for while the French were strong in the hope of speedy delivery, they felt that there was no safety till the tents of the invader had vanished from their shores and his ships from their river. "What we knew," says one of them, "of the character of M. Wolfe, that impetuous, bold, and intrepid warrior, prepared us for a last attack before he left us."

Wolfe had been very ill on the evening of the fourth. The troops knew it, and their spirits sank; but, after a night of torment, he grew better, and was soon among them again, rekindling their ardor, and imparting a cheer that he could not share. For himself he had no pity; but when he heard of the illness of two officers in one of the ships, he sent them a message

of warm sympathy, advised them to return to Point Levi, and
offered them his own barge and an escort. They thanked him,
but replied that, come what might, they would see the enterprise to an end. Another officer remarked in his hearing that
one of the invalids had a very delicate constitution. "Don't
tell me of constitution," said Wolfe; "he has good spirit, and
good spirit will carry a man through everything." An immense
moral force bore up his own frail body and forced it to its work.

Major Robert Stobo, who, five years before, had been given
as a hostage to the French at the capture of Fort Necessity,
arrived about this time in a vessel from Halifax. He had long
been a prisoner at Quebec, not always in close custody, and
had used his opportunities to acquaint himself with the neighborhood. In the spring of this year he and an officer of rangers
named Stevens had made their escape with extraordinary skill
and daring; and he now returned to give his countrymen the
benefit of his local knowledge. His biographer says that it was
he who directed Wolfe in the choice of a landing-place. Be
this as it may, Wolfe in person examined the river and the
shores as far as Pointe-aux-Trembles; till at length, landing on
the south side a little above Quebec, and looking across the
water with a telescope, he descried a path that ran with a long
slope up the face of the woody precipice, and saw at the top a
cluster of tents. They were those of Vergor's guard at the
Anse du Foulon, now called Wolfe's Cove. As he could see
but ten or twelve of them, he thought that the guard could
not be numerous, and might be overpowered. His hope would
have been stronger if he had known that Vergor had once been
tried for misconduct and cowardice in the surrender of Beausé-
jour, and saved from merited disgrace by the friendship of
Bigot and the protection of Vaudreuil.

The morning of the seventh was fair and warm, and the
vessels of Holmes, their crowded decks gay with scarlet uniforms, sailed up the river to Cap-Rouge. A lively scene
awaited them; for here were the headquarters of Bougainville,
and here lay his principal force, while the rest watched the
banks above and below. The cove into which the little river

runs was guarded by floating batteries; the surrounding shore was defended by breastworks; and a large body of regulars, militia, and mounted Canadians in blue uniforms moved to and fro, with restless activity, on the hills behind. When the vessels came to anchor, the horsemen dismounted and formed in line with the infantry; then, with loud shouts, the whole rushed down the heights to man their works at the shore. That true Briton, Captain Knox, looked on with a critical eye from the gangway of his ship, and wrote that night in his Diary that they had made a ridiculous noise. "How different!" he exclaims, "how nobly awful and expressive of true valor is the customary silence of the British troops!"

In the afternoon the ships opened fire, while the troops entered the boats and rowed up and down as if looking for a landing-place. It was but a feint of Wolfe to deceive Bougainville as to his real design. A heavy easterly rain set in on the next morning, and lasted two days without respite. All operations were suspended, and the men suffered greatly in the crowded transports. Half of them were therefore landed on the south shore, where they made their quarters in the village of St. Nicolas, refreshed themselves, and dried their wet clothing, knapsacks, and blankets.

For several successive days the squadron of Holmes was allowed to drift up the river with the flood tide and down with the ebb, thus passing and repassing incessantly between the neighborhood of Quebec on one hand, and a point high above Cap-Rouge on the other; while Bougainville, perplexed, and always expecting an attack, followed the ships to and fro along the shore, by day and by night, till his men were exhausted with ceaseless forced marches.

At last the time for action came. On Wednesday, the twelfth, the troops at St. Nicolas were embarked again, and all were told to hold themselves in readiness. Wolfe, from the flagship "Sutherland," issued his last general orders. "The enemy's force is now divided, great scarcity of provisions in their camp, and universal discontent among the Canadians. Our troops below are in readiness to join us; all the light artillery and tools are embarked at the Point of Levi; and the troops will land where the French seem least to expect it. The first body that gets on shore is to march directly to the enemy and drive them from any little post they may occupy; the officers must be careful that the succeeding bodies do not by any mistake fire on those who go before them. The battalions must form on the upper ground with expedition, and be ready to charge whatever presents itself. When the artillery and troops are landed, a corps will be left to secure the landing-place, while the rest march on and endeavor to bring the Canadians and French to a battle. The officers and men will remember what their country expects from them, and what a determined body of soldiers inured to war is capable of doing against five weak French battalions mingled with a disorderly peasantry."

The spirit of the army answered to that of its chief. The troops loved and admired their general, trusted their officers, and were ready for any attempt. "Nay, how could it be otherwise," quaintly asks honest Sergeant John Johnson, of the fifty-eighth regiment, "being at the heels of gentlemen whose whole thirst, equal with their general, was for glory? We had seen them tried, and always found them sterling. We knew that they would stand by us to the last extremity."

Wolfe had thirty-six hundred men and officers with him on board the vessels of Holmes; and he now sent orders to Colonel Burton at Point Levi to bring to his aid all who could be spared from that place and the Point of Orleans. They were to march along the south bank, after nightfall, and wait further orders at a designated spot convenient for embarkation. Their number was about twelve hundred, so that the entire force destined for the enterprise was at the utmost forty-eight hundred. With these, Wolfe meant to climb the heights of Abraham in the teeth of an enemy who, though much reduced, were still twice as numerous as their assailants.

Admiral Saunders lay with the main fleet in the Basin of Quebec. This excellent officer, whatever may have been his views as to the necessity of a speedy departure, aided Wolfe to the last with unfailing energy and zeal. It was agreed between them that while the general made the real attack, the admiral should engage Montcalm's attention by a pretended one. As night approached, the fleet ranged itself along the Beauport shore; the boats were lowered and filled with sailors, marines, and the few troops that had been left behind; while ship signalled to ship, cannon flashed and thundered, and shot ploughed the beach, as if to clear a way for assailants to land. In the gloom of the evening the effect was imposing. Montcalm, who thought that the movements of the English above the town were only a feint, that their main force was still below it, and that their real attack would be made there, was completely deceived, and massed his troops in front of Beauport to repel the expected landing. But while in the fleet of Saunders all was uproar and ostentatious menace, the danger was ten miles away, where the squadron of Holmes lay tranquil and silent at its anchorage off Cap-Rouge.

It was less tranquil than it seemed. All on board knew that a blow would be struck that night, though only a few high officers knew where. Colonel Howe, of the light infantry, called for volunteers to lead the unknown and desperate venture, promising, in the words of one of them, "that if any of us survived we might depend on being recommended to the general." As many as were wanted—twenty-four in all—soon came forward. Thirty large bateaux and some boats belonging to the squadron lay moored alongside the vessels; and late in the evening the troops were ordered into them, the twenty-four volunteers taking their place in the foremost. They held in all about seventeen hundred men. The rest remained on board.

Bougainville could discern the movement, and misjudged it, thinking that he himself was to be attacked. The tide was still flowing; and, the better to deceive him, the vessels and boats were allowed to drift upward with it for a little distance, as if to land above Cap-Rouge.

The day had been fortunate for Wolfe. Two deserters came from the camp of Bougainville with intelligence that, at ebb tide on the next night, he was to send down a convoy of provisions to Montcalm. The necessities of the camp at Beauport, and the difficulties of transportation by land, had before compelled the French to resort to this perilous means of conveying supplies; and their boats, drifting in darkness under the shadows of the northern shore, had commonly passed in safety. Wolfe saw at once that, if his own boats went down in advance of the convoy, he could turn the intelligence of the deserters to good account.

He was still on board the "Sutherland." Every preparation was made, and every order given; it only remained to wait the turning of the tide. Seated with him in the cabin was the commander of the sloop-of-war "Porcupine," his former school-fellow, John Jervis, afterwards Earl St. Vincent. Wolfe told him that he expected to die in the battle of the next day; and taking from his bosom a miniature of Miss Lowther, his betrothed, he gave it to him with a request that he would return it to her if the presentiment should prove true.

Towards two o'clock the tide began to ebb, and a fresh wind blew down the river. Two lanterns were raised into the maintop shrouds of the "Sutherland." It was the appointed signal; the boats cast off and fell down with the current, those of the light infantry leading the way. The vessels with the rest of the troops had orders to follow a little later.

To look for a moment at the chances on which this bold adventure hung. First, the deserters told Wolfe that provision-boats were ordered to go down to Quebec that night; secondly, Bougainville countermanded them; thirdly, the sentries posted along the heights were told of the order, but not of the countermand; fourthly, Vergor at the Anse du Foulon had permitted most of his men, chiefly Canadians from Lorette, to go home for a time and work at their harvesting, on condition, it is said, that they should afterwards work in a neighboring field of his own; fifthly, he kept careless watch, and went quietly to bed; sixthly, the battalion of Guienne, ordered to take post on the Plains of Abraham, had, for reasons unexplained, remained encamped by the St. Charles; and lastly, when Bougainville saw Holmes's vessels drift down the stream, he did not tax his weary troops to follow them, thinking that they would return as usual with the flood tide. But for these conspiring circumstances New France might have lived a little longer, and the fruitless heroism of Wolfe would have passed, with countless other heroisms, into oblivion.

For full two hours the procession of boats, borne on the current, steered silently down the St. Lawrence. The stars were visible, but the night was moonless and sufficiently dark. The general was in one of the foremost boats, and near him was a young midshipman, John Robison, afterwards professor of natural philosophy in the University of Edinburgh. He used to tell in his later life how Wolfe, with a low voice, repeated Gray's "Elegy in a Country Churchyard" to the officers about him. Probably it was to relieve the intense strain of his thoughts. Among the rest was the verse which his own fate was soon to illustrate,—

"The paths of glory lead but to the grave."

"Gentlemen," he said, as his recital ended, "I would rather have written those lines than take Quebec." None were there to tell him that the hero is greater than the poet.

As they neared their destination, the tide bore them in towards the shore, and the mighty wall of rock and forest towered in darkness on their left. The dead stillness was suddenly broken by the sharp *Qui vive!* of a French sentry, invisible in the thick gloom. *France!* answered a Highland officer of Fraser's regiment from one of the boats of the light infantry. He had served in Holland, and spoke French fluently.

À quel régiment?

De la Reine, replied the Highlander. He knew that a part of that corps was with Bougainville. The sentry, expecting the convoy of provisions, was satisfied, and did not ask for the password.

Soon after, the foremost boats were passing the heights of Samos, when another sentry challenged them, and they could see him through the darkness running down to the edge of the water, within range of a pistol-shot. In answer to his questions, the same officer replied, in French: "Provision-boats. Don't make a noise; the English will hear us." In fact, the sloop-of-war "Hunter" was anchored in the stream not far off. This time, again, the sentry let them pass. In a few moments they rounded the headland above the Anse du Foulon. There was no sentry there. The strong current swept the boats of the light infantry a little below the intended landing-place. They disembarked on a narrow strand at the foot of heights as steep as a hill covered with trees can be. The twenty-four volunteers led the way, climbing with what silence they might, closely followed by a much larger body. When they reached the top they saw in the dim light a cluster of tents at a short distance, and immediately made a dash at them. Vergor leaped from bed and tried to run off, but was shot in the heel and captured. His men, taken by surprise, made little resistance. One or two were caught, and the rest fled.

The main body of troops waited in their boats by the edge of the strand. The heights near by were cleft by a great ravine choked with forest trees; and in its depths ran a little brook called Ruisseau St.-Denis, which, swollen by the late rains, fell plashing in the stillness over a rock. Other than this no sound could reach the strained ear of Wolfe but the gurgle of the tide and the cautious climbing of his advance-parties as they mounted the steeps at some little distance from where he sat listening. At length from the top came a sound of musket-shots, followed by loud huzzas, and he knew that his men were masters of the position. The word was given; the troops leaped from the boats and scaled the heights, some here, some there, clutching at trees and bushes, their muskets slung at their backs. Tradition still points out the place, near the mouth of the ravine, where the foremost reached the top. Wolfe said to an officer near him: "You can try it, but I don't think you'll get up." He himself, however, found strength to drag himself up with the rest. The narrow slanting path on the face of the heights had been made impassable by trenches and abattis; but all obstructions were soon cleared away, and then the ascent was easy. In the gray of the morning the long file of red-coated soldiers moved quickly upward, and formed in order on the plateau above.

Before many of them had reached the top, cannon were heard close on the left. It was the battery at Samos firing on the boats in the rear and the vessels descending from Cap-Rouge. A party was sent to silence it; this was soon effected, and the more distant battery at Sillery was next attacked and taken. As fast as the boats were emptied they returned for the troops left on board the vessels and for those waiting on the southern shore under Colonel Burton.

The day broke in clouds and threatening rain. Wolfe's battalions were drawn up along the crest of the heights. No enemy was in sight, though a body of Canadians had sallied from the town and moved along the strand towards the landing-place, whence they were quickly driven back. He had achieved the most critical part of his enterprise; yet the success that he coveted placed him in imminent danger. On one side was the garrison of Quebec and the army of Beauport, and Bougainville was on the other. Wolfe's alternative was victory or ruin; for if he should be overwhelmed by a combined attack, retreat would be hopeless. His feelings no man can know; but it would be safe to say that hesitation or doubt had no part in them.

He went to reconnoitre the ground, and soon came to the Plains of Abraham, so called from Abraham Martin, a pilot known as Maître Abraham, who had owned a piece of land here in the early times of the colony. The Plains were a tract of grass, tolerably level in most parts, patched here and there with cornfields, studded with clumps of bushes, and forming a part of the high plateau at the eastern end of which Quebec stood. On the south it was bounded by the declivities along the St. Lawrence; on the north, by those along the St. Charles, or rather along the meadows through which that lazy stream crawled like a writhing snake. At the place that Wolfe chose for his battle-field the plateau was less than a mile wide.

Thither the troops advanced, marched by files till they reached the ground, and then wheeled to form their line of battle, which stretched across the plateau and faced the city. It consisted of six battalions and the detached grenadiers from

Louisbourg, all drawn up in ranks three deep. Its right wing was near the brink of the heights along the St. Lawrence; but the left could not reach those along the St. Charles. On this side a wide space was perforce left open, and there was danger of being outflanked. To prevent this, Brigadier Townshend was stationed here with two battalions, drawn up at right angles with the rest, and fronting the St. Charles. The battalion of Webb's regiment, under Colonel Burton, formed the reserve; the third battalion of Royal Americans was left to guard the landing; and Howe's light infantry occupied a wood far in the rear. Wolfe, with Monckton and Murray, commanded the front line, on which the heavy fighting was to fall, and which, when all the troops had arrived, numbered less than thirty-five hundred men.

Quebec was not a mile distant, but they could not see it; for a ridge of broken ground intervened, called Buttes-à-Neveu, about six hundred paces off. The first division of troops had scarcely come up when, about six o'clock, this ridge was suddenly thronged with white uniforms. It was the battalion of Guienne, arrived at the eleventh hour from its camp by the St. Charles. Some time after there was hot firing in the rear. It came from a detachment of Bougainville's command attacking a house where some of the light infantry were posted. The assailants were repulsed, and the firing ceased. Light showers fell at intervals, besprinkling the troops as they stood patiently waiting the event.

Montcalm had passed a troubled night. Through all the evening the cannon bellowed from the ships of Saunders, and the boats of the fleet hovered in the dusk off the Beauport shore, threatening every moment to land. Troops lined the intrench-ments till day, while the general walked the field that adjoined his headquarters till one in the morning, accompanied by the Chevalier Johnstone and Colonel Poulariez. Johnstone says that he was in great agitation, and took no rest all night. At daybreak he heard the sound of cannon above the town. It was the battery at Samos firing on the English ships. He had sent an officer to the quarters of Vaudreuil, which were much nearer Quebec, with orders to bring him word at once should anything unusual happen. But no word came, and about six o'clock he mounted and rode thither with Johnstone. As they advanced, the country behind the town opened more and more upon their sight; till at length, when opposite Vaudreuil's house, they saw across the St. Charles, some two miles away, the red ranks of British soldiers on the heights beyond.

"This is a serious business," Montcalm said; and sent off Johnstone at full gallop to bring up the troops from the centre and left of the camp. Those of the right were in motion already, doubtless by the governor's order. Vaudreuil came out of the house. Montcalm stopped for a few words with him; then set spurs to his horse, and rode over the bridge of the St. Charles to the scene of danger. He rode with a fixed look, uttering not a word.

The army followed in such order as it might, crossed the bridge in hot haste, passed under the northern rampart of Quebec, entered at the Palace Gate, and pressed on in headlong march along the quaint narrow streets of the warlike town: troops of Indians in scalp-locks and war-paint, a savage glitter in their deep-set eyes; bands of Canadians whose all was at stake,—faith, country, and home; the colony regulars; the battalions of Old France, a torrent of white uniforms and gleaming bayonets, La Sarre, Languedoc, Roussillon, Béarn,— victors of Oswego, William Henry, and Ticonderoga. So they swept on, poured out upon the plain, some by the gate of St. Louis, and some by that of St. John, and hurried, breathless, to where the banners of Guienne still fluttered on the ridge.

Montcalm was amazed at what he saw. He had expected a detachment, and he found an army. Full in sight before him stretched the lines of Wolfe: the close ranks of the English infantry, a silent wall of red, and the wild array of the High-landers, with their waving tartans, and bagpipes screaming defiance. Vaudreuil had not come; but not the less was felt the evil of a divided authority and the jealousy of the rival chiefs. Montcalm waited long for the forces he had ordered to join him from the left wing of the army. He waited in vain. It is said that the governor had detained them, lest the English should attack the Beauport shore. Even if they did so, and succeeded, the French might defy them, could they but put Wolfe to rout on the Plains of Abraham. Neither did the garrison of Quebec come to the aid of Montcalm. He sent to Ramesay, its commander, for twenty-five field-pieces which were on the Palace battery. Ramesay would give him only three, saying that he wanted them for his own defence. There were orders and counter-orders; misunderstanding, haste, delay, perplexity.

Montcalm and his chief officers held a council of war. It is said that he and they alike were for immediate attack. His enemies declare that he was afraid lest Vaudreuil should arrive and take command; but the governor was not a man to assume responsibility at such a crisis. Others say that his impetuosity overcame his better judgment; and of this charge it is hard to acquit him. Bougainville was but a few miles distant, and some of his troops were much nearer; a messenger sent by way of Old Lorette could have reached him in an hour and a half at most, and a combined attack in front and rear might have been concerted with him. If, moreover, Montcalm could have come to an understanding with Vaudreuil, his own force might have been strengthened by two or three thousand additional men from the town and the camp of Beauport; but he felt that there was no time to lose, for he imagined that Wolfe would soon be reinforced, which was impossible, and he believed that the English were fortifying themselves, which was no less an error. He has been blamed not only for fighting too soon, but for fighting at all. In this he could not choose. Fight he must, for Wolfe was now in a position to cut off all his supplies. His men were full of ardor, and he resolved to attack before their ardor cooled. He spoke a few words to them in his keen, vehement way. "I remember very well how he looked," one of the Canadians, then a boy of eighteen, used to say in his old age; "he rode a black or dark bay horse along the front of our lines, brandishing his sword, as if to excite us to do our duty. He wore a coat with wide sleeves, which fell back as he raised his arm, and showed the white linen of the wristband."

The English waited the result with a composure which, if not quite real, was at least well feigned. The three field-pieces sent by Ramesay plied them with canister-shot, and fifteen hundred Canadians and Indians fusilladed them in front and flank. Over all the plain, from behind bushes and knolls and the edge of cornfields, puffs of smoke sprang incessantly from the guns of these hidden marksmen. Skirmishers were thrown out before the lines to hold them in check, and the soldiers were ordered to lie on the grass to avoid the shot. The firing was liveliest on the English left, where bands of sharpshooters got under the edge of the declivity, among thickets, and behind scattered houses, whence they killed and wounded a considerable number of Townshend's men. The light infantry were called up from the rear. The houses were taken and retaken, and one or more of them was burned.

Wolfe was everywhere. How cool he was, and why his followers loved him, is shown by an incident that happened in the course of the morning. One of his captains was shot through the lungs; and on recovering consciousness he saw the general standing at his side. Wolfe pressed his hand, told him not to despair, praised his services, promised him early promotion, and sent an aide-de-camp to Monckton to beg that officer to keep the promise if he himself should fall.

It was towards ten o'clock when, from the high ground on the right of the line, Wolfe saw that the crisis was near. The French on the ridge had formed themselves into three bodies, regulars in the centre, regulars and Canadians on right and left. Two field-pieces, which had been dragged up the heights at Anse du Foulon, fired on them with grape-shot, and the troops, rising from the ground, prepared to receive them. In a few moments more they were in motion. They came on rapidly, uttering loud shouts, and firing as soon as they were within range. Their ranks, ill ordered at the best, were further confused by a number of Canadians who had been mixed among the regulars, and who, after hastily firing, threw themselves on the ground to reload. The British advanced a few rods; then halted and stood still. When the French were within forty paces the word of command rang out, and a crash of musketry answered all along the line. The volley was delivered with remarkable precision. In the battalions of the centre, which had suffered least from the enemy's bullets, the simultaneous explosion was afterwards said by French officers to have sounded like a cannon-shot. Another volley followed, and then a furious clattering fire that lasted but a minute or two. When the smoke rose, a miserable sight was revealed: the ground cumbered with dead and wounded, the advancing masses stopped short and turned into a frantic mob, shouting, cursing, gesticulating. The order was given to charge. Then over the field rose the British cheer, mixed with the fierce yell of the Highland slogan. Some of the corps pushed forward with the bayonet; some advanced firing. The clansmen drew their broadswords and dashed on, keen and swift as blood-hounds. At the English right, though the attacking column was broken to pieces, a fire was still kept up, chiefly, it seems, by sharpshooters from the bushes and cornfields, where they had lain for an hour or more. Here Wolfe himself led the charge, at the head of the Louisbourg grenadiers. A shot shattered his wrist. He wrapped his handkerchief about it and kept on. Another shot struck him, and he still advanced, when a third lodged in his breast. He staggered, and sat on the ground. Lieutenant Brown, of the grenadiers, one Henderson, a volunteer in the same company, and a private soldier, aided by an officer of artillery who ran to join them, carried him in their arms to the rear. He begged them to lay him down. They did so, and asked if he would have a surgeon. "There's no need," he answered; "it's all over with me." A moment after, one of them cried out: "They run; see how they run!" "Who run?" Wolfe demanded, like a man roused from sleep. "The enemy, sir. Egad, they give way everywhere!" "Go, one of you, to Colonel Burton," returned the dying man; "tell him to march Webb's regiment down to Charles River, to cut off their retreat from the bridge." Then, turning on his side, he murmured, "Now, God be praised, I will die in peace!" and in a few moments his gallant soul had fled.

Montcalm, still on horseback, was borne with the tide of fugitives towards the town. As he approached the walls a shot passed through his body. He kept his seat; two soldiers supported him, one on each side, and led his horse through the St. Louis Gate. On the open space within, among the excited crowd, were several women, drawn, no doubt, by eagerness to know the result of the fight. One of them recognized him, saw the streaming blood, and shrieked, "*O mon Dieu! mon Dieu! le Marquis est tué!*" "It's nothing, it's nothing," replied the death-stricken man; "don't be troubled for me, my good friends." ("*Ce n'est rien, ce n'est rien; ne vous affligez pas pour moi, mes bonnes amies.*")

NOTES

The letter reprinted here in its entirety was written in 1868 to Parkman's friend, Dr. George E. Ellis, enclosed in a sealed envelope, and inscribed, "Not to be used during my life." The letter from which excerpts are printed was written in 1886 to his friend Martin Brimmer and was accompanied by instructions that the document should not be used until Parkman's death, after which it should be presented to the Massachusetts Historical Society for preservation. For full details of the places where these letters are available, see the Bibliography of this volume.

It is apparent, then, that Parkman wanted these facts to be preserved. Why did he? For one thing, probably, because he was not at all sure that he should live to complete his histories; his physicians repeatedly predicted speedy death for him. His conscience pricked him, and he wanted the world to know that his failure to do the work he had set for himself was the fault of causes beyond his control. Again, the letters reflect the self-analysis and introspection common among New Englanders and especially sons of the Puritans. And, finally, Parkman may have felt that physicians of the future might wish to know the facts which so puzzled physicians of his own time.

Some of his friends have regretted that he left these letters (see Farnham's biography, p. 316). They have felt that the letters reveal too many intimate details and that they give an impression of morbidness foreign to Parkman's nature. Yet an age used to psychological studies and deeply personal autobiographies is not inclined to think Parkman's letter very personal. And the letters are not morbid; it is the facts of the case which are morbid.

EARLY ADVENTURES IN LITERATURE

Nature

This class theme was written in August, 1839, when Parkman was not quite sixteen, and is the earliest composition from his pen which has been preserved. It illustrates two leading interests of his boyhood, nature and science (chemistry, at this time). The attraction of nature never waned for him, as his books abundantly testify; but the interest in science which was expressed in his adolescent years by countless experiments in his home laboratory, and by the making of "shock machines" and pyrotechnic displays for his friends, became in later life an interest in the new scientific knowledge of the day (Darwinian evolution, for instance) and in the botanical, geological, and geographical settings for his histories.

The New-Hampshire Ranger

This poem appeared in the *Knickerbocker Magazine* (XXVI, 146–8, August, 1845). It illustrates young Parkman's interest in natural scenes and romantic events of the "Old French War." His determination to "woo this mistress" in verse was soon abandoned, however.

Satan and Dr. Carver

This sketch appeared in the *Knickerbocker Magazine* for December, 1845 (XXVI, 515–25). It was the last of five contributions to that magazine, four in prose and one in verse. Perhaps the best of the five was a tale called "The Scalp-Hunter," about which the editor of the *Knickerbocker* wrote to him enthusiastically:

"I thank you most cordially for your excellent sketch, 'The Scalp-Hunter,' which you were so good as to send us. It is truly a thrilling story, and, to my mind, the closing scene is worthy of Cooper's pen."

And later:

"I must again cordially thank you for the 'Scalp-Hunter.' I am an 'old stager' in matters of the sort; and it must be something *really* 'thrilling' to keep me awake at night, after reading a proof sheet. . . . "

"The Scalp-Hunter" is a thrilling tale, perhaps more thrilling to that day than to ours; we have become accustomed to Wild West movies. For that reason and because "Satan and Dr. Carver" represents one of the infrequent appearances of humor in Parkman's work, it has seemed better to reprint that tale than the earlier and more exciting one.

Two years after "Satan and Dr. Carver" appeared, Parkman sent the first instalment of *The Oregon Trail* to this same editor, and it was, needless to say, accepted.

A Storm at Sea

This is chapter XLVIII of his novel *Vassall Morton*, published in 1856.

The novel was not a success. It sold poorly, and Parkman was afterward somewhat ashamed of the book and never mentioned it among his works. However, the book does not deserve the oblivion into which it has been cast. George William Curtis, in a contemporary review in *Putnam's Monthly*, said that it was by far the best of late American novels (among the late American novels were *The Scarlet Letter* and *Moby Dick!*) but that it was sketchy, as though tossed off in intervals of more serious study. The book still reads well. For the student of Parkman it is interesting because it is Parkman's last attempt at fiction and his only major attempt, because it reveals his way of making use of his own experience, and because it illuminates so many corners of his own philosophy of life. For the last, see the Introduction to this volume. For a hint of the second, compare this chapter with Parkman's account of his own experiences at sea, reprinted in this volume from his diary (pp. 65–70 above).

Another American historian, Motley, also wrote novels, and with similar lack of success. Motley's novels were *Morton's Hope* (1839), and *Merry Mount* (1849).

The chapter here reprinted describes the death of the villain who, brought at last to account for his evil practices (he had the hero wrongfully imprisoned for many years and at last won the heroine's hand and fortune for himself, only to have the hero escape and re-assert himself), had absconded with money from a trust in his charge and was fleeing to Europe. He was traveling under an assumed name and was well on his way to safety when the storm arose.

THE ROMANCE OF TRAVEL

An Adventure in the Mountains

This narrative from Parkman's diary illustrates the impetuosity and vigor of his youth and also the nature of some of his vacation trips.

A Vacation Trip

Parkman very early fixed upon the plan for his lifework and combined pleasant vacations with research which later went into his books. Throughout these adventures he has his eyes open for battlefields, "the lines of Montcalm," old forts, sunken men-of-war, Indian trails. He was learning to know these forests through which Indians slunk on border raids and through which marched the armies of both England and France. At the same time he was heartily enjoying and keenly analyzing the people he met, and he was having his fill of forest life and adventure.

A Trip to Europe

This is one of the most revealing parts of Parkman's diary. Compare it with other famous trips to Europe—Emerson's, for instance, as he describes it in his journals, and the one which Mark Twain hilariously describes in *Innocents Abroad*. There is a certain similarity among all these accounts. All three men went with a healthy skepticism, determined not to be "taken in" by the older civilizations they were to see, and especially fortified against the monuments of Old World religion they were to see. Yet all three of them admitted, rather grudgingly, one or another of the fascinations of this ancient world, and all three (especially Emerson and Parkman) profited greatly by the experience.

Even on this trip, Parkman was indefatigably gathering notes for his histories and incidentally (as we can see by a comparison of his journal at sea with the chapter reprinted here from *Vassall Morton*) for his novel. He was especially interested in what he saw of the Catholic Church, because he realized how large a part the church played in the history of North America and how much he would have to write about ecclesiastical history. Therefore, he even secured admission to a Passionists' convent in Rome. The irreverence of his comments illustrates his rational and Protestant bias which his Catholic critics have so much deplored. Mark Twain and Emerson displayed, in different degrees, the same bias.

Selections from The Oregon Trail

The great trip in Parkman's long course of preparation for writing took him westward over the Oregon Trail. He stopped far short of Oregon. With a map of the prairie and Rocky Mountain states we can easily follow his route. He fitted himself out with equipment in St. Louis. Then he took a boat up the Missouri, past Jefferson City, to Westport, which is near the outskirts of modern Kansas City. From here he traveled the military road to Fort Leavenworth. This was the frontier, the "jumping-off-place" for the western country. Here was the end of roads and the end of military protection. He turned his course northwest across the prairie toward Fort Laramie, about 700 miles away. His route was the famous Oregon Trail, marked by bleached bones and rude graves. He crossed the Big Blue river on a raft and finally reached the Platte river, probably not far from the present city of Kearney, Nebraska. This stream led him almost to Fort Laramie. From Fort Laramie he made a wide circle toward the northwest among the spurs of the Rockies which he called the Black Hills, but which are really south and west of the ranges now known as the Black Hills. In fact, there is no evidence that Parkman ever got into Dakota; the states he traveled were the ones we now know as Missouri, Kansas, Nebraska, Wyoming, and Colorado. Parkman's adventurous circle brought him back to Fort Laramie, whence he rode south along the ranges, looking at Pike's Peak on his way, went through Pueblo, and stopped a while at Bent's Fort, east and a little south of Pueblo. There he used the Arkansas River as a guide and turned eastward. Somewhere near the present Great Bend and Ellinwood, Kansas, he left the Arkansas and headed straight across the plain to Westport. Then back down the river to St. Louis, and the trip was over.

To modern automobilists, especially those who have paralleled parts of the Oregon Trail in their trips over the Lincoln Highway, Parkman's journey may not seem to be much of a trip. But take the automobiles off the prairie, take off the roads and the highway stations, the grocery stores and the lunch counters, and populate the plains with savage Indians and wild buffalo, and you will have a different situation. For 1846, and for a young man fresh from Harvard, Parkman's journey was an adventure indeed.

The Oregon Trail was serialized in the *Knickerbocker Magazine*, beginning in 1847, and first published in book form in 1849.

Indian Domestic Life

A portion of chapter XII of *The Oregon Trail*.

This is another episode Parkman witnessed in the Indian village. It shows what intimate details of the Indian life he was enabled to observe.

A Close View of Indian Warfare

A portion of chapter XVI of *The Oregon Trail*.
This is an example of the material Parkman was collecting for future vivid descriptions of Indian battles.

Hunting the Buffalo

A portion of chapter XXIV of *The Oregon Trail*.
This exciting buffalo hunt occurred near the Arkansas river in western Kansas or eastern Colorado.
P. 106. *"Oui, monsieur, oui."* Yes, indeed, sir.
P. 106. *"Oui, bien chargé; you'll kill, mon bourgeois; yes, you'll kill—c'est un bon fusil."* Yes, well loaded. You'll kill, my master; yes, you'll kill—it is a good gun.
This was the last major adventure of the trip. The group continued down the Arkansas, struck out across the prairie, and finally arrived—not without reluctance—at civilization once again.
Notice throughout these selections how admiration for the Spartan qualities of the Indians is contending in Parkman's mind with his dislike of their savage emotionality and lack of rationality.

Westward over the Oregon Trail

Chapter VI of *The Oregon Trail*.
P. 110. *The St. Joseph Trail*—connecting Fort Leavenworth with the Oregon Trail proper.
Pp. 110 ff. *Emigrants.* Parkman's unfavorable attitude toward the emigrants is a familar illustration of his dislike for democracy in the raw (for a discussion of which, see the Introduction to this volume, pp. lxi-lxiv).
P. 111. *"Are ye for Oregon or California?"* The routes to Oregon and California diverged beyond the mountains, one going northwest and the other southwest. Many of the forty-niners traveled this route, and Parkman's publishers later capitalized on the sudden interest in California gold by calling the book *The California and Oregon Trail.*

Scenes at Fort Laramie

Chapter IX of *The Oregon Trail*.
Fort Laramie was built, like many other forts, not so much for military advantage as for protection of traders. It was located at a focal point for the fur-trading industry, and its walls—six feet thick and fifteen feet high—enclosed stores, shops, storage houses, and dwellings.
P. 127. *Catlin.* George Catlin, who spent eight years among the Indians, painting portraits of their famous chiefs.
P. 133. *Spanish flies.* Dried and powdered beetles, applied as a means of raising blisters on the skin.

Scenes at an Indian Camp

Chapter XI of *The Oregon Trail.*

An occasional view of and chance acquaintance with Indians on the prairie was not enough for Parkman's educational purpose. Therefore, he arranged to live with a village of Indians. Here he learned many of the habits of the tribes, which he described so vividly in his books. Here also he contracted dysentery, which very nearly put an end to his trip, if not his life. Some of the effects of this disease are vividly described in this chapter.

P. 138. *King Philip, Pontiac, Tecumseh.* Three famous chiefs who led bloody but unsuccessful revolts against the white men. King Philip led his tribe against the New England colonies in 1675–6, Pontiac laid siege to Detroit and ravaged the nearby frontier in 1763–4, and Tecumseh was defeated at Tippecanoe in 1811.

A BOOK ON ONE'S HOBBY

The Rose

Pages 95–98 of *The Book of Roses.*

When his weak eyes and his neurotic symptoms would not permit him to work on his history, Parkman turned—as Prescott had already done for a similar reason—to horticulture. The rose was his favorite and his specialty. He pursued its cultivation as thoroughly as he did everything else, so thoroughly that he became one of the most famous American rose fanciers of his time and was appointed to a professorship in Harvard's Bussey Institute. His best known creation was the *Lilium Parkmani* (Parkman's lily), which he sold to an English florist for $1,000. In general, however, his horticulture brought him little income. It was a labor of love and a satisfaction for his craving for action.

The passage here reprinted is one of the philosophical sections with which the otherwise technical book is liberally sprinkled. *The Book of Roses* is still a good textbook for an amateur floriculturist, and it is still pleasant reading.

ADVENTURES IN POLITICS AND EDUCATION

Parkman seldom entered the lists on contemporary problems, preferring to conserve his enfeebled energies for his lifework, but occasionally he spoke out, and when he did he spoke with all the vigor of one of his martial heroes or his Puritan ancestors. The three essays here reprinted show his opinions on education, on democratic suffrage, and on the position of women. His viewpoint toward education was strikingly liberal, whereas his viewpoint toward woman suffrage was declared to be old-fashioned and reactionary. His opinion of universal suffrage, expressed in the second essay, is an interesting revelation of his distrust of democracy, which meant to him mob rule and rule by demagogues. He was a natural aristocrat. At the same time, however, he distrusted absolutism and despotism of every sort. For a discussion of his political attitude see the Introduction to this volume, pp. lx–lxxvii.

The Tale of the "Ripe Scholar"

Published in the *Nation* for December 23, 1869 (IX, 558-60).

This consideration of democratic education is astonishingly modern. Parkman wrote in the days when the great expansion of the universities was beginning and when some people were worrying about the usefulness and depth of mass education. We have the same problem today, and Parkman's answer is prophetic of many of the most trustworthy modern answers. More deep thinking, says Parkman, is what we need—not more schools or more students. His solution to the educational problems of America would probably have been much like Jefferson's (whom Parkman distrusted because of his allegiance to French democracy)—an aristocracy of talent arrived at by providing free and sound higher education for the boys of greatest ability.

The Failure of Universal Suffrage

Published in the *North American Review*, July-August, 1878 (CXXVII, 1–20).

This trenchant essay is another one with modern implications, for we hear much of mob rule and demagoguery today. Parkman's answer was that we want good government, and that whether it is attained by a monarchy or by a democracy is a matter of lesser importance. The result is the important thing; the votes do not matter of themselves. Parkman's own choice of government, as was made clear in the introduction, is a constitutional republic, avoiding autocracy on one side and complete democracy on the other.

The Woman Question

Published in the *North American Review*, October, 1879 (CXXIX, 303–21).

Constitutional amendment has gone against Parkman's position on this question, and yet his essay is interesting for its revelation of his political viewpoint and the tenacity with which he clung to it. He wrote three essays on this subject, the second ("The Woman Question Again") a reply to critics of the essay here reprinted, and the third (*Some of the Reasons against Woman Suffrage*) a pamphlet which digested the previous material.

LITERARY CRITICISM

Parkman wrote no formal literary criticism, but he put a great deal of both literary and political criticism into his reviews. He is known to have written at least twenty-five book reviews for leading Eastern magazines. The content of these is summarized briefly in the Bibliography and discussed in the Introduction to this volume. The selections reprinted here are representative ones.

The Works of James Fenimore Cooper

Published in the *North American Review*, January, 1862 (LXXIV, 147–61).

Given the task of reviewing a revised edition of Cooper's works, Parkman was able to write what amounted to an essay on Cooper. The review as nearly approximated a critical essay as any of Parkman's writings.

Conflicting loyalties must have swayed Parkman as he planned this review. Cooper was one of his earliest favorite authors, from whom he had learned much. On the other hand, his own experience on the Oregon Trail had led him to doubt the validity of some of Cooper's most famous characters, and his own histories had already begun to appear with pictures of the Indian radically different from Cooper's Indians. Therefore, he was compelled to separate what he considered the good from the bad in Cooper and to weigh each volume carefully. His conclusion was that Cooper's Indians were not real, but that the books are vivid and vigorous. He especially admires Cooper's nationalism.

Charlevoix's History of New France

Published in the *Atlantic Monthly*, July, 1867 (XX, 125).

In one of his bibliographical notes, Parkman advises the reader to turn to Charlevoix's history for a point of view exactly opposite to Parkman's own. The review is, therefore, an example of how generous Parkman could be toward a writer who disagreed with him. Another interesting feature of the review is Parkman's praise of the translator for supplying the history with documentation and in some cases correcting Charlevoix's errors. Parkman was a great believer in full documentation (see the section on "His Theory of Historical Writing" in the Introduction, pp. l ff.).

Casgrain's Book on Acadia

Published in the *Nation*, March 14, 1889 (XLVIII, 232–3).

Perhaps nothing Parkman wrote so antagonized French Catholics as his treatment of the expulsion of the Acadians by the English (the same episode which Longfellow has romanticized in *Evangeline*). One of the answers to Parkman came from the Abbé Casgrain, who, in a book which ostensibly recorded "a pilgrimage" to the land of Acadia, took strong exception to Parkman's interpretation. This intense and cutting review of Casgrain's book was Parkman's reply. Casgrain and Parkman remained firm friends.

THE FIRST HISTORY

Pontiac was the first product of Parkman's studies in Indian history and his first attempt at formal historical writing. The book made a great impression in its day (1851), although the perspective of history has put it low among Parkman's books and Parkman himself later condemned it as "turgid and rhetorical."

The book tells the story of the dramatic revolt of the Ottawa chief Pontiac, who sent out the war belt and gathered in the tribes to attack the white men in 1763 and 1764. The English outpost at Detroit was to be the first point of attack. When the siege here was thwarted, the Indians were reduced to attacking lesser posts and frontier dwellings, and finally had to accept peace. Pontiac met death a little later at the hands of one of his own race.

Pontiac deals with the time immediately following the British conquest of Canada. If it is to be considered a part of *France and England in North America*, therefore, it is the last volume in the series. There is grave doubt that Parkman intended it to belong to this series, however, and certainly France appears in Pontiac's war only through rumor and implication.

The Indian Character

This famous characterization is a part of the long introductory chapter of *Pontiac*, which chapter Mrs. Parkman pronounced "incredibly dull."

The Indians Prepare for War

This narrative of the gathering of ominous war clouds is made up of the latter part of chapter VI, and all of chapters VII and VIII of *Pontiac*.

P. 228. *Wampum.* Parkman includes in his text a long note on wampum, explaining that it is made from shells, and that it is used for ornaments. An Indian orator delivered a belt of wampum for every clause of his speech. War belts were either red or black, depending on the tribe, whereas a peace belt was white.

The Council at the River Ecorces

Chapter IX of *Pontiac*.

This vivid scene depends greatly on Parkman's own life with the Indians. It serves to introduce Pontiac, a chief whom Parkman admired for his vigor, character, and bravery, although he was keenly aware of his cruelty. Pontiac approached more nearly Parkman's ideal of the rational leader than did most Indians; he tried to lead his people wisely, and might have won the battle of Detroit except for some unforeseen occurrences.

The Attack on Detroit

This selection (the last pages of chapter X and all of chapter XI of *Pontiac*) continues the story. It gives Parkman an opportunity to do what he always loved to do—describe a battle. In this case he is scrupulously exact in his description of the Indian method of warfare, although he is still able to catch the glamor and drama of the scene.

Captives of the Indians

A few pages from chapter XXII of *Pontiac*.

Balked in their assault on Detroit, the Indians turned on more vulnerable victims—the smaller posts, the interior garrisons, and the isolated pioneer dwellings. Many white men and women they scalped at once; others they carried away with them as captives. The plight of these captives was not enviable. Here Parkman has discussed the matter, in an excellent combination of his own experience with a vivid imagination.

The Death of Pontiac

Chapter XXXI of *Pontiac*.

Detroit was invulnerable, and the Indian warriors grew tired of devastating the frontiers; the Indian was never able to stick to one war for any length of time. Furthermore, the white armies were ready to deal out punishment. Pontiac was forced, therefore, to submit to a council with the British envoy and to accept peace. A little later he was slain by an Illinois Indian, possibly out of mere bravado, possibly because the murder was incited by the English. The reference at the end of the selection is to the revenge which Pontiac's countrymen took on the nation of the murderer. Almost the whole Illinois nation was exterminated.

THE GREAT HISTORY

Parkman's "great history," the record of *France and England in the New World*, began with the earliest settlements in Florida and extended to the fall of Quebec in 1759. It may be interesting to set down here the relative chronology of selections reprinted in this volume.

Wolfe before Quebec, 1759
The Battle on the Plains of Abraham, 1759

(The selections include two analytical chapters to which no date can readily be assigned.)

The student should allocate these dates in relation to others which may be more familiar. For example:

Reign of Queen Elizabeth, 1558–1603

Founding of Jamestown, 1607; Plymouth, 1620; Boston, 1630

Death of Shakespeare, 1616; Milton, 1674

Harvard founded, 1636

Commonwealth in England, 1649–60

William Penn colonizes Pennsylvania, 1682

Increase Mather died, 1723; Cotton Mather, 1728

Edwards born, 1703; Franklin, 1706; Washington, 1732; Jefferson, 1743

For a complete list and characterization of the volumes in Parkman's great series see the bibliographical section of this volume.

France and England in North America

This is from the introduction to *Pioneers of France in the New World*. Written before 1865, it states the point of view from which the whole series grew.

". . . At this hour, half a million of bayonets are vindicating the ascendency of a regulated freedom." A reference to the War between the States which was in progress while the book was being written. Parkman was opposed to disruption of the union over slavery and said that he would rather have all the slaves knocked over the head, but when the war started his martial spirit caused him no end of regret that he was unable to join the armies. "A regulated freedom" is an interesting reference to Parkman's political ideas (see the discussion of his political theory in the Introduction to this volume, pp. lx–lxxvii).

Parkman's footnotes are omitted from these selections. His books are extremely well documented with references to the sources of his information and occasional commentaries.

Early Spanish Adventure

Chapter I of *Pioneers of France in the New World*.

Parkman begins his book with an account of early Spanish exploration in Florida because it was in Florida that France made her only extensive experiment with Huguenot (Protestant) settlers. Huguenots were excluded from Canada, and Parkman thought that was a serious error in French colonial policy.

Fame long overdue has recently come to one of the four "wretched followers" of Narvaez who escaped. This one was Cabeza de Vaca, whose diary was before Parkman when he wrote. The diary is a remarkable story. It tells how the refugees lived for years among the Indians, crossed the Mississippi near Memphis, followed the Arkansas and Red rivers to New Mexico and Chihuahua, and finally reached the Gulf of California and the Spanish settlements in Mexico.

Menendez

Chapter VII of *Pioneers of France in the New World.*

Menendez was one of the most vigorous of the Spanish guardians of Florida. Spain had two reasons for wishing to keep the Huguenots out. In the first place, Spain wanted Florida for herse f, and the Huguenots were French; in the second place, while Spain was strongly Catholic the Huguenots were Protestant, and the Spanish were anxious to keep heresy out of the New World. As Parkman points out, the battles over Florida took on almost the likeness of a crusade.

Cartier and the St. Lawrence

A part of chapter I of the second part of *Pioneers of France in the New World.*

This chapter illustrates not only Parkman's genius for vivid description and his keen relish for such romantic events as the first sight of Quebec and Montreal, but also the way he combined his own thorough observation of the St. Lawrence with his historical imagination, thus arriving at a convincing picture of how the river must have looked to Cartier.

Champlain at Quebec

Chapter IX of *Pioneers of France in the New World.*

The reference to Aeneas is, of course, to the hero of Vergil's *Aeneid*, whose descendants founded Rome.

Lake Champlain

Chapter X of *Pioneers of France in the New World.*

The action of Champlain in joining the war party was of especial significance because it established a precedent for the long enmity between French and Iroquois. The five nations of the Iroquois were incomparably the strongest and most advanced tribes with whom the French and English came into contact. Single-handed, they determined the balance of power between English and French. Their strength and cunning kept the French from overrunning New York and the Middle West. Usually they sided with the English, harrying the French outposts and sometimes carrying the warfare to the very gates of Quebec. Formidable opponents, indeed, for Champlain to antagonize so early in the history of French settlement.

Daily Life of the Missionary Priests

A part of chapter XI of *The Jesuits in North America.*

The Jesuits were important in the history of New France for three reasons: their part in the religious history of the colony, their services in exploration, and their influence in the political struggle for North America. Indians whom the Jesuits had converted would naturally side with Catholic France against Protestant England.

Brébeuf and His Associates

Chapter VI of *The Jesuits in North America.*

This is another charming illustration of Parkman's ability to illuminate matter-of-fact chronicles with his vivid imagination and style.

Parkman's skepticism toward supernatural manifestations in these chapters on the Jesuits is balanced by his sincere regard for the heroism of the priests. His accounts of Brébeuf and other missionary priests had much to do with the canonization of these men.

The Founding of Montreal

A part of chapter XV of *The Jesuits in North America.*

Romance like this was a kind that Parkman loved to write. Here for a few pages he could forget his political thesis and his philosophical reservations and write pure pageantry after the fashion of his early favorites, Scott and Cooper. His final question, "Is this true history, or a romance of Christian chivalry?" is one which many readers have asked, and his answer—"It is both"—rests upon unassailable documentation.

The Ruin of the Hurons

Chapter XXVII of *The Jesuits in North America.*

The Hurons were the Indians among whom the Jesuits had been able to do the most effective work of conversion. The Iroquois, on the other hand, had provided few converts, and, ever since Champlain's first war party, they had shown little sympathy for the French and their allies. When the Hurons were routed, therefore, the French lost at once their most faithful Indian allies and their best converts.

Brébeuf and Lalemant later died the deaths of martyrs among the Indians.

P. 334. *Dutch guns.* The Iroquois were able to exchange furs for guns, powder, and ammunition sent from the Dutch colony of New Netherlands.

The Failure of the Missionaries

A part of chapter XXXIV of *The Jesuits in North America.*

Here Parkman summarizes the importance of the disaster to the Hurons, and blames the failure of the Jesuits' huge plan of conversion on the tomahawks and Dutch guns of the Iroquois. Thus that first venture of Champlain's assumes an even greater importance.

The Discovery of the Mississippi

Part of chapter V of *La Salle and the Discovery of the Great West.*

P. 336. *Talon.* Intendant, or representative, of the French king in Canada. The French government tried to divide up the power in its colonial government so that no one man could secure an ascendancy and so that the real commands could always come from Versailles.

Joliet and Marquette apparently descended the Mississippi about as far as the present Rosedale, Mississippi—about half way between Memphis and Vicksburg.

P. 347. *Kaskaskia.* Later name for fort in vicinity of Vincennes. The town here referred to was near the present city of Ottawa, Illinois.

An Illinois Village

A part of chapter XVI of *La Salle and the Discovery of the Great West.*

This, like most of Parkman's descriptions of scenery, depended largely on notes made by the historian himself on the spot. For his adventures in finding the scene of this village see the Introduction to this volume (pp. xlix–l) and *La Salle,* pp. 239–41.

La Salle Reaches the Mouth of the Mississippi

Chapter XX of *La Salle and the Discovery of the Great West.*

Parkman portrays La Salle as a strong, ambitious man who had to face almost insurmountable obstacles and political opposition. His great triumph was the discovery of the Mississippi's mouth. Returning with an expedition by sea, he sailed past the delta and landed far to the west. After a vain search for the great river, he established his colony in Texas. Hardships followed, and La Salle was assassinated on his way to seek help from the French settlements. The colony perished.

Bishop Laval

A part of chapter IX of *The Old Régime in Canada.*

This chapter shows Parkman's awareness of the gulf between his viewpoint and that of his Catholic readers. He tries to tread softly and at the same time tell the truth as he sees it.

This characterization of Laval compares interestingly with the longer characterization by Willa Cather in her novel, *Shadows on the Rock* (1931).

Heroes of the Long Saut

Chapter VI of *The Old Régime in Canada.*

This is another episode in the century-long war with the Iroquois. It shows in what terror these nations kept the French settlers, and how strong a weapon they proved against eventual French domination.

The Canadian Frontier

Chapter XVII of *The Old Régime in Canada.*

This is one of those chapters from that remarkable last half of *The Old Régime* where Parkman came as near writing social history as he ever did. Later specialists have sketched in details of his picture, but they have not made it more vivid. This chapter describes frontier life and the kind of Canadians it developed.

It may be interesting to recall that the census of 1667 gave 447 as the population of Quebec; Montreal, 766.

The Importance of Absolutism in Canada

Chapter XXIV of *The Old Régime in Canada*.

This is the concluding chapter in *The Old Régime*, the chapter in which Parkman sums up his point of view. He has discussed at length the social and political organization of the new colony, followed minutely the influence of absolutism on Canada and Canadians. Now he draws his conclusions.

Such arguments as these brought from Parkman's enemies the accusations of both Anglo-Saxon prejudice and anti-Catholic prejudice. The student can decide whether the accusations are justified.

Frontenac and Phips: A Puritan Crusade against Quebec

A part of chapter XII and the whole of chapter XIII of *Frontenac and New France under Louis XIV*.

This famous New England expedition is described by Cotton Mather in his *Magnalia*. A comparison of Parkman's account with Mather's shows that Parkman told the story with little or no Anglo-Saxon or New England bias. Mather's account is fervid with praises of Phips and his soldiers; Parkman's is calm, detached, factual. Parkman may have exhibited such a prejudice, as some of his critics say, but not in this place.

This selection also gives a good picture of Frontenac (another man who is interestingly characterized in Willa Cather's *Shadows on the Rock*). Parkman respected Frontenac for his strength and for his ability to inspire trust and allegiance in men. Certain other features of Frontenac, as the chapter reveals, he did not like.

The incidents here narrated took place in 1690.

The Combatants

Chapter I of *Montcalm and Wolfe*.

Here Parkman sets the stage for the last great drama of his chronicle. Fifty years have passed since the events concerning Frontenac, fifty years of border warfare (described in *A Half-Century of Conflict*). Now the clouds of a new war are gathering. It is the Seven Years' War which is to end with England triumphant in North America. In the last pages of this selection, Parkman sets out with great clarity the issues involved and his explanation of the result.

Wolfe before Quebec

Chapter XXV of *Montcalm and Wolfe*.

By 1759 the war had reached a stage where the safety of New France depended on the safety of its last and greatest stronghold, Quebec. Outnumbered, outsailed, outsupplied, the armies of France gradually with-drew to this fortress above the St. Lawrence, one of the strongest natural positions in the world. Montcalm was the commanding officer, Levis and Bourlamaque his principal subordinates. Vaudreuil was governor of the colony. When this chapter opens they are expecting an attack from the British fleet and armies, led by Wolfe.

The Battle on the Plains of Abraham

Chapter XXVII of *Montcalm and Wolfe*.

This is the last act in the drama. Wolfe's fleet and army have lain long and unsuccessfully before Quebec. Their guns have shattered and burned many buildings, but the walls and cliffs still stand. Their assaults have been repulsed. They are pessimistic about their chances of taking the city, despite the fact that the French are known to be in need of supplies. Soon winter will come, and they must sail home. And so they try a desperate plan.

In such a situation as this Parkman is in his element. Stirring action, personal bravery, military movements, grand natural scenery, the future of two countries depending on the results—he could do his best with such material.

Some of Parkman's critics have produced evidence to indicate that he undervalued Lévis, and it seems true that Lévis at least shared the hero's honors with his superior, Montcalm.